MAHARISHI'S PROGRAMME TO CREATE WORLD PEACE

GLOBAL INAUGURATION

Maharishi's Programme to Create World Peace

GLOBAL INAUGURATION

Demonstrating the Mechanics to Create Coherence in World Consciousness, the Basis of World Peace

1987

Thirteenth Year of the Age of Enlightenment
Maharishi's Year of World Peace

World Capital of the Age of Enlightenment, Maharishi Nagar, U.P. 201307, India.

Published jointly by Maharishi European Research University, Vlodrop, Holland, and Age of Enlightenment Press, Washington, D.C., U.S.A.

Copyright © 1987 International Association for the Advancement of the Science of Creative Intelligence (Switzerland). All rights reserved.

Library of Congress Cataloging-in-Publication Data
Mahesh Yogi, Maharishi.
    Maharishi's programme to create world peace.

    1. Transcendental Meditation. 2. Peace--
Miscellanea. I. Title
BF637.T6 8M3 455 1986   327.1'72   86–32102

ISBN 0–89186 052–5

ACKNOWLEDGEMENT: The editors express gratitude for reprint permission to all the publishers and broadcasters of the press reports and accounts of flying that appear in this book. In addition, the editors specifically acknowledge permission to reprint the articles on the following pages: page 512, reprinted with permission of *Dallas Morning News*; page 515, reprinted by permission of the *Denver Post*; page 519, reprint courtesy of the *Fort Worth Star-Telegram*; page 468, © 1986 New York News, Inc., reprinted with permission; page 457, © The New York Times Company, reprinted by permission; page 534, © the *Sacramento Bee* 1986; and pages 470 and 535, © *San Francisco Chronicle* 1986, reprinted by permission.

Printed in U.S.A. by Age of Enlightenment Press.
Publication number U1-10108-389.

GROUPS OF EXPERTS at the Maharishi World Capital of the Age of Enlightenment and in many other places on earth are creating coherence in world consciousness through their twice daily collective practice of the TM-Sidhi 'yogic flying' technique. As these groups grow larger day by day, coherence is rising in world consciousness and bringing more success and happiness to individuals, greater progress and invincibility to nations, and perfect health, harmony, and peace to the family of nations.

World-wide competitions in TM-Sidhi 'yogic flying' inaugurated Maharishi's Programme to Create World Peace. The success of these inaugurations, narrated in this book, has inspired annual competitions in Maharishi's practical and powerful technology for world peace.

Every year, competitions in TM-Sidhi 'yogic flying' will be held

- for each family on 1 May, in the family's home;
- for each city on 15 May, in that city;
- for each state or province on 1 June, in the state or provincial capital;
- for each nation on 15 June, in the national capital;
- for each continent on 1 July, at the Maharishi Continental Capital of the Age of Enlightenment: for Asia, in Maharishi Nagar, India; for Australia and the Pacific, in Cremorne, NSW, Australia; for Europe, in Vlodrop, Holland; for Africa, in Nairobi, Kenya; for Latin America and the Caribbean, in Brasilia, D.F., Brazil; and for North America, in Washington, D.C., U.S.A.; and
- for the whole world on Guru Purnima Day, the full-moon day in July dedicated to the tradition of great teachers, at the Maharishi World Capital of the Age of Enlightenment, Maharishi Nagar, India.

As coherence in world consciousness rises, the TM-Sidhas will fly farther and faster. With each higher flight, the world will celebrate a new height of health, happiness, prosperity, and peace. This is the significance of the annual 'yogic flying' competitions.

HIS HOLINESS
MAHARISHI MAHESH YOGI

Founder of Transcendental Meditation (1957); the Science of Creative Intelligence (1971); the Maharishi Technology of the Unified Field (1982); Maharishi International University, United States (1971); Maharishi European Research University, Switzerland (1975) and Germany (1982); Maharishi University of Natural Law, England (1982); Maharishi Veda Vigyan Vidya Peeth, India (Vedic University for Asia, 1983); Maharishi Vedic University, Europe and the United States (1985); six Continental Capitals of the Age of Enlightenment (1985); the World Government of the Age of Enlightenment, a non-political, non-religious, global organization with sovereignty in the domain of consciousness, authority in the invincible power of natural law, and activity in purifying world consciousness with the participation of the people of over 120 countries (1976); the World Federation of Ayurveda (1985); Maharishi's World Plan for Perfect Health (1985); the Maharishi World Centre for Perfect Health, India (1986); and Maharishi's Programme to Create World Peace (1986).

'It needed a scientific age for the world to appreciate the significance of the philosophy of Yoga and its practical application in creating integrated individuals, integrated nations, and an integrated world family.

'Yoga means union, the union of the individual awareness with the unified field of all the laws of nature in the state of transcendental consciousness. "Yogic flying" demonstrates the ability of the individual to act from the unified field and enliven the total potential of natural law in all its expressions—mind, body, behaviour, and environment. "Yogic flying" presents in miniature the flight of galaxies in space, all unified in perfect order by natural law.

'The mind-body co-ordination displayed by "yogic flying" shows that consciousness and its expression—the physiology—are in perfect balance. Scientific research has found maximum coherence in human brain functioning during "yogic flying". As the coherently functioning human brain is the unit of world peace, "yogic flying" is the mechanics to make world peace a reality, and thereby bring world health, world happiness, world prosperity, a world free from suffering—heaven on earth in this generation.'

—*Maharishi*

MAHARISHI'S PROGRAMME TO CREATE

TABLE OF

INTRODUCTION 1

MAHARISHI'S INAUGURAL ADDRESS 4

A BRIEFING FOR THE WORLD PRESS 11

INAUGURATING MAHARISHI'S PROGRAMME
   TO CREATE WORLD PEACE—WASHINGTON, D.C., U.S.A.,
   AND NEW DELHI, INDIA 31

PRESS CONFERENCES ON MAHARISHI AYURVEDA
   AND THE MAHARISHI UNIFIED FIELD BASED
   INTEGRATED SYSTEMS OF HEALTH, DEFENCE,
   AND ADMINISTRATION 46

INAUGURATING MAHARISHI'S PROGRAMME
   TO CREATE WORLD PEACE—

   ASIA 63
      China, Hong Kong, India, Indonesia, Japan, South Korea, Macao, Malaysia, Pakistan, Philippines, Singapore, Taiwan, Thailand

   AUSTRALIA AND THE PACIFIC 185
      Australia, New Zealand

WORLD PEACE • GLOBAL INAUGURATION

CONTENTS

AFRICA AND THE MIDDLE EAST 193
   Cyprus, Egypt, Ghana, Israel, Lebanon, South Africa, Turkey

EUROPE 247
   Austria, Belgium, Britain, Denmark, Finland, France, West Germany, Greece, Holland, Hungary, Iceland, Ireland, Italy, Norway, Poland, Portugal, Spain, Sweden, Switzerland, Yugoslavia

LATIN AMERICA AND THE CARIBBEAN 381
   Argentina, Bolivia, Chile, Colombia, Dominica, Ecuador, El Salvador, Guadeloupe, Guatemala, Jamaica, Mexico, Netherlands Antilles, Panama, Peru, Puerto Rico, St Lucia, Suriname, Trinidad and Tobago, Uruguay, Venezuela

NORTH AMERICA 435
   Canada, United States

APPENDICES—

   A. MAHARISHI'S PHILOSOPHY OF WORLD PEACE 560

   **B. THREE STEPS TO PERMANENT WORLD PEACE—
       THE GLOBAL MAHARISHI EFFECT** 568

   C. EXPERIENCES AND ACCOUNTS OF FLYING 570

MAHARISHI'S PROGRAMME TO CREATE

WORLD PEACE • GLOBAL INAUGURATION

INTRODUCTION

With the dangerous rivalry of the superpowers and the rise of international terrorism, concern for world peace grows more acute each year. To answer this urgent need of our time, His Holiness Maharishi Mahesh Yogi has developed a programme to create coherence in world consciousness as the basis for immediate and lasting peace.

In July, August, and September of 1986, Maharishi inaugurated his programme to create world peace. In 108 countries, 10,000 experts in the Maharishi Technology of the Unified Field demonstrated the TM-Sidhi 'yogic flying' technique—the mechanics to eliminate war and terrorism without loss of life.

Nearly twelve years earlier, in December 1974, Maharishi was told the result of sociological research conducted by scientists at Maharishi International University in Fairfield, Iowa, U.S.A. Crime, accident, and sickness rates were falling unexpectedly in four cities that had one per cent of their populations practising the Transcendental Meditation technique.

On the basis of this scientific finding, Maharishi said, 'We have found the formula for the Age of Enlightenment. When crime can be quietly reduced in four cities, the same programme, given to all cities in the world, will bring the sunshine of the Age of Enlightenment.'

On 12 January 1975, Maharishi inaugurated the Dawn of the Age of Enlightenment for all mankind. During the first five months of that year, he toured the world inaugurating the Dawn of the Age of Enlightenment in each of the five major continents.

On 12 January 1976, Maharishi founded the World Government of the Age of Enlightenment.[*] He said the function of the World Government is to administer and perpetuate the Age of Enlightenment by bringing life everywhere in accord with natural law. The sovereignty of the World Government, Maharishi said, is in the domain of consciousness, its authority in the invincible power of natural law, and its activity in purifying world consciousness.

In the same year, Maharishi began training teachers of the Transcendental Meditation programme to be Governors of the Age of Enlightenment. Their role, he said, is to govern the trends of time from the field of consciousness by enlivening the evolutionary power of natural law through their twice daily practice of the TM-Sidhi programme. In 1977, Maharishi offered the TM-Sidhi programme to people everywhere who had learned the Transcendental Meditation technique.

In 1978, Maharishi launched his Ideal Society Campaign in 108 countries. Newly-trained TM-

---

*The World Government of the Age of Enlightenment is a non-political, non-religious, global organization with the participation of the people of more than 100 countries. It does not usurp any of the functions of existing governments, nor does it replace them in any way. The programmes of the World Government of the Age of Enlightenment offer to every government ideal administration patterned on the flawless government of nature, by which everything is evolutionary and harmonious.

MAHARISHI'S PROGRAMME TO CREATE

INTRODUCTION

Sidhas joined in the campaign with Governors of the Age of Enlightenment to help reduce crime and conflict and improve the quality of life. Later that same year, teams of Governors of the Age of Enlightenment travelled to the most troubled areas of the world and calmed the violence through their silent, self-referral performance of the Transcendental Meditation and TM-Sidhi programme.

In the winter of 1983-84, 7,000 TM-Sidhas—the square root of one per cent of the world's population at that time—assembled at MIU to create coherence in world consciousness from one place on earth. This gathering was called the Taste of Utopia Assembly, and it did bring a sample taste of utopia to the world. For the three weeks of that assembly, international conflicts, crime, sickness, and accidents dropped and global economic indicators improved. Since then, three more world peace assemblies of comparable size have been held, two in the U.S.A. and one in Holland. They, too, proved as good as their name, creating an upsurge of peace in the world.

By 1986, more than 50,000 people had learned the TM-Sidhi programme. Groups of TM-Sidhas were practising together in nearly every country on earth.

On 25 May 1986, Maharishi announced his programme to create world peace. He said, 'Time demands the rise of the supreme power in the world which can have authority over the dangerous rivalry of the superpowers and can act like a dear mother to all nations. Ten thousand experts in the Technology of the Unified Field together in India can create coherence in world consciousness, which will positively dominate over the dangerous rivalry of the superpowers. Everyone in the world family will rise together under an indomitable strength of evolutionary power of natural law. Every nation coming to the level of fulfilment will be no damage to the fulfilment of any other nation. This is what will establish a permanent state of world peace.'

On 9 July, Maharishi launched his programme to create world peace at the First North American 'Yogic Flying' Competition, held at the Capital Convention Center in Washington, D.C., U.S.A.

On 21 July, Maharishi held the First International 'Yogic Flying' Competition at Indira Gandhi Indoor Stadium, New Delhi, to spread his message from India throughout the world.

Then, on 15 August, TM-Sidhas demonstrated for the press and the leaders of their nations Maharishi's technology to create coherence in national and world consciousness. In Beijing and Guangzhou, Delhi and Madras, Bangkok and Manila, Sydney and Caracas, Washington and Ottawa, Johannesburg and Cairo, Lisbon and Oslo, Belgrade and Budapest, Vienna and Warsaw, Geneva and Paris, Beirut and Jerusalem—in 1,000 cities, TM-Sidhas demonstrated 'yogic flying', the mechanics to create world peace.

WORLD PEACE • GLOBAL INAUGURATION

INTRODUCTION

This book narrates these events of 1986. It begins with Maharishi's address on 9 July, in which he set forth the principles of his programme. Next, it discusses the scientific theory and experimental evidence that validate Maharishi's plan for world peace. A third chapter outlines the applications of Maharishi's technology to different areas of society. The book's major part describes the demonstrations of TM-Sidhi 'yogic flying'. More than 350 reports in 23 languages from 56 countries document the enthusiastic response of the world press to Maharishi's bold initiative, and appendices on Maharishi's philosophy of world peace, Maharishi's three steps to create world peace, and experiences and accounts of flying down through the ages show the range and completeness of Maharishi's programme.

Maharishi has said, 'World peace is the personal and immediate requirement of every significant man in the world today.' Now, with the Maharishi Technology of the Unified Field, the means to fulfil this requirement is available. This book is an invitation to every individual to create world peace today without waiting for tomorrow. □

MAHARISHI

Maharishi's Programme to Create World Peace
INAUGURAL ADDRESS

In a one-hour discourse, recorded on videotape at the World Capital of the Age of Enlightenment, Maharishi Nagar, India, and delivered on 8 July 1986 to more than 3,000 experts in the Maharishi Technology of the Unified Field gathered at the Capital Convention Center, Washington, D.C., U.S.A., for the World Assembly on Perfect Health, Maharishi summarized his programme to create world peace. The following passages have been excerpted from that historic address.

The Call of Our Time

It is really fulfilling today to inaugurate an effective programme for lasting world peace. It is very fulfilling to respond to the call of our time, which demands the rise of a supreme power in the world that can have real control over the dangerous rivalry of the superpowers. The whole world family has been under fear continuously for decades in the past. The political history in the world has not been very worthwhile, with all the wars and now with something worse than war—the present state of terrorism. Terrorism can burst out at any place at any time, and terrorism involving the superpowers has created a terrible time for the whole human race. The only thing that could rescue mankind today is the rise of a power greater than that now being displayed by the superpowers.

WORLD PEACE • GLOBAL INAUGURATION

MAHARISHI'S INAUGURAL ADDRESS

Holistic Programme to Create World Peace

Both of the superpowers aspire to create world peace. Their strength and the strength of their approaches to create world peace and happiness in life are based on the electronic, chemical, and nuclear levels of nature's functioning. These are specific, relative levels of natural law. Our programme to create world peace is holistic. It is from the most fundamental level of natural law, the unified field of all the laws of nature, that field from where all diverse laws of nature emerge and which maintains all the different values in the universe. The electronic, chemical, and nuclear levels—all the different levels of energy in nature have their source in the self-interacting dynamics of the unified field. It is a platform from where different streams of natural law are continuously promoted and nourished.

What Is Important Is the Level of Consciousness

The different levels of natural law have both values, creative and destructive. How they are used depends upon the level of consciousness of the user. Arms are useless only if the owner is peaceful. It's not the number of missiles that is important, it's the level of consciousness of the user—how nourishing or how destructive is that level of consciousness. The level of consciousness is influenced by the environment. That is why all the wise men have been saying, 'Reduce arms, reduce arms, reduce arms.' Looking to the history of the world, one might feel that if all the arms were not there then the world would be in peace. But think of a time a few thousand years ago when there were no guns and bombs. Was life on earth free from battles? There have been cruel fights. What is important is the level of consciousness, whether it's destructive or creative. We want to produce that quality of world consciousness where destructive tendencies will simply not arise and whatever such tendencies may exist will get extinguished.

DISCOVERY OF THE UNIFIED FIELD
Unification of the Four Fundamental Forces of Nature

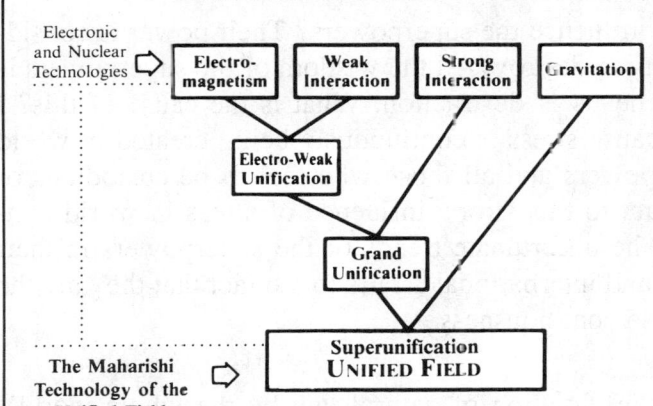

As the figure shows, all fundamental forces of nature are unified at the level of superunification.

The conclusion is that the Maharishi Technology of the Unified Field, being the technology of the most basic level of natural law, is superior to and more powerful than electronic, nuclear, and all other technologies at any level of nature's activity.

Another conclusion is that the future of all scientific research lies in the unified field, and the future progress of all mankind in the Maharishi Technology of the Unified Field, which is the technology of the subjective aspect of life—the basis of all objectivity in nature.

MAHARISHI'S PROGRAMME TO CREATE

MAHARISHI'S INAUGURAL ADDRESS

Unified Field Is Always Evolutionary

I want to emphasize that the nature of the unified field is only evolutionary. The power of the unified field is only nourishing. Destruction is non-existent in the unified field. This is a very important point. There is no danger of any destructive capability in the unified field. It is absolutely safe in the hands of those who know how to use it. Those knowers of the unified field, those who are practising the TM-Sidhi programme, have the skill of using the self-interacting dynamics of consciousness. They promote liveliness of the unified field in their own consciousness, and in groups they enliven the dormant self-interacting dynamics of the unified field to create harmony and an evolutionary influence in world consciousness. They promote coherence in world consciousness, and this spontaneously eliminates destructive trends and tendencies in life. Our means of establishing world peace are absolutely evolutionary, and therefore we feel absolutely safe in launching a programme to create peace in our dear world family.

Creating an Evolutionary Influence in World Consciousness

Here is a programme to skilfully use the total creative potential of natural law and create a very powerful evolutionary influence in world consciousness, so that destructive tendencies and thoughts will simply disappear, as darkness disappears with the onset of light. It's really very fulfilling for us to launch upon a programme which will eliminate the possibility of war without loss of life.

Raise National Law through Natural Law

Every country has its own natural law, and every nation is governed by its own national law. Our programme to create harmony in the world on the basis of the total potential of natural law can only create a powerful influence of coherence in every nation. It is our joy that this programme will raise national law in every nation through that evolutionary influence of natural law which is always nourishing to everyone. On that basis we see the reality that our programme will be the fulfilment of the aspirations of all nations, including the superpowers, for world peace.

Unfortunate Trends of the Superpowers Due to Stress in World Consciousness

How will this programme influence the superpowers? Their power is considered in terms of their ability to destroy. All the wisdom of the superpowers is focused on creating new means of destruction. What is the cause of this? I would say this is only because stress is continuously being created in world consciousness. The superpowers and all those who feel to be custodians of the world family must react to this strong influence of stress in world consciousness. I attribute all the unfortunate trends of the superpowers in their policies of administration and international affairs to the fact that they are the victims of the stress in world consciousness.

This stress is caused by the violation of natural law by the whole world's population. Why is that happening? Because nowhere is education dedicated

WORLD PEACE • GLOBAL INAUGURATION

MAHARISHI'S INAUGURAL ADDRESS

Objective Approach Does Not Train a Person to Act in an Evolutionary Way

to training the people to not violate the laws of nature. Education does not train the people to think and act spontaneously according to natural law. This is because modern scientific thinking has laid emphasis on the objective approach to unfolding the knowledge of natural law. Gaining the knowledge of electrons and protons in an objective way leaves a choice for the knower to use that knowledge for positive or negative results.

Pure Subjectivity— the Self-Interacting Dynamics of Consciousness

Very fortunately now, the sense of objectivity will be replaced by a very profound sense of subjectivity. Those few scientists who are probing into the nature of the unified field have glimpsed the total potential of natural law in terms of self-interacting dynamics. Self-interacting dynamics means subjectivity functioning within itself and promoting different laws of nature, which then promote matter and creation. These scientists are beginning to feel that objectivity is really an aspect of pure subjectivity.

Pure subjectivity means the self-interacting dynamics of consciousness, or pure intelligence. That is the basis of all creation, and that unified field we have located from the knowledge of the Veda, Vedic science, the science of pure knowledge. We have understood that reality to be a perpetual state of unity embedded in the nature of absolute peace in infinite dynamism.

Three-In-One Structure of the Unified Field

In that self-referral transcendental consciousness, in that peace where consciousness is fully awake, consciousness knows itself; it is the knower. Knowing itself, it is the known and the process of knowing—all three values in the structure of unified wholeness. This three-in-one structure is available to us from Rig Veda Samhita, the Samhita of Rishi, Devata, and Chhandas. The same three-in-one structure of the unified field is detailed by the supersymmetric unified field theories of quantum physics.

Enlivening the Evolutionary Power of the Unified Field in World Consciousness

This is pure subjectivity; and now we have the technology of the unified field, whereby pure subjectivity can be enlivened in world consciousness. That means the evolutionary power of the unified field is enlivened in world consciousness. That will never be in favour of destroying, because subjectivity will be nourished and become more and more powerful. Subjectivity becoming more and more powerful, what will prevail is increasing satisfaction in life on earth, increasing dignity of life, and increasing ability to nourish everything. This is what we want to promote in world consciousness, and this is the programme we are launching today.

A Power Greater than the Strength of the Superpowers

The only thing that can rescue mankind today is the rise of a power greater than the strength being displayed by the superpowers. The rise of this supreme, nourishing capability in world consciousness will transform the destructive tendencies of the superpowers. Their destructive abilities will remain, but their tendencies will be transformed and they will find a way to

MAHARISHI'S INAUGURAL ADDRESS

not use their knowledge of the electronic, nuclear, and chemical levels of natural law to destroy life. They will find ways to promote life through their knowledge of these levels of nature's functioning and will use their power to nourish all mankind.

Every Nation Will Rise in Fulfilment

We will see that the superpowers will naturally change their trends and there will be no terrorism, no threat of war, and no fear in the world family. Every nation will rise in fulfilment. Every government will experience real freedom. Whatever wars are seen here and there—the Iran-Iraq war, so much misfortune in South Africa and in Lebanon—all these negative things which should not be there will simply disappear. What will prevail is goodwill, cordiality, friendship. Everyone will be helpful to everyone. Every nation will be loving to every other nation. This is the kind of world family we will soon create.

Already, trends are seen in this direction. This has resulted from the purifying influence in world consciousness generated by such world assemblies as we have here today.

World Peace Is Holistic

During the last 30 years we have seen that all the different values of life—all areas of education, health, rehabilitation, defence, agriculture, trade, industry —all could be enhanced and raised to fulfilment through the help of natural law. On this basis, today we are inaugurating a programme in the name of world peace. World peace is a holistic value. Having seen that all different aspects of life can be individually handled and nourished through the technology of the unified field, today we are blowing the trumpet for a collective influence to create permanent peace in the world.

All Values of Individual Enrichment Offered in this Programme to Create World Peace

Launching this programme for permanent peace in the world is fulfilling for all the different programmes that we have launched through all these years. In 1978, we raised a voice for invincibility for every nation. There was the Year of Ideal Society, when we began a programme to create ideal society in 108 countries. In 1986, this Year of Perfect Health for All Mankind, we have developed our World Plan for Perfect Health to which so many nations are now responding. Today we sum up all those values of individual enrichment through our technology of the unified field and proclaim them all together in terms of the programme to create world peace.

Victory Before War

This is very, very fulfilling for us, because it's going to bring satisfaction to the greatest powers on earth. All these power blocs are going to fulfil their aspirations. Every military in the world would like to have a victory without fighting. Here is a programme for world peace through the technology of the unified field, whereby every military in the world will be invincible. Both the power blocs will enjoy victory before war, and every nation in the world will be invincible.

WORLD PEACE • GLOBAL INAUGURATION

MAHARISHI'S INAUGURAL ADDRESS

Individual Must Create Coherence in World Consciousness

The state of world peace will be perpetual when the unified field is lived in all the different aspects of daily life of all the people on earth. For that we need to create an influence of coherence in world consciousness. Then we will see how beautifully friendly the superpowers will be to each other. The individuals of the world must create that coherence in world consciousness on the basis of which the superpowers will become such great, close friends that they will join hands in nourishing all nations.

If the superpowers are not succeeding in becoming friends, this is because of the intense stress in world consciousness which we, through this technology of the unified field, must neutralize. This is how we are responding to the call of our time. We will be creating that beautiful atmosphere of cordiality in which the superpowers can only be friends and never enemies. Every nation in the world will cease to have any enemy. The whole world family will be united.

'The World Is My Family'

This is the ideal of life in India. In India they say, 'Vasudevah Kutumbakam'—'the world is my family'. Because of this value of life in India to embrace all mankind as one's own family, and because of India's history as a common friend to all nations all the time, we have decided to create a group of 7,000 in India.

Rise of that Supreme Power Which is Only Evolutionary and Nourishing

The fulfilment of the requirement of our time will be the rise of that supreme power which will have only an evolutionary, nourishing ability. In a natural way, most silently, it will not allow anything that would be destructive to life. I am quite sure the superpowers will be happy that now pure knowledge from modern science and Vedic science is rising to help them to accomplish their cherished goal of nourishing life everywhere. Very soon, capitalism in the world will find fulfilment—all the people will have affluence in life. All the cherished goals of communism to destroy poverty, improve creativity, and have no conflict—all these cherished goals will be fulfilled. The beautiful goals of all political values and all values of religion will be fulfilled. Today we have a very full heart overflowing for all mankind to bring fulfilment to all philosophies, old and new, and to raise our human race to a level of life which may be heavenly on earth.

7,000 Experts in the Technology of the Unified Field to Enliven the Evolutionary Power of Natural Law

World peace on a permanent basis is the requirement of the time; it is the requirement of life. What is required to make world peace permanent is the maintenance of one group of 7,000 experts in the technology of the unified field in one place on earth, and then, in time, a few groups of 7,000 practising this technology in all the continents. These groups of 7,000 will enliven the evolutionary influence of natural law in world consciousness. They will create a natural situation in which negative trends and destructive tendencies will simply not arise.

MAHARISHI'S PROGRAMME TO CREATE

MAHARISHI'S INAUGURAL ADDRESS

World Peace—the Personal and Immediate Requirement of Every Significant Man in the World Today

What I see is that world peace is the personal and immediate requirement of every significant man in the world today, and that means anyone who loves his life and the life of his neighbour. I invite every significant man in the world to rise to his responsibility and not postpone the creation of groups of 7,000 on earth for tomorrow. Every today is important, and every tomorrow is going to be important. We have the knowledge, and we should be able to give the gift of this knowledge to all mankind.

All glory to Guru Dev, whose teachings have given us this ability to free mankind from suffering, and whose blessings have made us capable of bringing fulfilment to all the nations in the world. That is our joy, with which we are inaugurating our programme to create world peace. □

WORLD PEACE • GLOBAL INAUGURATION

One of the largest non-political news conferences in Washington history: more than 120 journalists crowd a conference room at the Capital Convention Center, Washington, DC, for a briefing on Maharishi's Programme to Create World Peace.

'We want to give you a glimpse today of the new technology to create maximum coherence in brain functioning as the foundation for permanent world peace'—Dr Vinton Tompkins opening the 9 July news conference.

Maharishi's Programme To Create World Peace
A BRIEFING FOR THE WORLD PRESS

9 July 1986 • Capital Convention Center, Washington, D.C., U.S.A.

Dr Vinton Tompkins

MODERATOR: Eighty-three years ago and a few hundred miles from this place, man made his first powered flight: 120 feet, airborne for only 12 seconds. That hop at Kitty Hawk demonstrated the first stage of flying, and we all know what it has led to. Today, everyone accepts flight as commonplace, forgetting that the Wright Brothers' achievement was greeted with much skepticism.

We have called this press conference because we don't want such history to repeat itself. We want to give the world a preview now of what is in store from a vastly more powerful technology than that which propelled the first aircraft—a technology of the unified field of all the laws of nature. We hope to give you a glimpse today of the potential of the Maharishi Technology of the Unified Field for creating maximum coherence in brain functioning and, on that basis, coherence in the whole of world consciousness as the foundation for permanent world peace.

This morning's conference will be conducted in three stages. First, we will explain the principles of Maharishi's Programme to Create World Peace and the scientific research results that validate the effectiveness of its application. Then, we will demonstrate the technology to create coherence in world

MAHARISHI'S PROGRAMME TO CREATE

A BRIEFING FOR THE WORLD PRESS

consciousness as the basis of world peace. This will be done at the finals of the North American 'Yogic Flying' Competition. After that, members of the press will have an opportunity to question the scientists, the winners, and some of the 3,000 other 'yogic flyers' who are here in Washington attending the World Assembly on Perfect Health.

To begin the briefing, it's my great pleasure to introduce Dr Bevan Morris, President and Chairman of the Board of Trustees of Maharishi International University in Fairfield, Iowa, U.S.A.

DR MORRIS: Today is the inauguration of a programme to create world peace through a technology which creates coherence in collective consciousness and neutralizes the stress in society.

No solution has ever been found to the problem of world peace. Treaties, international organizations, disarmament conferences, use of arms—none of the solutions that have been tried have ever worked. Even as we speak, wars rage in the world. The world is covered by a pall of fear of war and terrorism and of the consequences in this nuclear age of the rivalry between the superpowers. What will be presented here today is evidence of a practical programme to fulfil the need for world peace—group practice of the Maharishi Technology of the Unified Field.

Dr Bevan Morris

Stress Is the Basic Cause of War

According to His Holiness Maharishi Mahesh Yogi, the founder of this programme, and according to the tradition of Vedic science from which Maharishi comes, war is caused by the build-up of stress in the collective consciousness of nations. Every day in every nation, people are violating the laws of nature. That means that they are performing actions which injure themselves, their neighbours, and their environment. These wrong actions cause stress in the individual and society as a whole. According to Maharishi's philosophy of world peace, stress in society can build up only to a certain point before the society explodes into some kind of calamity.

Transcendental Meditation Releases Stress

Many people in the world are well aware that the Transcendental Meditation programme relieves stress in the individual by creating extraordinarily deep mental and physical rest and relaxation. It produces a more coherent, orderly, and efficient style of functioning of the nervous system, which increases creativity and intelligence, improves health, and results in greater harmony with the laws of nature and fewer mistakes in daily life. All this is well supported by hundreds of scientific studies.

What we are adding to this today is the knowledge that practice of Maharishi's programme by many people together in the same place at the same time relieves not only the individual's stresses but can relieve the stress in society

WORLD PEACE • GLOBAL INAUGURATION

A BRIEFING FOR THE WORLD PRESS

as a whole. This is especially the case with the advanced programme of Transcendental Meditation, called the TM-Sidhi programme. The TM-Sidhi techniques enhance the effect of Transcendental Meditation in improving co-ordination between mind and body. When these more powerful techniques are practised by people together in groups, a coherent and orderly collective consciousness is created in society. The stress and incoherence in the life of the nation, which is the basic cause of world war, is eliminated.

TM-Sidhi 'Yogic Flying'

The most powerful of all these TM-Sidhi techniques is called the 'yogic flying' technique. At the moment when the body is about to lift up during 'yogic flying', optimal coherence of brain functioning occurs. Research has shown that group practice of this technique produces what is called the Maharishi Effect, an effect which spreads coherence throughout the society from the individuals practising the technique. This has been found to create peace even in the midst of war-torn environments where nothing else has worked.

Unified Field of All the Laws of Nature

How is this possible? It is because of the unified field of all the laws of nature. At this level of nature's functioning, all the matter and all the forces of nature are unified, and from this level all the laws of nature in the universe arise. This most fundamental field of nature is now being glimpsed by modern science through supersymmetric unified quantum field theories. But the unified field has been known in the ancient tradition of Vedic science for thousands of years.

Enlivening the Evolutionary Qualities of the Unified Field in the Entire Society

Vedic science describes the human brain as so sophisticated that it is possible for human consciousness to directly identify itself with this basic field. The human mind can experience this field through Transcendental Meditation and enliven it through the TM-Sidhi programme. Because this field is a field of infinite correlation, it connects all of us together. When you enliven this field, you enliven everywhere its basic qualities—unity, harmony, coherence—and the evolutionary influence thus generated instantaneously spreads from a small group of individuals who are practising the technique throughout the entire society, neutralizing negative tendencies and stresses.

7,000—the Formula for World Peace

This is called the Maharishi Effect. It has been found that the square root of one per cent of the world is what is necessary to produce the Maharishi Effect globally. The square root of one per cent of the world's population is about 7,000 people. Our immediate aim is to have a permanent group of at least 7,000 people practising this technology in India. Once groups of 7,000 TM-Sidhas have been established not only in India but in every continent, and once the square root of one per cent of the population of every nation and every city is practising Maharishi's technology, world peace will be perpetual. This, in essence, is Maharishi's programme to create world peace.

I would now like to introduce Dr R. Keith Wallace, President of Maharishi

MAHARISHI'S PROGRAMME TO CREATE

A BRIEFING FOR THE WORLD PRESS

Vedic University here in Washington and Chairman of the Department of Physiological and Biological Sciences at MIU. Dr Wallace is an authority on the physiological research on the Maharishi Technology of the Unified Field. He will give a brief description of research findings indicating coherence in individual physiology and psychology through the Transcendental Meditation and TM-Sidhi programme.

Dr R. Keith Wallace

DR WALLACE: Over 360 different scientific studies in 27 countries at more than 160 independent universities and research institutions have demonstrated the benefits of the Maharishi Technology of the Unified Field. Many of these studies have been published in leading journals, including *Science, American Journal of Physiology, Electroencephalography and Clinical Neurophysiology, International Journal of Neuroscience, Psychosomatic Medicine, British Journal of Psychology, Education, Criminal Justice and Behavior, Academy of Management Journal*, and many more.

These studies have found an integrated physiological response during practice of the Transcendental Meditation and TM-Sidhi programme. They describe a profound state of rest with many unique metabolic changes, including an entire redistribution of blood flow, changes in levels of certain hormones, a reduction of blood lactate, and many others.

Improved Physiological and Psychological Performance in Activity

This programme has comprehensive effects on activity. Even though a state of deep rest is achieved during the technique, outside of meditation the individual has a faster reaction time; faster recovery of certain spinal reflexes; improved perceptual-motor performance; improved cognitive function as seen in improved memory, intelligence, creativity, and academic performance; and a number of beneficial changes in the personality. In short, the programme creates coherence and integration of functioning at all levels, which improve the overall performance of the physiology and psychology.

Better Health

This is clearly seen in the field of health. A number of studies at major medical institutions have shown reductions in blood pressure in hypertensive patients, reductions in cholesterol, better recovery and adaptation to stress, and improvement in a variety of different stress-related conditions such as asthma and insomnia.

Reversal of Ageing

Perhaps the most interesting studies are those which have shown a reversal of the ageing process itself, particularly in long-term practitioners of the TM and TM-Sidhi programme. They have biological ages that are 12 to 15 years younger than their chronological ages. In addition, longitudinal studies show that the biological age is one-and-a-half years less after one-and-a-half years practice of this programme. A study that will be presented at a neuroscience conference in Washington, D.C., in November 1986 shows that one of the

WORLD PEACE • GLOBAL INAUGURATION

A BRIEFING FOR THE WORLD PRESS

best biochemical markers of the ageing process, serum dehydroepiandrosterone sulfate (DHEAS), which is a hormone that decreases from about age 20 to age 70 in a very linear fashion, remains at high levels in people practising this technique, particularly at the older ages. Another study looked at medical insurance utilization and found that both the in- and out-patient services required by people practising the TM and TM-Sidhi programme were half those of the norms.

But something more than good health and development of mental potential is offered by Maharishi's programme. It creates high coherence in the physiology, particularly in the functioning of the brain. This is especially true of the TM-Sidhi 'yogic flying' technique. I would like to ask Dr David Orme-Johnson to tell you about this and related effects. Dr Orme-Johnson is Chairman of the Department of Psychology at MIU and Co-director of the MIU Doctoral Programmes in Psychology and the Neuroscience of Human Consciousness.

Dr David Orme-Johnson

DR ORME-JOHNSON: From electroencephalographic (EEG) research we have found that the Transcendental Meditation technique produces a very coherent and simple style of brain functioning, and that the TM-Sidhi 'yogic flying' technique integrates this with dynamic activity. Our theory is that the experience of the simplest style of brain functioning, which is also the simplest state of our own awareness, constitutes the direct experience of the unified field of all the laws of nature, which is integrating and harmonizing in its essential character. When the individual practises the 'yogic flying' technique, he enlivens these qualities of the unified field and radiates that influence throughout society. I would like to describe briefly the coherence in individual brain functioning that occurs during the TM and TM-Sidhi programme and discuss the effects of this coherence radiating in society.

Coherence in Brain Functioning

When one examines the EEG of a non-meditator, one sees simple, synchronous activity in some parts of the brain and more complex, desynchronized activity elsewhere. In TM meditators, one sees a high level of synchrony during practice of the Transcendental Meditation technique across all the areas of the brain. This has been studied using a measure called 'coherence'. Coherence is determined through a sophisticated computer analysis of the brain wave data that identifies episodes of highly synchronized patterns of electrical activity from different parts of the brain. Such computer programmes monitor specific electrical cycles and look for peaks on the computer print-out that represent a coherence greater than 95 per cent between the wave forms of the electrical activity of different parts of the brain. Long-term TM meditators show very high levels of coherence. During the TM-Sidhi 'yogic flying' technique, one sees maximum coherence. Brain wave coherence also increases longitudinally. Measure the EEG of a TM meditator today, in three

Maximum Coherence during 'Yogic Flying'

months, and again after a year, and you will see increasing coherence in the different brain areas compared with control groups. (Please refer to the charts on page 17.)

Significance of Brain Wave Coherence

The functional significance of high coherence has been proven in our laboratory and in many other laboratories around the world. Individuals with higher levels of brain wave coherence are more creative, have higher levels of moral judgement, are more intelligent, and can assimilate information from the environment more efficiently.

Coherence in the Midst of Dynamic Activity— the Uniqueness of TM-Sidhi 'Yogic Flying'

During the experience of transcendental consciousness, the direct experience of the unified field, brain functioning becomes most coherent. This coherence first appears strongly in the alpha frequency band and through regular practice spreads to the slower and faster frequencies as well. During the TM-Sidhi 'yogic flying' technique, the same experience of high coherence across all brain wave frequencies is enjoyed in the midst of dynamic activity—the hopping phenomenon characteristic of the first stage of 'yogic flying'. Comparing the effects of the same individuals voluntarily jumping or practising the TM-Sidhi 'yogic flying' technique, researchers found that only 'yogic flying' produces this strong brain wave coherence together with dynamic activity.

Maharishi Effect

This brings us to the most fascinating research findings on the TM and TM-Sidhi programme, which are obviously relevant to Maharishi's Programme to Create World Peace. When individuals enliven the unified field of natural law through practice of the Maharishi Technology of the Unified Field, everyone in the environment shares the benefits. Like a wave coming in from the ocean on which everything bobs up and down together, the coherence generated from the level of the unified field by a few people enriches the lives of all and of the population as a whole. This is called the Maharishi Effect.

Improved Quality of Life

7,000 to Create the Global Maharishi Effect

Thirty-one studies on the Maharishi Effect have shown that practice of the Transcendental Meditation and TM-Sidhi programme by a small proportion of the population improves the quality of life throughout society. These studies have analyzed data from objective public data sources using the most advanced statistical techniques, and they have demonstrated on a day-by-day or week-by-week basis that changes in the size of the coherence-creating group practising the TM and TM-Sidhi programme create changes in the quality of life. With a group of 7,000 TM-Sidhas—approximately the square root of one per cent of the world's population—the quality of life throughout the world is improved. Likewise, the square root of one per cent of the population of a city or nation practising the TM-Sidhi 'yogic flying' technique together in one place creates the Maharishi Effect for that city or nation.

Before reviewing the results of the many studies on the Maharishi Effect, I

WORLD PEACE • GLOBAL INAUGURATION

A BRIEFING FOR THE WORLD PRESS

EEG RESEARCH LOCATES THE UNIT OF WORLD PEACE IN THE HUMAN BRAIN

The coherence spectral array (COSPAR) displays coherence of the EEG, the electrical activity of the brain. The COSPARs of individuals practicing the Maharishi Technology of the Unified Field show sharp increases in orderliness even for the first session of practice, and they exhibit a progressive increase as the practice advances. Figure 6 shows a pattern closely similar to that of a 15-year practitioner occurring during the TM-Sidhi "yogic flying" technique in a subject who had been practicing it for less than two years.

Coherence of the EEG rhythms between different brain areas suggest greater orderliness in brain functioning. These studies summarize the increase in orderliness in brain functioning arising from experience of the unified field in the state of transcendental consciousness. Through repeated experience the individual develops the habit to project thought and action from this simplest form of awareness, making thought and action most natural and therefore spontaneously evolutionary—fully in accord with all the laws of nature, free from suffering, mistakes, and problems. By enlivening the unified field at the basis of all life, the individual practicing the Maharishi Technology of the Unified Field is creating a powerful influence of coherence in world consciousness, transforming the trends of time and laying the foundation for permanent world peace.

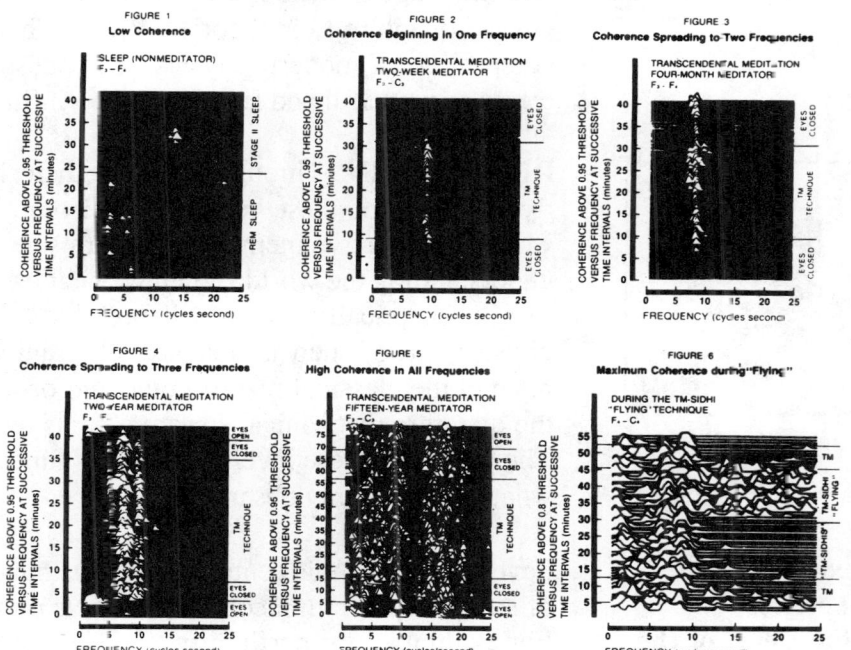

Creating Coherence in World Consciousness and Locating the Seat of World Peace in the Coherently Functioning Brain Physiology of the Individual

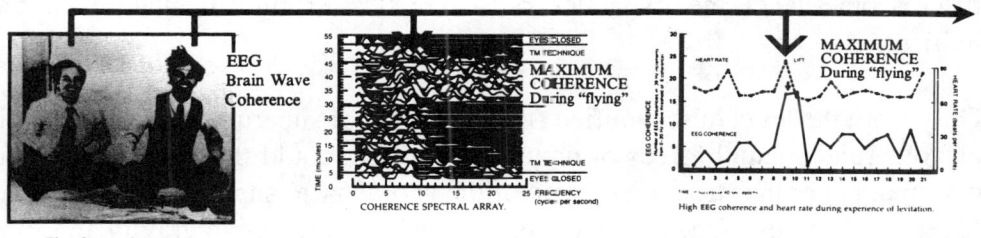

Maximum coherence in brain waves accomplishes the specific ability. In the case of the "flying" ability, the body lifts up at the point of maximum coherence.

Optimum brain functioning, as indicated by maximum coherence (orderliness) in brain wave activity during the TM-Sidhi practice of the Maharishi Technology of the Unified Field, creates the perfect conditions for the frictionless flow of awareness towards the fulfillment of its desire. The principle of least action, which governs all activity in nature and uses the skill of nature to quietly accomplish everything, is available in its optimum value when brain wave coherence is maximum and awareness is in its simplest state—transcendental consciousness.

In one aspect of the TM-Sidhi program, called the "flying" technique, at the moment of maximum coherence in brain wave activity the body lifts up and begins to hop (the first stage of "flying"). Simultaneously, the person experiences waves of exhilaration and profound stabilization of the silent level of awareness, the experience of the unified field of all the laws of nature, the total potential of natural law. In this way the "flying" technique accelerates evolution to enlightenment—the state of fulfillment in which life is lived in full accord with natural law, free of suffering and problems.

The phenomenon produced by the TM-Sidhi procedure of "flying" gives the experience of bliss and generates coherence between consciousness and matter in the body. EEG studies have shown that during this phenomenon, when the body lifts up in the air, matter and consciousness are completely integrated. This integration takes place at the level of the unified field of natural law, which has the character of infinite correlation. The impulse of coherence from this level instantly reconstructs the discordant tendencies in nature to become coherent.

In this way the phenomenon of coherence spreads, neutralizing the negative tendencies in the whole creation. This is how modern science confirms the prediction of Maharishi Patanjali, who said in his Yoga Sutras:

Tat sannidhau vairatyagah
"In the vicinity of coherence (yoga), hostile tendencies are eliminated."

One group of 7000 will generate a sufficiently strong influence of coherence to radiate globally and purify the whole world consciousness. This explains Maharishi's mechanics of creating world peace and shows how perfect is Maharishi's approach to world peace, both as it is understood and applied through ancient Vedic Science and as it is verified by modern science.

This is the scientific basis of Maharishi's program to create world peace and of the decision to create the Maharishi World Peace Fund to establish and maintain a group of ten thousand experts in the Maharishi Technology of the Unified Field.

MAHARISHI'S PROGRAMME TO CREATE

A BRIEFING FOR THE WORLD PRESS

would like to introduce the Chairman of the Department of Physics at MIU, Dr John Hagelin, who is a world leader in the development of supersymmetric unified quantum field theories. We will hear from Dr Hagelin how, from the perspective of modern physics, it is possible for Maharishi's technology to create so powerful and far-reaching an influence of coherence.

DR HAGELIN: Through the ages there have been many accounts of men flying. Most of these reports date from before the last few hundred years when the objective method of modern science has dominated our approach to understanding the world. When we hear of flying in this scientific age we tend to ask, skeptically, How is it possible? Wouldn't flying be a violation of physical laws, such as the law of gravity? But science today has looked beyond the classical macroscopic and observable levels of nature to glimpse the quantum mechanical structure of its most fundamental space-time scales. The picture at these levels of nature's functioning is a very different one from what we commonly observe.

Dr John Hagelin

Maximum Coherence at the Level of the Unified Field

Several times in this century physicists have been surprised by the appearance of striking quantum mechanical effects on the observable, macroscopic level. For example, in superfluidity, fluids display zero viscosity and will continue to flow indefinitely once set in motion. Such phenomena appear to contradict the laws of nature, but actually they give us a glimpse of the nature of physical reality at fundamental space-time scales. 'Yogic flying' demonstrates on the macroscopic level the dynamics of nature's most fundamental level, the unified field.

Quantum Gravity and 'Yogic Flying'

Only from the level of the unified field, the level of superunification, at which all four fundamental forces of nature are unified, could there be that natural command over the structure of space-time geometry to support 'yogic flying'. Classical theories of gravitation, theories such as Newtonian gravity and Einstein's general relativity, cannot explain 'yogic flying'. However, quantum gravity can. Quantum gravity is a theory of gravity which ordinarily applies to the nature of physics at the scale of the unified field. This is a level of nature's functioning which is prior to classical space-time geometry. At this level, space-time geometry is dynamically generated. It is possible, through the generation of a sustained coherent influence at the level of the unified field, to modify the local curvature of space-time geometry described in general relativity in such a way that the body flies up, or to the left, or forward, or in any possible direction. On the basis of currently conceivable ideas in physics, it is only through a technology of the unified field that 'yogic flying' is possible.

Functioning at the Level of the Unified Field

The demonstration of 'yogic flying' illustrates that the individual human nervous system has sufficient, integrated complexity to function at the level of the unified field. It proves the nervous system's capability to function at the level at which all the laws of nature are unified. From this perspective, the brain wave coherence which is maximum during 'yogic flying' represents an upsurge of coherence from the level of the unified field itself.

'Yogic Flying' and the Maharishi Effect

How does this understanding of 'yogic flying' relate to the Maharishi Effect? From a physical standpoint, ordinary influences among people are dominated by electromagnetism. They are of insufficient strength to explain the propagation of coherence throughout society over the distances seen in the Maharishi Effect. Therefore, it is necessary to invoke an understanding of nature which is prior to the understanding of classical space-time geometry, and this is the level of the unified field. 'Yogic flying' demonstrates the ability to function at this most fundamental scale. It is precisely this mastery that is required to explain the Maharishi Effect.

Infinite Correlation— a Quality of the Unified Field

One quality of the unified field which helps to explain the Maharishi Effect is infinite correlation. A somewhat technical explanation of infinite correlation is this: The scale of superunification at the level of the unified field is associated with a fundamental phase transition in the structure of natural law from a diversified state to a completely unified state. In physics, the defining characteristic of a phase transition is that the 'correlation length', which is a measure of the connectedness or correlation of different components of a system, becomes infinite. At the scale of superunification, all aspects of natural law at every point in the universe become infinitely correlated with each other. This means that a delicate impulse at one point in the system can create a precipitous change throughout the entire universe. This long-range correlation explains how action on the level of the unified field can have an influence that spreads anywhere and everywhere throughout the universe. In this way, the phenomenon of coherence spreads, neutralizing negative tendencies in the whole creation.

Danger of Fragmented Knowledge of Natural Law

Creating Peace on the Basis of Holistic Knowledge of Natural Law

The unified field is completely holistic in its nature. Only from this unified fountainhead of natural law can a completely holistic influence be produced. Such a holistic influence cannot be achieved through a partial, fragmented knowledge of nature's functioning. History records the dangerous effects of activity based on the knowledge of the more superficial electronic and nuclear levels of nature's dynamics. Only from the level of the unified field could an influence of harmony and peace, an influence of wholeness, be generated in the world. By demonstrating the capability of the human nervous system to function from the level of the unified field, 'yogic flying' demonstrates its ability to generate a holistic influence of coherence in world consciousness, the basis of world peace.

World peace can be achieved by as few as 7,000 experts practising the Maharishi Technology of the Unified Field together in one place. The power,

Principle of Constructive Interference

or intensity, of a field is proportional to the square of the amplitude of the field. This coherent summation of amplitudes by many sources is a principle known in physics as constructive interference. We make use of this principle at the level of the unified field through group practice of the Maharishi Technology of the Unified Field, giving us the formula of the square root of one per cent to create the Maharishi Effect.

Scientific Research on the Maharishi Effect

I hope that these brief remarks from the perspective of physics have provided some insight into Maharishi's Programme to Create World Peace. Earlier in this conference, Dr Orme-Johnson introduced on the research on the Maharishi Effect. Over 30 consecutive studies have documented this remarkable finding, which has already become one of the most thoroughly established sociological phenomenon ever studied. I would like to ask Dr Orme-Johnson to review the results of some of these studies, which document the Maharishi Effect on the city, state, national, and world levels.

Dr David Orme-Johnson

DR ORME-JOHNSON: Research has found repeatedly that a very small proportion of a city's population practising the Transcendental Meditation technique—as little as one per cent distributed throughout the population—creates the Maharishi Effect in the city. This has been measured in terms of reduced crime and accident rates and reduced problems of mental health.

The first study on the Maharishi Effect in cities was conducted by Landrith and others in 1976. They compared changes in crime rate from 1972 to 1973 in 11 U.S. cities that had more than one per cent of their populations practising the TM technique with 11 control cities matched for population size, college population, and geographic region. They found an 8.2 per cent drop in crime rate in the TM cities and an 8.3 per cent increase in the control cities, the latter being typical of the nation-wide trend at that time: in short, a relative drop of 16.5 per cent in crime rate in the TM cities that was statistically significant to less than one in one thousand. They also found that this decrease in crime rate could not have been attributed to year, population, region, or initial crime rate. Hatchard (1977) and Dillbeck (1978) further showed that decreased crime rate in high-TM cities was not due to year, income, police protection, or a number of other possible demographic variables.

Maharishi Effect Is Multi-Dimensional

Landrith and Dillbeck (1983) were the first to demonstrate that the Maharishi Effect was multi-dimensional—not just crime but suicides and auto accidents were less in one per cent TM cities. In a study the next year, Dillbeck, Landrith, Polanzi, and Baker took the enquiry a step further, using causal analysis to show that the percentage of TM participants in large samples of U.S. cities and metropolitan areas predicted decreased crime in the following years. This was additional evidence for a causal influence on decreased crime associated

WORLD PEACE • GLOBAL INAUGURATION

A BRIEFING FOR THE WORLD PRESS

with practice of the TM technique.

Maharishi Effect Calms the Violence of War in Lebanon

Crime is one kind of incoherence in a city; another is the greater turbulence of civil war. Abou-Nader, Alexander, and Davies (1984) analyzed the effects of the TM programme in the Lebanese community of Baskinta, which lay in an area of on-going armed conflict. Unlike other villages in the same war zone, Baskinta was fortunate to have more than one per cent of its population trained in the TM technique by July 1982. The researchers examined the amount of shelling and property damage in Baskinta and the neighbouring communities for a baseline period from October 1978 to June 1982 and the experimental period from July 1982 to March 1984. They also looked at casualties in Baskinta during the two periods. They found highly significant decreases in all these three dependent variables in Baskinta during the experimental period, both compared to its own baseline period and to each of the control villages. It was becoming clear that the TM technique not only reduced crime and accident rates in a city but also calmed the violence of war. Scientific evidence to support Maharishi's solution to the problem of world peace was emerging.

TM-Sidhi Programme and the Extended Maharishi Effect

The progress towards a practical formula for world peace had taken a giant leap forward in 1976-77, when Maharishi introduced the TM-Sidhi programme. As we heard from Dr Wallace, scientists found this programme produced even more dramatic effects of coherence and integration in individual physiology and psychology than did the TM technique. Accordingly, they suggested that far fewer than one per cent of a population practising this programme—in particular, the 'yogic flying' technique—would produce the Maharishi Effect. And if these TM-Sidhas were congregated in one place, their influence should be more powerful, meaning that an even smaller number would produce the same effect. As we heard from Dr Hagelin, the intensity or power of a coherent system grows as the square of its number of elements. One per cent was the empirically determined constant ascertained from the previous studies on the Maharishi Effect. Therefore, the scientists hypothesized that as little as the square root of one per cent of the population practising the TM-Sidhi programme together in one place would be enough. Various examples of coherent physical and biological systems, such as the laser, lent further credence to what they called the Super Radiance Effect, or the extended Maharishi Effect.

Research on the Ideal Society Campaign

In 1983, Dillbeck, Foss, and Zimmerman verified the extended Maharishi Effect in a study of Rhode Island state in the U.S.A. Looking at total crime, mortality, traffic fatality, and auto accident rates, and at pollution, unemployment, and other parameters, they found that 300 TM-Sidhas in Rhode Island during the Ideal Society Campaign, 12 June to 12 September 1978, significantly improved the quality of life in the state. Similarly, Dillbeck, Cavanaugh, and Berg (1983) found an 11 per cent drop in crime when a large group of

TM-Sidhas participated in the Vedic Science Course in the Union Territory of Delhi, India, from November 1980 to March 1981. During that period, there were neither significant changes in police procedure or policy nor any seasonal changes to account for the improvement. Both of these studies used time series analysis to control for possible cyclical patterns in the data and to accurately measure the extended Maharishi Effect.

Extended Maharishi Effect on a National Scale

Another study the same year demonstrated the extended Maharishi Effect on a national scale. Burgmans, Burgt, Langenkamp, and Vestegen examined crime trends in Holland and found significant decreases in crime rate during three one-month assemblies of TM-Sidhas numbering more than the square root of one per cent of the country's population. The researchers also found a significant decrease in traffic accidents.

Extended Maharishi Effect Improves Quality of Life in the U.S.A.

From July to August 1979, 2,500 TM-Sidhas assembled in Amherst, Massachusetts, U.S.A., to demonstrate the extended Maharishi Effect for the first time in a country of large population. Davies and Alexander (1983) found statistically significant drops in traffic fatalities, violent crimes, and air fatalities for the entire U.S.A. during this period. The decreases were even larger in the state of Massachusetts.

In the following year, Orme-Johnson and Gelderloos studied the percentages of 12 major quality of life indicators for the U.S.A. over a 25-year period, including crime, infectious diseases, suicide, cigarette and alcohol consumption, real gross national product, patent applications, academic degrees conferred, divorce, and auto fatalities. They found that year by year through the 1960s and early 1970s the quality of life in the U.S.A. as a whole was getting worse. In 1976, there was a sudden rise in the number of TM meditators in the U.S.A.—about 40,000 beginning the practice of the TM techniqueevery month—and the quality of life in the nation began to improve. Then, on numerous occasions in 1982, 1983, and 1984, the number of people practising the TM-Sidhi programme together in the Golden Domes of Pure Knowledge at Maharishi International University rose to more than 1,600. This was approximately the square root of one per cent of the nation's population, and the quality of life in the U.S.A. improved at an unprecedented rate.

To see if this change was being produced from MIU, the investigators used time series analysis. In this procedure, one obtains daily and weekly data over an extended period and then looks at the specific relationships between the fluctuations in the number of TM-Sidhas practising together and the changes in the data.

For example, Orme-Johnson, Cavanaugh, and Kreiger used time series analysis in a 1983 study of U.S. economic trends. Gathering daily data on the

WORLD PEACE • GLOBAL INAUGURATION

A BRIEFING FOR THE WORLD PRESS

Research Finds that 1,600 TM-Sidhas at MIU Led U.S. Economic Recovery

stock market and U.S. Treasury bonds, they found that 1,600 TM-Sidhas at MIU had a significant impact on both. The stock market generally leads economic recoveries, and the MIU Super Radiance group led the market, helping to catalyze the dramatic U.S. economic recovery of 1982-83. Every time there was a sudden rise in the number of TM-Sidhas in MIU's Golden Domes, bringing that number over the threshold of 1,600, the stock market increased sharply in the following weeks. In fact, 80 per cent of the increase during the bull market at the end of 1982 and during 1983 occurred in 20 per cent of the time, which were the one-week periods immediately following the rapid rises in the number of TM-Sidhas at MIU to over 1,600. A similar study by Dillbeck, Larimore, and Wallace (1984) using time series analysis found a significant decrease in U.S. national daily traffic fatalities in the days immediately after there were 1,600 TM-Sidhas at MIU.

In their study of the effect of the TM-Sidhi programme on overall quality of life in the U.S.A., Orme-Johnson and Gelderloos showed a similar result. Declines in infectious diseases, traffic fatalities, infant mortality, divorce, and the use of distilled spirits for the U.S.A. were led in time by high numbers of TM-Sidhas at MIU. As had been found with the Amherst study, the effect was stronger nearer the coherence-creating group; that is, the results in Iowa were greater than the national effect.

Israel Peace Project

The extended Maharishi Effect for Lebanon has been studied four times. In August and September of 1983, a group equivalent to the square root of one per cent of the population of Israel was gathered together in Jerusalem to test the hypothesis that a coherence-creating group of TM-Sidhas of sufficient size in Israel would actually decrease conflict in neighbouring Lebanon. The research project was undertaken jointly by MIU and Harvard University with support from the Fund for Higher Education, a non-profit organization independent of the TM movement.

Orme-Johnson, Alexander, Davies, Chandler, and Larimore (1984) found that when the group in Jerusalem was sufficiently large, war deaths in Lebanon dropped by as much as 70 per cent. As the size of the group varied over two months in a virtually random fashion, the number of war deaths in Lebanon varied inversely: when the group was larger there were fewer war deaths, and when it was smaller war deaths increased. Time series analysis revealed that the reduction in war deaths could not have been anticipated from any trends or cycles in the data. The reduction was unprecedented, and had been predicted in advance by the research team to an independent group of scientists in Israel and the United States. The effect of 'yogic flying' on creating peace was predicted to occur, and it did in fact occur.

When the coherence-creating group grew larger, not only did war deaths drop in Lebanon but the quality of life improved in Israel. Many complex sociological variables showed simultaneous improvement. There were fewer traffic fatalities, a lower crime rate, increases in the stock market, and improvements in the national mood.

Creating Progress towards Peace in Lebanon

Alexander, Abou-Nader, Cavanaugh, Davies, Dillbeck, Kfoury, and Orme-Johnson (1984) found marked reductions in the intensity of the Lebanese conflict on three other occasions: during two international assemblies of TM-Sidhas—one at MIU in the winter of 1983-84 and another in Yugoslavia in April 1984—and one course in Lebanon for 17 days in March 1984. With the onset of each of these assemblies, there was a dramatic drop in war deaths and injuries and significant progress towards peace. But at the end of each assembly, when the coherence-creating group disbanded, negative trends returned.

Time series analysis revealed that the improvements in Lebanon could not have been determined by the prior history of the conflict. Nor did the news media have any explanation; in fact, some journalists called these changes 'miraculous'.

Philippines Studies

Two other time series studies in the Philippines replicated the extended Maharishi Effect. The first study (Dillbeck and Castillo, 1985) examined a composite of the most reliable measures of national quality of life available, including crime, fetal deaths, and all other deaths, and found a significant improvement following the establishment of a large group of TM-Sidhas in December 1979. As the size of the coherence-creating group of TM-Sidhas decreased in time, the positive effect also decreased. The second study (Dillbeck, Shabl, and Glenn, 1985) found a decrease in crime in Metro Manila when a large group of TM-Sidhas was present there.

And in Great Britain, Beresford and Clements (1983) found a significant increase in the British stock market index during periods when enough TM-Sidhas were practising together in that country to affect the national quality of life.

Maharishi's World Peace Project

In 1985, Orme-Johnson, Dillbeck, Bousquet, and Alexander evaluated the results of Maharishi's World Peace Project, which had been held seven years earlier. Teams of one to two hundred TM-Sidhas had gone for about ten weeks in 1978 to five major trouble-spot areas of the world: Nicaragua and elsewhere in Central America, Lebanon, Iran, Thailand (to try to keep the war in Kampuchea from expanding), and southern Africa—specifically Zimbabwe (then Rhodesia) and Zambia. There they practised the TM-Sidhi 'yogic flying' technique in groups at their hotels and had no interaction with the local population. The research found a reduction in violence in each of these areas

WORLD PEACE • GLOBAL INAUGURATION

A BRIEFING FOR THE WORLD PRESS

during their stay.

Using an independent data source, the Conflict and Peace Data Bank, and with a baseline going back ten years, the investigators also discovered significant reductions in hostile acts and verbal hostility and increases in positive and co-operative events world-wide during Maharishi's World Peace Project. Their research controlled for factors like time of year as well as other forms of seasonality and systematic trends in the data. Essentially, the study showed that during the periods that groups of TM-Sidhas stayed in major conflict areas they created coherence that was measurable as a reduction in the total amount of international conflict.

Taste of Utopia Assembly

Global Maharishi Effect

A group of 7,000 TM-Sidhas, approximately the square root of one per cent of the population of the entire world, would be the most efficient way to create world peace. It could be located at one place anywhere in the world to create the Global Maharishi Effect. From 17 December 1983 to 6 January 1984, MIU held the Taste of Utopia Assembly, gathering over 7,000 Sidhas to test for this effect. Through news content analysis of major daily newspapers, Orme-Johnson, Cavanaugh, Alexander, Gelderloos, Dillbeck, Lanford, and Abou-Nader (1984) found increased progress by heads of state in reversing negative trends and accelerating positive ones, increased positivity in trouble-spot areas, increased progress towards peace in Lebanon, and decreased international conflicts world-wide during the assembly, as compared with the prior and subsequent three-week periods and with changes during comparable periods in previous years. In addition, during the assembly crime and infectious diseases decreased in the U.S.A. and Australia (on the opposite side of the globe) as well as in other countries. Auto fatalities in countries on three continents and air fatalities world-wide both decreased. All these findings of global improvement were highly statistically significant.

In a study of the effects of the Taste of Utopia Assembly on stock prices, Cavanaugh, Orme-Johnson, and Gelderloos (1984) analyzed daily data for the five months preceding and the six months following the assembly. They found a rise during the assembly by 2.2 times of the World Stock Index, an index of stock prices in 19 countries. By explicitly allowing for the impact of long-term interest rates and by using sophisticated statistical techniques, they rigorously demonstrated the Global Maharishi Effect.

Positive Effects of the World Assembly on Vedic Science

A further study by Orme-Johnson, Dillbeck, Alexander, Chandler, and Cranson (1985) replicated the Taste of Utopia results. For ten days in July 1985, 5,600 TM-Sidhas attended the World Assembly on Vedic Science in Washington, D.C. The researchers found that during this assembly international conflicts, infectious diseases (U.S.A.), and fires in Washington, D.C., all decreased, and the Dow Jones stock average and the World Stock Index in-

MAHARISHI'S PROGRAMME TO CREATE

A BRIEFING FOR THE WORLD PRESS

FIRST EXPERIMENT OF MAHARISHI'S PROGRAMME TO CREATE WORLD PEACE

This assembly, at Maharishi International University, Fairfield, Iowa, U.S.A., produced coherence in world consciousness for the three weeks of its duration, from 17 December to 6 January 1984.

Scientific research on the global effects of this assembly verified that coherence was created in world consciousness, marked by decreased negativity and increased positivity in the international fields of politics and economics.

This was the assembly which clearly demonstrated the possibility of creating world peace through the Maharishi Technology of the Unified Field. Later, similar assemblies were held in The Hague, Holland, and Washington, D.C., which confirmed the findings of the assembly.

When this powerful effect of coherence in world consciousness is generated permanently by a group of 10,000 experts in the Maharishi Technology of the Unified Field, a permanent state of peace will be enjoyed by all mankind.

7000 experts in the Maharishi Technology of the Unified Field in the presence of His Holiness Maharishi Mahesh Yogi creating a Taste of Utopia for all mankind, Maharishi International University, Fairfield, Iowa, U.S.A., 17 Dec. 1983 to 6 Jan. 1984.

Increased Positivity of Events in Situations of International Conflict

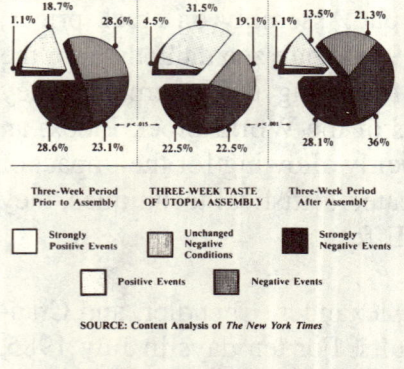

SOURCE: Content Analysis of *The New York Times*

During the Taste of Utopia Assembly the balance of negative to positive events in trouble-spot areas of the world shifted towards greater positivity, indicating increased progress towards normalizing of international relations through peaceful means. After the assembly the balance of events reverted towards greater negativity.

Simultaneous Increase of Major Stock Market Indices

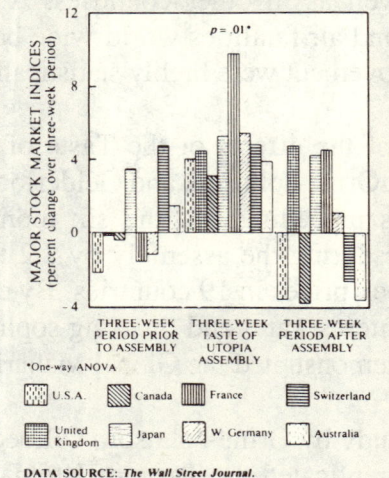

DATA SOURCE: *The Wall Street Journal*.

The eight major national stockmarkets of the world increased simultaneously during the Taste of Utopia Assembly, indicating balanced economic growth worldwide. After the assembly these stock markets reverted to a pattern similiar to that seen prior to the assembly, with some increasing and some decreasing.

Decreased Incidence of Infectious Diseases (Australia and U.S.A.)

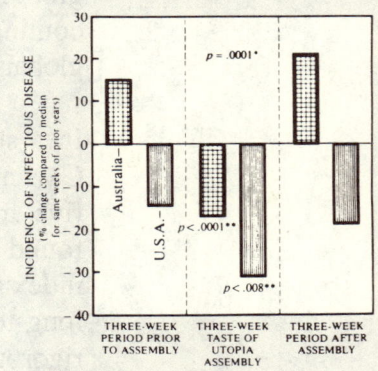

*Fisher's formula for combined probability
**Randomization test

DATA SOURCES: Center for Disease Control, U.S.A.; Department of Health, Commonwealth of Australia. (Number of previous years considered—4 years for Australia, 5 years for U.S.A.)

During the Taste of Utopia Assembly the incidence of all categories of notifiable infectious diseases decreased markedly in the USA and Australia compared to the mean for corresponding weeks during previous years. After the assembly the incidence of infectious diseases began to rise again towards levels comparable to previous years.

creased. In the case of both the Taste of Utopia Assembly and the World Assembly on Vedic Science, the specific improvements in quality of life were predicted in advance.

Different Maharishi Effect Groups Have Independent Impacts on Local Populations

Two more studies on the Maharishi Effect should be discussed, because they illustrate two additional points relevant to Maharishi's Programme to Create World Peace. In 1984, Bandy and Landford examined the effect of maintaining at least 400 TM-Sidhas practising together in Washington, D.C. Looking at local police and FBI crime statistics from August 1980 to November 1983, they found that the group had a significant impact on decreasing violent crime in the greater Washington metropolitan area. Also, this decrease was not accounted for by weather, police coverage, population age changes, or neighbourhood watch programmes. They also found that the group of 400 increased the Washington index of stock prices. What was new was the following: while the group of 1,600 at MIU also improved the Washington stock market during the same time period, the researchers demonstrated that its effect was independent of that of the Washington group. This was the first evidence that national and local extended Maharishi Effect groups have independent impacts on local populations. In another study, Reeks, Landford, and Stryker (1985) examined weekly data for the U.S.A. on 20 infectious diseases. They found that with 7,000 Sidhas at MIU incidences of all diseases decreased immediately, except for one, which had a lag of one week. With 1,600 at MIU, five diseases decreased at their incubation periods—usually one or two weeks. With the larger group, the drop in incidences of diseases was four times as great. Similarly, a time series analysis comparing the reduction in U.S.A. auto fatalities with 1,600 and 7,000 showed an eight-fold improvement during the 7,000 assembly. Thus the larger the size of the coherence-creating group, the more immediate and pronounced the improvements in quality of life.

The Larger the Coherence-Creating Group, the More Immediate and Pronounced the Improvements

Evaluating the Maharishi Effect as the Causal Factor in Positive Societal Change

In looking at the many studies on the Maharishi Effect, one sees that a variety of normally unrelated indices of quality of life are improving at the same time. This suggests that a new factor of change is at work. But why conclude it is the influence of the TM and TM-Sidhi programme and not something else? Time series analysis shows that the improvements could not have been expected from the previous behaviour of the indices being assessed and that these improvements are significantly correlated in time with the TM and TM-Sidhi programme interventions. Statistical techniques are used to rule out other mechanisms that might explain the results. In several studies, causality is strongly indicated by the finding that the increase in the size of the TM and TM-Sidhi programme group is followed closely in time by beneficial changes in society—that is, the cause precedes the effect. In some cases, the studies confirmed predictions lodged prior to the interventions. Finally, many of the findings replicated the results of previous studies on the Maharishi Effect.

MAHARISHI'S PROGRAMME TO CREATE

A BRIEFING FOR THE WORLD PRESS

But, one might say, world peace is an enormous undertaking, requiring continuous adjustment over an infinitely complex range of different factors on a global scale. Can one technique accomplish so much?

Maharishi Effect—One Simple Approach to Handle All Problems

Taken together, the studies show that the Maharishi Effect is multidimensional, simultaneously improving many different factors of quality of life; it is an accurate director of balanced, positive societal change. Once the critical threshold is crossed and the Maharishi Effect begins, it continues to improve the quality of life over time. The larger a group of TM-Sidhas is, the greater its impact in a given population. If the group disbands, or if the percentage of the population practising the TM and TM-Sidhi programme drops below the required level, the Maharishi Effect stops and the rapid pace of improvement subsides. Maharishi's programme has been shown to work in all parts of the world, whether North America, Latin America, Europe, Africa, the Middle East, Asia, or Australia and the Pacific. Moreover, global, national, and local groups of TM-Sidhas have been found to have independent impacts on improving the quality of life in the locality.

Prevention Is Better than Cure

The strategy to use Maharishi's technology most effectively to create world peace is simply expressed in the old saying, 'Prevention is better than cure'. Instead of fighting the fires of conflict once they are ignited, establish permanently in one place a large group of people practising the TM-Sidhi 'yogic flying' technique—10,000 TM-Sidhas to perpetually avert international conflict and continuously improve the quality of individual, national, and global life. As the group of 'yogic flyers' at Maharishi Nagar in India grows to 10,000, similar groups are rising in many countries and cities to accomplish simultaneously all three steps of Maharishi's Programme to Create World Peace.

Dr Morris will now briefly explain our plans to establish these coherence-creating groups and will introduce today's demonstration of 'yogic flying'.

Dr Bevan Morris

DR MORRIS: From Maharishi's perspective, we never wanted to publicly display 'yogic flying'. But now there are two reasons to do so. First, it has become obvious that by using this technique to experience and enliven the self-interacting dynamics of the unified field, we can stimulate its evolutionary nature in world consciousness, giving a positive direction to the trends of time and creating world peace. Second, with the rise of terrorism in the world and the dangerous rivalry of the superpowers, Maharishi and all of us feel a very urgent and pressing need to apply this technology to create world peace for the sake of all mankind.

Our aim is to create groups of 7,000 to make world peace a reality for the first time in human history, and to make that reality permanent. The initial step in

WORLD PEACE • GLOBAL INAUGURATION

A BRIEFING FOR THE WORLD PRESS

10,000 Vedic Pandits in India

our endeavour to create groups of 7,000 is to establish a group of 10,000 Vedic Pandits in India at the World Capital of the Age of Enlightenment, Maharishi Nagar, just outside New Delhi. Having 10,000 will ensure that 7,000 are always available. We want to establish an endowment fund to permanently support those 10,000 Vedic Pandits. They will practise the Maharishi Technology of the Unified Field twice a day, generating the Global Maharishi Effect to purify world consciousness and create peace on earth.

Two 7,000 Groups in the U.S.A.

In the U.S.A., we have a similar plan: to create two groups of 7,000, one here in Washington, D.C., and one in Fairfield, Iowa. Already, we have about 1,000 TM-Sidhas in Washington and nearly 3,000 in Fairfield.

World Peace through Maharishi's Programme

We appreciate, and Maharishi appreciates, all the efforts of all of the organizations that are trying to create world peace. But we also recognize that world peace has not been created, and there is no sign that through traditional means it is going to be created. Throughout human history there have been those who opposed wars, but still wars happen in the world. We believe, on the basis of all that we have experienced and the scientific evidence, that we will achieve world peace through Maharishi's programme.

Three Stages of 'Yogic Flying'

I would now like to invite our guests and the members of the news media to come upstairs to see the demonstration of 'yogic flying'. According to the classical texts of Vedic literature, 'yogic flying' proceeds in three stages. In the first stage, the body hops up into the air. The second stage is hovering, and the third stage is sustained flight. Today, what we will be demonstrating is the first, or hopping stage.

'Yogic Flying' Competitions

This will be demonstrated in a competition with four events—the yogic 25-metre hurdles, the yogic 50-metre race, and the yogic long and high jumps. Before each event, the competitors will practise the Transcendental Meditation technique for a few minutes to identify their conscious awareness with the unified field, from which level the phenomenon of 'yogic flying' occurs.

The Real Champions— Those Who Generate Coherence in World Consciousness

Separate events will be held for men and ladies, and medals will be awarded to the top three winners in each event. Certainly, the medals will be awarded to those 'yogic flyers' who go the fastest, the highest, and the farthest. Timekeepers, rulesmen, and judges are at the foam track upstairs ready to evaluate the performances. But all the competitors are demonstrating today with a deep awareness that the real competition is not in the outer display. Rather, it is in generating the most delicate impulse in the unified field to accomplish 'yogic flying' on the ground of the Self, the ground of pure silence, which is the unified field of natural law. The real champions are they who go most profoundly into the Self and generate most powerfully that beautiful, coherent influence on the level of the unified field which is the basis for creating coher-

MAHARISHI'S PROGRAMME TO CREATE

A BRIEFING FOR THE WORLD PRESS

World Peace

ence in world consciousness and world peace. I think you will feel the influence of coherence even as you are witnessing the remarkable phenomenon of 'yogic flying'. □

WORLD PEACE

7000

7,000 experts practising the Maharishi Technology of the Unified Field together twice a day will create coherence in world consciousness and establish peace on earth.

WORLD PEACE • GLOBAL INAUGURATION

Inaugurating Maharishi's Programme to Create World Peace
WASHINGTON, D.C., U.S.A., and NEW DELHI, INDIA

In the spring of 1986, the *International Herald Tribune* and many Indian newspapers carried a quarter-page announcement with a remarkable headline: 'Maharishi's Programme to Create World Peace—Eliminating the Basis of Terrorism and War without Loss of Life—Ensuring Permanent Success through the Maharishi World Peace Fund.'

The announcement declared, 'The principle to create world peace is to create coherence in world consciousness.... This is achieved through the Maharishi Technology of the Unified Field.... With 7,000 experts in the Maharishi Technology of the Unified Field gathered in one place creating coherence in world consciousness, peace on earth will be powerful and power on earth will be peaceful.'*

First North American 'Yogic Flying' Competition
Capital Convention Center, Washington, D.C., U.S.A.

Several months later, the *Wall Street Journal* and the *Washington Post* brought the same bold message to the people of North America.

On 25 June, a letter went from Maharishi Vedic University in Washington, D.C., to top leaders in the United States and Canada—government officials and politicians, business and labour leaders, eminent judges and lawyers, generals, university presidents, publishers, physicians, scientists, and scholars. The letter invited them to Washington's Capital Convention Center on 9 July for the North American inauguration of Maharishi's Programme to Create World Peace.

The letter said, 'We will demonstrate Maharishi's technology to create coherence in world consciousness, the basis for establishing world peace. This technology is the TM-Sidhi "yogic flying" technique, an aspect of the Maharishi Technology of the Unified Field.'

For the first time since Maharishi introduced his TM-Sidhi programme in 1976, 'yogic flying' was now going to be publicly demonstrated.

The letter continued, 'Maharishi's programme for world peace is an opportunity for those most concerned with the future of mankind to do something that really works. It is being inaugurated now with a deep awareness of the urgent need to accelerate the growth of real peace on earth and with great appreciation for all the efforts already undertaken for world peace.... We hope that you, as one of the leaders of our society, will be able to attend the inaugural ceremonies and gain insight into this programme which has the potential of at last fulfilling the aspiration for world peace that has been cherished by the wise throughout the ages.'

Foreign ambassadors in Washington and at the United Nations, as well as the international press corps, were also invited to the demonstration, with the purpose of promoting knowledge of Maharishi's programme world-wide.

A news conference on the morning of 9 July attracted more than 150 journalists. Every major North American television and radio network, all wire services, and most of the biggest newspapers and magazines were represented. Several newsmen remarked they be-

---
*Please refer to the newspaper announcement of Maharishi's Programme to Create World Peace on the following page.

MAHARISHI'S PROGRAMME TO CREATE

INTERNATIONAL 'YOGIC FLYING' COMPETITIONS

MAHARISHI'S PROGRAM TO CREATE WORLD PEACE
ELIMINATING THE BASIS OF TERRORISM AND WAR WITHOUT LOSS OF LIFE
Raising U.S. $100 Million to Ensure World Peace

His Holiness Maharishi Mahesh Yogi

"Time demands the rise of the supreme power in the world which can eliminate terrorism and have positive control over the destructive capability of the superpowers, which has been keeping mankind under constant fear for decades. Our program to create world peace will promote the rise of this supreme power—the invincible, evolutionary power of natural law—in world consciousness and free mankind from fear." —*Maharishi*

Efforts of 3,000 Years to Create World Peace

It is obvious to everyone that all means employed by man so far to achieve world peace have failed. Since 1000 B.C. there have been over 8,000 peace treaties, and each one lasted on average no more than nine years. The League of Nations was founded in 1920 to ensure that World War I was "the war to end all wars." Twenty years later World War II erupted. The United Nations was established in 1945 to end war and conflict between nations once and for all. Since then there have been more than 150 wars. It is clear that political negotiations, treaties, and use of arms have never and can never create a lasting state of world peace.

The Responsibility of the Individual

World peace was rightly considered to be the responsibility of governments. That is why traditionally it has not been the practice of individuals to take the initiative for world peace. Today the situation is different. With the onset of terrorism, governments are not succeeding in providing safety and security to life in any part of the world. Even the superpowers themselves are constantly in fear, and the dangerous rivalry between them is challenging the life of everyone.

Now it is time for the responsible individuals in the world to wake up and take the responsibility for creating and maintaining world peace.

"With the onset of terrorism, world peace is the personal and immediate requirement of any significant man in the world today and it must be fulfilled today, without waiting for tomorrow." —*Maharishi*

Maharishi's Principle to Create World Peace

Peace is secured in the orderly evolution of life. Orderly evolution requires unrestricted progress, which flowers on the ground of coherence.

The principle to create world peace is to create coherence in world consciousness. Only an indomitable strength of coherence in world consciousness will prevent the rise of stress in the world. This alone will root out terrorism without loss of life. This alone will eliminate the basis of crime, conflict, and war, and will gracefully bring to an end the dangerous rivalry of the superpowers.

Coherence in world consciousness can be produced only by creating coherence in individual brain physiology. This is achieved through the Maharishi Technology of the Unified Field—Transcendental Meditation, its advanced techniques, and the TM-Sidhi program.

This technology identifies the individual creativity of the human mind with the cosmic creativity of natural law. It cultures the human mind to operate from the self-interacting dynamics of the unified field of all the laws of nature, which is the source and governor of all values in the universe. Because the unified field has the character of infinite correlation, an impulse of coherence generated from this level instantly harmonizes discordant tendencies throughout the environment.

7,000 to Create World Peace

Scientific research has shown that 7,000 individuals (the square root of one percent of the world's population) practicing the Maharishi Technology of the Unified Field together in one place create a powerful influence of coherence in the whole world consciousness, producing an upsurge of positive trends and tendencies in life everywhere.

With this technology world peace is only a matter of maintaining a group of 7,000 to daily create coherence in world consciousness. With this formula in our possession, world peace is now only a matter of money to maintain the group of 7,000.

Seven thousand experts practicing the Maharishi Technology of the Unified Field together can be trained and modestly maintained in India with the annual income from a fund of 100 million dollars.

The Maharishi World Peace Fund

The Maharishi World Peace Fund has been established to raise this amount to create and maintain world peace.

The leaders and the wealthy, who have the real well-being of humanity at heart, are invited to examine closely Maharishi's principles and practical program to create world peace. By establishing the Maharishi World Peace Fund today, they can fulfill their responsibility of bringing peace to the world and thereby ensure tomorrow for all mankind.

"There are hundreds of organizations for peace all over the world. People are trying to create world peace from various different levels of approach. Our appreciation goes for every effort that is being made for world peace.

"However, only a new seed will yield a new crop. Only a new philosophy and new efforts based on new knowledge will fulfill the age-old dream of the wise for world peace.

"Our approach to world peace is holistic and most basic. It is from that most basic level of nature's functioning, the unified field of natural law, where eternal silence itself is the lively basis of the eternal dynamics of the universe—the self-interacting dynamics of the unified field of natural law—where peace upholds dynamism. That is why peace created from this level will be powerful, and power on earth will be peaceful." —*Maharishi*

Please address inquiries about Maharishi's Program to Create World Peace and the Maharishi World Peace Fund to:

Maharishi Continental Capital of the Age of Enlightenment for North America
5000 14th Street NW
Washington, D.C. 20011, U.S.A.

Maharishi European Continental Capital of the Age of Enlightenment
Station 24, 6063 NP Vlodrop
The Netherlands

Maharishi World Capital of the Age of Enlightenment
Maharishi Nagar
U.P. 201307, India

WORLD PEACE • GLOBAL INAUGURATION

INTERNATIONAL 'YOGIC FLYING' COMPETITIONS

lieved this was the largest non-political press conference in Washington's history.

The inauguration was held at the World Assembly on Perfect Health, which was chaired by Dr B.D. Triguna, President of the All-India Ayurveda Congress and Vice-Chancellor of Maharishi Vedic University, Europe. Dr Triguna was joined on the stage by many renowned Ayurvedic physicians. Dr Bevan Morris, President of Maharishi International University (MIU), U.S.A., served as master of ceremonies.

In preparation for the 'yogic flying' competition, an acre of polyurethane foam matting had been laid out on the floor of the largest hall at the Convention Center. It was covered with white sheets and divided into five lanes by long red ribbons.

Twenty-two competitors from seven countries—Canada, the U.S.A., Mexico, Guadeloupe, the Philippines, India, and Bermuda—entered the arena to enthusiastic applause from the audience of 1,000. They sat at one end of the foam track to practise the Transcendental Meditation technique for five minutes before beginning 'yogic flying'.

Twenty-five television camera crews and scores of photographers crowded the edges of the track to capture the 'yogic flying'. Silently, the spectators, press, and special guests settled in their seats to await the soft, electronic tone that would signal the end of the group meditation.

'Let the competition begin.' With these words, Dr Neil Paterson, Governor General of the World Government of the Age of Enlightenment for North America, formally opened the First North American 'Yogic Flying' Competition.

The competition was held in four events: the yogic 25-metre hurdles race, the yogic long and high jumps, and the yogic 50-metre race, all in the sitting position. The audience was asked to hold its applause until the end of the final event. As each hurdle was crossed and each new height and distance reached, the hall was flooded with a feeling of silent enthusiasm. The competitors' bright smiles before, during, and after each event showed that this was no ordinary athletic contest.

The *Washington Post* reported, 'When the final race, the 50-metre dash, was completed, the contestants were utterly animated. While the audience rose to their feet in applause, the hoppers remained seated, hopping vigorously among themselves....'

During the competition, scientists from MIU monitored the brain wave activity of 'yogic flyers'. Large colour television screens displayed graphic presentations of EEG patterns, showing the growing coherence the competitors were experiencing. The researchers demonstrated that the body lifts up at the moment of maximum coherence in brain activity. The TM-Sidhas themselves later described the subjective experience of coherence during 'yogic flying'.

Eddie Gob, a Governor of the Age of Enlightenment from Guadeloupe who won three of the four gold medals in the men's competition, was quoted in the *Washington Times* as saying to the audience, 'It's so blissful and exhilarating. You just want to go on and on. When I first learned "yogic flying" they had to tell me, OK, OK, you can stop now.'

Susan Weller, an architect from Fairfield, Iowa, who won three gold medals in the ladies' events, said, 'In the finals, I felt more and more joy inside. The longer the competition went on, the deeper I felt. Staying in that most settled state longer enhanced my ability.'

Ken Chandler, a member of the faculty at Maharishi International University, described the mastery of natural law demonstrated by 'yogic flying', 'When you experience the unified field during the TM-Sidhi programme, you have the sense that you can do anything, because the world is not outside the Self. Anything at all can be accomplished when you are functioning on that subtle level of infinite correlation.'

Jeffrey Klein, a Governor of the Age of Enlightenment from the U.S.A., explained mastery of natural law in terms of support of nature. 'The laws of nature organ-

MAHARISHI'S PROGRAMME TO CREATE

INTERNATIONAL 'YOGIC FLYING' COMPETITIONS

CHAMPIONS OF THE FIRST NORTH AMERICAN 'YOGIC FLYING' COMPETITION

MEN — *LADIES*

Yogic 25-metre Hurdles Race in Sitting Position

Gold:	Eddie Gob (Guadeloupe), 11.53 sec	Susan Weller (U.S.A.), 16.92 sec
Silver:	Ken Allen (U.S.A.), 11.60 sec	Nancy Lonsdorf (U.S.A.), 17.05 sec
Bronze:	David Pasco (U.S.A.), 11.77 sec	Barbara Briggs (U.S.A.), 17.80 sec

Yogic Long Jump in Sitting Position

Gold:	Eddie Gob (Guadeloupe), 70 in	Susan Weller (U.S.A.), 51.25 in
Silver:	Rod Falk (Canada), 66.5 in	NaNa Maynard (U.S.A.), 51 in
Bronze:	Jeffrey Klein (U.S.A.), 65.25 in	Nancy Lonsdorf (U.S.A.), 49 in

Yogic High Jump in Sitting Position

Gold:	Blaine Watson (Canada), 24.75 in	NaNa Maynard (U.S.A.), 19 in
Silver:	Rod Falk (Canada), 22.5 in	Barbara Briggs (U.S.A.), 18 in
Bronze:	Jeffrey Klein (U.S.A.) and Eddie Gob (Guadeloupe), 21.6 in	Susan Weller (U.S.A.), 17 in

Yogic 50-metre Race in Sitting Position

Gold:	Eddie Gob (Guadeloupe), 23.33 sec	Susan Weller (U.S.A.), 35.72 sec
Silver:	Tom Kirkendall (U.S.A.), 23.35 sec	Barbara Briggs (U.S.A.), 37.13 sec
Bronze:	John Tower (U.S.A.), 23.62 sec	Nancy Lonsdorf (U.S.A.), 38.21 sec

ize,' he said, 'and you just go.'*

Michael Dillbeck, Professor of Psychology at MIU

*Maharishi describes practice of the Transcendental Meditation and TM-Sidhi programme as 'research in consciousness as a field of all possibilities'. It is the most profound kind of research into the fine mechanics of nature's functioning.

and a finalist in the Washington competition, explained that 'The unified field is not only an objective reality described by physics, it is the pure subjective essence of life. As a psychologist, it is a joy to learn to function from that level of pure subjectivity and also to objectively investigate the effects of the experience on the

WORLD PEACE • GLOBAL INAUGURATION

INTERNATIONAL 'YOGIC FLYING' COMPETITIONS

individual and society.'

The theme of world peace was emphasized at every phase of the competition. For instance, Eddie Gob told the audience that 'The purpose of the competition was not to demonstrate "yogic flying" for its own sake, but to demonstrate the possibilities created by maximum coherence in the functioning of the individual brain, the basic unit of world peace.'

At the awards ceremony that evening, Dr Paterson rang a great silver bell, the Maharishi Bell of Invincibility, saying, 'This is to symbolize invincibility to every nation through Maharishi's Programme to Create World Peace. A ceremonial Maharishi Bell of Invincibility will be awarded to every head of state when he creates peace in his own country through Maharishi's programme as an essential step towards creating, strengthening, and perpetuating world peace.'

Dr Morris and Dr Triguna awarded the winners gold, silver, and bronze medals.

'This has been a very historic day,' Dr Morris said at the awards ceremony. 'We have demonstrated that the technology for world peace is now in hand and has only to be used.'

Dr Paterson lit a candle on a large cake decorated with a map of the world to symbolize the hope kindled for all mankind by the day's competition.

'We feel absolutely confident,' he said, 'that with this programme we can create world peace.'

Reports of the First North American 'Yogic Flying' Competition made headlines throughout the world. More than 60 media organizations reported the news, and their accounts were printed in hundreds of publications and broadcast on scores of radio and television stations.

National Public Radio's 'All Things Considered', one of America's most respected radio news programmes, told listeners throughout the U.S.A., 'The point of TM and "yogic flying" is to promote greater brain wave coherence and hence coherence in world consciousness, the basis of world peace. Governments have failed to do this ... and that has made it necessary to have the public demonstration.'

The *Washington Times* explained that 'Theoretically, a yogic flyer has very orderly brain waves, fluid co-ordination between mind and body. Consciousness and matter become completely integrated, and all the coherence can spread around the world if enough meditators gather at the same time and place.'

The message was summarized by a quote from Dr Morris in the *Los Angeles Times*: 'Yogic flying can bring peace to the world.'

A practical, simple technique to eliminate the root of terrorism and war and foster harmony among nations had been demonstrated. Millions of people were inspired with fresh hope for world peace. As the many Gannett newspapers throughout the U.S.A. and Canada asked their readers on 10 July, 'Did you feel more peaceful on Wednesday? Maybe it was because of 22 flying yogis....'

First International 'Yogic Flying' Competition
Indira Gandhi Indoor Stadium, New Delhi, India

At the conclusion of the awards ceremony in Washington, Dr Morris told the assembly, 'As every activity of Maharishi and his world-wide movement has always been undertaken in the name of his spiritual master, His Divinity Swami Brahmananda Saraswati Maharaj, Jagadguru Shankaracharya of Jyotir Math, Himalayas, Maharishi will inaugurate for the whole world his programme to create world peace on 21 July, Guru Purnima Day—the full-moon day dedicated to the spiritual master, Shri Guru Dev—at the Indira Gandhi Indoor Stadium in New Delhi, India.

'From this Guru Purnima Day, efforts will begin to gather 10,000 TM-Sidhas at Maharishi Nagar, near

MAHARISHI'S PROGRAMME TO CREATE

INTERNATIONAL 'YOGIC FLYING' COMPETITIONS

New Delhi. This will ensure that 7,000 are available at all times practising the Maharishi Technology of the Unified Field together to create and maintain world peace.'

The most accomplished 'yogic flyers' from all continents, including the winners from North America, were invited to New Delhi for the inauguration and also to compete in the First International 'Yogic Flying' Competition.

Administrators at the World Capital of the Age of Enlightenment in Maharishi Nagar had already begun sending out letters and telexes about the inauguration to India's leaders. These messages said, in part, 'Time demands the rise of a supreme power in the world which can have authority over the destructive capabilities of the superpowers and have the ability to control terrorism without loss of life. In response to this call of time, Maharishi is starting a yogic programme to enliven the evolutionary power of natural law in world consciousness, which will nourish all life on earth and eliminate all negative tendencies everywhere in the world.... His Holiness Jagadguru Shankaracharya Swami Vishnudevanand Saraswati* has consented to preside over the programme.'

Two days before the event, leaders of Maharishi Ved Vigyan Vidya Peeth (Maharishi Vedic University for Asia) and professors from the European and North American campuses of Maharishi Vedic University gathered at the Hans Plaza Hotel in central New Delhi to address a news conference on Maharishi's Programme to Create World Peace. The conference, which lasted two-and-a-half hours, was attended by more than 100 members of the press, including reporters from all the national newspapers and broadcast media of India, the international wire and television news services, and many of the principal newspapers and magazines of the world.

The next morning, the *Times of India* announced the international inauguration with the headline, 'Attaining peace through "Yogic flying"'. The *Hindustan Times* reported, 'The demonstration [on 21 July] is to show Maharishi's Transcendental Meditation-Sidhi "Yogic Flying" technique. It is an aspect of his "technology of the unified field", which will create coherence in world consciousness. The Maharishi, the delegation said, hopes to use the programme to establish and permanently maintain world peace.'

The *Patriot* wrote, '[They said] the Transcendental Meditation-Sidhi programme of yogic flying was the "only thing that worked" because it took recourse to the "power of the unified field"—something which was more potent than nuclear power.'

That same day a full-page announcement from Maharishi Ved Vigyan Vidya Peeth appeared in all the Hindi- and English-language national papers. At the top of the announcement were photographs of Maharishi and the Shankaracharya. The headlines read, 'Inauguration of Maharishi's Programme to Create World Peace—Eliminating the Basis of Terrorism and Negativity in the World Family—Demonstration of the Principles to Create World Peace from Maharishi's Vedic Science in the Light of Modern Science'. The text summarized the principles of Maharishi's programme and invited the people of India to Indira Gandhi Indoor Stadium to witness the technique to apply them.

On Tuesday, 21 July, 10,000 people accepted that invitation, streaming through the stadium gates prior to the 5:00 p.m. starting time. As they took their seats, filling the stadium to its highest rows, a news conference was just ending in a nearby room. Brahmachari Nandkishore, Chief Minister of the Ministry of Natural Law and Order of the World Government of the Age of Enlightenment, explained to 160 members of the New Delhi press corps the purpose of what they were about to observe.

He began by quoting Maharishi: 'Peace is secured in orderly evolution of life. Orderly evolution requires unrestricted progress, which flowers on the ground of coherence. The principle to create world peace is to create coherence in world consciousness.'

Brahmachari Nandkishore then explained that coher-

---
*The present Shankaracharya of Jyotir Math.

WORLD PEACE • GLOBAL INAUGURATION

INTERNATIONAL 'YOGIC FLYING' COMPETITIONS

ence in world consciousness can be produced only by creating coherence in individual brain physiology, which is achieved through the Maharishi Technology of the Unified Field.

He introduced a new theme that would be central to Maharishi's message of world peace in the coming months. 'World peace,' Brahmachari Nandkishore said, 'will be a by-product of bliss rising in the individual and society.' The bliss generated by Maharishi's technology, he said, will eliminate stress and thereby root out the cause of violence and war.

As the news conference adjourned, 1,700 young Vedic scholars from Maharishi Ved Vigyan Vidya Peeth filed into the stadium and filled the tiers of seats behind the speakers' platform. They and the rest of the audience overlooked a stage draped with flower garlands and golden streamers and adorned with jewel-like lights. As the Shankaracharya entered, the young Vedic Pandits began a recitation from the Vedic literature, their voices reverberating harmoniously throughout the vast stadium dome.

Then came the procession of champions: 70 finalists in TM-Sidhi 'yogic flying' from 38 countries, walking in ranks across the vast expanse of sheeted foam and standing, facing the stage, as the names of their countries were read out.

The Shankaracharya formally opened the ceremonies. He was followed by Dr Morris who, in his keynote remarks, described Maharishi's Programme to Create World Peace as 'well-founded on the most advanced scientific knowledge with its roots deep in the perfect knowledge of natural law present in the ancient Vedic literature.'

Pt Ram Chandra Malviya, Vice-Chancellor of Maharishi Ved Vigyan Vidya Peeth, and other distinguished Vedic Pandits amplified this theme, and modern scientists brought out central principles from their respective disciplines, establishing the scientific basis of Maharishi's Programme to Create World Peace and of the decision to create the Maharishi World Peace Fund.

On this foundation of knowledge, the First International 'Yogic Flying' Competition began. As the four events took place, the press filmed and photographed, crowding four or five rows deep around the yogic long jump and high jump and lining the sides of the 25- and 50-metre races.

After the events, while the judges were tabulating their results, dignitaries inaugurated three new institutions for the study and application of Maharishi's Vedic Science: the Maharishi World Centre for Ayurveda and the World Hospital of Ayurveda, inaugurated by Dr Triguna; the Maharishi World Centre for Jyotish, inaugurated by Dr B.V. Raman, an internationally acclaimed Jyotishi*; and the Maharishi World Centre for Gandharva Veda, inaugurated with a performance of music selected from the Gandharva Veda.

Before awarding the medals for 'yogic flying', Dr Paterson summarized the major events in the 30-year history of Maharishi's world-wide movement and said, 'Maharishi's activity in the world mirrors the sequential and spontaneous character of nature's functioning. This functioning is described by unified quantum field theories in terms of "sequential dynamical spontaneous symmetry breaking", whereby the unified field creates from within its own self-referral dynamics.

'In the *Bhagavad Gita*,' Dr Paterson said. 'this is expressed in the verse, "Prakritim Svam Avashtabhya Visrijami Punah Punah" ("Curving back on my own nature, I create again and again"). In this natural process, the programme to create world peace has emerged from the source of pure knowledge in one individual, His Holiness Maharishi Mahesh Yogi, and it is already hastening the establishment of a unified field based perfect civilization on earth.'

Dr Morris concluded the New Delhi inauguration by emphasizing that Maharishi's programme can be used only for good. At the level of the unified field, he said,

---

*An expert in the traditional science of accurately predicting and preventing future imbalances in the individual and society

INTERNATIONAL 'YOGIC FLYING' COMPETITIONS

CHAMPIONS OF THE FIRST INTERNATIONAL 'YOGIC FLYING' COMPETITION

	MEN	LADIES

Yogic 25-metre Hurdles Race in Sitting Position

Gold:	Matt Boutrin (Martinique), 14.81 sec	Susan Watterson (U.S.A.), 23.65 sec
Silver:	Ken Allen (U.S.A.), 15.34 sec	Nicola Menges (West Germany), 24.65 sec
Bronze:	Bom Thapa (India), 15.37 sec	Susan Weller (U.S.A.), 26.69 sec

Yogic Long Jump in Sitting Position

Gold:	Eddie Gob (Guadeloupe), 163 cm	Susan Watterson (U.S.A.), 132.08 cm
Silver:	Frits Commandeur (Holland), 154 cm	NaNa Maynard (U.S.A.), 117.86 cm
Bronze:	Jeffrey Klein (U.S.A.), 151 cm	Susan Weller (U.S.A.), 114.30 cm

Yogic High Jump in Sitting Position

Gold:	Blaine Watson (Canada), 60 cm	Susan Watterson (U.S.A.), 41 cm
Silver:	Leslie Davis (Britain), 53 cm	NaNa Maynard (U.S.A.) and Susan Weller (U.S.A.), 31 cm
Bronze:	Jeffrey Klein (U.S.A.), Stephen Benson (Britain), and Rod Falk (Canada), 51 cm	

Yogic 50-metre Race in Sitting Position

Gold	Matt Boutrin (Martinique), 25.89 sec	Susan Watterson (U.S.A.), 37.83 sec
Silver:	Stephen Benson (Britain), 27.50 sec	Nancy Lonsdorf (U.S.A.), 43.79 sec
Bronze:	Tom Kirkendall (U.S.A.), 27.79 sec	Nicola Menges (West Germany), 47.38 sec

peace upholds dynamism and dynamism upholds peace, immortality, self-sufficiency, and invincibility.

'Destruction is non-existent in the eternal continuum of the unified field,' Dr Morris said. 'The nature of the unified field is only evolutionary. There is no danger of any destructive capability arising from the Maharishi Technology of the Unified Field. Maharishi's programme is absolutely evolutionary, and for that reason it is absolutely safe as a global

WORLD PEACE • GLOBAL INAUGURATION

INTERNATIONAL 'YOGIC FLYING' COMPETITIONS

programme to create peace in the world family.'

Dr Morris described world peace as a holistic achievement requiring that all areas of life become positive and evolutionary. 'As world peace rises,' he said, 'all areas of human concern will rise towards perfection through the Maharishi Unified Field Based Integrated Systems of Health, Education, Administration, Economics, Agriculture, Rehabilitation, and Defence.'

The next day, the national press published throughout India the news of Maharishi's inauguration. The *Navbharat Times* proclaimed, 'Many wonders of yoga'; the *Indian Express* told its readers, 'Yogis flying—a hopping success'; the *Times of India* wrote of the 'Bouncy highway to bliss'; the *Punjabi Kesari* called the programme 'a unique effort to establish world peace'; and the Press Trust of India said it was 'an incredible show of yogic prowess' which 'enthralled thousands of spectators' in 'an awe-struck audience'.

Maharishi's clear message was also carried with enthusiasm from Delhi throughout the world by scores of press organizations. The Associated Press, in a report published by newspapers and broadcast media from Hong Kong to London, said, 'When large groups of people meditate together ... [they] can exert a powerful force to overcome discord, international terrorism, and even superpower rivalry, organizers say. They say that about 7,000 people—the square root of one per cent of the world's population—can create a powerful global force for peace and happiness if they apply the TM technology in one place.' □

MAHARISHI'S PROGRAMME TO CREATE

INTERNATIONAL 'YOGIC FLYING' COMPETITIONS

First North American Yogic

An audience of 1,000 people assembled for the competition.

Twenty-five television camera crews and scores of photographers wait silently at the edge of the foam.

With each stroke of the TM-Sidhi practice, individual awareness enlivens infinite dynamism on the ground of perfect silence in the unified field of natural law. Mind-body coordination is maximum; with each intention to fly the body goes up into the air. Here, four champions spontaneously rise up together, blissfully flying to radiate coherence in world consciousness, the basis of world peace.

WORLD PEACE • GLOBAL INAUGURATION

INTERNATIONAL 'YOGIC FLYING' COMPETITIONS

FLYING COMPETITION•FINALS

Five minutes of group meditation prepare the TM-Sidhas for the practice of 'yogic flying'.

The competition begins; scene during the long jump.

Established deep in the Self, Blaine Watson of Canada rides waves of bliss in the 25-metre hurdles.

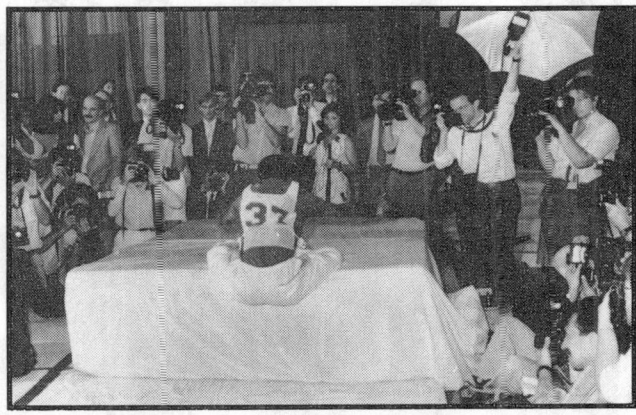

At the high jump event, 30 fascinated photographers crowd space enough for 10.

Eddie Gob of Guadeloupe wins the long jump with a distance of 70 inches.

In the final event, the 50-metre race in sitting position, Blair Butterfield of Bermuda flies down the red-ribboned lanes in long, light hops.

MAHARISHI'S PROGRAMME TO CREAT

First International Yogic

On 21 July 1986, 10,000 people attended the First International 'Yogic Flying' Competition, held at the Indira Gandhi Indoor Stadium in New Delhi, India.

Dr Bevan Morris, President of Maharishi International University (MIU), U.S.A., and master of ceremonies at the First International 'Yogic Flying' Competition.

Pt Ram Chandra Malviya, Vice Chancellor of Maharishi Ved Vigyan Vidya Peeth, India, presents Maharishi's programme from the perspective of ancient Vedic science.

Dr John S. Hagelin, Chairman, Department of Physics, Maharishi International University, presents Maharishi's programme from the perspective of modern science.

Dr R. Keith Wallace, President, Maharishi Vedic University, U.S.A., and Chairman, Department of Biology, MIU, presents scientific research on Maharishi's programme.

WORLD PEACE • GLOBAL INAUGURATION

Flying Competition •Finals

The men finalists.

Meditating before the competition.

MAHARISHI'S PROGRAMME TO CREATE

INTERNATIONAL 'YOGIC FLYING' COMPETITIONS

Evaluating coherence in brain functioning during 'yogic flying'.

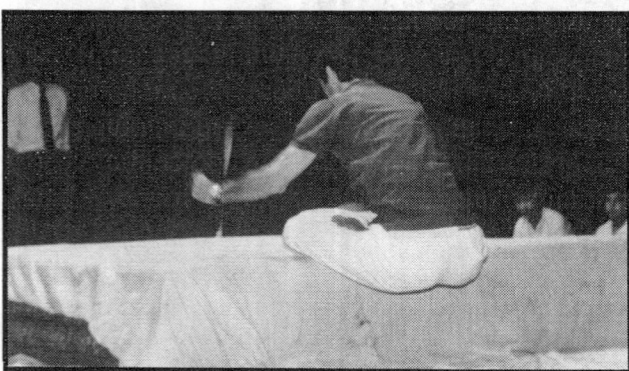
The yogic high jump in sitting position.

The yogic 25-metre hurdles in sitting position.

The yogic long jump in sitting position.

The yogic 50-metre race in sitting position.

WORLD PEACE • GLOBAL INAUGURATION

INTERNATIONAL 'YOGIC FLYING' COMPETITIONS

Demonstration of 'yogic flying' by the students of Maharishi Ved Vigyan Vidya Peeth.

Dr Neil Paterson, Governor General of the World Government of the Age of Enlightenment for North America, announces the winners of the First International 'Yogic Flying' Competition.

Governor of the Age of Enlightenment Matt Boutrin of Martinique receives congratulations from Dr Morris and Dr Hagelin after winning two gold medals.

Governor of the Age of Enlightenment Susan Watterson is awarded her fourth gold medal by Leona Bock, national leader of Maharishi's movement in Canada.

More than 100 members of the New Delhi press corps gathered on 25 July 1986 at the Hans Plaza Hotel for the first of three news conferences on Maharishi's unified field based approach to creating world peace.

Raj Vaidya B.D. Triguna, President, All-India Ayurveda Congress, and Director, Maharishi World Centre for Ayurveda, explains the significance of Maharishi Ayurveda for world peace, as Dr Shiv Sharma, Executive Secretary, All-India Ayurveda Congress, looks on.

Maharishi's Programme to Create World Peace

PRESS CONFERENCES

on Maharishi Ayurveda and the Maharishi Unified Field Based Integrated Systems of Health, Defence, and Administration

Many members of the Delhi press corps had been at Indira Gandhi Stadium on 21 July. They had seen 'yogic flying' and had heard the scientific presentation of Maharishi's Programme to Create World Peace. The plan presented was simple and practical, and the atmosphere of lively silence generated by the demonstration was profound. The journalists were fascinated. They came away thoughtful, and many were inspired.

Their reports were published around the world in thousands of newspapers. Millions of people in Thailand, the Philippines, Brazil, the U.S.A., Britain, Holland, Switzerland, India, and many other countries watched 'yogic flying' on television. World consciousness was stirred. Editors wired their correspondents in Delhi to send more reports and photographs, and they dug into their files for the notices published in previous years by Maharishi's movement.

These announcements offered an invincible defence strategy to every nation. They invited governments to solve their problems through the Maharishi Technology of the Unified Field and recommended Maharishi's Unified Field Based Integrated Systems of Education, Health, Defence, Administration, Economics, Rehabilitation, and Agriculture as effective means to achieve an ideal society.

WORLD PEACE • GLOBAL INAUGURATION

PRESS CONFERENCES ON MAHARISHI'S UNIFIED FIELD BASED APPROACH

Articles about Maharishi's programmes had recently been appearing in scores of periodicals in many countries. Japan's leading business paper, *Nihon Keizai Shimbun*, published a ten-article series on the benefits of unified field based management. A book entitled *Super Meditation, the Miracle of TM* topped the best-seller lists in Tokyo and Osaka. Passengers on the North American transcontinental flights of United, the world's largest commercial airline, watched a documentary about TM in business. The use of Maharishi's programme for effective rehabilitation in the prisons of Brazil, Guatemala, and 11 other countries was reported world-wide, including a story in the Sunday edition of *The New York Times*. People around the globe read articles on how Maharishi's unified field based approach to education is enabling schools in India and the U.S.A. to rank among the top in their nations. Maharishi's World Plan for Perfect Health had just been presented to the Minister of Public Health of China, to physicians and medical scientists at the U.S. National Institutes of Health, at leading medical schools in the U.S.A. and Britain, and to medical authorities in Australia and New Zealand.

Never before had there been such wide-spread interest in the Maharishi Technology of the Unified Field and its applications to different areas of society. The press at the International 'Yogic Flying' Competition wanted to know how all these initiatives related to Maharishi's Programme to Create World Peace, and they had many questions. To answer them, scientists and experts in the Maharishi Technology of the Unified Field convened a press conference four days later at the Hans Plaza Hotel in central New Delhi. It was the first of three conferences related to world peace held over the following two weeks. It focused specifically on Maharishi Ayurveda and the Maharishi Unified Field Based Integrated System of Health.

Press Conference on Maharishi Ayurveda and the Maharishi Unified Field Based Integrated System of Health

25 JULY 1986 • NEW DELHI, INDIA

Present at the press conference were Dr Morris, Dr Hagelin, Dr Wallace, and Dr Orme-Johnson, as well as 22 medical doctors from 10 nations, all expert in the Maharishi Technology of the Unified Field and its application to health.

World Experts in Maharishi Ayurveda

The principal speaker was Dr Brihaspati Dev Triguna, President of the All-India Ayurveda Congress and one of India's most renowned Ayurvedic physicians. Dr Triguna had recently become Director of the Maharishi World Centre for Ayurveda at Maharishi Nagar. Dr Shiv Sharma, Executive Secretary of the Congress, and Dr Girendra Mahapatra, Secretary General of the World Federation for Ayurveda, joined Dr Triguna and the scientists on the platform.

More than 100 journalists attended, representing major newspapers of India and leading international news and television services.

Dr Morris introduced the conference by relating world peace to health. He

PRESS CONFERENCES ON MAHARISHI'S UNIFIED FIELD BASED APPROACH

Invincibility—the Key to World Peace

began with the first point of Maharishi's philosophy of world peace: Invincibility is the key to world peace; only if all nations are invincible will world peace be stable.

'The collective consciousness of an invincible nation is self-sufficient and integrated,' Dr Morris said. 'When national consciousness is integrated, the life-supporting desires of all the different groups in the nation are upheld by the evolutionary power of natural law. No group remains frustrated in achieving its goals; every part of the nation and the nation as a whole are fulfilled.

Perfect Health for the Nation

'This is perfect health for a nation,' Dr Morris said. 'Only a perfectly healthy nation will enjoy self-sufficiency and invincibility.'

Dr Morris said that all problems in a nation—economic failures, social unrest, crime, conflict, epidemics, environmental imbalances—all national problems are basically disorders of collective health, which is the health of all the individuals in the nation.

'The health of the nation and the health of the individual are intimately connected,' Dr Morris said. 'A healthy individual is able to contribute fully to society, and a healthy society provides the nourishing and strengthening environment essential for the individual to rise to perfect health.'

Perfect Health Is Perfect Balance

Dr Morris defined perfect health as perfect balance of mind and body and of the individual with his environment. The technology to achieve balance, he said, is Maharishi Ayurveda.

'According to Maharishi,' Dr Morris said, 'all disease indicates fundamental imbalance in the system, caused by violation of the laws of nature.

Imbalance is Caused by Violation of Natural Law

'Violation of natural law was inevitable,' he continued, 'as long as knowledge of natural law was incomplete. Now, with the discovery of the unified field of all the laws of nature by modern science, there is no reason why any man need continue to violate natural law. Maharishi Ayurveda provides the complete knowledge and practical technology of the unified field to bring life fully in accord with natural law. It creates balance between spiritual, intellectual, and material values of life.

Maharishi Ayurveda Offers Perfect Health

'Maharishi Ayurveda,' Dr Morris said, 'offers perfect health to the individual and perfect collective health to all mankind—world health, which necessarily includes world peace, world prosperity, world happiness, and an ideal family of nations.'

A health writer asked what distinguished Maharishi Ayurveda from Ayurveda.

Dr Triguna replied that Maharishi Ayurveda is 'complete Ayurveda', in conformity with the ancient Ayurvedic texts and including all avenues of life—consciousness, physiology, behaviour, and environment.

PRESS CONFERENCES ON MAHARISHI'S UNIFIED FIELD BASED APPROACH

He added that Maharishi Ayurveda not only handles all these values of individual and collective health in the present, but also secures perfect health for the future.

A Disease-Free Society

'This feature of Maharishi Ayurveda is unique,' Dr Triguna said. 'It offers the possibility to create a disease-free society in every country and a world free from suffering.'

Dr Hagelin pointed out to the journalists that the glamour of the modern scientific approach to knowledge was primarily responsible for the decline of almost all ancient traditional values of life in this century. He said that the field of medicine was inevitably affected by this objective approach, which largely disregarded the subjective value of life. As a result, natural medicine was neglected in every nation, including India, the land of Ayurveda.

The Unified Field—the Field of Pure Subjectivity

'But today, modern science has glimpsed the field of pure subjectivity—the unified field of natural law,' Dr Hagelin said. 'With his Technology of the Unified Field, Maharishi has provided a new opportunity for all ancient traditions based on the value of life, the value of subjectivity, to regain vitality.'

The Re-Awakening of Ayurveda

Dr Triguna commented that the resurgence of the traditional value of life governed by natural law is seen in the present re-awakening of Ayurveda. He said that Maharishi's revival of this most ancient system of perfect health comes at a time when there is growing dissatisfaction with modern medicine. Medical research and the experience of people throughout the world have brought to light the harmful side effects of modern medicine and its lack of success in preventing illness, he said.

'Maharishi Ayurveda is the fulfilment of the world-wide search for a more effective system of health, one which is free from harmful side effects, prevention-oriented, and capable of eliminating disease at its source,' Dr Triguna said.

Maharishi's World Plan for Perfect Health

Dr Wallace then described Maharishi's World Plan for Perfect Health, which, he said, offers self-sufficiency in health care to every nation through Maharishi Ayurveda. With the implementation of this plan, Dr Wallace said, the goal of the World Health Organization—'Health for All by the Year 2,000' —could be achieved well before its target date.

Dr Wallace explained that Maharishi's plan calls for establishing perfect health in every nation by utilizing each country's own medicinal flora and by creating coherence in the brain physiology of its people.

'Human brain physiology is the most precious resource of any country,' Dr Wallace said. 'It holds the potential for infinite freedom and invincibility through mastery of natural law. In the human brain lies the capability of functioning spontaneously in accordance with all the laws of nature so that thought, action, and behaviour are always evolutionary.

'As a result, life will be free from suffering and continuously lived in waves of bliss and fulfilment,' Dr Wallace said. 'This is the goal of Maharishi's World Plan for Perfect Health, which will perpetuate the Age of Enlightenment.'

Maharishi Ayurveda Is Universal

Dr Mahapatra said that Maharishi's plan can achieve its goal because Maharishi Ayurveda is universal. Its principles are absolute, he said. They are based on natural law and therefore are applicable to the people and medicinal flora of every country.

'Ayurveda provides complete knowledge of how to identify and use medicinal plants,' Dr Mahapatra said. 'These principles are expounded in the classical texts and materia medica of Ayurveda in India, where this science has been preserved throughout the ages. Today, Maharishi's insights have inspired the foremost experts in Ayurveda to put this precious knowledge to practical use in all parts of the world through his world plan for perfect health.

'Ayurveda states that the medicinal plants growing in any country are most effective for maintaining the perfect health of the people living there,' Dr Mahapatra continued. 'The traditional skills of Ayurvedic experts in identifying medicinal values in plants, together with the use of local plants in different countries—the practice of folk medicine—are completely competent to bring self-sufficiency in health care to any nation.'

Holistic Approach of Maharishi Ayurveda

In this regard, Dr Mahapatra contrasted the fragmented approach of modern medicine, which focuses primarily on isolating and treating the symptoms of disease, with the holistic approach of Maharishi Ayurveda, which deals with the origin of disease. He also noted that modern medicine takes pride in isolating the active ingredient of a plant.

'But this disconnects the active ingredient from the balancing power of nature available within the whole plant,' Dr Mahapatra said. 'Maharishi Ayurveda uses the whole plant to promote balance in individual physiology and so eliminate disease.'

Maharishi Technology of the Unified Field

One journalist asked about the connection of the Maharishi Technology of the Unified Field with Maharishi Ayurveda.

Dr Wallace replied that the Maharishi Technology of the Unified Field is the approach to perfect health from the angle of consciousness.

'The Maharishi Technology of the Unified Field develops coherence in brain functioning by allowing the conscious mind to identify itself with the unified field,' he said. 'Through the Maharishi Technology of the Unified Field, the total potential of natural law contained in the unified field is put to use in practical life.'

WORLD PEACE • GLOBAL INAUGURATION

PRESS CONFERENCES ON MAHARISHI'S UNIFIED FIELD BASED APPROACH

Higher States of Consciousness

Dr Wallace explained that regular practice of the Maharishi Technology of the Unified Field develops higher states of consciousness, in which brain functioning is optimal. This ensures that thinking and action are spontaneously in tune with natural law, he said.

'Numerous scientific research studies have found that the development of higher states of consciousness through the Maharishi Technology of the Unified Field is accompanied by extensive benefits for physical and mental health,' Dr Wallace said. 'These include reduction of major risk factors for disease, improvement in a wide variety of clinical disorders, reduced requirements for medical care, and reversal of the ageing process.'

Long Life Should Be a Common Experience

Dr Triguna commented that the word 'Ayurveda' means the Veda of Ayu—the knowledge of the complete range of life, extending from the shortest to the longest life-span.

'All Ayurvedic procedures serve to reconnect life to its immortal source in the unified field,' Dr Triguna said. 'They enliven the link between the changing values of physiology and their unchanging origin in the unified field. In this way, they ensure that perfect balance is maintained under all circumstances. According to Ayurveda, long life is within the reach of every human being and should certainly be a common experience.'

Maharishi Ayurveda Rasayanas

Dr Wallace then briefly reviewed scientific research on the programmes of Maharishi Ayurveda showing prevention and reversal of the ageing process. He also described the revival, under Maharishi's guidance, of the highly sophisticated science of the preparation and use of herbal and mineral substances known as Rasayanas.

Dr Wallace said that research studies in the U.S.A. and India are now verifying the ancient Ayurvedic understanding that Rasayanas are effective in strengthening the immune system, preventing cancer and cardiovascular disease, enhancing neurological recovery, and preventing the deterioration of the body's tissues that usually occurs with ageing.

'Heart disease, cancer, and stroke are the main causes of mortality in most countries today,' Dr Wallace said, 'so it is not surprising that this research has already attracted considerable interest. This hope for prevention is entirely credited to Maharishi's systematic approach to the revival of the complete knowledge of Ayurveda as the scientific system of perfect health.'

Prevention Is Better than Cure

Dr Triguna said that *prevention* is the principal focus of Maharishi Ayurveda. He recounted that during his recent world tours he had become keenly aware of the urgent demand in all countries for a holistic, cost-effective system of preventative medicine. He said that since Maharishi Ayurveda is based on the totality of natural law, it offers a truly holistic approach to prevention, encompassing all the factors that influence susceptibility to disease. Maharishi

MAHARISHI'S PROGRAMME TO CREATE

PRESS CONFERENCES ON MAHARISHI'S UNIFIED FIELD BASED APPROACH

Ayurveda programmes increase resistance to disease by improving the efficiency of the immune system and by maintaining balance in all parts of the body, he said.

Dr Triguna added that Maharishi Ayurveda provides effective methods to detect and correct imbalances before disease arises. He said that through pulse diagnosis the most expert Ayurvedic physicians are capable of detecting any existing or forthcoming disease or imbalance.

Balanced Diet and Nutrition according to Constitutional Type

Maharishi Ayurveda also recognizes the need for balanced diet and provides a thorough understanding of nutrition according to constitutional type, Dr Triguna said. To ensure that nutrition is complete, Maharishi Ayurveda offers a comprehensive range of natural food supplements, both for prevention and for use in specific disorders, he said. These supplements are prepared according to the precise procedures described in the classical Ayurvedic texts, and they play a key role in balancing the physiology, increasing vitality, and preventing illness, he said.

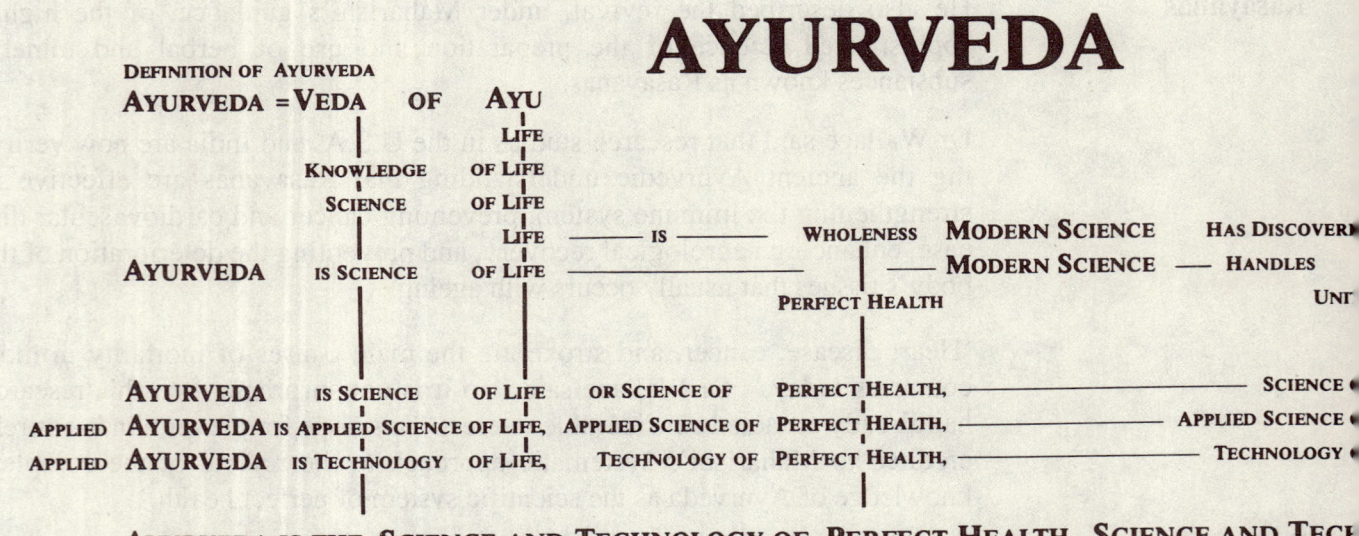

AS SUPERSYMMETRIC UNIFIED QUANTUM FIELD THEORIES
THE LAWS OF NATURE, AYURVEDA HAS BEEN REALIZED AS T

AYURVEDA

AYURVEDA IS THE SUPREME SCIENTIFIC SY

Brought to light by His Holiness Maharishi Mahesh Yogi during

WORLD PEACE • GLOBAL INAUGURATION

PRESS CONFERENCES ON MAHARISHI'S UNIFIED FIELD BASED APPROACH

Maharishi Ayurveda Prevention Centres World-Wide

Several physicians present at the news conference described the development of Maharishi Ayurveda in their countries. They said that Maharishi Ayurveda Prevention Centres have already been opened in countries on all continents, including Australia, the Philippines, Thailand, Sri Lanka, Kenya, Italy, Austria, Switzerland, West Germany, France, Holland, Denmark, Finland, Sweden, Norway, Great Britain, Ireland, Canada, the U.S.A., and Brazil, with initiatives underway in many more countries. Practitioners of modern medicine in 22 countries have been trained in Maharishi Ayurveda.

The physicians said that 12,000 medical doctors throughout the world have learned the Maharishi Technology of the Unified Field and many more recommend it to their patients. In addition, an active programme of biochemical, pharmacological, physiological, immunological, and clinical research on Maharishi Ayurveda is underway at leading scientific institutions world-wide.

Maharishi World Centre for Ayurveda

At the time of the press conference, the Maharishi World Centre for Ayurveda was being established at Maharishi Nagar. With 1,200 beds, the Centre's hos-

---

OF MODERN PHYSICS HAVE GLIMPSED THE UNIFIED FIELD OF ALL
TECHNOLOGY OF THE UNIFIED FIELD FOR PERFECT HEALTH

MODERN SCIENCE

See Unified Field charts on:
- Physics
- Chemistry
- Mathematics
- Computer Science
- Physiology, etc.

WHOLENESS — IN THE UNIFIED FIELD OF ALL THE LAWS OF NATURE
WHOLENESS — IN THE UNIFIED FIELD OF ALL THE LAWS OF NATURE
CONSCIOUSNESS — IMMORTALITY, INFINITY, INVINCIBILITY, SELF-SUFFICIENCY
(REVERSAL OF AGEING PROCESS, SEE CHART...) (EXPANSION, COSMIC INDIVIDUAL, ENLIGHTENMENT) (UNRESTRICTED SUCCESS) (FREEDOM AND FULFILMENT)

Introduction of Ayurveda will enliven these values in the life of the nation.

WHOLENESS — SCIENCE OF THE UNIFIED FIELD OF ALL THE LAWS OF NATURE
WHOLENESS, APPLIED SCIENCE OF THE UNIFIED FIELD OF ALL THE LAWS OF NATURE
WHOLENESS — TECHNOLOGY OF THE UNIFIED FIELD OF ALL THE LAWS OF NATURE

LOGY OF THE UNIFIED FIELD OF ALL THE LAWS OF NATURE

Introduction of Ayurveda in the life of all the people will provide holistic health—life according to natural law—life in happiness, free from suffering.
Maharishi Ayurveda Prevention Centres will render the nation invincible, to enjoy the perpetual sunshine of the Age of Enlightenment.

TEM OF NATURAL MEDICINE

ternational Conference on Natural Medicine, 20 March – 12 April 1985, Brasilia

pital will be the world's largest facility for treatment, teaching, and research in Maharishi Ayurveda.

One member of the press asked how Maharishi's Programme to Create World Peace related to his World Plan for Perfect Health and Maharishi Ayurveda. He asked what it contributes to world health.

Creating World Peace through the Balancing Principle of Maharishi Ayurveda

Dr Orme-Johnson replied that Maharishi envisioned the possibility of creating world peace through the BALANCING PRINCIPLE of Ayurveda. EEG research had shown that this principle is practically available through the Maharishi Technology of the Unified Field, Dr Orme-Johnson said. The performance of 'yogic flying' was found to produce maximum coherence in individual brain physiology and in the collective consciousness of society as a whole, and sociological research had found that the square root of one per cent of a population practising this technology together in one place produces sufficient coherence in collective consciousness to significantly improve the quality of life in the whole society.

For three weeks in the winter of 1983-84, a group of 7,000 individuals had practised Maharishi's technology together and produced this effect on a global level for the first time, Dr Orme-Johnson said.

7,000 TM-Sidhas —the Best Medicine for Global Health

'Scientific research on this assembly showed that 7,000 TM-Sidhas are the best medicine for global health,' he said. 'Their practice creates balance in the collective physiology of all nations. Therefore, Maharishi Ayurveda prescribes group practice of the Maharishi Technology of the Unified Field—specifically, the technique of "yogic flying"—for perfect health and peace in the world. Establishing a permanent group of 7,000 to create the Global Maharishi Effect is an essential step of action in Maharishi's World Plan for Perfect Health.'

The next day, a reporter for the *Statesman*, one of India's national newspapers, paraphrased Dr Triguna: 'Ayurveda has a lot to contribute towards improving world health, and Maharishi Mahesh Yogi has made commendable efforts in spreading this knowledge world-wide.'

Press Conference on the Maharishi Unified Field Based Integrated System of Defence

2 AUGUST 1986 • NEW DELHI, INDIA

Another topic of global concern, defence, was the theme of the second press conference, held ten days later, on 2 August. Beneath a banner that read, 'Enlightenment to the Individual and Invincibility to Every Nation', Dr Wallace explained the connections between health, defence, and world peace.

Defence in Terms of Immunity

Physiologists, he said, discuss defence in terms of immunity. 'The immune system protects the physiology against threats to its integrity,' Dr Wallace said. 'The dimensions of immunity range from defence against invading pathogens to resistance to stress, from positive health habits to improved mental health. Anything that increases coherence or integration in the physiology enhances its immune status. All strategies to strengthen the self-referral feedback mechanisms that maintain balance in the body's functioning are strategies in its defence and promote its health and longevity.'

Reduction of Ageing Shows Liveliness of the Body's Defences

Dr Wallace described one research study in the U.S.A. showing that TM meditators had a 68.8 per cent lower hospital admissions rate than the mean for the U.S. population as a whole. They also had much less of an increase in health insurance utilization with age. He said this finding suggests a slowing of the ageing process through regular practice of the TM programme.

'Several other studies have shown that the Maharishi Technology of the Unified Field reduces ageing—a holistic expression of the liveliness of the body's defences,' Dr Wallace said.

Dr Orme-Johnson commented that this understanding of defence in terms of immunity can be extended to society. He referred to 31 sociological studies as showing that the Maharishi Technology of the Unified Field improves the resistance of a whole society to disorders of collective health, including social, economic, and political problems.

When National Consciousness Is Coherent, the Nation Is Invincible

'Just as the individual mind or consciousness affects the functioning of the individual immune system, so the collective consciousness of the whole society affects the immunity of society,' Dr Orme-Johnson said. 'When national consciousness is coherent and integrated, the nation is invincible. It is secure from both external enemies and the internal threats of crime, poverty, and all negative tendencies. It is healthy and at peace.'

An Invincible Armour for the Nation

Dr Orme-Johnson said that the application of Maharishi's Invincible Defence Strategy creates an invincible armour for the nation.

'The Vedic literature speaks of Rashtriya Kavach, national armour,' he said. 'This means integrated national consciousness. Through the use of the Maharishi Technology of the Unified Field, national consciousness becomes integrated and strong. National life is promoted in accordance with natural law. The nation radiates a life-supporting influence throughout the world, automatically preventing an enemy from arising. This radiance of friendliness and harmony is its invincible armour. A sword is not even raised against it. That is its invincible strength—the danger is prevented.'

Dr Triguna commented that Maharishi's Programme to Create World Peace

Avert the Danger before It Arises

utilizes two key aspects of Maharishi Ayurveda, Yoga and Jyotish, to keep danger away from the individual and society. Jyotish is the scientific approach to accurate prediction and prevention of imbalances. It secures the future by prescribing Yoga, the Maharishi Technology of the Unified Field, to create coherence in individual and collective consciousness. To underline his point, Dr Triguna quoted from the *Yoga Sutras* of Maharishi Patanjali: 'Heyam Dukham Anagatam' ('Avert the danger before it arises').

Dr Morris emphasized that Maharishi's approach is the opposite of destructive means of defence, which leave the enemy fearful and only postpone confrontation.

Maharishi's Invincible Defence Strategy Can Never Be Destructive

'History records that destructive means of defence have always proved suicidal for any nation,' Dr Morris said. 'Maharishi's Invincible Defence Strategy can never be destructive to life because it works from the level of the unified field, which in its very essence is only creative and evolutionary.'

A journalist said that nations deploy destructive means of defence out of fear of other nations. He asked how Maharishi's programme neutralizes this fear.

Stress Is the Real Enemy of the Nation

Dr Morris replied that fear is caused by stress, and that stress has its basis in violation of the laws of nature.

'Stress in the citizens' physiology is the real enemy of the nation,' he said. 'Since education does not train the people to think and act spontaneously in accordance with natural law, the whole population is violating the laws of nature, causing stress, weakness, and fear and creating the need for defence. The Maharishi Technology of the Unified Field cultures the physiology of the individual and nation to remain stress-free, removing the basis of fear and weakness and thus eliminating the very need for defence.'

Another journalist asked how Maharishi's approach improves upon existing means of defence.

Dr Wallace replied that defence ministries have relied upon electronic and nuclear technologies for defence.

Establishing Peace through the Creative Power of Natural Law

'But peace in the world has been overshadowed by fear of the destructive power on the electronic and nuclear levels of natural law,' Dr Wallace said. 'Now peace can be easily established through the application of the creative power of natural law, which lies at more fundamental levels. The most fundamental, most creative level of nature's functioning is the unified field. It is much more powerful than the nuclear and electronic levels. Stimulating the unified field, in Maharishi's words, "promotes the rise of the supreme power in world consciousness that will free mankind from fear."'

Several journalists questioned the speakers closely about the programme's ef-

WORLD PEACE • GLOBAL INAUGURATION

PRESS CONFERENCES ON MAHARISHI'S UNIFIED FIELD BASED APPROACH

Eliminating Terrorism through Maharishi's Programme to Create World Peace

fect on terrorism.

'Terrorism is international,' Dr Morris commented. 'Any approach to combat it must be global in impact. Fortunately, with Maharishi's Programme to Create World Peace, any nation can eliminate international terrorism by assembling a group of 7,000 experts in the Maharishi Technology of the Unified Field. Such a group would eliminate stress and fear and would enliven the evolutionary qualities of the unified field on a global scale.'

Dr Morris summarized Maharishi's programme as 'creating world peace through the power of silence'.

Creating World Peace through the Power of Silence

'We know from both ancient Vedic science and the most advanced theories of modern quantum physics that the Veda—the unified field of natural law—is a field of perfect silence with infinite dynamism,' he said. 'Eternal silence upholds the self-interacting dynamics of the unified field—peace upholds dynamism. In Maharishi's words, "Peace on earth created from this level will be powerful and power on earth will be peaceful."'

Victory before War

Dr Morris ended the press conference with a vision of what defence will be like when Maharishi's Programme to Create World Peace has been implemented: 'Maharishi's unified field based approach has raised defence from the ground of ignorance and cruelty to the heights of wisdom and compassion. Nourishing the hearts of all nations, every nation will enjoy invincibility. Victory before war is the clarion call of unified field based defence.'

Press Conference on the Maharishi Unified Field Based Integrated System of Administration

7 AUGUST 1986 • NEW DELHI, INDIA

A third press conference was held on 7 August, eight days before the global demonstration of Maharishi's Programme to Create World Peace.

In his opening statement, Dr Morris said that, according to one historian, in the past 55 centuries there have been only 292 years without warfare.

'For at least 95 per cent of recorded history man has been fighting with himself,' Dr Morris commented. 'Throughout this time world peace has been the responsibility of governments. In view of this, it isn't reasonable for individuals to rely on governments for peace.'

'This is not a criticism of governments,' Dr Morris added. 'They are the highest authorities in a nation and always deserve respect, support, and appreciation. Rather, this demonstrates a basic principle about governments—that they are not independent entities.

Maharishi's Absolute Theory of Government

'According to Maharishi's Absolute Theory of Government, a government, no matter what its system, is, in Maharishi's phrase, "an innocent mirror of the nation". It simply reflects the quality of the collective consciousness of all the people.

'A government's destiny is designed by the collective consciousness,' Dr Morris said. 'A government cannot design its own destiny any more than a machine driven by electric power can influence the power in the power lines.'

Using another analogy, Dr Morris compared a government to a hand that is writing. Behind the hand is the mind, he said. If the mind is turbulent, the handwriting will be disorderly. Likewise, if the collective consciousness of a nation is violent, the performance of its government will display violence.

Creating Coherence in National Consciousness

'Governments so far have lacked the knowledge of how to create coherence in national consciousness, because there has been no holistic concept of life, no knowledge of the total potential of natural law,' Dr Morris said.

'In this scientific age, we have begun to understand that basic level of creation from which everything emerges and from where everything could be controlled,' he said. 'This is the unified field of natural law. The concept of handling the collective consciousness of a nation from this holistic level of life is an ancient Vedic concept, restored by Maharishi in his formulation of Vedic science. Now the technology to improve national consciousness is available. The technique is to identify individual consciousness with the unified field.'

Raising Individual Consciousness to Improve National Consciousness

Dr Morris explained that since individual consciousness is the unit of national consciousness, raising the consciousness of the individual is the direct way to improve national consciousness. This will improve the performance of the government and make it competent to maintain world peace.

'World peace, once created by individuals, can certainly be maintained by governments,' Dr Morris said.

One journalist asked how Maharishi's approach related to the day-to-day administration of government.

Governing with the Supreme Efficiency of Nature

Dr Morris responded that the Maharishi Technology of the Unified Field 'offers to every government that supreme efficiency with which nature governs the universe, without altering the present system of government in any way.'

He explained that all trends and tendencies in every country are fundamentally governed by natural law. The unified field, being the fountainhead of all the laws of nature, underlies all aspects of national life and, as such, is available

WORLD PEACE • GLOBAL INAUGURATION

PRESS CONFERENCES ON MAHARISHI'S UNIFIED FIELD BASED APPROACH

A Nation's Most Precious Resource—the Brain Physiology of Every Citizen

everywhere. The means to enliven the unified field in national consciousness are also available everywhere, in the brain physiology of every individual. Therefore, every government has within its power all it could ever need to make life fulfilling and the nation ideal.

'It is just a matter of knowing how to use the nation's most precious resource—the brain physiology of every citizen,' Dr Morris said.

Maharishi's Unified Field Based Approach Brings Fulfilment to Every System of Government

A reporter with one of the international news services asked if the Maharishi Technology of the Unified Field favoured one system of government over another.

Dr Morris replied that the unified field favours all equally. 'It is the only level of life universal enough to bring fulfilment to every system of politics, economics, and religion, while simultaneously harmonizing them all,' he said.

Another journalist commented that many leaders advocate increased communications between peoples—cultural exchanges, athletic contests, and the like—to promote international harmony. He asked what makes Maharishi's programme more effective than this approach.

'The prerequisite for effective communications between people is to raise their level of consciousness,' Dr. Morris said. 'Talk may temporarily alleviate fear, and information may relieve uncertainty for a time, but unless national consciousness is raised, fears and doubts will return to trouble international relationships.

'If the road joining two villages is falling apart, it is not enough to patch its surface,' Dr Morris said. 'One must repair the foundation. We may not have known before how to work at the level of the foundation, but now we do.

Developing Higher States of Consciousness Is Vital to Accomplishing World Peace

'Developing higher states of consciousness is vital to accomplishing world peace,' Dr Morris continued. 'Narrowness of vision and inability to accomplish one's desires cause uncertainties, loss of self-confidence, and all the unwanted values that make life cry for peace.'

Dr Morris explained that direct experience of the unified field develops consciousness. Growing purity of consciousness, he said, stimulates spontaneous use of finer levels of natural law. This ultimately leads to the use of the full potential of natural law in unity consciousness, the highest state of consciousness. With growth of consciousness comes broader vision and comprehension and greater ability to fulfil desires. Naturally this is accompanied by increasing satisfaction and happiness.

'Peace depends on happiness,' Dr Morris said. 'Happiness, fulfilment, satisfaction—these depend on progress. Because the nature of life is to grow and evolve, stagnancy at any level leads to frustration and unhappiness. For world peace to be a reality, life everywhere must be lived under the direct influence

Reinforcing the Evolutionary Power of Natural Law in World Consciousness to Create World Peace

of the evolutionary power of natural law. Reinforcement of that power in world consciousness is the only effective way to bring satisfaction to everyone and neutralize all kinds of negativity in the world.'

Dr Morris said that the full evolutionary power of natural law can be located at the level of the unified field. He said that physics describes the dynamics of the unified field as self-interacting. Acting only with itself, the unified field creates all the forms and phenomena of the universe.

Maharishi Technology of the Unified Field Creates Peace as a By-Product of Increasing Bliss

'The unified field is self-evolutionary,' Dr Morris said. 'It needs nothing outside itself. In subjective terms, the unified field is a state of fulfilment, of bliss —a level of unshakable satisfaction. Anything that can identify itself with the unified field spontaneously gains that evolutionary and blissful character. When approached by human awareness, the unified field stimulates human awareness in the evolutionary direction and fills it with the experience of bliss. Negative tendencies are spontaneously neutralized, and fulfilment is lived in life. This is how the Maharishi Technology of the Unified Field creates peace as a by-product of increasing bliss.'

One member of the press asked if Maharishi's programme was directed to specific individuals, or was he inviting anyone to implement it.

The Role of the Individual

Dr Morris replied that 'There are many, many individuals who care deeply for their fellow man. Our appeal is to them. They have always wanted to find the best way to translate their concern into effective action. Now they can eliminate the basic cause of fear and weakness in the world. Maharishi has provided a technology that will do much more than they had even hoped possible. Like watering the root of a plant to bring nourishment to all its branches, leaves, flowers, and fruits, the Maharishi Technology of the Unified Field enlivens the root of world consciousness in the unified field to let the world garden blossom in peace.'

Dr Morris added that those creative individuals who employ large numbers of people and enjoy raising the national economy through their efforts stand at the basis of the collective consciousness of their people.

'Their activities and personal interests frequently are global,' he said. 'They are feeling increasing pressure from the rivalry of the superpowers and the unpredictable violence of terrorism. For their own pleasure and even their own survival and progress, these wealthy people, and indeed all leaders, must formulate a successful plan and take action for world peace.'

7,000 Experts in the Maharishi Technology of the Unified Field to Enliven the Evolutionary Power of Natural Law in World Consciousness

Maharishi's plan, Dr Morris said, calls for 7,000 experts in the Maharishi Technology of the Unified Field practising together in one place.

'Such a group will generate a very strong influence of positivity to purify world consciousness day by day,' he said.

WORLD PEACE • GLOBAL INAUGURATION

PRESS CONFERENCES ON MAHARISHI'S UNIFIED FIELD BASED APPROACH

Dr Morris quoted Maharishi: 'World peace, arising from the growing purity of world consciousness, will enliven and release all the evolutionary power of natural law which is dormant in world consciousness. This will bring about the full blossoming of positivity and infinite creativity in the national consciousness of every country. With this, the governments of all countries will rise to their supreme dignity, which they have always deserved, and will enjoy self-sufficiency and freedom from limitations.'

Demonstrations of Maharishi's Programme in 1,000 Cities in 108 Countries

Dr Morris said that 'The sooner a group of 7,000 is established, the sooner the world will enjoy peace and every nation will be invincible.'

He emphasized that this was not just another plan to bring attention to the need for peace. 'It isn't simply an event to build awareness about peace,' he said. 'It is a programme to physically create world peace.'

Dr Morris said there are 50,000 'yogic flyers' throughout the world. On 15 August, in 1,000 cities in 108 countries, several thousand of them would present Maharishi's programme.

Awakening a New Optimism for World Peace

'We hope their demonstrations of Maharishi's technology will awaken everywhere a new optimism for world peace,' Dr Morris said.

The reports and press clippings on the following pages show that this hope was realized. They tell of the enthusiasm the TM-Sidhas inspired in communities all around the world. Each demonstration began with a videotaped introduction and review of scientific research by Maharishi and faculty of Maharishi International University and Maharishi Vedic University. With an understanding of how Maharishi's technology creates coherence in world consciousness, the audiences were prepared to see in 'yogic flying' much more than a person hopping up into the air. They became the first generation in history to witness the technique to create immediate and lasting world peace. □

Inaugurating Maharishi's Programme to Create World Peace

NARRATIVES AND PRESS REPORTS

ACKNOWLEDGEMENT

Gratitude is expressed to the many publishers and broadcasters of the press reports printed in this section, first for hastening the rise of world peace by bringing the news of Maharishi's beautiful programme to so many members of our world family, and second for granting permission to reprint their reports in this book.

WORLD PEACE • GLOBAL INAUGURATION

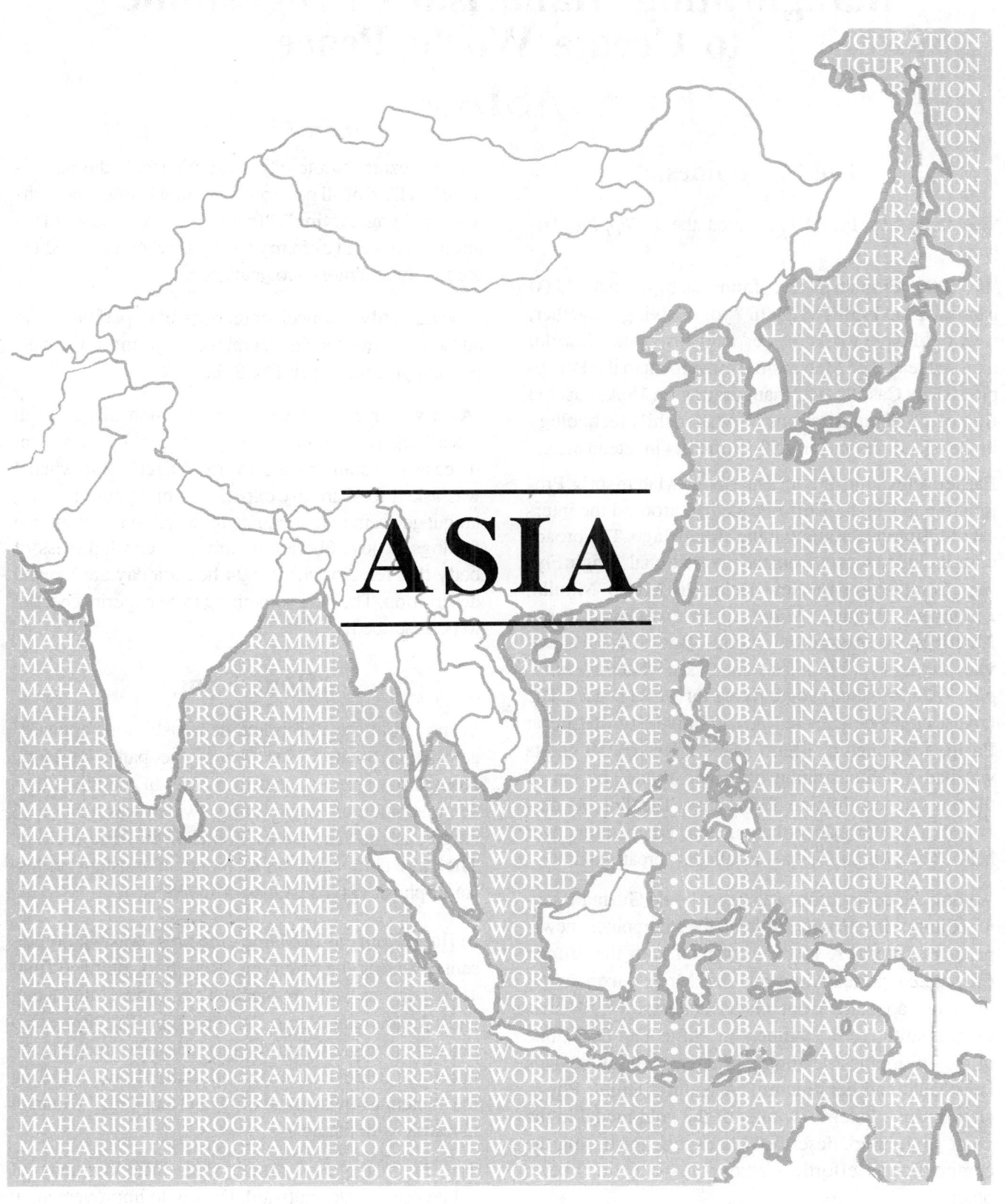

ASIA

Inaugurating Maharishi's Programme to Create World Peace
ASIA

The Philippines

'See how they FLY,' exclaimed the *Philippine Tribune*.

'If 7,000 Filipinos, one from each of our 7,000 islands, practised TM-Sidhi 'yogic flying' together, we would have world peace,' said Josephine Castillo, national leader of Maharishi's movement in the Philippines. Mrs Castillo was inaugurating on 15 August the first of 13 demonstrations of Maharishi's technology in the island nation, with 50 journalists in attendance.

Earlier television broadcasts about Maharishi's Programme to Create World Peace had aroused the interest of Filipinos throughout the archipelago. The broadcasts included scenes from the International 'Yogic Flying' Competition in New Delhi. In **Metro Manila, Lingayen, Baguio, Malolos, Santa Cruz, Trece Martires, Maragondon, Cebu, Bacolod,** and **Davao,** hundreds of Filipinos came to see what the *Philippine Tribune* called 'yogic flying for world peace'. The largest audience gathered at the University of Life in **Pasig,** a borough of Metro Manila, where 250 guests watched a demonstration of 'yogic flying' by ten of the most expert Filipino TM-Sidhas. The *Tribune* described it as 'probably the quietest competition ever held.' The *Manila Chronicle* called it 'breath-taking'.

Among the competitors was Cornelio de Guzman, senior editor of the *Manila Bulletin*, the Philippines' newspaper of record. A fellow newsman with the *Manila Chronicle* reported with pride that Mr de Guzman 'got the most applause from media colleagues'. Medals were awarded to the winners by Jullie Yap Daza, one of the Philippines' leading journalists, who three days later headlined her column, 'A Natural High'. Physician Enrique Paterno, winner of the gold medal in the yogic high jump, described his experience during the competition as 'effortless, enjoyable—a feeling like no other'.

Mr de Guzman wrote of his experience, 'I did not believe in a field of all possibilities until I learned the technique of "yogic flying". "Incredible" was the word uttered in my mind or in my thoughts when I hopped for the first time almost two years ago.

'The humanly inconceivable, blissful experience is so attractive to me that I never miss a single morning or afternoon practice of my TM-Sidhis.

'As a writer of 27 years I never found difficulty in describing various human experiences. I found them so easy to communicate to my readers. But when I was asked to share my experience on "yogic flying", language seemed inadequate to describe it. I think the feelings of joy, liberation, strength, and lightness of body that remain with me 24 hours a day are beyond description. They are something to be experienced, not to be described.'

Hong Kong

Scenes from the Philippine demonstrations appeared across the South China Sea in the pages of **Hong Kong's** newspapers, next to reports of the city's own demonstration of 'yogic flying', which was held on 15 August at the Jade Lotus Room of the Hilton Hotel. The three demonstrators included an assistant professor of physics at the Chinese University.

In Hong Kong, as in Manila, the press was well represented among the observers. Reporters attended from 16 papers, as well as Radio-Television Hong Kong and Commercial Radio. A report in *Tai Kung Pao* noted that 'yogic flying' is a technique to integrate the mind and achieve alliance with natural law, fulfilling the ancient Chinese ideal of 'Tien Ren He Yi' ('man in harmony with nature').

The *Tai Kung Pao* article said, 'The harmony of coherence radiates outward, leading to improvement in

INAUGURATING MAHARISHI'S PROGRAMME TO CREATE WORLD PEACE—ASIA

the quality of life in the city, society, and even in the whole world.' The *Tin Tin Daily News* carried the headline, 'Transcendental Meditation yogic flying. World-wide demonstrations by all affiliated organizations. The goal—world peace.'

The *Business Standard* published an Associated Press report that said, 'TM teaches that world peace can be achieved by orderly activity of the human brain through deep meditation. Meditating together in large groups, adherents say, can neutralize negative and disruptive forces, like terrorism.'

The *South China Morning Post* reported, 'You can fly —and improve humanity's collective disposition while you're at it.'

Macao

At **Macao's** Hotel Royal, 'yogic flying' was demonstrated for the public and representatives from six newspapers, as well Macao television and radio.

The Macao *Daily News*, in its Sunday edition, said that 'Hopping in the air gave the audience a new vision of life and broadened their awareness.' The *Si Man Pao* explained that through 'yogic flying' 'a powerful influence of positive coherence is generated, which influences others and creates a peaceful atmosphere. In this way, the goal of eliminating wars and cruelty and establishing world peace can be achieved.'

China

Interest in Maharishi's Programme to Create World Peace was awakened in China by scenes of the First International 'Yogic Flying' Competition, shown on a 23 July nation-wide television broadcast. Ten days later, the *Physical Culture Post*, a popular Chinese sports magazine, ran a photograph of 'yogic flying' with a short descriptive article. Thus the stage was set for a team of TM-Sidhas from Hong Kong, led by Governors of the Age of Enlightenment Miss Chan Wei Wah and Miss Siu Kit Foon, to begin a tour of 14 principal Chinese cities.

Starting on 15 August, their tour took them to eight provinces, from Heilongjiang in the far north to Guangdong, mainland China's southernmost state. Their 15 presentations were attended by more than 5,000 people, many of them leaders of Chinese society. Ten television and three radio programmes broadcast the news throughout the country, and more than 30 newspapers—national, provincial, and local—reported on the events. Ten of the articles appeared with photographs on the front page.

In North China

In **Beijing**, Maharishi's programme was inaugurated at the National Research Institute of Sports Science. The event was organized by the Beijing Research Association for the Maharishi Technology of the Unified Field, which has a membership of more than 350 Beijing residents who practise the Transcendental Meditation and TM-Sidhi programme.

Among the 400 guests in Beijing were many prominent Chinese scientists, as well as vice chairmen, bureau directors, directors, and party leaders from several national organizations, including the State Science and Technology Commission, the Ministry of Public Health, and the State Commission for Physical Culture and Sports.

The TM-Sidhas later commented, 'We had never seen so many cars parked outside a function as we saw that night in Beijing.'

The dignitaries were seated at the front of the hall. The stage was padded with foam rubber mats covered with white sheeting. To one side was a podium, and on the wall behind the stage a long red banner with gold characters read, 'Yogic Flying Demonstration, Introducing the Mechanics to Create World Peace through Creating Coherent Brain Functioning.' Seventy-inch television monitors displayed a videotape of Maharishi and scientists from Maharishi International University, Maharishi Vedic University, and Maharishi University of Natural Law explaining the mechanics of the programme to create world peace.

The principal national media of China—State Televi-

INAUGURATING MAHARISHI'S PROGRAMME TO CREATE WORLD PEACE—ASIA

sion, the *People's Daily*, the *Guangming Daily*—were represented. Three other national publications—the *Health Newspaper*, the *Sports Newspaper*, and the *New Athletics Magazine*—also sent reporters, as did many local Beijing press organizations. The next day State Television broadcast a report of Maharishi's programme on the 7:00 p.m. and 10:00 p.m. national news.

In every city the TM-Sidhas visited throughout China they were hosted by a prominent university, government organization, or political party. Their host in **Tianjin** was Tianjin University, one of China's leading technical schools, and the recently retired president of the university was among the audience of 70 faculty and students.

The first of two demonstrations in **Dalian**, an industrial city on China's northern coast, was hosted on 29 August by the Dalian Municipal Committee of the China Known Kung Democratic Party (CKKDP). The CKKDP is one of seven democratic political parties in China co-existing with the Communist Party. Its membership is made up of senior medical professionals, engineers, and professors.

Three hundred people came to the Dalian Institute of Technology for the 29 August demonstration. As the guests arrived they were welcomed by CKKDP officials, who presented them with packets of literature on 'yogic flying' and the Maharishi Technology of the Unified Field. During the demonstration, several of the scientists present attempted to evaluate the physiology of 'yogic flying' by using a remote control device to monitor the heart rate of the TM-Sidhas.

The second demonstration was held on 9 September at the Hall of the Dalian Municipal Committee of the Chinese Peoples' Political Consultative Conference (CPPCC), a national organization whose role is to harmonize all the political parties of China. Officials of seven political groups were present, as were leaders of many of Dalian's most important organizations, including the Communist Committee, the People's Congress, the Dalian Municipal Government, and the CPPCC. Also among the 300 guests were eminent scientists, artists, educators, and physicians from throughout the city.

Professor Yang Lie Yu, Member of the National Committee of the CPPCC, Vice-Chairman of the Dalian Municipal People's Congress, and Chairman of the Dalian Municipal Committee of the CKKDP, welcomed the demonstrators. His remarks were characteristic of the warm welcome accorded the visitors by leading officials throughout China.

'According to *World News* magazine, *Jiefang Daily*, Shanghai's *Living Weekly Journal*, and *New Athletics Magazine*,' Professor Yang said, 'a new and widespread health practice—the Transcendental Meditation technique—has charmed the world. In over 120 countries, several million people are practising this technology.

'Over 350 scientific studies conducted at more than 160 universities and research institutions since 1970 have shown that this technology can develop mental potential, improve health, establish a stable state of psychology, and also fully enliven man's natural self-healing ability in order to normalize blood pressure and eliminate the psychosomatic diseases caused by physical fatigue and mental stress.

'This technology was founded and taught by Maharishi Mahesh Yogi.... He states that it is a scientific meditation, which is definitely not a religion and is different from the Chinese Qigong practice.

'He has established Maharishi International University in Iowa, U.S.A., and Maharishi European Research University in Switzerland and Holland. Taiwan, Hong Kong, and Macao also have similar organizations of teaching and research in this technology.

'...We, the Dalian Municipal Committee of the CKKDP, for the sake of promoting contacts, establishing friendship, and exchanging information with Hong Kong, Macao, and national and overseas areas, have specially invited leaders, comrades, and friends of our municipality to come and witness this demonstration of the effects this technology produces.'

WORLD PEACE • GLOBAL INAUGURATION

INAUGURATING MAHARISHI'S PROGRAMME TO CREATE WORLD PEACE—ASIA

The TM-Sidhas' hosts expressed great enthusiasm after the presentation of Maharishi's programme and gave them letters of introduction to affiliated organizations throughout China.

In **Shenyang**, 200 people watched Maharishi's lecture on six television monitors placed around the demonstration hall. That evening, Shenyang city television broadcast scenes of 'yogic flying', and the next day a report was published on the front page of the Shenyang *Daily News*. The headline read, 'Wonderstruck by Yogic Practice—Hong Kong Ladies Can Sit and Levitate from the Ground!'

The Shenyang *Evening News's* report began, 'The legendary Xun Wu Kung sat on clouds and moved through the mist. Is this a fairy tale? Not long ago, a "yogic flying" competition was held in New Delhi, India. Yogic Olympians levitated by mere thought-impulse and made forward hops. Once this piece of news went out in the newspapers, people were wondering, Can man really fly as the great saint Xun Wu Kung did?

'On the afternoon of 13 September, at the audio-visual centre of the Liaoning Provincial College of Traditional Chinese Medicine, Miss Chan Wei Wah and Miss Siu Kit Foon ... demonstrated the amazing "yogic flying" in front of scholars, experts, and reporters. The two ladies sat in lotus posture on a piece of foam, and, after ten minutes of meditation, they shook a little and then their bodies bounced up into the air and kept hopping unceasingly.'

The Shenyang *Daily News* commented that the ladies looked 'relaxed and natural throughout the demonstration.'

In **Harbin**, 300 people filled the theatre of the Institute of Health Education at the Heilongjiang Provincial Ministry of Public Health. The distinguished audience included the Chairman of the Standing Committee of the Heilongjiang People's Congress and top officials from many provincial associations, commissions, and ministries.

Front page headlines the next day in the Harbin *New Evening Post* said, 'Extraordinary practice proves its effect—the body lifts up.' According to the article, 'All in the audience were amazed.'

The Harbin *Living Post* wrote, 'One person in the audience exclaimed, "Incredible!", as he saw two delicate ladies, after ten minutes of meditation in the sitting posture, lift off the ground again and again.... Their demonstration brought great amazement as well as great interest to the several hundred scholars and scientists present.... Experts are now investigating into the physiological mechanics and scientific basis of the phenomenon.'

In **Wuhan**, the capital of Hubei province, 140 faculty and students attended a presentation of Maharishi's programme at Wuhan University.

In **Xi'an** the presentation was hosted jointly by the Xi'an Municipal Committees of the CPPCC and the CKKDP. It was held in the CPPCC meeting hall.

'Our hosts organized everything,' Miss Chan and Miss Siu said. 'They hired three cars to transport the foam mats, arranged a large video screen, invited the public and all the VIP's, and served us a lavish banquet after it was over.'

The next day, the Xi'an *Daily News* printed on its front page a photograph of a smiling 'yogic flyer' in mid-air.

In East China

In the east China city of **Hangzhou**, known as 'heaven on earth' for its scenic beauty, 400 students and faculty attended the presentation at Zhejiang University.

The Hangzhou *Daily News* reported, 'Yesterday noon, a fascinating and unprecedented 'yogic flying' demonstration was held in the Health Hall of Zhejiang University.... According to the [TM-Sidhas], during the demonstration their brains were in a state of absolute silence, their bodies felt relaxed, and they hopped nimbly by mere intention. The hopping is not based on physical effort. After their performance, they felt totally relaxed and happy. They said that the practice of "yogic flying" not only maximizes coherence in brain functioning and improves health, but also increases creativity, self-confidence, optimism, and harmonious social life.'

In **Shanghai,** the *Worker's Post* reported, 'On a hard floor with neither springboard nor springs, how can a human being lift up in the air? We personally witnessed a new and extraordinary demonstration of "yogic flying".'

One hundred and fifty other people also witnessed the Shanghai demonstration, which was hosted by the Research Association for the Maharishi Technology of the Unified Field of East China Normal University and held in the university's main office building. Faculty and students from two other leading Shanghai universities, Fudan and Shanghai Jiaotong, were also present.

The *People's Daily* commented, 'In Shanghai, researchers in the fields of natural and social science were very interested in the demonstration.'

China News Service was among the six press organizations represented, and its photograph and report were published by the overseas edition of the *People's Daily*, by the *Liberation Daily*, and by six newspapers in Hong Kong and Macao. Several days after the demonstration, Shanghai television showed scenes of the New Delhi 'yogic flying' competition to the 12 million people of China's largest city.

In Central China

The Science and Technology Commission of **Chengdu,** capital of Sichuan Province, became so interested in Maharishi's programme that they not only offered to host the demonstration, but also made all the necessary arrangements in a single day. Two hundred people responded to the commission's invitation and came to see 'yogic flying' on 17 September at the theatre of the Sichuan Opera.

In **Chongqing,** an article on 18 September in the *Evening News* described the Transcendental Meditation programme and the Science of Creative Intelligence in detail: '[Transcendental Meditation] achieves a profound state of wakeful rest, which is different from waking or sleeping. EEG testing has found that in this state the electrical activity of the left and right cerebral hemispheres and the central and peripheral parts of the brain is coherent and synchronized....

'Synchrony of brain waves indicates a profound increase of flexibility and coherence of the brain functioning, which not only benefits the physiology and releases fatigue but also improves memory, intelligence, creativity, and learning ability.

'Transcendental Meditation is related to disciplines such as physics, chemistry, physiology, and psychology, and many scholars and experts have validated from the angles of their own disciplines the benefits of TM for health, development of intelligence, balanced psychology, and increased creativity, thus giving rise to a new science—the Science of Creative Intelligence.'

The Chongqing Municipal Committee of the CKKDP displayed a giant wall painting and posted 50 smaller signs in the city centre to announce the demonstration. The announcement read, 'Warmly Welcome the Hong Kong Foundation of the Science of Creative Intelligence to Demonstrate in Chongqing the Extraordinary Performance of "Yogic Flying"'.

More than 1,000 people came on 19 September to the Chongqing Grand Sports Stadium. Among the many prominent guests were two Vice Chairmen of the Chongqing Municipal People's Congress and the Chairman of the Advisory Committee of the Chongqing Communist Party. Journalists from local television, radio, and press, as well as Xinhua, China's national news agency, reported the event.

In South China

To illustrate the theme of the event in **Guangzhou,** south China's largest city, Guangdong provincial television began its report by slowly panning the characters on the long red and gold banner in the hall—'"Yogic Flying" Demonstration—Introducing the Mechanics to Create World Peace.' The report

WORLD PEACE • GLOBAL INAUGURATION

INAUGURATING MAHARISHI'S PROGRAMME TO CREATE WORLD PEACE—ASIA

showed a videotape recording of Maharishi explaining the principles and practice of his programme, and then scenes of the International 'Yogic Flying' Competition in New Delhi and of the five Chinese TM-Sidhas demonstrating 'yogic flying' in Guangzhou.

In **Xiamen,** an important trading port on the South China Sea and one of China's special economic zones, the *Daily News* published on 24 September a long article on the Maharishi Technology of the Unified Field. After briefly recounting a history of Maharishi's worldwide movement and the scientific research on his technology, the article described the visit to China in 1982 of over 70 scientists of different disciplines from MIU and its affiliated universities. The article said that 'their exchanges on this technology with researchers, scientists, and medical experts of our country aroused a great interest in the academic field.'

The report noted that several research associations for the Maharishi Technology of the Unified Field had already been established in China. 'In the near future,' the paper said, 'this newly established international health practice will be promoted more speedily in all parts of our country.'

Several days earlier, officials of the CPPCC, the CKKDP, and the Xiamen Commission for Physical Culture and Sports had jointly sent out a letter to the principal organizations of the city, inviting them to a presentation of Maharishi's programme on 26 September at the People's Sports Stadium. The letter urged leaders to 'organize members of your institution to participate in this event.'

The article and invitations drew 600 people. Xiamen's deputy mayor, who was the chief guest, announced the timings for the preliminary meditation and 'yogic flying' demonstration. After the programme, a formal banquet was given in honor of the team of TM-Sidhas by the chairmen of the provincial committees of the CPPCC and the CKKDP.

In **Fuzhou,** the demonstration was held in the hall of the Fujian Provincial Committee of the CKKDP. Among the 300 guests were leaders from several provincial colleges and political and professional organizations. The Fujian *Evening News* reported on its front page that 'the whole audience applauded and marvelled at the demonstration.'

The Fuzhou *Daily News* said of the demonstrators, 'They did not use physical effort, they used consciousness, and they hopped lightly.... They say that everyone, man or lady, old or young, can master this technique by learning from a qualified teacher.'

The demonstration in Fuzhou concluded the TM-Sidhas' remarkable tour. Within the space of little more than one month, 'yogic flying' had become a well-known phenomenon in China, and Maharishi's Programme to Create World Peace had been introduced to millions of people in the world's most populous nation.

Taiwan

Across the Taiwan Strait, journalists from five newspapers and two national television stations gathered at **Taipei's** Hotel China to watch a group of TM-Sidhas, among them a retired army general, fly for world peace. That evening, on the 11:00 p.m. news, Taiwan television brought Maharishi's programme to people throughout the island. Four days later, a half-hour special on the event was aired, entitled 'Tamen hsiang fei' ('They wish to fly').

South Korea

In South Korea, at **Seoul's** Shilla Hotel, 15 reporters from all the major national newspapers as well as KBS Television joined 20 other guests for a two-hour presentation on 'yogic flying', the Maharishi Effect, and world peace.

Japan

In Japan, presidents of corporations, university professors, and more than 40 journalists, including representatives from two of the country's largest television networks, were among the audience at a demonstration in **Tokyo's** Hotel Otani. The organizers reported that many of the guests 'laughed with joy and delight' dur-

INAUGURATING MAHARISHI'S PROGRAMME TO CREATE WORLD PEACE—ASIA

ing the 'yogic flying'.

The joy was even greater for the demonstrators. One TM-Sidha said, 'I felt an expansion of consciousness, and my body was very light and blissful. I am sure the powerful effect generated by this technique is capable of creating coherence throughout the world.'

Six weeks later, another demonstration was held on **Okinawa**, and scenes of the 'yogic flying' there were broadcast on Okinawa television.

Singapore

Among Southeast Asian nations, Singapore, Indonesia, Malaysia, and Thailand all hosted inaugurations of Maharishi's Programme to Create World Peace. Three hundred people crowded the ballroom of the Shangrila Hotel in **Singapore** on 15 August to see one TM-Sidha demonstrate 'yogic flying'. The organizers said that other Sidhas had decided merely to sit on the foam mat behind the demonstrator, but, when the performance began, the impulse to fly was so strong that spontaneously they also began to hop.

Malaysia

Three hundred fifty spectators, including 20 journalists, attended a demonstration at the Hotel Dayang in **Petaling Jaya**, Malaysia. The proceedings there ended with the ceremonial cutting of a large cake and wishes for 'Peace to our nation and through our nation to the world.'

Reports on the inauguration appeared in many of Malaysia's Chinese-language newspapers. Their headlines conveyed the inspiration the audience had felt: '300 spectators call it a miracle—"yogic flying" demonstration'; 'Returning to nature and going to Utopia—the miracle of Transcendental Meditation'; 'Twenty minutes of Yoga is better than eating ambrosia'; 'Promotes mind-body co-ordination—Transcendental Meditation technique in Malaysia is sprouting and growing'.

The *China Press* wrote that at least 3,000 people in Malaysia have learned the TM technique and some 200 practise the TM-Sidhi programme. That article said, 'The founder of the Transcendental Meditation and TM-Sidhi programme and the Science of Creative Intelligence is Maharishi Mahesh Yogi. Beginning in 1958, Maharishi promoted and spread this meditation to the whole world.... For the past 20 or 30 years, medical and scientific studies have shown benefits for the development of mind and body. Due to this the technique has gained popularity at all levels of society. In 1976, the TM technique was brought into Malaysia under the Malaysian Foundation of the Science of Creative Intelligence by one of the founding members, Mr Ong Teong Beng.'

An article in **Tong Bao** noted, 'The technique of Transcendental Meditation is also called the "technology of peace", because, through practice of the technique, waves of peace and positivity spread throughout the surroundings, influencing the atmosphere and people and promoting peace in the world.'

Indonesia

The Indonesian Press Agency was among the media at the demonstration on 15 August in **Bandung**, Java. At the demonstration on **Bali**, world peace was described by the master of ceremonies as 'already achieved in principle and soon to be accomplished in practice through Maharishi's unprecedented plan.'

Thailand

Over 200 guests, including businessmen, teachers, and several government officials, attended the two-hour **Bangkok** inauguration of Maharishi's Programme to Create World Peace.

One television station and six newspapers reported on what the *Bangkok Post* called, 'The physically uplifting side of meditation.'

The *Nation* began its 16 August article: '"At this time ... a Transcendental Meditation (TM) Sidhi Flying contest is being held by TM centres all over the world," said Police Major General Phat na Pomphet to an audience of TM practitioners, enthusiasts, and observers at the President Hotel's Madura Room. "But

WORLD PEACE • GLOBAL INAUGURATION

INAUGURATING MAHARISHI'S PROGRAMME TO CREATE WORLD PEACE—ASIA

for Thailand, this is the first of its kind. Let me assure you that we are not attempting to show any miracles from the Transcendental Meditation Sidhi Flying; what you will witness today is purely scientific.'"

Were the demonstrators tired after 'yogic flying'? the *Nation* asked. "'Not at all...,' replied one competitor. "After all, it was ... brain power.'" The article concluded with a quotation from Maharishi: 'Let us eliminate the possibility of war without loss of life.'

Pakistan

At the Intercontinental Hotel in **Karachi**, Pakistan, writers for the capital's principal English dailies joined an audience of 90 to watch a demonstration of 'yogic flying' by a Pakistani TM-Sidha who had just completed training as a teacher of the Transcendental Meditation programme. A videotape of the demonstration was later shown to large audiences in Pakistan.

India

In India, the 'Land of the Veda', 15 August was Independence Day. Fifty-one teams of 11 young student Vedic Pandits travelled from Maharishi Ved Vigyan Vidya Peeth (Maharishi Vedic University for Asia) in Maharishi Nagar, outside New Delhi, to 35 cities throughout the length and breadth of the subcontinent. From **Jammu** in the Himalayan northwest to **Nagarcoil** far in the tropical south, the young Pandits presented Maharishi's Programme to Create World Peace. Dressed in the Dhoti, Kurta, and cap traditionally worn by Vedic scholars, they began their demonstrations by reciting from the Vedic literature and then performed the TM-Sidhi 'yogic flying' technique.

At important locations in each city, the teams of Pandits also conducted Vedic performances to enliven the evolutionary trends of natural law in the locale. Their presence and presentations inspired people everywhere with a strong desire to fully own the profound knowledge of natural law from Vedic science, as brought to light by Maharishi.

Large Audiences

Large audiences attended the inaugurations. Four thousand came in **Lucknow**; in **Haridwar**, the gateway to the Himalayas, 2,500 people from throughout Haridwar and Rishikesh attended; in **Simla**, there were 1,500 guests.

Fourteen hundred people came to the Geeta High School in **Kurukshetra**, not far from the battleground immortalized in the *Bhagavad Gita*. In **Ambala**, 1,000 guests attended the presentation, and in **Jammu**, 900. In **Bhopal**, 800 people came despite a heavy rain on the day of the event. Eight hundred also came in **Rajkot**. Just as the demonstration in Rajkot started, a gentle, cooling rain began, moderating the very hot weather that had been oppressing the city.

Demonstrations in **Ahmedabad, Ayodhya, Mathura, Vallabhvidyanagar**, and **Nagpur** each drew approximately 700 people. In **Patna**, 600 attended; in **Allahabad, Muzaffarnagar, Jaipur**, and **Jabalpur**, 500; and in **Madras, Ajmer**, and **Sriganganagar**, 400.

Distinguished Guests

Distinguished spiritual leaders, state cabinet ministers and legislators, justices, judges, advocates and district magistrates, inspectors general of police and other government officials, eminent physicians and scientists, engineers, managers, bankers and businessmen, school principals, university vice-chancellors, and several nationally renowned educators were among the many leaders of society who attended the demonstrations by the young Vedic Pandits.

All the presentations began with audio- or videotape recordings of Maharishi speaking on his programme to create world peace. Then the chief guest was introduced and invited to comment on the significance of Maharishi's programme.

In **Allahabad**, Sri Chandra Mohan Srivastava, Principal of K.P. Inter College, said Maharishi had 'restored the practical teaching of Vedic science with a simple, easy, natural, spontaneous, and effortless

INAUGURATING MAHARISHI'S PROGRAMME TO CREATE WORLD PEACE—ASIA

process for the upliftment of the individual and society.'

In **Kanpur**, the chief guest, Sri Shambhu Saran Tripathi, said that Maharishi had brought the Age of Enlightenment to mankind. He called Maharishi's programme 'a harbinger of new life to be experienced by the people of all continents.'

In **Hyderabad**, 50 TM-Sidhas competed in 'yogic flying'. In **Bangalore**, at the Maharishi Institute of Creative Intelligence, 250 people watched in 'pin-drop silence', according to the organizers, as TM-Sidhas demonstrated 'yogic flying' and journalists from the *Deccan Herald*, *Indian Express*, and *Prajavani* took photographs and notes. The flying in Bangalore lasted for 15 minutes, but, wrote one reporter, 'There was no sign of fatigue on the faces of the demonstrators.'

Transforming Effect

The young Vedic Pandits themselves said that the 'yogic flying' generated 'much bliss, great inner happiness.' In every city, the demonstration of 'yogic flying' had a transforming effect on the audience. In **Dehra Dun**, one guest remarked, 'You have profoundly enriched my feelings and opened my eyes to a fuller vision of the world.'

The chairman of the **Ayodhya** inauguration, Pt Baij Nath Dwivedi, said that the bliss and peacefulness experienced during the demonstration showed what daily life is like when it is based on knowledge of the Veda, the unified field of natural law.

'Mankind', he said, 'will be relieved from problems and suffering, and will enjoy heaven on earth.'

After witnessing the demonstration in **Nagpur**, a guest commented of the 'yogic flying', 'If the Vedic students do this every day, world peace will come soon.'

A beautiful feature of every presentation was the sweet and profoundly coherent influence produced by the Pandits reciting from the Vedic literature. In **Varanasi**, the renowned centre of Vedic learning, several leading educators commented how impressed they were by the performance of the young students. In many cities, guests expressed their appreciation and respect for the Vedic curriculum of Maharishi Ved Vigyan Vidya Peeth and said they wanted their children to gain the value of this knowledge by enrolling as students at the school.

Enthusiastic Response

In cities throughout the country, including **Jodhpur**, **Rohtak**, **Hisar**, and **Coimbatore**, audiences responded with long applause to the suggestion that the programme be repeated in the coming years. The most frequently asked question was, When can we begin practice of the Transcendental Meditation technique?

Inspired by the presentations, distinguished leaders in many cities rallied the audiences to support Maharishi's initiative. In **Bhiwani**, advocate Mr V.K. Sharda called the programme 'a matchless and extraordinary campaign which requires whole-hearted support from all of us.' After the presentation in **Madurai**, one businessman said he wanted to donate a building for the establishment of a Maharishi Ayurveda hospital, and, at a general meeting, Madurai government officials and politicians passed a resolution that implementation of the TM-Sidhi programme be accelerated effectively in all the villages of the city.

In **Delhi**, all the national daily newspapers, both Hindi and English, featured large announcements of the 17 demonstrations of Maharishi's Programme to Create World Peace to be given by the Vedic students in the capital city. The scholars were joined for these demonstrations by expert TM-Sidhas from other countries—Governors of the Age of Enlightenment and members of the Thousand-Headed Purusha Programme who were at Maharishi Nagar conducting research in Vedic science.

The Delhi 'yogic flying' demonstrations were held in community halls and state guest houses in different parts of the city. Altogether, approximately 3,000 people attended, including diplomats, government officials, and many leading citizens. At most sites the auditoriums were filled to capacity or were overflowing. The sound of the Vedic recitations drew people from the streets into the halls, particularly in Chandnichowk, one of old Delhi's market districts, where the entire performance was aired outdoors by loudspeaker. Together the recitations and 'yogic flying' created what one guest called a 'soft, sweet, family feeling'.

A press conference held prior to the demonstration at Himachal Bhavan, the guest house for Himachal state, drew 20 journalists from Indian, foreign, and international news organizations.

Wide Press Coverage

The local press throughout India gave the demonstrations wide coverage. In **Ambala**, articles appeared in *Punjabi Kesari*, the *Daily Review*, *Navbharat Times*, and *Hindustan*. Both the *Muzaffarnagar Bulletin* and the *Uttam Bulletin* published reports. Journalists from the *Times of India*, *Navbharat Times*, *Dainik Jagran*, *Hindustan Samachar*, *Amrit Prabhat*, and the Press Trust of India attended the demonstration in **Allahabad**. *Jan Morcha* and *Shree Ram Janma Bhumi* were represented at the demonstration in **Jaunpur**, and in **Varanasi** three local papers printed articles.

The inaugurations in **Jabalpur** and **Indore** were reported in a number of newspapers, including *Navbharat Samachar*, *Indore Samachar*, *Nai Dunia*, and *Swadesh Samachar*, several under the headline, 'Yogic flying for world peace'. One article said that the possibility of 'yogic flying' can be understood from theories of quantum gravity and that the flying technique itself is described in the Yoga Sutras of Maharishi Patanjali. Thus, it said, 'yogic flying' is appreciated from the perspectives of both modern science and ancient Vedic science.

Hyderabad's *Dainik Hindi Milap* noted that the reality of 'yogic flying' is validated by many records in the Vedic literature and has now been presented scientifically by Maharishi. The article quoted Pt Ram Chandra Malviya, Vice-Chancellor of Maharishi Ved Vigyan Vidya Peeth, saying that the Vedic literature presents the principles to create world peace and that those principles have been practically applied by Maharishi to make world peace an achievable reality.

The Public Relations Society of India sponsored the inauguration in **Bhopal**, which had been announced in advance in the *Madhya Pradesh Chronicle* under the headline, 'Human "flying" miracle in Bhopal Aug. 15'.

The article began, 'Experts in Maharishi Mahesh Yogi's now world-famous programme on Transcendental Meditation will demonstrate publicly the benefits of yoga in Madhya Pradesh. This will be the first ever such live demonstration [of 'yogic flying', in which] the meditator's brain waves become orderly to the point where co-ordination between mind and body is maximum and the body rises off the ground.'

The Bhopal demonstration was written up in both *Dainik Jagran* and *Dainik Bhaskar*.

In **Meerut**, both *Punjabi Kesari* and *Dainik Jagran* published reports. The latter explained how through 'yogic flying' mind-body co-ordination increases and brain functioning becomes coherent.

'With coherent brain functioning,' the article said, 'the individual is orderly, society is orderly, the nation is orderly, and world consciousness is coherent. With coherent world consciousness, balance is maintained in the world as the basis for permanent world peace.' Maharishi's approach to creating world peace, the article continued, is 'very fundamental, totally original and holistic. Through it all negative trends in society can be removed and terrorism completely eliminated.'

In another article, printed in Bombay's *Society* magazine, Dr Girendra Mahapatra, Secretary General of the Maharishi World Federation of Ayurveda, explained Maharishi's approach to creating world peace: 'One man in the village is good enough to ensure clean clothes for the entire village. Similarly, if some 7,000 people are brought together for TM they can act like the washerman' for world consciousness.

The article explained that the group of 7,000 TM-Sid-

INAUGURATING MAHARISHI'S PROGRAMME TO CREATE WORLD PEACE—ASIA

has, by creating a powerful influence of coherence in collective consciousness, eliminates the stress in world consciousness and world peace spontaneously results.

India—the Host of Peace for the Whole World Family

Guests at all the demonstrations on 15 August received a pamphlet, *Maharishi's Programme to Create World Peace—Removing the Basis of Terrorism and War*. In this document Maharishi comments, 'It is interesting to observe that the Vedic Pandits of this generation—the remnants of the Vedic civilization, the most ancient civilization in the world—are rising up to be the pioneers of world peace, and India, the all-time common friend of all nations, is rising to be the host of peace for the whole world family.'

The young students of Maharishi Ved Vigyan Vidya Peeth, on their tours throughout the Land of the Veda, brought home to the people of India the realization that Maharishi's technology, which has its roots deep in the Vedic tradition, offers a genuine hope for world peace. They said that although their group at Maharishi Nagar now numbers 2,000, Maharishi's programme calls for 10,000 to create coherence in the whole world consciousness. Whenever people urged the visiting students to come again, they replied that they wanted to return on Independence Day 1987 with the news that they are now 10,000 and world peace has been created. □

WORLD PEACE • GLOBAL INAUGURATION

INAUGURATING MAHARISHI'S PROGRAMME TO CREATE WORLD PEACE—ASIA

Mr Ong Teong Beng, national leader of Maharishi's movement in Malaysia, inaugurates his country's first 'yogic flying' demonstration.

Malaysian TM-Sidha 'yogic flyers' who demonstrated the mechanics of Maharishi's Programme to Create World Peace.

Demonstrating the first stage of 'yogic flying' in the Philippines.

At the Grand Sports Stadium, Chongqing, China. The top banner reads, 'Warmly welcome the Hong Kong Foundation of the Science of Creative Intelligence to demonstrate in Chongqing.' The lower banner says, 'Yogic flying competition—introducing the mechanics to create world peace through creating coherent brain functioning.'

MAHARISHI'S PROGRAMME TO CREATE

INAUGURATING MAHARISHI'S PROGRAMME TO CREATE WORLD PEACE—ASIA

At the demonstration in Xiamen, China.

After a banquet hosted by political leaders of Shenyang.

At the Dalian Institute of Technology, Dalian, China.

At the inauguration in Chengdu, China.

At the inauguration in the CPPCC Hall, Dalian, China.

At the demonstration in Hangzhou, China.

WORLD PEACE • GLOBAL INAUGURATION

INAUGURATING MAHARISHI'S PROGRAMME TO CREATE WORLD PEACE—ASIA

The demonstration at Himachal Bhavan, New Delhi.

Scholars of Maharishi Ved Vigyan Vidya Peeth meditate before demonstrating 'yogic flying' at Green Park Community Centre, New Delhi.

Pt Ramakrishna Shastry (seated, centre) chairs the inauguration of Maharishi's Programme to Create World Peace at Maharishi Institute of Creative Intelligence, Bangalore.

At the demonstration of the mechanics to create world peace, World Sociology Congress, New Delhi, 22 August 1986.

Second row, from left: Pt Pravar Ram Gulam Pande, Pt Pravar M.M. Ram Vilas Shukla, Pt Pravar Ram Chandra Malviya, with the 11 scholars of Maharishi Ved Vigyan Vidya Peeth who demonstrated 'yogic flying' in Jammu, India.

MAHARISHI'S PROGRAMME TO CREATE

INAUGURATING MAHARISHI'S PROGRAMME TO CREATE WORLD PEACE—ASIA

At the demonstration in Jammu, India.

The team of Vedic Pandits in Bhiwani, India.

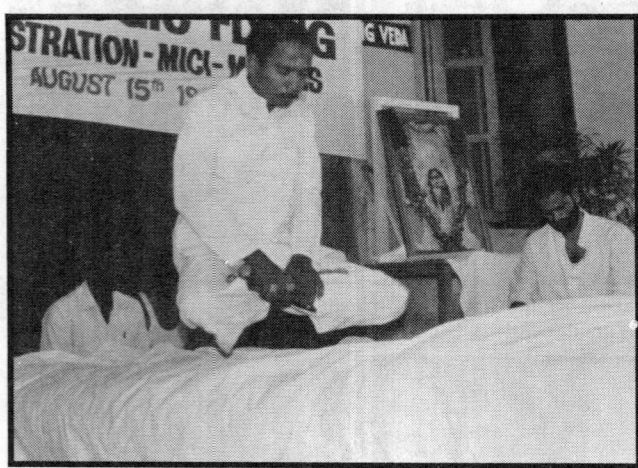
At the demonstration in Madras, India.

The inauguration in Madras, India.

At the demonstration in Ambala, India.

'Yogic flying in Vallabhvidyanagar, India.

WORLD PEACE • GLOBAL INAUGURATION

PRESS REPORTS FROM ASIA

China • *The Physical Culture Post*
New Delhi 2 August 1986 (Chinese)

坐地腾起半米多

首届瑜珈腾空赛在新德里举行

本报讯 7月21日，在印度首都新德里举行了首届国际"瑜珈腾空"比赛。五位瑜珈信徒单凭着意念，使身体腾离地面，并向前空移一步。

瑜珈信徒们称，目前只达到第一阶段——跳跃。不久将进入第二阶段——腾空和第三阶段——飞行。

这次比赛在新德里的甘地体育馆内进行，来自18个国家的50位选手，参加了50米冲撞、25米跳栏、跳远和跳高四个项目的比赛。

所有参赛者均采取莲式坐姿。与此同时，场外的一队科学家们，则忙于利用量规、转盘和电子仪器统计各种数据，并测量参赛者的脑电波。

（黎明京）

加拿大瑜珈运动员布兰·华生离地二十二点五英寸，获得「跳高」冠军。

PRESS REPORTS FROM ASIA

China • *Guangdong television*

Guangzhou, Guangdong   17 August 1986   (Chinese)

(*English translation*)

Broadcaster: Compatriots from the Hong Kong Foundation of the Science of Creative Intelligence demonstrated Transcendental Meditation 'Yogic Flying' for the press and leaders of society here in Guangzhou at a press conference on 17 August.

The Transcendental Meditation 'Yogic Flying' technique was founded by Maharishi Mahesh Yogi, the Indian scientist and educator who integrated an ancient system of meditation from India with the unified field theory of modern science to create a scientifically validated technique for optimizing coherence in brain functioning.

Over 350 scientific studies have shown that Transcendental Meditation is beneficial for improving physical and mental health, increasing learning ability and creativity, releasing stress and tension, eliminating psychosomatic diseases, and even reversing ageing.

Several million people from over 120 countries are practising this technique.

In New Delhi, an international 'yogic flying' competition was held on 21 July.

WORLD PEACE • GLOBAL INAUGURATION

PRESS REPORTS FROM ASIA

China • *Jiefang Ribao*
Shanghai 23 August 1986 (Chinese)

图片新闻

香港创智科学基金会陈慧华女士和萧洁欢女士，二十日晚在华东师大礼堂示范瑜珈腾空术。她俩在一块不大的地毯上作莲花坐姿，静默十分钟左右，然后稍微抖动一下，身体便腾空而起，向前跳跃几步。本市自然科学和社会科学界人士对此均极感兴趣。图为陈慧华在示范。

China • *People's Daily* (Overseas Edition)
Shanghai 23 August 1986 (Chinese)

凝神蓮花坐　陡然騰空起
港女士在滬表演瑜珈奇功

中新社上海八月二十一日電　香港創智科學基金會的陳慧華、蕭潔歡兩位女士，昨晚在這裏表演了瑜珈騰空術。

兩位女士在一塊不大的地毯上作蓮花坐姿，靜默十分鐘左右，然後稍微抖動一下，身體便騰空彈起，向前跳躍幾步。

據兩位女士介紹，這是瑜珈飛行的第一階段——跳躍，進一步便是凌空升起和空中飛行，不過到目前為止，還沒有人能達到第二、第三個階段。她們說，超覺靜坐、瑜珈飛行技術能造就最高度協調有序的大腦生理機能，而使人的頭腦清醒、神經鎮靜並減輕人的壓抑感。上海一些從事自然科學和社會科學研究的人士對這次表演極感興趣。

PRESS REPORTS FROM ASIA

China ● *Hangzhou Ribao*

Hangzhou, Zhejiang 25 August 1986 (Chinese)

看瑜珈飞行表演

八月二十四日，香港创智科学基金会陈慧华、肖洁欢女士，应浙江大学气功协会的邀请，在浙江大学健身房作了一次别开生面的"瑜珈飞行技术表演。"

瑜珈功，是印度古老的健身养性之术，与中国的气功有异曲同工之妙，并称为世界两大奇功。本世纪五十年代末，印度一位物理学家、哲学家玛哈礼师，根据物理学中"物质运动均有一个统一场"的原理，揭示了人的大脑表层思维都统一于更深更完美的层次，类似物理学的"大统一场"的观点。为此，他把古老的瑜珈功与现代科学相结合，开创了"玛哈礼师统一场技术"，即"超觉静坐技术"。

世界上已有一百二十多个国家，数以百万计的人在学习、运用这种简单实用的健身法。

"瑜珈飞行"是"超觉静坐技术"的最高境界，分为三个阶段：跳跃、空中停留、空中飞行。陈、肖两位女士表演的是第一阶段：先在厚厚的海绵垫上盘起双腿，闭目打坐十分钟，然后在身体向上腾起的同时向前跳动，一起一落，反复来回，约七八分钟。跳动中双腿始终盘屈，保持坐姿。据表演者介绍，在整个过程中，她们的大脑处于一种绝对安宁平静的状态，身体自由放松，在一种潜意识的支配下，轻灵地腾跳，而不依靠肌肉的运动。作完之后，浑身显得愉快轻松。她俩还说，练习"瑜珈飞行"不仅可提高人的大脑功能，增强身体健康，而且能提高人的创造力、自信心和乐观精神等，协调人的社会生活。

陈、肖两位女士均为香港创智科学基金会"超觉静坐技术"教员，她俩计划在一定的时候来杭州开办这类培训班，以传授超觉静坐技术。

云 影

瑜珈飞行表演
昨在浙大举行

昨天中午，一场饶有趣味、别开生面的"瑜珈飞行技术表演"，在浙江大学健身房举行。表演者香港创智科学基金会陈慧华、肖洁欢女士，是应"浙大"气功协会邀请来杭的。

（冯）

WORLD PEACE · GLOBAL INAUGURATION

PRESS REPORTS FROM ASIA

China • *Harbin New Evening News*
Harbin, Heilongjiang   9 September 1986   (Chinese)

奇功显效腾空起
——访香港陈慧华、肖洁欢女士

九月六日晚，在省卫生宣传教育所剧场，两位年轻的女士闭目盘坐在舞台上。约十分钟光景，两位女士睁开双眼的同时，身体轻轻弹起，在离地约五、六寸高处向前跳跃。台下观众无不称奇。

省气功科学研究会的同志向记者介绍说，这是他们特邀香港创智科学基金会陈慧华、肖洁欢两位女士，专程来我省进行"超觉静坐"和"瑜伽飞行"表演。

怀着一种好奇心，记者借机采访了这两位女士。今年三十岁的陈慧华女士，操着"粤味"很浓的普通话，侃侃而谈。

她说，所谓"超觉静坐"，是当代印度哲人玛哈礼师于一九五八年首先传授世界各地的。七年前，这位印度科学家兼教育家又使瑜伽飞行问世。陈慧华女士解释说，"瑜伽飞行"，是"超觉静坐"的最深境界，即身体与脑功能达到最高诉调性时，身体会自动升起，共分为三个阶段：首先是"跳跃"，就是刚才我们所表演的；其二是"凌空升起"；第三是"空中飞行"。目前，全世界已有一百多个国家的三百万人练习"超觉静坐"，但据权威人士分析，就人的潜力来说，是有可能达到后两个阶段的。

在与两位女士谈话间，记者无意中燃起一支烟。二十七岁的肖洁欢女士当即劝道："吸烟是很不利健康的呀！如果你能练习'超觉静坐'，我保管你能把烟戒掉！"

接着，两位女士介绍说："超觉静坐"和"瑜伽飞行"，不单是自然、自动和自发地开发人的创造性潜力，使思维条理化，促进身心健康，更重要的是能使人的大脑各部分都达到高度协调、和谐。"超觉静坐"是一个简单易学的精神技术，不要特别的坐姿，也没有性别和年龄限制，在合格的老师传授下，经过七个简单的步骤，数小时便可掌握。

临辞别时，两位女士向记者透露，她们已接受省气功科学研究会的邀请，十月将再次来我市，传授"超觉静坐"和"瑜伽飞行"的功法。
　　本报记者 张瑶

陈慧华（上）肖洁欢（下） 张瑶摄

China • *Harbin Living Post*
Harbin, Heilongjiang   10 September 1986   (Chinese)

港女士在哈表演瑜珈腾飞奇功

一位观者脱口而出："简直不可思议。"当看似弱不禁风的两位女子，取"莲花座"姿，静思十分钟后，身子微抖，拔地而起，一次次跳跃。香港创智科学基金会的陈慧华和肖洁欢女士，六日在哈瑜珈"腾空飞行"术的表演，既令在场省内数百名学者、科研工作者和气功爱好者为之震惊，也引起了他们浓郁的兴趣。

这种在全世界有三百多万人学练的"瑜珈飞行"术，是通过大脑的意念控制，来达到身心的协调，其究竟有何生理机制和科学依据，有关专家正进行研究和探讨。因为两位香港小姐腾空而起。（本报记者 罗健摄影报道）

PRESS REPORTS FROM ASIA

China • *Shenyang Ribao*
Shenyang, Liaoning   14 September 1986   (Chinese)

香港瑜珈术专家在沈表演"腾空"功

本报讯 应中国农工民主党沈阳市委和辽宁中医学院的邀请，香港创智科学基金会信托人、玛哈礼师国际大学技术导师陈慧华、肖洁欢两位女士，九月十三日在沈为一百多位气功爱好者和社会、自然科学工作者做了一次别开生面的"瑜珈飞行"表演。

表演是在辽宁中医学院电化教室里一块长六米、宽两米的软垫上进行的。只见两位女士取"观音坐莲"姿势，两眼微闭，静默约十分钟后，身子微微抖动，接着身体腾空弹起约二、三百厘米，落下，又弹起，连续四、五分钟，整个过程中，两女士始终盘屈，保持坐姿，轻松自然。

瑜珈功是印度古代健身养性之术。据陈慧华女士介绍，超觉静坐技术，可造就最高度协调有序的大脑生理机能，而使人头脑清醒，使思维条理化，增加创造能力，促进身心健康，并有防老化的神奇功效。

China • *Shenyang Wanbao*
Shenyang, Liaoning   16 September 1986   (Chinese)

瑜珈功令人惊诧 香港两女士竟能坐地腾空

本报讯 孙悟空能够腾云驾雾，这只是神话吗？前不久，在印度首都新德里举行了国际"瑜珈腾空"比赛，五位瑜珈运动员单凭着意念，竟使身体腾离地面，并向前空多一步。这一消息经报载传开后，给人们带来了一团不解的谜——人果真能如孙大圣般腾飞吗？

九月十三日下午，在辽宁中医学院电教室内，来自香港创智科学基金会的陈慧华、肖洁欢女士，当着数十名学者、专家、新闻记者表演了令人迷惑不解的"瑜珈飞行技术"。只见两位女士以莲花坐姿于软垫子上，静默十分钟后，轻轻抖动一下，接着，身体便腾空弹起，不停地向前跳跃。

瑜珈功，是印度古老的健身养性之术，同中国气功。本世纪五十年代末，印度一位物理学家、哲学家玛哈礼师，根据物理学中"物质运动均有一个统一场"的原理，揭示了人的大脑表层思维都统一于更深更完美的层次，类似物理学的"大统一场"的观点。为此，他把古老的瑜珈功与现代科学相结合，开创了"玛哈礼师统一场技术"，即"超觉静坐技术"。如今世界上已有一百二十多个国家，数以百万计的人在学习、运用这种简单实用的健身法。

据两位香港女士谈其整个过程的感受时说，她们的大脑处于一种绝对安宁平静的状态，身体自由放松，其灵巧地腾跳，不是依靠肌肉运动而是在一种潜意识的支配下完成。作完之后，浑身显得轻松愉快。她们讲，练习"瑜珈飞行"能提高人的大脑功能，增强身体健康和人的创造力、自信心和乐观精神。

陈、肖两位女士从八月十五日起已于北京、广州、上海、杭州等八个城市进行了表演。这次来沈表演，是由沈阳市农工民主党辽宁中医学院气功协会接待的。
（照铭）

图为在印度新德里一运动员在作瑜珈腾空表演。
慧华 洁欢供稿

WORLD PEACE • GLOBAL INAUGURATION

PRESS REPORTS FROM ASIA

China • *Chongqing Wanbao*
Chongqing, Sichuan   18 September 1986   (Chinese)

世界推行的"超觉静坐技术"
——玛哈礼师统一场技术

近年来，世界上有一百二十多个国家数以万计的人在学习、运用一种简单实用的健身法——"超觉静坐技术"。

"超觉静坐技术"又名"玛哈礼师统一场技术"。它的创始人是印度裔物理学家玛哈礼师，他是把印度古代的一种静坐法，同现代物理学中的统一场论结合起来而创立的。

人体健康程度、精力和情绪的好坏，在很大程度上取决于大脑皮层的机能，即取决于大脑主交感神经与副交感神经是否平衡。"超觉静坐技术"训练有素者，能使主、副交感神经的兴奋与抑制迅速趋向平衡同步，达到一种既非清醒、亦非睡眠的积极休息状态。此时用脑电波显示仪测试，发现大脑的前后部、左右半球间以及中部与大脑支层之间，都产生明显的同步趋向（这与用脑电波测试我国气功师结果一致）。

脑电波趋于同步，表明大脑各部位的神经中枢之间的灵活性、协调性大大增强，从而使大脑功能得以改善。这不仅直接影响机体，消除疲劳，还有助于增强记忆力、智力、创造力和学习能力。

"超觉静坐技术"涉及到物理、化学、生物学、控制论、信息学以及心理学等等。许多专家学者分别从各自的科学领域证明它对人体健康、智力开发、心理平衡、创造力提高所起的促进作用，形成了一门新兴学科——创智学。

香港陈慧华、肖洁欢女士明日在我市表演「瑜珈腾空」术

本报讯 香港创智基金会瑜珈飞行代表、"超觉静坐"技术导师、玛哈礼师国际大学中国区代表陈慧华女士同该大学技术导师肖洁欢女士，将于明日晚上在市体育馆表演"瑜珈腾空"术。此前她们曾在北京、广州、上海、杭州、大连、成都进行了表演。

（欧道义）

China • *Chongqing Ribao*
Chongqing, Sichuan   20 September 1986   (Chinese)

香港陈慧华肖洁欢女士来渝
表演"超觉静坐——瑜珈飞行"

本报讯 （记者李元胜）来自香港创智科学基金会的陈慧华、肖洁欢女士昨晚在市体育馆表演"超觉静坐——瑜珈飞行"。这次活动是由中国农工民主党重庆市委和市体委主办的。

据陈慧华介绍，印度籍科学家、教育家玛哈礼师于一九五八年向世界各地传授了源于印度古代吠陀的超觉静坐功法，一九七九年又传授"瑜珈飞行"。这些功法有助于协调大脑生理机能，消除神经紧张，促进创造能力。目前，全世界有一百多个国家的三百万人练习。

昨晚八点四十许，两名女士开始了表演。她们穿着宽大的练功服，在铺有垫子的一张乒乓球桌上闭目盘腿作"莲花坐"。十分钟后，她们身体微微抽动，身体向前上方冲出，腾空数寸后落下。三分钟的连续跳跃中，她们面带微笑，神情轻松。

三十岁的陈慧华女士和二十七岁的肖洁欢女士学习这项功法已经六年，她们八月下旬以来陆续在上海、杭州、哈尔滨、沈阳进行过表演。

PRESS REPORTS FROM ASIA

China • *Chongqing Wanbao*

Chongqing, Sichuan   20 September 1986   (Chinese)

昨晚八点四十分，市体育馆内并连铺有垫子的乒乓台上，两位身穿练功服的女士闭目盘腿"莲花坐"，十分钟后，身体向上、向前冲起，腾空数寸一起一落，似跳跃向前，往返数次，轻松自如。这就是香港陈慧华、肖洁欢女士表演的"超觉静坐——瑜珈飞行术"。这种功法有助于协调大脑生理机能、消除精神紧张，促进创造能力。图为表演时的情景。赵克摄影

China • *Xian Wanbao*

Xian, Shaanxi   24 September 1986   (Chinese)

盘腿打坐 意念腾空
香港女士在我市表演瑜珈奇功

本报讯 香港创智科学基金会的陈慧华、肖洁欢女士昨晚在市政协礼堂表演的"超觉静坐"——"瑜珈飞行"使古城数百观众惊奇不已。

陈、肖二位女士先在铺有毯子的桌子上盘腿打坐，犹如老僧入定。十分钟后，身体微微晃动，向前上方冲出，腾空数寸后落下。一起一落、反复来回约五分钟。腾越跳动时，身体始终保持"莲花坐"姿，二位女士自始至终面带微笑、神态轻松自如。（之沪）

WORLD PEACE • GLOBAL INAUGURATION

PRESS REPORTS FROM ASIA

China • *Laodong Bao*

Shanghai　20 September 1986　(Chinese)

"瑜伽腾空"目睹记

沈鹤　李淳

在一无跳板、二无弹簧的硬地板上，人是怎么凌空腾起的呢？我们亲眼目睹了一场瑜伽腾空的新奇表演。

二十日晚上，在华东师大办公楼小礼堂，来自香港的陈慧华和肖洁欢小姐为本市新闻单位和一些科研部门作示范表演。

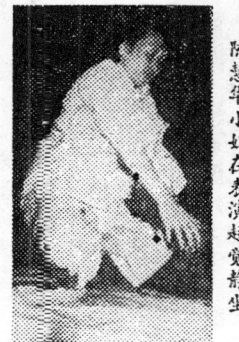

陈慧华小姐在表演超觉静坐。　姜敏　摄

"我们表演的这项技术叫超觉静坐，源于印度古代吠陀科学（即瑜伽术），训练人的脑生理。印度籍科学家和教育家玛哈礼师把这门古科学同现代科学相结合，发展成为玛哈礼师统一场技术。"陈小姐用带有广东口音的普通话，配合电视录像向大家介绍超觉静坐技术。

接着，两位小姐开始表演超觉静坐飞行。她们换上白底蓝花无领中式布上衣和镶着宽条花边的绸裤，显得十分清淡、素雅。在草绿色的地毯上她们两脚相枷，盘成莲花座，双目微闭，渐渐入静止状态。陈小姐开始头向下低垂，又慢慢抬起，然后又向下低垂，如此不断反复，而肖小姐则抬头静止不动。

十分钟后，陈小姐浑身开始抖动，忽然只见她双手上升，身体也随之向上腾起30厘多，并向前平移了一步的位置，然后落下，又腾起、平移。肖小姐也浑身抖动，开始腾跃。肖、陈两位在长八米、宽四米多的地毯上腾跃……

八分钟内，两位小姐各自腾跃了50多次，在观众热烈的掌声中，她们从地毯上站起来。记者马上对肖小姐进行测试，心跳为一百十多次。

"是的，腾跃时身体仍处活动状态。"陈小姐解释道，"超觉静坐后，人的各种生理机能达到高度的和谐和统一，自我感觉身体变得很轻很轻，稍用意念，就会在不知不觉中腾起。我们只是超觉静坐瑜伽飞行的第一阶段，即空中腾跃，第二阶段人能达到在天空静止，第三阶段人能在空中飞行，但是，目前全世界练习瑜伽飞行的人只能达到第一阶段。"

坐在前排观赏的市气功科学研究会（筹）负责人丁公量和裴锡荣两位老人说："'瑜伽腾空'虽不同于中国的气功，但在某些方面很象中国气功中的自发动功，是可信的。"主持会议的师大生理学家周绍慈说，"我对气功、瑜伽术等全是外行，看了表演后，我相信这是事实，不是作假。人体的每种活动都可以找到其生理原理，相信'瑜伽腾空'也是如此。一般人的跳跃是靠小腿腓肌的收缩，而瑜伽腾空却调动了股肌腰肌，这是一般人难以做到的，这两位弱女子真是不简单。"

临结束前，她俩直言不讳地说："此次来上海的目的是在于：造福个人、创造脑功能协调，造福人类、建立世界和平。"她们相信，在中国会有更多的人能够学习并掌握"超觉静坐"统一场技术。

PRESS REPORTS FROM ASIA

China • *Shaanxi Ribao*

Xian, Shaanxi 24 September 1986 (Chinese)

图为陈慧华在作"腾空"表演。

本报记者 郭凤展摄

香港陈慧华肖洁欢女士在西安表演瑜珈腾空术

本报讯 香港创智科学基金会的陈慧华、肖洁欢女士二十三日晚在西安市政协礼堂表演"超觉静坐——瑜珈飞行"。

瑜珈功,是印度古老的健身养性术。目前世界上已有一百二十多个国家,数以百万计的人练习这种功法。

在昨晚的表演中,二位女士身着练功服,先在一块不大的软垫上盘腿莲花坐,闭目静默十分钟后,只见她们身体微微抽动,接着向前上方腾空弹起。在她们数分钟的连续跳跃中,面带微笑,神清轻松。

(本报记者 张治华)

China • *Xiamen Ribao*

Xiamen, Fujian 27 September 1986 (Chinese)

香港陈慧华肖洁欢来厦作"超觉静坐"技术示范表演

本报讯 昨晚,香港创智科学基金会陈慧华、肖洁欢两位女士在市体育场羽毛球馆为我市数百名观众作了"超觉静坐——瑜珈飞行"技术示范表演。

在一块不大的地毯上,两位女士取莲花坐姿,静默约十分钟,然后身体稍微抖动一下,便腾空而起,向前腾跃几步。她们精彩的表演引起了在场观众的极大兴趣。

据两位女士介绍,"超觉静坐"是目前风行于世界的一种健身术。"超觉静坐"技术,目的还在于通过创造协调有序的大脑功能,使人们能够和谐、愉快、健康地工作和生活。

陈慧华、肖洁欢两位女士是在北京、上海、广州、武汉等十二个城市作"超觉静坐"、"瑜珈飞行"的表演之后,应我市政协"三胞"联谊会、农工民主党厦门市委会和市体委的邀请来到我市的。

(异之、公羽)

WORLD PEACE • GLOBAL INAUGURATION

PRESS REPORTS FROM ASIA

China • *Xiamen Ribao*

Xiamen, Fujian 25 September 1986 (Chinese)

超觉静坐——风靡世界的新兴健身术

在印度北部喜玛拉雅山麓一带的村落里，自古流传着一种独特的静坐健身法。本世纪五十年代末，一位名叫玛哈礼师的印度现代物理学家发现并研究了它。玛哈礼师运用现代物理学中的统一场论，和这种古老的静坐法结合起来，经过十多年的努力，终于创立起一整套完整的"超觉静坐技术"（英文简称「TM」），又称为"玛哈礼师统一场技术"。关于这项技术的研究，逐步形成了一门独立的学科，即所谓"创智科学"。

一九七〇年，玛哈礼师到了美国，与哈佛大学著名生物学家华莱士博士合作，对「TM」在改变人的生理状况等作用方面进行了大量的实验工作，提出了一系列富有说服力的报告。从那时起到现在，在国际科学论坛上，已有四十三个国家的一百五十多所大学和研究机构，提出了六百多篇研究报告和论文，证实了「TM」对于人类生理、心理、社会以及生态上的显著效益。目前，"超觉静坐"已风靡欧美，及于全球。据统计，全世界约有一百二十多个国家和地区共三百多万人正在学习、运用这门新兴的健身术。

超觉静坐技术简单易行。人们可以通过短期的学习掌握它。不过学习时必须在受过专门训练的老师指导下，按照规定的程序进行。静坐的练习每日二次，每次约二十分钟。静坐时神经系统充分放松，保持最低限度的兴奋，慢慢进入一种既非清醒，亦非睡眠的积极休息状态，即所谓"超觉"状态。据研究，人在这种状态中，可获得优于熟睡时两倍质量的休息。而静坐后的精力良好状况，可维持六至八小时。

有关实验结果表明：实行超觉静坐，不但能大大提高人的大脑功能，而且能使人体天然的医疗本能得到高度的发挥，对于降低血压和胆固醇，防治心血管疾病，对于消除机体疲劳、精神压抑、情绪紧张，以及由上述原因导致的生理、心理性疾病，有着极为良好的功效。一个人，如果长期坚持实行这种静坐，则能有效，逆退生理老化过程。

我国从一九八二年开始接触"玛哈礼师统一场技术"，先后有国外有关学者来华讲学及开办「TM」学习班。玛哈礼师本人也于一九八二年连同七十多位各国科学家前来我国，与中国科学院等有关方面的科研工作者和医学专家交流了这门技术的科研概要，引起国内学术界的浓厚兴趣。目前，在北京已成立了"统一场技术研究会"。上海的复旦、交大、华东师大二医等高校也都曾举办过有关的介绍讲座或传授课。可以预计，不久的将来，超觉静坐这门国际性的新兴健身术，将会在我国各地得到较快的推广。

本月二十六日，玛哈礼师国际大学中国区代表和技术导师香港创智科学基金会超觉静坐专家陈慧华、肖洁欢女士一行，将在我市为社会各界人士举行一场"超觉静坐技术"表演。

异之

PRESS REPORTS FROM ASIA

China • *Fujian Ribao*
Fuzhou, Fujian 30 September 1986 (Chinese)

香港陈慧华肖洁欢女士来榕

表演超觉静坐瑜珈飞行奇功

本报讯 九月二十八日晚，在省政协八楼会议室里，香港陈慧华、肖洁欢女士作了别开生面的"超觉静坐——瑜珈飞行"表演，观众莫不拍手称奇。

陈慧华年届"而立"，肖洁欢芳龄廿七。她俩是香港创智科学基金会的"超觉静坐——瑜珈飞行"术的教师。表演时，两位女士身着练功服，闭目静默，盘腿而坐。十分钟后，似观音莲花座，身子微抖，一起腾升而起，离座数寸，似跳跃向前，一落，往返数次，轻松自如。

"这不是气功，更不是魔术。"陈女士对记者介绍说，"超觉静坐"又称"它"。"玛哈礼师统一场论"一种静坐法同现代物理学中的古代统一场论结合起来而创立的"瑜珈飞行"是"超觉静坐"高技术。即脑功能达到最协调时，身体会自动腾起，分三个阶段发展：一是腾跳；二是空中浮动；三是空中飞行。"超觉静坐"使人的主、副交感神经的兴奋与抑制迅速趋于平衡同步，协调大脑生理功能，消除精神紧张，达到既清醒又积极休息状态理化，促进创造能力；还可达到使衰老迎退，有益身心健康。目前，已有一百多个国家的三百多万人练习"超觉静坐"。我国北京、上海分别成立了玛哈礼师统一场技术研究会。

陈、肖两位女士是应省政协"三胞"工作委员会、农工党省委会、中华全国体育总会福建分会的邀请前来福州表演的。这之前，她们已到北京、上海、大连、西安、重庆和厦门等十三个城市表演。

（本报记者李彬）

China • *Fuzhou Wanbao*
Fuzhou, Fujian 30 September 1986 (Chinese)

陈慧华、肖洁欢来榕表演瑜珈飞行技术

二十八日晚，数百名观众在省政协大楼礼堂惊奇地观看了香港创智科学基金会陈慧华、肖洁欢两位女士所作的瑜珈飞行表演。 林一平

PRESS REPORTS FROM ASIA

China • *Fuzhou Wanbao*

Fuzhou, Fujian　7 October 1986　(Chinese)

凌空腾跃显神功
—— 观瑜珈飞行表演

9月28日晚，在省政协八楼会议室里，来自香港的陈慧华、肖洁欢两位女士在软垫上闭目盘腿，取"莲花坐姿"。凝神端坐约十分钟后，身体微微抖动，忽而向上前方腾空跃起数寸，落下，又跃起，连续四五分钟，她们始终保持坐姿，脸带微笑，轻松自然。这两位女士表演的是"超觉静坐——瑜珈飞行"技术。他们的表演，引起了在场的专家、学者和观众的极大兴趣。

表演前，两位女士通过电视录像和幻灯向观众介绍了这种技术。"超觉静坐技术"又名"玛哈礼师 统一场技术"。它是由印度物理学家、哲学家玛哈礼师在本世纪五十年代末，将印度古老的瑜珈功与现代科学相结合而创立的。"瑜珈飞行"是"超觉静坐"的最深境界。她们表演的是瑜珈飞行的第一阶段——跳跃。第二和第三阶段是空中停留和空中飞行。不过目前为止，还没有人能达到后两个阶段。

据陈、肖两位女士介绍，练习"超觉静坐——瑜珈飞行"技术，能造就最高度协调有序的大脑生理机能，使人的头脑清醒，思维敏捷，减轻压抑感，调动潜能，增加创造能力，促进身心健康，可以协调人的社会生活。它的原理，正在被现代科学所论证。

当记者问到她们腾起的感觉时，陈慧华女士说，她们的心境很轻松，很平静，有一种开心、幸福的感觉。她们不依靠肌肉的运动，而是在一种潜意识的支配下轻灵地跳跃的。

陈慧华今年三十岁，肖洁欢二十七岁。她们是香港创智科学基金会的"超觉静坐"技术教员。她们说，在合格教师的指导下，无论男女老幼，人人皆可学会这种技术。来福州前，她们已先期在北京、上海、广州、杭州、天津、厦门等地作过表演。

（本报记者　林一平）

MAHARISHI'S PROGRAMME TO CREATE

PRESS REPORTS FROM ASIA

Hong Kong • *South China Morning Post*
Hong Kong   16 August 1986   (English)

Devotees of the Maharishi display their world-saving yogic flying.

By NICOLA PARKINSON

THROW away your Superman suit and listen to this.

You can fly – and improve humanity's collective disposition while you're at it.

But one step at a time.

Yogic flying, as it is called, comes in three stages. You've got to hop, before you can hover, before you can fly.

An envelope containing a photo of two smiling young men in white shirts sitting in the lotus position a good half metre off the ground, and an invitation to a display, was enough to pique my curiosity.

On mattresses laid down on the floor of the Hilton's Jade Lotus Room, three local devotees of his holiness Maharishi Mahesh Yogi – a Chinese University professor, an American businessman and an employee of Cable and Wireless – sat poised for yogic flight.

In a silence broken only by the clicking of cameras, and with their legs in a yogic twist, they meditated, inert and as full of promise as unpopped corn.

With the ring of a small bell, up went the first cross-legged kernel, hopping and

WORLD PEACE • GLOBAL INAUGURATION

stopping, apparently in a state of complete spontaneity.

Depending on how adept they were at maintaining a delicate level of consciousness called "the unified field," the longer they could keep hopping.

If yesterday's exhibition was anything to go by, the road to world peace is paved with mattresses populated by would-be hoppers neutralising their own and the world's stress.

"The beauty" of the Maharishi principle was explained by visiting Dutchman Dr Robert Croughs, professor at the Maharishi European Research University in Switzerland, which is like any other university except that students and teachers meditate twice a day.

The practitioner of the technique is endowed with unbounded awareness and experiences a taste of Utopia, the source of thought itself, said Dr Croughs.

This all seems to result in "bubbles of bliss" which super-radiate, gobbling up all that is negative in the atmosphere.

If enough people did this the world wouldn't be in such a mess, he said. It could bring about world peace and put an end to terrorism – and of course, that's why the Maharishi needs US$1 million (about HK$7.8 million) to maintain a permanent army of 7,000 to achieve his program for world peace.

When performed by enough people, the technique had been shown to reduce crime and suicide rates, road accidents and illness, and even raise stock prices, said Dr Croughs, a former professor in Greek at Amsterdam University who left Spartacus for the Maharishi 10 years ago.

To be sure, nobody yesterday got beyond the hopping stage of flight or even knew anyone at stage two of levitation or beyond.

But that didn't mean anything, they said.

The technique was hundreds of years old, and there had been many masters in that time, surely.

Unfortunately the stress of this modern age is impeding, overwhelming even, but full levitation is achieved by some – in private.

Hong Kong • *Business Standard*

Kowloon   16 August 1986   (English)

Meditating for peace

NEW DELHI: Thousands of meditators in 108 countries were to levitate simultaneously yesterday to contribute to world peace and try to fight terrorism.

The *yogic flyers* around the world are practitioners of transcendental meditation, or TM, as taught by the Maharishi Mahesh Yogi.

TM teaches that world peace can be achieved by ordering activity of the human brain through deep meditation. Meditating together in large groups, adherants say, can neutralise negative and disruptive forces, like terrorism.

Practitioners claim that about 7,000 people meditating together in the same place can have a significant positive effect on the environment, reducing illness, crime and other problems, including terrorism.

They say 7,000 can influence the rest of the world because the number is about one percent of the square root of the world's population. — AP

PRESS REPORTS FROM ASIA

Hong Kong • *Sing Pao*

Hong Kong   16 August 1986   (Chinese)

苦練超覺異術
人類自會騰飛

專家示範強調終有一天實現

本報特訊 人類騰空飛行的夢想，可能由練習瑜伽飛行的人士首先實現。

不過，即使是練習瑜伽飛行的人，亦未能預言人類何時能達致騰飛的境界，他們是憑信念及推測而確信有這一天的來臨。

廿九歲中醫學生陳耀南昨示範完瑜伽飛行第一階段的盤膝跳躍後表示，現時世界上仍未有人能做到第二階段的騰空及第三階段的一飛沖天，不過，他相信人類可達到這些境界。

瑜伽飛行可經由超覺靜坐完美課程而實現。陳耀南說，一個人先要修習七日的超覺靜坐課程，經半年自行練習後，才可修讀超覺靜坐完美課程。

學生陳耀南昨示範完瑜伽飛行第一階段的盤膝跳躍後表示，現時世界上仍未有人能做到第二階段的騰空及第三階段的一飛沖天，不過，他相信人類可達到這些境界。

分鐘的練習，便可達致飛行境界。

他又說，資深的學生可以連續廿分鐘不停盤膝跳躍。

陳耀南練習超覺靜坐及瑜伽飛行已經有五年，他說希望藉此而進步滲透中醫的病理。

圖為陳耀南示範盤膝跳躍

WORLD PEACE • GLOBAL INAUGURATION

PRESS REPORTS FROM ASIA

Hong Kong • *Wah Kiu Yat Pao*
Hong Kong   16 August 1986   (Chinese)

本港新聞

實習超覺靜坐 身體凌空跳躍
令大腦協調和諧達到世界和平

（特訊）兩位本港華人及一位外籍商人，昨午在希爾頓酒店舉辦了「瑜珈飛行」示範會，雖然他們憑實習超覺靜坐祇達到「凌空跳躍」的第一階段，但已令在塲人士耳目一新，大開眼界。

自一九六五年担任瑪哈禮師歐洲研究大學的教授指出：「瑜珈飛行」分階段，第一階段是凌空跳躍，第二階段是凌空靜止，第三階段是凌空飛行，但迄今仍未有人類能夠達到第二階段的功力」。

由本地飛行者示範「瑜珈飛行」的人士，包括有任職電報局的徐士禮，曾任中大物理系助教，現修讀中醫的陳耀南和「香港實習瑪哈禮師統一場技術商界人士協會」主席艾朗士。艾朗士表示：實習「超覺靜坐」和「瑜珈飛行」技術不單止很自然產生酒能，而我們的全部創造性潛能，而更重要是這技術能我們的大腦各部份協調、和諧起來，而散發開去的這種協調腦電波，可使整個城市，社會甚至令世界各方面領域都得以改善。

香港創智科學基金會主任陳敏賢席上宣佈，這個示範會是同時在一百零八個國家同時舉行的一個全球性行動，旨在顯示造就世界和平的基礎樞紐，而這也就是造就世界和平的協調，而這也就是造就世界和平的協調。

她表示：「這次示範是歷史性的和獨一無二，為世界和平而舉行，而世界上如此多個國家超過一千多個城市示範第一階段的「瑜珈飛行」——是人類歷史上史無前例的」。

參加示範的陳耀南表示，實習「瑜珈飛行」時，當腦部活動達到最高的協調性的一剎那（在腦電波圖上顯示出來），身體騰空飛起，開始跳躍。

他指出：在第一階段時「瑜珈飛行」是體驗到意識與身體上的物資之間的協調性，是來自一切自然律的統一塲的層次。因為統一塲具有無限關連性的特性，故這層次產生出來的協調，迅即中和大自然各處的不和諧傾向，使他們和諧起來。這樣，協調性擴展，整個世界傾向和平。

瑪哈禮師創立的「瑜珈飛行」技術，是一塲科技的一部份，實習這技術時，身體在腦功能達到最高協調性時令自動升起。

（區）

（本報記者攝）

PRESS REPORTS FROM ASIA

Hong Kong ● *Tah Kung Pao*
Hong Kong   16 August 1986   (Chinese)

人果真可以飛？

昨日有三人為此向記者示範，結果……

實習記者 陳素娟

人可以不借助外物飛行？這種飛行可為世界帶來和諧，消除恐怖主義和戰爭對人類的威脅？

昨日希爾頓酒店有個別開生面的記者招待會，題目名為：「宣慶全球性瑪哈禮師造就世界和平的計劃」，由該計劃東亞區超覺靜坐完美課程大使羅拔柯負責解釋「瑜伽飛行」、「超覺靜坐」的原理，和與世界和平的關係。

他說，所謂「超覺靜坐」，即用靜坐方式達致精神的專一，與外界環境相結合，激發身體內部的潛能，及使大腦各部分協調、和諧起來，而這種協調的腦電波散發開去，會使整個城市、社會甚至全世界的各方面領域得到改善。

他還說，「瑜伽飛行」是腦部活動達到最高協調性的一刹那，身體便會騰空飛起，此種飛行可分三個階段：第一階段是跳躍，第二階段是空中停留，第三階段是空中飛行。

在記者招待會中，有三位本地「飛行者」示範「瑜伽飛行」的第一階段。只見三位男士一同坐在約十張床墊排起來的「台」上，閉目打坐約五分鐘後，由羅拔柯「叮」一聲打了一下鐘，他們開始全身顫抖，繼而便坐着跳躍，三人中，有人跳得遠些，有人只原地跳起，再原地降落。終於，他們最少跳了一圈後，便停止，其中一位「飛行者」更發出輕微的喘息聲。其中一位「飛行者」——據稱曾任中大物理系助教，現修讀中醫的陳耀南，在接受記者訪問時表示，在「起飛」的一刹那，好像有種輕鬆、舒適的感覺，推動他前進：但那一刹很快便完結，所以，他可能在不知不覺間出了點力。

他表示，這超覺靜坐只學七晚便會，其中有三年練了五年，至於「瑜伽飛行」學超覺靜坐完美技術，卻只學了一個月而已。他說，自他學了超覺靜坐後，覺得身體好了，精神充足。

至於現今的「瑜伽飛行」第二及第三階段究竟有沒有人做到呢？他表示，現在未有，但照書上顯示，應是人類可能達到的階段。

記者曾就「瑜伽飛行」問及對物理學有認識的人士，他表示，在理論上，如果人能發出如噴射器般大的能量，便可抗拒地心吸力而停留於空中。但問題是：人不借助外物，這般大的能量從何而來？

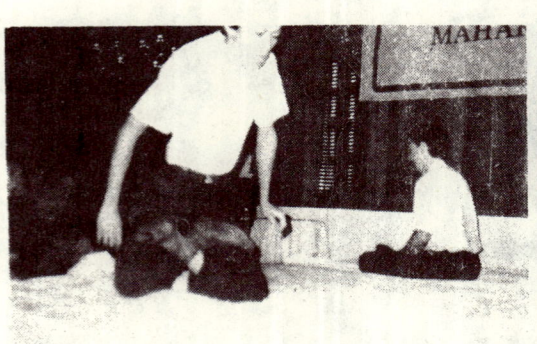

（攝報本）　那刹一的跳起「者行飛」

WORLD PEACE • GLOBAL INAUGURATION

PRESS REPORTS FROM ASIA

Hong Kong • *Business Standard*
Kowloon 16 August 1986 (English)

It's Fly-day, so hop for the best...

The camera never lies — but photographer Sam Tsui used a fast shutter speed to make this 'Yogic Flyer' appear to hover.

by **Carolyn Watts**

It was seven years ago that followers of the bearded, beaded Indian guru known as the Maharishi, first revived the ancient art of "Sidhic Flying", which has three stages: hopping, hovering and "flying out of the window over Hongkong harbour."

Known to many as the leader of the worldwide school of Transcendental Meditation (TM), the Maharishi seized upon the technique of "flying" — similar to levitation — as a way of furthering the cause of inner and outer peace.

According to ancient Indian teachings, "flying" is a technique higher than ordinary meditation and gives a person total control over body and mind. It links him into the field of universal consciousness and acts as a strong force for peace.

Yesterday's "flying" event at the Hilton Hotel marked the inauguration of the Maharishi's worldwide programme to eliminate terrorism and war and create world peace. And while three local TM practitioners meditated and undertook the "first stage" of yogic flying, other TM experts in 1,000 cities around the world were also flying....

Hongkong's meditators were Mr Ed Irons, Mr Chui Shi-lai and Mr Chan Yui-nam.

Mr Irons, who began meditating 10 years ago, said that whatever it might look like, hopping was an exhilarating experience.

"It's a very overwhelming sensation that goes through every cell of your body. It's a feeling of great happiness."

And flying?

"We're still evolving towards that. I haven't seen anybody do it so far," he said.

PRESS REPORTS FROM ASIA

Hong Kong • *Fai Pao*
Hong Kong 16 August 1986 (Chinese)

超覺靜坐可達致世界和平
瑜伽飛行昨三人示範
發電腦波後開始跳躍
第二第三階段昇起與飛行尚未有人突破

（快報消息）由於世界各地都有恐怖事件及戰爭發生，一位印度老禪師遂發明一種稱為「超覺靜坐」的意念，可以從心境中領會到忘我的境界，達致世界和平的靜坐，謂之「超覺靜坐」是當代印度哲人瑪哈禮師於一九五八年，首先將它傳授到世界各地。

香港創智科學基金會昨日舉辦「瑜伽飛行」示範，據瑪哈禮師瑞士歐洲研究大學羅拔柯博士解釋，「瑜伽飛行」是「超覺靜坐」的最深境界，其中分為三個階段：（一）跳躍；（二）凌空昇起；（三）在空中飛行。不過，到現時為止，練習「瑜伽飛行」的人士，都只能做到第一階段，第二及第三層次尚未有人突破。

昨日作「瑜伽飛行」示範有三位人士，他們閉眼在靜坐的十分鐘之後，就開始跳躍，然後十分鐘左右停止，事後其中一位示範者陳耀南表示，他在每次跳躍的時候心情都非常開朗、輕鬆，他說，靜坐的周圍環境，定要寧靜，他個人學習超覺靜坐已經有五年，以致能發出一正面的腦電波，他們的組織會在世界各地舉行集體超覺靜坐，最大規模的為七千人一起靜坐，他認為這樣大幅的腦電波場可以令該地的其他人也感受到，而營造一個平靜氣氛，進而達到世界和平的目的。

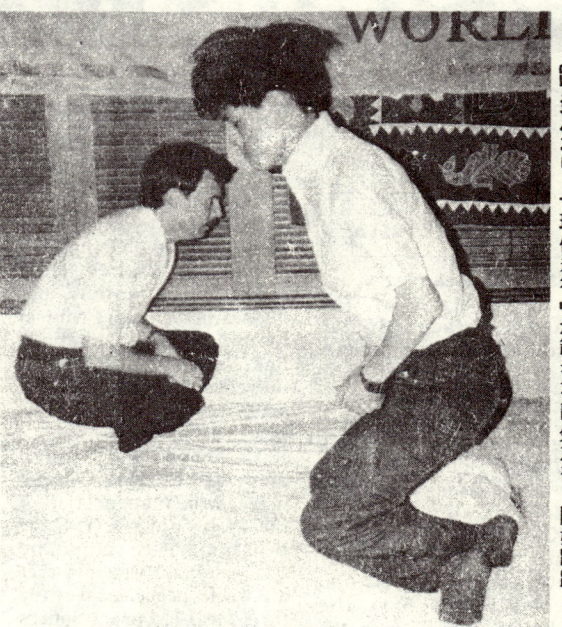

跳多少高，「瑜伽飛行」示範者在靜坐之後，開始跳躍。

WORLD PEACE • GLOBAL INAUGURATION

PRESS REPORTS FROM ASIA

Hong Kong • *Ming Pao*
Shanghai 22 August 1986 (Chinese)

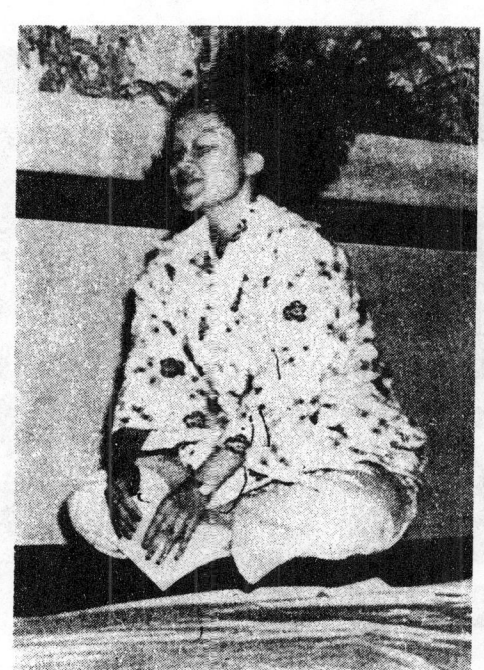

香港女士表演瑜珈騰空

香港創智科學基金會的陳慧華、蕭潔歡兩位女士，二十日晚上在上海華東師範大學禮堂表演了瑜珈騰空術。她們表演時，坐在地毯上，先作蓮花坐姿，靜默十分鐘左右，然後稍微抖動一下，身體立即騰空彈起，向前跳躍幾步。圖為陳慧華女士表演。

Hong Kong • *Ta Kung Pao*
Shanghai 22 August 1986 (Chinese)

陳慧華示範瑜珈騰空
（中新社傳真）

香港兩位瑜珈師在滬表演騰空術

【中國新聞社上海二十一日電】香港創智科學基金會的陳慧華、蕭潔歡兩位女士，昨晚在華東師範大學禮堂表演了瑜珈騰空術。

兩位女士在一塊不大的地毯上作蓮花坐姿，靜默十分鐘左右，然後稍微抖動一下，身體便騰空彈起，向前跳躍幾步。

上海一些從事自然科學和社會科學研究的人士對這次表演極感興趣。

PRESS REPORTS FROM ASIA

India • *Amrit Bazar Patrika*

Calcutta 18 July 1986 (English)

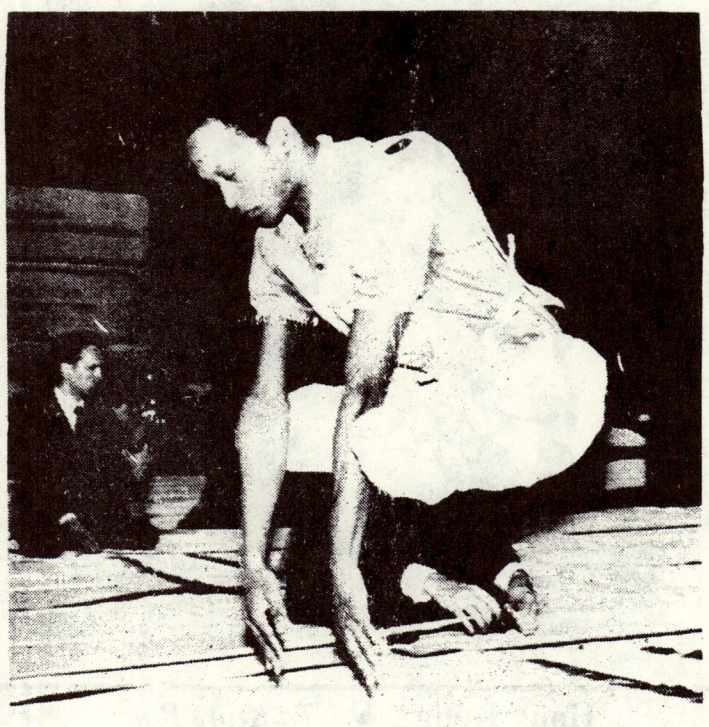

Eddie Gob demonstrating the TM-Sidhi "Yogic Flying" technique, an aspect of the Maharishi Technology of the Unified Field founded by Maharishi Mahesh Yogi, at the Washington Convention Centre.

WORLD PEACE • GLOBAL INAUGURATION

PRESS REPORTS FROM ASIA

India • *The Statesman*
New Delhi   19 July 1986   (English)

MORE THAN A FLIGHT OF FANCY

Eddie Gob (left) and Blaine Watson demonstrating the effect of "yogic flying" in Washington D.C.

PRESS REPORTS FROM ASIA

India • *Navbharat Times*
New Delhi   20 July 1986   (Hindi)

वेद-विज्ञान पर आधारित विश्व शांति अभियान

—नगर संवाददाता—

नई दिल्ली, १९ जुलाई। विश्व में शांति स्थापित करने और अपने देश को आतंकवाद से मुक्त कराने के लिए महर्षि महेश योगी २१ जुलाई से वेद-विज्ञान पर आधारित विश्व शांति अभियान प्रारम्भ कर रहे हैं। इसका उद्घाटन ज्योतिर्मठ के शंकराचार्य जगद्गुरु स्वामी विष्णुदेवानंद सरस्वती करेंगे।

महर्षि के अनुयाइयों द्वारा आज यहां आयोजित एक संवाददाता सम्मेलन में यह जानकारी दी गई कि इस अभियान की शुरुआत इंदिरा गांधी स्टेडियम में यौगिक विद्या 'आकाश गमन सिद्धि' के प्रदर्शन और प्रतियोगिता से होगी। इसमें एशिया, यूरोप, उत्तर और दक्षिण अमेरिका, आस्ट्रेलिया तथा अफ्रीका के सैकड़ों योगाभ्यासी भाग लेंगे। ये योगाभ्यासी महर्षि के भावातीत ध्यान और सिद्धि कार्यक्रम में पारंगत हैं।

स्टेडियम में आयोजित किए जा रहे प्रदर्शन में इलेक्ट्रो इन सिफेलोग्राफ मशीन भी लगाई जाएगी, जिसमें दर्शक ध्यानकाल के दौरान योगाभ्यासियों की मस्तिष्क क्रिया में होने वाली संबद्धता को वीडियो पर्दें पर देख सकेंगे। इस प्रदर्शन में ही योगाभ्यासियों की पद्मासन में बैठे हुए ५० मीटर की दौड़, ऊंची कूद और बाधा दौड़ की प्रतियोगिता होगी, जिसमें महाद्वीपीय ट्राफियां और विश्व चैम्पियनशिप प्रदान की जाएंगी।

कई प्रयोग और परीक्षण के बाद महर्षि इस निष्कर्ष पर पहुंचे हैं कि जब किसी जनसंख्या के एक प्रतिशत का वर्गमूल किसी स्थान पर भावातीत ध्यान और सिद्धि कार्यक्रम का अभ्यास करता है, तो समस्त जनसंख्या में सत्व का प्रभाव घना होता है। हत्या, अपराध, अनाचार, दुर्घटनाएं, अभाव, असंतोष और प्रदूषण आदि विघटनकारी वृत्तियों का विनाश होता है। पर इसके लिए जरूरी है कि सात हजार व्यक्तियों का एक स्थाई समूह एक स्थान पर नियमित रूप से भावातीत ध्यान और भावातीत ध्यान सिद्धि का अभ्यास करे।

उल्लेखनीय है कि महर्षि ने विश्व के सभी देशों से स्थाई विश्व शांति स्थापित करने के आह्वान के साथ 'महर्षि नगर' (नोएडा) में दस हजार वैदिक पंडितों का एक स्थाई समूह बनाने और उसके लिए १२० करोड़ रुपए के महर्षि विश्व शांति कोष स्थापित करने की घोषणा की है।

यह भी उल्लेखनीय है कि 'महर्षि नगर' पिछले कुछ दिनों से खुद ही विवादास्पद बना हुआ है और नोएडा-प्रशासन के साथ उसकी खींचतान चल रही है।

बहरहाल विश्व शांति अभियान में भाग लेने कई विदेशी औरत मर्द राजधानी पहुंच चुके हैं और हंस-प्लाजा होटल के ३५ कमरे एक महीने के लिए बुक करा लिए गए हैं। एक कमरे का दैनिक किराया ५२५ रु. है।

WORLD PEACE • GLOBAL INAUGURATION

PRESS REPORTS FROM ASIA

India • *Hindustan*
New Delhi   20 July 1986   (Hindi)

हिन्दुस्तान, रविवार, २० जुलाई, १९८६

पद्मासन में लम्बी दौड़

(हमारे कार्यालय संवाददाता द्वारा)
नई दिल्ली, १९ जुलाई। आगामी सोमवार को यहां इंदिरा गांधी स्टेडियम में एक अनूठी प्रतियोगिता होगी जिसमें पद्मासन में बैठे योगाभ्यासी ५० मीटर की लम्बी दौड़ ऊंची कूद, लम्बी कूद और बाधा दौड़ में हिस्सा लेंगे। इसमें २२ देशों के लोग भाग लेंगे तथा विजेताओं को ज्योतिर्मठ के जगद्गुरू शंकराचार्य स्वामी विष्णु देवानन्द सरस्वती द्वारा पुरस्कार वितरित किए जाएंगे।

इस आयोजन के बारे में जानकारी देते हुए महर्षि इंटरनेशनल युनिवर्सिटी, फ्येर फील्ड, इओवा अमरीका के न्यास मंडल के अध्यक्ष श्री बेवान मोरिस ने कहा कि इसका मूल उद्देश्य यह प्रदर्शित करना है कि विश्व शांति स्थापित करने का एक अभिनव तरीका भावातीत ध्यान योग है। यह कार्यक्रम देश को आतंकवाद से मुक्ति दिलाने सहित विश्व में शांति स्थापित करने के लिए महर्षि महेश योगी के वेदविज्ञान पर आधारित विश्व शांति अभियान का हिस्सा है।

इस अवसर पर वर्ल्ड गवर्नमेंट आफ द एज आफ एंलाइटमेंट की नेचुरल लॉ एंड आर्डर मिनिस्ट्री के चीफ मिनिस्टर ब्रह्मचारी नन्द किशोर ने कहा कि समष्टि की चेतना के समन्वय से विश्व शांति लाना संभव है। उन्होंने कहा कि इस बारे में भारत के लोगों का विशेष दायित्व है।

वैज्ञानिक डा. जोन एस. हेगलिन ने विश्व शांति के लिए मानसिक संगति पर जोर दिया।

संवाददाता सम्मेलन में बताया गया कि आकाश गमन सिद्धि का शिव-संहिता और पातंजलि योग दर्शन में वर्णन हुआ है और महर्षि महेश योगी ने भारत की हजारों वर्ष पुरानी इस विधा को पुनः अपनी भावातीत ध्यान और भावातीत ध्यान सिद्धि कार्यक्रम की सरल योग विद्या से सर्व सुलभ बना दिया है।

India • *Janmorcha*
Jaunpur, Uttar Pradesh   26 August 1986   (Hindi)

विश्व शांति की स्थापना के लिए महर्षि महेश योगी के यौगिक अभियान

जौनपुर, २० अगस्त। महर्षि वेद विज्ञान विश्व विद्यापीठ के बच्चों ने अपना यौगिक प्रदर्शन किया जिसे देखकर लोगों में काफी हर्ष हुआ। अपनी सिद्धी अभ्यास की प्रदर्शन में बच्चों के हॉपिंग बहुत ही सुन्दर हुआ जिसे देखने के लिए लोगों की बहुत भीड़ थी। इस अवसर पर उ०प्र० के सहकारिता मन्त्री श्री अरुण कुमार सिंह ने विद्यापीठ के बच्चों द्वारा वैदिक मन्त्रों उच्चारण से बहुत प्रसन्न हुए तथा सभी बच्चों को धन्यवाद ज्ञापित किये। इस अवसर पर स्थानीय संस्था के प्रभारी श्री हीरा जी उपाध्याय ने विश्व शांति एवं देश के सार्व भौमिक विकास हेतु सभी को भाषातीत ध्यान एवं नियमित सिद्धि अभ्यास करने का आवाहन की।

PRESS REPORTS FROM ASIA

India • *The Times of India*

New Delhi   20 July 1986   (English)

Attaining peace through 'Yogic flying'

By A Staff Reporter
NEW DELHI, July 19.

SEVERAL dozen acolytes of the 'Maharishi' Mahesh Yogi will be demonstrating what they call 'Yogic flying, Stage I,' at the Indira Gandhi Indoor Stadium on Monday at 5 p.m.

Dubbed the first international competition of Yogic flying, they say it forms the inauguration of his programme to create world peace.

The competitors (there will be a Yogic 50 m. race, a 25 m. hurdles and a Yogic Long & High Jump) will not actually be flying. That, explained Mr Bevan Morris, head of the Maharishi International University, US, at a press conference here today, is Stage III. Stage I, is only hopping; while meditating, to make the body hop the length in the lotus position, on six-inch foam.

How is that to lead to world peace? Meditation of this kind, intone Mahesh Yogi's followers, leads to growing 'coherence' (it is a favourite word in their lexicon) of brain waves. At the point of maximum coherence, the body lifts off.

India • *Indian Express*

New Delhi   20 July 1986   (English)

Yogic flying competition

Express News Service
NEW DELHI, July 19.

An international yogic flying competition will take place at the Indira Gandhi stadium on Monday evening in which devotees of transcendental meditation will demonstrate the meditation techniques to achieve optimal coherence so that a person can rise two feet in the air in the lotus position.

The competition is the formal inauguration of a global programme to achieve world peace, a spokesman of the Maharishi Mahesh Yogi Age of Enlightenment News Service told reporters on Saturday.

He said about 100 people would participate in the demonstration.

WORLD PEACE • GLOBAL INAUGURATION

PRESS REPORTS FROM ASIA

India • *Patriot*
New Delhi   20 July 1986   (English)

Our Staff Reporter

.... The much-publicised "yogic flying" demonstration at the Indira Gandhi Indoor Stadium on Monday evening... is going to be "yogic hopping" — the first stage in the Maharishi's "technology" to create coherence in world consciousness.

Speaking to newsmen Saturday afternoon at one of the New Delhi's posh hotels, one of the devotees of the Maharishi said "flying" was the final stage and one which could be achieved only "when the individual and collective stress levels" had been brought down to near-zero.

Monday's participants, who are reportedly coming by planeloads from North America, South America, Africa, Europe, Australia and the Pacific to take part in yogic 50 metres, yogic 25 metres, yogic high jump and long jump events that will be recorded by 100 news organisations and 17 TV networks, have not reached that advanced stage as yet.

Brahmin boys

The Yogi's recipe for world peace, explained Brahmachari Nand Kishore - "the chief minister of natural law and order in the world government" of the Yogi, were "seven thousand Brahmin boys sitting together and through transcendental meditation, affecting the stress level of each participant and the world at large". One such session in Maharishi International University, USA, succeeded in "producing optimistic trends in the world stock market", he said....

Mr Bevan Morris, president and chairman of the board of trustees at Maharishi International University, Iowa, said the transcendental meditation-Sidhi technique of yogic flying was the "only thing that worked", because it took recourse to the "power of unified field" — something which was more potent than nuclear power.

India • *Vir Arjuna*
New Delhi   20 July 1986   (Hindi)

'एज आफ एन्लाइनमैंट' के सदस्य विश्व और व्यक्तिगत चेतना के सामंजस्य की विधियों में से एक 'योगीय उड़ान' का प्रदर्शन करते हुए। बांयें से नेपाल के बोम थापा, गुआडेलॉप के एडी गोव, कनाडा के ब्लेन वाटसन तथा अमेरिका के रिचर्ड लामारिटा।

PRESS REPORTS FROM ASIA

India • *Jansatta*
New Delhi   20 July 1986

पद्मासन में ही दौड़-कूद होगी
जनसत्ता संवाददाता

नई दिल्ली, १९ जुलाई । सिद्धियों के सौदागर महेश योगी विश्वशांति अभियान की शुरुआत सिपुरंग लगे गद्दों पर उछाल भरने वाले साधकों की प्रतियोगिता से परसों २१ जुलाई को इंद्रप्रस्थ स्टेडियम में करेंगे । महर्षि महेश योगी इसे आकाशगमन सिद्धि की प्रथमावस्था कहते हैं ।

महर्षि की विश्व सरकार के प्रवक्ता ने आज होटल हंस की इक्कीसवीं मंजिल पर पहुंचे हुए संवाददाताओं को बताया कि ज्योतिर्मठ के शंकराचार्य स्वामी विष्णुदेवानंद सरस्वती महाराज इस प्रतियोगिता का उद्घाटन करेंगे । एशिया, यूरोप, उत्तरी अमेरिका, दक्षिणी अमेरिका, आस्ट्रेलिया इसमें हिस्सा लेंगे ।

प्रवक्ता ने दावा किया कि विश्व में अब तक लगभग ३० लाख लोग भावातीत ध्यान और पचास हजार से ज्यादा भावातीत सिद्धि में प्रशिक्षित किए गए हैं ।

प्रवक्ता के अनुसार आकाशगमन सिद्धि में पद्मासन लगा कर बैठे साधक का आसन उठता है तो चेतनामन व जड़ शरीर के बीच सामंजस्य स्थापित होता है । इस सामंजस्य को वीडियो के पर्दे पर भी देखा जा सकता है ।

प्रवक्ता के अनुसार पद्मासन वाली अवस्था में ही योगाभ्यासियों की बाधा दौड़, ऊंची कूद व लंबी कूद प्रतियोगिता होगी ।

India • *The Daily Punjab Kesari*
New Delhi   21 July 1986   (Hindi)

'आकाश गमन सिद्धि' प्रदर्शन आज से

नई दिल्ली, 20 जुलाई (वि.): विश्व में वेद विज्ञान के प्रकाण्ड विद्वानों और आधुनिक विज्ञान के अग्रणीय वैज्ञानिकों ने एक स्वर से शंखनाद किया है कि विश्व शांति का सपना विश्व चेतना में सम्बद्धता लाकर ही साकार किया जा सकता है और महर्षि महेश योगी की योग विद्या के सामूहिक अभ्यास से विश्व चेतना में आसानी से सम्बंद्धता उत्पन्न की जा सकती है ।

वेद विज्ञान के प्रकाण्ड पण्डित और विश्व के अग्रणीय वैज्ञानिक कल यहां संवाददाताओं को संबोधित कर रहे थे । इंदिरा गांधी स्टेडियम में आकाशगमन सिद्धि का प्रदर्शन सोमवार को होगा ।

संवाददाताओं के प्रश्नों का जवाब देते हुए महर्षि अन्तर्राष्ट्रीय विश्वविद्यालय फेयरफील्ड (आर्योवा) अमरीका के अध्यक्ष डा. बेविन मोरिस ने कहा कि इतिहास गवाह है कि प्रथम और द्वितीय विश्व युद्ध के बाद हुई संधियों और शांति पत्रों से विश्व शांति स्थापित करने में कोई मदद नहीं मिली । उल्टे तब से लेकर अब तक 150 युद्ध हुए और अन्तर्राष्ट्रीय स्तर पर सौहार्दयता की बजाए टकराहट ही अधिक मुखर हुई । इसका कारण यह है कि समाज का जीवन प्राकृतिक नियमानुसारी नहीं हुआ । डा. मोरिस ने कहा कि महर्षि प्रणीत "भावातीत ध्यान" और "भावातीत ध्यान सिद्धि कार्यक्रम" से मनुष्य के मस्तिष्क की क्रिया में वह सम्बद्धता और परम शांति आती है जो आधुनिक भौतिक विज्ञान की नवीनतम खोज "यूनीफाइड फील्ड" और भारतीय शास्त्रों में वर्णित "शुद्ध चेतन सत्ता" (ब्रह्म सत्ता) का मुख्य गुण है ।

WORLD PEACE • GLOBAL INAUGURATION

PRESS REPORTS FROM ASIA

World-wide • *The Associated Press*

New Delhi 21 July 1986 (English)

Meditators Hop for Peace in First World 'Yogic Flying' Olympics

By Victoria Graham

About 70 meditators, including an American magician, hopped, bounded, and frog–leaped Monday in the First World 'Yogic Flying' Competition to help fight terrorism through 'levitation.'

The men and women contestants from about 18 countries bounded and bumped their way blissfully across a bed of mattresses in Indira Gandhi Stadium.

One of [India's] holiest men...presided over what organizers called the first stage of flying, or levitation, to promote peace and world harmony. India was chosen as the site since it is the cradle of ancient Vedic Science which teaches the achievement of harmony with the universe.

The entrants were awarded gold, silver, and bronze medals in four events: 25-meter hurdles, 50-meter race, long jump, and high jump.

Matt Boutrin of Martinique and Susan Waterson of the United States won gold medals for the 25-meter hurdles with times of 14.81 seconds and 23.65 seconds, respectively.

Eddie Gob of Guadeloupe won the long jump with 163 centimeters, Blaine Watson of Canada won the high jump with 60 centimeters, and Matt Boutrin won the 50-meter race.

The other women's standings were not immediately available.

'We are not doing anything miraculous,' said Watson, 31, a TM teacher. 'Flying is a perfect feeling but you can do it after six months.

'This (flying) is the mechanism of world peace,' he said. 'Only a new seed and new approach will yield a new crop of harmony and brotherhood.'

The contestants are practitioners of Transcendental Meditation (TM) which teaches that 'flying' is possible when the body lifts off and begins to hop at the moment of maximum harmony of brain waves. Meditators must hop before they can fly and they say the second stage is floating or hovering. The third stage is actual flight.

When large groups of people meditate together, their brain waves are synchronized, they tap into a universal energy source and can exert a powerful force to overcome discord, international terrorism, and even superpower rivalry, organizers say.

The flyers are followers of Maharishi Mahesh Yogi. Maharishi, who lives outside of New Delhi, has been teaching Transcendental Meditation for 30 years. He was not present Monday.

The competition was staged to inaugurate Maharishi's Programme to Create World Peace and World Peace Fund.

TM organizers announced that 10,000 skilled meditators and flyers soon would take up permanent residence at one of Maharishi's schools outside New Delhi.

They will be the first of similiar meditation groups on all continents, each one of them in tune with cosmic rhythms and spreading global happiness, organizers said.

TM organizers say that about 7,000 people—the square root of one percent of the world's population—can create a powerful global force for peace and happiness if they apply the TM technology in one place. Studies show that similiar groups on national and city levels also have positive effects in reducing crime rate and disease and boosting the stock market, they say.

The First North American 'yogic flying' competition was held July 9 in Washington, D.C.

'For thousands of years man has tried to achieve peace through treaties, disarmament, international organizations, and building up arms. All methods have failed and today the need is urgent,' said Dr. Bevan Morris, president of Maharishi International University in Fairfield, Iowa, U.S.A.

'Governments never have and never can create world peace, yet the rise of terrorism, wars, and rivalry between the superpowers has made peace imperative as never before,' he said in an opening address.

Doug Henning, a famous magician from Los Angeles, took part in the competition and said, 'This is real magic. For years I have been performing levitation through illusion. But this is the greatest thing the world has ever seen as magic.'

WORLD PEACE • GLOBAL INAUGURATION

Henning, 39, who has staged Broadway magic shows and developed magic effects for Michael Jackson, said, 'I feel light, free, and refreshed when I "fly."'

'If you ever wanted to fly on a magic carpet or be on Cloud Nine, this is it,' he said. Yossef Yaakovl, an Israeli student studying computer science in the United States, said, 'Flying is like a lift taking you up. It is a perfect feeling. The mind says to the body, "go to the air," and the body does.'

Hidekatu Kitarmura, an acupuncture practioner from Japan, said, 'Meditation and TM helps in my profession. TM is more enjoyable than Zen and it helps me understand the subtle activity of the body.'

TM practitioners routinely hop twice every day as they meditate. Flying previously was a very private affair, but organizers say they have decided to go public because of increasing turbulence in the world.

India • *Press Trust of India*

New Delhi   21 July 1986   (English)

Yogic Flying Demonstration

At an incredible show of yogic prowess, followers of Maharishi Mahesh Yogi this evening enthralled thousands of spectators at the Indira Gandhi National Stadium with 'bliss-induced yogic flying', apparently defying the fundamental principles of physical laws.

The devotees of Transcendental Meditation hopped, bounced, or levitated atop polyethylene mats in their first public demonstration of 'yogic flying' in the country.

To an awe-struck audience, they demonstrated a 25-metre hurdles race, yogic long jump, yogic high jump, and 50-metre dash, all sitting in lotus position. The practised meditators' 'yogic flying' is part of their leader's programme for generating 'coherence in world consciousness, the basis of world peace'.

Theoretically, a yogic flyer has very orderly brain waves and fluid coordination between mind and body. Consciousness and matter become completely integrated and all this 'coherence'—a favourite term among meditators—can spread peace around the world if enough meditators gather at the same place and time, Dr John S. Hagelin, a noted U.S. scientist, told newsmen.

He said 'yogic flying', essentially, is a demonstration of the same coherence phenomenon at a more fundamental level of nature's functioning, the level of the unified field itself. Classical theories of gravitation, theories such as Newtonian gravity and Einstein's general relativity, did not support 'yogic flying'. However, modern quantum gravity theory has brought forth a deeper understanding of nature's functioning which supports such a performance. Dr Hagelin said, 'Quantum gravity is a coherent theory of gravity which ordinarily applies to the nature of physics at the scale of the unified field.'

Organisers said that usually Maharishi has closed the flying session to the press, but with the rise in terrorism and the tension between the world powers, Maharishi agreed to this first 'yogic flying' in the country. Dr Bevan Morris, president of Maharishi International University, U.S.A., and master of ceremonies at the flying demonstration, said, 'We have found clearly that this technique can create world peace ... and the decision for this display was compelled by a need for world peace.'

Shri Jagad Guru Shankaracharya, Jyotir Math, Swami Vishnu Devanand Saraswati Maharaj, who inaugurated the 'yogic flying' demonstration, was of the view that it could help in bringing world peace. On this occasion, the First International Yogic Flying Competition was also organised in which devotees of Maharishi Mahesh Yogi participated from 28 countries including India.

India • *Press Trust of India Television*
New Delhi   21 July 1986   (English)

A vast concourse gathered at the Indira Gandhi Indoor Stadium this evening to witness competitors from 38 countries demonstrate what was billed as 'TM-Sidhi Yogic Flying Competition'. Jagadguru Shankaracharya of Jyotir Math inaugurated the competition. Finalists from the competitions held earlier this month in all continents demonstrated the technique in four events—Yogic 50m race, Yogic 25m hurdle, Yogic long jump, Yogic high jump, all in the Sidhi Sadhana position.

The technique perfected by Maharishi Mahesh Yogi claims to create coherence in brain function. The body lifts and begins to hop at the moment of maximum brain coherence. The unique characteristics of 'TM-Sidhi Yogic Flying' is the presence of alpha and theta activity during flying, which is not seen during voluntary physical jumping performed in the ordinary state of consciousness.

According to the organizers, the yogic hopping demonstrated today was the first stage. If the technique is perfected, they claim, the body can be suspended and eventually considerable distances can be covered by levitation.

WORLD PEACE • GLOBAL INAUGURATION

PRESS REPORTS FROM ASIA

India • *United News of India*

New Delhi   21 July 1986   (English)

An international yogic centre of Maharishi's followers is to be established at NOIDA in Ghaziabad district, adjoining the capital.

It will house 10,000 people.

This was stated at an international yogic flying competition here in which yogis from several countries took part.

The Jagad Guru Shankaracharya of Jyotir Math presided over the competition that took place at the Indira Gandhi Stadium.

World-wide • *United Press International*

New Delhi   21 July 1986   (English)

By Marc Prager

About 50 followers of Maharishi Mahesh Yogi Monday took a step—or more precisely a hop—closer to their goal of lifting their bodies off the ground using only their minds while helping the cause of world peace.

The First International 'Yogic Flying' Competition, a curious blend of...science and sports, was probably one of the most good-natured sporting events ever.

The stated purpose of the competition, which follows by almost two weeks a similar meet held in Washington, D.C., was to draw attention to what some claim is the power of Transcendental Meditation to ensure world peace and end terrorism.

Followers of the system to achieve total relaxation founded by Maharishi Mahesh Yogi say they hope to establish a permanent group of 7,000 meditators hopping up and down in unison which they say will create coherence in world consciousness and bring about world peace.

Some 10,000 spectators at New Delhi's Indira Gandhi Indoor Stadium watched about 50 competitors from 18 countries vie for gold, silver, and bronze medals in four events—50-metre dash, 25-metre hurdles, long jump, and high jump.

Everyone competed in the lotus position—sitting with the feet tucked beneath the knees.

Meanwhile, a team of scientists in white coats busied themselves with an impressive array of gauges, dials, and electronic hardware designed to measure the brain waves of the participants.

At the start of the first event, the 25-metre hurdles, a hush fell over the crowd as the competitors, at one end of a long expanse of foam mattresses, sat in the lotus position with their eyes closed and sank into a trance-like state.

Some sat still with ear-to-ear grins while others shook their heads back and forth in synchrony with some internal rhythm as their 'minds began expanding to infinity,' as one participant described it.

A bell signaled the end of the five-minute warm-up session, and the competitors' bodies began quivering, twitching, and shaking.

One by one they began popping up and down, like Mexican jumping beans, and bouncing down the foam track.

More than 100 reporters and photographers jostled for an unobstructed look at the competitors, including American magician Doug Henning, hopping down the track.

Eddie Gob of Gaudeloupe, who won three gold medals in Washington, D.C., won only one event Monday, the long jump with a hop of 64 inches (163 cm). He blamed his performance on jet-lag and the noise of the crowd which disrupted his concentration.

Gob, 27, who took up Transcendental Meditation almost nine years ago, said it was only 'a matter of time' before he progressed to the second stage of 'yogic flying'—hovering.

Blaine Watson of South Ontario, Canada, the winner in the high jump with a mark of 24 inches (60 cm), described what he felt at the start of each event.

'Just before the point of lift-off, the different areas of the brain begin to act in symmetry,' he said. 'The coherence of the brain is the maximum at the lift-off.'

A beaming Watson, still in a 'state of bliss,' sat while a scientist attached electrodes to his head to measure his brain waves.

'They say I smile all the time,' said Watson, smiling.

WORLD PEACE • GLOBAL INAUGURATION

PRESS REPORTS FROM ASIA

India • *Indian Express*

New Delhi   22 July 1986   (English)

Yogis' flying—a hopping success

A Mahesh Yogi follower performs long jump during the International Yogic Flying Competition at Indira Gandhi Stadium on Monday — Express photograph.

PRESS REPORTS FROM ASIA

India • *Andhra Patrika*

Vijayawada   22 July 1986   (Telugu)

గాలిలో తేలిన అధ్యాపకులు

డాసీపెట్టుకుని కూడ్చుని (పద్మాసనం వేసుకుని అన్నమాట) గాలిలోకి ఎగిరి కింపకి దిగటం తేలిక కాదు కాని ఈ మధ్య కొత్త ఢిల్లీలో కెనడా నుంచి వచ్చిన ఇద్దరు యోగాసనాల అధ్యాపకులు అంతపసీ చేసి చూపించాడు.

వాడు నిజంగా గాలిలోకి ఎగిరారా లేకపోతే తేలారా ? చెప్పటం కష్టమే !

ఈ అధ్యాపకుల పేర్లు ఎడ్డిగాఢ్, బ్లెయిన్ నాట్సన్. వీడు ప్రేక్షకులలో కొందరిని కూడా పిలిచి వారిచేత ఎగిరేట్టు చేశారు.

అందరి మెదడులసి ఎలక్ట్రిక్ ఎన్సెఫెల్ గ్రాఫ్ (ఇ. ఇ. జి.) ద్వారా పరిశీలించి చూడగా ప్రేక్షకుల నుంచి వచ్చినవాడు ప్రయాసపడుతున్నట్టు, యోగాసనాల అధ్యాపకులు నిద్రలో ఉన్నట్టూ ఆ "ఇ. ఇ. జి." చిత్రాలు తెలిపాయిట.

"ఇదంతా మీ దేశం నుంచి వచ్చినదే, పతంజలి యోగ సూత్రాల ద్వారా నేర్చుకున్నదే" అని కెనడా యోగులు అంటున్నారు.

అసలు ఎలాగ ఎగరగలిగారు, అన్న ప్రశ్నకి వారి సమాధానం _

"ప్రకృతిలో ఉండేదంతా ఒక ఐక్యక్షేత్రం నుంచి ఉద్భవించినదే. కంటికి కనిపించే పదార్ధాల అణువుల కన్న సూక్ష్మమయిన స్థాయి ఒకటి ఉంటుందని శాత్రజ్ఞులు అంటున్నారు. ఐక్యక్షేత్రం టినికన్న సూక్ష్మమయిన స్థాయికి చెందిన దన్నమాట. అణువుల లోపల చాలా శక్తి దాగి ఉన్నప్పటే ఐక్య క్షేత్రంలో ఇంకా చాలా ఎక్కువ శక్తి దాగి ఉన్నది.

"యోగాభ్యాసం ద్వారా మనస్సు ఈ ఐక్యక్షేత్రాన్ని అందుకోగలదు."

"అప్పుడు ఎగిరే శక్తి దేహానికి వస్తుంది."

అధ్యాపకులు ఇద్దరూ ఐక్యక్షేత్రం ద్వారా ప్రపంచ కాంతిని పెంచవచ్చు అంటున్నాడు. మహర్షి మహేష్ యోగి చెప్పిన అతీత ధ్యానం ద్వారా అంతా సాధించవచ్చుని వారి సూచన. (స్టేట్స్ మెన్ పత్రిక వార్త ఆధారంగా.)

WORLD PEACE • GLOBAL INAUGURATION

PRESS REPORTS FROM ASIA

India • *The Times of India*

New Delhi   22 July 1986   (English)

Bouncy highway to bliss

Two glimpses of the world's first 'yogic flying' competition held in Delhi on Sunday by followers of Maharishi Mahesh Yogi—the 25m. hurdles (left) and the 'yogic' long jump (right).

PRESS REPORTS FROM ASIA

India • *Navbharat Times*
New Delhi   22 July 1986   (Hindi)

योग के अनेक करतब : महेश योगी का अभियान

—नगर संवाददाता—

नई दिल्ली, २१ जुलाई। अड़तालीस देशों के योगाभ्यासियों ने पद्मासन में ५० मीटर की दौड़ के साथ आज शाम इंदिरा गांधी स्टेडियम में विश्व शांति के लिए महर्षि महेश योगी द्वारा वेद-विज्ञान पर आधारित अभियान का प्रारम्भ किया।

शंखनाद के बीच इसका उद्घाटन ज्योतिर्मठ के शंकराचार्य जगद्गुरू स्वामी विष्णु देवानंद सरस्वती ने किया। महर्षि महेश योगी खुद इस अवसर पर उपस्थित नहीं थे। उनके प्रतिनिधि के रूप में अमेरिका स्थित महर्षि अंतरराष्ट्रीय विश्वविद्यालय के अध्यक्ष डा. बेवान मौरिस थे।

इस अवसर पर ज्योतिर्मठ के शंकराचार्य ने कहा कि महर्षि महेश योगी के इस अभियान से आतंकवाद सिर्फ इस देश से ही नहीं बल्कि पूरी दुनिया से खत्म हो जाएगा और मानव खुशहाल हो जाएगा।

महर्षि के प्रतिनिधि डा. मौरिस ने भी यही कहा कि 'कल रात महर्षिजी से मेरी बात हुई थी। हमारा लक्ष्य तमाम दुनिया को खुशहाली प्रदान करना है। और इस खुशहाली की आधारशिला यौगिक विद्या 'आकाश गमन सिद्धि' है।'

डा. मौरिस ने कहा : महर्षि अब तक इस विद्या को प्रदर्शित करने से सकुचा-शर्मा रहे थे मगर भारत में बढ़ते आतंकवाद और विश्व में हथियारों की होड़ ने उन्हें मजबूर कर दिया। आकाश गमन सिद्धि विश्व-शांति की पहली सीढ़ी है।'

उन्होंने कहा कि महर्षि महेश योगी अपने इस अभियान में जोरशोर से लगे हुए हैं। इसके लिए वह नौएडा में दस हजार वैदिक पंडितों का एक स्थाई समूह बना रहे हैं।

इन दस हजार वैदिक पंडितों में से नमूने के तौर पर लगभग दो हजार बाल-पंडितों की झलक इंदिरा गांधी स्टेडियम में दिखाई गई। १० से १८ साल के ये पंडित पीली धोती, पीला कुर्ता और पीली-सफेद टोपी पहने थे। इसके लिए सिर्फ 'पंडित' या 'ब्राह्मण' ही क्यों ? इसके उत्तर में महर्षि का कहना है यह विद्या (आकाश गमन सिद्धि) भारत की है। 'शिव-संहिता' और 'पतंजलि योग दर्शन' में इसका उल्लेख है। और इसीलिए भारत के वैदिक पंडितों में योग-विद्या के बीज उनकी आनुवंशिकी में पहले से ही मौजूद है।

महर्षि के अभियान के उत्सव में आज इंदिरा गांधी स्टेडियम में १० हजार से अधिक लोग मौजूद थे। उन्होंने पहली अंतरराष्ट्रीय यौगिक उड़ान प्रतियोगिता को बड़ी उत्सुकता और धैर्य से देखा। विभिन्न देशों के प्रतियोगियों ने ५० और २५ मीटर की दौड़, लम्बी कूद और ऊंची कूदों के आकर्षक कार्यक्रम पद्मासन मुद्रा में प्रस्तुत किए।

फूलों के पहाड़ पर रखी चांदी की कुर्सी और उस कुर्सी पर विराजमान थे ज्योतिर्मठ के शंकराचार्य। उनके दाएं-बाएं खड़े सेवक चंवर डुला रहे थे।

महर्षि महेश योगी के एक विदेशी अनुयाई सोमवार को दिल्ली स्थित इन्दिरा गांधी स्टेडियम में पद्मासन की मुद्रा में छलांग लगाते हुए।

WORLD PEACE • GLOBAL INAUGURATION

PRESS REPORTS FROM ASIA

India • *Punjab Keshari*
New Delhi   3 August 1986   (Hindi)

विश्वशांति कायम करने का एक अनूठा प्रयास

ज्योतिर्मठ के जगद्गुरु शंकराचार्य स्वामी विष्णु देवानंद सरस्वती इंदिरा गांधी स्टेडियम में गुरू पूर्णिमा के अवसर पर आकाशगमन सिद्धि प्रतियोगिता का अवलोकन करते हुए ।

पिछली 21 जुलाई को गुरु पूर्णिमा के पावन अवसर पर नई दिल्ली स्थित इन्दिरा गांधी स्टेडियम में विश्व में स्थायी शांति के लिए वेद विज्ञान पर आधारित महर्षि महेश योगी के जिस कार्यक्रम का प्रदर्शन किया गया, वह आध्यात्मिक क्षेत्र में निःसन्देह एक सराहनीय प्रयास है ।

विश्व में अशांति एवं आतंक का वातावरण प्राकृतिक नियमों के लगातार उल्लंघन का परिणाम है । प्राकृतिक नियमों के निरन्तर अतिक्रमण से सारे संसार में प्राकृतिक विषमता का फैलाव बढ़ रहा है, जिससे हर कहीं तनाव संचित हो रहा है । ये तनाव किसी भी समय आतंकवाद या अन्य विस्फोटक स्थिति धारण कर सकते हैं ।

उक्त आयोजन चेतना विज्ञान के क्षेत्र में विश्व को एक नई दिशा प्रदान करने वाले महर्षि महेश योगी की प्रेरणा से किया गया था । विश्व से आतंकवाद को जड़ से समाप्त करने, आसन्न युद्ध की विभीषिका से मानव मात्र को मुक्त करने के लिए यह प्रदर्शन अपने आप में अद्वितीय था । स्टेडियम में महर्षि के पचास से अधिक वेद विज्ञान में दक्ष लोगों ने भाग लिया । इनमें भाग लेने वालों में समस्त विश्व के लगभग अड़तीस देश शामिल थे । पद्मासन लगाकर 50 मीटर की दौड़ तथा 25 मीटर की बाधा दौड़ के साथ ही लम्बी और ऊंची कूद के शानदार प्रदर्शन द्वारा इन विशेषज्ञों ने दर्शकों को यह दिखा दिया कि इस यौगिक क्रिया से क्या कुछ सम्भव है । हजारों दर्शकों में आध्यात्मिक चेतना का संचार करने वाले इस प्रदर्शन का गहरा प्रभाव समस्त दर्शकों पर पड़ा । यौगिक अभ्यास का यह कार्यक्रम उन लोगों को जरूर कुछ अटपटे लगे होंगे, जिनके दृष्टिकोण नितांत भौतिकवादी हैं, लेकिन जो इसकी आध्यात्मिक गहराई को समझते हैं, वे इसे अत्यन्त उपयोगी और महत्वपूर्ण मानते हैं ।

इस पावन अवसर पर ज्योतिर्मठ के शंकराचार्य जगद्गुरु विष्णु देवानन्द सरस्वती ने वेद विज्ञान पर आधारित महर्षि अभियान का उद्घाटन करते हुए कहा—"अब वह समय दूर नहीं, जब यौगिक चेतना पर आधारित भावातीत ध्यान से विश्व की धरती पर से आतंकवाद का नामोनिशान मिट जाएगा ।" उन्होंने जीवन के चार प्रमुख तत्वों की चर्चा करते हुए कहा—"शांति, शक्ति, प्रीति और भक्ति के माध्यम से व्यक्ति चाहे जिस देश, धर्म या सम्प्रदाय का हो, वह संसार में व्यक्तिगत चेतना, सामूहिक चेतना और राष्ट्रीय चेतना में नई स्फूर्ति पैदा कर सकता है । हर व्यक्ति शांति चाहता है । हर व्यक्ति की यह इच्छा होती है कि वह शक्तिवान हो लेकिन यह शक्ति, यह प्रीति और भक्ति तभी विकसित होंगे, जब चेतना जागृत होगी । जब तक यह चेतना जागृत नहीं होती, तब तक नातंकवाद, हिंसा तथा युद्ध का वातावरण रहेगा । उनका विचार है—"आतंकवाद को समाप्त करने के लिए आतंकवादी बनने की आवश्यकता नहीं है । किसी का दमन करके शांति नहीं मिल सकती । शांति तो

—राजेन्द्र प्रसाद श्रीवास्तव

प्रेम और भक्ति से प्राप्त होती है । प्रेम वहीं होता है, जहां अपनत्व होता है । हिंसा या आतंकवाद का वहां कोई स्थान नहीं है ।" जगद्गुरु ने कहा—"शक्ति के लिए तप की जरूरत होती है । शक्ति हथियारों से प्राप्त नहीं की जा सकती है । वह मनुष्य की चेतना में अजेयता का भाव उदय होने से आती है ।"

स्वामी विष्णु देवानन्द जी ने इस बात पर हर्ष व्यक्त किया कि महर्षि विश्व में शांति कायम करने और समस्त देशों को शक्तिशाली बनाने के लिए जिस योजना को शुरू करने जा रहे हैं, उसमें किसी अस्त्र-शस्त्र की आवश्यकता नहीं होगी । वह मानव चेतना में ही ऐसा संस्कार प्रवाहित करेगी कि मनुष्य में ही परिवर्तन घटित हो जाएगा ।

आतंकवादी या विध्वंसकारी तत्वों को जड़ से समाप्त करने की इस प्रक्रिया में किसी प्रकार की धन-जन की हानि नहीं होगी । महर्षि वेद विज्ञान के माध्यम से यह एक ऐसा परिवर्तन होगा, जो नितांत सात्विकता और नैसर्गिकता के माध्यम से जन-जन में स्वतः स्फूर्त होकर व्यक्त होगा । जगद्गुरु ने अपनी विचारधारा को अधिक स्पष्ट करते हुए—"सत् (प्रकृति), चित् (विकृति) तथा आनन्द (संस्कृति) की प्राप्ति यौगिक चेतना पर आधारित भावातीत ध्यान के माध्यम से ही प्राप्त हो सकती है ।" उन्होंने यह विश्वास व्यक्त किया कि भावातीत ध्यान से विश्व में आतंकवाद तथा भय का वातावरण समाप्त होगा और स्थायी विश्व शांति कायम होकर रहेगी । इस भौतिक विज्ञान के चरमोत्कर्ष के सामने सिवा इस मार्ग को अपनाने के दूसरा विकल्प है ही नहीं ।

इस अवसर पर महर्षि वेद विज्ञान विद्यापीठ के उपकुलपति पण्डित रामचन्द्र मालवीय ने भारत की प्राचीन गुरु परम्परा के गौरव की चर्चा करते हुए कहा—"महर्षि महेश योगी का यह यौगिक अभियान

गत दिनों राजधानी स्थित इंदिरा गांधी स्टेडियम में महर्षि महेश योगी के आध्यात्मिक कार्यक्रम का प्रदर्शन किया गया। पद्मासन लगाकर **50 मीटर की दौड़, 25 मीटर** की बाधा दौड़, लम्बी और ऊंची कूद के प्रदर्शन द्वारा वेद विज्ञान में दक्ष विशेषज्ञों ने दिखा दिया कि यौगिक क्रियाओं द्वारा क्या कुछ नहीं किया जा सकता ।

अत्यन्त पुनीत और विशुद्ध वेद विज्ञान से ओत-प्रोत है और इस अभियान में सभी को सहयोग देने की आवश्यकता है ।

उनका कहना है कि विश्व में हर जगह अशान्ति का वातावरण है और यह अशान्ति एवं कलह परिवार के स्तर से लेकर विश्व चेतना के समस्त स्तरों को कलुषित कर रहा है । महर्षि के शान्ति प्रयासों की सराहना करते हुए मालवीय जी ने शान्ति के उन दो उपायों का जिक्र किया, जो महर्षि की दृष्टि में अत्यन्त महत्वपूर्ण हैं । उन्होंने कहा कि ज्ञान का स्रोत वेद विद्या है ।

इसका अधिकाधिक प्रचार होना चाहिए । दूसरा योग विद्या है, जिसके माध्यम से विश्व शान्ति की स्थापना सम्भव हो सकती है । उन्होंने योग विद्या के अन्तर्गत ही महर्षि वेद विज्ञान की भावातीत प्रणाली के मुख्य उद्देश्यों का भी जिक्र किया । यौगिक चेतना पर आधारित भावातीत ध्यान से न केवल व्यक्तिगत शान्ति मिलती है, बल्कि उससे आसपास का वातावरण भी शान्तमय हो जाता है ।"

समारोह का संचालन अमरीका स्थित महर्षि इन्टरनैशनल यूनिवर्सिटी के अध्यक्ष डा. बेवन मॉरिस ने किया । इस अवसर पर उन्होंने कहा—"आकाश गमन सिद्धि से, जो विश्व शान्ति की दिशा में पहली सीढ़ी है, मस्तिष्क क्रिया में अधिकतम समानुगति की स्थिति पैदा होती है । उस क्षण मन और शरीर का समन्वय अपने सर्वोच्च स्थिति में रहता है ।

यदि इस समानुगति स्थिति को मानव स्वभाव स्थायित्व मिल जाए तो विकारों के पैदा होने का प्रश्न ही नहीं उठेगा । वह स्वतः समूल नष्ट हो जाएंगे ।"

इस अवसर पर कई प्रमुख वैज्ञानिकों, वैदिक विद्वानों, वैद्याचार्यों, डाक्टरों, ज्योतिषाचार्यों, संगीतज्ञों आदि ने महर्षि के अनुरूप व्याख्या करके यह सिद्ध किया कि महर्षि वेद विज्ञान सभी दृष्टियों से वेद विज्ञान की अभिव्यक्ति है और वैज्ञानिक होने के साथ-साथ मनुष्य के अन्तर्मन को सतत सतर्क, विवेकशील, जागृत और स्वतः स्फूर्ति देने वाली है ।

इस अवसर पर महर्षि गान्धर्व वेद विश्व विद्यापीठ, ज्योतिष विद्यालय एवं महर्षि आरोग्य धाम का भी उद्घाटन समारोह सम्पन्न हुआ ।

आकाशगमन सिद्धि में एक प्रतियोगी 50 मीटर की दौड़ में भाग लेते हुए ।

WORLD PEACE • GLOBAL INAUGURATION

PRESS REPORTS FROM ASIA

India • *The Hindustan Times*

New Delhi   4 August 1986   (English)

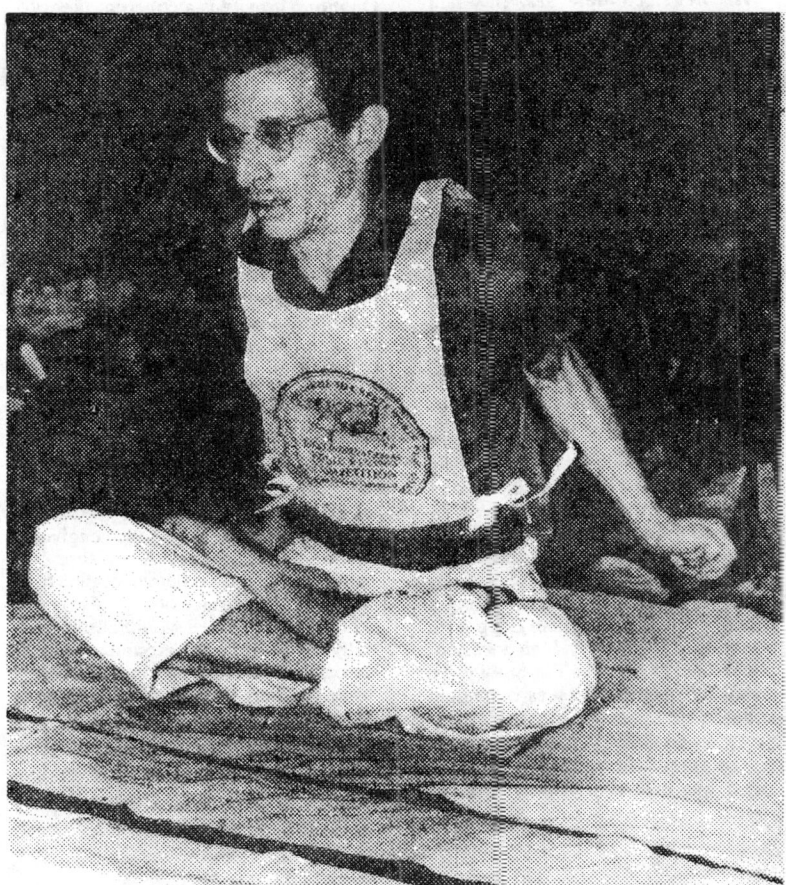

MAN taking flight is a subject of such fascination to the human psyche that even today when we are poised to enter the 21st century and are in an era of science and technology, thousands of people make it a point to at least visit the place where such marvels are claimed to take place. Who knows man may take flight?

One such venue where thousands gathered to watch the historic event was the Indira Gandhi Indoor Stadium in Delhi on July 21 wehre Maharashi Mahesh Yogi's programme to create world peace was to be inaugurated along with the first international Yogic flying competition.

More than a hundred newsmen, journalists, photographers, television crew, broadcasting crew, turned up at the Press conference preceding the inaugural ceremony, not to miss the theoretical aspect of the great event.

Dr Bevan Morris, president and chairman of the Board of Trustees of Maharishi International University in Fairfield, said that during the last several thousand years many methods had been tried to end war in the world and bring about world peace but none of the methods had succeeded. All the existing methods primarily relied upon Governments to bring about peace which is "quite foolish", and now in order to give a new approach something new had to be tried.

He said according to Maharishi Mahesh Yogi war is caused by the buildup of stress in the collective consciousness of nations. Every day in every nation of the world people are violating the laws of nature. That means they are performing actions which injure themselves, their neighbours, and their environment. These wrong actions cause stress in the individual and society.

According to Maharishi's philosophy of world peace, just as in an individual stress can only build up so far, before he falls phsically or mentally sick, so in societies stress can build up only to a certain point before the society explodes into some kind of catastrophe.

And this is where, he explained, Transcendental meditation programme came in. As the TM progam relieved stress in the individual by creating extraordinarily deep mental and physical rest and relaxation, and by producing a more coherent, orderly, and efficient style of functioning of the nervous system, which increases creativity and intelligence, improves health, and results in greater harmony with the laws of nature and fewer mistakes in daily life; the advanced program of TM, called the TM-Sidhi program, in which many people practised TM together at the same time and same place relieved not only the individual's stressed but can relieve the stresses in society as a whole.

The most powerful of these TM-Sidhi techniques is the "yogic flying" technique. At the moment when the body is about to lift up during "yogic flying" optimal coherence of brain functioning occurs.

Research has shown that group practice of this technique can spread coherence from the individuals practising the technique to the whole society eliminating stress and bringing about peace in society.

How does this work? It works on the principles of a law, which is more powerful and fundamental than any known to science. It is the unified field of all the laws of nature.

The power of the unified field is much greater than the power of the nuclear and electronic levels of natural law. The Maharishi technology of the unified field shows it is possible for human consciousness to directly identify itself with this basic field where all the matter and all the forces of nature are unified and from which all the laws of nature in the universe arise.

The identification with this field during TM or TM-Sidhi program leads to harmony and coherence in the incivual and also spreads coherence and harmony in society, neutralizing negative tendencies, and stresses.

To produce the effect of TM-Sidhi

MAHARISHI'S PROGRAMME TO CREATE

program for world peace and progress it needed the square root of one percent of the total population of the world to practice the program. This crucial figure today is about 7,000 people.

This has given the formula for creating world peace, groups of 7,000 practising the Maharishi technology of the unified field togehter.

The first permanent group of this kind is to be created in India at the World Capital of the Age of Enlightenment, Maharishi Nagar, just outside New Delhi. A group of 10,000 Vedic pandits is to be set up so that there is always at 7,000 of them.

He said we want to establish an endowment fund to permanently support those 10,000 vedic pandits practising these techniques for creating world peace.

The literature given to the Press mentioned the exact amount, "Ten thousand experts practising the Maharishi Technology of the Unified Field together can be trained and modestly maintained in India with the annual income from a fund of 120 crore". It said, "the leaders and the wealthy who have the well being of humanity at heart, are invited to examine closely Maharishi's principles and practical programme to create

By Satyen Mohapatra

world peace. By establishing the Maharishi World Peace Fund, the leaders and the wealthy can fulfil their responsibility to themselves, their families their neighbours, their country, and their world. They can bring peace to the world today and thereby ensure every tomorrow for all mankind."

The newsmen were also shown a videotape of bio-electrical activity of the brain. Using scientific jargon it was explained by experts that the unique characteristic of TM-Sidhi, Yogic flying was the presence of alpha and theta activity during flying, in the EEG records, which was not seen during ordinary voluntary jumping. Alpha and theta activity usually are seen when the mind is in an inward, restfully alert state, and are particularly predominant in the experience of transcendental consciousness during TM technique when the individual mind is identified with the unfied field of natural law.

It was explained that when you examine the EEG of a non-meditator you see simple, synchronous activity in some parts of the brain and more complex desynchronisation elsewhere. In meditators what you see is a high level of synchrony during transcendental meditation across all the areas of the brain. This has been studied using a measure called coherence. Long term meditators show very high levels of coherence. During the TM-Sidhi yogic flying technique, one sees maximum coherence.

The final bastion of the skeptical mind was probably broken with the statement of Dr John S. Hegelin, who said that classical theories of gravitation, theories such as Newtonian gravity and Einstein's general relativity, would not support yogic flying.

However quantum gravity can. Quantum gravity is a coherent theory of gravity which ordinarily applies to the nature of physics at the scale of the unified field.

The yogic flying demonstrates the capability of individual nervous system to function at the level of the unified field at which all the laws of nature are unified.

This is a level of nature's functioning which is prior to classical space-time geometry. The level of the unified field is a level at which space time geometry is dynamically generated. It is possible through the generation of a sustained coherent influence at the level of the unified field, the scale of quantum gravity, to modify in such a way the local curvature of space time geometry described in general relativity that the body flies up, or to the left, or forward, or in any possible direction.

The media men were however given a little warning note. A spokesman said what would be demonstrated today was the first stage of yogic flying in which the individual would automatically rise up from the ground and hop across a certain distance and then continue hopping; the second stage would be rising up in the air and floating or hovering for some time; and the third and final stage would be real flying in the air ....

WORLD PEACE • GLOBAL INAUGURATION

PRESS REPORTS FROM ASIA

India • *Patriot*

New Delhi   5 August 1986   (English)

Levitation: Fact or fantasy

By Suresh Chopra

ON 21 JULY, all roads led to the Indira Gandhi Indoor Stadium in New Delhi thousands crammed into the 25,000 capacity stadium to witness a fare that promised to be nothing short of a miracle: men and women levitating, or as the ad said, a feat of 'yogic flying'.

The occasion was the First International Yogic Flying Competition organised by Maharishi Mahesh Yogi as part of the inaugural function of his programme to 'create world peace'. Eighty odd competitors from various parts of the world took part, including men and women, and the World Press was in full attendance for this was the first time there was going to be a public demonstration of the Maharishi's much talked about ability to make people levitate through transcendental meditation....

To begin with it would be worth pointing out that levitation is an age old phenomenon which has fascinated man for centuries. One school of thought (which includes Maharishi Mahesh Yogi) holds forth the view that levitation is not a supernatural phenomenon or some kind of miracle as is generally believed. The mysterious process by which a person rises and floats about in the air is within the power of every human being, according to this school of thought.

They point out to the mass of historical evidence, all duly recorded and authenticated, to support their viewpoint. Most of these instances concern ascetics and holy men who had succeeded in establishing complete control over themselves and the forces of nature. Even in today's world, it

Demonstrating the first stage of 'yogic flying — Patriot photo

is held, there are several little-known places like isolated Tibetan monastries and little known Hindu ashrams where the lamas and yogis levitate as a matter of routine. Nobody hears about them for the simple reason that these individuals are devoid of any desire to seek publicity of any kind having attained a state of mind where worldly recognition, money, fame etc. etc. are considered to be meaningless.

Further, these practitioners of levitation do not look upon their ability to levitate as anything extraordinary. To them it is within the reach of every human being and is just a question of total self-mastery and controlling the various forces as work in the universe.

It is pointed out that the ancients were fully conversant with the art of levitation and with the passage of time decadance set in and man lost this power along with a host of other so-called miraculous abilities like extrasensory perception (ESP), telepathy, psychokinesis (the ability to move objects with mindpower) and other such 'siddhis' or gifts.

A telling point made by the claimants of this theory is that of all the miracles attributed to saints there is none so persistent as that of their ability to rise in the air in total defiance of the laws of gravitation. Isn't it just possible, ask these claimants, that what has been described as a miracle was nothing else than the ability to levitate? This group points to the case of St Joseph of Copertino, who died in 1663, which is the best authenticated case in Christian literature....

Indeed the stories of people levitating are many and come from many lands. From ancient China comes the story of the two daughters of Emperor Yao who were seen flying around to every corner of the kingdom by the populace. From Greece there is the legend of Daedalus who escaped from confinement along with his son Icarus by flying to freedom.

During their rituals shamans are alleged to sometimes fly about like birds. In Christian legend Simon Magus was able to sail through the air, and was brought down by the prayers of St Peter. One of the greatest Tibetan lamas, Milarepa (1058-1120) was seen flying across the sky on a number of occasions.

These are, of course, just the recorded and well authenticated cases on which there is no dispute. As pointed out earlier lamas and yogis levitate as a matter of routine in their monasteries and ashrams, their activities being beyond the public gaze. And now we have Maharishi Mahesh Yogi claiming to be able to teach these same powers to the modern world. Is it possible that he is in the know of the same secret knowledge as the lamas and yogis by which man can suspend the laws of gravitation?

World-wide • *United Press International*

New Delhi   15 August 1986   (English)

Followers of Maharishi Mahesh Yogi Friday bounced on mattresses in New Delhi and reportedly in hundreds of cities around the world to demonstrate 'Yogic Flying' which they say will bring world peace and an end to terrorism.

Organizers of the demonstration, which they claimed was held simultaneously in 1000 cities in 108 countries, claim groups of meditators practising 'Yogic Flying' in unison can bring about a positive change in world consciousness.

They say efforts to achieve world peace through conventional means have failed, and that the only way to end wars is by hopping in the lotus position with the feet tucked behind the knees.

Hopping is the first stage of 'Yogic Flying' and the only one ever demonstrated in public. Followers of Mahesh Yogi said no one has yet achieved the subsequent stages—hovering and flying.

The practitioners of Transcendental Meditation, the system to achieve total relaxation made popular by Mahesh Yogi, claim only 7000 'levitators'—one per cent of the world's population—are needed to establish and maintain world peace.

WORLD PEACE • GLOBAL INAUGURATION

PRESS REPORTS FROM ASIA

World-wide • *The Associated Press*

New Delhi   14 August 1986   (English)

Meditators in 108 Countries to Levitate Friday for Peace

Thousands of meditators in 108 countries will levitate simultaneously Friday to contribute to world peace and try to fight terrorism.

The 'Yogic Flyers' around the world are practitioners of Transcendental Meditation, or TM, as taught by the Maharishi Mahesh Yogi.

TM teaches that world peace can be achieved by ordering activity of the human brain through deep meditation. Meditating together in large groups, adherents say, can neutralize negative and disruptive forces, like terrorism.

Practitioners claim that about 7000 people meditating together in the same place can have a significant positive effect on the environment, reducing illness, crime and other problems, including terrorism.

They say 7000 can influence the rest of the world because the number is about one percent of the square root of the world's population.

TM teachers also claim that instructing large groups of people to meditate in Lebanon, the Philippines, Nicaragua, Sri Lanka, Iran and elsewhere produced positive short-term effects in calming the tense situations.

The Maharishi launched his program for world peace in New Delhi last month with a public exhibition of 'Yogic Flying', in which participants lifted off the ground, apparently hopping, while meditating. Practitioners say they will one day be capable of actual directed flight.

The Maharishi says that if people can hop, they can fly. Flying together, he claims, will achieve world peace.

India • *Muzaffar Nagar Bulletin*

Muzaffar Nagar, Uttar Pradesh   24 August 1986   (Hindi)

। इस अवसर पर महर्षि नगर गाजियाबाद से आए महर्षि महेश योगी द्वारा संचालित महर्षि वेद विज्ञान विद्यापीठ के ग्यारह विद्यार्थियों द्वारा जिला अधिकारी महोदय के सम्मान में स्वस्ति वाचन किया गया । इसके बाद स्वामी कल्याण देव जी महाराज ने वृक्ष का महत्व समझाते हुए अपने सारगर्भित विचारों से लोगों को लाभान्वित किया । इस अवसर पर जिले के बहुत आदमी उपस्थित थे । अन्त में प्राचार्य महोदय श्री सिद्दीकी ने सभी उपस्थित लोगों का एवं जिला अधिकारी महोदय का आभार प्रकट किया । इस कार्यक्रम का संचालन श्री रामपाल जी द्वारा किया गया ।

PRESS REPORTS FROM ASIA

India • *Madhya Pradesh Chronicle*

Bhopal, Madhya Pradesh   15 August 1986   (English)

Blaine Watson from Toronto, Canada, demonstrates the first stage of "yogic flying," where the body lifts up and begins to hop at the moment of maximum brain wave coherence. "Yogic flying" is an aspect of the Maharishi Technology of the Unified Field, which creates coherence in individual and world consciousness, the basis for world peace.

'Human Flying' miracle in Bhopal on Aug. 15

The ... world of "human flying" through Vedic methods will be demonstrated by the Maharishi Mahesh Yogi Centre, New Delhi, at the Rotary Bhawan, T T Nagar, Bhopal on independence day. Eminent Journalist and Patron of Public Relations Society of India, Madhya Pradesh Chapter, Nagarshri KP Narayanan, will be the chief guest.

Yogic flying was recently demonstrated to a gathering of over 8000 people at the Indira Gandhi Indoor Stadium, in New Delhi, under the blessings of Shankaracharya of Jyotirmath.

Maharshi Mahesh Yogi's now world famous programme on transecedental meditation will demonstrate publicly the benefits of Yoga. In Madhya Pradesh, this would be the first ever such live demonstration revealing the secrets of yogic studies. The programme is being sponsored by the Public Relation Society of India's Madhya Pradesh Chapter.

The flying experiment would be conductred by 11 children in the age group of fifteen.

Maharshi Mahesh Yogi's yogic philosophy is to bring about world peace through mediation, as meditation helps ease tension. When one meditates, theoretically, the meditator's brain waves become orderly to the point where fluid coordination between mind and body is complete. At this point, the body rises off the ground.

Recently in Delhi flying through meditation were conducted where 25 metre hurdles and 50 metre high and long jumps were conducted and scientific study.

Meditation helps build a sound mind to bring about pure knowledge. It is extremely beneficial to students. The MP Chapter of Public Relations Society of India and Maharshi Mahesh Yogi Institute invites all citizens to witness this rare phenomena on 15th August at the Rotary Bhawan between 11 am and 12 pm.

India • *Dainik Jagran*

Haridwar, Uttar Pradesh   15 August 1986   (Hindi)

महेश योगी का विश्व शान्ति अभियान

हरिद्वार, १५ अगस्त। विश्व शान्ति स्थापना की प्रबल योजना को लेकर श्री महेश योगी द्वारा चलाये गये वेद-विज्ञान पर आधारित अभियान का आयोजन आज पुण्य स्थली हरिद्वार के जयराम आश्रम में हुआ। इस भव्य आयोजन की अध्यक्षता श्री देवेन्द्रस्वरूप जी ने की यद्यपि इस अवसर पर श्री महेश योगी उपस्थित नहीं थे, कार्यक्रम में वी०डी०ओ० फिल्मों के माध्यम से भौमातीत ध्यान एवं वेद, आयुर्वेद का भी प्रचार प्रसार किया गया, हजारों की संख्या में उपस्थित लोगों ने कार्यक्रम देखा व लाभान्वित हुये। स्मरणीय हो कि पिछले माह २० जुलाई को दिल्ली के इन्दिरा गांधी स्टेडियम में ज्योतिर्मठ के शंकराचार्य जगदगुरू स्वामी वेदानन्द जी सरस्वती ने महेश योगी द्वारा विश्व शान्ति के लिये वेद-विज्ञान पर आधारित अभियान का उद्घाटन किया था।

इस अवसर पर शंकराचार्य जी ने कहा था कि महर्षि महेश योगी के इस अभियान से आतंकवाद सिर्फ इस देश से ही नहीं बल्कि पूरी दुनिया से खत्म हो जायेगा और मानव खुशहाल हो जायेगा।

MAHARISHI'S PROGRAMME TO CREATE

PRESS REPORTS FROM ASIA

India • *India Today*
New Delhi   15 August 1986   (English)

The Maharishi (left); and yogic 'flying'

India • *Bharat Janin*
Rohtak, Hariyana   16 August 1986   (Hindi)

रोहतक में महेश योगी के शिष्यों द्वारा
विभिन्न कार्यक्रमों का प्रदर्शन

रोहतक, 16 अगस्त। श्री रामदास शास्त्री से प्राप्त जानकारी के अनुसार, उनके संरक्षण में रोहतक आए शिष्यों ने गत 15 अगस्त को प्रातः 5 बजे से 8 बजे स्वामी परमानन्द के 'मोड़हम्' आश्रम में रुद्राभिषक एवं भावातीत ध्यान तथा दुर्गा भवन में सायं 5 बजे गुरु पूजन, प्रथमेशीर्ष विष्णु सूक्त, सूर्य सूक्त, रुद्र सूक्त, का वेद-पाठ किया एवं इनके द्वारा प्राणायाम, आसन, भावातीत ध्यान आदि का प्रदर्शन किया।

इसके अतिरिक्त उपस्थित दर्शकों को महर्षि महेश योगी की विश्व चेतना, विश्वशान्ति योजना की जानकारी दी गई जिसके अनुसार सात हजार छात्रों को सभी सुविधाओं सहित विश्व विद्यालयों की स्थापना करने और विश्व में क्रांति लाने का कार्यक्रम है। इसी योजना के अन्तर्गत आरोग्य धाम एवं आयुर्वेद विद्यालय तथा संगीत विद्यालय खोलने की बात भी कही गई है।

बताया गया है कि 15 अगस्त के अवसर पर महर्षि महेश योगी संस्थान की ओर से एक-एक आचार्य के नेतृत्व में ग्यारह-ग्यारह छात्रों की टोलियां देश के 108 विभिन्न स्थानों पर ऐसे कार्यक्रम प्रस्तुत करने के लिए भेजी गई है।

WORLD PEACE • GLOBAL INAUGURATION

PRESS REPORTS FROM ASIA

India • *Indian Express*
Bangalore   16 August 1986   (English)

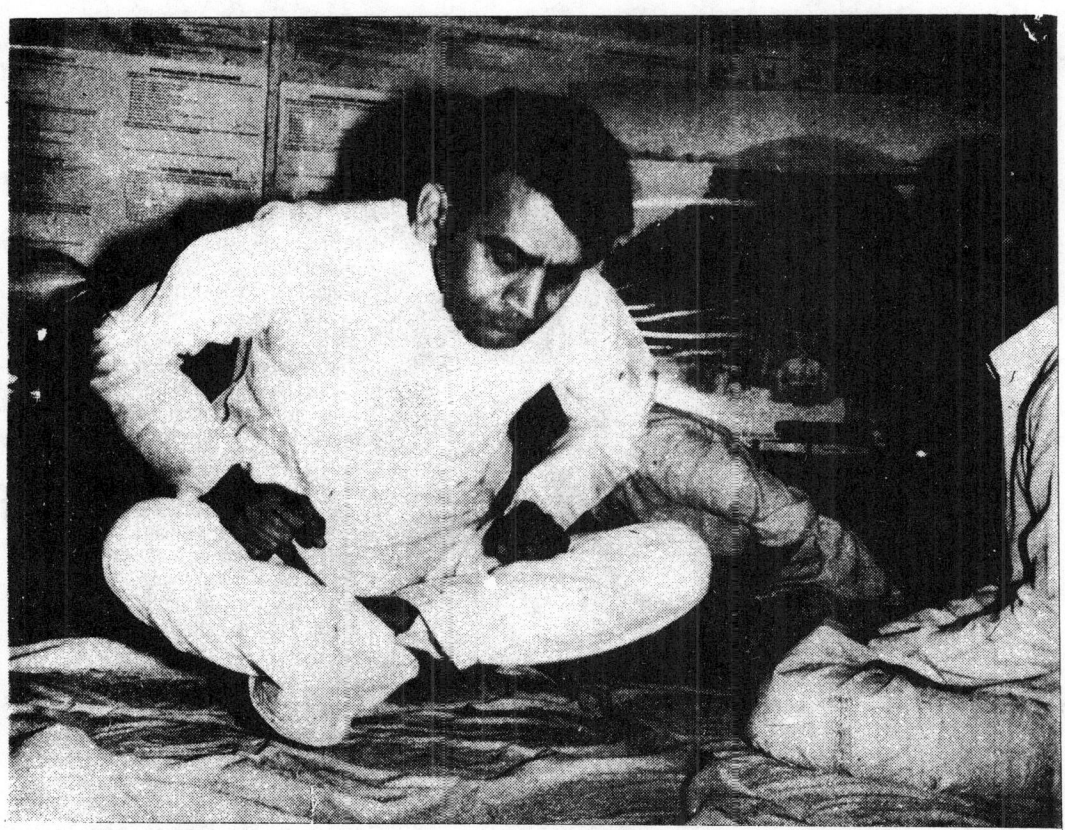

Flying, the maharishi way...

'Yogic flying' in City

Express News Service

Bangalore, Aug. 15: They just sat with their eyes closed for about 20 minutes on a specially prepared mattress and, when the small gathering showed signs of impatience, changed their position to "Padmasana". Ready for "take-up," the five disciples of Maharishi Mahesh Yogi started ... hopping like rabbits.

This was what they called yogic levitation and the show was held at the Maharshi Institute of Creative Intelligence here on Friday....

This feat, they claimed later, would create a sense of harmony among the performers which can collectively raise the level of consciousness of entire humanity, ensuring better health, peace and prosperity.

Mr. Prabhakar, in-charge of the MICI here, explained that hopping was the first stage of levitation, and could be made graceful and effective with regular practice of the Siddhi technique of transcendental meditation.

PRESS REPORTS FROM ASIA

India • *Deccan Herald*
Bangalore   16 August 1986   (English)

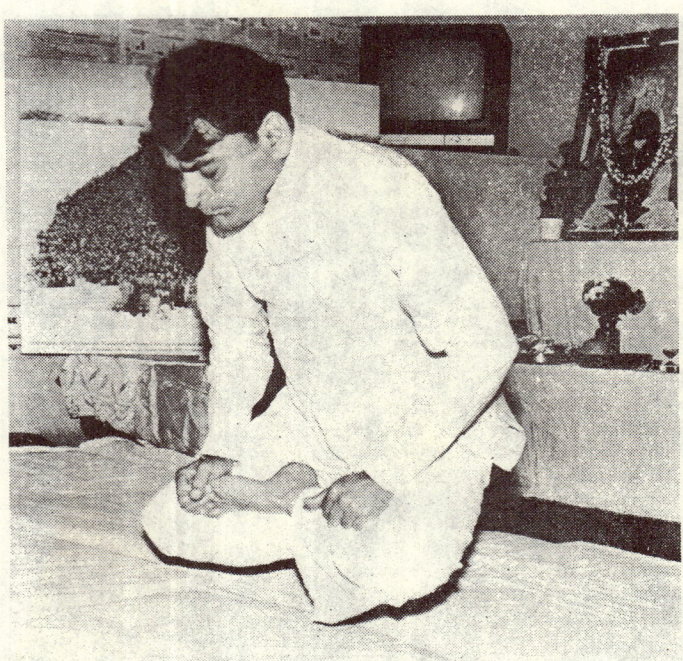

A practitioner of Transcendental Meditation (TM) demonstrating "yogic hopping" in Bangalore on Friday

Yoga goes 'hopping'

By Our Staff Reporter

BANGALORE, Aug. 15. — Five Indian devotees of Maharshi Mahesh Yogi's Transcendental Meditation here today gave a demonstration of "yogic flying" or "hopping" in the lotus position.

At the programme, organised by the local Trancendental Meditation Centre at the Langford Gardens here, the "hoppers" meditated for 20 minutes on a mattress about 10 feet by 20 feet spread on the ground, while a small audience, including mostly TM practitioners meditated along, and others looked on curiously.

Before the event, however, the "yogic hoppers" made it clear to the audience that "yogic hopping" was only the first stage of "flying." "Hopping" preceded "hovering" and ultimately "flying," they contended. In which case expectations were at something of a low ebb. Twenty minutes past the deadline, the meditators … hopped about the mattress, lifting themselves about four to six inches above the mattress with each hop, sometimes bumping precariously into each other.

The hoppers hopped vigorously, pausing at intervals, for about 10 to 15 minutes, but did not seem fatigued.

TECHNIQUE: Announcing their intentions of the exercise, the practitioners said "hopping" was a prelude to "yogic flying", an advanced meditation technique that could bring peace to the world. The theory states that during the "yogic flying" technique, at "the moment of maximum coherence in brain activity as measured by Electro Encephelo Graph (EEG) the body lifts up and begins to hop". "The coherence between consciousness and matter in the body that is experienced during the first stage of yogic flying originates at the level of the unified field of all the laws of nature" they said.

The "step to world peace", the Maharshi contended on video tape shown before the performance, was "the positivity generated through the efforts of a group of at least 7,000 which would transform strife into peace on the international level to create world peace. Simultaneously groups of the square root of one per cent of the population practising the "Maharshi Technology of the Unified Field" together in every country will bring peace to the nation by creating coherence in national consciousness.'..

WORLD PEACE • GLOBAL INAUGURATION

PRESS REPORTS FROM ASIA

India • *Prajavani*

Bangalore   16 August 1986   (Telugu)

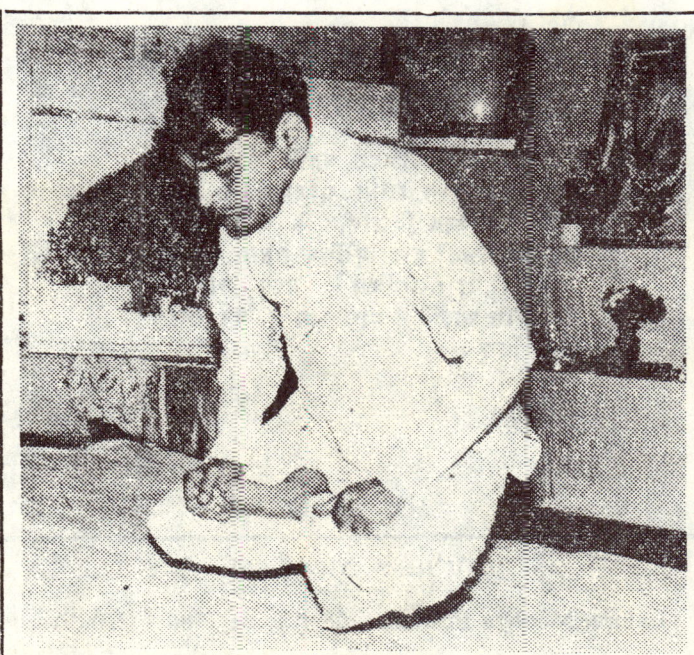

ಕುಳಿತೇ ಕುಪ್ಪಳಿಸುವ ಅಪೂರ್ವ ಪ್ರದರ್ಶನ

ಬೆಂಗಳೂರು, ಆ. 15– ಪದ್ಮಾಸನ ಭಂಗಿಯಲ್ಲಿ ಕುಳಿತುಕೊಂಡು ಕುಪ್ಪಳಿಸುವ ಅಪೂರ್ವ ಪ್ರದರ್ಶನ ಇಂದು ಇಲ್ಲಿ ನಡೆಯಿತು.

ಮಹರ್ಷಿ ಮಹೇಶ್ ಯೋಗಿ ಅತೀಂದ್ರಿಯ ಧ್ಯಾನ ಕೇಂದ್ರದ ಐದು ಮಂದಿ ಈ ಯೋಗ ಸಾಧನೆಯನ್ನು ಪ್ರದರ್ಶಿಸಿದರು.

ಇಲ್ಲಿನ ಲ್ಯಾಂಗ್‌ಫರ್ಡ್ ಗಾರ್ಡನ್‌ನಲ್ಲಿ ಅತೀಂದ್ರಿಯ ಧ್ಯಾನ ಕೇಂದ್ರದಲ್ಲಿ ಈ ಪ್ರದರ್ಶನ ನೀಡುವ ಮುನ್ನ ಅವರು ನೆಲದ ಮೇಲೆ ಹಾಸಿದ ಚಾಪೆಯಲ್ಲಿ ಕುಳಿತು ಸುಮಾರು 20 ನಿಮಿಷ ಧ್ಯಾನಸಕ್ತರಾಗಿದ್ದರು.

ಯೋಗ ಸಾಧನೆಯ ಮೂಲಕ ಕುಪ್ಪಳಿಸುವುದು ಮೊದಲ ಪಂಥ. ನಂತರ ಗಾಳಿಯಲ್ಲಿ ತೇಲಾಡುವುದು. ಕೊನೆಯದಾಗಿ ಹಾರಾಟ ಎಂದು ಅವರು ವಿವರಿಸಿದರು.

ಸುತ್ತ ನೆರೆದಿದ್ದ ವೀಕ್ಷಕರು ಕಾತುರದಿಂದ ನೋಡುತ್ತಿದ್ದಂತೆಯೇ ಸುಮಾರು 20 ನಿಮಿಷಗಳ ಧ್ಯಾನ ಮುಗಿಸಿದ ಪ್ರದರ್ಶಕರ ಮುಖ ಹಾಗೂ ಮೈಯಲ್ಲಿ ಲಘು ಕಂಪನ ಕಾಣಿಸಿಕೊಂಡಿತು. ಪದ್ಮಾಸನ ಭಂಗಿಯಲ್ಲಿ ಕುಳಿತಿದ್ದವರು ಮೊಣಕಾಲ ಮೇಲೆ ಕೈಊರಿ ಕುಪ್ಪಳಿಸಿದರು.

ಪ್ರತಿ ಕುಪ್ಪಳಿಕೆಯಲ್ಲೂ ಅವರ ಮತ್ತು ಚಾಪೆಯ ನಡುವಣ ಅಂತರ ಸುಮಾರು ಆರು ಅಂಗುಲದಷ್ಟಿತ್ತು. ಸುಮಾರು 10 ರಿಂದ 15 ನಿಮಿಷಗಳ ಕಾಲ ಕುಪ್ಪಳಿಸಿದ ನಂತರಪೂ ಅವರು ಆಯಾಸಗೊಂಡಂತೆ ಕಾಣಿಸಲಿಲ್ಲ.

ಮಿದುಳಿನ ಚಟುವಟಿಕೆಗಳಲ್ಲಿ ಪರಿಪೂರ್ಣ ಹೊಂದಾಣಿಕೆ ಸಾಧಿಸಿದಾಗ ಮಾತ್ರ ಈ ಯೋಗ ಕ್ರಿಯೆ ಸಾಧ್ಯ ಎಂದು ಅವರು ವಿವರಿಸಿದರು.

ವಿಶ್ವಶಾಂತಿಗೆ ಇದು ಮಾರ್ಗಸೂಚಿ ಆಗಬಲ್ಲದು ಎಂಬ ಮಹರ್ಷಿಯ ವಾಣಿಯನ್ನು ವಿಡಿಯೋ ಮೂಲಕ ಬಿತ್ತರಿಸಲಾಯಿತು.

PRESS REPORTS FROM ASIA

India • *Samachar*

Indore, Madhya Pradesh   26 August 1986   (Hindi)

विश्व शांति के लिए यौगिक उड़ान

आजादी के पर्व पर महर्षि महेश योगीजी द्वारा छेड़े विश्व शांति अभियान के तहत, महर्षि वेद विश्व विद्यापीठ के योग शिक्षकों एवं विद्यार्थियों द्वारा यौगिक उड़ान का सफल प्रदर्शन किया। कार्यक्रम के मुख्य साक्षी श्री श्रीनिवास शास्त्री ने योग साधना पर विचार व्यक्त किए।

India • *Swedesh*

Indore, Madhya Pradesh   18 August 1986   (Hindi)

विश्व शांति हेतु यौगिक उड़ान

इन्दौर। महर्षि वेद विज्ञान विश्व विद्यापीठ महर्षि नगर उ. प्र. से आये भावातीत ध्यान योग साधकों के द्वारा स्थानीय सी. तुकोगंज स्थित ध्यान पीठ पर आकाश गमन सिद्धि की प्रथम अनुभूति का सफल प्रदर्शन किया गया।

भारत के स्वतंत्रता दिवस पर महर्षि महेश योगी ने अपनी 'यूनिफाइड फिल्ड सिद्धांत प्रक्रिया' अन्तर्गत विश्व के एक हजार केन्द्रों पर विश्व शांति हेतु यह कार्यक्रम निश्चित किया है। ध्यान साधक अपनी साधना के दौरान पतंजलि योग सूत्रों को 'संयम' करते हैं, परिणाम स्वरूप साधक न्यूटन सिद्धांत के परे क्वान्टम ग्रेविटि सिद्धांत का पालन करते हैं। साधकों के प्रदर्शन को आमन्त्रित साक्षियों ने अचम्भित होते हुए सराहा।

प्रमुख साक्षी श्री श्रीनिवास शास्त्री ने योग साधना का आज की परिस्थितियों में एकमात्र शांति उपाय बताते हुए विस्तृत विवेचना की।

११ ब्रह्मचारी पण्डित रुद्राभिषेक एवं यज्ञ आदि अनुष्ठान हेतु स्थानीय यजमानों के लिये भी उपलब्ध रहेंगे। जिनसे महर्षि ध्यान विद्यापीठ सा. तुकोगंज नाथ मंदिर रोड़ से सम्पर्क साधा जा सकता है।

WORLD PEACE • GLOBAL INAUGURATION

PRESS REPORTS FROM ASIA

India • *Danik Prabhat*

Meerut, Uttar Pradesh   26 August 1986   (Hindi)

विश्वशांति की स्थापना हेतु महर्षि का यौगिक अभियान

मेरठ (वि)। स्वतंत्रता दिवस की पावन बेला पर महर्षि चेतना विज्ञान संस्थान एवं भावातीत ध्यान योग केन्द्र, शास्त्री नगर मेरठ के तत्वावधान में महर्षि महेश योगी द्वारा विश्वशांति की स्थापना हेतु यौगिक अभियान के अन्तर्गत "आकाश गमन" सिद्धि के प्रथम चरण का प्रदर्शन नानक चंद डिग्री कालेज के सभागार में सम्पन्न हुआ। प्रदर्शन महर्षि वेद विज्ञान विश्व विद्यापीठ महर्षि नगर से आये बाटुक ब्रह्मचारियों द्वारा किया गया। ज्ञातव्य है कि इस अभियान के अन्तर्गत इस ही दिन विश्व के एक हजार शहरों में एक ही समय सायं ५ बजे से यह प्रदर्शन शुरू किया गया। श्री रामहजारी गौतम आचार्य के नेतृत्व में सम्पन्न हुए इस प्रदर्शन की लोगों ने भूरि-भूरि प्रशंसा की।

कार्यक्रम का शुभारम्भ करते हुए ध्यान योग प्रशिक्षक एवं केन्द्र प्रभारी श्री हरीश चन्द्र घस्माना ने बताया कि प्रदर्शन उस सिद्धान्त का प्रदर्शन है, जिसके द्वारा मनुष्य के मस्तिष्क की क्रियाओं में सौम्य गुण उत्पन्न करके विश्व चेतना में सतोगुण का संचार किया जा सकता है। विश्वशांति की स्थापना की जा सकती है। हिंसात्मक प्रवृत्तियों का निराकरण किया जा सकता है व आतंकवाद जड़ से समाप्त किया जा सकता है।

कार्यक्रम की रुपरेखा बताते हुए श्री घस्माना जी ने बताया कि इस सिद्धांत का प्रदर्शन वाशिंगटन (अमेरिका) व इंदिरा गांधी स्टेडियम (दिल्ली) में भी हो चुका है, जिसकी वीडियो फिल्म भी कार्यक्रम में सम्मिलित की गई है। महर्षि आडियो-वीडियो प्रवचन, वेद सूक्तों का पाठ, यौगिक-प्रदर्शन कार्यक्रम के विशेष अंग रखे गये हैं।

इस आयोजन हेतु राष्ट्रीय मुख्यालय "महर्षि नगर" से पधारे ध्यान सिद्धि प्रशासक श्री भुवनेश शर्मा ने कहा कि "आकाश गमन सिद्धि" का अभ्यास करते समय चेतन मन का जड़ शरीर से बाढ़ा सामंजस्य स्थापित हो जाता है, जिससे मस्तिष्क के करोड़ों तन्तुओं की क्रियाओं में सम्बद्धता उत्पन्न हो जाती है। इस प्रदर्शन की उपयोगिता मानव मस्तिष्क के भीतर साम्य उत्पन्न करना है। विश्वशांति तभी होगी जब समस्त विश्व में साम्य होगा। आपने जनसमूह के किए गए प्रश्नों का भी समाधान किया।

इस अवसर महर्षि महेश योगी आडियो-वीडियो टेप सुनाया गया, जिसमें उन्होंने कहा कि विश्व की कोई भी सरकार आतंकवाद को समाप्त करने में समर्थ नहीं है महाशक्तियां भी भय से आक्रांत हैं। अब प्रत्येक व्यक्ति को शांति बनाए रखने का उत्तरदायित्व लेना होगा। विश्वशांति के लिए अनेक संगठन हैं, जो विभिन्न स्तरों से विश्वशांति के लिए प्रयास कर रहे हैं। हम सभी के प्रयत्नों की सराहना करते हैं। विश्वशान्ति के लिए हमारा तरीका अधिक मौलिक व पूर्णता लिए हैं।

आयोजन में अनेक गणमान्य व्यक्तियों ने भाग लिया। श्री भुवनेश्वर प्रसाद बहुगुणा ध्यान शिक्षक का कार्यक्रम की सफलता में विशेष योगदान रहा। अन्त में श्री घस्मानों ने आगन्तुकों का आभार व्यक्त किया।

PRESS REPORTS FROM ASIA

India • *The Patriot*

New Delhi   2 September 1986   (English)

WORLD PEACE • GLOBAL INAUGURATION

PRESS REPORTS FROM ASIA

India • *Society*

Bombay   September 1986   (English)

... After the First Olympics of the Age of Enlightenment at the Washington Convention Centre, the advanced practitioners of TM congregated for another round at the Indira Gandhi stadium in Delhi.

As the competition began in a well dressed stadium, the Yogis took to the air, in what was essentially a flying competition. The power to levitate allegedly comes from the Sidh Yoga technique. The experience is described as unique by almost every person who tried it out. "There is tremendous bliss in flying...(says Richard LaMarita, finalist), who was one of the six hundred Americans who flew down on an aircraft this time to Delhi for the event. "You just have a very deep silence inside. It is difficult for a spectator to understand the feeling until he has experienced it himself. When I heard about a 'flying competition' in Washington my first reaction was to laugh. I thought no one was ever going to believe that. But the press conference before the event turned out to be the

Dr. Anna Alvarez.

Richard LaMarita.

largest non-political conference in the history of Washington. *People* magazine gave us a two page story. The reports were very positive and the level of skepticism is declining."

The flying is really a three part process. It starts with hopping, goes on to a low hovering and climaxes with a longer term flying in the air. While people have only seen and experienced the first stage of hopping so far, they are convinced that the next stages will follow naturally. "It is written in the Vedas that it is possible," says Brahmachari Shailendra, a physicist who bumped into TM on a cycling trip across Europe. "And it is like following a map. When the first few stops have come you know that the final destination will arrive. How can you be sure of anything? We are following the path and right now we are on schedule."...

"And there is more to flying than just the immediate round of pleasure it affords. The main aim is to ensure world peace, to keep super nuclear powers in check. The Maharishi contends that if one percent of the world population got together, disasters of every kind can be averted. And if his flying technique is adopted it can even be the square root of that one percent. "It is like a washerman in a village," explains Dr.Mohapatra, who has shifted to Maharashtra after a degree in MBBS from Delhi University. "One man in the village is good enough to ensure clean clothes for the entire village. Similarly if some seven thousand people are brought together for TM they can act like the washerman." Adds Steve Schulte, "It sounds mystical when you first hear about it but there is a lot of proof that it works." Bouncing around on the thick foam mats at Indira Gandhi Stadium, many of the participants do feel responsible for world peace. "But the immediate pleasure it gives to you is more important," says Zoran, a student of law from Yugoslavia. "There are a very

WORLD PEACE • GLOBAL INAUGURATION

large number of people going in for it in my country as well. On August 15th we demonstrated 'flying' in Belgrade and the function was organised by one of the largest newspapers in the country.... Altogether Yugoslavia has some three hundred fliers and over a thousand TMers."

In fact, foreigners have been following the movement with tremendous zeal and a large number of the participating fliers had just aeroplaned in for the programme in Delhi. "We're not doing it because I want to replace an aeroplane, it is not to make travel easier," smiles Brahmachari Shailendra, "but we believe in the power it has, and it gives us." "I don't think people do things totally altruistically," adds Steve Schulte, a teacher of TM at Washington University, "to just go thousands of miles just to help the world, or just because Maharishi says it is good. I don't think all these people would be doing it just for that reason. There is a tremendous freedom in it, just lifting off from the ground is a very powerful experience. It's a very real phenomenon."

Dr. Anna Alvarea is young flier from Spain who is here to study ayurveda which she feels has many advantages over allopathy. "I have been flying for six months," she says, having learnt yoga in Brazil, Holland and India. "And the experience has given me complete bliss. I have never felt something so infinite in all my life."

Hoppings, or flying as it is called, is not an easy affair but is not physically impossible either. Having computed the difference in the two, scientifically, Brahamachari Shailendra says, "There is a difference between plain hopping and yogic flying. We have recorded the EEG of the brain in both cases. In normal jumping there is no cohesion between the different centres of the brain but with TM Siddhi they all start going in step. The body and mind are integrated together as the body lifts with the help of the mind. All of us are fliers here. It is like floating on the waves of bliss."

"Collective thought has tremendous power," says Dr. Mohapatra, "each person's individual thought has varying power, like a ripple in an ocean can move

Dr. Mahapatra (left) and Brahmachari Shailendra.

MAHARISHI'S PROGRAMME TO CREATE

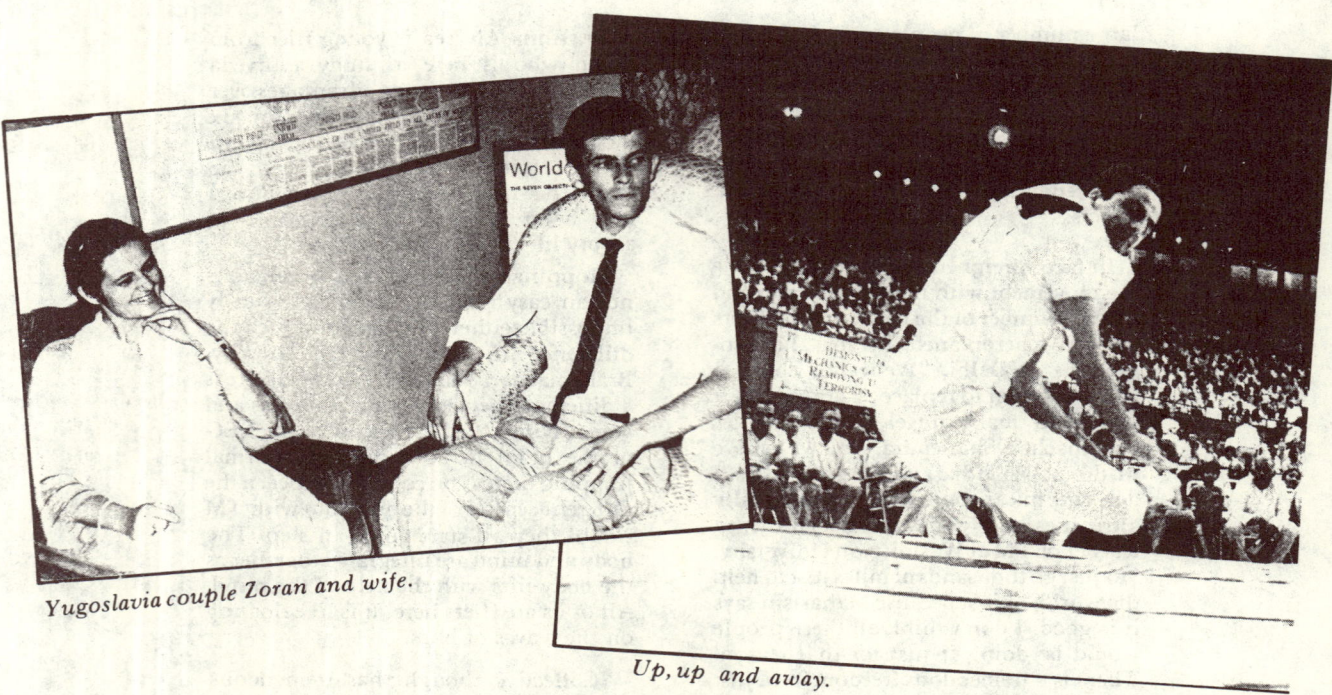

Yugoslavia couple Zoran and wife.

Up, up and away.

a mosquito, and in another person's minds, a wave can upturn a ship. The TM Siddhi programme is like the might of an ocean. If you desire it from inside your mind, you can even transform gravity."

And transcendental meditation, it appears, has stepped into many lives almost in the role of a saviour. It is easy to do, it does not require renunciation of the world, and can be done on a subway on the way to work. TMers insist that it gives them greater happiness and help the stressful days along, and the movement has gathered the support of a variety of professionals. Hagelin, a physicist, on a visit to Maharishinagar also endorses its scientific treatment, "I think TM has great potential. It is very popular in the States."

Mahesh Yogi had been trained under the Shankaracharya of the *Jyotirmath* of Allahabad, and then decided to give humankind something to help them along. A few years later the Beatles discovered him and Mahesh Yogi's relationship with the West began with a big bang. His institute opened across Europe and America and many well known names come to be included in the list of TMers. Pierre Trudeau has TM in common with Ramnath Goenka, Clint Eastwood, Faye Dunaway, Stevie Wonder and Shirley McClaine. And Maharshi Mahesh Yogi has eventually made a base near Delhi which has aptly been called Maharishinagar. Many miles out of the Capital's six hundred acres of green belt area are now engulfed in the silence of meditation. The sprawling complex is still settling in with its ayurvedic hospital still under construction and the Veda Vigyan Vidyapeeth, a school for Brahmin boys is nearly complete.

The Veda Vigyan Vidyapeeth contains a flying school with a difference. The boys instructed in the Vedic services, are taught the art of transcendental meditation, and many of them are 'flying' as well. In a mass demonstration hundreds of these dhoti-kurta clad little yogis displayed their 'special ability'. Most of these boys, coming from poor rural areas, are given free meals and accomodation. Once they enroll, a minimum of 7,000 Brahmin boys, Maharishi's 'peace tank' will be established. If 7,000 people get together to practise the Siddhi yoga, he has promised phenomenal results.

WORLD PEACE • GLOBAL INAUGURATION

Questioned whether the Brahmin boys can fly better than other people, the answer is, "Probably. There is more tradition in them."

As far as the Flying Olympiads are concerned, it seems this is only the beginning. They have other such events planned for the future where yogis would fly higher and higher. The winners of these competitions are awarded medals. "just like the Olympics," says Richard who participated at New Delhi, "and they are not really important. The main thing is participation—and if you don't win a prize you know that your mind-body co-ordination is not good enough." It must be granted that even if it's hopping, they did it well. And as the *Washington Post* comments: "if this competition was any indication, the road to world peace is paved with rubber mats, divided into five lanes and populated by would-be hoppers neutralizing their own and the world's stress."

Mayuri Chawla

South Korea • *The Daily Sports*

Seoul   17 August 1986   (Korean)

PRESS REPORTS FROM ASIA

Macao • *Macao Daily News*

Macao　17 August 1986　(Chinese)

瑜伽飛行 表演昨日舉行
凌空跳躍令觀眾耳目一新
最高境界凌空昇起及飛行未有人做到

【本報消息】來自香港的兩名華人及一名外籍商人，昨日下午在皇都酒店舉行了「瑜伽飛行」表演，而得到「凌空跳躍」，但已令在場的觀眾耳目為之一新。

「瑜伽飛行」是「超覺靜坐」的最高境界。「超覺靜坐」是當代印度哲人瑪哈禮師基於世界各地都有恐怖事件及戰爭發生而於一九五八年首先將它傳授到世界各地

雖然他們目前只能做到人類不需借助外物而騰空飛行的第一步「凌空跳躍」，但已令在場的觀眾耳目為之一新。

昨日來澳作「瑜伽飛行」示範表演的人士包括任職香港電報局的徐禮士，曾任香港中大物理系助教、

「瑜伽飛行」現修讀中醫的陳耀南，謂若以「超覺靜坐」的意念，可以從心所謂正和平的靜坐中領會師統一場技術商界人士協會主席艾朗士。據他們表示，當他們在「超覺靜坐」時心目中只有一個意念，而當他們跳躍離開地面的時候心情是無比的舒暢和喜悦。他們又表示實習「超覺靜坐」及「瑜伽飛行」不單只是自然、自動、自發地開發人們的創造性潛能，更重要的是能使大腦各部分都達到協調、和諧，而由此散發開去的這

種協調、和諧更能使「整個城市、社會甚至世界各個領域都得以改善，即所謂正向性增加，負向性減低」，據了解該會開設兩、三個星期後來澳加。聽起來有點令人不可思議。

據瑪哈禮師造就世界和平的計劃之東亞區「超覺靜坐」完美課程大使羅拔柯教授解釋：「瑜伽飛行」包括三個過程：一是「瑜伽飛行」，二是凌空昇起，三是在空中飛行。不過到目前為止，還沒人能得第二及第三跳躍。

階段。

香港方面目前已成立「創智科學基金會」，活動是七千人一起靜坐。昨日作「瑜伽飛行」的三人，他們示範前首先閉眼靜坐約十分鐘，然後開始跳躍，約十分鐘後停止。

城市舉行示範表演。過去曾經一次最大的兩日在全世界一千一百八十個國家，

「瑜伽飛行」表演昨舉行，圖為示範者表演凌空跳躍。

WORLD PEACE • GLOBAL INAUGURATION

PRESS REPORTS FROM ASIA

Macao • *Jornal "Va Kio"*
Macao   17 August 1986   (Chinese)

香港創智科學基金會
昨來澳介紹瑜珈飛行
三人示範作蓮花座後跳躍

【專訪】一種以「超覺靜坐」而推動世界和平的「全球性瑪哈禮師造就世界和平計劃」，於本月十五、十六兩日在世界一百零八個國家超過一千個城市中以示範「瑜珈飛行」的方式舉行。據主辦單位表示，根據社會研究學論中，只要在世界上有七千人同時同地作超覺靜坐，其腦電波的協調條及和諧，將可使世界上的「負向性」（罪案、交通意外、戰爭等）降低。

就該項和平計劃，香港創智科學基金會及有關負責人，昨日在皇都酒店舉行記者招待會及即場示範「瑜珈飛行」。

今次記者招待會的主持者包活了陳敏賢（香港創智科基金會主任）、EDWARD IRONS（香港實習瑪哈禮師統一場科技商界人士協會主席）以及羅拔柯博士（瑪哈禮師瑞士歐洲研究大學及東亞區TMSIDHI負責人。

陳敏賢歡迎嘉賓蒞臨，並稱這示範會其實是同時在一百零八個國家同時舉行的一個全球性行動，旨在顯示造就世界意識更為協調的機制，而這也就是造就世界和平的基礎樞紐。

自然很自動自發地開發了我們的全部創造性潛能；更重要的是這技術能同時使我們的大腦各部份協調，和諧起來，所發開去的這種協調腦電波使整個城市、社會甚至全世界的各方面領域，都得到改善。」

隨後，會任荷蘭阿姆斯特丹大學教授，自一九七五年至今任瑪哈禮師歐洲研究大學的柯教授，詳細解釋了超覺靜坐（

「瑜珈飛行」由本地飛行者示範，他們有任職於六頁電報局的徐士禮、會任中大物理系助教，現修讀中醫的陳耀南和

「瑜珈飛行」是人類歷史上史無前例的，是如此多個國家，超過一千多個城市示範第一階段的「瑜珈飛行」是歷史性的和獨一無異的，為世界和平而在世界上的示範。

「香港實習瑪哈禮師統一場技術商界人仕協會」主席EDWARD IRONS，EDWARD IRONS表示對在他和其他講者都誠意邀請所有希望改善自己個人、香港社會工商界工作的人仕來說，「創造性」是首要的，而創造性幹勁、眼光和超凡的記憶力及健康都是有恆地實習瑪哈禮師統覺靜坐技術的必然副產品。他說：「實習超覺靜坐（TM）和TMSIDHI技術不單止很

TM）和TMSIDHI技術，特別是「瑜珈飛行」如何能為世界和平帶來貢獻。

他和其他講者都誠意邀請所有希望改善自己個人、香港社會以至世界的生活質素，和平的人參加一個免費的「超覺靜坐」介紹講座，該講座定於八月十九日星期二在希爾頓酒店印度廳舉行。

「瑜珈飛行」的傳世已有七

圖中表演者斯德里的一次示範中，將可身體自動升起，做瑜珈飛行。

MAHARISHI'S PROGRAMME TO CREATE

年之久，創辦人爲瑪哈禮師（MAHARISHI），「瑜珈飛行」是分爲三個程序：（一）跳躍。（二）停留空中。（三）飛行。在上述三個程序中，由於受到環境所限制，故此停流半空及飛行的兩個程序現今於世仍未有人能夠做到，但並不表示不可爲，因爲主要是人類現今仍未能將意識運用至無驚性而使之超越萬有引力，故此才被環境及意念所影响。「瑜珈飛行」亦並非什麼奇蹟，瑪哈禮師會謂世上沒有所謂奇蹟，只是人類還未有窺通其竅門。

昨天在「瑜珈飛行」示範中，有三人作表演，他們一個一個地在作蓮花坐姿（雙跏跌）之後，靜坐五分鐘左右，然後有人敲一下鐘聲，於是便見他們整個身體輕微地彈起，向前跳寫整個人示範時，是在一幅地氈上進行。地氈長約三四尺，靜坐者跳四五次便到盡頭。用手轉身又再跳回原地。三個人每人示範一次，跳躍離地最高的約五六吋，向前移動半尺左右。

Macao • *Si Man Pao*

Macao   17 August 1986   (Chinese)

瑜伽消息

〔本報專訊〕：據瑪哈禮師之信徒―瑞士籍羅拔柯博士解釋：「超覺靜坐」的最深境界係「瑜伽飛行」術。

據羅拔柯之所釋：「超覺靜坐」術，係可分三個階段：第一階段爲跳躍，第二階段爲騰界，第三階段爲空中飛行，不過，至目前爲止，練習「瑜伽飛行」術者，都祇能做到第一階段跳躍而已，第二及第三階段尙未有人突破。

昨日表演的三名信徒是EDWARD RONS、陳耀南及徐士禮，他們在地氈上，閉目靜坐，兩足相盤，約十分鐘後，倒跳躍行走，猶如蛤蟆跳躍，沒有一個有騰界之本力達到該境界。

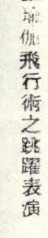
▲瑜伽飛行術之跳躍表演

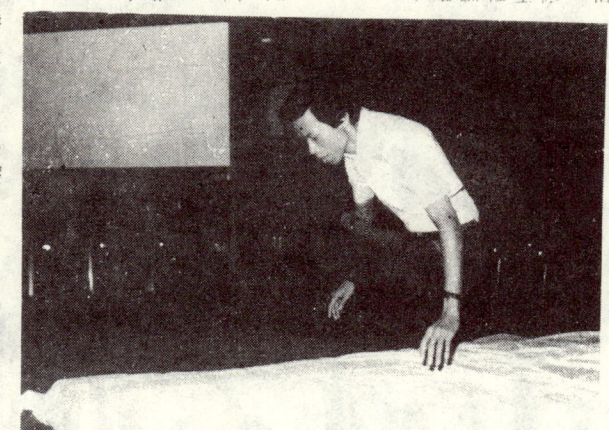

「但他表示「瑜伽飛行」他將朝對於防疫服務。

完美之課程，若要學「瑜伽飛行」得先學「超覺靜坐」術，可使人們心境寧靜，協調和諧，降低負向性（罪惡、疾病）上升，正向性（和諧協調）上升。由於靜坐時腦電波協調，以致能發出正面電波，如果人如此，可組成一個幅度之正腦電波塲，令其他人也感受到，營造一個平靜氣氛，進而達一個寶現。信徒陳耀南，因研習中醫，他希望藉此機會，進一步滲透中醫消除戰爭、暴戾，使世界和平的目的。至於人類苦練超覺靜坐術後日後腦飛行了，可組成一個幅度之正腦電波塲，病理。

WORLD PEACE • GLOBAL INAUGURATION

PRESS REPORTS FROM ASIA

Malaysia • *Chinese Press*

Kuala Lumpur 16 August 1986 (Chinese)

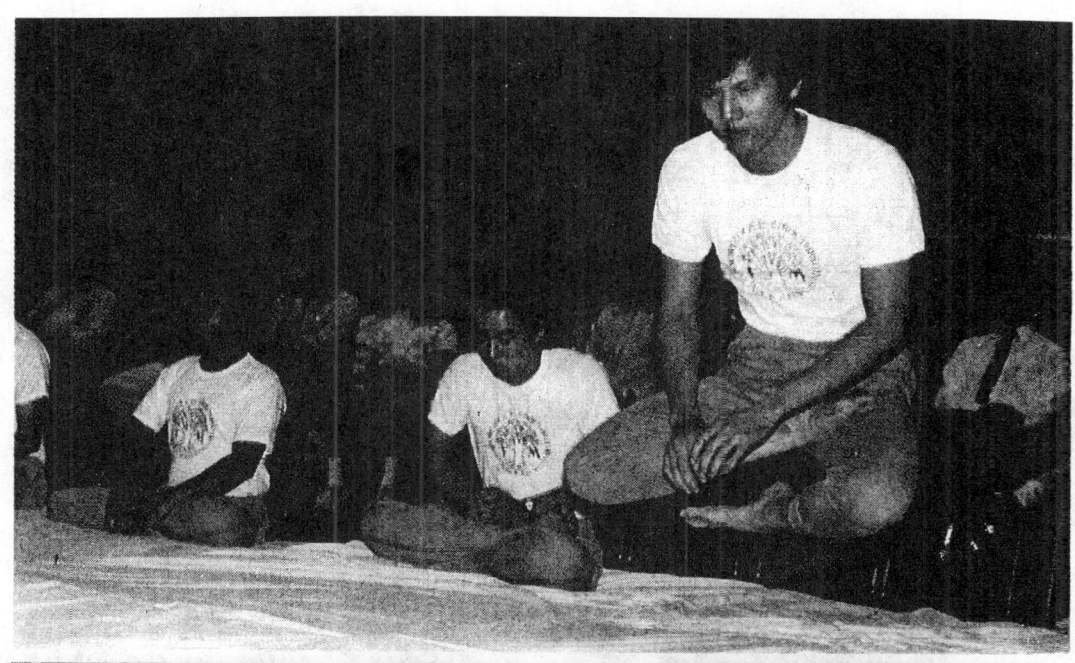

空中飛人！ 他們在做什麼？給人催眠嗎？不，原來他們的瑜珈術已經到了新的境界，能夠凌空飛舞。

才見他們盤膝打坐，凝神貫注一會，突然整個身體飛躍而起。像下圖這位仁兄，一「飛」高達一呎半哩。

共有七個瑜珈高手昨晚在八打舞再也一間酒店表演，吸引不少觀眾。

PRESS REPORTS FROM ASIA

Malaysia • *Nanyang Siang Pan*
Kuala Lumpur　17 August 1986　(Chinese)

這不是天方夜譚！
我國有二百人練瑜伽飛行術

名学员在示范瑜伽飞行术，图为他的一个飞跃动作。

马来西亚创造智慧的科学基金会主席达摩达兰医生。

吉隆坡十六日讯 专心打坐可以使人体跃起，浮在空中，甚至如在天方夜谭中坐在飞毡上般飞行。

他们称之为"瑜伽飞行术"。

他们昨日甚至在此间达洋酒店示范表演他们都是马哈里西马昔瑜伽术的学员。

他们希望藉打坐将积极思想的脑波传递出去。为世界带来和平。

马哈里西马昔瑜伽术导师王忠明说，这是古代艺技，创办人是马哈里西马昔圣人。在六十年代开始受到科学家及当代社会的拥护，而延续至今。

他说，马哈里西马昔瑜伽术分为两个阶段：（一）基本超常打坐，及（二）昔迪超常打坐。

基本超常打坐旨在消除个人在现实社会上所承受的压力及紧张，同时促进人体健康。它的学习过程是先聆听导师的介绍演说及预习演

之后，学员即合格进入第二阶段——昔迪超常打坐，瑜伽飞行术是其中一部份，而瑜伽飞行术则分成三个步骤：弹，浮及飞。

王忠明说：学员进展视个人对杂念的克制，目前全球据说仅有两人已达致浮的水平。

他说，马来西亚人是在十年前开始有机会学习到这种瑜伽术，当时成立的马来西亚创造智慧的科学基金会，目前已有三千名学员

他说，全马共有十名导师，前来学习的学员皆献捐出他一个星期的薪水。

马来西亚创造智慧的科学基金会主席是达摩达兰医生。

他说，令人遗憾的是在众多学员中，仅有二百人学习瑜伽飞行术

他说，如果马来西亚人中有一巴仙学习瑜伽飞行术，这个国家将是和平安宁的仙境

他表示，当这些人集中精神打坐，他们将中和消极思想，突出积极思想，同时将有规律的思想传达予周围的人，甚至扩大及全国人民。

他透露，他将在本月廿一日星期四晚上七时四十五分在达洋酒店公开演讲，欢迎公众人士出席。

WORLD PEACE • GLOBAL INAUGURATION

PRESS REPORTS FROM ASIA

Malaysia • *Tong Bao*
Kuala Lumpur   18 August 1986   (Chinese)

促進腦細胞及心智和諧
超覺靜坐技術在馬萌芽茁長

這位超級靜坐的學員只達到了靜坐的第一階段，在進入狀態的會自動彈離地面。

（八打靈十七日訊）「超覺靜坐」——一種據說能促進腦細胞及心智和諧的技術經開始在我國萌芽茁長。

這種源自印度的「超覺靜坐」技術也被稱為「和平技術」，因為它能通過人體散發出的「和平及積極微波」，感染週圍的空氣和人們，進而為世界帶來和平。

大馬創智科學基金會主席王忠明昨晚在一項「超覺靜坐」技術示範表演儀式上說，在目前世界超級強國相斗，戰爭烽火處處及恐怖主義升級的當兒，「超覺靜坐」將扮演其角色，感化世界每個人民及促進世界和平。

他指出，「超覺靜坐」並不需要任何的信仰，因其既非宗教，亦非是哲學的一門，只是一種能讓人民澈底進入深度休息，使身心清新的一種技術。

他說，學習「超覺靜坐」將使人體發揮精神潛能，增進健康，建立穩定的心理，並促使世界人類普遍的和諧。

他說，「超覺靜坐」可以說是既簡單而又不費神思的技術，每日只需晨昏練習兩次，每次十五至二十分鐘。在這期間，身體便能獲得比睡眠更能令人鬆弛的充分休息，但仍保持清醒和富警覺性。

他說，這項技術在世界各國，特別是美國，經有眾多的學員。在大馬，練習這種技術的約有二百人。

這種「超覺靜坐」技術的創始人是來自印度的瑪赫里西。他在美國創辦了一間瑪赫里西大學，在該大學，「超覺靜坐」是其中的一項課程。

王忠明表示，為了有效地感染及塑造世界和平「氣氛」，國際超覺靜坐會的目標是要教導至少七千人學習這種技術。而在我國，這項指標是至少四百人。

王氏指出，國際超覺靜坐會在世界一百零八個國家的一千城市裡，同時進行「超覺靜坐」示範表演，以促起人們對這項技術的注意。

他說，「超覺靜坐」共分為三個階段，首個階段學習者將能坐著騰跳，次階段能凌空升起，而最後階段則能在空中移動。

MAHARISHI'S PROGRAMME TO CREATE

PRESS REPORTS FROM ASIA

Malaysia • *Shin Min Daily News*
Kuala Lumpur   18 August 1986   (Chinese)

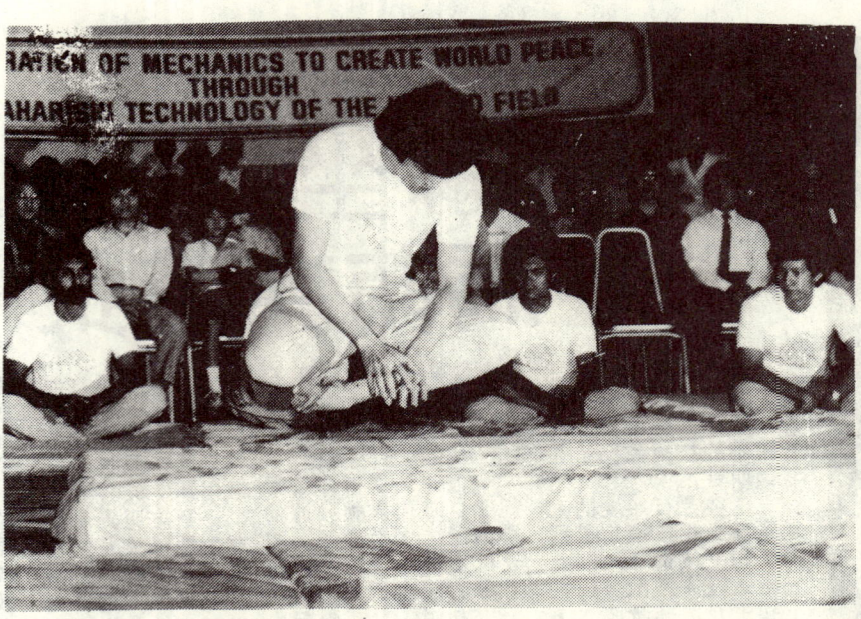

一名示範者在施行瑜珈"飛行術"。

「瑜珈飛行術」表演

（吉隆坡十七日訊）馬來西亞創智科學協會日昨于八打靈達揚酒店舉行一項"瑜珈飛行術"示範，吸引了約三百名公衆人士到場觀看。

這種由瑪哈禮師所研創的"飛行術"並非是真正的飄浮在空中，示範者只不過是盤膝跳動而已。它的另一個名稱為"超覺靜坐"。

據該協會的執委羅雅蘭女士表示，自從她學了這種瑜珈術後，整個人就像脫胎換骨，不但從前所患的疾病不藥而癒，她的思考力也大大的增加。

她說，超覺靜坐除了能使人增加記憶力之外，也能够直接改善學習能力。

羅雅蘭女士也是光華中學的一名教師。她指出，當一名瑜珈者在打坐時，其感受就像飄忽于空中一樣。那種暢快的感受是非筆墨能以形容的。

她接着說，超覺靜坐也能大大減低入睡之時間，使失眠徹底消除，而且絕無服食安眠葯之副作用。

WORLD PEACE • GLOBAL INAUGURATION
PRESS REPORTS FROM ASIA

Malaysia • *Tong Bao*
Kuala Lumpur　31 August 1986　(Chinese)

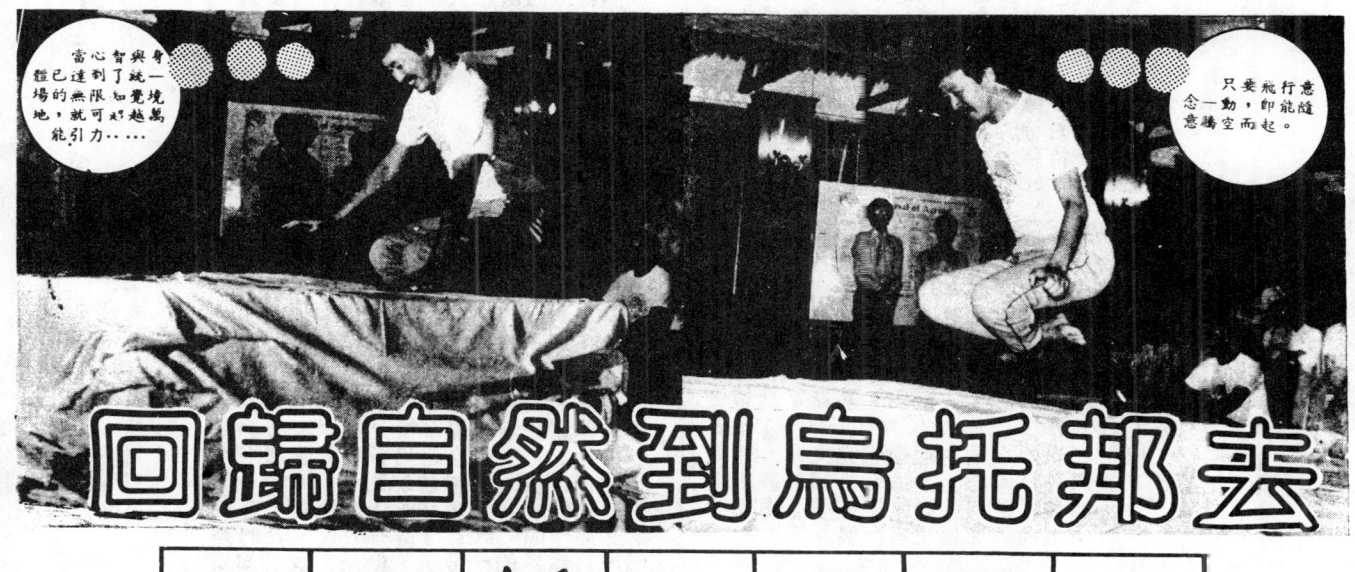

當心智與身體已達到了統一場的無限知覺境地，就可跨越萬能引力……

只要飛行意念一動，即能隨意騰空而起。

回歸自然到烏托邦去
超覺靜坐的奇蹟

盤足坐在軟墊上的凡人竟能騰空飛起，身體停留在空中。這不是法術，也不是輕功，而是瑜伽的超覺靜坐法。修練超覺靜坐，可運用腦電波致使周圍產生和諧氣氛，據說甚至可減少天災人禍疾病，促進世界和平，信不信由你！

瑜伽術能使人飛行？
八月十五日，大馬創智科學中心假八打靈達洋酒店，舉行馬來西亞首次的飛行示範。共有七名瑜伽飛行者當眾示範，包括華、巫、印三種族。他們盤足坐在軟墊上作騰空示範，臀部離開軟墊騰高呎餘，令公衆人士嘖嘖稱奇。
大馬創智科學中心主席達摩達蘭醫生指出，這種騰起，是瑜伽飛行的第一步。

大馬創智科學中心之所以舉行這個超覺靜坐飛行示範，是希望藉靜坐將積極思想由腦波傳遞出去，為世界帶來和平。

根據創智科學中心表示，為了有效地感染及塑造世界和平氣氛，國際創智科學會在世界一百〇八個國家的一千個城市裏，同時進行「超覺靜坐」，以期獲得集體靜坐的超然效果。

這七位飛行者一邊面露喜色，身體一邊此起彼落地騰升。超覺靜坐負責人指出，騰起者會感受到歡暢的喜悅與美妙的感覺。

歷史深遠

超覺靜坐是科學的，而且被介紹到歐美各國，所以很多人認為是一種較新的靜坐法，其實，它的歷史極為深遠。

超覺靜坐發源自至少有五千年以上的古代VEDA，梵文是「知識」的意思，是指關於創造宇宙所有的完全知識。VEDA是隱藏於創造宇宙泉源的純淨意識。……

一九四一年，瑪哈利西・瑪赫西．

瑜義（MAHARISHI MAHESH YOGI）修完物理學，畢業於阿拉哈拔大學，接受GURU DEV 大師指導十三年之久，繼承這種靜坐法，印度的瑜伽創始者被稱爲聖人巴丹沙利，他是由 VEDA 所出敎師之一。所以超覺靜坐也可以說是瑜伽的源頭。

自一九五八年，瑪赫西開始將這種靜坐法廣傳到美國及世界各國。瑪赫西為明確的分別多種瞑想與這種純淨的靜坐法，特將之命名爲TRANSCENDENTAL MEDITATION，簡稱TM，也就是超覺靜坐。

一九六一年，第一次的超覺靜坐教師討論會在印度召開。一九七一年，引進超覺靜坐的四年制瑪赫西國際大學（MIU）宣告創立。同年，瑪赫西又確立了「創智科學」（SCIENCE OF CREATIVE INTELLIGENCE）。

一九七二年，羅勃・基斯瓦烈博士（ROBERT KEITH WALLACE）發表有關超覺靜坐的生理學研究文章，登載於美國科學雜誌上。由此，超覺靜坐很快的開始在美國知識階層或學生中廣傳，科學上的研究也更有發展。

今年，瑪赫西已經計劃在五大洲設立大學。目前，這種教育機關在一百四十國內約有一千五百個中心，而超覺靜坐的教師已經達到大約兩萬人。練習超覺靜坐的人約超過三百五十萬人。

根據中國文化大學出版部印行的「超覺靜坐的奇蹟」（日本東京瑪赫西研究所原著）一書，超覺靜坐被喻為人類歷史中最古老而且最純淨的，也可以說是最奧妙、最科學的靜坐法。

此書也指出，科學家們經進行了種種實驗，如超覺靜坐中的生理狀態變化，腦波變化，血液中的成份或荷爾蒙的變化，記憶力或智能指數的變化等，深入研究關於超覺靜坐的效果。如此，經數十年由哈佛大學、史丹佛大學等一流研究所，以不同的角度搜集的各種資料整理後，超過九百種的研究論文，已經由瑪赫西歐洲研究大學分為四卷的論文集發刊。

「超覺靜坐的奇蹟」書中也說，在美國已經有五千名的醫師以超覺靜坐為預防醫學的有效方式。而以色列的內政部由一九八二年開始也推荐超覺靜坐。

超覺靜坐的做法是順其自然而且很簡單，小孩子也能學習。其坐法是坐姿完全可以隨心所欲。坐在椅子上，沙發上都可以，盤腿而坐或坐禪似地結跏趺坐，伸腳坐也可，總之選擇個人最舒適的坐姿。

一九八三年十二月十七日至八四年一月六日共三星期，在美國愛荷華州費城的瑪赫西國際大學曾舉行公開實驗，共有七千八百人參與這個命名為「七○○○烏托邦的嘗試」大會。

根據「超覺靜坐的奇蹟」，這期間，車禍率竟減少一半，傳染病的發生率也減少卅巴仙，發明新專利的提案增加十五巴仙，報章上對改善社會光明的記載增加近兩倍。各國元首的發言內容正性向改進者，達全體的七十巴仙。當時最不安定的中東黎巴嫩紛爭也驟減，被恐怖份子殺害的人數銳減到等於零。

消除壓力

⋯大馬創智科學中心的領導人王忠明暨全職超覺靜坐導師接受本報專訪。王忠明說：「接受過超覺靜坐與瑜伽飛行術的訓練後，我們體驗到生活的新一面，尤其體會到人是可能活得快樂，可以享受工作的，因為身為一個人，我們是屬於自然界的一份子。但是，我們知道自然與創造意識境界是有多種層次的，如果我們能利用超覺靜坐的技巧平靜下來，就能漸漸地進入所有自然規律最純淨意識（即快樂與智慧）的泉源（見插圖），是無限寧靜的，在這活動的階層，假如我們違反自然界的規律，我們就有壓力的產生。」⋯

王忠明說：「人們不能享受快樂的一個理由是，當我們工作後，在我們的區限性知識階層不斷增加壓力（例如疲勞、生活緊張是增加壓力的原因之一），這是我們會衰老的原因。科學研究證明通過超覺靜坐，能消除生活上的壓力和緊張，就有轉換老化的境界。簡單地說，一棵樹要每天澆水，否則它會枯萎。」

統一場

常常我們聽到不同的靜坐法，超覺靜坐是那一種呢？

王忠明指出，超覺靜坐是最自然的，這種技巧不必推敲，不用集中精神，就連四歲的小孩也可練習。它不是宗教或信仰，沒有特別的衣著與食物的禁忌，不必思索也不必改變生活方式。⋯

什麼是統一場？

「在自然界中，每一樣東西都直接與統一場有關連。從科學的量子物理學方面來看，所有的力是由四種基本力能產生的，即電磁力，弱相互作用，強相互作用和地心吸力。電力與滋力這兩種力能，各別看來是沒有關連的，但當我們從更深一層看，它們都是從電滋力產生的。」

「愛因斯坦也知道，除了電力與磁力，還有電磁力的存在。倘若我們更深入地研究，就會發現上述這四種基本力，都是來自統一場。」…

他繼續說，超覺靜坐讓我們沉潛到統一場和體驗統一場的存在，更深一級的瑜伽飛行術則活化統一場的經驗。馬赫西強調瑜伽飛行技術的原因是，當一組人在進行瑜伽飛行術時，就會影响周圍環境的氣氛。

王忠明再舉例道：「普通電燈光的電波是沒有和諧性的，而激光之所以有這麼強的威力，是因為發出的光有和諧性，一百火的電燈光只能發出一百火的光力，而一百火的激光却能發出一百平方火（即一萬火）的光力。瑜伽飛行員就如激光一樣，能散發出最和諧的電波。在這整個世界裡，有將近五十億人口，因此只需要七千人集體進行瑜伽飛行術，那麼他們所發出的和諧性，就能消除世界的負性向，減少犯罪率，提昇正性向的氣氛，從而提高人類集體意識，帶來和平。

王忠明做了以下這個結論。

他說：「自然境界有很多規律，大自然有很多智慧規律，種瓜得瓜，種豆得豆，遠至宇宙，星球也有其規律，地球繞着太陽，地球自轉，月亮繞着地球。人類是宇宙的一份子，那麼我們也是自然規律的一份子。我個人認為造物者對人類特別關照，我們有自由做任何事，包括為非作歹，違反自然界，使到世界出現混亂的局面，除了破壞以外我們當然有權力導循自然界規律，生活在和諧的自然界中。」

「在我們意識中，有各階層的潛能和自然的規律。但所有自然規律都在統一場裏頭，沒有煩惱，只有人性向善的改變與光明的一面。人類之所以痛苦，是因為沒有領悟到真我，通過超覺靜坐，可以使人類領悟真我，發揮真我，使我們生活在和諧的自然界中。」

第 四 意 識

羅雅蘭夫婦與三名孩子都云學超覺靜坐，並認為這是終身受用不盡的技術。

在一九八二年十月，羅雅蘭大學的同學參加過超覺靜坐後覺得很好，告訴她種種好處，如消除精神壓力、增加工作效率等，羅雅蘭感到有趣，便抱着好奇的態度學習。她說：「超覺靜坐是種享受。」

「以前我的身體一向來很弱，每天早上鼻涕直流，一定要拿紙巾出門的，睡覺時還要叠高枕頭，否則呼吸就不順暢，學習了超覺靜坐約兩個月後，以上現象都消逝了！」…

「超覺靜坐並不難，只要晨昏有規律的靜坐廿分鐘，就會覺得精神飽滿了。」羅雅蘭說。

或許你也要懷疑地問，能長時間保持精神奕奕，是否一種透支？

根據科學報告，人只用了五至十巴仙的智力，簡單地說，我們通常體驗的意識共有三種：「醒覺時的意識」、「作夢時的意識」與「睡覺時的意識」，而超覺靜坐能使我們沉潛到第四意識狀態，即是超覺意識。

和 諧 電 波

羅雅蘭說：「講起來超覺靜坐是很簡單且容易進行的。它共分七個階段學習，只要六天就可完成「超覺靜坐」課程。她指出，功效是因人而異的，它符合自然界的規律。「不過，當你學後段時期再回想起來就會知道這技巧帶給我們的效果是那麼的奧妙，總而言之，這超覺靜坐技巧可幫助我們消除神經系統的所累積的壓力。當我們的神經系統淨化後，我們的心智和身體就會健全，意識自然擴張，生活就會符合自然的規律而暢順愉快；每天精力充沛，工作愉快。在體質上，確有返老還童的功效。」

在練習「超覺靜坐」兩個月後，般上就能做「瑜伽飛行術」（TM-SIDHI）…

這種躍起，根據瑪赫西說，是「瑜伽飛行」的第一步，第二步是浮在空中，第三步驟是飛行。她說：「瑜伽飛行技術的修習，重點不在外在的型象（即是躍起），而是在躍起時腦電波達到最高的統能境界（MAXIMUM COHERENCE）而產生和諧的電波，這和諧電波能影響我們的週圍環境，使到大家的集體意識提高。

瑜伽飛行技術之所以令人起飛是…

因為修習者心智和身體已達到了統一場的無限知覺的境地，超越了萬能引力，因此飛行意念一動，即能隨意躍起。

MAHARISHI'S PROGRAMME TO CREAT

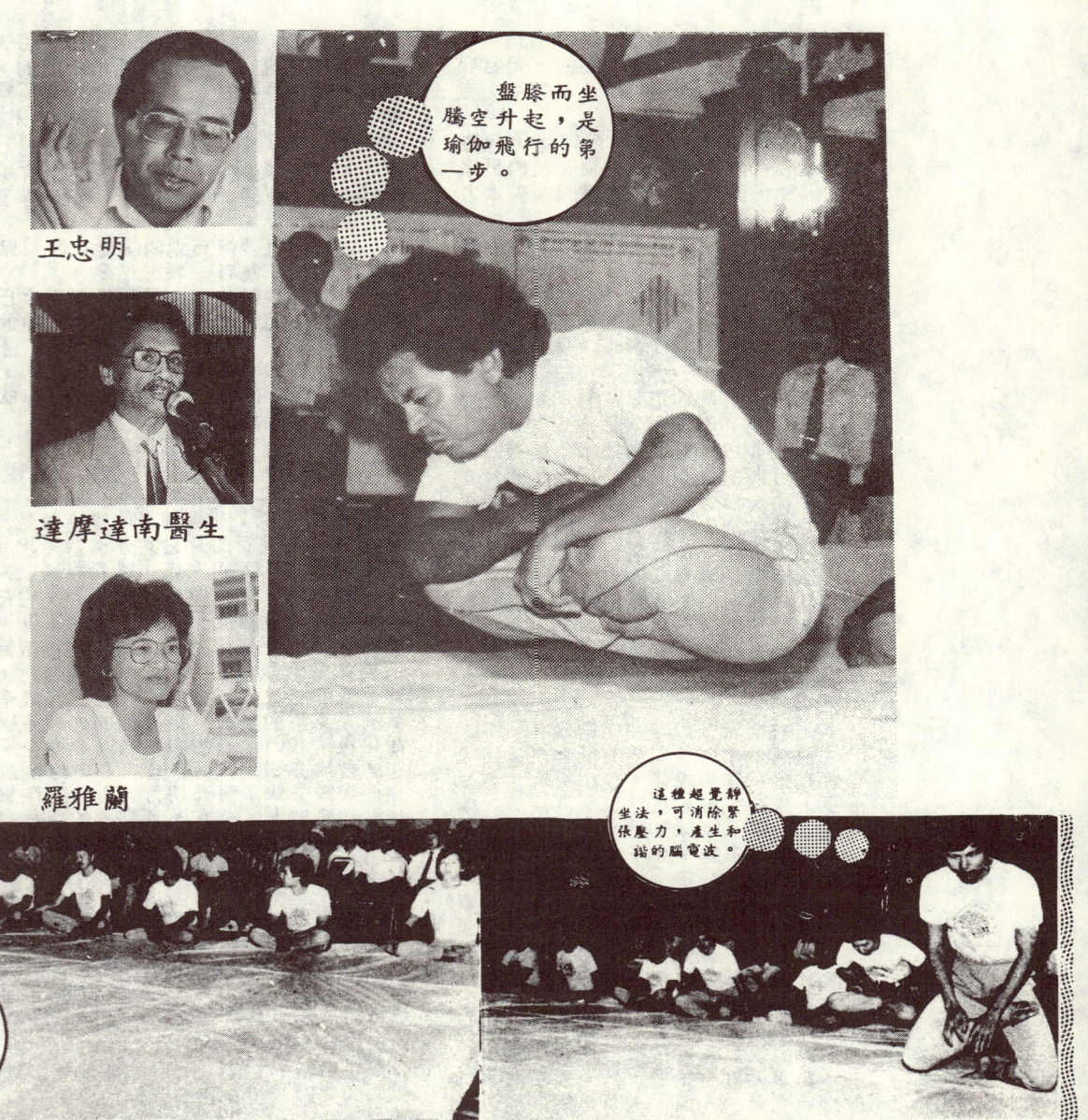

王忠明

達摩達南醫生

羅雅蘭

盤膝而坐騰空升起，是瑜伽飛行的第一步。

七位瑜伽飛行者，盤足坐在軟墊上進行騰空示範。

這種超覺靜坐法，可消除緊張壓力，產生和諧的腦電波。

文：水月　圖：阮順成

WORLD PEACE • GLOBAL INAUGURATION

PRESS REPORTS FROM ASIA

Malaysia • *China Press*
Kuala Lumpur 6 September 1986 (Chinese)

廿分鐘學瑜珈
好過吃仙丹

△王添明為「瑜珈來表演大會」主持切糕儀式。壁上掛着瑪赫西大師的照片。

一群人盤膝打坐，閉目凝神，口中喃喃自語，突然整個身體飛躍而起，凌空飛舞……。

觀衆驚為觀之，全場騷動，難得有機會觀賞我國七名瑜珈術高手空前的公開表演。

這種「瑜珈凌空術」（YOGIS FLYING）是「瑪赫西統一場技術」（MAHARISHI TECHNOLOGY OF THE UNITIED FIELD）的最高境界。凡修練至此境界者，都能隨心所欲，凌空飛舞。

「瑪赫西統一場技術」分為二個層次，一為初級的超覺靜坐（TRANSCENDENTAL MEDITATION，簡稱TM），第二層次是超覺靜坐高級意識技術（TM－SIDHI）。目前全球超過一百四十個國家，共有三百五十萬人學習TM。在大馬約有三千人學習TM，只有二百多人進入第二個層次。

追求精神熱潮領域
無我境界。第四意識

這種超覺靜坐及創智科學的創始人是當代印度哲人瑪赫西大師（Maharishi Mahesh Yogi）。在一九五八年，瑪赫西才開始將這種靜坐法廣傳到美國及世界各國去，所以許多人都認為它是一種較新的靜坐法。其實超覺靜坐早在五千年前已存在了，但由於缺乏教導及傳播，加上沒有先進的科學儀器來証明其效能，它一直被人們給忽略了，直到近二三十年來，許多先進國家的醫學家証實超覺靜坐是種醫治身心的現代科學後，此技術才普遍起來，深受各階層人士的喜愛。

一九七六年，超覺靜坐才正式流傳至我國。

馬來西亞創智科學基金的創辦人之一的王添明受訪時說，超覺靜坐是人類歷史中最古老且最純淨，同時又是最奧妙、最科學的靜坐法。

他說，從一九七零年開始，全球一百多間大學和研究所，提出四百多項科學報告，證實了超覺靜坐能發揮精神潛能、增進健康、建立穩定的心裡，改善人際關係，並且可導致世界人類普通的和諧。

王添明說在目前這個科技發達、物質生活愈富裕的時代里，人們就愈會感覺到人的內在價值及精神生活的重要性，因此全球各地都興起了追求精神世界的熱潮，比如學禪、瑜珈、打坐、密宗等。

「歸根究底，人們是在尋求人類精神的發源池，因為那是人類生存的一切活動的原動力。」

一旦進入「純淨意識」境界時，任何思想與物質都不存在，那是一種超越時間、空時所有現象的狀態。這種狀態禪稱為「空的境界」或「無我的境界」，而科學家稱之為「第四意識」。

超覺靜坐經七步驟
持之以恆。方可見效

他說，超覺靜坐法可使人們輕易體驗以上的境界，它與禪、密宗等在形式上不同吧，所追求的目標却是一致的。

王添明說，超覺靜坐是種簡單、容易、自然及毫不費力的技術。它不分宗教、膚色、種族、性別，連四歲小童也可學習。

「超覺靜坐的坐法是選最舒適的坐法，不須集中或控制精神，一切順其自然，精神放鬆。當然它有一定的「方程式」必須遵守。一般人只需每天早晚練習一次，每次練習約廿分鐘，只要持之以恆，方可見效。」

超覺靜坐是必須經過「七個步驟」：
①超覺靜坐介紹演講。
②預備演講。
③個別面談。
④個別指導。
⑤第一天的檢驗。
⑥第二天的檢驗。
⑦第三天的檢驗。

經過六天共約十個小時的指導課程後，每個人都可以循序學到。

至於收費方面，王添明說，由於各人的薪水有異，他們只收學習者四分之一的月薪，作為費用。王添明強調說，據「TM一巴仙效果」來說，只要全球人口有一巴仙人在練習TM，人類社會就能自然而然地達致和諧的境地。

減緩人體老化速度
增強記憶。消除疲勞

他舉例說，雷射光廣泛被利用是因它不同於一般光線，其光芒整齊而有規律，首尾一貫，照射到某種原子就會放射出新的光線，這種光線又照射到下一個原子，再放射出新的光線。這種循環的「誘導放射」使全部的原子更有規律。同樣的，若一巴仙人學習TM，其和諧的腦波將會一個個傳出去，逐漸擴大到四處，進而塑造一個美好和諧的社會。

最後，王添明說，日內於八打靈所表演的「瑜珈凌空術」目的是要影响更多公眾人士學習TM。

「FLYING不是我們所強調的，我們要的是TM的效能。」

其中一名「飛人」威廉受訪時說，學習TM后，使他比較樂觀，心胸開闊，眼光較遠。

他學習TM已有四年了，家中大小成員都是TM練習者。他說，TM能使一個人生活更有規律，身心愉快，提高工作效率，同時也能增進人際關係，造福人群社會。

現年四十歲的安沙里說，學習TM好處很多，除了消除疲勞、鬆弛精神、減緩人體老化的速度外，還可加強記憶力，提高工作效率，信心增加，對前景更具樂觀。

他說，有機會接觸到TM是他人生中最大的幸運，其效能好處很多，不能言傳，就像飲水一樣，冷暖只有飲者才能真正體會到。

他非常鼓勵人們學習TM，他說：「不學是你的巨大損失啊！」

報導／本報何書忠
攝影／本報余萬隆

- 他所能夠凌空升起，
- 追求超時空的熱潮，
- 全馬三千人在學習，
- 減緩人體老化精神。

△安沙里：消除疲勞，加強信心，提高工作效率。

△威廉：TM可使生活更有規律。

WORLD PEACE • GLOBAL INAUGURATION

△口中喃喃自語後，整個人便飛躍起來。

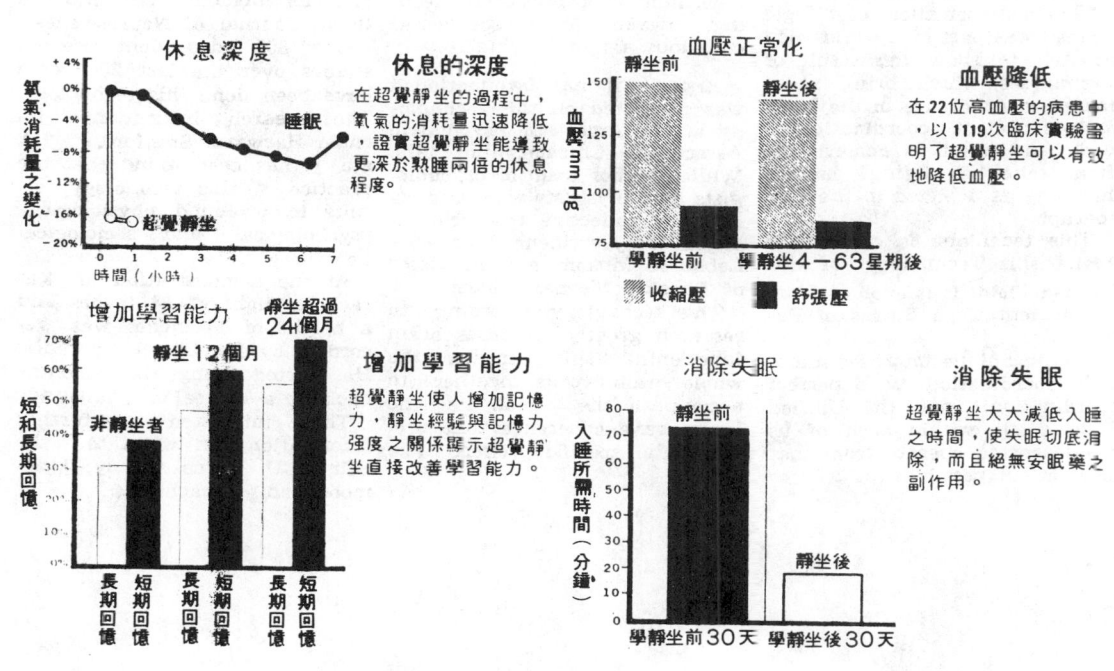

休息的深度
在超覺靜坐的過程中，氧氣的消耗量迅速降低，證實超覺靜坐能導致更深於熟睡兩倍的休息程度。

血壓降低
在22位高血壓的病患中，以1119次臨床實驗證明了超覺靜坐可以有效地降低血壓。

增加學習能力
超覺靜坐使人增加記憶力，靜坐經驗與記憶力強度之關係顯示超覺靜坐直接改善學習能力。

消除失眠
超覺靜坐大大減低入睡之時間，使失眠徹底消除，而且絕無安眠藥之副作用。

PRESS REPORTS FROM ASIA

Pakistan • *Morning News*

Karachi   1 September 1986   (English)

YOGIC FLYING

Higher functioning of mind demonstrated

By Our Staff Reporter

The capability of the higher functioning of the mind was demonstrated here recently. About 90 people witnessed a Pakistani expert take off about 18 inches from the ground and hop on foam without physical effort.

This demonstration organised by the Society for the Science of Creative Intelligence was held at the Pearl Continental Hotel.

It was to prove that such mental development resulted in capacities to influence matter (like our body) to achieve seemingly superhuman results.

This demonstration of "Yogic flying" was part of a world wide attempt to show the result of techniques which bring about increased coherence in the brain and sufficient coordination of body and mind to achieve the first stage of flying namely hopping, as depicted in the photograph.

This technique is called the Maharishi Technology of the Unified Field. It is evolved from the ancient Yoga Sutras of Patanjali.

This technique improves mind-body coordination. With perfect coordination, from the Unified Field deep within each of us one learns to operate from that level of all possibilities....

Recent scientific studies have indicated that this is a practical technology to create world peace. When these techniques are practiced collectively from any single point on the globe an influence of harmony and positivity radiates throughout the city, nation and world. If one has a thought for the body to lift up the body lifts up. This first stage of flying is accompanied by an inner experience of great bliss and happiness.

By studying the EEG of the brain a neurophysiologist can determine if a person is sleeping, awake, in transcendental consciousness or "flying".

A paper it may be mentioned was presented on this technology at the American Psychiatric Association, Chicago, June 1979. While another team of psychologists and physisists who presented their collective research, included Dr. Kerridene Badaowi, a Lebanese Muslim and Professor of Physics, Marne, France.

This technology according to research greatly optimises brain functioning. This means the whole brain works together to accomplish the goal. Its the brain wave coherence that produces the specific effect like flying.

There is a statistically measurable influence of purity, harmony and order in the surrounding society.

This has been experimentally verified more than 30 times, with the involvement of government agencies and scientists from top universities around the world. It has been used in experimental interventions to calm down disorder and violence in hot spots in many different countries. Two of the most important studies on this phenomenon have already been published in respected research journals including the International Journal of Neuroscience.

Over 300 independent research studies over the last 25 years have been done this technology. The research institutions include Harward, Stanford, UCLA etc. It has been found that the practice of this technology results in profound physiological, psychological and sociological benefits

At the demonstration in Karachi a flight of 64 inches and a height of 18 inches was recorded, by Mr Lionel Andrades. He started flying six months back at a course in Thailand.

Those interested in further information can write to the SCI, 24-D, Cyrus Colony, Mahmoodabad, Karachi 44.

WORLD PEACE • GLOBAL INAUGURATION

Yogic flying technique demonstrating the capacity of the mind to lift the body without any physical effort, shown at Pearl Continental Karachi recently. This is part of the technology of the unified field to generate coherence in brain functioning.

(The above photo also appeared in *The Leader,* Karachi, 27 August 1986.)

PRESS REPORTS FROM ASIA

Philippines • *Philippines News Agency*

New Delhi   6 August 1986   (English)

The Philippines will be one of the 108 countries where a yogic flying competition will be held on August 15, 1986, according to a Philippine representative of the Maharishi Technology of the Unified Field now in New Delhi.

Josephine Castillo, who is attending a worldwide conference of Maharishi experts at Maharishi Nagar, NOIDA, India, said that the demonstration of the TM Sidhi 'yogic flying' technique will celebrate the inauguration of the Maharishi Programme to Create World Peace and eliminate terrorism and war.

Maharishi's formula aims to create coherence in world consciousness by creating coherence in individual brain physiology. This is achieved through Transcendental Meditation and the TM-Sidhi programme.

In this technique, the body lifts up at the moment of maximum coherence in brain functioning. Coherence radiates from the level of the unified field, the most fundamental level of nature, neutralizing negative tendencies and creating harmony throughout the environment.

Previous competitions of the flying technique have been held, first, in Washington D.C. Convention Center last July 9 and, second, at the Indira Gandhi Indoor Stadium, New Delhi, on July 21, 1986. The competition included the yogic 50-meter race, the 25-meter hurdles, the high jump and the yogic long jump, all in the lotus position.

Other Filipinos who attended the conference besides Josephine Castillo and her husband Poli are Atty. Vicente Santos and family, Nora Llamas and Linda Penalosa.

WORLD PEACE • GLOBAL INAUGURATION

PRESS REPORTS FROM ASIA

Philippines • *Philippines News Agency*

New Delhi   12 August 1986   (English)

Fly high and fly happy was the message of Maharishi Mahesh Yogi to Filipinos competing in the coming 15 August yogic flying competition.

Technology of the Unified Field founder Maharishi gave the message to Josephine Castillo, national leader in the Philippines of the Age of Enlightenment Movement who recently enplaned for the Philippines in time for the event.

The 15 August flying contest will also be held in all major cities of India and in centres of 108 countries worldwide, including the Philippines.

The competition was first held in Washington, D.C., U.S.A. last 9 July and at the Indira Gandhi Indoor Stadium, New Delhi, 21 July to launch a global programme for world peace.

The New Delhi event consisted of participants in the classic lotus position at one end of a 50-metre foam mattress. At the tinkle of a bell, they hopped like rabbits to the other end. Some rose about four inches and several of them, a foot.

According to Dr. Bevan Morris, Minister of Education and Enlightenment in Maharishi's World Government, they are only demonstrating the first stage of yogic flying. The second stage, floating and the ultimate stage, flying, have not been demonstrated yet.

Maharishi is now concentrating his operations in India with headquarters at Noida, a few minutes ride from New Delhi. His 600-acre Maharishi Nagar has several buildings and more infrastructures are being constructed.

Being built is a school building for 1200 students training in the Vedic sciences and a 1200-bed Ayurveda hospital for treating patients and conducting research in traditional medicines. Also planned is a giant fibreglass roofed flying hall for 7000 people practicing Transcendental Meditation.

PRESS REPORTS FROM ASIA

Philippines • *News Herald*

Manila 16 August 1986 (English)

TWO PARTICIPANTS in the First Yogic Flying Competition hosted by the Maharishi Technology of the Unified Field hop over the hurdles along a 25-meter foam track in a meet at the University of Life in Pasig yesterday. The competitors in the Yogic Flying Competition demonstrated the mechanics for what the group claimed as the possible achievement of World Peace through the Maharishi Technology of the Unified Field.

NH photo by Egay Montaña

WORLD PEACE • GLOBAL INAUGURATION

PRESS REPORTS FROM ASIA

Philippines • *The Philippine Tribune*

Manila   16 August 1986   (English)

Yogic flying for world peace

By ELVIRA MATA

IT WAS probably the quietest competition ever held.

Nine competitors, dressed in white T-shirts and loose pants tucked their feet over their thighs and meditated for five minutes. The crowd, instead of cheering or eating pop-corn, meditated along with them.

A bell tinkled and away they hopped on five-inch thick foam tracks with a series of raised bumps.

It was the men's 25-meter hurdle, the first event in the First Philippine Yogic Flying Competition held yesterday at the University of Life.

There were three other events, the long jump, the high jump and the 50-meter dash, performed in the same lotus position, or in the free-style or semi-lotus position.

The flying competition was held to inaugurate Maharishi's program to create world peace. Maharishi teaches that if 7,000 people (the square root of one percent of the world population) all meditate at the same time, the world will be at peace. "because of the coherence on all levels of mind, body and environment."

Josephine Castillo, president of the Age of Enlightenment Foundation of the Philippines, said war is caused by a build-up of stress in society and the world. Meditation is known to relieve stress in individuals.

"Meditation by more people who practise yogic flying techniques can collectively relieve world stress," she said.

In yogic flying, the body spontaneously lifts off from the ground at the point of maximum coherence of brain waves, spreading a super radiance effect on the people who are not participating in the joint meditation.

What was demonstrated at the University of Life was just the first stage of flying, which is hopping. As a student of TM advances, he begins to hover or float, then fly.

Outleaping the other yogic hoppers were Benjie Lacsamana, 28, who teaches TM at the Age of Enlightenment and Iking Paterno, 25, a chemical engineer working with a fertilizer company.

Philippines • *People's Journal*

Manila   16 August 1986   (English)

Hop for peace

FILIPINO "yogic flyers" yesterday joined thousands of meditators in 108 countries who levitated and hopped simultaneously to contribute to world peace and try to fight terrorism. Practitioners claim that about 7,000 people meditating together in the same place can have a significant positive effect on the environment, reducing illness, crime and other problems, including terrorism.
Picture: JEFFREY TIANGCO

WORLD PEACE • GLOBAL INAUGURATION

PRESS REPORTS FROM ASIA

Philippines • *The Manila Chronicle*
Manila   16 August 1986   (English)

Defying gravity. *Alex Tuason, his legs locked in a lotus position, appears to be suspended in mid-air as he competes in the long-jump event of the first Filipino Yogic Flying competition at the University of Life. Nine siddhis, or yoga experts, took part in the contest.*

PRESS REPORTS FROM ASIA

Philippines • *Manila Bulletin*

Manila   16 August 1986   (English)

FLYING TILT. The Maharishi yogic flying contest was held yesterday at the University of Life. Two contestants — Rober Lucero (5) and Andrew Ella (8) — are shown crossing barriers during the contest. (Bob Dungo)

Philippines • *Philippine Daily Enquirer*

Manila   16 August 1986   (English)

YOGIC FLYING? Rene Saguita, representing Manila, demonstrates "yogic flying", actually more like hopping, during the first Philippine competition of "yogic flying" held yesterday at the University of Life in Pasig, Metro Manila.

WORLD PEACE • GLOBAL INAUGURATION

PRESS REPORTS FROM ASIA

Philippines • *The Philippine Star*

Manila   16 August 1986   (English)

FLYING CONTEST

Benjie Laxamana topped the first Philippine yogic flying competition by winning two gold, one bronze and one silver medals at the ULTRA yesterday. Other winners were Enrique Paterno, with a gold and three silver medals; and Peter Lee, with a gold and two bronze medals.

PRESS REPORTS FROM ASIA

Philippines • *The Manila Chronicle*
Manila   17 August 1986   (English)

TM EXHIBITION

For seasoned photographers like the Garcia brothers, Albert and Luis (Gamma and Tempo), Exequiel Tee and Ed Tapan (Tribune), Bob Dungo (Manila Bulletin) and Luis Liwanag (Agence France Presse), last Friday's yogic exhibition at the University of Life Convention Hall must have been the strangest "sports" event in recent memory.

Even at the last minute, no one in the audience, except perhaps advance practitioners of transcendental meditation (TM), a technique preached by Maharishi Mahesh Yogi, knew what to expect. Not until the North American Yogic Flying Competition last July 9 in Washington D.C. was a long-concealed art revealed to the public.

Why the demonstration?

As explained in the handouts distributed by nervous but smiling TM organizers, "Governments have failed to create world peace. Today, with the onset of terrorism, they are not providing safety to the people in any part of the world. Even the superpowers are constantly in fear, and the rivalry between them in challenging the life of every individual. Now is the time for responsible individuals in the world to take the responsibility for creating and maintaining world peace.

"As Maharishi has said, 'World peace is a personal and immediate requirement for any significant man in the world today.'"

The point of TM and yogic flying is to promote greater brain wave coherence in one's surroundings, and ultimately the world consciousness, which directly creates over-all peace.

Yogic flying is differentiated from the layman's usual concept of "levitation." The method comes in three distinct stages, with the day's participants attempting only stage one. For now, the nine young men who had signed up for the hurriedly organized event, which was happening simultaneously in 108 other countries, were concentrating on the hopping stage, propelled, they believed, by nothing more than their spiritual awareness.

Garbed in identical tri-color T-shirts and loose pants, the new Olympians sat motionless, legs crossed in the familiar lotus position, and meditating. Before them stretched a sea of foam mattresses divided into hopping lanes by red satin ribbons.

Across the room, on the far stage, governors of the Age of Enlightenment Foundation with visiting TM leaders from Martinique, Mr. and Mrs. Philippe Desbordes, watched serenely. Not a sound was heard from the audience.

At first, nothing. Not even a shiver....
Up went the first cross-legged meditator. He was off and hopping in the first event, the 25-meter dash. The crowd's excitement at witnessing such a phenomenon was palpable and very real. The tension was relieved only when all the participants had reached the finish line and applause was finally permitted.

The next three events — the high jump onto elevated mattresses, the long jump and the 50-meter dash — were spectacles — no less breathtaking. Standouts were longtime TM practitioners Benjie

WORLD PEACE • GLOBAL INAUGURATION

Andrew Ela in the long jump

Lacsamana (No. 4), who later placed gold in all heats but the high jump, Iking Paterno (No. 11) and Andrew Ela (No. 5).

Asked to describe the feeling, consistent placer Paterno, 28, a veterinarian, says, "Flying thrills the body. It's effortless. It's enjoyable and a feeling like no other."

Paterno, who seems eternally good-natured, has been hooked on TM for 10 years. Says he, "I decided to dedicate myself to the teaching of TM because I saw how good its effect was on the environment and on myself. It made me a better person."

Flying, he says, is best done in large groups. "The sensation is stronger."

A surprise number of the program was a special demonstration by 'Manila Bulletin' senior editor Cornelio "Kune" de Guzman and Philippe Desbordes. De Guzman naturally got the most applause from media colleagues and TM advocates Julie Daza (Tribune), Alex Dacanay (Panorama) and Margie Logarta (Chronicle) who wouldn't have missed the one-time event for anything.

Next year's competitions, though, should be better, TM members promised brightly. Says Paterno. "Then, we just might really fly."

(M. T. LOGARTA)

Iking Paterno attempting the high jump

Photos by: Jess Fonseca

WORLD PEACE • GLOBAL INAUGURATION

PRESS REPORTS FROM ASIA

Philippines • *The Philippine Tribune*
Manila 18 August 1986 (English)

A natural high

HOW high can a human being fly without wings?

If you ask a ballerina like Anna Villadolid, one flies as high as one's legs, toes and training can take her. If you ask a TM teacher like Iking Paterno, it takes a few months' discipline of meditation and exercises.

And they're off:

At the University of Life last Friday morning five lanes of foam mattresses were laid out end to end from one end of the convention hall to the other. Their total length: 25 meters. In the next 60 minutes or so, following a five-minute meditation, the "yogic fliers" were showing to journalists and others gathered in the hall how "coherence" triggers the phenomenon called hopping. It begins with a twitch, then a gentle series of shudders like an electrical or chemical impulse, and then the body lifts off to varying heights, from a few inches to more than a foot — and just keeps going.

In a sitting position, with their legs folded under them in the lotus style, they hopped like grasshoppers or rabbits, but not all at the same time, not all with the same speed or at the same height, proving that the "pilot" stills controls the "plane".

Hopping, which is the first stage (to be followed by hovering or floating in the air, and then flying through the air), was revealed to the public last month in Washington, D.C., where an army of media skeptics filmed the proceedings and showed them on TV or splashed the news in the news or features pages of the biggest dailies. The phenomenon, however, is not new; it is as ancient as the Vedic knowledge, and

MEDIUM RARE
• JULLIE YAP DAZA

those fairy tales of magic carpets sailing through the air, when the world was more childlike and less cynical and much more supportive to man's spirituality, probably contain more truth than fiction.

What does the "flier" feel when he or she takes off lke a dragonfly? According to my colleques Jo Garcia and Kune de Guzman of the Bulletin, "it's like unloading an elephant, taking it off our back". (Alcoholics and drug addicts unload a mere monkey when they have been dried out.)

Kune even obliged his colleques with a special demonstration after the awarding of prizes at the UL by hopping the entire 25 meters of the mattress lane. And the guy was not even properly positioned: instead of folding his legs under and in front of him, they were crossed and folded behind him....

To transcend — ah, that is the secret. Not so much to defy the physical laws of nature, as to transcend them, like a ballerina, like a pasha on on a magic carpet. It's a natural high. No wonder, ballet dancers move with an airy grace, and meditators radiate their sense of bliss, like there's nothing in the world to stop them from enjoying life.

PRESS REPORTS FROM ASIA

Philippines • *Manila Bulletin*
Manila 21 August 1986 (English)

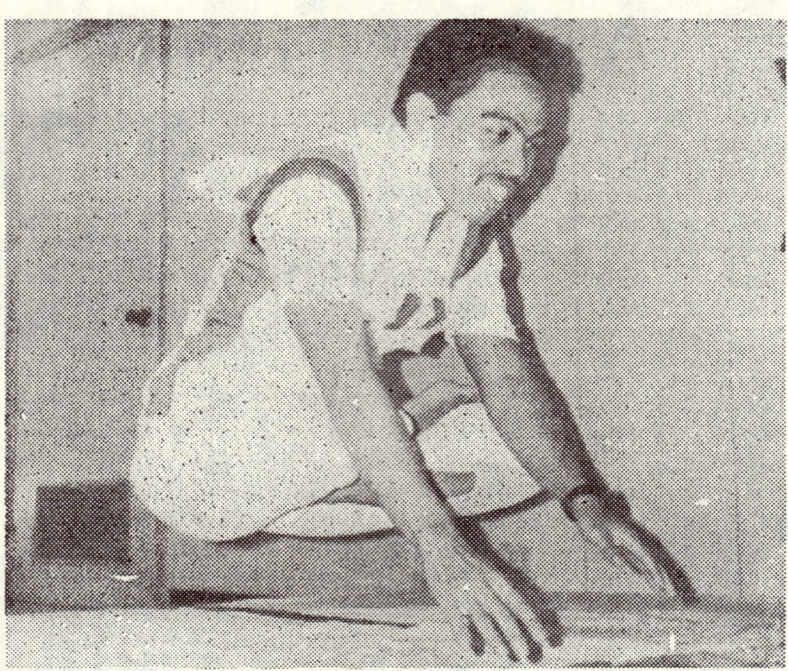

UP UP IN THE AIR. Iking Paterno demonstrates the first stage of 'yogic flying' where the body lifts up and begins to hop at the moment of maximum brain wave coherence. 'Yogic flying' is an aspect of the Maharishi Technology of the Unified Field which creates coherence in individual and world consciousness, the basis for world peace. A public demonstration of 'yogic flying' will be held on Saturday, Aug. 23, 2 p.m. at Conference Room No. 4 of the Philippine International Convention Center.

WORLD PEACE • GLOBAL INAUGURATION

PRESS REPORTS FROM ASIA

Philippines • *Malaya*

Manila   22 August 1986   (English)

Yogic flying contest
Hopping for world peace?

By ROMY TANGBAWAN
Staffmember

Silence filled the air as 9 contestants — clad in white cotton pants and numbered shirts — meditated for five minutes, their legs crossed in classic lotus position.

At the sound of a bell, three of them at the forefront started shaking their heads and bodies, hissed, bounced, then sprung forward like frogs, still cross-legged, racing through the 25-meter foam-rubber track lined with red ribbons.

Thus began the First Philippine "Yogic Flying" Competition last August 16 at the University of Life Convention Hall in Pasig, Metro Manila, sponsored by the Age of Enlightenment Foundation of the Philippines.

The all-male participants were advanced practitioners of Transcendental Meditation (TM), a kind of meditation started by Maharishi Mahesh Yogi.

Contrary to general perception, the contestants did not "fly" literally. They hopped with their legs tucked over their thighs.

But to followers of Maharishi, hopping is only the first stage of the TM-Sidhi "Yogic Flying." As explained by Josephine Castillo, a leading practitioner of TM who bagged a gold medal in the 25-meter hurdle race during the First International "Yogic Flying" Olympics held in India on July 21 this year, they are still trying to reach the second stage wherein they can hover or float, and eventually the last stage wherein they can fly through the air.

"Yogic Flying," says Castillo, is the highest form of transcendental meditation. It can only be achieved if one's "brain and body perform coherently."

THERE THEY GO... Contestants in the First Philippine "Yogic Flying" competition.

Enrique Paterno, a 28-year-old physician from Quezon City, won silver medals in the 25-meter hurdles, 50-meter dash and long jump, plus a bronze in the high jump category. *(Art Son)*

"Since 1,000 B.C., numerous treaties have been forged among nations with the hope of achieving peace, but these never lasted long," Castillo told some 200 spectators, most of whom are meditators themselves. A significant number consisted of reporters and photographers ....

Quoting Maharishi, Castillo said "governments have failed to create world peace, and that terrorism continues to rise. Even superpowers are constantly in fear and the rivalry between them is challenging the life of every individual."

Only then can world peace be achieved if the "world stress" is released, she contended.

"To release world stress, all you need is the right number of people superradiating in a state of transcendental, meditative bliss."

And the right number is 7,071, the cube root of one per cent of the world population. If people reach a pure state of meditation, enabling them to fly, then they can "transform strife into peace on the international level."

"The reason we only hop is because there is still stress left in our systems from various damaging experiences," Castillo echoed Bevan Morris, head of the Maharishi International University in Iowa, United States ....

Peter Lee, 24, explained that hopping in the "Yogic Flying" style is impossible to perform unless one learns TM. "You cannot force yourself to hop. There must be a coherence of the mind and body, and this is obtained through TM."

"The less stressful you are, the easier you hop," said Lee.

Laxamana had the most "coherent" mind and body, edging out his opponents in the 25-meter hurdles, 50-meter dash and long jump events.

Paterno, a 28-year-old doctor, grabbed silver medals in the 25-meter hurdles, 50-meter dash and long jump, plus a bronze in the high jump contest.

Lee garnered third place in the 25-meter hurdles, long jump and 50-meter dash; while 39-year-old Lucero reaped a silver medal in the high jump squabble and a bronze in the freestyle long jump ....

"This is just the start. We hope more competitions will follow," said Castillo.

The competition is patterned after the Olympic games which originated in Greece hundreds of years ago. Castillo said both the Greek Olympic games and the "Yogic Flying" olympics are similar in that they are both aimed at fostering world peace through sports competitions.

"The only difference, and it is a very great difference," she said, "is that in our case, the winner is not one who hops faster or jumps higher or longer but one who reaches the deepest stage of meditation, which is needed for the achievement of a lasting, powerful global peace."

WORLD PEACE • GLOBAL INAUGURATION

PRESS REPORTS FROM ASIA

Philippines • *The Philippine Tribune*
Manila   23 August 1986   (English)

See how they FLY!

A BELL tinkles and signals the start of the yogic flying competition. The contestants, dressed in loose clothes, their legs crossed in a lotus position, meditate at the starting line of 6-inch thick foam tracks.

Toes twitch, the body trembles, then bounces in place gaining momentum before the meditator hops, hops and away he goes.

They call it yogic flying and believers in Maharishi Mahesh Yogi and transcendental meditation demonstrated it last week at the University of Life and yesterday afternoon at the PICC. Organizers are encouraging people to learn yogic flying to create coherence in world consciousness, which is the basis of the Maharishi's program to establish and permanently maintain world peace.

Yogic flying demonstrates superior mind-body coordination inherent in the human nervous system. Anyone can easily learn yogic flying, they say. The first stage of which is hopping, followed by levitating, then the meditator takes off and flies. *Whee!*

MAHARISHI'S PROGRAMME TO CREATE

ANDREW Ela, opposite; Robert Lucero, silver medalist, high jump (10")

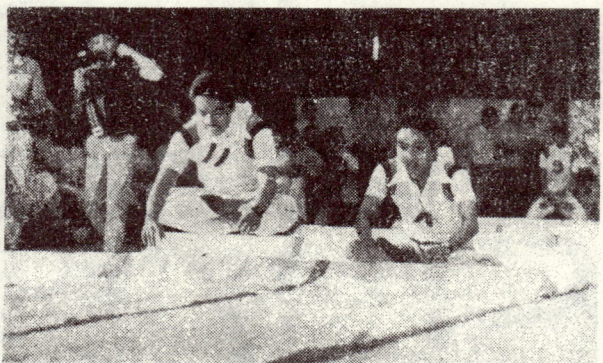

IKING Paterno, gold medalist, high jump (15"); Benjie Lacsamana, gold medalist 25-m dash (17 seconds)

PETER Lee, bronze medalist, 50-m dash (65 seconds) and 25-m dash (30 seconds)

RENE Salita

WORLD PEACE • GLOBAL INAUGURATION

PRESS REPORTS FROM ASIA

Philippines • *Radio DWRT*

Manila   31 August 1986   (English)

Interviewer: Members of the Transcendental Meditation movement seem to fly their way to peace and order by practicing 'yogic flying'. 'Yogic flying' is a remarkable experience where the physical body gets off the ground seemingly violating the law of gravity. A member of the TM movement, Ed Cabagnot, confirms that 'yogic flying' is not a myth.

Ed Cabagnot: This is real, the body can lift off the ground physically....

Interviewer: 'Yogic flying' is indeed an expression of some kind of union or reunion. The Sanskrit term 'yoga', like its English relative 'yoke', refers to the return of the individual self to an original state in which its being and nature are perfect. According to the president of the Age of Enlightenment Foundation of the Philippines, Inc. and the leader of TM in the Philippines, Josephine Castillo, 'yogic flying' is an aspect of the Transcendental Meditation programme and TM-Sidhi programme. It is an activity that creates maximum coherence in the brain physiology of an individual.

Josephine Castillo: It's a technique which provides the system with a very deep, profound state of rest, and eliminates stress, tensions, anxiety, and depression. All this stress which is in the physiology is removed through the Transcendental Meditation programme. And what the person experiences is unbounded awareness, a state of restful alertness. The person is deeply rested inside and yet remains awake.

Interviewer: The person performing 'yogic flying' does not look like superman zooming in the sky. Hopping is more the term than flying. For Josephine Castillo hopping in air is a headstart.

Josephine Castillo: We are not yet completely flying just as we would want to. But, if you remember, when the first airplane flew it didn't really fly, it just hopped; it took off for 12 seconds and hopped about 120 feet. So now even if we are just hopping, it is a breakthrough in human potential. We are illustrating now the capacity of the mind and the body to be so intimately co-ordinated that the body can naturally take off.

Interviewer: Ed Cabagnot of the TM movement supports Josephine Castillo's claim that at present no one actually has flown in the sky just like superman or supergirl would.

Ed Cabagnot: No one is flying at this point. But there are three steps to real flying. First is hopping, the second step is hovering, and the third step is honest to goodness, bona fide flying. At present collective consciousness is not so pure. So most of the people in the world, most of the Sidhas, can only hop; which means that when you are sitting in the lotus position on a mattress you can hop 7 metres away and go around the room.

Interviewer: 'Yogic flying' is not as difficult as it sounds. Even ... an adult as old as 90 can do it. An expert of the Maharishi Technology of the Unified Field, Josephine Castillo, points out that this exercise that Maharishi Mahesh Yogi discovered is effortless and yet it provides numerous benefits.

Josephine Castillo: You will definitely have deep rest. You will definitely have reduction of oxygen consumption, reduction of breath rate, reduction of high blood pressure.

Interviewer: The state of tranquility may be obtained by Transcendental Meditation, according to Josephine Castillo. During this state of placidity achieved through TM one can actually utilize one's maximum human potential.

Josephine Castillo: When we do the TM technique we begin to know that there is so much more of ourselves within us. It is just like if you are a wave in the ocean and you do not even realize that if you just settle down you can also be just as unbounded as the ocean. So when you practise TM, just by settling down your own mind you begin to realize your true self, your own complete total potential.

Interviewer: The movement offers two basic programmes. One is the Transcendental Meditation programme and the other is the TM-Sidhi course. In the Transcendental Meditation programme, one learns how to meditate, while in the TM-Sidhi course, one learns how to fly. To non-practitioners, meditation is nothing but a state of motionlessness. But, for a practitioner, in Transcendental Meditation there is activity in passivity. Ed Cabagnot believes Transcendental Meditation is such a wonderful experience.

Ed Cabagnot: If I had to describe meditation—unless you're meditating, to other people, it's just like possibly people sitting down in a corner, not doing anything—but for the person meditating, it's hard to describe that experience; a person is getting acquainted with his real Self, or that infinite silence of the unified field.

Interviewer: According to Ed Cabagnot, under the Transcendental Meditation programme, one gets acquainted with silence, while in the TM-Sidhi course, one learns how to behave inside stillness.

Ed Cabagnot: That's why we learn how to fly, because at a certain level of very deep meditation we are taught some keys that are really subjective to ourselves, and our body lifts off naturally off the ground.

Interviewer: It is surprising that experts in the TM field claim that an amazing activity such as 'yogic flying' can be learned in about two months time. Before, 'yogic flying' was kept within practitioners only. Outsiders were not allowed to witness the event, but as years went by, Maharishi, the founder of this movement, decided to go public. 'Yogic flying' competitions were held in various parts of the world. And, recently, a contest consisting of categories such as a 50-metre dash, high jump and hurdles was held in the Philippines. How were the winners chosen? Ed Cabagnot responds.

Ed Cabagnot: At the risk of sounding very competitive, since we're trying to create unity and not competition, the winners in the 'yogic flying' competition were judged quantitatively. That is, the highest, how many metres you could jump in your flying, how well you can fly around. They didn't judge for gracefulness, not yet.

Interviewer: The purpose of these competitions is to show the world how vast the human mind is. Is everything really possible in this world?

WORLD PEACE • GLOBAL INAUGURATION

PRESS REPORTS FROM ASIA

Philippines • *Panorama*
Manila 7 September 1986 (English)

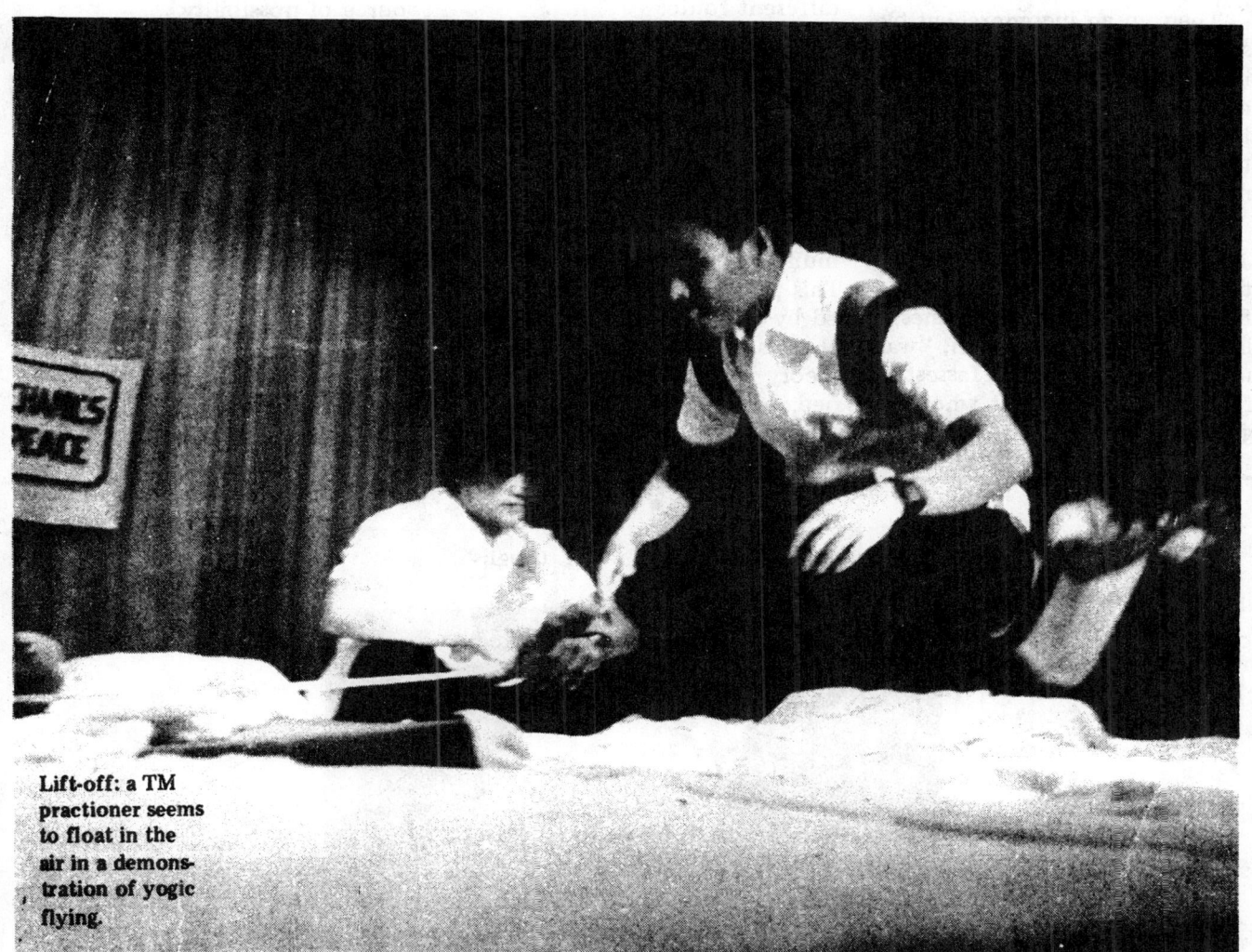

Lift-off: a TM practioner seems to float in the air in a demonstration of yogic flying.

Another kind of flying

By ALEX DACANAY

... Nine "siddhas" (those who have taken the "flying course" of Maharishi) were enlisted in a mind-over-matter contest which duplicated the yogic demonstrations held in India and the US last July. Clad in loose pants and uniform tricolor shirts, they lined up behind a long stretch of linen-covered foam cushions divided into lanes with bright red ribbons. Extra foam hurdles marked several lanes of the "track."

At a signal, the contestants dropped on the foam, crossed their legs in the traditional lotus pose and began to meditate.

While the audience watched with mute enthusiasm and curiosity, the process that yoga experts know so well started to take place, invisibly, in each athlete's nervous system. When a bell tinkle signalled the end of meditation and the start of flying, the racers started to twitch and jerk convulsively.

Then, in an incomprehensible surge of energy, the contestants bounded up and started to hop down the lane like rabbit. When the inspiration wore off, one had to stop and summon a fresh signal.

The race's purpose, said Josephine Castillo, president of the Age of Enlightenment Foundation of the Philippines, in an introductory speech, "was not to see who can go fastest or farthest or highest but who can go deepest."...

Just as the original Olympics had for its goal the attainment of peace, the yogic Olympics seeks the same goal but via a different route.

The key, say TM experts, is brain coherence.

In a pamphlet titled "EEG Research Locates the Unit of World Peace in the Human Brain," Maharishi followers claim that "the body lifts off the ground at the point of maximum coherence of brain waves." This possibility is neither sustained by Newtonian or Einsteinian physics. Only in a unified field theory is the phenomenon justified.

"Flying" exemplifies the coherence between matter and consciousness in the body and is traceable to the unified field of all the laws of nature—an infinite source of possibility ....

Incidentally, "hopping" is only the first stage, and TM organizers claim the next year or two will see the demonstration of "hovering" and actually, "flying" yogis.

At the outset, "hopping" is all we need. Harmonious activity into the brain (through an even distribution of alpha, beta, gamma and delta waves) is thought to create similar ripples throughout nature—thanks to infinite correlation at the level of the unified field. ●

Taiwan • *China Post*

Taipei 12 July 1986 (English)

Eddie Gob demonstrates "Yogic Flying" at the Washington Convention Center Wednesday. Gob demonstrated the TM-Sidhi "Yogic Flying" technique, an aspect of the Maharishi Technology of the United Field founded by his Holiness Maharishi Mahesh Yogi. (AP)

WORLD PEACE • GLOBAL INAUGURATION

PRESS REPORTS FROM ASIA

Taiwan • *China Post*

Taipei   16 August 1986   (English)

Meditators in 108 countries to levitate for world peace

NEW DELHI

New Delhi, India, Aug. 14 (AP) Thousands of meditators in 108 countries will levitate simultaneously Friday to contribute to world peace and try to fight terrorism.

The "yogic flyers" around the world are practitioners of Transcendental Meditation, or TM, as taught by the Maharishi Mahesh Yogi.

TM teaches that world peace can be achieved by ordering activity of the human brain through deep meditation. Meditating together in large groups, adherants say, can neutralize negative and disruptive forces, like terrorism.

Practitioners claim that about 7,000 people meditating together in the same place can have a significant positive effect on the environment, reducing illness, crime and other problems, including terrorism.

They say 7,000 can influence the rest of the world because the number is about one percent of the square root of the world's population.

TM teachers also claim that instructing large groups of people to meditate in Lebanon, the Philippines, Nicaragua, Sri Lanka, Iran and elsewhere produced positive short-term effects in calming the tense situations.

The Maharishi launched his program for world peace in New Delhi last month with a public exhibiton of "yogic flying," in which participants lifted off the ground, apparently hopping, while meditating. Practitioners say they will one day be capable of actual directed flight.

The Maharishi says that if people can hop, they can fly. Flying together, he claims, will achieve world peace.

PRESS REPORTS FROM ASIA

Thailand • *Siamrath Daily News*

Bangkok   12 July 1986   (Thai)

เอ็ดดี้ ก็อป กำลังสาธิตวิธีการเหาะด้วยพลังจิตชุด "โยคีลอยฟ้า" ในการประชุมที่วอชิงตันเมื่อ วันพุธ เทคนิคในการลอยตัวขึ้นได้จากพื้นนี้เป็นศาสตร์ที่สั่งสอนกันในสำนักยูไนเต็ด ฟิลด์ ซึ่งก่อตั้งโดยโยคีมหาฤษี มเหส   (เอพี)

WORLD PEACE • GLOBAL INAUGURATION

PRESS REPORTS FROM ASIA

Thailand • *The Nation*
Bangkok 16 August 1986 (English)

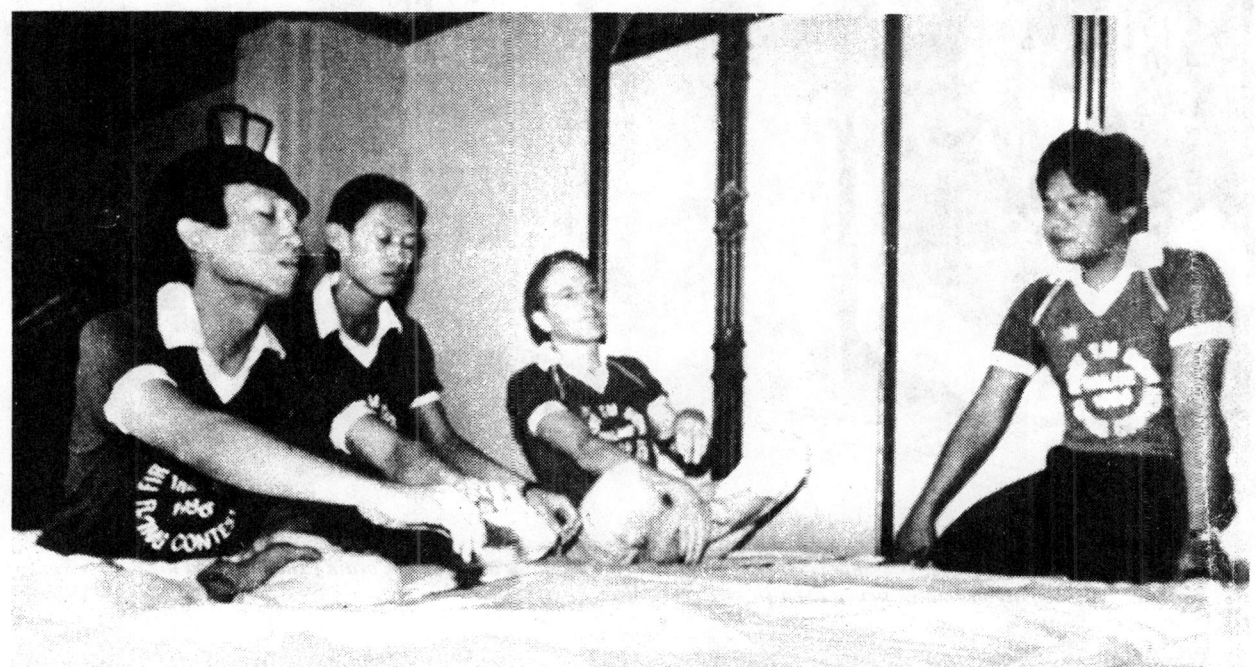

TM teachers practice group meditation prior to their 'flying exercises.'

Promoting peace through meditation

By Promporn Pramualratana

"AT this time, all over the world, a transcendental meditation (T.M.) Sidhi Flying Contest is being held by T.M. centres all over the world," said Police Major General Phet na Pomphet to an audience of T.M. practitioners, enthusiasts and observers at the President hotel's Mayura room. "But for Thailand, this is the first of its kind. Let me assure you that we are not attempting to show any miracles for the T.M. Sidhi flying which you will witness today is purely scientific," he said.

MAHARISHI'S PROGRAMME TO CREATE

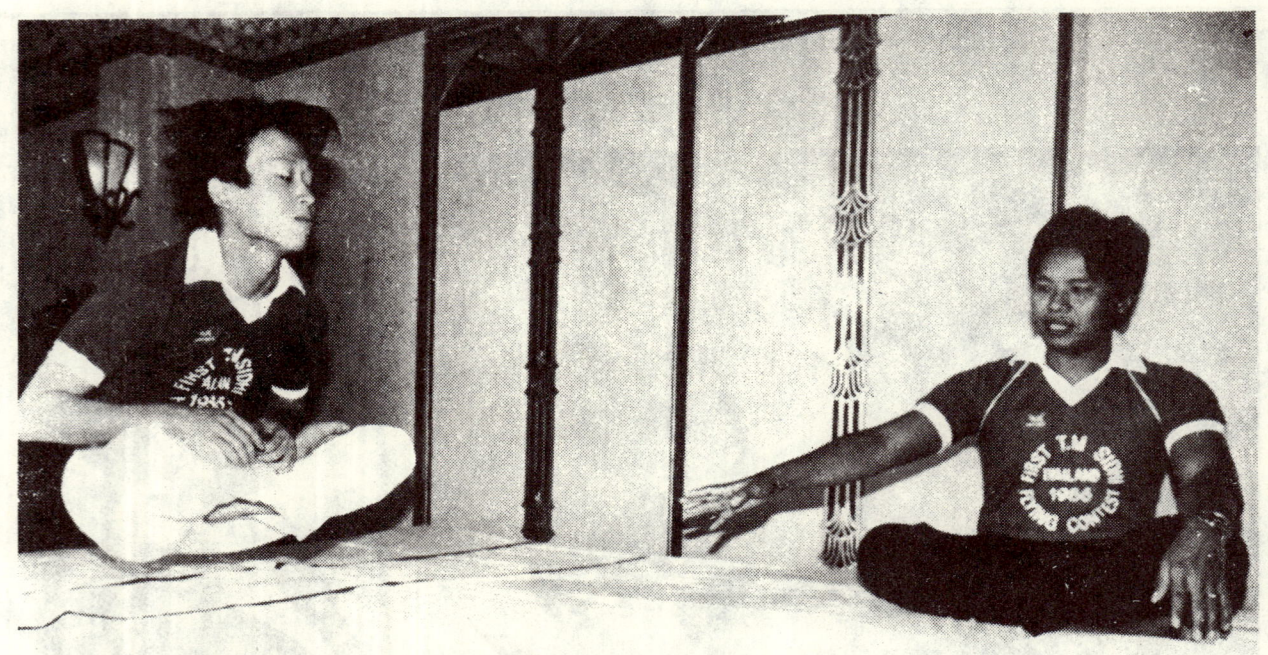

TM SIDHI FLYING: *"... that is when the highest coordination between the brain functions and the cells occur. This activity promotes peace even in an atmosphere of terrorism."*

The time was 11.20 am and the contestants wearing warm-up outfits with T.M.T-shirts had gathered on the stage, first to practice communal meditation along with the approximately 200 participants, and then to demonstrate the 7 metre dash the high jump in the sitting position, and the long jump.

T.M. President (Bangkok) Krirkchai Charoen-rajapark, 33, the energetic son of Le Meridian President chairman, Khunying Somsri, his voice, calm and smooth said, "We shall observe a moment of silence, together with the demonstrators, so that they can meditate and gather up the energy to practice yogic flying." All was still for five minutes except for the clicking of camaras.

Having revved up the required energy, the demonstrators, mostly teachers at the T.M. Centre, began to show signs of their newly gathered force one by one, their noses, eyes, jawbones, heads, necks, shoulders, twitched and jittered and jiggled. Said Tassanee Chantara, 27, a teacher at the T.M. Centre; "They're not doing that consciously — the movement is purely the muscles acting of their own accord, through the deep relaxation due to T.M; this is the energy which they will use in order to float.

After the deep relaxation produced by T.M., 'alpha' brain waves will occur; simultaneously the T.M. 'beta' waves, brought about by the active state of consciousness, occurs. During there is a systematic coordination of these waves and levitation becomes possible.

As their breathing becomes more audible, the demonstrators spring up and down along the mattress that has been prepared on the small stage. In the first level of T.M. Sidhi Flying, as the practitioners sit in the cross-legged yogic posture, they are able to attain some levitation. The movement will appear like a cross-legged jump. In the second level of levitation, the body will be able to float upwards, and unlike the jump, in mid-air, it will be still. The third level of levitation, and the highest level is when the body rises upwards and is able to propel itself in the air; this is in actual fact, floating. Presently because of the unhealthy world situation, the practitioners have not been able to float. Tassanee said.

According to Dr Neil Patterson, an American T.M. professor who aired his views in the documentary entitled, "Maharishi Programme to Create World Peace", yogic flying is actually the systematic and coordinated system of the brain.

The T.M. practitioners on the Mayura room stage later demonstrated the "high jump in the sitting position".

Revving up their energies again, the demonstrators started to seemingly shake and jiggle all their muscles before 'floating' up and down towards two very thick mattresses upon which they wouldl and in the high jump. Some made it while others didn't. Were the 'floating sportsmen' tired after the 'flying exercise's. "Not at all," said one of the T.M. teachers. "After all, it was all brain power."

In the Maharishi foundation film, Patterson, the T.M. expert, expressed his desire to one day hold an Olympic T.M. Sidhi Flying Contest. According to the T.M. experts, the ancient vedics had discovered the forces of universal energy, thousands of years ago. It was only recently, twenty five years ago, that scientists technically confirmed this as 'the unified field'.

President Krirkchai cited Albert Einstein as one of the earlier proponents of this energy. If we as human beings make contact with this source of energy, we will be able to promote health, productivity, well being, and peace within ourselves and among others. T.M. is presently being practised in Japan at national corporations such as Mazda, Toyota and Sumitomo.

It was found that when Sumitomo employees practiced T.M., productivity increased. The reasons being reduced absenteeism and health care costs, as well as a more active performance among employees, "It's refreshing and restores vitality!" remarked a chief engineer at a leading Japanese firm in the film presented by the Bangkok TM Centre, entitled, "Building High Performance People."

The director of a Detroit manufacturing company thought that T.M. would make his employees more passive. But on the contrary, it made them more coherent, improved their performance and increased the company's productivity. "T.M. is our secret weapon," he said. "It gives our company a hard core stability."

In a high pitched voice, through half meditating eyes and through his long white beard, His Holiness Maharishi Mahesh Yogi appears in this same film calling out for world peace: "....it's really fulfilling for me to respond to the call of time — to inaugurate effective programme for world peace ... So we can have real control of the threats which the world faces. Let us eliminate the possibility of war without loss of life."

PRESS REPORTS FROM ASIA

Thailand • *Matichon*

Bangkok　16 August 1986　(Thai)

"ที.เอ็ม." โชว์ลอยตัว
อนาคตกะลอยเหาะ

ที.เอ็ม.ไทย โชว์ลอยตัวเหนือพื้น ชี้เป็นผลจากการฝึกจิต ไม่ใช่ไสยศาสตร์ เตรียมส่งแข่งขันระดับโลก ตั้งเป้าลอยนิ่งเหนือพื้น–ลอยเหาะในอนาคต

เมื่อเวลา 10.00 น. วันที่ 15 สิงหาคมนี้ ที่ห้องมยุรา โรงแรมเมอริเดียน-เพรสิเดนท์ สมาคมแห่งยุคภูมิปัญญารุ่งโรจน์ประเทศไทย ได้จัดให้มีการแสดงผลการวิจัยและการฝึกจิตแบบ 'ที.เอ็ม. (Transcendental Meditation) โดยได้มีการนำแผ่นป้ายแสดงแผนภูมิ, ภาพถ่าย, วิดีโอเทป เกี่ยวกับความเป็นมาของการฝึกจิตดังกล่าว

ตัวแทนของสมาคมได้กล่าวถึงผลการวิจัยเกี่ยวกับเทคนิค ที.เอ็ม. ว่า ได้มีการวิจัยเรื่องนี้มากกว่า 350 อย่างจาก 160 มหาวิทยาลัย ใน 27 ประเทศ อาทิ สหรัฐ, แคนาดา, อังกฤษ เยอรมนี, อินเดีย, สหภาพแอฟริกาใต้, ออสเตรเลีย ว่าส่งผลที่ดีต่อสุขภาพ, สังคม, ได้ใช้จิตอย่างเต็มที่ และก่อให้เกิดสันติสุขแก่โลกในที่สุด มีจุดแรกเริ่มมาจากพระอินเดียชื่อ มหาริชชี มเหธ โยคี นำเผยแพร่ต่อชาวตะวันตก

นอกจากนี้ตัวแทนของสมาคมยังกล่าวอีกว่า หลังการฝึกเทคนิคที.เอ็ม.จนสามารถพัฒนาไปฝึกในขั้นเทคนิคการลอยตัว ที.เอ็ม.สิทธิได้แล้ว ผู้ฝึกจะสามารถลอยตัวได้ 3 ขั้นตอนคือ ขั้นแรก ร่างกายของผู้ฝึกจะยกขึ้นและตกลงมาคล้ายการกระโดด, ขั้นที่สอง จะเป็นการลอยตัวนิ่งกลางอากาศ และ ขั้นสุดท้ายจะเป็นการลอยกลางอากาศและเคลื่อนที่ไป-มาได้

"ผมก็กลัวเหมือนกันว่า ถ้ามีการฝึกกันจริงจัง อีกหน่อยนึกอยากจะไปเชียงใหม่ก็เหาะไป การบินไทยจะขาดทุนเอา" ตัวแทนของสมาคมกล่าวติดตลก

ต่อมาในเวลาประมาณ 11.45 น. ได้จัดให้มีการสาธิตการลอยตัวบนเวทีที่จัดไว้ซึ่งมีพื้นเป็นที่นอนสาธิตปูอยู่ จากนั้นได้มีสมาชิกของสมาคม 7 คนขึ้นไปบนเวทีเตรียมการสาธิต แต่ผู้ประกาศแจ้งว่าจะมีผู้สาธิตเพียง 3 คนเท่านั้น เป็นชาวต่างชาติ 1 คน ไทย 2 คน

หลังจากตัวแทนพร้อม นายเกริกชัย เจริญรัชตภาคย์ นายกสมาคมได้นำผู้ร่วมในห้องทำจิตที.เอ็ม.ให้ทุกคนนั่งนิ่งคล้ายการทำสมาธิ เมื่อผ่านไป 5 นาที จึงได้เริ่มการสาธิต

ผู้สาธิตการลอยตัวสามคนเริ่มต้นนั่งขัดสมาธิสักครู่หนึ่งจึงมีอาการสะบัดหน้าตา แล้วมีการกระโดดขึ้นคล้ายกบจากจุดริมหน้าหนึ่งของที่นอน เมื่อสุดอีกหนึ่งก็หยุดลง และมีบางคนที่สามารถกระโดดอยู่กับที่ได้โดยไม่เคลื่อนที่ไปข้างหน้า จากนั้นได้มีการนำที่นอนหนา 2 ชั้นมาวางกลางเวทีให้ผู้สาธิตกระโดดลอยตัวในท่านั่งสมาธิขึ้นไป ระยะแรกไม่สามารถโดดขึ้นได้ แต่ได้มีความพยายามลองซ้ำก็สามารถทำได้ตามที่ต้องการสาธิต

นายเกริกชัย เจริญรัชตภาคย์ นายกสมาคมกล่าวกับ "มติชน" ว่า จุดเริ่มต้นของเทคนิคที.เอ็ม.มาจากอินเดียในปีค.ศ. 1971 มีครูจากการฝึกของมหาริชชีครั้งแรก 2,000 คน และในปัจจุบันมีสาขาอยู่ทั่วโลกมีครูผู้ฝึกสอนกว่า 30,000 คน โดยเทคนิคที.เอ็ม.นี้ไม่ใช่เรื่องไสยศาสตร์ เป็นวิทยาศาสตร์ที่ผ่านการพิสูจน์มาแล้วไม่เหมือนการเข้าญาณ เป็นการใช้ธรรมชาตินำจิตสู่ภายใน ซึ่งในการสาธิตวันนี้ก็ได้มีการขออนุญาตจากมหาริชชีทำพร้อมกันทั่วโลก

อย่างไรก็ตาม จากการสังเกตของช่างภาพและผู้สื่อข่าวซึ่งนั่งชมอยู่ด้านหน้าสุดพบว่า ระหว่างที่มีการทำสมาธิแบบที.เอ็ม.สิทธินั้น ผู้สาธิตแอบเปิดตามองผู้ชม ระหว่างการสาธิตก็มีการกระโดดลอยตัวชนกัน จนผู้สาธิตเองก็หัวเราะ เมื่อลอยตัวขึ้นที่นอนสองชั้นไม่ได้ก็หัวเราะลืมถากาในทันที ทั้งในด้านระยะการลอยตัวก็เหมือนกับผู้สาธิตจะทราบว่าจะลอยจากจุดใดไปสิ้นสุดที่จุดใด ไม่มีการพลาดตกจากที่นอนที่เตรียมพร้อมไว้บนเวทีแล้ว

WORLD PEACE • GLOBAL INAUGURATION

PRESS REPORTS FROM ASIA

Thailand • *Neawna*
Bangkok   16 August 1986   (Thai)

๒ สาวชี้ประโยชน์ของการฝึกทีเอ็ม.
เผยฝึกสำเร็จสามารถลอยตัวได้

สมาคมแห่งยุคภูมิปัญญารุ่งโรจน์ประเทศไทย โดยมีเกริกชัย เจริญรัชตภาคย์ เป็นนายกสมาคมฯ จัดให้มีการฝึก ที.เอ็ม.พร้อมสาธิตการลอยตัวของสมาชิก ที่โรงแรมเพรสิเด้นท์ เมื่อ ๒ วันก่อน

จากการเปิดเผย ทัศนีย์ จันทร วัย ๒๗ ปี ผู้ชนะเลิศในการฝึกที.เอ็ม.ลอยตัวได้ ๘ เมตรใน ๗ วินาที จบคณะอักษรศาสตร์จากจุฬาลงกรณ์มหาวิทยาลัย ปริญญาโทจากมหาวิทยาลัยมิชิแกน กล่าวว่าทั้งครอบครัวฝึก ที.เอ็ม. ทั้งหมดประมาณ ๑๑ คนโดยเริ่มจากคุณแม่ซึ่งเพื่อน ๆ แนะนำให้เข้าฝึกที.เอ็ม. หรือการทำสมาธินั่นเองแต่เป็นการฝึกที่ไม่ได้มีกำหนดอะไรมาก เพียงแต่ฝึกในช่วงเช้าขณะที่เพิ่งตื่นนอนและในช่วงเย็นก่อนทานข้าว การฝึกที.เอ็ม.ให้ประโยชน์ในแง่ของการพักผ่อนที่ลึกมากกว่าการนอนหลับเพราะเมื่อฝึกแล้วจะทำให้มีความรู้สึกสดชื่นแจ่มใส ซึ่งสามารถทำให้เราปฏิบัติภารกิจที่ดีมีจิตใจดีต่อผู้อื่นด้วย

การฝึกที.เอ็ม. นั้นถ้าฝึกได้ถึงขั้นที่สามารถรวมจิตและกายให้เป็นจุดเดียวกันแล้วก็จะสามารถลอยตัวได้ ซึ่งแบ่งการลอยตัวได้ ๓ ระดับได้แก่ การลอยกระโดด, การลอยตัวนั่งและขั้นสุดท้ายคือการลอยตัวที่สามารถลอยไปไหนมาไหน การฝึกที.เอ็ม.ไม่ใช่เป็นเรื่องของความเชื่อทางไสยศาสตร์ หรืออวิชาใด ๆ แต่เป็นเรื่องของวิทยาศาสตร์ที่มีการพิสูจน์แล้ว การลอยนั้นเป็นเรื่องของพลังจิตและร่างกายที่รวมตัวกันเท่านั้น

วัธราพร ร้างใหญ่ วัย ๒๗ ปีจบการศึกษาจากพณิชยการเจ้าพระยา ทำงานที่บริษัทชันชาย การเม้นท์ เปิดเผยว่าที่หันมาฝึกที.เอ็ม.ก็เพราะว่ามีปัญหาส่วนตัว ซึ่งทำให้เกิดอาการเครียดทางจิต จึงคิดจะหาทางสงบของจิตแรก ๆ ก็ไปฝึกนั่งสมาธิ

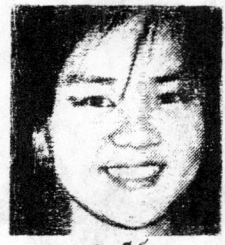

ทัศนีย์

ตามพุทธสถาน แต่เนื่องจากหลักเกณฑ์ที่พุทธศาสนาวางไว้จึงทำให้ไม่สามารถจะฝึกสมาธิได้ ประกอบกับสมาคมฯ ตั้งอยู่ใกล้บ้านจึงทดลองฝึก ซึ่งก็ฝึกได้ง่ายกว่า แต่ทำที.เอ็ม.อยู่ประมาณ ๘ เดือนก็เลิกเพราะติดภารกิจ

การฝึกที.เอ็ม.ทำให้เกิดผลดีหลายอย่าง อาทิทำให้สงบเยือกเย็นมากขึ้นสามารถควบคุมพฤติกรรมของเราได้ เพราะการฝึกที.เอ็ม.เป็นพลังงานหนึ่งในลักษณะของพลังงานนิ่งในตัวเราไม่ใช่เรื่องของไสยศาสตร์ แต่เป็นวิทยาศาสตร์ที่ต้องมีเทคนิคหรือหลักเกณฑ์ในการฝึกสามารถทำได้ง่ายและทำได้ทุกสถานที่

การฝึกที.เอ็ม.นั้นถือว่าเป็นการพักผ่อนทางจิตเหมาะสำหรับสังคมที่ยุ่งวุ่นวายในปัจจุบันนี้เพราะจะทำให้สามารถต่อสู้กับงานที่เครียดได้ดีมาก ก็คิดว่าจะกลับมาฝึกต่อ และไม่กลัวว่าใครจะดูถูกในเรื่องนี้ด้วย

PRESS REPORTS FROM ASIA

Thailand • *Bangkok Post*
Bangkok 18 August 1986 (English)

The physically-uplifting side of meditation

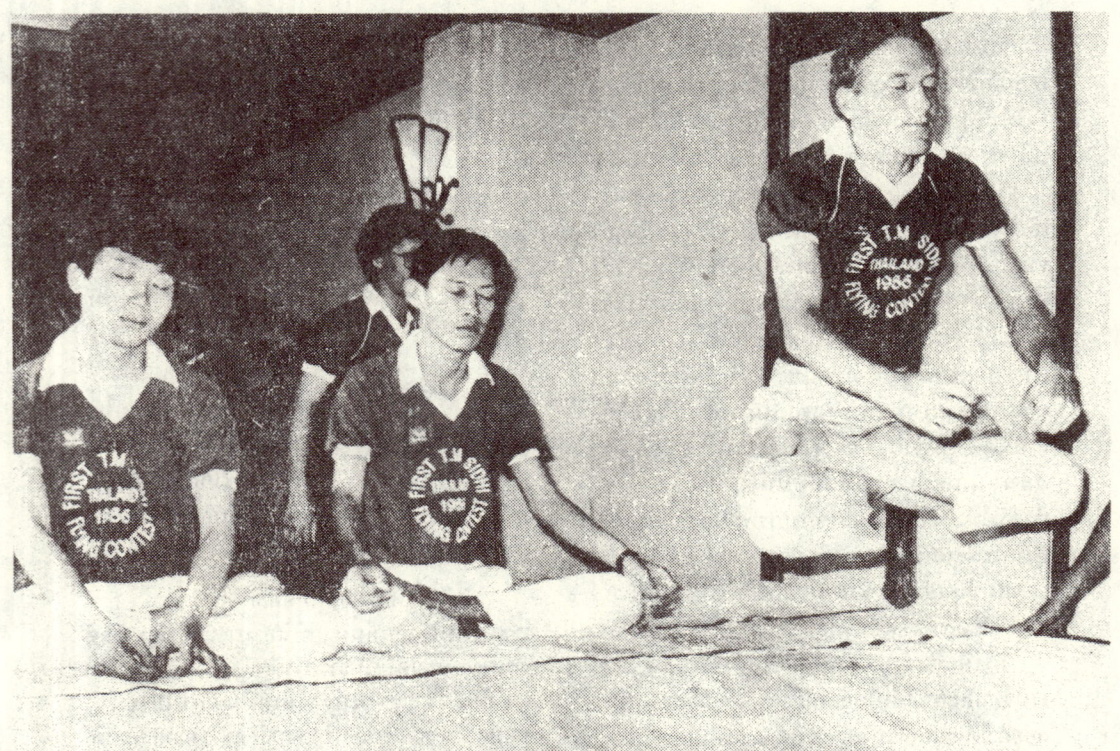

How meditation can keep you a jump ahead of the rest.

MEDITATION is uplifting. Spiritually, no one can dispute that. But physically well? Um...

Don't feel bad if you are hesitant about the whole thing. Certainly you aren't the only one.

Realising this, the Transcendental Meditation Centre in Thailand organised "Thailand's First TM Sidhi Flying Contest" a body-floating contest among its "Sidhi" members at the President Hotel to erase lingering doubts that deep meditation can lift one up physically.

According to the centre, floating in space is not a miracle but a simple skill achieved through deep meditation practices.

There are three different stages of body-floating, the centre asserts. The first is a hop-like step when the body will float upwards and then fall immediately back to the ground.

What makes this a hop with a difference is one's steady brain waves which enable the mind and body to receive a deep rest.

The second stage is when one's body can stay afloat, while in the third stage one can move the body in different directions.

A demonstration and contest only showed the hop-like floating stage. The centre, however, promised to hold a future demon-

WORLD PEACE • GLOBAL INAUGURATION

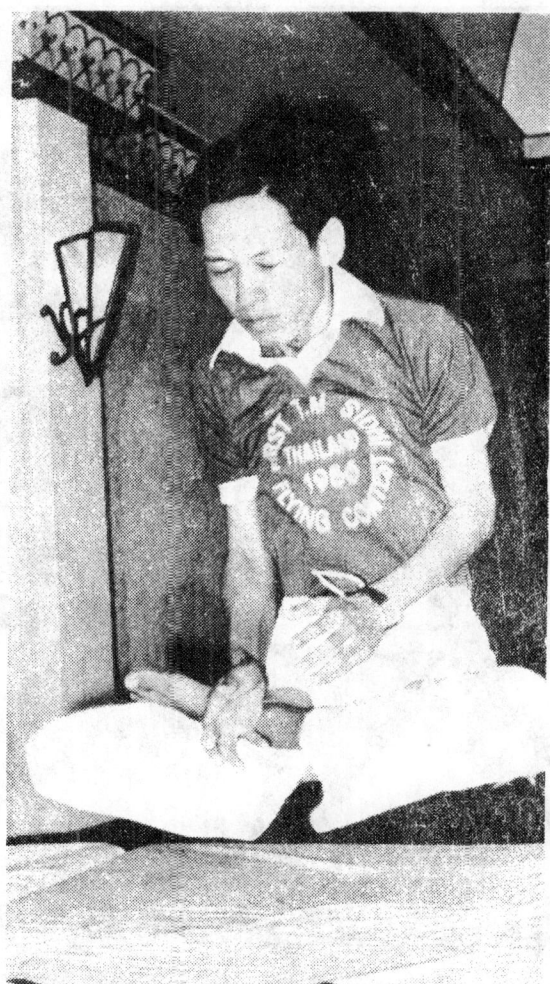

Concentration... and lift-off.

stration of advanced body-floating when its members have acquired greater skills through transcendental meditation.

This form of meditation, introduced by Maharishi Mahesh Yogi, is being promoted worldwide as one of the spiritual means of achieving world harmony. Meditation, says the centre, can reduce depression and anxiety while increasing work efficiency.

MAHARISHI'S PROGRAMME TO CREAT

PRESS REPORTS FROM ASIA

World-wide • *The Associated Press*

New Delhi   21 July 1986   (English)

ASSOCIATED PRESS

GETTING A LIFT—Two contestants in the international "yogic flying" competition, to be held in Indira Gandhi Stadium in New Delhi, practice for the opening of the contest, where 100 meditators from 18 countries will try to hop across mattresses while in blissful levitation.

AUSTRALIA AND THE PACIFIC

Inaugurating Maharishi's Programme to Create World Peace
AUSTRALIA and the PACIFIC

Australia

From **Brisbane** and Sydney in the east to Perth in the far west, 15 August in Australia was celebrated with demonstrations of the technique to create fully integrated national consciousness and world peace.

In **Melbourne**, where 12 metres of foam had been laid out in the conference room of a downtown hotel, TM-Sidhas soared and, according to one spectator, generated a 'light and creative' atmosphere. Subsequently, the Australian Broadcasting Company aired the performance twice on both television and radio. The *Sun*, Melbourne's principal daily, carried a report on its second page with the headline, 'Maharishi plan for peace set to take off', and the TM-Sidhas described the effects of 'yogic flying' to the people of Melbourne on local radio. Three days later, the leaders of the Melbourne Capital of the Age of Enlightenment hosted a large world peace banquet to celebrate the enthusiasm generated in their city for Maharishi's programme.

Sydney's demonstration was held at the Continental Capital of the Age of Enlightenment for Australia and the Pacific, with Dr Byron Rigby, Governor General of the World Government of the Age of Enlightenment for the continent, presiding. All four Sydney television stations reported the news, one noting that the atmosphere during the 'yogic flying' was 'very silent and very lively'.

In **Adelaide**, four stations chronicled the demonstration. The leading television news programme of Western Australia, 'A State Affair', broadcast a seven-minute report of the 'yogic flying' held at **Perth's** Merlin Hotel. The report featured prominent citizens in the audience who practise the Transcendental Meditation technique.

New Zealand

Across the Tasman Sea in New Zealand, the conference room at **Auckland's** South Pacific Hotel was crowded with journalists on 15 August. Television New Zealand, Radio New Zealand, Radio International, *East City News*, and the *Star*—Auckland's largest daily newspaper—all sent journalists to cover the event. The *Star* described the setting in its report: 'In a velvet-draped room in one of Auckland's better hotels, aglare with television lights, we gathered to witness a startling initiative for world peace.' The *Star's* account was also published in the *Napier Daily Telegraph* and the *Timaru Herald*. The *East City News* ended its report with this suggestion, 'Perhaps the hope of the world lies with young men on rubber mattresses and officials with stop watches.' □

WORLD PEACE • GLOBAL INAUGURATION

PRESS REPORTS FROM AUSTRALIA AND THE PACIFIC

Australia • *Channel 7 TV*

Sydney, Australia   15 August 1986   (English)

Reporter: Organizers say, 'Ten thousand people to fly.'... The idea springs from the Maharishi and his Transcendental Meditation. They say it's the only weapon against terrorism and nuclear war.

Maharishi: It is really fulfiling today to inaugurate an effective programme for lasting world peace.

Reporter: The solution is, to fly. For when the mind is without stress, the body levitates. The transcendentalists say they've been forced by the state of the world to reveal a ten-year secret. They call it 'yogic flying'. Gravity, they admit, still curbs their euphoria. But they say it's hard to keep a dedicated TM flyer down. They hope to achieve full levitation soon. However, the flyers says it's what's going on in the mind that's of real importance, and when hundreds of minds combine, awesome power is released. That's why 10,000 meditators in 108 countries climbed into their yogic machines today....

The flyers say in January 1983 they broke the drought in Australia, and they're having another mass gathering next Easter to solve the problem-beset Australian economy....

Broadcaster: Around the corner, the problems of the world will come to an end when we get together and levitate.

Reporter: ...'Yogic flying' is an advanced form of Transcendental Meditation. It's an experience of happiness.

Maharishi: This time demands the rise of a supreme power in the world.

Reporter: To the flyers, it's all really quite simple.

TM-Sidha: The coherence we produce has an effect on the whole environment. It harmonizes natural law. Negative trends take a downward dive when we're producing this effect.

Reporter: Hopping is only stage one. At level three, people fly around the room, although no one has ever filmed this. But the most remarkable aspect is, if we all get together and fly, our thoughts can reduce the crime rate, drug usage, improve the stock exchange, and bring world peace.

TM-Sidha: The effect of this advanced technique of Transcendental Meditation is to radiate peace to a greater extent than the usual practice of TM....

MAHARISHI'S PROGRAMME TO CREATE

PRESS REPORTS FROM AUSTRALIA AND THE PACIFIC

Australia • *The Sun*

Melbourne   16 August 1986   (English)

By ANDREW STEPHENS

THEY told us they were going to fly, and our hopes were high.

Yesterday was the world launch of the Maharishi program to create world peace.

And the highlight was to be real-life levitation.

When the big moment came, our hearts fluttered.

We perched on the edge of our seats, watching four men in green tracksuits.

They meditated, willing their bodies off the ground.

They convulsed, sitting cross-legged on a row of foam-rubber mattresses.

You could see it in their faces — they were ready for takeoff.

We watched, they twitched ... then hopped.

Like gleeful frogs they bounced from one end of the mattresses to the other and back.

This was yogic flying, they told us ... a happy end to global conflict, terrorism and violence.

It's called the transcendental meditation Sidhi technique, discovered by His Holiness Maharishi Mahesh Yogi, of Beatles fame.

Was it a rouse? No, said leaper Ian Crooks.

Hopping would lead to the "inevitable consequence of floating or flying".

"The most beautiful thing about this meditation is that it allows the mind to settle down and come into contact with a broad field of consciousness," he said.

"I started using the technique in 1977 and the initial experience was very profound.

"It makes one realise there is so much more in existence, a whole field of consciousness."

According to theory, Sidhi meditation and so-called flying drains stress from the body.

Practitioners believe that if a big enough group of people meditates at the same time, the stress-reduction effect washes over other people.

Devotees claim large-scale meditations, involving up to 7000 people, have caused reductions in stress, crime, terrorism and illness — and have even boosted stock-exchange activity.

They say if 10,000 people perform Sidhi meditation in one place, the outcome would be world peace.

But why fly, or hop?

"When you meditate, you feel yourself move," Mr Crooks said.

"The experience is enlivening and enriching."

Yesterday's demonstration was held in 108 countries.

Devotees say sociological and scientific studies have shown the technique causes world harmony by tapping a unified field of consciousness ....

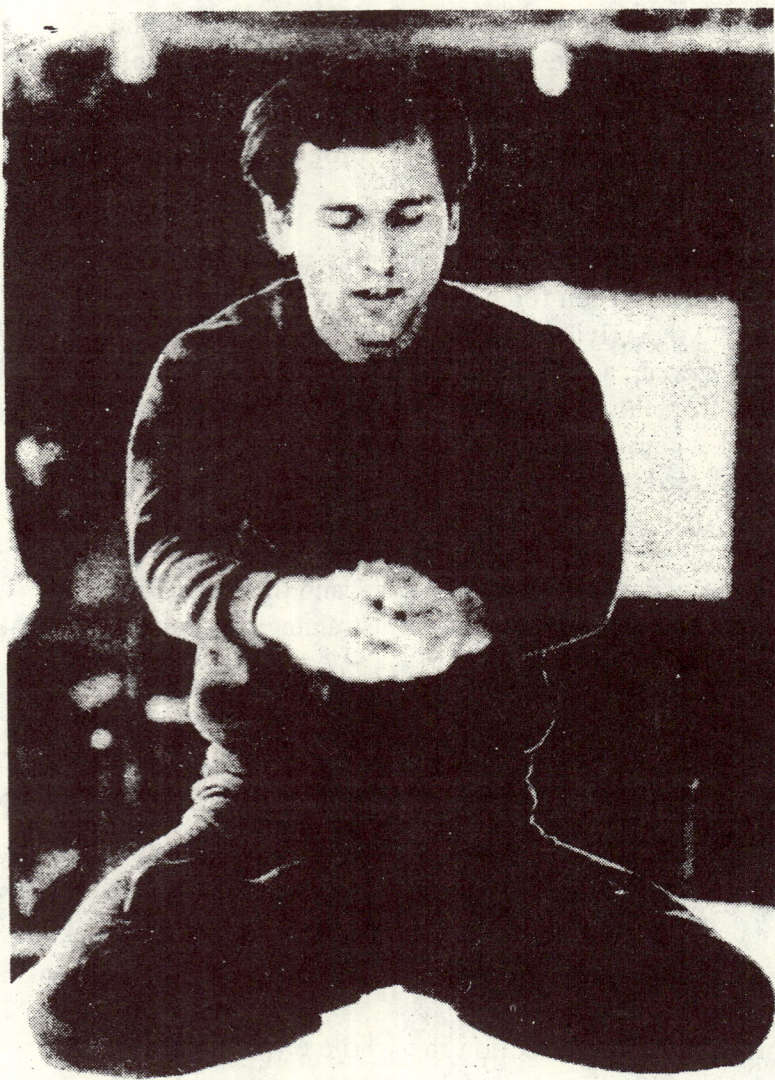

● Robert Hody demonstrates the Sidhi technique of "flying". Picture: FIONA HAMILTON

WORLD PEACE • GLOBAL INAUGURATION

PRESS REPORTS FROM AUSTRALIA AND THE PACIFIC

Australia • *Western Mail*

Perth   16-17 August 1986   (English)

Caught on the hop

ALL things are possible — even flying by the seat of your pants — according to the gospel of yoga.

And here is the living proof in the shape of David Wroth.

He and his yoga off-sider Derek D'Cruz were showing how its done at a Perth hotel.

David is caught on the hop as Derek does some deep meditating.

It seems that if you practise little hops often enough you get higher and higher.

Who knows, perhaps the sky's the limit?

Picture: NIC ELLIS

MAHARISHI'S PROGRAMME TO CREATE

PRESS REPORTS FROM AUSTRALIA AND THE PACIFIC

New Zealand • *Sunday Star*
Auckland   17 August 1986   (English)

Peace for the world...and yogis might fly

By PRUE DASHFIELD

In a velvet-draped room in one of Auckland's better hotels, aglare with television lights, we gathered to witness a startling initiative for world peace.

Clean-cut followers of the Maharishi Mahesh Yogi told us the TM-Sidhi technique of yogic flying would succeed where 8000 peace treaties since 1000BC, the League of Nations and the United Nations had failed.

The Maharishi's Programme to Create World Peace is being inaugurated in 108 countries around the world. He has decided that politicians are entirely ineffectual and with the parlous state of international relations, the time has come to show the way.

They told us that just 1% of the square root of the world's population practising the technique can radiate sufficient coherence into world consciousness to eliminate terrorism and war.

No more nuclear threat, no more car bombs, no more murders or rapes, no more disappointing dips in the stock market. Henry Kissinger, eat your heart out.

After lengthy oral, written and video explanation of the phenomenon, including a message from the venerated Maharishi taped at his World

Capital of the Age of Enlightenment in India, the five demonstrators of the TM-Sidhi technique of yogic flying emerged from behind a wooden screen, settled themselves on foam mattresses in the lotus position and warmed up for their exertions with 10 minutes of meditation.

Most of the gathering supportively closed their eyes in an effort to maximise cohesiveness in room consciousness. A baby gurgled. Non-meditators, impatient for lift-off, tapped their toes.

At last, the two umpires reached for stop-watches and tape measures and national director of the New Zealand Maharishi Foundation Bryan Lee tinkled a little brass bell by way of a starting gun.

This had a very interesting effect on the five flyers, four of whom work in the computer industry. They began minor convulsions, snorting, sniffling and a bit of preliminary bouncing on the spot before bounding at high speed down the mattresses on their bottoms.

At maximum altitude they were perhaps 30cm aloft, but yogic flyers have not yet conquered gravity and any notions we had of white-garbed yogis soaring and swooping about the rafters of the South Pacific Hotel were straightened out by Mr Lee and his clinical psychologist off-sider in the briefing session.

They had explained the three stages of yogic flight. So far nobody has mastered the second step — hovering — or the third, full flight. What we would be observing was stage one, hopping.

Ian Smillie (38), who attended the recent International Yogic Flying Competition in India excelled on the hopping dash up the mattresses.

A 1.2m bottom-up, knees-down long hop earned him a peck on the cheek from Mrs Lee and a wrapped prize which, she said later, was symbolic in nature.

But he did not perform so well on the high hop. Ken Thomas (37), the most convulsive demonstrator sprang 335mm on to a wad of sheets sandwiched between two foam mattresses, a feat which delighted foundation officials and astonished himself.

PRESS REPORTS FROM AUSTRALIA AND THE PACIFIC

New Zealand • *East City News*

Auckland   20 August 1986   (English)

Doing the peace hop

By Barbara Weil

Last week five transcendental meditators demonstrated the latest technique to achieve lasting world peace.

"Yogic Flying" is still in its infancy — the best its practioners can yet achieve is "hopping."

They hopped at Auckland's South Pacific Hotel for a special press briefing last Friday.

It was billed as "a new approach to physically create world peace by creating coherence in brain functioning and radiating coherence throughout the environment."

A cause like that must be worth pursuing.

And a representative gathering of media people with cameras at the ready waited for the revelation.

Even TVNZ's Rod Vaughan was there, secure in the knowledge that such a peaceful gathering was a good deal safer than tracking pugilistic party leaders fishing in Turangi.

The demonstration was organised by the Mararishi Foundation of New Zealand and follows the first "Yogic Flying Olympics" in the United States last month.

The set up looked like a sales' seminar with videos and microphones ready for the pitch.

The only difference was the white mattresses along one side of the room.

A very earnest young man in an impeccable grey suit introduced the programme....

The room went silent. Only the eyes of the media people remained open.

As we waited one or two of the meditators momentarily opened an eye only to close it quickly when they found another watching them.

In the silence a baby began to alternately cry and gurgle. Would this interfere with the alpha and theta waves?

However Bryan rang the bell indicating that the long-awaited demonstration was about to begin.

...Then one by one they hopped the length of the room on the white mattresses, in the lotus position. Bryan asked for a round of applause.

Then it was time to sort out the "winners." The U.S.A. held the inaugural "Yogic Flying Olympics" last month. The level there is advanced enough to have categories such as the 50 metre dash, and long and high jump as well as hurdle events.

The New Zealand events awarded prizes in two events, time and distance. The winners were presented with gift wrapped parcels.

The benefits of TM for individual practitioners are undeniable....

Perhaps the hope of the future lies with young men on rubber mattresses and officials with stop watches.

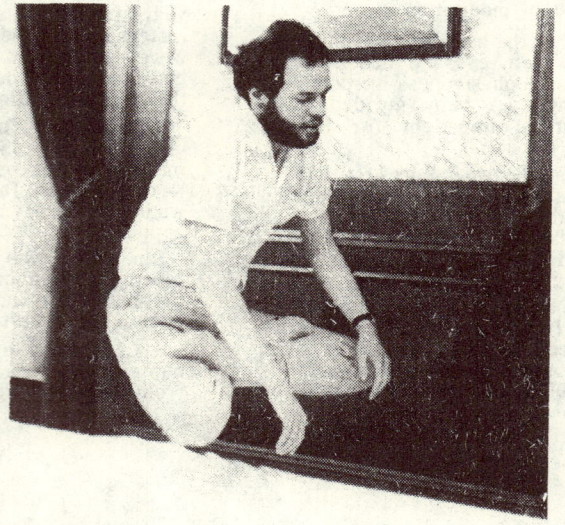

One of the winners, Brian Hurst, who works in computers "hopping for peace".

WORLD PEACE • GLOBAL INAUGURATION

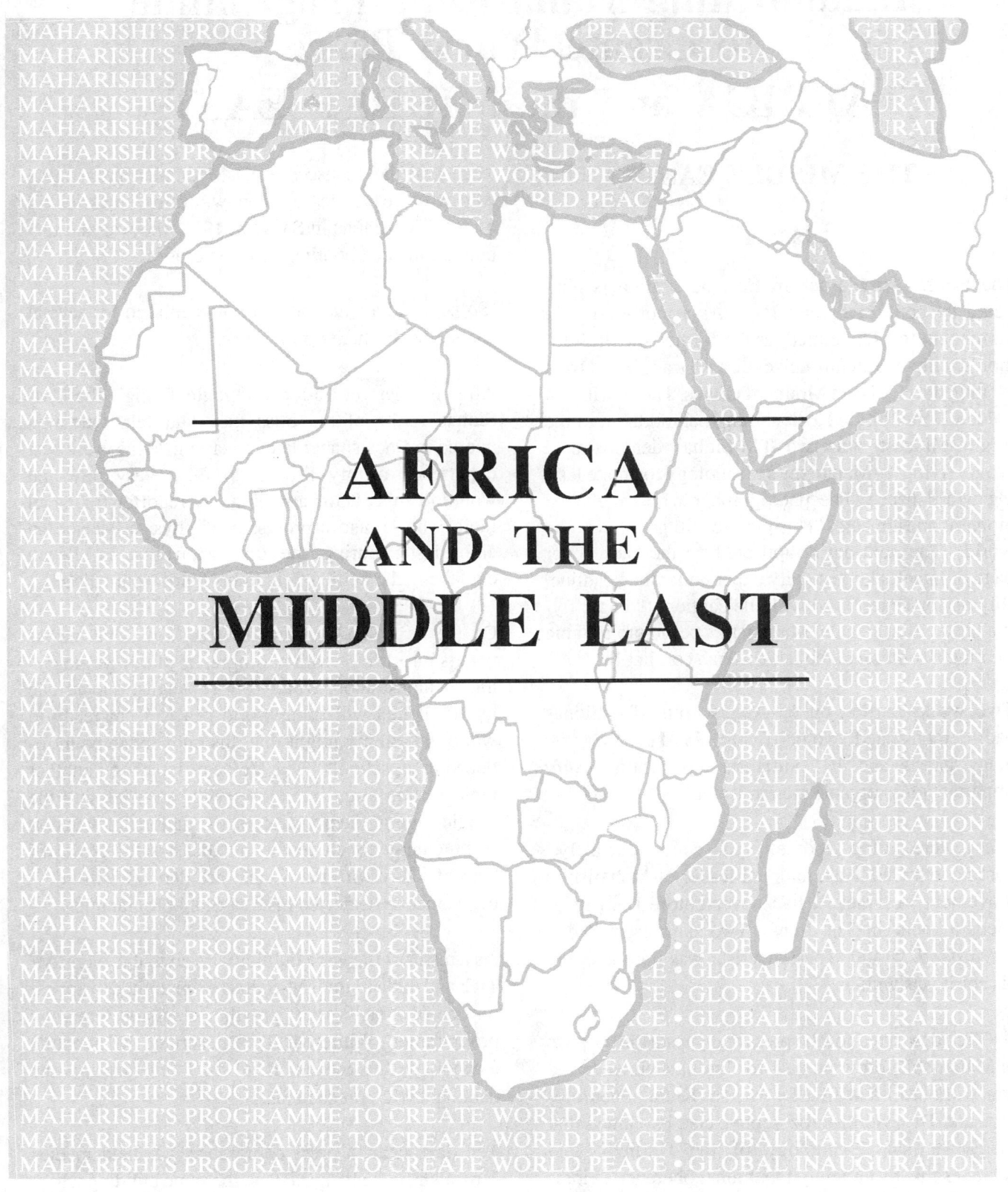

AFRICA AND THE MIDDLE EAST

Inaugurating Maharishi's Programme to Create World Peace
AFRICA and the MIDDLE EAST

THE MIDDLE EAST

Israel

The Dome of the Rock in **East Jerusalem** is honoured by both Arabs and Jews. As a mosque it is a monument to Mohammed; as the former site of Solomon's temple it memorializes Jewish tradition. Overlooking the city is the Mount of Olives. There, with the golden Dome of the Rock shining behind them in the bright Mideast sun, two TM-Sidhas demonstrated 'yogic flying'—Maharishi's technology to create lasting world peace. The photographer who caught the moment on film said, 'This picture will go all over the world.' The next day it appeared on the back cover page of Israel's largest daily paper under the headline, 'Flying for Peace', and with the caption, '"Yogic flying" is the first stage in Maharishi's peace programme to bring a solution to the Israeli-Arab conflict.'

Two weeks earlier, on 15 August, nine TM-Sidhas had demonstrated 'yogic flying' in **Tel Aviv** for many guests and 19 journalists representing every important press organization in Israel.

'They were sitting so quietly you could hear a fly,' commented Gad Tick, national leader of Maharishi's movement in Israel. 'I had never before been in so silent a room in Tel Aviv.' Two days later *Yediot A'Haronoth* wrote, 'The Maharishi was not there, but his spirit was with us.'

Mr Tick described for the press and guests the purpose of Maharishi's programme—to eliminate violence and war without loss of life. Dr Miriam Kutai, a neurologist, and Dr Eylon Meroz, a physicist, explained that the Maharishi Technology of the Unified Field achieves this by creating maximum coherence in individual brain functioning, the unit of world peace. A teacher of the Transcendental Meditation programme who was present described how, during an assembly of 400 TM-Sidhas in Safad in 1978, the war and turbulence in neighbouring Lebanon ceased.

'So peaceful a situation had not been seen for several years,' the teacher told the press.

After the demonstration of 'yogic flying', the TM-Sidhas spoke of the bliss they had felt. One was quoted in a newspaper later as saying, 'This is the best experience of my life. I do this every day and wouldn't miss it for anything.' A reporter for Israel radio who is also a professor of physics became so enthusiastic during the discussion that he began explaining the unified field to his fellow journalists.

On the next Sunday, four of Israel's national newspapers ran articles with photographs of the 'yogic flying' demonstration. *Hotam* on 22 August quoted one guest: 'If this will bring world peace, I am ready to work with all my might that this knowledge be introduced in all schools.' The Voice of Israel and another radio station aired interviews with Mr Tick and the 'yogic flying' demonstrators. A national television commentator concluded his broadcast with, 'Now, if I hear of a day with many road accidents, I will know that someone neglected his TM-Sidhi programme.'

As a result of the wide publicity given to the event, Mr Tick and three of the TM-Sidhas were invited to appear on one of Israel's most popular television interview programmes. While Mr Tick described Maharishi's technology, the Sidhas 'flew' on foam mats for the national television cameras.

Ten days later, a press conference was held in East Jerusalem at the Palace Hotel, the same building where TM-Sidhas had stayed during the Israel Peace

WORLD PEACE • GLOBAL INAUGURATION

INAUGURATING MAHARISHI'S PROGRAMME TO CREATE WORLD PEACE—AFRICA AND THE MIDDLE EAST

Project.* Sixty guests came, including, in the words of one demonstrator, 'many dignitaries in big cars from Bethlehem, Amala, and the West Bank.' They were joined by 16 reporters from the Associated Press, United Press International, the BBC, VIZ News, and several Arabic and Hebrew publications.

Mr Tick described the conference: 'The audience was fascinated. They felt, maybe this can bring peace, so let's do it. That was the tone.' The Arab TM-Sidha among the demonstrators was interviewed for Arab radio and press. One article in *Ashaab* on 5 September was headlined, 'The most modern way to solve the crisis in the Middle East'. 'Now', a TM-Sidha said afterwards, 'we want to demonstrate in the Arab universities in Bethlehem and elsewhere.'

The photograph on the Mount of Olives was taken the day following the press conference in East Jerusalem. Later that afternoon, 150 people assembled for a third demonstration, this one held at the TM-Sidha kibbutz in north Israel as part of its fifth anniversary celebration.

Lebanon

In neighbouring Lebanon, a press release was circulated to all the national press, and the details of Maharishi's programme were reported by local **Beirut** television. At a special news conference for the major Lebanese magazines, one of the TM-Sidhas told journalists, 'What the bombs and kidnappings have produced in Lebanon is terror and fear in the whole population. But our experience is that the Maharishi Technology of the Unified Field has proved to be very efficient in neutralizing all kinds of negative tendencies in society. Whenever there were gatherings of experts in the technology big enough to have an effect on the whole world, these were the only periods in Lebanon's recent history when we had some relief in our situation. So what we need now is to implement this technology immediately. This global demonstration has given a fresh wave of hope for the world and especially for Lebanon.'

*Please refer to page 23.

L'Orient de Jour, the major Lebanese French-language newspaper, printed a full description of Maharishi's programme, calling 'yogic flying' 'a new formula for peace'. 'The positivity engendered by group flying will transform the international conflict into world peace,' the paper reported. 'In the quest for peace, here is an original formula ... and if it succeeds?'

Turkey

In other Middle Eastern countries that did not have demonstrations on 15 August, the press nonetheless reported on Maharishi's programme. Representatives of the Islamic Republic Press Agency, Iran's official news-gathering service, had attended the First International 'Yogic Flying' Competition in New Delhi and two later press conferences and had filed a report to Tehran. An article in Turkey's *Hayat* magazine asked, 'Is it possible for men to fly...?' The magazine responded, 'For years, the possibility of levitation has been a subject of public discussion world-wide, but a few days ago there was a demonstration of this interesting phenomenon in Washington at the First North American "Yogic Flying" Competition.... Scientists and people who perform "yogic flying" say that anybody can use this technique very easily, and by means of it world peace will be established permanently and scientifically.' On 9 October, Turkey held its first demonstration of Maharishi's programme. Two hundred people attended the event in **Ankara**, including several journalists.

Cyprus

In Cyprus, 60 members of the public came to a 'yogic flying' demonstration at the Hilton Hotel in **Nicosia**, and three national papers reported on this mechanics to create world peace. An article in *Agon* announced, 'Where politics fail ... Yogic knowledge starts.' The text began, 'Collective efforts of 7,000 people can create a coherent influence strong enough to radiate globally, purifying world consciousness and converting hostilities and warfare into peace on the international level.'

Thirty-five people came to a demonstration in **Limassol**, Cyprus' principal business centre, and 25 to one in **Paphos**. Two reporters from the Kimon Press News Agency were among the 40 people who watched 'yogic flying' in **Larnaca**. A long article in the *Cyprus Mail* presented a detailed account of Maharishi's programme, and an article in *Alitheia* on 10 October commented, 'We hope for the good of Cyprus that Maharishi's proposal is implemented....'

Following a large mailing of special invitation cards to leaders of society in Cyprus, a second demonstration of 'yogic flying' held at the Hilton Hotel in Nicosia was attended by 250 people, including many dignitaries. Members of the press from eight newspapers were present, and the response was highly enthusiastic.

AFRICA

Maharishi Ayurveda was also the topic of two articles written by the New Delhi correspondent of Global Foto and wired to many daily newspapers throughout the Middle East and North, Central, and East Africa. A third article, which appeared in several newspapers, including the Nairobi *Sunday Standard*, described in detail Maharishi's Programme to Create World Peace. The article noted, 'In Africa, the movement is strongest in Kenya where its continental headquarters are located.'

Jeune Afrique, in a report on 7 September, informed readers throughout French-speaking Africa, 'By using meditation we enliven a unified field inside the individual and the world, and the environment becomes coherent. In this way, peace can gain ground.'

Egypt

In **Cairo**, Egypt, a videotaped report of the demonstrations in Washington and New Delhi was played to several journalists and interested guests.

Ghana

In the first week of September, photographs of 'yogic flying' and articles on Maharishi's Programme to Create World Peace appeared in the *Ghanaian Times* and the *Mirror*, two leading newspapers in **Accra**, Ghana.

The headline in the *Mirror* read, 'Ghana to host "flying Olympics"'. The article quoted a Ghanaian Governor of the Age of Enlightenment: 'Now is the time for the responsible individuals in the world to take responsibility for creating and maintaining world peace.' The Governor noted that while the world needs 7,000 'yogic flyers' to achieve peace, Ghana needs only 360 'to bring prosperity to the country'.

The newspaper reports invited members of the public to 'The First Ghana "Yogic Flying" Demonstration'. Several hundred people responded, filling the Arden Hall of Accra's Ambassador Hotel on 14 September. On a stage decorated with flowers, in front of a long banner that read, 'Inauguration—Maharishi's Peace Plan in Ghana', leaders of Maharishi's movement in Ghana and elders of Accra society introduced the programme. A physicist related quantum physics to the Maharishi Technology of the Unified Field, and a medical doctor explained Maharishi's World Plan for Perfect Health. Then four Ghanaian TM-Sidhas demonstrated 'yogic flying'. The inauguration concluded with a formal candle-lighting and cake-cutting ceremony, symbolizing 'the fruits of world peace from Maharishi's programme, generation after generation'.

South Africa

In **Johannesburg**, South Africa, 30 journalists representing 16 stations and publications came to the conference centre of the Sandton Sun, a leading hotel in the area, for an introduction to Maharishi's programme. Six TM-Sidhas demonstrated 'yogic flying'. One guest said, 'The silence in the room was profound ... it was a deep and wonderful experience.'

Reports were published in the *Sunday Times*, the *Citizen*, and the *Star*, which has the largest circulation of all newspapers in the country, and were broadcast on Radio 702, reaching the largest radio audience. The article in the *Sunday Times* began, 'Just 130 volunteers—willing to levitate through Transcendental Medi-

WORLD PEACE • GLOBAL INAUGURATION

INAUGURATING MAHARISHI'S PROGRAMME TO CREATE WORLD PEACE—AFRICA AND THE MIDDLE EAST

tation—could bring peace to crime-ridden Soweto, says TM instructor George Khoza.... "Through TM, [Khoza says] you can achieve inner peace and influence those around you to feel the same...."'

The *Citizen* noted, 'They believe a group of 600 people collectively practising the programme of "yogic flying" two times a day will be required for lasting peace' in South Africa.

The response to the presentation led representatives of Maharishi's movement in South Africa to conclude that there is 'a new readiness in collective consciousness here to expand beyond present boundaries in thinking and accept both the principle of "yogic flying" and the concept of coherence being generated in the collective consciousness of society.... We feel that a great step forward has been taken.' □

At the demonstration of 'yogic flying' in Nicosia, Cyprus.

MAHARISHI'S PROGRAMME TO CREATE

INAUGURATING MAHARISHI'S PROGRAMME TO CREATE WORLD PEACE—AFRICA AND THE MIDDLE EAST

Mr Gad Tick, national leader of Maharishi's movement in Israel, introduces the 'yogic flying' demonstration in Tel Aviv.

At the inauguration in Accra, Ghana.

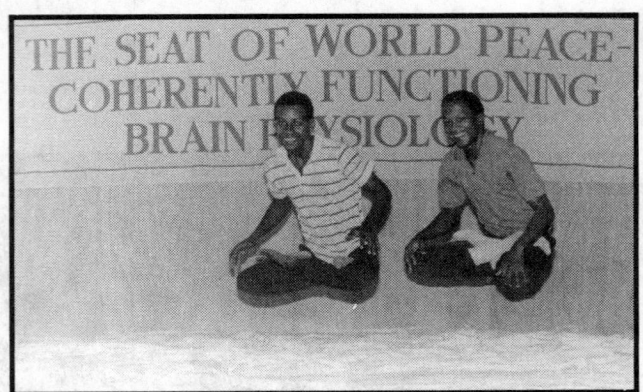

The bliss of 'yogic flying' for world peace.

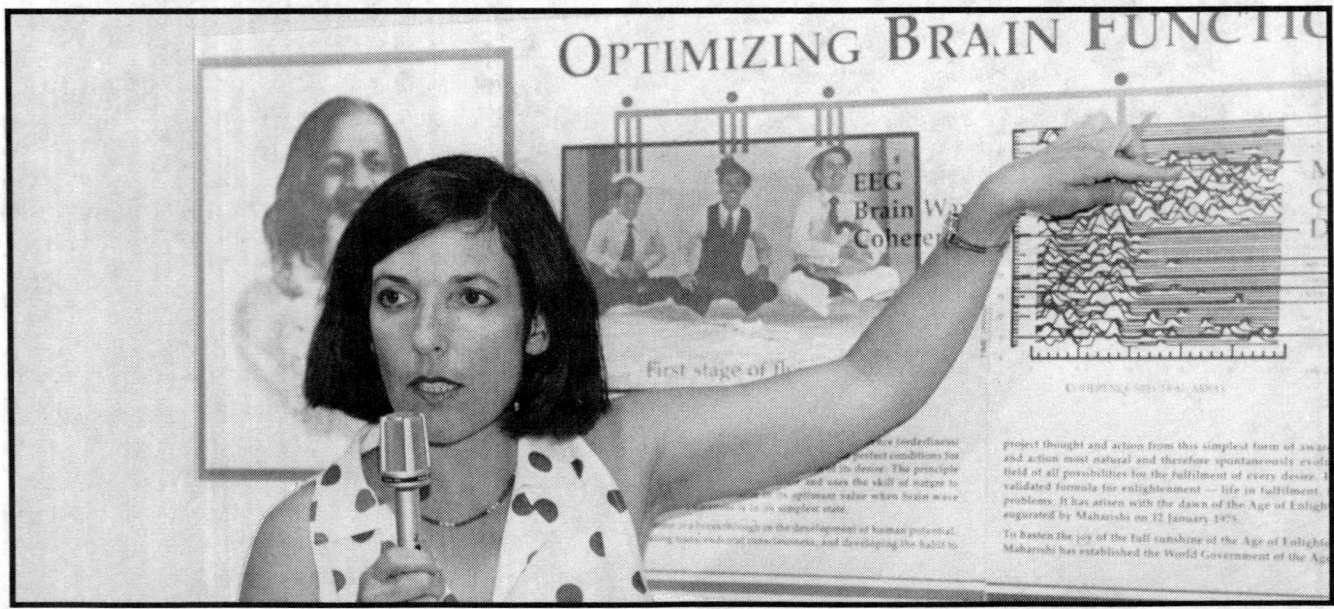

Neurologist Dr Miriam Kutai explains at Tel Aviv demonstration how 'yogic flying' creates coherence in individual brain physiology.

WORLD PEACE • GLOBAL INAUGURATION

PRESS REPORTS FROM AFRICA AND THE MIDDLE EAST

Cyprus • *Philelefcheros*
Nicosia 19 August 1986 (Greek)

Η μέθοδος Μαχαρίσι για παγκόσμια ειρήνη

Την περ. Παρασκευή το πρόγραμμα του Μαχαρίσι, Μάχες Γιόγκι, για παγκόσμια ειρήνη, εγκαινιάσθηκε ταυτόχρονα σε 108 χώρες του κόσμου συμπεριλαμβανομένης και της Κύπρου.

Μέρος των εγκαινίων ήταν και η επίδειξη της μηχανικής για δημιουργία της παγκόσμιας ειρήνης. Αυτή η Τεχνολογία για δημιουργία συνάφειας στην παγκόσμια συνείδηση είναι η τεχνική ΥΔ-ΣΙΝΤΙ «Γιογκικό πέταγμα» μια άποψη της τεχνολογίας Μαχαρίσι του Ενοποιημένου Πεδίου.

Αναφέρουν σχετικά οι οργανωτές:

«Η Ιστορία είναι μάρτυρας της ανικανότητας των κυβερνήσεων για δημιουργία παγκόσμιας ειρήνης και σήμερα οι κυβερνήσεις είναι ανίκανες να προσφέρουν ασφάλεια στον κόσμο σ' οποιοδήποτε μέρος της γης. Ακόμα και οι υπερδυνάμεις είναι σε συνεχή φόβο και η αναμέτρηση μεταξύ τους θέτει σε κίνδυνο την ζωή κάθε ατόμου. Τώρα είναι η ώρα υπεύθυνων ατόμων στον κόσμο που να αναλάβουν την ευθύνη δημιουργίας παγκόσμιας ειρήνης και να τη διατηρήσουν.

Επιστημονικές έρευνες επανειλημμένα υπέδειξαν ότι 7000 ειδικοί ασκούντες την τεχνική ΥΔ-ΣΙΝΤΙ «Γιογκική πτήσης» μαζί σε ένα τόπο στη γη διενεργούν αρκετά δυνατή επίδραση συνάφειας, ώστε να εκπέμπουν σ' όλη τη γη και να εξαγνοποιούν την παγκόσμια συνείδηση.

Αυτή η παγκόσμια εκπομπή συνάφειας είναι η έμπνευση και η επιστημονική βάση του προγράμματος Μαχαρίσι για δημιουργία παγκόσμιας ειρήνης».

■ Στη φωτογραφία επίδειξη της τεχνικής της γιογκικής πτήσης. Το σώμα σηκώνεται και αρχίζει να αιωρείται. «Ο συντονισμός μεταξύ συνείδησης και ύλης στο σώμα που παρατηρείται στο πρώτο στάδιο της γιογκικής πτήσης πηγάζει από το επίπεδο του ενοποιημένου πεδίου όλων των νόμων της φύσης», λέγουν οι οπαδοί της θεωρίας αυτής».

PRESS REPORTS FROM AFRICA AND THE MIDDLE EAST

Cyprus • *Simerini*
Nicosia 24 August 1986 (Greek)

Εκεί που αποτυγχάνει η πολιτική, αρχίζει η... γιογκική φιλοσοφία!

Η ΣΥΛΛΟΓΙΚΗ προσπάθεια επτά χιλιάδων ατόμων μπορεί να παράγει αρκετή δυνατή επίδραση συνάφειας ούτως ώστε ν' ακτινοβολήσουν παγκόσμια και να εξαγνίσουν τη συνείδηση του κόσμου μετατρέποντας τις διαμάχες σε Ειρήνη σε διεθνές επίπεδο.

Αυτά επαγγέλλεται για την Παγκόσμια Ειρήνη η Τεχνολογία Μαχαρίσι του Ενοποιημένου Πεδίου που έχει σαν άμεσο στόχο τη βελτίωση της ποιότητας της ζωής σε όλη την κοινωνία. Σύμφωνα με το Μαχαρίσι «Ακόμη και οι υπερδυνάμεις συνέχεια φοβούνται και η αντιπαράταξη μεταξύ τους θέτει σε κίνδυνο τη ζωή του κάθε ατόμου. Η συνάφεια που δημιουργείται στην Παγκόσμια Συνείδηση από την ομαδική εξάσκηση της Τεχνολογίας του Ενοποιημένου Πεδίου θα ενισχύσει την ειρήνη στη γη».

ΤΕΧΝΙΚΗ ΤΗΣ ΓΙΟΓΚΙΚΗΣ ΠΤΗΣΗΣ

Μια άποψη της Τεχνολογίας αυτής, την τεχνική του Υπερβατικού Διαλογισμού και της Γιογκικής Πτήσης επέδειξε και στην Κύπρο μια ομάδα ειδικών στις 15 Αυγούστου στο ξενοδοχείο «ΧΙΛΤΟΝ» στα πλαίσια των Παγκοσμίων Εγκαινίων του Προγράμματος Μαχαρίσι για τη Δημιουργία Παγκόσμιας Ειρήνης.

Ο Μαχαρίσι είπε «Αυτό το υπερακτινοβόλημα παγκόσμια είναι η επιστημονική βάση για τα εγκαίνια σε όλες τις έξι Ηπείρους της πρωτοβουλίας για παγκόσμια ειρήνη».

ΑΛΛΑ, πως η Γιογκική Πτήση δημιουργεί συνάφεια στην Παγκόσμια Συνείδηση; Επιστημονικές έρευνες κατέδειξαν ότι:

Κατά τη διάρκεια της τεχνικής της γιογκικής πτήσης τη στιγμή του μέγιστου συγχρονισμού στα κύματα της δράσης του μυαλού, όπως μετρούνται από το EEG το σώμα σηκώνεται και αρχίζει να πηδά. Ο συντονισμός μεταξύ συνείδησης και ύλης στο σώμα που παρατηρείται στο πρώτο στάδιο της γιογκικής πτήσης πηγάζει από το επίπεδο του ενοποιημένου πεδίου όλων των νόμων της φύσης. Επειδή το ενοποιημένο πεδίο έχει το χαρακτήρα της άπειρης συσχέτισης, μια ώθηση συνάφειας προερχόμενη από αυτό το επίπεδο, ομαλοποιεί αμέσως δυσαρμονικές τάσεις σ' όλη τη φύση. Έτσι εξαπλώνεται η συνάφεια, εξουδετερώνοντας αρνητικές τάσεις σ' όλη τη δημιουργία.

Το πρόγραμμα Μαχαρίσι υποδεικνύει τρία βήματα για παγκόσμια ειρήνη.

● **Η ΘΕΤΙΚΟΤΗΤΑ** που θα παραχθεί από τις προσπάθειες της ομάδας των 7000 θα μετατρέψει τις διαμάχες σε ειρήνη σε διεθνές επίπεδο. Αυτό θα δημιουργήσει παγκόσμια ειρήνη.

● **ΤΑΥΤΟΧΡΟΝΑ** ομάδες του 1% του πληθυσμού ασκώντας την Τεχνολογία Μαχαρίσι του Ενοποιημένου Πεδίου συλλογικά σε κάθε χώρα θα επιφέρουν ειρήνη στο έθνος με το να διμιουργήσουν συνάφεια στη συνείδηση του έθνους. Αυτό θα δημιουργήσει Εθνική Ειρήνη σε κάθε χώρα και θα ΕΝΔΥΝΑΜΩΣΕΙ ΤΗΝ ΠΑΓΚΟΣΜΙΑ ΕΙΡΗΝΗ.

● **ΜΙΑ ΟΜΑΔΑ** που θα αριθμεί το 1% του πληθυσμού των πόλεων όλων των χωρών ασκούντες την Τ.Μ.Ε.Π. σε ένα τόπο συλλογικά για 15—20′ ημερησίως και ανεβαίνοντας σε ψηλότερα επίπεδα συνειδήσεως θα διατηρήσουν ένα ψηλό επίπεδο συνάφειας στην πόλη για πρόοδο χωρίς περιορισμούς στην εκπλήρωση κάθε οικογένειας και ομαλή διαχείριση των διαφόρων υποθέσεων της πόλης γενικά. Αυτό θα δημιουργήσει ειρήνη σε κάθε πόλη, σε κάθε χώρα και θα διαιωνίσει την ΠΑΓΚΟΣΜΙΑ ΕΙΡΗΝΗ.

WORLD PEACE • GLOBAL INAUGURATION

Ο **Blaine Walson** από το Τορόντο του Καναδά επιδεικνύει το μηχανισμό δημιουργίας Παγκόσμιας Ειρήνης, εξάλειψης της τρομοκρατίας και των πολέμων με την τεχνική της ιογκικής πτήσης, στα εγκαίνια του προγράμματος στο Νέο Δελχί στις 21 Ιουλίου

PRESS REPORTS FROM AFRICA AND THE MIDDLE EAST

Cyprus • *Cyprus Mail*
Nicosia 2 September 1986 (English)

Maharishi's world peace programme

"NOW it is up to individuals to take the initiative for world peace. World peace is the immediate and personal requirement of every significant man in the world today" - Maharishi.

The mechanics to create world peace through the TM-Sidhi "Yogic Flying" technique will be demonstrated and Maharishi's programme to create world peace by enlivening coherence in individual brain physiology will be explained at Paphos tomorrow at the Cypria Maris Hotel; Limassol: Friday September 5 at the Apollonia Beach Hotel- Larnaca: Tuesday September 9 at the Golden Bay Hotel; Nicosia: Wednesday September 10 at the Hilton Hotel, all at 7.30pm.

The inauguration of Maharishi's Programme to Create World Peace has been conducted on every continent, along with the historic first World's International "Yogic Flying" competitions, in New Delhi, India on July 21, 1986. Recently, on August 15, the mechanics to create coherence in World Consciousness was demonstrated in 108 countries and over 1,000 cities. This week, demonstrations of the mechanics to create world peace through the TM-Sidhi "Yogic Flying" Technique will be conducted in Cyprus.

"This practice creates a more orderly style of functioning in the brain physiology, as indicated by the EEC coherence. At the point of maximum EEG coherence, when mind-body coordination is greatest, the body lifts up due to the intention of the mind. This phenomenon is understood with help from modern physics," says a press release.

Awareness

"Physics describes the basis of all matter and energy in the universe as a unified field of natural law. When the unified field of natural law is enlivened in the simplest form of awareness then all the evolutionary qualities of the unified field such as Infinite Creativity Perfect Orderliness, Harmonizing and Infinite Correlation are also enlivened for the whole society. The individual radiates harmony, coherence and peace to the rest of the world.

"Over 31 sociological studies have been conducted on the coherence creating effect of the Maharishi Technology of the Unified Field. These studies indicate a minimum threshold of natural law such as crime, sickness and accidents in a given population. The formula requires that a group equal to the square root of 1 per cent of the population be practicing the TM-Sidhi "Yogic Flying" Technique in one place.

"Research on the city, national and world levels verifies that negative tendencies due to violations of natural law decrease in the life of society at large. These findings have led

WORLD PEACE • GLOBAL INAUGURATION

■ Maharishi Mahesh Yogi

to the three step plan of Maharishi to create permanent world peace.

"Step I - establishment of a group of 7000 in at least one place on earth to radiate coherent harmonious tendencies throughout society. This will create world peace.

"Step 2 - establishing groups of the square root of 1 per cent of the nations population practicing Maharishi Technology of the Unified Field to strengthen world peace.

"Step 3 -- creating groups equal to the square root of 1 per cent of the population in each city to insure that the coherence and progress of the society is maximized and world peace is permanent.

"The estabilishment of the "Maharishi World Peace Fund" has come about to fulfill the need of the time for a permanent group of 7000. It is expected that with 100 million dollar a group of 10,0000 Vedic students can be established permanenty in one place so that they may be trained to apply Maharishi's Programme ot Create World Peace."

PRESS REPORTS FROM AFRICA AND THE MIDDLE EAST

Cyprus • *Cyprus Mail*

Nicosia 10 September 1986 (English)

Meditating on the prospects for world peace

THE Maharishi Mahesh Yogi's Programme to create World Peace has been put together to try to eliminate the basis of terrorism and war wihtout loss of life.

The Maharishi's programme was inaugurated for the whole world on July 21 this year in New Delhi, India. The inauguration included a demonstration of 'Yogic Flying', the mechanics to create coherence (a much-used word here) in world consciousness, the basis of world peace. But in answer to my question to Lothar Pirc and Ted Pizanis, who themselves gave a demonstration of this 'flying' technique at the Apollonia Hotel in Limassol on Friday evening, as to whether anyone had got past the first stage of 'Yogic Flying' to the second stage of actual levitation and **staying** there, or to the third and final stage of 'flying', the answer was no....

Theoretically, a yogic flyer has very orderly brain waves and fluid co-ordination between mind and body. Consciousness and matter become completely integrated and all this 'coherence' can, it seems, spread peace around the world if enough meditators gather together at the same place and time. This was told to newsmen at the New Delhi demonstration by Dr. John S. Hagelin, a noted U.S. scientist.

The phenomenon produced by the TM-Sidhi procedure of 'flying' gives the experience of bliss and generates coherence between consciousness and matter in the body. EEG studies have shown that during this phenomenon, when the body lifts up in the air, matter and consciousness are completely integrated. This integration takes place at the level of the unified field of natural law, which has the character of infinite correlation. The impulse of coherence from this level instantly reconstructs the discordant tendcencies in nature to become coherent.

Coherence in world consciousness can be produced only by creating coherence in individual brain physiology. This is achieved through the Maharishi Technology of the Unified Field (Transcendental Meditation, its advanced techniques and the TM-Sidhi programme.

Scientific research has apparantely shown that 7,000 individuals (the square root of one per cent of the world's population) practicing the Maharishi Technology of the Unified Field together in one place create a powerful influence of coherence in the whole world consciousness, producing an upsurge of positive trends and tendencies in life everywhere.

Lothar Pirc is a lecturer in this technology, and Ted Pizanis BSCI, MBA is the Cyprus Representative of International Programmes, and after completing their course of demonstrations at the Golden Bay Hotel in Larnaca yesterday and at the Hilton Hotel, Nicosia tonight, they hope to have aroused enough interest to start courses in TM here in Cyprus.

Helen Stylianou

■ Yogic flying by Lothar Pirc at the Apollonia

WORLD PEACE • GLOBAL INAUGURATION

PRESS REPORTS FROM AFRICA AND THE MIDDLE EAST

Cyprus • *The Cyprus Weekly*
Nicosia   12-18 September 1986   (English)

Yogis put the bounce into meditation

Ted Pizanis bounces into action at the Hilton on Wednesday

Pictures by Masis der Parthogh

HOUSEWIVES, a judge, lawyers, artists, businessmen, actors and children all packed into the Hilton on Wednesday evening and craned their necks for the demonstration of yogic flying or levitation.

The grouping may not have been as large as that which gathered in Washington a month ago to witness the launching of Maharishi Yogi's programme for world peace through yogic flying, but they were equally intrigued.

And though the levitators, three young men in crisp suits, emphasised that the importance of the demonstration did not lie in its spectator value but in the effect it has on the individual and on society some of those who turned up clearly did so for the spectacle.

The demonstration did not start straight away. There was first a detailed lecture on why and how transcendental meditation helps both the individual and the cause of world peace.

There were slides, and a video tape to drive home what the group considers central to its message - that the beneficial results of TM can be proved scientifically.

The programme of world peace, they explained, and the latest effort to combat world terrorism combines ancient Vedic teaching and modern science.

Yogic flying - which is more like bouncing in its first stage, can contribute to this end, they said.

It necessitates the total coherence of the brain, and brings about what they described as 'a very beautiful uplift". When carried out by a groups it creates a super radiance effect, and spreads peace to society, they explained.

Total silence was the first prerequisite, so that the three, Lothar Pirc, Andreas Moritz and Ted Pizanis could begin meditating.

Yogic flying came, as they explained when the mind managed to control the body completely. The three sat meditating on a row of yellow mats. The signal to begin came from another member of the Cyprus Association for the Advancement of the Science of Creative Intelligence, and seemed to resemble hopping, while still crosslegged.

PRESS REPORTS FROM AFRICA AND THE MIDDLE EAST

Cyprus • *Agon*

Nicosia   13 September 1986   (Greek)

Η γιογκική φιλοσοφία κάμνει ό,τι δεν μπορεί να κάμει η πολιτική

● Της Στάλως Χαραλάμπους

Ο,τι δεν επιτυγχάνει η πολιτική το επιτυγχάνει η... γιογκική φιλοσοφία. Η συλλογική προσπάθεια επτά χιλιάδων ατόμων ανά τον κόσμο, μπορεί να παράγει αρκετή δυνατή επίδραση συνάφειας, ούτως ώστε να ακτινοβολήσουν παγκόσμια και να εξαγνίσουν την συνείδηση όλου του κόσμου. Εξαγνίζοντας έτσι την συνείδηση του κόσμου μετατρέπονται οι διαμάχες σε ειρήνη, σε διεθνές επίπεδο!

Αυτά διακηρύττει γιά την Ειρήνη στον κόσμο, η Τεχνολογία του Μαχαρίσι. Στόχος της τεχνολογίας αυτής είναι η βελτίωση της ποιότητας της ζωής του ανθρώπου, και η επικράτηση της ειρήνης σε όλη την κοινωνία.

Την τεχνολογία του Μαχαρίσι επέδειξαν και στη Λάρνακα τρεις ειδικοί οι Ted Pitanis, Lothar Piro, Andreas Moritz σε πλήθος Κυπρίων και ξένων στο ξενοδοχείο «ΓΚΟΛΤΕΝ ΜΠΕΫ» στη Λάρνακα.

Μιλώντας προς τους δημοσιογράφους ο κ. Ted Piranis είπεν ότι μια άποψη της τεχνολογίας αυτής που είναι η τεχνική του Υπερβατικού Διαλογισμού και της «Γιογκικής πτήσης», δημιουργούν μια συνάφεια, μια βάση για την Παγκόσμια ειρήνη.

Επιστημονικές έρευνες έδειξαν ότι: Κατά τη διάρκεια της γιογκικής πτήσης την στιγμή του μέγιστου συγχρονισμού στα κύματα της δράσης του μυαλού, όπως μετρούνται από το EEC, το σώμα σηκώνεται και αρχίζει να πηδά. Ο συντονισμός μεταξύ της συνείδησης και ύλης στο σώμα που παρατηρείται στο πρώτο στάδιο της «γιογκικής πτήσης», πηγάζει

Ασκηση «Γιογκικής πτήσης...» Με αυτή - σύμφωνα με την φιλοσοφία του Μαχαρίσι - επιτυγχάνεται η Ειρήνη στην ματοβαμμένη υφήλιο...

από το επίπεδο του ενοποιημένου πεδίου όλων των νόμων της φύσης. Επειδή τώρα το ενοποιημένο πεδίο έχει το χαρακτήρα της άπειρης συσχέτισης, μια ώθηση συνάφειας προερχόμενη από αυτό το επίπεδο ομαλοποιεί αμέσως δυσαρμονικές τάσεις σ' όλη την δημιουργία.

Το πρόγραμμα του Μαχαρίσι όπως δήλωσε ο κ. Ted Pitanis αναφέρεται σε τρία βήματα: Την

α) Θετικότητα: Αυτή θα παραχθεί από τις προσπάθειες μιας ομάδας 7000 ατόμων και θα μετατρέψει τις διαμάχες σε ειρήνη στο διεθνές επίπεδο, δημιουργώντας έτσι ΠΑΓΚΟΣΜΙΑ ΕΙΡΗΝΗ.

Το β) ταυτόχρονα, ομάδες του 1% του πληθυσμού, ασκώντας την Τεχνολογία του Μαχαρίσι του Ενοποιημένου Πεδίου συλλογικά σε κάθε χώρα ξεχωριστά, θα επιφέρουν ειρήνη στο έθνος με το να δημιουργήσουν παγκόσμια ειρήνη. Τούτο θάχει σαν αποτέλεσμα να δημιουργηθεί η εθνική ειρήνη και κατά συνέπεια θα ενδυναμωθεί και η Παγκόσμια ειρήνη. Και το γ) ΜΙΑ ΟΜΑΔΑ ασκώντας σ' ένα τόπο συλλογικά για 20' περίπου την «Γιογκική πτήση» και ανεβαίνοντας σε ψηλότερα επίπεδα συνειδήσεως θα διατηρήσουν ένα ψηλό επίπεδο συνάφειας στην πόλη για την πρόοδο γενικά. Και αυτό θα διαιωνίσει πάλι την Παγκόσμια Ειρήνη.

Το πρόγραμμα του Μαχαρίσι όπως δήλωσε στο «ΚΙΜΩΝ ΠΡΕΣΣ» ο κ. Ted Piranis παρουσιάστηκε σε 108 χώρες και σε πάνω από 1000 πόλεις έγιναν επιδείξεις του φαινομένου αυτού. Και γιαυτό θέλουμε να δώσουμε στον κόσμο να καταλάβει ότι υπάρχει ένα μέσο, και ένας τρόπος να εξουδετερωθούν όλες οι αρνητικές τάσεις που υπάρχουν στον κόσμο όπως π.χ. η τρομοκρατία που παρουσιάζει στις μέρες μας έξαρση και συνεχώς αυξάνεται σε όλα τα επίπεδα, σε όλες τις χώρες του κόσμου. Και η φιλοσοφία του Μαχαρίσι αυτές τις αντιδράσεις θέλει να εξαλείψει για να δημιουργήσει την Παγκόσμια Ειρήνη».

WORLD PEACE • GLOBAL INAUGURATION

PRESS REPORTS FROM AFRICA AND THE MIDDLE EAST

Cyprus • *Periodiko*
Nicosia   4 October 1986   (Greek)

ΕΝΑΣ Ινδός Μαχαρίσι ισχυρίζεται πως με τη συγκεντρωτική διαστημική προσπάθεια 7,000 μυημένων οπαδών μπορεί να ακτινοβολήσει στον κόσμο την ειρήνη και την ευημερία. Γι' αυτή την προσπάθεια θα απαιτηθεί ένα ποσό 100 εκατομμυρίων δολαρίων. Στελέχη της κίνησης του Μαχαρίσι έδωσαν πρόσφατα στην Κύπρο δημοσιογραφική διάσκεψη κι έκαμαν επίδειξη των υπερβατικών ικανοτήτων τους. Για τη φιλοσοφία του Μαχαρίσι μιλούν στο «ΠΕΡΙΟΔΙΚΟ» και τέσσερις από τους 150 Κύπριους οπαδούς του.

Της ΜΑΡΙΝΑΣ ΣΤΕΦΑΝΙΔΟΥ

ΜΑΧΑΡΙΣΙ ΜΑΧΕΣ ΓΙΟΓΚΙ: «Με 7,000 κεφάλια και 100 εκ. δολάρια θα γαληνέψει ο κόσμος»

ΚΑΤΩ από την απειλή ενός πυρηνικού αφανισμού, στον αιώνα των διαταραχών και της τρομοκρατίας, ο Ινδός επιστήμονας και καλόγερος Μαχαρίσι Μαχές Γιόγκι ενώνει την αρχαία επιστήμη και φιλοσοφία των Βεδών με τη μεγαλύτερη επιστημονική ανακάλυψη της σύγχρονης φυσικής σε μια συλλογική προσπάθεια των λαών για παγκόσμια ειρήνη.

Όπως ο ίδιος ισχυρίζεται, με την άσκηση της τεχνολογίας του ενοποιημένου πεδίου, η συλλογική προσπάθεια 7 χιλιάδων ατόμων μπορεί να παράξει αρκετά δυνατή επίδραση, ώστε ν' ακτινοβολήσει παγκόσμια και να εξαγνίσει τη συνείδηση του κόσμου, μετατρέποντας τις διαμάχες σε ειρήνη, στο διεθνές επίπεδο.

Μπορούμε, λοιπόν να ελπίζουμε στην πραγματοποίηση της ουτοπίας; Θα μπορέσει ποτέ να υπάρξει ο ιδανικός κόσμος της αρμονίας και της ειρήνης. Γι' αυτό το θέμα, μίλησαν πρόσφατα στην Κύπρο 2 Γερμανοί και ένας Αμερικανός, αντιπρόσωποι του Μαχαρίσι και δάσκαλοι των τεχνικών του ενοποιημένου πεδίου. Στη διάλεξη —την οποία ακολούθησε επίδειξη του πρώτου σταδίου της τεχνικής του Υ.Δ σίντι

207

προγράμματος— αναλύθηκαν οι τεχνικές της τεχνολογίας Μαχαρίσι του ενοποιημένου πεδίου, οι εκτενείς ωφέλειες τους προς το άτομο που τις εξασκεί και προς την κοινωνία μέσω της συλλογικής συνείδησης και η δημιουργία ειρήνης στην παγκόσμια σφαίρα.

Η τεχνολογία Μαχαρίσι του ενοποιημένου πεδίου βασίζεται στην ανακάλυψη από τη σύγχρονη φυσική, του ενοποιημένου πεδίου όλων των νόμων της φύσης. Στα βαθύτερα του επίπεδα, αυτό το πεδίο όπου οι 4 θεμελιώδεις δυνάμεις: Ο ηλεκρομαγνητισμός, η βαρύτητα, οι αδύνατες και δυνατές δυνάμεις ενώνονται, αποκτά τις ιδιότητες της απόλυτης αυτοεπίδρασης, αυτάρκειας και του απέραντου δυναμισμού.

Αυτές οι μοναδικές ιδιότητες είναι οι ίδιες που χαρακτηρίζουν το πεδίο της απόλυτης και αγνής συνείδησης όπως περιγράφεται από το Μαχαρίσι. Για να καταφέρει κανείς το μοναδικό αυτό βίωμα της απόλυτης συνείδησης πρέπει ν' αναπτύξει ένα εξευγενισμένο επίπεδο νευροφυσιολογικής λειτουργίας. Κι αυτό το επιτυγχάνει κανείς με τις διαδικασίες της τεχνολογίας του ενοποιημένου πεδίου που εισήγαγε ο Μαχαρίσι. Τον Υπερβατικό διαλογισμό και το Υ.Δ. σίντι πρόγραμμα.

Πώς γίνεται

Η τεχνική του υπερβατικού διαλογισμού είναι μια απλή πνευματική διαδικασία. Δεν κινείται μέσα σε πλαίσια ειδικού τρόπου ζωής και δεν σχετίζεται με θρησκείες, φιλοσοφία, πίστη ή διάθεση. Είναι ένα εικοσάλεπτο πρόγραμμα, που επαναλαμβάνεται δυο φορές την ημέρα και που δεν απαιτεί να έχεις τα πόδια σου σταυρωμένα στη στάση του λωτού. Χρησιμοποιεί την έμφυτη ικανότητα του νευρικού συστήματος να εξευγενίζει τη λειτουργία του και ν' αναπτύσσει το ολικό των δυνατοτήτων του. Κατά τη διάρκεια της πρακτικής, μ' ένα αυθόρμητο και φυσικό τρόπο, το άτομο φτάνει στο επίπεδο της τέταρτης συνείδησης, όπου παραμένει χωρίς σκέψεις ή αισθήματα, αλλά μόνο με την εμπειρία της ζωντανής απόλυτης γνώσης. Μέσα από τη φυσική αυτή περιπλάνηση των επιπέδων της σκέψης και της συνείδησης, ο νους ακολουθεί τη φυσιολογική του πορεία προς τη μεγαλύτερη απόλαυση και ευτυχία.

Το 1976, δεκαπέντε περίπου χρόνια μετά την εισαγωγή του Υπερβατικού Διαλογισμού, ο Μαχαρίσι άρχισε να διδάσκει τις προηγμένες τεχνικές του Υ.Δ. σίντι προγράμματος. Η χρησιμοποίηση αυτού του προγράμματος αναπτύσσει μια εξαιρετική ψυχοφυσιολογική λειτουργία κι ένα συντονισμό μυαλού και σώματος. Σταθεροποιεί επίσης την εμπειρία της απόλυτης συνείδησης, οδηγώντας έτσι σε υψηλότερα επίπεδα συνείδησης.

Τα τρία στάδια της τεχνικής του Υ.Δ. σίντι προγράμματος είναι τα «πηδήματα», η «αιώρηση του σώματος στον αέρα» και η «γιογκική πτήση διά μέσου του αέρος». Αν και το φαινόμενο της πτήσης δεν έχει ακόμα επιτευχθεί πλήρως, η τεχνική του Υ.Δ. σίντι προγράμματος έχει αποδειχθεί σαν εξαιρετικά δυναμική όσον αφορά τα φυσιολογικά αποτελέσματα και την προσωπική εμπειρία.

Αποτελέσματα στις φυσιολογικές λειτουργίες του οργανισμού, με την πρακτική του Υπερβατικού Διαλογισμού και του Υ.Δ. σίντι προγράμματος είναι η προώθηση της μακροζωίας και η βελτίωση της βιολογικής ηλικίας σε σχέση με τη χρονολογική ηλικία.

Την τεχνική του Υ.Δ. και του Τ.Δ. σίντι προγράμματος, μπορούν και είναι σε θέση να εξασκήσουν όλοι, οι άνθρωποι, ανεξαρτήτως ηλικίας (ακόμα και παιδιά) και ανεξαρτήτως επαγγέλματος, θρησκείας ή κουλτούρας.

Βελτίωση στην ποιότητα της κοινωνίας διά μέσου της συλλογικής συνείδησης.

Όταν το ενοποιημένο πεδίο του φυσικού νόμου αναζωογονείται στην πιο απλή μορφή επίγνωσης, όλες οι εξελικτικές του ιδιότητες: τέλεια τάξη, αρμονικότητα και ο άπειρος συσχετισμός— αναζωογονούνται για ολόκληρη την κοινωνία, διά μέσου της συλλογικής συνείδησης.

Έτσι, με την εμπειρία της απόλυτης συνείδησης δεν βελτιώνεται μονάχα η συμπεριφορά του ατόμου αλλά και η συλλογική συνείδηση και η συμπεριφορά ολόκληρης της κοινωνίας.

«Τώρα» —λέει ο ίδιος ο Μαχαρίσι— «έχουμε εισάξει ένα πρόγραμμα, για τη δημιουργία μιας δυναμικής επίδρασης συνάφειας στην παγκόσμια συνείδηση, με την οποία, ο επικίνδυνος ανταγωνισμός των υπερδυνάμεων, μπορεί να ουδετεροποιηθεί, και όλα τα έθνη να απελευθερωθούν από το συνεχή φόβο... Ένα πρόγραμμα το οποίο θα εξαλείψει την τρομοκρατία, χωρίς να χαθούν ζωές και θα εκμηδενίσει την πιθανότητα πολέμου...».

«Εκείνο που χρειαζόμαστε» —συνεχίζει ο Μαχαρίσι— «είναι μια ομάδα 7.000 ατόμων που να εξασκούν συλλογικά την τεχνολογία του ενοποιημένου πεδίου, για να αναζωπυρώσουν την εξελικτική επήρεια του φυσικού νόμου στην παγκόσμια συνείδηση. Έτσι θα δημιουργηθεί μια φυσική κατάσταση όπου οι αρνητικές και καταστροφικές τάσεις απλώς δεν θα υπάρχουν».

Κατά το Μαχαρίσι περισσότερες από 31 κοινωνιολογικές μελέτες που έγιναν πάνω στο αποτέλεσμα της δημιουργίας συνάφειας με την τεχνολογία Μαχαρίσι του ενοποιημένου πεδίου, έδειξαν ότι για τη μείωση των παραβιάσεων των φυσικών νόμων, όπως η εγκληματικότητα, οι αρρώστιες και τα δυστυχήματα, χρειάζεται άσκηση της τεχνολογίας από ένα μίνιμουμ αριθμό ατόμων. Ο αριθμός αυτός είναι ίσως με το τετράγωνο της τετραγωνικής ρίζας του πληθυσμού της γης και ισοδυναμεί με 7.000 άτομα.

Μια τέτοια παγκόσμια συγκέντρωση έγινε στην Αμερική μεταξύ της 17ης Δεκεμβρίου του 1983 και της 6ης Ιανουαρίου 1984. 7.000 ειδήμονες στην τεχνολογία Μαχαρίσι του ενοποιημένου πεδίου, που συγκεντρώθηκαν στο Διεθνές Πανεπιστήμιο Μαχαρίσι στην Αϊόβα, έδωσαν στον κόσμο την πρώτη

Στιγμιότυπο από την επίδειξη της τεχνικής του Υ.Δ. Σίντι προγράμματος από τους προσκεκλημένους αντιπροσώπους και δασκάλους της τεχνολογίας Μαχαρίσι του ενοποιημένου πεδίου.

WORLD PEACE • GLOBAL INAUGURATION

γεύση ουτοπίας.

Εκτεταμένη επιστημονική έρευνα, που έγινε κατά την διάρκεια της συγκέντρωσης, ντοκουμέντανε τα λόγια του Μαχαρίσι με τις επιπτώσεις: Αυξημένη αρμονία στις διεθνείς σχέσεις, αυξημένη οικονομική ευημερία, πιο θετικές και εξελίξιμες δηλώσεις και πράξεις των ηγετών κρατών, πρόοδο όσον αφορά ειρηνικές λύσεις συγκρούσεων, μειωμένα δυστυχήματα, ασθένειες και εγκληματικότητα και αυξημένη εθνική δημιουργικότητα σε πολλά έθνη.

Το σχέδιο Μαχαρίσι για τη δημιουργία της μόνιμης παγκόσμιας ειρήνης διαμορφώνεται σε τρία βήματα.

• **Πρώτο βήμα** που θα συμβάλει στη δημιουργία της Παγκόσμιας Ειρήνης, είναι η δημιουργία ομάδας 7.000 τουλάχιστον ατόμων σ' ένα τόπο στη γη για ν' ακτινοβολούν, με την εφαρμογή της τεχνικής, συνάφεια και αρμονία διά μέσου της κοινωνίας.

• **Δεύτερο βήμα** είναι η δημιουργία ομάδων, αριθμητικά ίσων με το τετράγωνο της τετραγωνικής ρίζας του 1% του πληθυσμού των χωρών που ασκούν την τεχνολογία του ενοποιημένου πεδίου για να συμβάλουν στην ενίσχυση της παγκόσμιας ειρήνης.

• **Τρίτο βήμα** είναι η δημιουργία ομάδων αριθμητικά ίσων με το τετράγωνο της τετραγωνικής ρίζας του 1% του πληθυσμού κάθε πόλεως για να εξασφαλίσουν την μέγιστη συνάφεια και πρόοδο της κοινωνίας και τη μόνιμη παγκόσμια ειρήνη.

Τώρα η παγκόσμια ειρήνη είναι απλώς ζήτημα χρημάτων. Αναμένεται ότι με 100 εκατομμύρια δολάρια δαπάνη θα είναι δυνατή η μόνιμη εδραίωση σ' ένα τόπο μιας ομάδας 10.000 ατόμων τα οποία θα εκπαιδευθούν στην εφαρμογή του προγράμματος του Μαχαρίσι για τη δημιουργία της Παγκόσμιας Ειρήνης.

Και στην Κύπρο

Από τα 3 εκατομμύρια άτομα που εξασκούν σήμερα διεθνώς την τεχνολογία ενοποιημένου πεδίου, τα 130 βρίσκονται στην Κύπρο. Ο Κυπριακός Σύνδεσμος για την Ανάπτυξη της Επιστήμης της Διάνοιας, ιδρύθηκε στην Κύπρο το 1984.

Ξεκίνησε με 20 μέλη και σήμερα έχει φτάσει τα 130 μέλη, από τα οποία το μεγαλύτερο είναι 70 ετών και το μικρότερο 9. Μια φορά τη βδομάδα τα μέλη συγκεντρώνονται στο οίκημα του συνδέσμου όπου διαλογίζονται ομαδικά, ακούνε μαγνητοφωνημένες ή παρακολουθούν ζωντανές διαλέξεις. Συχνά επισκέπτονται τον Σύνδεσμο, εκπαι-

Από αριστερά ο κ. Γιώργος Ψυχής και ο κ. Γιώργος Χατζηγεωργίου. Δυο από τα ιδρυτικά στελέχη του Κυπριακού συνδέσμου για την ανάπτυξη της επιστήμης της διάνοιας.

δευμένοι δάσκαλοι στην τεχνολογία Μαχαρίσι του ενοποιημένου πεδίου, οι οποίοι διδάσκουν σε νέα ή παλαιά μέλη τις πνευματικές διαδικασίες του Υπερβατικού Διαλογισμού και του Υ.Δ. σίντι προγράμματος.

Ένα από τα ιδρυτικά μέλη του συνδέσμου είναι ο κ. Γιώργος Χατζηγεωργίου, ο οποίος ασχολείται με τον υπερβατικό διαλογισμό, εδώ και 10 χρόνια, και ο οποίος λέει χαρακτηριστικά «Θα ήταν άδικο να προσπαθήσω να περιγράψω με λόγια την ακριβή εμπειρία και το αίσθημα της ευτυχίας. Αλλά θα το σύστηνα σε όλους...».

Ο κ. Γιώργος Ψυχής, δεύτερο ιδρυτικό στέλεχος του Συνδέσμου, μιλά για την πρώτη του εμπειρία με την τεχνολογία Μαχαρίσι, όταν δυο χρόνια πριν παρακολούθησε μια διάλεξη που δόθηκε από πέντε δασκάλους, αντιπροσώπους του Μαχαρίσι «Δεν κατάλαβα τότε και πολλά πράγματα. Από ένστικτο όμως ένιωσα ότι κάτι υπήρχε...».

Ο Υπερβατικός Διαλογισμός άλλαξε σημαντικά τη ζωή του κ. Ψυχή: «Όταν μετά από πολλές εμπειρίες, λέει, αντιλήφθηκα ότι σκοπός της ζωής ήταν η εξέλιξη, χρειάστηκα τα κατάλληλα μέσα γι' αυτήν την εξέλιξη. Για μένα, ο Υπερβατικός Διαλογισμός και το Υ.Δ. σίντι πρόγραμμα είναι η απόλυτη ευτυχία που τίποτα δε μπορεί να την αντικαταστήσει».

Προσφώνηση της διάλεξης από τον κ. Γιώργο Χατζηγεωργίου. Από αριστερά ο κ. Λόταρ Πιρκ, ο κ. Τεντ Πιζάνης και ο κ. Αντρέας Μόριτζ.

«Σταμάτησα το τσιγάρο, είχα πιο ομαλή εγκυμοσύνη, έχω περισσότερη υπομονή με τα παιδιά μου και είμαι πολύ πιο ενεργητική», λέει η κα Σωτηρούλα Χατζηγεωργίου. «Η ζωή μου άλλαξε. Με το σύζυγο μου νιώθουμε πιο κοντά ο ένας στον άλλο, βρίσκουμε περισσότερη κατανόηση ο ένας από τον άλλον... Υπάρχει μια εκπληκτική, ασυνήθιστη αγάπη μεταξύ μας. Θα έλεγα ότι είναι το κάτι άλλο και θα σύστανα τον Υπερβατικό Διαλογισμό και το Υ.Δ. σίντι πρόγραμμα σε όλα τα ζευγάρια».

Από τα 130 μέλη του συνδέσμου, τα 9 έχουν διδαχθεί πρόσφατα το Υ.Δ. σίντι πρόγραμμα. Μέχρι στιγμής τα 7 είχαν καταφέρει το πρώτο στάδιο, που είναι τα πηδήματα. «Σκοπός μας» —λέει ο κ. Χατζηγεωργίου— «είναι να συγκεντρωθεί μια ομάδα από 500 μέλη που να εκπαιδευθούν στον Υ.Δ. και Υ.Δ. σίντι πρόγραμμα, ώστε να μπορέσει με τη συλλογική τους ταυτόχρονη προσπάθεια να επέλθει ειρήνη στην Κύπρο και Μέση Ανατολή».

Άλλος σκοπός του Συνδέσμου είναι η ίδρυση πανεπιστημίου Μαχαρίσι στην Κύπρο, όπου θα διδάσκονται οι πνευματικές τεχνικές και συν τω χρόνω και διάφορα μαθήματα «Το MIU (Maharishi International University) στην Αϊόβα», λέει ο Ted Pizanis, ένας από τους προσκεκλημένους του συνδέσμου, δασκάλους και εκπροσώπους του Μαχαρίσι στην Κύπρο. Είναι πλήρως αναγνωρισμένο και μπορεί κανείς ν' αποφοιτήσει σε διάφορα θέματα. Προσωπικά έχω μεταπτυχιακό δίπλωμα (MSc) μάστερς ντιγκρί στο Business Administratios».

Επίσης σκοπός του πανεπιστημίου Μαχαρίσι στην Κύπρο θα είναι και η προμήθευση χώρου και κατάλληλης εκπαίδευσης γι' αυτή την ομάδα των 500 ώστε να μπορεί να διαλογίζεται συλλογικά για την ακτινοβόληση ειρήνης και συνάφειας στην Κύπρο και Μέση Ανατολή.

Το νεαρώτερο μέλος του συνδέσμου είναι η 9χρονη Άντρη Χατζηγεωργίου η οποία ασχολείται με τον υπερβατικό διαλογισμό από τα 7 της χρόνια λέγει σχετικά: «Με βοηθά να είμαι προσηλωμένη στα μαθήματα μου και να έχω ιδέες. Επίσης με βοηθά να είμαι πιο ευγενική με τις φίλες μου. Θα ήθελα όλα τα παιδιά στο σχολείο μου να έκαναν Υ.Δ. Τότε θα ήταν όλα πιο ευγενικά και δε θα τσακωνόμαστε κάθε μέρα.

Κι αν όλος ο κόσμος ήταν διαλογιζόμενος θα είμαστε όλοι πιο ευγενικοί, πιο καλοί, πιο αγαπημένοι και πάντα πάντα, πάντα ειρηνικοί».

Δημοσιογράφοι, φωτορεπόρτερς και πλήθος κόσμου παρακολουθούν τη διάλεξη και την επίδειξη της πρώτης τεχνικής του Υ.Δ. Σίντι προγράμματος.

WORLD PEACE • GLOBAL INAUGURATION

PRESS REPORTS FROM AFRICA AND THE MIDDLE EAST

Ghana • *The Mirror*

Accra   6 September 1986   (English)

Ghana To Host 'Flying Olympics'

EBEN C. SAM

THE Arden Hall of the Ambassador Hotel in Accra will be the venue of a rare feature — the global inauguration of world peace through "yogic flying" demonstration on Sunday, September 14, 1986.

This demonstration also called Transcendental Meditation (TM) which will be the first in the country involves deep meditation — at the moment of maximum coherence and with complete harmony in the brain functioning, the body lifts up into the air and begins to hop.

The aim of the demonstration is to use the "yogic flying" technique, an aspect of the Maharishi Technology of the Unified Field to physically create world peace.

Similar demonstrations in the form of athletic events at which medals were won have been held in the United States of America (USA) and India, followed by demonstrations in 108 countries.

Explaining the rationale behind the show the director of the Maharishi International University in Ghana, Nii Padi said, the "flyers", followers of Maharishi Mahesh Yogi founder of the Transcendental Movement have been doing this since 1975 as a very private thing but now feels bound to bring it out because of the turbulent times — super power areas build up, threat of war and worse still, terrorism.

He said from the beginning the aim was to create an ideal individual so they documented scientific researches on how the brain waves synchronize as one practices the "TM and TM-SIDHI" programme; the brain synchrony produced profound health benefits for the body.

Then it moved to creating an ideal society because of what they call "group dynamics effect of their 'super-radiance" — the act of "flyers" flying together in one place.

Now their target is to physically create world peace. He said "now is the time for the responsible individual in the world to take the responsibility for creating and maintaining world peace".

TM, Nii Padi said the world needs 7,000 "flyers" to achieve world peace while Ghana needs only 360 "flyers" to bring prosperity to the country.

The first proof of this was when 7,000 followers met at Fairfield in Iowa, USA for 21 days; world trends became very positive; economics, international relations, scientific discoveries, decrease in negative trends, increased balance in nature like stabilization of world weather patterns were recorded.

TM Nii Padi further said the Transcendental Meditation Movement also intends establishing a 100 million dollar World Peace Fund to maintain 10,000 "flyers" in this regard.

MAHARISHI'S PROGRAMME TO CREATE

• The first stage of "yogic flying", where the body lifts up and begins to hop at the moment of maximum brain wave coherence. Governors of the Age of Enlightenment demonstrate the technology for creating coherence in individual and world consciousness, the basis of world peace.
From left: Bom Thapa from Nepal, Eddie Gob from Guadeloupe, Blaine Watson from Canada, and Richard LaMarita from the U.S.A.

Ghana • *The Ghanian Times*

Accra   16 September 1986   (English)

T.M. inaugurated

THE Ghana Branch of the Maharishi's World Peace Plan was inaugurated at the Arden Hall of the Ambassador Hotel in Accra on Sunday.

Thhe Maharishi's World Peace is a movement dedicated to the establishment of world peace through a process of Transcendental Meditation (TM).

Nii Padi national chairman of the movement, explained that the goal of the TM was the achievement of a "unifying level of consciousness between peoples of the world."

He explained that the unifying level was an essential element for the achievement of coherence and a peaceful atmosphere for communication between people holding opposing views in the world.

According to him this was a direct means of restructuring society overnight. —GNA.

WORLD PEACE • GLOBAL INAUGURATION

PRESS REPORTS FROM AFRICA AND THE MIDDLE EAST

Israel • *Ha'Aretz*

Tel Aviv   17 August 1986   (Hebrew)

"תעופה יוגית תוכל להבטיח את ההרמוניה במזרח-התיכון"

לפי תוכנית השלום של מהרישי מהש יוגי

מאת נורית אמיתי, סופרת "הארץ"

ביום שישי, בשעה 10:30, "התעופפו", לרבות ישראל, מאות אנשים המאוגדים באגודה הבידלאומית למדיטציה טרנסנדנטלית. המבצע אורגן במסגרת תוכנית השלום של מהרישי מהש יוגי.

גם בישראל ביקשו להדגים תשעה גברים, את "המכניקה למניעת טרור וליצירת שלום עולמי, באמצעות טכניקת התעופה"; במסיבת עיתונאים בתל אביב הודגש, כי ב"תעופה היוגית" יש שלושה שלבים: קפיצות, ריחוף ותעופה. ההדגמה השלושה כללה קפיצות, כשרוב הכדוגמים ישבו בישיבת לוטוס, כשכפות רגליהם מונחות מעל בר כיהם. גד תיק, יושב ראש האגודה הסביר, שכאשר יש קבוצה המתרגלת טכנולוגיה זו ביחד, היא מסוגלת למנוע תופעות חברתיות שליליות ברמה לאומית ובידלאומית ולבסס מצב של שלום עולמי. הכוונה היא, ששבעת אלפים בני-אדם יבצעו את התרגיל ביחד, ואז ישפיע הדבר על ההרמוניה העולבית.

במזרח-התיכון נחוץ כי רק מאתיים איש יתרגלו את ה"תעופה היוגית" פעמיים ביום במטרה לשמור על ההרמוניה באוירנו וניטרול תופעות שליליות, סבורים ראשי האגודה.

הפיסיקאי אילון מרוז הסביר, כי "התעופה היוגית" היא טכנולוגיה חדישה בפיסיקה המודרנית, וד"ר מרים ברמדקוטאי, רופאה נירולוגית ציינה, כי בזמן ה"תעופה היוגית" נוצר תואם (קוהורנטיות) מרבי בפעילות של גלי המוח, כפי שהיא נרשמת על ידי מכשיר האיא"ג, ואז הגוף מתרומם ו"קופץ".

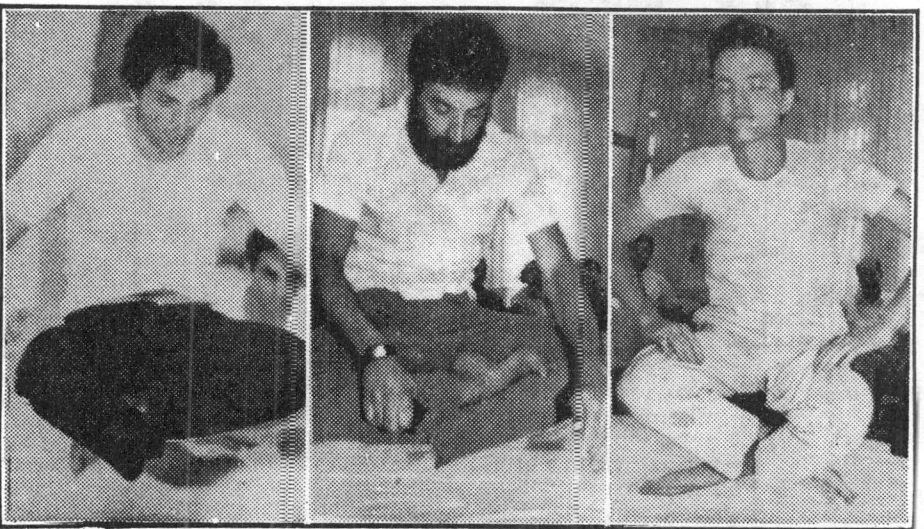

שלושה מהמדגימים בפעולה: (מימין לשמאל): אריה שרגא (26) מתל-אביב, אריאל עוז (28) ממעלה אדומים, מיכאל גולדשמיט (29) מקיבוץ יחד.

PRESS REPORTS FROM AFRICA AND THE MIDDLE EAST

Israel • *Al-Hamishmar*

Tel Aviv   17 August 1986   (Hebrew)

אנשים ואירועים

"תעופה יוגית"

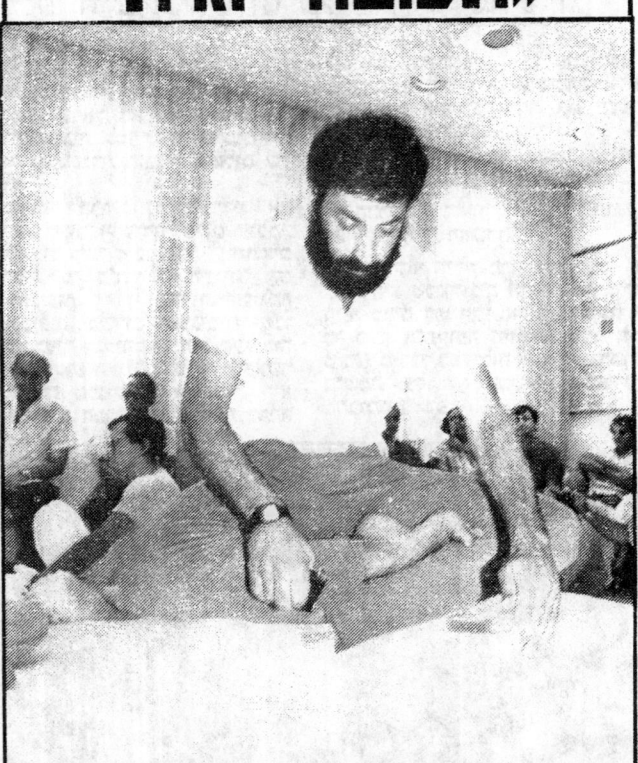

9 גברים הדגימו אתמול את טכניקת "התעופה" של המדיטציה הטרנסנדנטלית, שהיא היבט של טכנולוגיית "השדה המאוחד" של מהרישי. בטכניקה זו, הגוף מתרומם ברגע שנוצר תואם (קוהרנטיות) מירבי בתפקיד המוח. התואם קורן מרמת "השדה המאוחד", הרמה הבסיסית ביותר של הטבע, ומנטרל השפעות שליליות ויוצר הרמוניה בכל הסביבה... זהו ההסבר של היוגים לתופעה – אריאל עוז ממעלה אדומים מציג את "ריחופו" באוויר.

ד"ר מרים ברמן-קוטאי, רופאה נירולוגית, הסבירה כי בזמן התעופה היוגית נוצר תואם מירבי (קוהרנטיות) בפעילות גלי המוח, כפי שהיא נרשמת ע"י מכשיר האלקטרו אנצפלוגרף (א.א.ג.), ואז הגוף מתרומם ומתחיל לקפוץ. הד"ר קוטאי הסבירה כי קוהרנטיות היא רמת התואם בין תדירויות שונות של גלי המוח הנמדדת מאזורים שונים על פני קליפת המוח. במדידות שנערכו בשעת קפיצות רציניות לא התגלו תופעות קוהרנטיות המושגות בזמן "תעופה יוגית".

(שע"ה)

WORLD PEACE • GLOBAL INAUGURATION

PRESS REPORTS FROM AFRICA AND THE MIDDLE EAST

Israel • *Yediot A'Haronoth*

Tel Aviv   31 August 1986   (Hebrew)

התעופה היוגית רוצה להביא שלום לאיזור

— מאת יצחק רביחיא, כתב "ידיעות אחרונות"

תוכנית חדשה לפיתרון הסיכסוך היהודי-ערבי, בשיטת המדיטציה הטרנסצנדנטלית, תוצג השבוע בירושלים, בפני עשרות נכבדים ערבים ממזרח-העיר, ראשי ערים ונציגי העיתונות. את השיטה תציג האגודה הבינלאומית למדיטציה בישראל.

תוכנית השלום אותה הגה ומפיץ בעולם המהרישי מהש יוגי, מבוססת על טכנולוגיה של השדה המאוחד: מושג בפיסיקה המודרנית שפרשו "הרמה של כוחות הטבע הפועלים בשיתוף פעולה".

לדברי נציגי האגודה, אם יבצעו כ־200 איש (שורש ריבועי של אחוז אחד מהאוכלוסיה) את לב הראשון של התוכנית, הנקראת "התעופה היוגית", יבוא שלום אמיתי לאיזור.

Israel • *Ashaab*

Jerusalem   5 September 1986   (Arabic)

احدث طريقة .. لحل ازمة الشرق الاوسط !؟

القدس — عقد صباح امس مؤتمر صحفي لحل مشكلة الشرق الاوسط عن طريق استخدام اسلوب «التأمل الذهني» وذلك باشراف الجمعية العالمية للتفكير والتأمل في اسرائيل.

وعند تحدث في المؤتمر الصحفي كل من جاك وايلون ميروز وميريام بيرمان كيتي فاعطوا فكرة عن نشوء الجمعية وارتباطها بافكار الحاخام الهندي مهراشي يوغي وهي عبارة عن تمرينات ذهنية عقلية تساعد على الصفاء النفسي والسلام الداخلي وتنعكس بالتالي على العلاقات الطيبة مع الاخرين.

وقد عرض عدد من الاشخاص حركات رياضية عقلية وهي تمرين «الطيران» قال عنها خليل جدعون احد اعضاء الجمعية انها تهدف الى الوصول الى مصدر التفكير مما يجعل الانسان ينسجم بصورة طبيعية مع قوانين الطبيعة وهذا يؤدي الى راحة عميقة تمكن الجهاز العصبي من التخلص من «الشوائب» التي تدفع الى التوتر والعصبية.

وعن الجمعية قال جدعون ان هدفها هو احلال السلام في الشرق الاوسط عن طريق استخدام اسلوب التأمل الذهني والقضاء على التوتر لدى الانسان وهذا يساهم في احلال السلام مع الاخرين حتى ولوكانوا قبل ذلك اعداء.

واضاف جدعون ان السلام الحقيقي هو الذي يكون بين الافراد سواء كانوا عرب ام يهودا فعندما يكون لدى الانسان سلام داخلي فان هذا كفيل باحلال السلام العام في المنطقة.

واشار جدعون الى انه يوجد في انحاء العالم اليوم حوالي مليوني شخص يمارسون هذا النوع من التفكير الذهني.

MAHARISHI'S PROGRAMME TO CREATE

PRESS REPORTS FROM AFRICA AND THE MIDDLE EAST

Israel • *Yediot A'Haronoth*
Tel Aviv   5 September 1986   (Hebrew)

ה„מרחפים" למען השלום

WORLD PEACE • GLOBAL INAUGURATION

PRESS REPORTS FROM AFRICA AND THE MIDDLE EAST

Israel • *Akhbar Mahailieh*
Jerusalem   5 September 1986   (Arabic)

مؤتمر صحفي في القدس
لحل مشكلة الشرق الأوسط «بالتأمل»!

القدس ــ عقد صباح أمس في فندق بالاس بالقدس مؤتمر صحفي لحل مشكلة الشرق الأوسط عن طريق استخدام أسلوب «التأمل الذهني» وذلك باشراف الجمعية العالمية للتفكير والتأمل في إسرائيل.

وقد تحدث في المؤتمر الصحفي كل من جاد تيك وايلون ميروز ومريام بيرهان كيتي فاعطوا فكرة عن نشوء الجمعية وارتباطها بأفكار الحاخام الهندي مهراتشي يوغي وهي عبارة عن تمرينات ذهنية عقلية تساعد على الصفاء النفسي والسلام الداخلي وتنعكس بالتالي على العلاقات الطيبة مع الاخرين!

وقد عرض عدد من الاشخاص حركات رياضية عقلية وهي تمرين «الطيران»

قال عنها خليل جدعون أحد اعضاء الجمعية أنها تهدف الى الوصول الى مصدر التفكير مما يجعل الانسان ينسجم بصورة طبيعية مع قوانين الطبيعة وهذا يؤدي الى راحة عميقة تمكن الجهاز العصبي من التخلص من «الشوائب» التي تدفع الى التوتر والعصبية.

وعن الجمعية قال جدعون أن هدفها هو احلال السلام في الشرق الأوسط عن طريق استخدام أسلوب التأمل الذهني والقضاء على التوتر لدى الانسان وهذا يساهم في احلال السلام مع الاخرين حتى ولو كانوا قبل ذلك أعداء!

وأضاف جدعون أن السلام الحقيقي هو الذي يكون بين الافراد سواء كانوا عربا أم يهودا عندما يكون لدى الانسان سلام داخلي فان هذا كفيل باحلال السلام العام في المنطقة!

وأشار جدعون الى أنه يوجد في أنحاء العالم اليوم حوالي بليوني شخص يمارسون هذا النوع من التفكير الذهني!

∙∙

PRESS REPORTS FROM AFRICA AND THE MIDDLE EAST

Kenya • *Sunday Standard*

Nairobi   14 September 1986   (English)

Meditators compete in floating in the air

CAN human beings defy the laws of gravity? On July 21, more than 100 journalists from around the world and about 8,000 spectators witnessed a demonstration in New Delhi, India, that would seem to indicate the answer is yes.

The occasion was the first-ever international competition in levitation. It was organised by followers of Maharishi Mahesh Yogi, founder of the Transcendental Meditation movements.

The movement has a worldwide following embracing the entire economic spectrum from peasants and workers, through businessmen and professionals, right up to army generals, high court judges and government ministers.

Story and pictures by Amin Kassam

In Africa, the movement is strongest in Kenya where its continental headquarters are located. Although Kenya did not participate in the New Delhi competition, it had done so in earlier stages leading to the finals but had been knocked out.

The evening was billed as an exhibition of 'yogic flying" with the events being a 25-metre-hurdles race, a high jump, a long jump and a 50-metres dash — all performed while sitting in the cross-legged lotus meditation position.

The "tracks" for the races were rows of foam-rubber mattresses covered with white sheets and divided into lanes by red ribbons. During the speeches leading up to the races, skeptical members of the press made a point of casually walking over the matresses or sitting on them to check for extra "spring." They were ordinary foam rubber.

Meditation

The first race of the evening was the 25-metre hurdles in which the hurdles were 15-centimetre high rolls of cloth. A hush fell over the crowd in the Indira Gandhi National Indoor Stadium as the row of competitors lined up, dressed in loose white drawstring pants and brightly-coloured short-sleeved shirts.

With still and video cameras trained on them, under bright floodlights, the competitors shut their eyes. A few minutes of meditation were followed by a shiver among some of the competitors — reminiscent of the behaviour of a car shaking into life as a crack was turned, before the advent of the electric ignition. Then came a few hops in place and the race was on.

"Flying" was a misnomer because progress was made in a series of low hops averaging around a metre in length. Some of the meditators kept their hands in the air, others gripped their feet to prevent them trailing and a few used their hands for balance as they came down at the end of each hop. However, the hands touched lightly on the mattresses and could not have provided much propulsion.

Some spectators interviewed afterwards felt the feat could have been duplicated by an intensively trained athlete. However, the organisers say the brain wave patterns of meditators change while they "fly;" but those of people hopping through deliberate muscular effort do not do so. Also, the faces of the competitors showed relaxation instead of the tension one would expect after physical effort.

Hopping is said to be the first stage of yogic flying. The second is increasing ability to hover in midair, while the third is controlled flight in any direction. All the competitors were in the first stage.

WORLD PEACE • GLOBAL INAUGURATION

Fascinating as the races were, the event had a more serious side to it. The levitation exhibition was the highlight of ceremonies to inaugurate the Maharishi's programme to create world peace.

According to the Maharishi, advanced meditation makes the human brain function more coherently. At "maximum coherence," when all sections of the brain are working in harmony, the body lifts up and begins to hop. The changes in the brain can be seen by attaching electrodes to the head of a meditator and connecting them to an electroencephalograph (EEG), an instrument used to record small electrical impulses produced by the brain.

The changes were demonstrated in this way at the stadium, with the traces on the screen showing increasing orderliness as the demonstrator went deeper into meditation.

Wars

At maximum coherence, says the Maharishi, the brain taps into the universal reservoir from which everything in nature flows, termed the "unified field." At this stage, with the right mental impulse, it is possible to manipulate the gravitational field immediately around the meditator. Since the unified field has infinite links within nature, harmony in one art, achieved through meditation, affects the whole of nature. Negative trends in human society, such as crime and violence, can thus be held in check.

The Maharishi contends that wars are not caused merely by the buildup of weapons. "Think of a time a few thousand years ago when guns and bombs were not available. Was life on earth free from battles? There were cruel fights. It is on the level of consciousness, whether it is destructive or it is creative," that the solution lies, he says.

The movement has a long list of studies from which it has concluded that if the square root of one per cent of the world's population — which comes to 7,000 people currently — meditate continuously in one spot, they can counteract negativity all over the world. The studies show a correlation between meditation and falling crime in several U.S. cities. The movement has made a start towards setting up such a group at Maharishi Nagar just outside Delhi.

Whether or not one accepts the validity of the Maharishi's theory, the demonstration of "yogic flying" showed that modern science cannot affort to reject out of hand what it cannot explain.

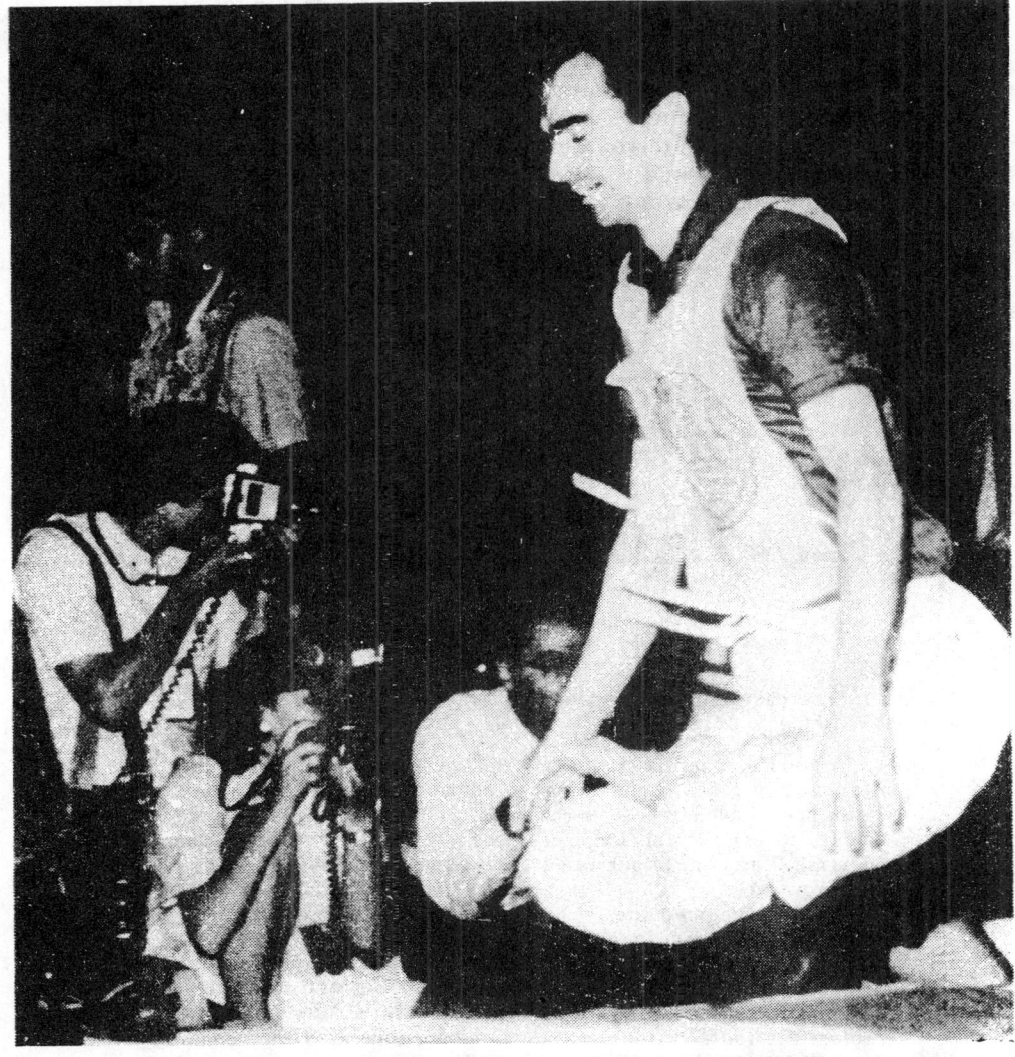

IN the lotus position, a participant in the levitation competition in New Delhi proceeds by leaps and bounds over hurdles.

PRESS REPORTS FROM AFRICA AND THE MIDDLE EAST

Lebanon • *Le Réveil*
Beirut 15 August 1986 (French)

Aujourd'hui, dans une centaine de pays
MAHARISHI PROPOSE SES TECHNIQUES YOGIQUES COMME MOYEN D'INSTAURER LA PAIX DANS LE MONDE

Maharishi Mahesh Yogi, un grand sage de l'Inde, qui propose pour ce faire sa technologie du «champ unifié» (4 millions d'experts à travers le monde) invite ce vendredi 15 août à une démonstration publique de ces techniques dans une centaine de pays. Démonstration qui tiendra lieu de réponse à l'interrogation suivante: peut-on venir à bout du terrorisme et instaurer la paix dans le monde par la pratique de certaines «techniques yogiques d'envol»).

Prise de vue de la compétition «d'envol yogique» en juillet 86 à Washington DC.

Mais d'abord qu'est-ce que le «champ unifié», quelles relations peut-il avoir avec les techniques de lévitation, et comment pourrait-il agir sur la guerre ou le terrorisme?

La physique moderne — du moins la mécanique quantique — a montré qu'à la base de la matière il existe un champ unifié où résident sous une forme potentielle toutes les lois de la nature. Les dernières découvertes de la physique avaient déjà réduit l'expression des lois de la nature à quatre forces fondamentales: l'électromagnétisme, l'interaction faible, l'interaction forte, la gravitation. Mais les savants sont aujourd'hui portés à croire, ou à considérer théoriquement que ces quatre forces fondamentales sont susceptibles d'être unifiées dans une théorie fondamentale dite du «champ unifié»

La «lévitation yogique»

Maharishi Mahesh Yogi dans la tradition des grands maîtres de l'Inde, a montré que la conscience humaine est en mesure d'accéder par le biais de techniques spéciales à ce «champ unifié», permettant ainsi d'agir sur toutes les lois de la nature. La lévitation entre autre ne serait qu'un aspect de la maîtrise d'une des lois de la nature. A ce sujet, le Pr. John Hagelin, un des plus grands physiciens des temps présents, écrit: «La différence entre la dynamique de la nature, aux niveaux fondamentaux, et au niveau classique macroscopique observable est simplement une différence de cohérence. La cohérence est l'attribut des phénomènes quantiques. La «lévitation yogique» est essentiellement une démonstration du même phénomène de cohérence à un niveau plus fondamental du fonctionnement de la nature, le niveau-même du «champ unifié». Les théories classiques de gravitation, telles que la gravitation de Newton et la relativité générale d'Einstein, ne peuvent expliquer la «lévitation yogique». Cependant, la gravitation quantique peut le faire. La gravitation quantique est une théorie cohérente de gravitation qui ordinairement, s'applique à la nature de la physique à l'échelle du champ unifié. La «lévitation yogique» prouve que le système nerveux de l'individu a suffisamment de complexité intégrée pour fonctionner au niveau du champ unifié».

Amélioration de la qualité de vie ou «l'effet Maharishi»

Le 9 juillet dernier, à Washington D.C, s'est déroulé devant un public représentant des médias internationaux les premières compétitions d'envol yogique en Amérique du Nord. Les finalistes de ces compétitions, hommes et femmes, ont montré

Pour une cohérence entre la conscience et la matière dans le corps.

à quel point l'individu pouvait maîtriser ces techiniques de lévitation comme en ont témoigné les nombreux commentaires de la presse mondiale et des télévisions.

Durant la technique d'«envol yogique» au moment de cohérence maximum de l'activité cérébrale telle que mesurée par l'électro-encéphalogramme, le corps s'élève en l'air et se met à rebondir. La cohérence entre la conscience et la matière dans le corps expérimentée au cours de cette première étape d'«envol yogique» s'origine au niveau du champ unifié de toutes les lois de la nature. Etant donné que ce champ est caractérisé par une corrélation infinie, une impulsion de cohérence engendrée à ce niveau harmonise instantanément les tendances discordantes dans tout l'environnement neutralisant ainsi les tendances négatives qui peuvent s'y trouver.

De nombreuses études sociologiques réalisées à travers le monde au cours des dix dernières années ont montré que la racine carrée du 1% d'une population pratiquant la technologie d'«envol yogique» améliore d'une manière sensible la qualité de la vie dans une société donnée. Cet effet a été baptisé l'«Effet Maharishi». Cette année, Maharishi Mahesh Yogi a décidé de lancer un «Programme pour établir la Paix Mondiale». Ce programme, qui a été inauguré à New Delhi aux Indes le 21 juillet dernier, comporte trois étapes devant mener à la paix mondiale.

Première étape: la positivité engendrée par l'envol commun d'un groupe d'au moins 7000 experts de cette technologie devrait transformer l'état de conflit au niveau international en paix mondiale.

Deuxième étape: simultanément des groupes d'«experts» représentant la racine carrée du 1% de la population de chaque pays apporteront la paix à leur nation en créant la cohérence dans la conscience nationale. Au Liban, ceci correspondrait à un groupe d'environ 200 «experts» en «envol yogique». La paix nationale ainsi établie renforcera la paix mondiale.

Troisième étape: l'«envol» pratiqué deux fois par jour en commun dans chaque ville permettra de corroborer cette influence pacifiante et de perpétuer par conséquent la paix mondiale.

PRESS REPORTS FROM AFRICA AND THE MIDDLE EAST

Lebanon • *Al-Ahrar*
Beirut 15 August 1986 (Arabic)

اليوغا في سبيل السلام
"الحقل الموحّد" والارتفاع عن الأرض

اول مرحلة من الطيران

الطيران الكامل.

هل بالامكان القضاء على الارهاب واحلال السلام في العالم من خلال ممارسة بعض تقنيات اليوغا ومنها تقنية الطيران؟ اجل.. يجيب مهاريشي يوغي حكيم كبير من الهند. وهو يقترح لذلك تطبيقا تكنولوجيا المعروف باسم الحقل الموحد والذي يمارسة اربعة ملايين خبير في العالم. وقد دعا مهاريشي الى تجربة علنية لهذه التقنيات تقام حاليا في اكثر من مئة بلد.

ولكن ما هو هذا الحقل الموحد وما هي علاقته بتقنية اليوغا للطيران وكيف يمكنه ان يؤثر على الحرب او على الارهاب؟

ان علم الفيزياء الحديث وبصورة خاصة الميكانيكية الكمية كشف انه في اساس المادة يقوم حقل موحد حيث تكمن بالقوة كافة قوانين الطبيعة لقد اختزلت الاكتشافات الفيزيائية الاخيرة كما هو معلوم ـ قوانين الطبيعة باربع قوى اساسية هي :

١) الالكترونية المغناطيسية
٣) Forte — Inter-action Faible
٤) Inter-action الجاذبية.

الا ان العلماء يحملون اليوم على الاعتقاد نظريا ان هذه القوى الاربع بامكانها ان تتوحد في نظرية اساسية تعرف باسم الحقل الموحد. لقد برهن مهاريشي ان يتصل بهذا الحقل الموحد، عن طريق تقنيات خاصة تسمح له بالتأثر على جميع قوانين الطبيعة. وليست تقنية الطيران اي ارتفاع الجسد عن الارض من دون مجهود سوى وجه من وجوه التحكم باحدى قوانين الطبيعة. في هذا الموضوع كتب البروفسور جون هاغلن احد كبار علماء الفيزياء في هذا العصر يقول : "

ان الفرق بين دينامية الطبيعة على مستوياتها الاولية ومستواها الكلاسيكي المرئي هو فرق في التناغم، فالتناغم هو صفة الظواهر الكمية وما الطيران اليوغي في جوهره الا برهان على ظاهرة التناغم على المستوى الاولي للطبيعة اي مستوى الحقل الموحد.

يضيف هاغلن : " ان النظريات الكلاسيكية في مجال الجاذبية ولا سيما نظريات نيوتن النسبية العامة عند اينشتاين لا يمكنها ان تفسر فعل الطيران اليوغي. في المقابل تستطيع ذلك نظرية الجاذبية الكمية. فالجاذبية الكمية نظرية متجانسة توافق طبيعة الفيزياء على مستوى الحقل الموحد ويشير هاغلن الى ان الطيران اليوغي يثبت ان الجهاز العصبي عند الانسان فيه ما يكفي من المركبات المجتمعة سويا للعمل على مستوى الحقل الموحد.

في التاسع من تموز الماضي وفي مدينة واشنطن الاميركية اقيمت امام جمهور من الصحافيين العالميين اول مباراة " لطيران اليوغا " في اميركا الشمالية وقد اثبت الرابحون بالفعل من رجال ونساء الى اي حد يستطيع الانسان التحكم بتقنية الطيران هذه على نحو

ما اشادت به وسائل الاعلام العالمية من صحافة واذاعات وتلفزيون.

اما عملية الطيران فتحدث في لحظة التناغم القصوى على مستوى تموجات الدماغ كما يظهر ذلك التخطيط الكهربائي للدماغ. ان التناغم بين الوعي والجسم في هذه اللحظة يتولد من الحقل الموحد لكافة قوانين الطبيعة علما بان هذا التناغم وفور حدوثه ينعكس انسجاما على جميع ما يحيط به ويلغي بالتالي كل الظواهر السلبية.

لقد اثبتت عدة دراسات سوسيولوجية اجريت في انحاء العالم خلال السنوات العشر الاخيرة ان الجذر التربيعي لواحد بالمئة ١٪ من السكان في مجتمع معين. وقد سمي هذا التأثير الايجابي بتأثير مهاريشي.

لقد قرر مهاريشي هذه السنة برنامجا لاحلال السلام في العالم. دشن في نيودلهي ـ الهند في ٢١ تموز الماضي يتضمن ثلاث مراحل من شأنها ان تؤدي الى السلام العالمي.

المرحلة الاولى : ان الايجابية المولدة بفعل الطيران الجماعي لسبعة الاف خبير في هذه التقنية من شأنها ان تحول الصراعات الدولية الى سلام عالمي.

المرحلة الثانية : وهي تقضي بان يجتمع في كل بلد فريق من الخبراء يمثل الجذر التربيعي لواحد بالمئة من سكان هذا البلد بمقدورهم احلال السلام لاتهم بمقدورهم على طريق خلق التناغم في الوعي الوطني.

هذا الامر يمكن ان يتم في لبنان بفضل مئتي " خبير بالطيران اليوغي ومن جراء حلول السلام في كل وطن يتعزز السلام العالمي.

المرحلة الثالثة : تقضي بان يمارس خبراء الطيران اليوغي مجتمعين تقنيتهم مرتين في اليوم حيثما وجدوا فيسهمون بذلك بتعزيز هذا التأثير السلمي وبتأمين استمرارية السلام العالمي.

PRESS REPORTS FROM AFRICA AND THE MIDDLE EAST

Lebanon • *Al Anwar*
Beirut   15 August 1986   (Arabic)

■ الجسد الطائر ... واليوغا المساعدة ■

هل بالامكان القضاء على الارهاب واحلال السلام في العالم من خلال ممارسة بعض تقنيات اليوغا ومنها تقنية الطيران؟ اجل، يجيب مهاريشي ماهيش يوغي حكيم كبير من الهند، وهو يقترح لذلك تطبيق التكنولوجية المعروفة باسم «الحقل الموحد»، والتي يمارسها اربعة ملايين خبير في العالم. وقد دعا مهاريشي الى تجربة علنية لهذه التقنيات تجري اليوم في اكثر من مئة بلد.

ولكن ما هو هذا «الحقل الموحد» وما هي علاقته بتقنية اليوغا للطيران وكيف يمكنه ان يؤثر على الحرب او على الارهاب؟
ان علم الفيزياء الحديث وبصورة خاصة الميكانيكية الكمية Mécanique Quantique كشف انه في اساس المادة يقوم حقل موحد حيث تكمن بالقوة كافة قوانين الطبيعة. لقد اختزلت الاكتشافات الفيزيائية الاخيرة ـ كما هو معلوم ـ قوانين الطبيعة باربع قوى اساسية هي:
١) الالكترونية
٢) المغناطيسية
٣) Inter-action Forte — Inter-action Faible
٤) الجاذبية.

الا ان العلماء يحملون اليوم على الاعتقاد نظريا ان هذه القوى الاربع بامكانها ان تتوحد في نظرية اساسية تعرف باسم «الحقل الموحد». لقد برهن مهاريشي ماهيش يوغي المتحدر من سلسلة كبار الحكماء في الهند انه بامكان الوعي الانساني ان يتصل بهذا «الحقل الموحد» عن طريق تقنيات خاصة تسمح له بالتاثير على جميع قوانين الطبيعة. وليست تقنية الطيران اي ارتفاع الجسد عن الارض من دون مجهود سوى وجه من وجوه التحكم باحدى قوانين الطبيعة. في هذا الموضوع كتب البروفسور «جون هيغلن» (John Hagelin) احد كبار علماء الفيزياء في هذا العصر يقول: «ان الفرق بين دينامية الطبيعة على مستوياتها الاولية ومستواها الكلاسيكي المرئي هو فرق في التناغم، فالتناغم هو صفة الظواهر الكمية وما الطيران اليوغي في جوهره الا برهان على ظاهرة التناغم على المستوى الاولى للطبيعة اي مستوى «الحقل الموحد».

ويضيف هيغلن: «ان النظريات الكلاسيكية في مجال الجاذبية ولا سيما نظريات نيوتن النسبية العامة عند اينشتاين لا يمكنها ان تفسر فعل الطيران اليوغي. في المقابل تستطيع ذلك نظرية الجاذبية الكمية. فالجاذبية الكمية نظرية متجانسة توافق طبيعة الفيزياء على مستوى الحقل الموحد ويشير هيغلن الى ان

الطيران اليوغي يثبت ان الجهاز العصبي عند الانسان فيه ما يكفي من المركبات المجتمعة سويا للعمل على مستوى الحقل الموحد.

في التاسع من تموز الماضي وفي مدينة واشنطن الاميركية جرت امام جمهور من الصحافيين العالميين اول مباراة «لطيران اليوغا» في اميركا الشمالية. وقد اثبت الرابحون بالفعل من رجال ونساء الى اي حد يستطيع الانسان التحكم بتقنية الطيران هذه على نحو ما اشادت به وسائل الاعلام العالمية من صحافة واذاعات وتلفزيون.

اما عملية الطيران فتحدث في لحظة التناغم القصوى على مستوى تموجات الدماغ كما يظهر ذلك التخطيط الكهربائي للدماغ. ان التناغم بين الوعي والجسم في هذه اللحظة يتولد من الحقل الموحد لكافة قوانين الطبيعة علما بأن هذا التناغم وفور حدوثه يعكس انسجاما على جميع ما يحيط به ويلغي بالتالي كل الظواهر السلبية.

لقد اثبتت عدة دراسات سوسيولوجية اجريت في انحاء عدة من العالم خلال السنوات العشر الاخيرة ان الجذر التربيعي لواحد بالمئة من السكان (%1 √) في حال ممارسة تقنية طيران اليوغا يحسن بشكل ملحوظ نوعية الحياة في مجتمع معين. وقد سمي هذا التأثير الايجابي «بتأثير مهاريشي».

لقد قرر مهاريشي هذه السنة برنامجا لاحلال السلام في العالم. هذا البرنامج الذي دشن في نيودلهي - الهند في 21 تموز الماضي يتضمن ثلاث مراحل من شأنها ان تؤدي الى السلام العالمي.

المرحلة الاولى: ان الايجابية المولدة بفعل الطيران الجماعي لسبعة الاف خبير في هذه التقنية من شأنها ان تحول الصراعات الدولية الى سلام عالمي.

المرحلة الثانية: وهي تقضي بان يجتمع في كل بلد فريق من الخبراء يمثل الجذر التربيعي لواحد بالمئة من سكان هذا البلد بمقدورهم احلال السلام لامتهم عن طريق خلق التناغم Cohêrence في الوعي الوطني. هذا الامر يمكن ان يتم في لبنان بفضل مئتي «خبير بالطيران اليوغي». ومن جراء حلول السلام في كل وطن يتعزز السلام العالمي.

المرحلة الثالثة: تقضي بأن يمارس خبراء الطيران اليوغي مجتمعين تقنيتهم مرتين في اليوم حيثما وجدوا فيسهمون بذلك بتعزيز هذا التأثير السلمي وبتأمين استمرارية السلام العالمي.

■ الحقل الموحد بمساعدة الروح الهائمة ■

PRESS REPORTS FROM AFRICA AND THE MIDDLE EAST

Lebanon • *L'Orient le Jour*

Beirut 26 August 1986 (French)

VOL YOGIQUE GRACE A LA M.T.

M. Robert Kfoury auquel la méditation transcendantale doit sa lancée au Liban, vient de participer à la compétition de «vol yogique», qui a eu lieu tout dernièrement à Washington D.C., aux Etats-Unis.

Appartenant à la raison pure, la méditation transcendantale se voit à présent non seulement une philosophie, mais également un moyen d'instaurer la paix dans le monde, de venir à bout du terrorisme, et ce par la pratique de certaines «techniques yogiques d'envol».

C'est là, du moins, l'avis de Maharishi Mahesh Yogi, un grand sage de l'Inde, qui propose pour ce faire, d'appliquer sa technologie du «Champ Unifié». «Qu'est-ce que donc que le «Champ Unifié»? Quelles relations peut-il avoir avec les techniques de lévitation? Et comment pourrait-il agir sur la guerre ou le terrorisme?»

La physique moderne a montré qu'à la base de la matière il existe un champ unifié où résident — sous une forme potentielle — toutes les lois de la nature. Les dernières découvertes de la physique avaient déjà réduit l'expression des lois de la nature à quatre forces fondamentales: l'électromagnétisme, l'interaction faible, l'interaction forte, la gravitation. Mais aujourd'hui, les savants sont portés à croire (ou à considérer théoriquement) que ces quatre forces fondamentales sont susceptibles d'être unifiées dans une théorie fondamenale dite du «Champ Unifié».

Maharishi Mahesh Yogi a montré — dans la tradition des grands maîtres de l'Inde — que la conscience humaine est en mesure d'accéder à ce «Champ Unifié» par le biais de techniques spéciales, permettant d'agir sur toutes les lois de la nature. La lévitation ne serait donc — entre autres — qu'un aspect de la maîtrise de l'une des lois de la nature.

With each stroke of the TM-Sidhi practice the awareness goes deeper into the unified field level of consciousness, enlivening infinite dynamism on the ground of perfect silence. Mind-body coordination is maximum; with each intention to fly the mind propels the body up into the air. Here four medalists spontaneously rise up together, blissfully flying to radiate coherence in world consciousness, the basis of world peace.

Il faudra.... s'élever de terre, pour obtenir la paix.

L'«envol yogique» ou... une nouvelle recette pour la paix.

Professeur John Hagelin, un des plus grands physiciens des temps présents, écrit que **«la différence entre la dynamique de la nature aux niveaux fondamentaux, et au niveau classique macroscopique observable est simplement une différence de cohérence. La cohérence est l'attribut des phénomènes quantiques. La «lévitation yogique» est essentiellement une démonstration du même phénomène de cohérence à un niveau plus fondamental du fonctionnement de la nature, le niveau même du «Champ Unifié».** Les théories classiques de gravitation, telles que la gravitation de Newton et la relativité générale d'Einstein, ne peuvent expliquer la «lévitation yogique», alors que la gravitation quantique elle peut le faire, car elle est une théorie cohérente de gravitation qui s'applique — d'ordinaire — à la nature de la physique à l'échelle du «Champ Unifié». La «lévitation yogique» prouve que le système nerveux de l'individu a suffisamment de **complexité intégrée pour fonctionner au niveau du «Champ Unifié».**

C'est dans ce cadre, que se sont déroulées dernièrement à Washington D.C. les premières compétitions d'envol yogique, les finalistes de ces compétitions (hommes et femmes) ont montré à quel point l'individu pouvait maîtriser ces techniques de lévitation: au cours de la technique «d'envol yogique», au moment de cohérence maximale de l'activité cérébrale telle que mesurée par l'électro encéphalogramme, le corps s'élève en l'air et se met à rebondir. La cohérence entre la conscience et la matière dans le corps, expérimentée au cours de cette première étape d'«envol yogique» prend son origine au niveau du champ unifié de toutes les lois de la nature. Le champ étant caractérisé par une corrélation infinie, l'impulsion de cohérence engendrée à ce niveau harmon se **instantanément** les tendances discordantes dans tout l'environnements, neutralisant ainsi les tendances négatives qui peuvent s'y trouver.

De nombreuses études sociologiques réalisées à travers le monde au cours des dix dernières années, montrent que la pratique de la technologie d'«envol yogique» améliore d'une manière sensible la qualité de la vie dans une société donnée; cet effet a été baptisé «L'Effet Maharishi».

Cette année, Maharishi Mahesh Yogi a décidé de lancer un «Programme pour établir la Paix Mondiale». Inauguré tout dernièrement à New Delhi (aux Indes) il comporte trois étapes qui devraient mener à la paix mondiale.

Première étape: La positivité engendrée par l'envol en commun d'un groupe d'au moins 7000 experts de cette technologie devrait transformer l'état de conflit (au niveau international), en paix mondiale.

Deuxième étape: Simultanément, des groupes d'«experts», représentant la population de chaque pays, apporteront la paix à leur nation en créant la cohérence dans la conscience nationale. (Au Liban, ceci correspondrait à un groupe d'environ 200 «experts» en «envol yogique»). La paix nationale ainsi établie renforcera la paix mondiale.

Troisième étape: «L'envol», pratiqué deux fois par jour en commun dans chaque ville, permettra de corroborer cette influence pacifiante, et de perpétuer par conséquent la paix mondiale.

Dans cette recherche désespérée de la paix, voilà une nouvelle recette bien originale.

Et si elle aboutissait???

Samia DIBO

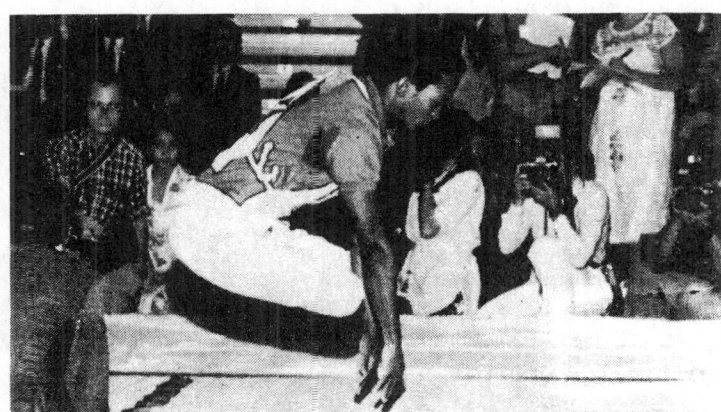

La positivité par l'envol en commun transformera le conflit international en paix mondiale.

PRESS REPORTS FROM AFRICA AND THE MIDDLE EAST

Lebanon • *An Nahar Arabe et International*
Beirut 8 September 1986 (Arabic)

ظاهرة

١٠٠ مليون دولار كلفة تحقيق السلام العالمي

المهاراشيون قادرون على تحقيق السلام في لبنان... وفي العالم كله!

اتباع مهاريشي التقوا في واشنطن وطاروا امام عدسات المصورين

يقول اتاتورك: "ان رجل السياسة الذي يحتاج الى احكام الدين ليبسط سلطته ليس الا جباناً". ولكن لبسط السلطة طرق اخرى قد تؤدي الى السلام العالمي، ان هي استعملت كما يجب.

في غمرة الصراعات الدائرة اجتمعت جماعة من اتباع مهاريشي المهندي في الولايات المتحدة، في واشنطن لعرض مشروع جديد لتحقيق سلام عالمي دائم عبر تبني مشروع مهاريشي للسلام.

ونحن في هذا التحقيق ندعوكم الى سماع ما قيل ومشاهدة ما جرى لتحكموا في الامر. فاننا في لبنان لسنا بعيدين عن هذه الظاهرة، لأن لمهاريشي اتباعاً في لبنان يراهنون على مشروعه للسلام العالمي وينتظرون، كما قالوا لنا، اليوم الذي يحصل فيه هذا السلام كي يفاخروا بأنهم كانوا اول من اقتنع بهذا الخط. وكما تعلمون فالحياة كلها رهانات: اما ان تربح كثيراً او تخسر كثيراً.

التأمل التجاوزي

"اذا رأيت مزارعاً ينثر البذور بين الاشواك، فانك تعتبره مغفلا. ومتى نبهته الى مما يفعل اجابك: "اني منشغل بالزراعة كما ترى، ولا وقت لدي لقلع الاشواك وتسوية التربة". فان كنت انت ايضاً تعتبر نفسك مشغولا جداً، بحيث لا تستطيع المشاركة في مشروع مهاريشي للسلام العالمي فانك تكون كذلك المزارع الاحمق، لا تعلم انه عليك ان تساعد اولا لخلق الظروف الملائمة لانجاح العمل الذي تقوم به. فلماذا لا تؤجل عملك، مهما كان، حتى نحصل على السلام العالمي؟ حينها يصبح اي عمل، مهما كان صعباً، سهل الانجاز"! هذا جزء مما قاله الدكتور كارليغ كينغ، المدير العام لـ"مهاريشي لقيادة العالم"، في افتتاح المباراة النهائية للطيران اليوغي، التي جرت في العاصمة الاميركية واشنطن، بتاريخ التاسع من تموز الماضي.

والواقع ان هذه المباراة "الغريبة" لم يكن القصد منها رياضياً بالمعنى المألوف. فان لهذا النوع من الرياضة دلالة خاصة لا يعرفها الا الذين يتقنون التأمل التجاوزي او هم مطلعون عليه.

والتأمل التجاوزي تقنية عقلانية بسيطة وطبيعية تهدف الى مساعدة انسان عصرنا على تحمل متطلبات الحياة اليومية وتخفيف حال التوتر الذي ينتج من نظام الحياة العصرية، السريعة الحركة والتي خلقت اناساً يركضون خلفها لاهثين. ويعتبر مهاريشي ماهش يوغي الاب الروحي لممارسي التأمل التجاوزي؛ فهو الذي

مهاريشي ماهش يوغي في صورة نشرت له عام ١٩٧٨.

WORLD PEACE • GLOBAL INAUGURATION

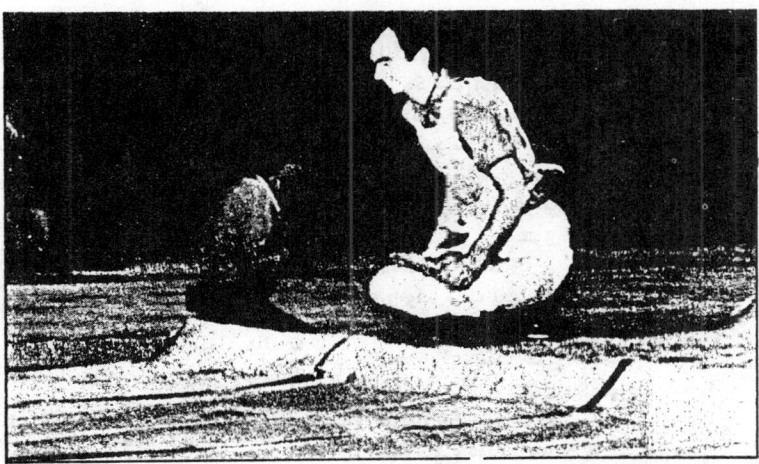
بلاين واتسون الكندي في طيران ٥٠ مترا من الحواجز.

بلاير باترفيلد من برمودا في طيران مسافة ٥٠ مترا.

٣٠ مصوراً يلتقطون اول صورة للقفز العالي اليوغي.

طوّر هذه التقنية عام ١٩٥٧ وطوّر علم الذكاء الخلاق عام ١٩٧١.

اما آخر منجزات هذا الحكيم الهندي فهي مشروع للسلام العالمي طرحه في التاسع من تموز ١٩٨٦، خلال اللقاء العالمي للصحة الكاملة الذي عقد في واشنطن وحضره ثلاثة آلاف خبير بالتقنية الجديدة التي اطلقها عام ١٩٨٢، تقنية الحقل الموحّد.

والحقل الموحد هو نتيجة اجتماع قوى الطبيعة الاربع الاساسية، كما اثبتتها الفيزياء الحديثة وهي:
- الكهرومغناطيسية
- التفاعل الضعيف
- التفاعل القوي
- التجاذب.

ويستعمل الخبراء في التأمل التجوزي، الذين يمارسون تقنيات الـ TM-Sidhis ، هذا الحقل الموحد ليصلوا الى تغيير في الامور، كل الامور، لأن الحقل الموحد هو في كل مكان كما يقولون.

خمسون الف خبير

يصل عدد الخبراء في التأمل التجوزي الى الخمسين ألفاً، وهم منتشرون في جميع انحاء الارض ويصل عددهم في لبنان الى زهاء الـ ١٧٥.

وبالعودة الى الكلمة التي عرضت في واشنطن، للحكيم مهاريشي، والتي سجّلها في "العاصمة العالمية لعصر الاستنارة"، ماهاريشي ناغار (الهند) فاننا نوجز منها النقاط الاساسية التي رها والتي تعتبر المرتكز الاساسي شروعه لاحقاق السلام العالمي.

يقول مهاريشي: "ان عصرنا يطالبنا امة قوة عظمى قادرة على ضبط راع الخطير بين القوى العظمى وجودة حامياً. لقد عانت العائلة لمية من الرعب المتواصل لسنوات يدة مضت. فالتاريخ السياسي حافل روب واخبارها. واليوم هناك شيء لر من الحرب وهو الارهاب. فالارهاب ن ان يضرب في اي مكان وفي اي ن وهو يهدد الجنس البشري، كل س البشري".

ويضيف، ان القوى العظمى تسعى، صنع السلام العالمي والسعادة على س الكترونية، كيميائية او نرية جودة في الطبيعة اصلا، ولكنما ضيقة اق.

229

MAHARISHI'S PROGRAMME TO CREATE

ويطرح ماهاريشي مشروعه على انه مشروع شامل يرتكز على قانون الطبيعة، الحقل الموحد لكل قوانين الطبيعة، الذي يشمل مني ما يشمل [...] الالكترونية والكيميائية [...]

ثم يبادر الى القول ان لكل مستوى من اسس الطبيعة وجهين: خلاقـاً [...] مرآ. واستعمال هذه الاسس يحمل [...] خطر التدمير. فالاسلحة تصبح [...] ان كان صاحبها مسالماً. فالمهم [...] عدد الصواريخ بل وعي المسؤول [...]. ويشير الى ان النزاعات لم تنشأ [...] وجود الاسلحة بل انها كانت نتيجة [...] وعي البشر لميولهم التدميرية. [...] باستعمال قانون الطبيعة كاملا [...] ينتهي الشر تماماً كما تختفي [...] مع بزوغ الفجر.

ويضيف انه خلال الثلاثين عاما [...] تبين ان كل القيم يمكن [...] الى اسمى مراتبها بمساعدة [...] الطبيعة. و"على هذا الاساس، [...] اليوم مشروعا باسم السلام [...]، الذي هو قيمة شاملة. وها نحن [...] في البوق للدعوة الى تأثير جماعي [...] سبيل خلق سلام دائم في العالم". ويأتي هذا المشروع بعد دعوة [...] عام ١٩٧٨ لخلق "المجتمع [...]"، وطبق طريقته في اكثر من [...] دول.

وهو يطمح من خلال مشروعه الى جعل [...] العظمى صديقة لان هذا هو [...] الاسمى في الهند. وكما يقول [...]: «Vasudevah عائلتي هو العالم Kutumbaka». ويدعو ماهاريشي الى [...] السبعة آلاف شخص الذين [...] العالم لتحقيق السلام.

٧ الاف لتحقيق السلام

وتعود قصة السبعة آلاف شخص الى اللقاء الذي جرى في جامعة ماهاريشي العالمية، في مدينة فيرفيلو، ولاية آيوا الاميركية في السابع عشر من كانون الاول ١٩٨٣ وحتى السادس من كانون الثاني ١٩٨٤.

وكانت الابحاث القائمة في المراكز التابعة لماهاريشي في العالم اثبتت انه حين يصبح ١٪ من سكان اية مدينة او اي بلد يمارسون التأمل التجاوزي، تزيد النزعة الى الايجابية في المجتمع كله. سواء على مستوى المدينة او على مستوى البلد.

وقد ثبت بعد تجارب اخرى ان الجذر التربيعي ((V)) للواحد في المئة من سكان اي بلد، متى مارسوا التقنيات المتطورة في التأمل التجاوزي المعروفة بـ TM-Sidhis ، في الوقت والمكان نفسهما، فانهم يعطون النتيجة نفسها التي تحصل عند ممارسة ١٪ من السكان للتأمل التجاوزي في الوقت نفسه.

وقد استعان ماهاريشي بهذه النظرية وعقد لقاء لسبعة آلاف شخص في الولايات المتحدة، وهم يمثلون الجذر التربيعي للواحد في المئة من سكان الارض. وحين مارس هؤلاء تقنيات استعمال الحقل الموحد بواسطة التأمل التجاوزي حصلت تطورات مهمة في العالم، على كل الصعد الاقتصادية والسياسية والاجتماعية. وقد اعدت مراكز الابحاث التابعة لجامعة ماهاريشي العالمية، رسوماً بيانية فصّلت نسبة النزعة الايجابية التي حصلت على كل الصعد.

والاطلاع على هذه الرسوم يمكن ملاحظة تأثير التناغم الذي حصل بين ٧٠٠٠ شخص، على وضع العالم.

وانطلاقا من هذه التجربة جدد ماهاريشي دعوته الى العالم للاعتماد على هذه الطريقة لتحقيق السلام العالمي.

وقد نشرت الـ"واشنطن بوست" والنسخة العالمية من الـ"هيرالد تريبيون" والـ"وال ستريت جورنال" اعلاناً عن هذه الحركة يدعو الى دعم مؤسسة ماهاريشي للسلام العالمي بمبلغ مئة مليون دولار، للمساهمة في تحقيق

السلام العالمي عن طريق تغطية مصاريف اقامة ١٠٧٠٠٠ انسان (الجذر التربيعي لـ١٪ من سكان الارض مع الاحتياط)، في الهند، لاستعمال الحقل الموحد في الوقت نفسه، عبر ممارسة التقنيات المتطورة من التأمل التجاوزي.

وفي الاعلان اشارة الى ان السلام العالمي اصبح مسؤولية الافراد بعد فشل الحكومات في كل دول العالم في تأمين السلام والطمأنينة للافراد.

ويدعو الاعلان الافراد الى اخذ المبادرة بمحاربة الارهاب عبر نشر السلام العالمي ودعم مشروعه؛ لأن السلام العالمي اصبح ضرورة شخصية وملحة لاي انسان في العالم.

وقد جاء هذا الاعلان بعد ختام "الالعاب الاولمبية للطيران اليوغي" التي جرت مبارياتها النهائية في واشنطن، يوم الاربعاء ٩ تموز الماضي. وشملت هذه الالعاب مباريات في "الطيران" بدون حواجز مسافة ٥٠ متراً، و"الطيران" مع حواجز مسافة ٣٥ متراً، و"القفز العالي" و"القفز الطويل". وقد شارك في المباريات النهائية عشرون رجلا وثلاث عشرة امرأة.

واراد المنظمون ان تأخذ هذه المباريات طابع العلنية، ليتمكنوا من لفت العالم الى الامكانات التي يمكن ان يفوز بها من يمارس التقنيات المتطورة من التأمل التجاوزي. فغطى المباريات ٢٥ فريقاً تلفزيونياً واكثر من مئة مصور.

وفي حفلة الافتتاح القى بضعة مسؤولين في جامعة ماهاريشي العالمية كلمات شددت على الحاجة الى السلام اليوم وعلى دور مشروع ماهاريشي في صنع السلام العالمي.

٨٠٠٠ معاهدة سلام

وكان الدكتور نيل باترسون، "الحاكم العام للحكومة العالمية لعصر الاستنارة في اميركا الشمالية" بدأ كلمة الافتتاح بالآتي:

"على مر الاجيال انصب اهتمام الشعوب على خلق السلام العالمي، ولكن يتبين للجميع اليوم ان كل الجهود التي بذلت لخلق السلام العالمي فشلت". استطاع احد علماء التاريخ ان يحصي ثمانية آلاف معاهدة سلام عقدت منذ القرن العاشر قبل الميلاد حتى اليوم،

لبنان: مهارشيو التأمل التجاوزي ٢٠٠٠ و ١٧٥٠ دهم يستطيعون الطيران!

٣ - على صعيد كل مدينة: الحاجة الى ممارسة الجذر التربيعي من ١٪ من السكان لهذه التقنيات فيحصل التقدم والاكتفاء لدى كل عائلة وتتحسن الادارة. ويؤدي تراكم السلام في المدن الى سلام على مستوى كل دولة ثم الى سلام عالمي.

روح الالعاب الاولمبية

بعد الدكتور كيرلغ، افتتح الدكتور باترسون المباريات بكلمة مقتضبة اثار فيها نقطة مهمة وهي انه ذكر بأن تقليد التنافس الذي حوله الاغريق الى العاب اولمبية عام ٧٧٦ قبل الميلاد، كان يهدف الى احلال السلام؛ وانه لسوء الحظ لم تنجح الالعاب الاولمبية في تحقيق الهدف منها، الهدف الاساسي؛ وتحولت مع الوقت الى تقليد رياضي لا قيمة سياسية له، وليس من اهدافه

واعطى الدكتور كينغ "العلامات" التي يمكن من خلالها معرفة نجاح الخطوات على الصعد الثلاثة المذكورة آنفاً:

١ - على صعيد العالم: وقف الحرب العراقية - الايرانية، الحوار بين القوى العظمى، نزع الارهاب، وقف التنافس بين القوى العظمى، نمو التجارة الدولية والصناعية.

٢ - على صعيد كل دولة: وقف الحروب الاهلية، دعم مجموعات الشعب للدولة، اغناء الحياة الوطنية، زيادة مصادر الدخل القومي، تنظيم الحياة على المستوى القومي بموجب قانون الطبيعة، ازدهار التجارة الداخلية والصناعية.

٣ - على مستوى كل مدينة: تحسن الادارات وقد باعمال ناجحة، عدم خرق القوانين، التصرف بايجابية من قبل جميع السكان.

احلال السلام العالمي.

ثم القى عدد من المسؤولين في جامعة مهاريشي كلمات دعت الى تحقيق السلام العالمي عن طريق تسهيل لقاء ٧٠٠٠ شخص في الهند عبر المساعدة (المادية).

وشرح الدكتور ر. كايث والاس رئيس اللجنة العالمية للصحة الكاملة ورئيس قسم العلوم الفيزيولوجية والبيولوجية في جامعة مهاريشي، الفرق بين ممارسي التأمل التجاوزي والآخرين. فقال ان ممارسي هذه التقنية يبدون.

لابن واتسون بطل القفز العالي (٢٤،٧٥ انش).

العلامة وقف حرب الخليج

تلاه في الكلام الدكتور كيرلغ كينغ، المدير العام لـ"معهد مهاريشي لقيادة العالم". وقد ركز الدكتور كينغ في كلمته على ما يريده مهاريشي من خلال طرحه لمشروع السلام العالمي. ففصل النقاط الثلاث الاساسية لصنع السلام واتناغم:

١ - على الصعيد العالمي: الحاجة الى ٧٠٠٠ شخص يمارسون دائماً التقنيات المتطورة للتأمل التجاوزي؛ وهذا مشروع مهاريشي ناغار في الهند.

٢ - على صعيد كل دولة: الحاجة الى ممارسة الجذر التربيعي من ١٪ من سكان كل دولة لهذه التقنيات لايجاد وعي قومي مما يوطد اسس السلام العالمي.

ولم تستمر اكثرها حظاً اكثر من تسع سنين. وفي نهاية الحرب العالمية الاولى انشئت عصبة الامم لتؤكد ان تلك الحرب كانت "حرب انهاء كل الحروب"؛ وبعد عشرين سنة اندلعت الحرب العالمية الثانية، وفي ١٩٤٥ انشئت هيئة الامم المتحدة لتضع حداً للحروب نهائياً، ومنذ ١٩٤٥ حتى اليوم، احصى احد علماء التاريخ مئة وخمسين حرباً".

واضاف: "لا المفاوضات السياسية ولا المعاهدات ولا استعمال الاسلحة قادرة على خلق حال سلام دائم".

ومن جملة ما قاله انه لا يجوز ان نسمح بأن يكرر التاريخ ذاته لان في هذا التكرار، هذه المرة، محوا للتاريخ.

وانهى كلامه بالقول: "اننا واثقون كلياً من قدرتنا على خلق سلام عالمي دائم، الآن".

تسلية بالارقام

يقولون ان كلفة جمع ١٠٠٠٠ شخص تبلغ سنوياً ١٠٠ مليون دولار، اي، اذا اعتبرنا الدولار بـ٤٥ ليرة: ٤،٥ مليارات ليرة لبنانية. فتكون كلفة الشخص الواحد يومياً: ١٢٣٢،٨٧ ليرة لبنانية.

فاذا كنا في لبنان نحتاج الى ٢٠٠ شخص لتحقيق السلام، تبلغ القيمة اليومية الواجب دفعها ٢٤٦٥٧٤ ليرة التي تساوي سنوياً ٨٩٩٩٩٥١١ ليرة لبنانية، فيكون المبلغ الواجب على كل لبناني ان يدفعه، اذا اعتبرنا ان سكان لبنان ٤ ملايين نسمة: ٢٢،٤٩ ليرة لبنانية، لنقل ٢٢ ليرة ونصفاً.

هل ان احداً من اللبنانيين لا يدفع هذا المبلغ لتحقيق السلام؟ انهم يصرفون على اللوتو واليانصيب والفانوس لسحري (البدعة الجديدة) اكثر عن هذا بكثير.

MAHARISHI'S PROGRAMME TO CREATE

عضواً، اصغر بـ١٢ سنة من عمرهم الحقيقي، خاصة متى كانوا في اعمار تقرب من الشيخوخة.

واشار الى ان عدد المرات التي يستعمل فيها ممارسو التأمل التجاوزي والتقنيات المتطورة منه (Sidhis) بطاقات تأمينهم الصحي ٥٠٪ اقل من الآخرين.

لبنان كمثال

ثم تكلم رئيس قسم علم النفس في الجامعة، الدكتور دافيد اورم - جونسون على فائدة التقنيات المتطورة للتأمل التجاوزي، من خلال عرضه لـ٣٢ دراسة اجريت في العالم عن تأثير هذه التقنيات على الوضع في العالم. واستشهد بمثل عن لبنان جاء فيه:

"في دراسة لاحداث الشرق الاوسط عام ١٩٨٣، وجدنا انه من تغير عدد ممارسي الطيران اليوغي في القدس كان لهذا تأثير على عدد قتلى الحرب في لبنان. فعندما كان الممارسون كثراً، كان عدد القتلى اقل. والعكس. وقد قمنا بدراسات عديدة على هذا الموضوع بالذات للتأكد من ان الامر ليس ممكناً حصوله فتوصلنا الى ان ما حصل هو امر جديد وغير متوقع. وكانت تجربة ناجحة جاءت بالنتائج التي كنا ابلغناها الى علماء في اسرائيل والولايات المتحدة...".

وتحدث رئيس قسم الفيزياء الدكتور جون هاجلين فبين الفرق بين الفيزياء الكلاسيكية والفيزياء الكمية. وقال ان نظريات التجاذب النيوتنية والنسبية الاينشتاينية لا تدعم الطيران اليوغي. وبين كيف ان الطيران اليوغي يبرهن على اهمية القوة الموجودة داخل النظام العصبي البشري. ورأى في هذه القوة اساساً صالحاً لتطبيق مشروع مهاريشي للسلام العالمي.

بعد كل هذه الكلمات المهمة لأنما تبين مختلف جوانب مشروع مهاريشي للسلام العالمي، بدأت المباريات النهائية العلنية لتبرهن للعالم على القدرة التي يمكن ان يصل اليها

الانسان في التحكم بالتفاعلات داخل جسمه. وكم كانت دهشة الصحافيين عظيمة حين بدأت اجسام المشاركين ترتفع في الهواء وتطير بقفزات متلاحقة.

هكذا يطيرون ولهذا

ولكن، قد يتبادر الى ذهن القارىء السؤال: كيف يتم الطيران؟ كيف يحقق السلام العالمي؟

في الفيزياء الكمية Quantique مبدأ يقول انه كلما انخفضت حرارة احد الاجسام تصل حركة العناصر الكهربائية الموجودة فيه الى الانتظام. وكلما اقتربنا من درجة الصفر المطلق (Zéro absolu)، التي تساوي - ٢٧٣ درجة مئوية نقترب من الانتظام الكامل للالكترونات.

وقد اجرى احد علماء الفيزياء ميسنر Meissner اختبارات على المعادن يهمنا منها الاختبار الآتي: اذا عرّضنا جسماً من معدن معين لحقل مغناطيسي فان الفوضى تدب في الالكترونات هذا الجسم. اما اذا كانت حرارته منخفضة حتى الصفر المطلق، فان الانتظام الموجود داخله يجعله في مأمن من تأثير الحقل المغناطيسي.

وهذا هو المبدأ المعتمد في شرح تأثير استعمال تقنيات الحقل الموحد: فالتناغم حين يحصل بين بضعة اشخاص يؤدي الى الطيران اليوغي ظاهرياً. ولكنه يؤدي بالفعل الى تناغم فكري يعمل فيه دماغ كل المشاركين على الموجة نفسها (بالمستوى نفسه) وهذا يجعلهم في مأمن من التأثيرات الخارجية.

وهناك مثال آخر مهم و مثال اللمبة والليزر. فمبدأ الاضاءة بين اللمبة والليزر واحد ولكن انتظام اقل من ١٪ من الالكترونات المكونة للمبة هو في اساس وجود الليزر. وهذا الانتظام اعطى الليزر تلك القوة في الاختراق والسرعة في الحركة. وهكذا فحين ينتظم ١٪ من السكان بواسطة التأمل التجاوزي يعطون نتيجة افضل من السكان الذي يعيشون في فوضى. ويكفي، كما قلنا، الجذر التربيعي (١٪) من السكان، في ممارسي الـ TM-Sidhis ليخلقوا نظاماً متناسقاً داخل المجتمع يصبح في مأمن من التأثيرات الخارجية.

هذا هو مشروع مهاريشي للسلام العالمي. وهو، كما ترى، مشروع جديد لأنه، كما يقول احد المسؤولين من جامعة مهاريشي: "كل الوسائل القديمة من معاهدات ومنظمات دولية، ومحادثات نزع السلاح وحتى امتلاك جيوش كبيرة العدد، اثبتت فشلها".

لبنان ليس بعيداً

اللبناني، كما هو معروف عنه، يحب الصرعات. لذا نراه السبّاق في المنطقة الى تبني كل التيارات الجديدة التي يسمع بها. ومن هذا المنطلق اصبح عدد "المهاريشيين" الذين يمارسون التأمل التجاوزي يربو على الالفين و١٧٥ منهم قادرون على الطيران بواسطة استعمال التقنيات المتطورة للتأمل التجاوزي TM-Sidhis.

ويقول السيد بيار بشارة، احد المدربين على تقنيات التأمل التجاوزي: "يلزمنا في لبنان ٣٠٠ خبير يمارسون التأمل التجاوزي المتطور Sidhis حتى تزيد الدفعة الايجابية في البلد وتنتهي الحرب". واعطى مثالاً على ذلك اجتماعاً حصل في احد الفنادق في برمانا في آذار ١٩٨٤، ضم ٧٥ خبيراً كانوا يمارسون معاً التقنيات المتطورة من ١ الى ١٧ آذار. وبنتيجة مراقبة الاوضاع في تلك الفترة لاحظوا وقف القصف عن المنطقة التي كانوا فيها وتحسن السياسة الداخلية وقيام دعوات حوار. ولكن المشكلة تكمن في انه يجب ان يكون ٣٠٠ شخص في مكان واحد وعلى مدار السنة ليحصل تناغم على مستوى البلد. وما يعوق جمع ٣٠٠ شخص هي كلفة المشروع. لهذا فانهم يسعون الى اجراء اتصالات بالاماكن التي تضم عادة اكثر من ٣٠٠ شخص في وقت واحد، كالمدارس والمصانع الكبرى، والثكن العسكرية والمستشفيات.. وهكذا تحل مشكلة جمع الاشخاص ونحصل على السلام.

ويستشهد بأن شركة "الجنرال موتورز" الاميركية تسمح لعمالها بالتوقف عن العمل مدة ساعة يومياً لممارسة التأمل التجاوزي صباحاً ومساء. وتشير الدراسات الى ان العامل حين "يتأمل" صباحاً فانه يعطي عملاً بنوعية افضل خلال ساعات عمله السبع. وتعتمد المصانع اليابانية هذه الطريقة. وتتبنى حكومة الصين الشعبية مشروعاً مماثلاً لادخاله على البرامج التربوية...

وهكذا نرى انه على رغم تزايد المادية في مجتمعنا الحديث ما زال هناك اشخاص يهتمون بالروحانيات، بل ويراهنون عليها لتحقيق اغلى امنية الا وهي السلام العالمي.

وان كان لا بد من كلمة اخيرة نشير

عصام عازوري

نتائج فيرفيلد كما نشرتها جامعة مهاريشي

الى ان نظريات مهاريشي تشبه اقوال كوبرنيك الذي قال وهو يموت: "ومع هذا فهي تدور" (الارض) حصراً على الاكتشاف الذي اضطهد بسببه والذي ثبت انه صحيح.

خلال اللقاء الذي حصل في فيرفيلد ولاية ايوا الاميركية بين السادس عشر من كانون الاول ١٩٨٣ والسادس من كانون الثاني ١٩٨٤، والذي ضم ٧٠٠٠ شخص يمثلون الجذر التربيعي لواحد في المئة من سكان الارض، تمت ملاحظة ايجابيات عديدة على صعيد السلام الدولي. وقد اصدرت جامعة مهاريشي دراسة علمية عن تطور الاوضاع قبل اللقاء وخلاله وبعده ووزعت رسوم بيانية تمثل نسبة تطور النزعات الايجابية بالمقارنة مع النزعات السلبية:

I ‏ تزايد الايجابية في الاحداث اللبنانية. (المصدر: جريدة "النهار" اللبنانية)

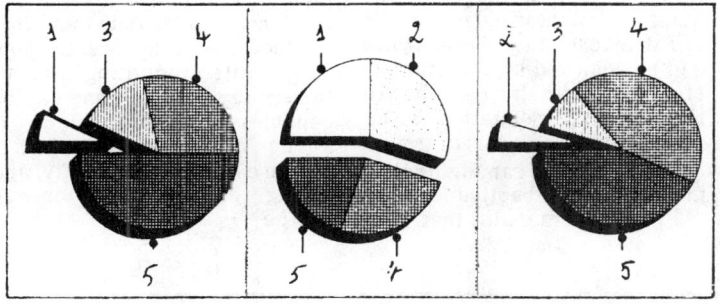

٣ اسابيع قبل اللقاء ‏- ٣ اسابيع خلال اللقاء ‏- ٣ اسابيع بعد اللقاء

1 ‏- احداث ايجابية جدا   3 ‏- شروط سلبية ثابتة   4 ‏- احداث سلبية
2 ‏- احداث ايجابية   5 ‏- احداث سلبية جدا

II ‏ تزايد الايجابية في الاحداث الدولية (المصدر: جريدة نيويورك تايمز).

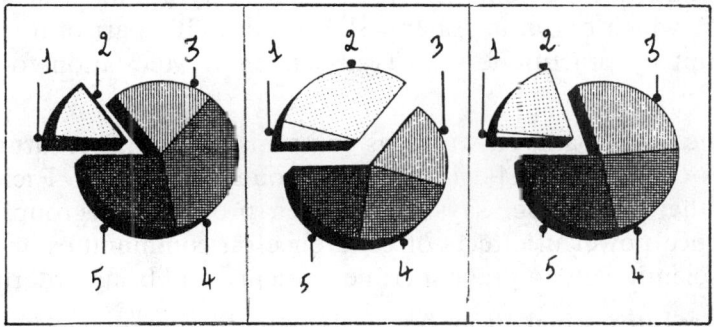

٣ اسابيع قبل اللقاء ‏- ٣ اسابيع خلال اللقاء ‏- ٣ اسابيع بعد اللقاء

MAHARISHI'S PROGRAMME TO CREATE

PRESS REPORTS FROM AFRICA AND THE MIDDLE EAST

South Africa • *The Star*

Johannesburg 15 August 1986 (English)

'Yogic flyers' are hopping for world peace

NEW DELHI — Thousands of meditators in 108 countries will levitate simultaneously today to contribute to world peace and combat terrorism.

The "yogic flyers" are practitioners of Transcendental Meditation, or TM, as taught by the Maharishi Mahesh Yogi.

TM teaches that world peace can be achieved by ordering activity of the human brain through deep meditation. Meditating together in large groups, adherants say, can neutralize negative and disruptive forces.

Practitioners claim that 7 000 people meditating together in one place can benefit the environment and reduce illness, crime and other world ills.

The Maharishi launched his programme for world peace in New Delhi last month with a public exhibition of "yogic flying," in which participants lifted off the ground, apparently hopping, while meditating. Practitioners say they will one day be capable of directed flight.

The Maharishi says that if people can hop, they can fly, and flying together will achieve peace.

South Africa • *Radio 702*

Johannesburg 15 August 1986 (English)

(....sounds of hopping.....)

Broadcaster: No, that is not a steam train or a heart afflicted by an erratic pacemaker, it's a very enthusiastic peacemaker. 702's Paul Gray attended a demonstration of "Yogic Flying" which began in Johannesburg today. It's part of a worldwide simultaneous attempt by practitioners of Transcendental Meditation to establish world peace.

Paul Gray: The participants sit with legs and arms crossed, feet turned up, and after a few minutes of meditation begin hopping around the floor....Richard Peycke, an instructor in the technnique, says it has been proved that groups yogic hopping together produce powerful effects of coherence on communities and he says it has been proved scientifically to prevent crime, violence and bring orderliness.

Richard Peycke: Interestingly, too, one finds an improvement in economic indicators.

Paul Gray: The programme to create world peace by Transcendental Meditation has been launched in 108 countries, and according to those in the know the hopping is the first stage to total hovering and eventual flight.

NOTE: Radio 702 is a popular music station and claims the largest listenership in South Africa (800,000 overall).

WORLD PEACE • GLOBAL INAUGURATION

PRESS REPORTS FROM AFRICA AND THE MIDDLE EAST

South Africa • *The Star*

Johannesburg 16 August 1986 (English)

Six men demonstrated how they could "fly" by means of transcendental meditation by hopping crosslegged on thick mats. There were similar demonstrations in 108 countries yesterday. ● Photograph: Garth Lumley.

Yogic 'hoppers' lift off to 'create world peace'

By Glenda Spiro

The first stage of people "flying" through transcendental meditation was launched in Johannesburg yesterday while similar demonstrations took place in 108 countries.

Six young men hopped crosslegged on mats, which they say is the first stage of Yogic flying. The next is hovering above ground and flying is the final stage. These have not yet been reached.

First the men meditated in front of a hushed audience. A soft bell rang and the men, seemingly in a trance started to twist and shake and then when the mood got them, bounced in the air backwards and forwards along nine thick mats.

They said they were completely aware of their actions while hopping and that it was a pleasurable sensation.

The aim of this unique exercise is ... to create world peace.

The Transcendental Meditation organisation says: "Maximum coherence in the brain functioning of individuals is created to radiate world consciousness, the basis for peace".

PRESS REPORTS FROM AFRICA AND THE MIDDLE EAST

South Africa • *The Citizen*

Johannesburg 16 August 1986 (English)

'Yogic flyers' hope to help bring peace

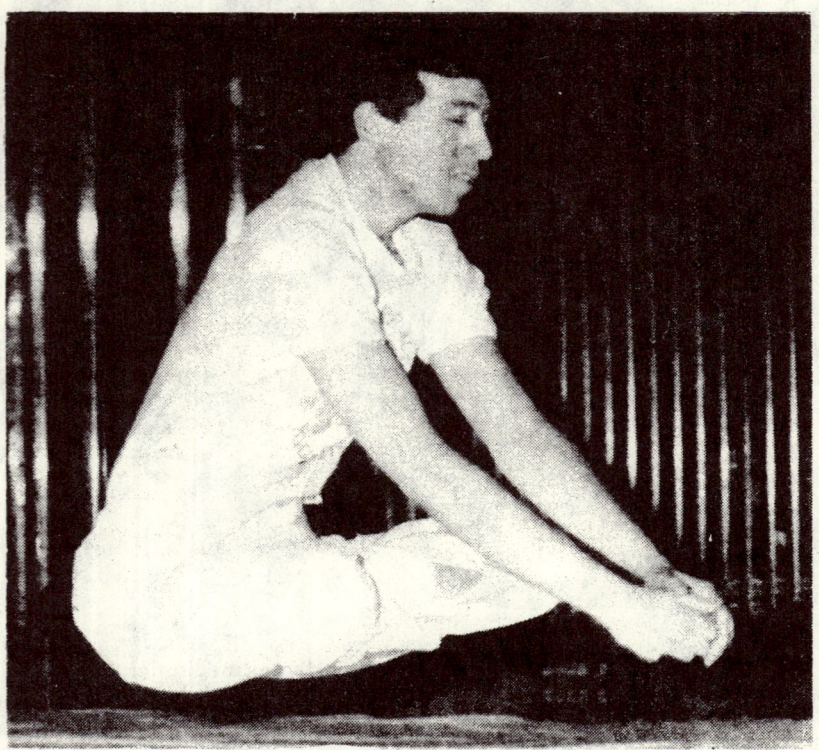

A young demonstrator goes through the technique of yogic flying while meditating, to bring permanent peace to the world. The programme was launched in over a 100 countries yesterday.

Citizen Reporter

THE desire for world peace and stability was the theme in 108 countries, including South Africa yesterday, when six young men from Transcendental Meditation organisation (TM) demonstrated for the first time the technique of "yogic flying".

The act of "flying" was created by "maximum coherance in the brain function of individuals "and the programme aims to meet the urgent need of our time to counteract violence and war and to create a constructive and peaceful interaction.

Members of the Press were given a demonstration of yogic flying at a Johannesburg hotel where the young men meditated for about five minutes and then bounded cross legged through the air.

The Citizen was told that the measured effects of yogic flying include reductions in violence, crime rates, hospital admissions and accident rates. In several countries progress towards peaceful resolutions of conflict had been measured.

The Press saw only the first stage of yogic flying — the hopping stage. The other two stages — which are much more difficult to execute, — are hovering while floating and finally actually flying.

The six demonstrators said they remained completely aware of their actions while hopping through the air and that they all felt a very pleasurable sensation.

The organisers said that to create a formula for peace in South Africa people needed to think more positively. They believe a group of 600 people collectively practising the programme of yogic flying twice a day would be required for a lasting peace.

WORLD PEACE • GLOBAL INAUGURATION

PRESS REPORTS FROM AFRICA AND THE MIDDLE EAST

South Africa • *Sunday Times*

Johannesburg   7 September 1986   (English)

BOUNCING UP: IT'S ALL IN THE MIND

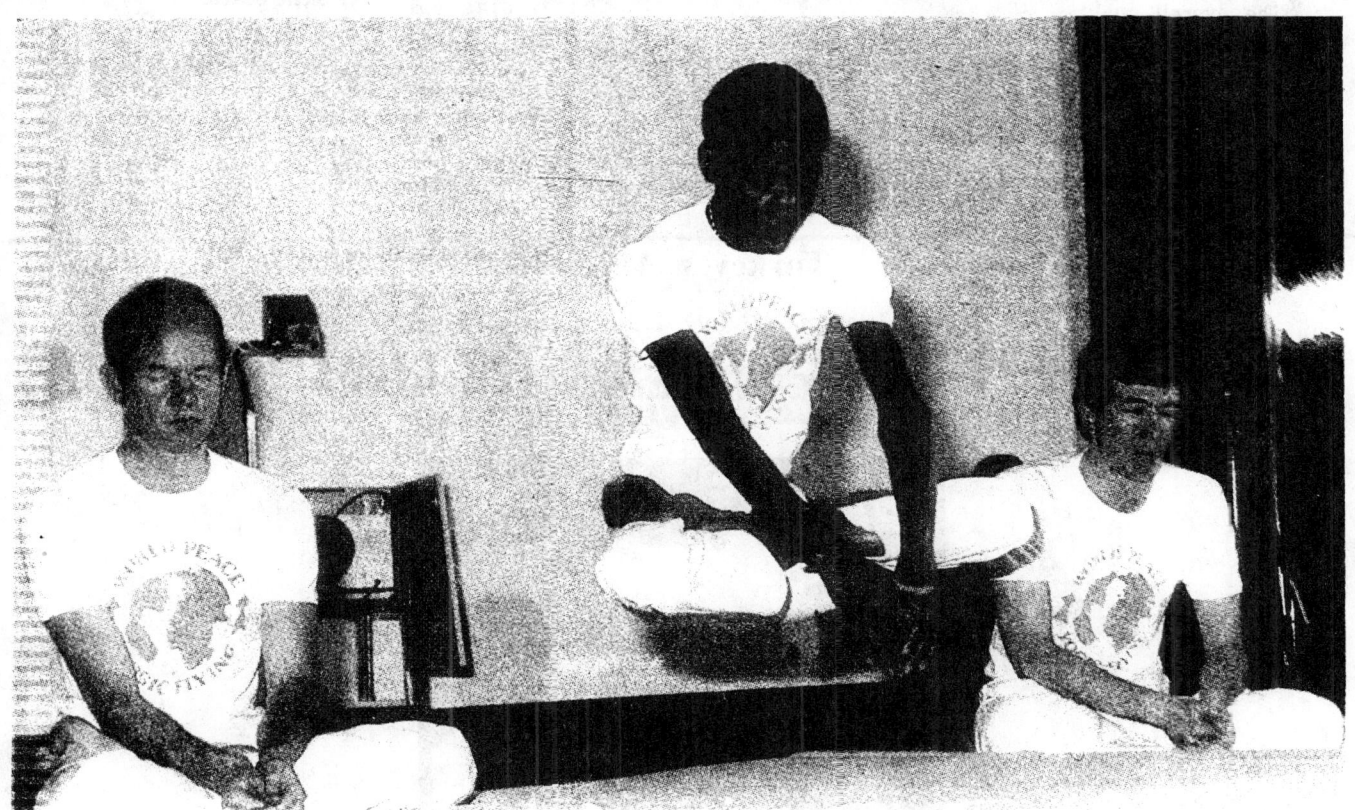

Airborne... George Khoza demonstrates the art of yogic flying

Wanted: 130 yogic fliers to beat Soweto crime

JUST 130 volunteers — willing to levitate through transcendental meditation — could bring peace to crime-riddled Soweto, says TM instructor George Khoza.

"It has been scientifically proved that by joining our classes you can influence the people around you to think as you do," he says.

"Through TM, you can achieve inner peace and influence those around you to feel the same.

"The aim is to bring permanent peace to the world by creating maximum coherence in the brain function of individuals."

Yogic flying was demonstrated in Johannesburg recently by several young men. Sitting cross-legged, they bounced up to hover briefly in the air — the first stage of levitation.

Practise

George says that people who practise this technique have found they are better able to cope with life — they become more dynamic, intelligent, clear-headed and balanced, and so more joyful.

MAHARISHI'S PROGRAMME TO CREATE

"Where several people in a community practise the technique, there has been a decrease in violence, crime, accidents, hospital admissions and other negative trends," he says.

"The overall quality of life in the society improves."

Another TM lecturer Mr Tom Mphatsoe, says: "Soweto needs only about 130 people practising yogic flying together twice a day to become the most creative peaceful, progressive and dynamic town in South Africa.

Pleasant

The men who demonstrated the yogic flying said they remained completely aware of their actions while in the air and added that it was a pleasant sensation.

George says: "It is obvious to everyone that all means used so far to achieve peace have failed.

"It is also clear that treaties, negotiations and bargaining can never create lasting peace in the world.

"Now we have a new and effective method which can bring peace to our country.

"The coherence of the brain produced when a person practises TM brings coherence in national consciousness, a sound basis for permanent peace.

"World peace is an age-old dream — only a new philosophy and new efforts can fulfil it," says George.

Turkey • *Milliyet*

Istanbul   11 July 1986   (Turkish)

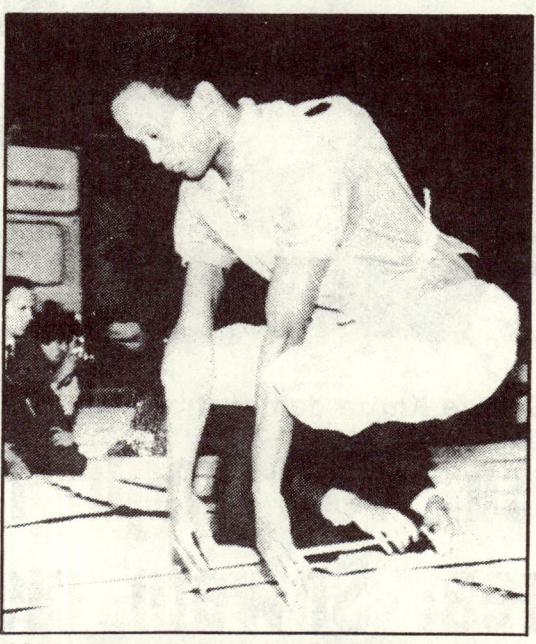

"Uçtu uçtu, adam uçtu"

UÇTU, uçtu, kuş uçtu" tekerlemesi artık değişti ve **"insan uçtu"** şeklini aldı. Washington'da düzenlenen bir gösteride **Eddie Gob** adındaki bir yogacı, çok sayıdaki gazetecinin önünde yerden 50 santim yükselmeyi başardı. Hint asıllı **Maharishi Mahesh Yogi** tarafından dünya çapında örgütlenen yoga kuruluşunun etkin üyelerinden olan **Gob**'un yer çekimini nasıl yok ederek bu işi başardığı konusunda fizikçilerin çok kafa yoracakları söyleniyor.

WORLD PEACE • GLOBAL INAUGURATION

PRESS REPORTS FROM AFRICA AND THE MIDDLE EAST

Turkey • *Günes*
Ankara   11 July 1986   (Turkish)

Yoga ile ayakları yerden kesildi

Uçan Amerikalı

GÖSTERİ sonrasında dakikalarca alkışlanan Gob, yoganın zihni ve bedeni dinlendiren en faydalı spor olduğunu söyledi

AMERİKALI ycgacı **Eddie Gob**, yüzlerce kişinin gözü önünde uçtu. Washington'da bir gösteri düzenleyen **Gob**'un ayakları yerden kesilirken, salondaki orta yaşlı birkadının bayıldığı bildirildi.

Uzun yıllardır yogayla uğraşan **Eddie Gob**, piri **Maharisni Mahesh Yogi**'nun bulduğu "**birleşik alan**" teknolojisinden örnekler verdiği gösterisinde "**IM-Sidhi**" uçuşunu büyük bir başarıyla uyguladı.

Gösteri sonrasında dakikalarca alkışlanan **Gob**, yoganın zihni ve bedeni dinlendiren en faydalı spor olduğunu söyledi. Çağımızın yaygın hastalığı stress ve bunalıma karşı yogayı öneren **Gob**, "**Bu işin içine gerçek anlamda giren, yoga huzurunun tadına varan biri, bir daha kolay kolay vazgeçemez**" dedi.

PRESS REPORTS FROM AFRICA AND THE MIDDLE EAST

Turkey • *Hayat*

Istanbul 25 August, 1986 (Turkish)

Uçan insanlar olimpiyatı

İnsanlar herhangi bir araç ve kas gücü kullanmadan uçabilir mi? Dünya kamuoyunda yıllardır merak konusu olan ve tartışılan bu nokta, geçtiğimiz günlerde Amerika'da çok ilginç bir gösteriye sahne oldu.

«1'inci Amerika Yogi Uçuşu Yarışması» adı altında gerçekleştirilen bu gösteride çeşitli kategorilerde altın, gümüş ve bronz madalyalar dağıtıldı.

Zaman zaman gazete ve dergiler, bazı özel zihinsel teknikler kullanan kişilerin yerden havalanabildikleri, uçtukları haberine resimli olarak yer veriyor. İnsanlar herhangi bir araç ve kas gücü kullanmadan uçabilir mi?

İlginç gösteri

Dünya kamuoyunda yıllardır merak konusu olan ve tartışılan bu nokta, geçtiğimiz günlerde Amerika'nın başkenti Washington'da «1'inci Amerika Yogi Uçuşu Yarışması» adı altında çok ilginç bir gösteriye sahne oldu. Pek çok ülkenin basın ve televizyonlarının da davet edildiği bu toplantıda, Transandantal Meditasyon Sidhi uçuş tekniğini kullanarak insanların da uçabileceği «Yogi Uçuşu» ile dünya basınına tanıtıldı.

«Yogi Uçuşu»nu gerçekleştiren kişiler ve bilim adamları, isteyen herkesin bu tekniği rahatlıkla uygulayabileceğini ve böylelikle dünya barışının bilimsel ve kalıcı bir şekilde gerçekleşebileceğini belirtiyorlar. Yandaki fotoğraflarda yarışmacılar uçuş esnasında görülüyor. Bu fotoğraflar tüm dünya basınında yayınlandı ve ilgiyle karşılandı.

(Lütfen sayfayı çeviriniz)

WORLD PEACE • GLOBAL INAUGURATION

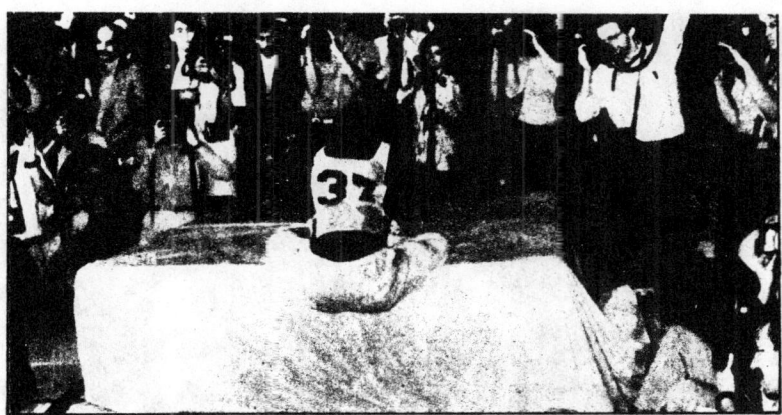

H 160'dan fazla üniversite ve araştırma enstitüsü, yaptıkları bilimsel araştırmalar ile, tekniğin hem kişi hem de toplum üzerine olan yararlarını inceliyor.

EEG beyin topografisi tabloları, beynin, işaretler ile belirtilmiş olan 4 EEG frekansından her biri için yukarıdan görülen ortalama bioelektriksel hareketini göstermektedir. Spektrum, giderek artan EEG sinyalinin gücünü belirten, mordan kırmızıya kadar bir sınır gösterir.

Nasıl uçuluyor?

TM-Sidhi «Yogi Uçuşu»nun eşsiz karakteristiği, uçuş sırasında, herhangi bir sıçrayış sırasında görünmeyen alfa ve teta dalgasının varlığıdır. Herhangi bir sıçrama derken, fiziksel güç kullanma kastedilmektedir. TM-Sidhi yogi uçuşunda ise (fiziksel güç kullanılmamakta) zihin en basit uyanıklık durumunda özel bir zihinsel teknik kullanmaktadır.

Kişisel yararları

TM ve TM-Sidhi programının gündelik yaşama çok güçlü etkileri olduğu belirtiliyor. Teknik sırasında derin bir dinlenmeye ulaşılması, daha sonra kişiye, çok hızlı bir tepki süresi, zekâ ve hafızada gelişme, yaratıcılıkta artış, akademik başarı, karakterde olumlu değişiklikler gibi yararlar sağladığı belirlenmiş. Kısaca, teknik fizyolojinin ve psikolojinin tüm performansını geliştiren, uyum ve tüm seviyelerdeki işlemlerde bütünlük ortaya çıkarıyor.

Dünya barışının bilimsel formülü

Uçuş sırasında, bedenin havalanacağı an, beyin çalışmasında en fazla uyum gerçekleşiyor. Araştırmalar, bu tekniğin grup halinde uygulanması ile, bireyin tekniği uygulamasından ortaya çıkan uyumun, tüm topluma, süper ışıma adı ile bilinen bir etki ile yayıldığını ortaya koymuş. Bu etkinin başka hiçbir şeyin etkileyemediği savaş zamanında bile barış ortamı sağladığı belirtiliyor.

Yetkililer, Türkiye'de tekniği öğrenmek isteyen kişilerin İstanbul'da Maharishi Birleşik Alan Teknolojisi Derneği'ne, Şair Nedim Cad. No: 78 Ceylan Apt. Beşiktaş (Tel: 158 69 43). İzmir'de, derneğin İzmir şubesine, Şair Eşref Blv. No: 58 Alsancak (Tel: 22 46 51). Ankara'da, Yaratıcı Zekâ Bilim ve Kültür Derneği'ne, Nergiz Sokağı 4/3 Çankaya (Tel: 27 67 26) başvurabileceklerini belirtiyorlar. Bu derneklerde halka açık konferanslar düzenleniyor ve teknik öğretiliyor.

Fizyoloji bölümü başkanı Dr. Keith Wallece (yanda) ve EEG beyin topografisi tabloları.

MAHARISHI'S PROGRAMME TO CREATE

Uçan insanlar olimpiyadı

Öğrenciler
Maharishi Uluslararası Üniversitesi öğrencileri üniversite başkanını dinlerken (yanda).

«Tarihi bir gün»
Üniversite başkanı Dr. Bevan Morris (sağda) konuşmasını yaparken, «Bu çok tarihi bir gün. Dünya barışı için gerekli olan teknolojinin elimizde olduğunu gösterdik» dedi...

WORLD PEACE • GLOBAL INAUGURATION

PRESS REPORTS FROM AFRICA AND THE MIDDLE EAST

Throughout Africa and the Middle East • *Global Photo*

New Delhi   21 August 1986   (English)

Editor's Note:

Ayurveda, the world's oldest scientific system of perfect heath, has been restored in its completeness by Maharishi. Maharishi Ayurveda includes all avenues of life—consciousness, physiology, behaviour, and environment. It offers perfect health for the individual and also perfect collective health for society, perfect collective health for the nation, and perfect collective health for all mankind—world health, which necessarily includes world peace, world prosperity, world happiness, and an ideal family of nations.

Maharishi Ayurveda recognizes that no problem in the world can be isolated from the field of health and that all problems of society are disorders of collective health. Such disorders, including economic failures, social unrest, crime, epidemics, international conflicts, and environmental imbalances, are identified by Maharishi Ayurveda as being caused by the violation of natural law by the individuals in society. In order to produce perfect health for the nation and the world as a whole, Maharishi Ayurveda prescribes group practice of the Maharishi Technology of the Unified Field—most specifically, the technique for 'yogic flying'.

Maharishi envisioned the possibility of creating world peace through the BALANCING PRINCIPLE of Ayurveda. As was discussed earlier in this book, scientific research has shown that this balancing principle is practically available through the Maharishi Technology of the Unified Field. The performance of 'yogic flying' reflects the perfect mind-body coordination displayed by an integrated individual and has been shown to produce maximum coherence in both individual brain physiology and in the collective consciousness of society as a whole.

The world-wide demonstrations of 'yogic flying' presented the balancing principle of Maharishi Ayurveda to create world peace. The following two articles on Maharishi Ayurveda were written in India at the time of the demonstrations there.

Maharishi Ayurveda— Medical Marvel Thousands of Years Old

By Amin Kassam

The Indian medical system of Ayurveda is thousands of years old. Today, under the guidance of Maharishi Mahesh Yogi, it is being revived in conformity with the ancient Ayurvedic texts as a complete system of health.

Ayurveda translates as 'the science of the knowledge of life', according to Dr. J. R. Raju, a prominent practitioner. The system uses herbal and mineral preparations which have the advantage of having no harmful side effects as do the artificial chemicals of modern medicine....

Ayurveda, Dr. Raju said, treats illness within a holistic framework. Herbal and mineral medicines are used to strengthen the body's defences for both prevention of illness as well as healing. In addition, there is a recognition that man is a part of nature and is affected by the biological and cosmic rhythms....

In Ayurveda, emphasis is also placed on improving the external environment through the advocacy of health-promoting practices on the individual as well as community level. Stress is combatted by encouraging meditation among patients.

The system seems to have been known internationally at one time. Western doctors have found similarities in theory and practice between Ayurveda and the Hippocratic tradition, including terminology that seems to have Vedic roots.

Throughout Africa and the Middle East • *Global Photo*

New Delhi   28 August 1986   (English)

Maharishi Ayurveda—
Your Pulse Tells More than You Think

By Amin Kassam

When you first meet Dr. R. J. Raju, the outstanding impression is of quiet humility. He seems to be bubbling with happiness and welcomes everyone without reserve.

He is a leading expert in the ancient medical system of Ayurveda, currently being restored to completeness by Maharishi Mahesh Yogi. There is nothing in his manner to indicate that he can perform feats which Western-trained doctors find astounding. He answers questions quietly, without holding back. As the interview unfolds, he gestures with animation, gazing straight back at you. He seems to have no secrets....

I ask him about Nadi Vigyana—pulse diagnosis, which enables an Ayurvedic doctor to diagnose illnesses without the use of medical instruments. He offers to demonstrate, takes my wrist, places three fingers on the artery and concentrates for a few seconds. Then he reels out a list of minor ailments I am suffering from at the moment—every one of them true. I watch him do the same thing for my companion, whom he has never met before, and one other person. Both confirm the correctness of his diagnosis.

It appears that none of us has serious problems. However, he has diagnosed serious illnesses before, even before there were symptoms to provide clues for Western-trained doctors.

What is the secret of Nadi Vigyana? Dr. Raju says all illnesses are caused by an imbalance in the Vata (nervous system), Pitta (metabolic system) or Kapha (physical constitution). An Ayurvedic practitioner listens to three different pulses on the wrist, using three fingers at the same time. Using a series of calculations, he can tell what part of the body is experiencing problems. At a finer level, other gradations are used to pinpoint diseases more exactly....

Dr. Balraj Maharshi, teacher of Dr. Raju, is a legend among Ayurvedic practitioners. He has given semi-public demonstrations of his pulse-reading skills in Western countries. But he is most noted for his ability to pick out herbal plants growing in the wild and specify their uses.

During a recent visit to Brazil, he is reputed to have walked through a forest with that country's leading herbalist, and to have not only identified plants already known to the herbalist but also others which the herbalist had known of through hearsay but which he had not been able to find.

Dr. Raju studied under Dr. Balraj Maharshi for eight years, as well as under other famous Ayurvedic specialists....

PRESS REPORTS FROM AFRICA AND THE MIDDLE EAST

Tunisia • *La Presse*

Tunis   7 September 1986   (French)

Au cours d'un concours international de lévitation en Inde, des hommes ont volé

GLOBALFOTO/NEWS, (NEW DELHI) — Un être humain peut-il défier la loi de la gravité ? Récemment à New Delhi en Inde, une centaine de journalistes et 8.000 spectateurs ont dû se rendre à l'évidence : il semble que la réponse soit oui.

C'était au cours du premier concours international de lévitation, organisé par des disciples du Maharishi Mahesh Yogi, fondateur de Mouvement de Méditation Transcendantale. Le mouvement attire des adeptes du monde entier et de toutes les couches sociales : du simple paysan en passant par l'homme d'affaires, le cadre professionnel, jusqu'au général d'armée et le ministre.

«Spectacle de danse yogique» annonçaient les affiches. Au programme de la soirée : un 25 mètres haie, saut en hauteur, saut en longueur et un sprint de 50 mètres, le tout à accomplir dans la position du lotus (position de méditation, assis les jambes croisées).

Des matelas en mousse recouverts de draps blancs séparés par des bandes rouges constituaient les «pistes» de course. Pendant les discours préliminaires au concours, certains journalistes peu crédules ont testé les matelas en marchant dessus dans l'espoir de découvrir quelque subterfuge. Mais les matelas étaient bel et bien des matelas ordinaires.

Par petits bonds d'un mètre

Un lourd silence s'abat sur la foule dans le stade couvert Indira Gandhi. La première course va commencer : le 25 mètres haie (les haies en l'occurrence sont des rouleaux de tissu de 15 cm de hauteur). Vêtus de grand pantalons blancs et chemises de couleur, les concurrents s'alignent pour le départ.

Tous les spots, les caméras et les vidéos sont braqués sur eux et les concurrents ferment les yeux. Quelques minutes de méditation et soudain certains se mettent en branle.

On ne peut pas dire qu'ils «volent» vraiment. Ils avancent plutôt par une série de petits bonds d'environ un mètre de longueur. Certains ont les bras en l'air alors que d'autres se tiennent les pieds pour les empêcher de traîner au sol. Quelques-uns s'appuient très légèrement sur les mains frôlant le sol après chaque bond. Mais les mains touchent à peine terre et ne peuvent donc pas les aider à se propulser en l'air.

Les spectateurs n'en croyaient pas leurs yeux, certains sont d'ailleurs resté sceptiques jusqu'au bout en disant que l'exploit pouvait être accompli par un athlète qui aurait suivi un entraînement intensif.

Selon les organisateurs du concours, des tests effectués à l'électroencéphalogramme (EEG-enregistrement de l'activité électrique du cerveau), ont révélé qu'il n'y avait aucun changement dans les courbes enregistrées chez les méditants lorsqu'ils se déplacent ainsi. Or si une personne effectue des «bonds» de la sorte grâce à la force physique et musculaire, un changement visible s'opère.

Dans l'apprentissage du «vol yogique», le déplacement par petits «bonds» est le premier stade. Les concurrents ont tous participé à cette épreuve. Pour les plus avancés, le second stade est la capacité de rester suspendu dans l'air. Plus difficile encore est de «voler» dans une direction précise.

Mis à part la curiosité suscitée par ces course extraordinaires, le concours avait un côté sérieux : il faisait partie d'une série de cérémonies qui ont marqué l'inauguration du programme pour la paix dans le monde élaboré par le Maharishi.

Une conférence maximum

Selon le grand maître, l'esprit fonctionne de manière plus cohérente grâce à la méditation poussée. Un individu atteint la «cohérence maximum», quand toutes les parties de son cerveau fonctionnent en harmonie. C'est à ce moment là que le corps peut s'élever du sol pour accomplir de petits «bonds».

Cette harmonie cérébrale est visible à l'EEG. Une démonstration a d'ailleurs été pratiquée au cours de cette soirée pour convaincre même les plus sceptiques. Sur un écran géant, les spectateurs ont pu voir que les courbes électroniques devenaient de plus en plus régulières à mesure que l'individu se plongeait dans une méditation de plus en plus profonde.

Au niveau de la cohérence maximale, le cerveau puise dans le «réservoir universel», appelé «champ unifié». C'est de là que découle toute chose de la nature, selon le Maharishi. Puisque la nature entière est reliée à ce «champ unifié», elle peut bénéficier de l'harmonie qui se dégage de la méditation.

Ainsi certaines tendances négatives au sein de la société tels le crime et la violence pourraient être contrecarrées, selon la théorie du grand maître.

Pour le Maharishi, les guerres qui sévissent dans le monde ne sont pas uniquement le résultat de la course moderne aux armements. «Pensez qu'il y a plusieurs siècles, les bombes et les fusils n'existaient pas. La terre était-elle sans conflit ? Il y avait de terribles batailles. Tout, le positif comme le négatif, se passe au niveau de la conscience», dit-il.

Des membres du mouvement dirigé par le Maharishi ont consulté une longue liste de documents d'où ils ont tiré le conclusion suivante : si la racine carrée d'un pour cent de la population — ce qui représente 7.000 âmes à l'heure actuelle — pratiquaient une méditation continue à un endroit précis, elles pourraient contrecarrer la négativité dans le monde entier.

Des études ont d'ailleurs révélé un lien entre la pratique de la méditation et une baisse du niveau de criminalité dans plusieurs villes des Etats-Unis.

Quand à la lévitation, elle ne peut être réalisée, selon les adeptes, que quant le méditant a atteint le niveau de cohérence maximale et se trouve en relation avec le «champ unifié».

Ce n'est qu'à ce moment là et avec la bonne impulsion mentale que le champ de gravité autour de l'individu peut être manipulé, d'où la lévitation.

Peu importe si l'on accepte ou non les théories du Maharishi, la démonstration de la «danse yogique» prouve bien que la science moderne ne peut rejeter d'emblée les choses qu'elle ne sait expliquer.

WORLD PEACE • GLOBAL INAUGURATION

EUROPE

Inaugurating Maharishi's Programme to Create World Peace
EUROPE

From Athens to Dublin and Warsaw to Lisbon, European experts in the Maharishi Technology of the Unified Field inaugurated Maharishi's Programme to Create World Peace.

Portugal and Spain

Two inaugurations in Portugal, one in **Lisbon** and another in **Oporto,** and demonstrations in **Madrid**, **Barcelona**, and **Vitoria,** Spain, brought Maharishi's formula for world peace to the people of the Iberian peninsula.

France

Across the Pyrenees, **Marseilles** was one of 14 cities in France that witnessed Maharishi's mechanics to eliminate terrorism and war. The next day, one of the Marseilles newspapers, *Le Meridional*, published an article under the headline, 'Hop! Hop! Hop! "Yogic Flying" for ... world peace'. Using words reminiscent of man's first moon landing, a newspaper in **Tours**, *Le Nouvelle République du Centre-Ouest,* captioned a photograph of 'yogic flyers' in mid-air, 'A little hop for a man, a great leap for mankind.'

People in **Rennes, Brest, Vesoul, Lille**, and **Nantes** first saw 'yogic flying' in mid-September, and by the end of the month the residents of six other cities in France had witnessed demonstrations. One publisher featured 'yogic flying' in the lead article of a new magazine and used the article nationally in radio and television promotional advertising.

At the **Paris** demonstration, journalists from many newspapers, including *Le Monde*, asked TM-Sidhas about the value of this technique for France. One Sidha replied, 'Scientists say that if a large group of people in a country practises 'yogic flying', coherence will increase in that nation. So many positive changes have occurred in my life since I started, I really feel that they can only be right. This is why I hope that such demonstrations in France and throughout the world will inspire more people to learn this practice.'

Switzerland

While the superpowers' negotiators in **Geneva** sought peace through nuclear arms control, an article in the *Tribune de Genève* offered a more practical and effective means to establish peace. Dated 23 July, the article was headlined, 'World competition—levitating for peace'. Reporting on the New Delhi competition held two days earlier, the article said, 'When a sufficient number of people practise meditation together ... they become capable of creating a powerful influence to eliminate disharmonies, international terrorism, and even the rivalry between the superpowers.'

Three weeks later, Geneva had its own demonstration of 'yogic flying'. It was attended by seven journalists, including representatives of the news services Agence France Presse and Schweiz Depeschen Agentur. Simultaneously, a demonstration in Seelisberg introduced Maharishi's programme to major media from throughout Switzerland. The largest French-language paper in the country, *24 Heures*, wrote, 'In their beautiful headquarters, Maharishi European Research University on Lake Lucerne, the practitioners of Transcendental Meditation ... have unveiled their secrets ... in a packed room where TV cameras and photographic flashes added to the atmosphere of great importance.'

Beneath an enormous banner reading, 'Maharishi's Programm zur Schaffung des Weltfriedens, Die Grundlage des Weltfriedens: Kohärentes Funktionieren der Gehirnphysiologie' ('Maharishi's Programme to Cre-

WORLD PEACE • GLOBAL INAUGURATION

INAUGURATING MAHARISHI'S PROGRAMME TO CREATE WORLD PEACE—EUROPE

ate World Peace; Coherently Functioning Brain Physiology, the Unit of World Peace'), eight TM-Sidhas flew for the cameras. A long report was aired that night on Swiss television's national evening news, and on 18 August a reporter wrote in *Il Dovere*, 'After five minutes of meditation, they succeeded in hopping, raising the body in the air with incredible jumps of 30-40 centimetres high and one metre in length with crossed legs and closed eyes.'

Said the *Tages-Anzeiger* of Zurich, 'After they landed, their faces had an expression of bliss. They were smiling and laughing.' Wondering whether the flying was a muscular or mental feat, the author wrote that he observed no perspiration on the 'yogic flyers'.

Commented one observer, 'The quality of silence that preceded the actual "yogic flying" demonstration was in itself a tremendous experience—very unique and very pacifying. The sight of these people taking off into the air and hopping so lightly and effortlessly, looking so serene and happy, was very inspiring, and one could feel the effect of their practice on the whole surroundings. From this I could imagine that a big group practising together must have the ability to create peace and harmony in the world.'

Italy

In Italy, the organizers called the demonstrations, 'Very successful—beyond any optimistic expectations.' At the inauguration in **Brunate** on Lake Como, the hall was decorated with many banners, including one that read, 'La Sede Della Pace Mondiale—La Fisiologia Del Cervello Che Funziona Coerentemente' ('The Seat of World Peace—Coherently Functioning Brain Physiology'). Among the 160 people in the hall was Brunate's mayor, Mr Angelo Donede, who spoke during the ceremonies. National Italian television and four of Italy's leading daily newspapers attended, as did members of the local press. Their headlines announced, 'TM to pacify planet', and 'Meditation and flying against stress and wars'.

Thirteen TM-Sidhas demonstrated 'yogic flying' in Brunate. One of them was a Catholic priest, who said of his experience during the demonstration, 'I felt great energy and experienced a deep sense of fellowship with everyone, including the audience.' He added, 'The journalists were very impressed by the joy that was obvious on our faces.'

After the demonstration one television journalist commented, 'I noticed that all the people in the hall, every one of them, were calm, serene, and happy. I had never seen that before at any place I have visited. I was very impressed.'

Il Giorno wrote, 'Observers were open-mouthed with amazement watching the people levitating.' Another article said, 'They were making hops 30-40 centimetres high and one metre long, but afterwards they appeared perfectly rested.'

Corriere della Sera said that one of the TM-Sidhas (a businessman), 'who hopped with perfect freedom, explained that this experience not only makes him happy but also more creative in his work.' Another article quoted a famous Italian football star who was present at the demonstration as saying, 'With TM I feel more light, clear, and calm. Everyone should meditate. They will find serenity.'

La Notte said, 'For some, the 15th of August in Brunate marked the beginning of a new age for mankind.'

At the special request of ANSA, the Italian news agency, and of other media that had been unable to attend the 15 August event, a second demonstration was held in Brunate. It was attended by 140 people, including local government officials. On 13 September, further demonstrations were given in **Torino**, **Trieste**, **Modena**, and **Firenze**, and on the following day in **Livorno**.

Greece

Across the Adriatic, demonstrations were given on 15

INAUGURATING MAHARISHI'S PROGRAMME TO CREATE WORLD PEACE—EUROPE

August in **Athens** and **Thessaloniki**, Greece.

Yugoslavia

In Yugoslavia, there were four events. In **Ljubljana**, the capital of Slovenia, 80 people attended a conference and press briefing on Maharishi's programme. It was preceded by a 20-minute interview with TM-Sidhas on one of Yugoslavia's most popular radio programmes. Two demonstrations were held in **Budva**, a vacation resort on the Adriatic coast: one attracted 250 people to the Zeta Film Hall and the second, sponsored by Sloveska Plaza, the tourist centre, drew 1,000 guests as well as members of the local press.

The grand event in Yugoslavia was held in **Belgrade's** principal conference hall, the Sava Congress Centre. It was jointly sponsored by TV Novosti, a newspaper, a Belgrade factory, and a department store. One hundred journalists came, including representatives from national television and radio. Radio broadcasts preceding the Belgrade demonstration helped to bring more than 2,500 Yugoslavs to see seven of their countrymen fly for world peace. The crowd grew so large that two additional wings of the hall had to be opened, and even then many people had to stand outside and watch through the doorways. TV Novosti reported the next day, 'It was unprecedented for Belgrade that so many people came for one lecture.'

Two neurophysiologists and a professor of political science from the local university introduced Maharishi's Programme to Create World Peace. Then came the 'yogic flying'.

'Almost unbelievably,' TV Novosti continued, 'at the request of the organizers, silence fell in the crowded hall for ten minutes as the seven practitioners were meditating with eyes closed.'

Then, the report said, 'A wonder happened! Three of them, to the great excitement of the visitors, without any movements of hips or legs and with straight spines, sitting in the Yoga position, suddenly started to lift up and land without any effort.... One visitor said, "To call it only hopping is nonsense and ridiculous. .." A journalist said, "I was looking carefully to the right of the stage. I saw one of them ... suddenly start to lift up ... with unbelievable ease, peacefully, without any contraction of muscles in hips or thighs.... Please congratulate that man for me."... [Said a judge from Italy,] "I came 500 kilometres for this demonstration and I feel very satisfied."'

After the Belgrade demonstration, TM-Sidhas and Yugoslav leaders of Maharishi's movement were interviewed twice for two hours each on 'Studio B', one of the nation's most popular radio interview programmes. They were also interviewed by TV Belgrade, TV Sarajevo, Radio Belgrade, Radio Bar, and Radio Vrnjacka Banja. In addition, short news reports were aired on Radio Titograd, Radio Bar, and Radio Hercegnon, and a two-hour presentation of Maharishi's programme was given to 100 people at the cultural centre in **Novi Sad**.

Austria

The **Vienna** demonstration was held in a grand hall near the presidential palace. Among the 50 guests were reporters from the Austrian Press Agency and other journalists. Several articles and two television reports subsequently appeared. In the following weeks, Maharishi's Programme to Create World Peace was inaugurated in **Dornbirn**, **Innsbruck**, **Bregenz**, and **Villach**.

Manfred Stuckler, a Governor of the Age of Enlightenment from Austria, commented, 'All the citizens of Austria are very concerned to create world peace, because Austria is a country that lies exactly on the borderline between East and West. At large assemblies with one or two thousand people practising the Maharishi Technology of the Unified Field together, one can feel so clearly the inner bubbling up of bliss and the intense happiness. I am convinced it should be possible to create peace on earth

INAUGURATING MAHARISHI'S PROGRAMME TO CREATE WORLD PEACE—EUROPE

through the inner peace created by this technology. The demonstrations in Austria have brought not only the knowledge of how to create peace but actual waves of peaceful influence to both eastern and western countries.'

Poland

Dr Johannes Stuckler, Manfred's brother, travelled from Austria to Poland to demonstrate 'yogic flying' at **Warsaw's** Hotel Victoria Intercontinental. His presentation was preceded by a broadcast on Polish television. The programme included scenes of 'yogic flying' from Washington, D.C., and an interview with Dr Stuckler, in which he called 'yogic flying' 'a very serious performance to create world peace.'

Two Warsaw newspapers published accounts of Maharishi's programme. *Polityka* reported on the International 'Yogic Flying' Competition in New Delhi, which had been attended by a Polish Press Agency correspondent. The second article, published in *Tribuna Lubu*, described the Warsaw demonstration.

Hungary

In **Budapest**, the demonstration of 'yogic flying' was held in a gymnasium and was videotaped by scientists from Eutvos Lorant University. More than 100 people attended, including physicians, physicists, psychologists, and psychiatrists. One Governor of the Age of Enlightenment demonstrated 'yogic flying', his hands folded in his lap to show that his arms were not helping him to hop. Later, the Governor commented that 'this historic event opened a new possibility of research in the field of consciousness for Hungarian scientists.'

So great was the interest generated by the presentation of Maharishi's programme and the performance of 'yogic flying' that questions continued afterwards for one-and-a-half hours, and, according to the organizers, many people were inspired to learn the Transcendental Meditation technique.

Three of the guests later celebrated the 'yogic flying' with poems. One said, 'You hop to the space above, and deep in my being I wing along with you.' Another spoke of 'the power of the inner experience, of the inside radiating out'.

Two articles with photographs chronicled the Hungarian event, one in the country's leading weekly magazine and one in a Budapest daily newspaper. At the end of its article the latter promised 'to continue the scientific analysis of this phenomenon in a future edition of this newspaper.'

West Germany

West Germany led all of Europe by holding 32 inaugurations on one day in different cities. Three regional television stations broadcast reports on the evening news, and many German newspapers published articles with photographs of 'yogic flying'.

At **Berlin's** Hotel Bristol-Kempinski, 13 TM-Sidhas demonstrated for an audience of 165 people, which included many journalists from the local and national press. In **Munich**, 100 guests attended, and one of Germany's principal newspapers, *Süddeutsche Zeitung*, interviewed several TM-Sidhas at the Munich Capital of the Age of Enlightenment. **Hamburg's** demonstration was the best attended: 250 guests, including 25 journalists, assembled at the city's Intercontinental Hotel.

Demonstrations were also held in **Cuxhaven, Lübeck, Bremen, Bad-Zwischenahn, Wittmund, Hannover, Braunschweig, Düsseldorf, Münster, Schledehausen, Bern, Paderborn, Köln, Aachen, Bonn, Frankfurt, Saarbrücken, Mannheim, Heidelberg, Stuttgart, Heilbronn, Kaiserslautern, Esslingen, Freiburg, Ulm, Regensburg, Kötzting, Nürnberg,** and **Veitshochheim.**

The *Weser Kurier* of Bremen said, 'Hopping for

INAUGURATING MAHARISHI'S PROGRAMME TO CREATE WORLD PEACE—EUROPE

peace—77 Bremen Maharishi followers work real miracles'. A headline in the *Neue Braunschweiger Zeitung* read, 'Flying for the peace of the world, Sidhas from Braunschweig take off....' Describing his personal feeling during the demonstration in Hamburg, a reporter for the *Hamburger Tagesanzeiger* wrote, 'This event, even though experienced in public, has transformed me most deeply inside.'

Holland

On 12 July the headline of an article in Holland's *De Volskrant* declared, 'In Washington they floated for peace.' One month later, Holland had its own inauguration of Maharishi's programme at the TM-Sidha Ideal Village in **Lelystad**. Fourteen experts demonstrated 'yogic flying' beneath a banner that said, 'De Maharishi Technologie van het Verenigd Veld' ('The Maharishi Technology of the Unified Field').

'Now the meaning of the Flying Dutchman has become clear,' remarked one TM-Sidha afterwards. 'This demonstration has given the citizens of the "low countries" a vision of rising above sea level by means of the field of all possibilities, the unified field of pure consciousness. It has inspired our youth and given satisfaction to the elderly.'

Fourteen journalists attended the demonstration. That evening, scenes of 'yogic flying' were shown on national television news. *NRC Handelsblad*, one of Holland's most respected daily newspapers, published a detailed account of the demonstration, headlined 'Hop, hop, hop, on the way to eternal world peace.'

Belgium

In neighbouring Belgium, seven articles and a national television report chronicled the 'yogic flying' demonstration in **Brussels**. 'It was first class,' remarked one of the 40 guests. 'It brought waves of peace and happiness from the heart of Belgium to Europe and the world.' The question-and-answer session with the guests and journalists lasted more than an hour.

Britain

Wearing shirts imprinted with a map of Britain and golden rays of coherence radiating out to the world, a dozen TM-Sidhas hopped high and far in England's first 'yogic flying' competition in **London**.

'Lively, enjoyable, inspiring' was the way one guest described the inauguration, held at the Royal Garden Hotel and attended by over 300 guests. Two eminent representatives of Maharishi's world-wide movement introduced the programme: Dr Bevan Morris, President of Maharishi International University, and Dr Geoffrey Clements, Vice-Chancellor of Maharishi University of Natural Law in Buckinghamshire and Governor General of the World Government of the Age of Enlightenment for the continent of Europe.

One hundred guests attended another demonstration at the TM-Sidha Ideal Village in **Skelmersdale**, near Manchester. Eighty attended in **Edinburgh**, and hundreds more witnessed 15 other demonstrations held in **Birmingham**, **Worcester**, **Liverpool**, **Oxford**, **Cambridge**, **Norwich**, **Leicester**, **Huddersfield**, **Cardiff**, **Bournemouth**, Swythamley Park Academy (in the Peak district), **Falmouth**, **Jersey** (in the Channel Islands), Roydon Hall (near **Maidstone** in Kent), and **Chelmsford**.

The British press took a lively interest in the demonstrations. Many of the main television networks reported, including the BBC and Granada, Central, and BBC Welsh TV, as did local, national, and international British radio, including the BBC World Service, BBC Radio 4, Radio Capital, Radio Oxford, Radio Cornwall, Radio Wales, and Radio Scotland. Many people heard a discussion of Maharishi's Programme to Create World Peace on Radio Yorkshire's 'Good Morning Yorkshire'.

Britain's best-known newspapers—*The Times*, the

WORLD PEACE • GLOBAL INAUGURATION

INAUGURATING MAHARISHI'S PROGRAMME TO CREATE WORLD PEACE—EUROPE

Telegraph, the *Guardian*, the *Scotsman*—all reported on Maharishi's programme. Said *The Times*, 'According to the Maharishi ... it needs only the square root of one per cent of the five billion world population to create sufficient coherence to spread throughout the globe.' The *Scotsman* carried a photograph of 'yogic flying' on its front page with the headline, 'World peace gets off to a flying start.'

By the end of September, 38 different articles had appeared in papers throughout Britain. The *Ormskirk Advertiser's* headline said, 'Hop in search of peace', while the *Ormskirk Star* stated, 'How Transcendental Meditation can lead to world peace'. With remarkable insight the *Worcester Evening News* headlined its story, 'It's self-raising power'. The *Western Mail* sedately told its readers, 'An ancient form of flying made its public debut in Wales yesterday.' In Cambridge, the *Evening News* said, 'Securing world peace may seem a rather out of this world ambition, but a group in Cambridge is rising to the challenge—literally.'

'The "yogic flying" demonstrations,' commented Nigel Grace, one of the national leaders of Maharishi's movement in England, 'brought a fresh wave of optimism to the whole nation.'

Ireland

Across the Irish Sea, the *Irish Independent* announced, 'There's less bother with a hover ... or a hop.' Its article began, 'A "flying" way to decrease the Northern troubles and the country's unemployment and economic problems was unveiled yesterday with hopes and hops. The "solution" will just take 300 Irish people meditating twice a day using the Maharishi's "yogic flying" method, it was announced in Dublin yesterday.'

The *Independent* was one of several newspapers represented at the **Dublin** demonstration. Dr Clements and Dr Morris, just arrived from London, gave the keynote speeches. Three national papers carried photographs of 'yogic flying' on the front page, and one Irish national television station provided a ten-minute report on the event. During the days following the Dublin demonstration, introductory lectures on the Transcendental Meditation programme were heavily attended throughout the country.

Denmark

Denmark's inauguration was held in **Copenhagen's** Lyngby Mall. It was chaired by the principal of the Danish Folk High School which applies Maharishi's unified field based approach to education. Seventeen journalists attended, representing Denmark's four largest daily newspapers, three national magazines, two departments of the state broadcasting service, and other media.

'Nyhedsmagasinet', a radio news programme, narrated, 'People from all levels of society—people in suits and ties and others in jogging suits, men and women, young and old—came to the presentation.... It is now nearly 4:30. We have heard about the intention behind "yogic flying" ... and it is time for the group who will be flying to come in.... Among other things, we have been told that the purpose of this demonstration is to begin a world peace initiative.... There is a group of five young men in white sitting on light blue mattresses ... looking ... very happy while they meditate. It doesn't seem that the people or press photographers bother them.... During the flying one can see that they are happy, even ecstatic.'

The radio journalist asked one TM-Sidha when the third stage of flying would be demonstrated. He replied that 'It is a question of coherence in the collective consciousness of this society and of the whole world. A world that is more peaceful, more harmonious, in greater accordance with natural law, will promote more advanced "yogic flying".'

Denmark's largest-circulation newspaper printed a long article with two photographs of 'yogic flying', and the country's oldest and most respected paper published its article on the back cover page, with a photograph spanning four columns.

The headlines of one article said, 'Maharishi Yogi's recipe for world peace—we hop and hop and hop—harmony and order'. The article explained, 'Through the practice of the yogic flying technique, the body lifts itself from the mattress and begins to hop at the moment the brain reaches a state of maximum coherence, which means harmony and order. This spreads from individual consciousness, or brain physiology, to the world and dissolves tensions in the collective consciousness.'

The article said that a permanent group of 10,000 TM-Sidhas, established by Maharishi in India to practise 'yogic flying' together, 'will create world peace. Paradise will be back on earth.'

Sweden

The Swedish national television broadcasting company responded with enthusiasm to an invitation to film 'yogic flying' for the evening news. Organizers proceeded to arrange a large hall in **Stockholm** for 15 August, and 50 guests, including eight journalists, attended. Many more came to other demonstrations in **Malmö, Norberg,** and **Norrtalje**.

One Swedish TM-Sidha commented, 'These "yogic flying" demonstrations removed any misconceptions people might have had about the TM-Sidhi programme being a mystical phenomenon. Many people in Sweden as well as in the rest of the world have now realized that the Maharishi Technology of the Unified Field is a practical, scientific method to create world peace.'

Finland

In **Helsinki**, Finland, to the applause of 60 guests, the fastest 'yogic flyer' in the yogic 25-metre hurdles in sitting position covered the distance in 12.3 seconds, just 0.45 seconds slower than the best time in New Delhi. Nine journalists were there, including reporters from both of the city's television stations.

Several days later, a television station reported on Maharishi's programme for six minutes immediately after the evening news. The report began, 'Last Friday, only two days after Linkola's programme of the Finnish Green Party had been made public, Maharishi Mahesh Yogi from India announced his own world peace programme....' The report explained that 'the square root of one per cent of the population practising the Maharishi Technology of the Unified Field ... will create peace in every city and every country and will perpetuate world peace. This is Maharishi Mahesh Yogi's programme for creating and maintaining world peace.'

Describing the demonstrators, a Finnish newspaper reporter wrote, 'And what about those eyes! They were just radiating bliss, which is not possible during hard muscular effort. When I looked at those eyes, I could tell what must have been the feeling inside the man.'

As a Finnish TM-Sidha commented, 'People of my country and the whole world should know the source of and real mechanics for happiness in life. The demonstrations on 15 August brought that knowledge to many, many people.'

Norway and Iceland

Norway's principal demonstration created, according to one guest, 'a strong atmosphere of serenity' in a setting of great cultural significance for Norway, the seafaring museum in **Bygdøy**. Diplomats, scientists, and 15 journalists were among the 200 guests present. The Magic Circle of Oslo became so fascinated by the phenomenon that it offered 100,000 Norwegian kroners to the first person who demonstrates the third stage of 'yogic flying'.

Two of Oslo's daily newspapers published articles on Maharishi's programme, and the Norwegian Broad-

WORLD PEACE • GLOBAL INAUGURATION
INAUGURATING MAHARISHI'S PROGRAMME TO CREATE WORLD PEACE—EUROPE

casting Corporation aired reports on radio.

At the banquet hall of the Hotel Norway in **Bergen**, 150 people attended a second inauguration, while across the North Atlantic in **Reykjavik**, Iceland, five TM-Sidhas demonstrated Maharishi's mechanics to create world peace.

'This solution to the problems of our time is now known by many of the responsible people of our countries, and we urge them to support Maharishi's programme,' said one Scandinavian TM-Sidha. 'We will continue to fly together to create peace, and as our numbers grow we will see peace blossom in the world.' □

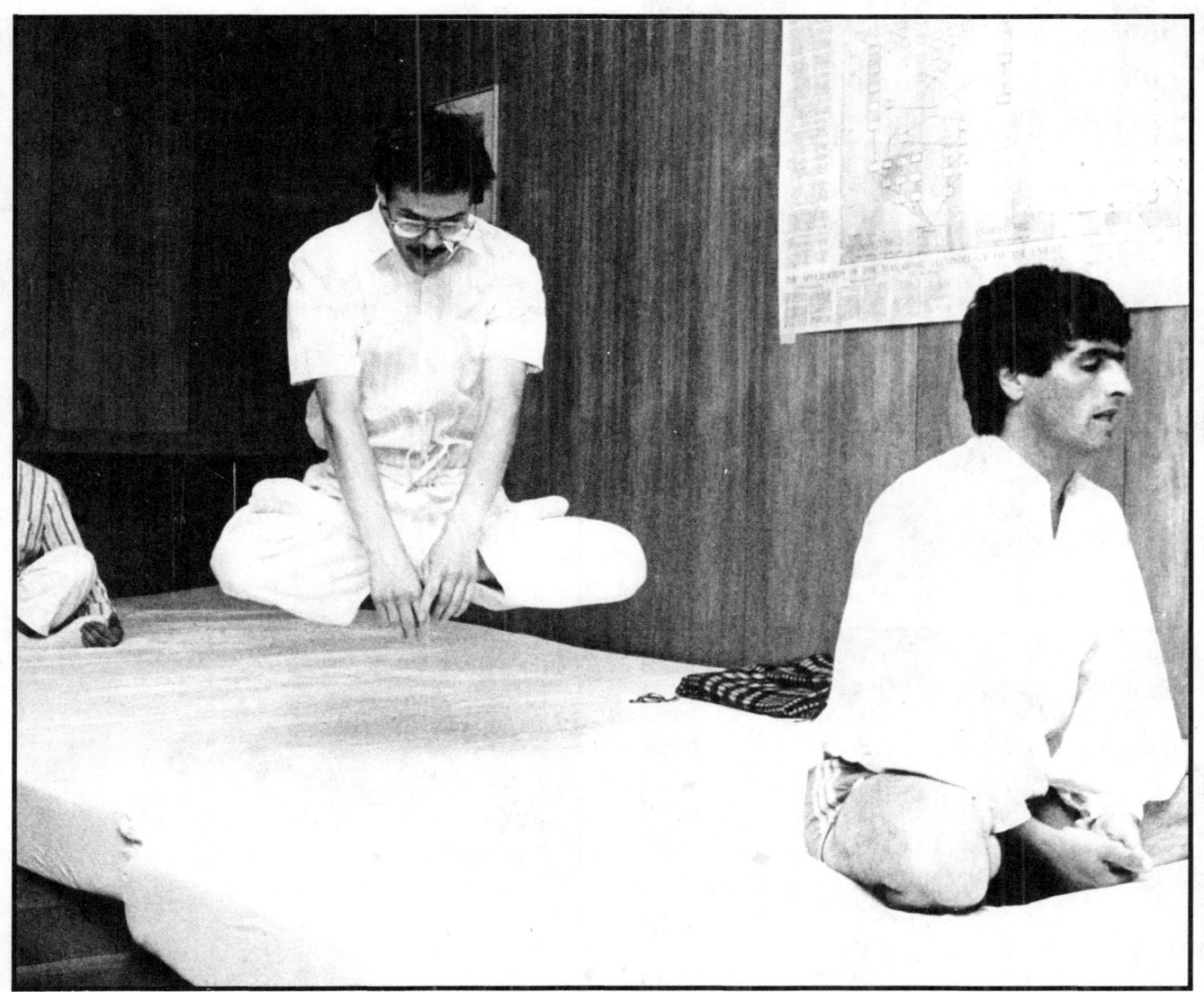

Demonstrating 'yogic flying' at the Congress Hall, Saarbrücken, West Germany.

MAHARISHI'S PROGRAMME TO CREATE

INAUGURATING MAHARISHI'S PROGRAMME TO CREATE WORLD PEACE—EUROPE

Introducing the 'yogic flying' competition at Maharishi European Research University in Seelisberg, Switzerland.

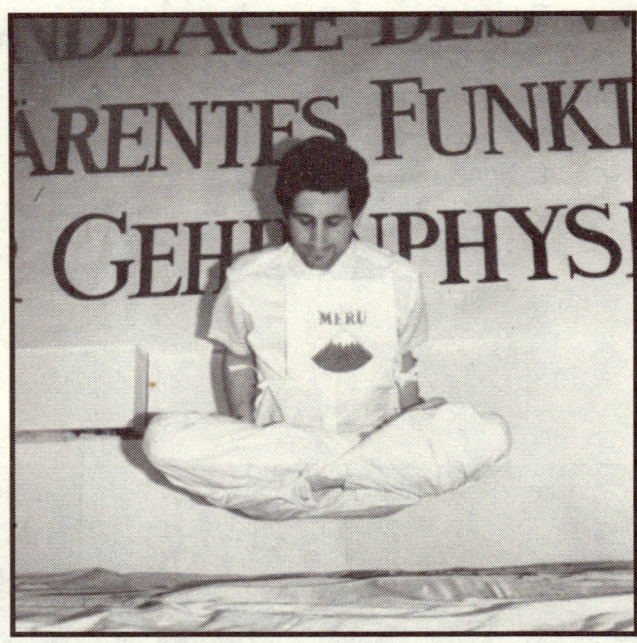

In Seelisberg, an effortless performance for world peace.

Photographers capture 'yogic flying' in Seelisberg.

The champions in Seelisberg.

At the demonstration in Vienna, Austria.

WORLD PEACE • GLOBAL INAUGURATION

INAUGURATING MAHARISHI'S PROGRAMME TO CREATE WORLD PEACE—EUROPE

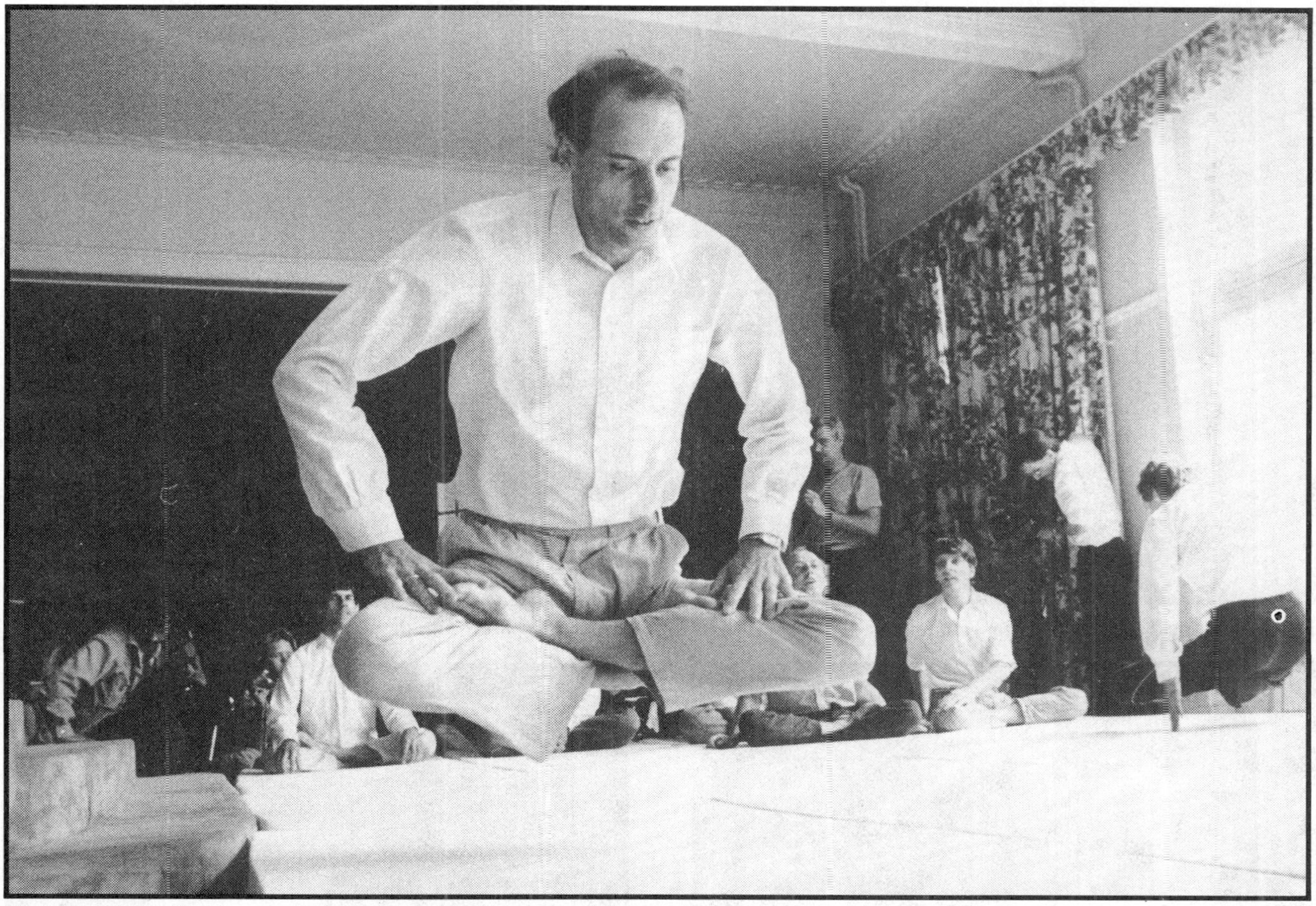

High flight in Holland—creating coherence for Europe and the world.

British National 'Yogic Flying' Competition underway in London.

In Thessaloniki, Greece, explaining the scientific principles at the basis of Maharishi's Programme to Create World Peace.

MAHARISHI'S PROGRAMME TO CREATE

INAUGURATING MAHARISHI'S PROGRAMME TO CREATE WORLD PEACE—EUROPE

Demonstrating 'yogic flying' in Denmark.

TM-Sidhas after the demonstration in Brunate, Italy.

A photograph of Martin Cullen, Irish Governor of the Age of Enlightenment, demonstrating 'yogic flying' at the Dublin inauguration (right), appeared on the front page of the *Irish Times* on 16 August (above). The front page of the *Irish Independent* (below Mr. Cullen's hand) also carried a large photograph of 'yogic flying.'

WORLD PEACE • GLOBAL INAUGURATION

PRESS REPORTS FROM EUROPE

Austria • *Wann & Wo*
Bregenz   11 September 1986   (German)

Sie fliegen für den Frieden. Obwohl es ihnen noch nicht gelungen ist zu schweben, sind diese Meditierenden zuversichtlich. „Vielleicht klappt's schon in einem Jahr." Wenn sie dann durch das Zimmer schweben, glauben sie auch, den Krieg endlich beseitigt zu haben. Die Jünger des Maharischi Yogi haben ein Friedensprogramm ausgearbeitet, das auf den hüpfenden Männern beruht. „7000, die meditieren, und es klappt", war die Kernaussage auf einer Pressevorführung des Vereins „Transzendentale Meditation" in Bregenz. Wollen wir's hoffen.   Foto: Günther Steiert

PRESS REPORTS FROM EUROPE

Belgium • *Le Vif / L'Express-Weekend*
Brussels   26 September – 2 October 1986   (French)

Maîtriser la pesanteur…

Passionné de recherches, ingénieur, futur docteur en biomécanique et travaillant à l'université d'Eindhoven, Jacques pratique en chambre le hopping mais ne cache plus son aptitude à maîtriser la loi de la gravitation universelle.

Après les modes successives de jogging, footing, surfing, bodybuilding et autres loisirs en -ing venus d'outre-Atlantique, on aurait pu croire que les Etats-Unis nous avaient mis au point une nouvelle discipline sportive. Il n'en est rien, car le hopping est le premier pas — ou plutôt le premier saut — vers le yogic flying, la lévitation. Il en est fait mention il y a déjà 2 000 ans dans le premier traité systématique sur le yoga, traité écrit par Patanjali, haute figure de l'antiquité indoue.

L'Inde, préoccupée bien avant la psychologie des profondeurs du XIXᵉ siècle, bien avant l'introspection et la contemplation méditative occidentale, de la structure de la condition humaine ne pouvait que séduire ce grand jeune homme de trente ans qui se penche en laboratoire sur les mystères de la vie et ses mécanismes complexes.

« Patanjali décrivait certains pouvoirs occultes, les siddhis, acquis lorsqu'on a choisi de se connaître, non pas le soi pétri de conditionnements physiques, sociaux, culturels, religieux,… mais le Soi originel. »

Parmi ces siddhis, la connaissance des existences précédentes, celle des états mentaux d'autres hommes, l'invisibilité, la disparition de la faim et de la soif, il y aurait la lévitation, celle-ci devant passer par deux stades avant de consister vraiment en un déplacement aérien : le sautillement et le flottement au-dessus du sol. Toutefois, l'essentiel des siddhis ne résidera pas dans leur extériorisation. Le siddha, celui qui s'adonne à la pratique des siddhis, n'est pas un magicien qui jette de la poudre aux yeux. Le travail le plus important est celui qui s'exerce au plus profond de lui, à la source de la pensée.

Tintin reporter et héros national ayant, lui, les pieds bien sur terre aurait pu s'éviter les frais d'un voyage au Tibet pour y voir un lama flotter au-dessus du sol. En effet, non loin de l'avenue Louise, dans un hôtel de maître discret du début du siècle, Jacques, qui n'a pourtant rien d'un phénomène de foire, a prouvé qu'il est, sinon au sommet de son art, du moins apte à maîtriser la pesanteur et à commander à son corps à être plus léger que l'air.

Simplement vêtu d'un tee shirt blanc et d'un training bleu, il prend place sur un des matelas de mousse qui jonchent le sol, se met en position de lotus et ferme les yeux durant quelques minutes, le temps pour lui de « transcender le niveau grossier de la réalité et d'atteindre celui, plus subtil, de la source de la pensée ». Soudain, il bondit. Les sauts se multiplient. Aller. Retour. Le voilà qui traverse plusieurs

Dans la foulée, de belges démonstrations : on transcende le niveau grossier de la réalité pour atteindre celui, plus subtil, de la source de la pensée. Rien de plus simple alors que de commander au corps de devenir plus léger que l'air.

fois la pièce sans être le moins du monde essoufflé. Bien au contraire, aucun rictus de fatigue ne se lit sur ses traits, mais un sourire radieux illumine son visage.

En soi, la performance physique réalisée n'a rien de spectaculaire — quoiqu'il ne soit pas évident du tout de franchir deux mètres en position de lotus, essayez donc vous aussi ! Par contre, la démonstration et les résultats prennent une toute autre dimension quand notre apprenti homme-oiseau nous certifie qu'« ils sont le fruit non pas d'un entraînement acharné, mais d'une gymnastique très douce du mental à des niveaux encore inexplorés de la conscience ». Et, dans la foulée, de rappeler les doutes émis quant à l'avenir de l'aviation lorsqu'en 1903, les frères Wright tentèrent pour la première fois de propulser un engin motorisé dans les airs.

Ce jour-là, ils ne s'arrachèrent de la piste d'envol que pour s'élever à 120 pieds durant 12 secondes, sous les yeux amusés des badauds qui étaient à mille feux de soupçonner que, dans le futur, les moyens de communication de l'époque seraient détrônés par l'avion. Et si, à son tour, celui-ci courait le risque d'être « dépassé » par les adeptes du hopping ? C'est la question que l'on se pose beaucoup ces temps-ci, paraît-il, au pays qui a pourtant vu naître Superman, Spiderman et autres volatiles humains.

Il faut dire que la « First North American Yogic Flying Competition » s'y est déroulée il y a peu et qu'une vingtaine de jeunes gens furent pris sur le vif en pleine action, pour ne pas dire en plein vol. Mais pourquoi donc rendre public aujourd'hui ce qui a jusqu'à présent été gardé confidentiel ? Notre belge yogi (gantois pour être précis) connaît la réponse : « Le hopping et le yogic flying sont des solutions de choc à tous les problèmes de violence et de terrorisme qui endeuillent le monde. Plus il y aura d'adeptes du hopping, plus la terre tournera rond. »

Matière à méditer

Les amateurs d'émotions fortes n'en auront pas pour leur compte. Si la lévitation pèse lourd dans la balance de l'équilibre guerre/paix, ce n'est pas aujourd'hui qu'on assistera au départ d'une flottille de tapis volants chevauchés par des fakirs occidentaux qui s'en vont bouter le diable et les cavaliers de l'Apocalypse.

L'embarquement se fait en chambre et l'unique instrument de vol est le

WORLD PEACE • GLOBAL INAUGURATION

Un meeting aérien du troisième type qui décoiffe : les trois médaillés pris sur le vif, au sommet de leur art, la maîtrise de la pesanteur. On nage bien comme un poisson dans l'eau, pourquoi ne planerait-on pas comme un oiseau dans l'air ? ?

corps avec, à son bord, seul maître d'équipage, le mental partant à la découverte de la conscience et expérimentant, à la source de la pensée, « le champ unifié de la physique moderne, celui d'où émergent les lois de la nature et notamment celle de la pesanteur par là même maîtrisée. » Vaste programme...

« L'organisateur de ces démonstrations est Maharishi Mahesh Yogi. A la fois authentique maître spirituel indien et scientifique puisque physicien de formation universitaire, celui-ci a assimilé le niveau de vide récemment entrevu au champ unifié de la conscience. » Le grand chercheur devant l'éternel qu'est Jacques est convaincu qu'ainsi science et conscience se trouvent enfin réconciliés, car le niveau de vide physique semble bien cohabiter avec le domaine du non-manifesté où tout est possible.

Mais, on est terre à terre ou on ne l'est pas : comment passe-t-on du « manifesté » que nous avons l'habitude d'expérimenter à l'état de veille, au « non-manifesté » ? « J'ai adopté une technique particulière de méditation que je pratique deux fois par jour durant vingt minutes. Les effets de celle-ci sont maintenant bien connus pour avoir été observés dans les laboratoires de plus d'une centaine d'universités de par le monde. Méditation à ne pas confondre avec concentration puisqu'on use d'un mantra (mot sanskrit) qui, en aidant à se libérer des pensées, facilite la plongée de l'individu vers la source de celles-ci. »

Pour être à la hauteur

Pour être bref, disons que les effets de la pratique de cette technique d'exploration convergent tous vers l'épanouissement de la personne : les nombreux tests pratiqués et les multiples études électroencéphalographiques réalisées attestent, et de l'amélioration physiologique — diminution du cholestérol, de l'hypertension, de l'acide lactique, autant de révélateurs de stress —, et de l'augmentation du potentiel mental, partant de ses manifestations — créativité, intelligence, rapidité d'esprit, mémoire — chez les sujets qui s'y sont essayés.

Too much ? Pas du tout ! « Il y a mieux encore. » En effet, lorsque de grands groupes de « techniciens » du champ unifié de la conscience se réunissent, on observerait soit une diminution inexplicable du taux d'accidents, de vols, de crimes dans l'environnement direct des lieux de rassemblement de ces groupes, soit une augmentation imprévisible de la majorité des valeurs boursières, indice d'équilibre mondial irréfutable.

De là à penser que de l'harmonie individuelle dépend la paix dans le monde... Et voilà ce bon vieux « gnoothi se auton » (connais-toi toi-même) de Socrate qui refait surface. Rien de nouveau sous le soleil ? Pas si sûr ! Plus que jamais, la paix est précaire et ce n'est pas de jouer son petit Candide qui empêchera des semis amoureusement plantés de se faire atomiser « aujourd'hui peut-être, ou alors demain ».

Jacques a choisi de faire face en allant au plus profond de lui persuadé de créer ainsi dans son sillage une atmosphère de positivité qui neutralisera le stress et l'agressivité environnante. « Ce à quoi ne parviendra jamais le plus musclé des athlètes produisant volontairement de tels bonds. » Ainsi conclut en s'en allant à grandes enjambées cet enthousiaste qui ne manque ni d'air ni d'humour.

PATRICIA HARDY ■

PRESS REPORTS FROM EUROPE

Denmark • *NYT Aspekt*

Copenhagen   November 1986   (Danish)

Hopla – vi flyver!

Demonstration af yogisk flyvning.

af Jan von Müllen

Den 15. august blev der i Lyngby Storcenter nord for København givet en offentlig smagsprøve på den meget omtalte »flyveteknik«, der er en del af det videregående TM-sidhi-program. Inden for Transcendental Meditation har man ellers hidtil holdt lav profil med hensyn til diverse yogiske evner, og det er altid blevet understreget, at de kun er et ydre biprodukt af den langt vigtigere indre forvandlingsproces.

Når man ved denne lejlighed trådte mere åbent frem, hænger det angiveligt sammen med et påtrængende aktuelt behov for hurtigst muligt at få etableret nogle store grupper, hvor man gennem fælles udøvelse af bl.a. flyveteknikken kan bidrage til at opløse stress i hele verdens kollektive bevidsthed. Et stigende antal sociologiske undersøgelser tyder på, at dette faktisk kan lade sig gøre, og under alle omstændigheder er der næppe nogle vågne og ansvarlige mennesker, der vil benægte, at de nuværende globale kriser skriger på helt nye og overraskende løsninger.

Som det vel kunne forventes, var budskabet lidt for specielt for i hvert fald nogle af de fremmødte journalister, der vist havde ventet at blive præsenteret for noget på linie med Supermans mellemgalaksiske soloflyvninger. At se de udvalgte fem kandidater i fuld lotusstilling hoppe let og elegant rundt mellem hinanden var ellers ikke kedeligt, og især var den gode stemning, der bredte sig i lokalet, særdeles mærkbar for de omkring 150 tilskuere.

Demonstrationen fandt i øvrigt sted samtidig med lignende arrangementer i ikke mindre end 108 lande og var et led i Maharishis nye verdensplan for fred. □

Maharishi udtalte for nylig: »Der eksisterer hundredvis af fredsorganisationer over hele verden. Forskellige mennesker søger at skabe fred ud fra forskellige synsvinkler og tilnærmelser. Vi værdsætter alle bestræbelser på at fremme verdensfreden.

Vores tilnærmelse til verdensfred er holistisk (helhedsorienteret) og virker fra det mest grundlæggende niveau. Den tager sit udgangspunkt i det mest grundlæggende plan af naturens aktivitet, hvor selve den evige stilhed er det levende grundlag for universets uendelige dynamik. Dette er det forenede felt for alle naturlove i dynamisk vekselvirkning med sig selv. Her danner fred grundlag for uendelig dynamik. Den verdensfred, som skabes fra dette niveau, vil derfor føre til vedvarende fremgang og udvikling for hele menneskeheden.«

Fysiologiske og psykologiske undersøgelser har vist, at Transcendental Meditation er en effektiv metode til at fjerne spændinger og stress hos den enkelte og til at forbedre den personlige livskvalitet. Sociologiske undersøgelser peger i dag på, at TM og specielt det videregående TM-Sidhi-program, som indbefatter »yogisk flyveteknik«, ikke blot bringer øget harmoni og positivitet til det enkelte menneske, men også til samfundet og verden som helhed.

Foto: Lars Borup.

WORLD PEACE • GLOBAL INAUGURATION

PRESS REPORTS FROM EUROPE

Denmark • *Ekstra Bladet*

Copenhagen 16 August 1986 (Danish)

Maharishi Yogis opskrift på verdensfred:

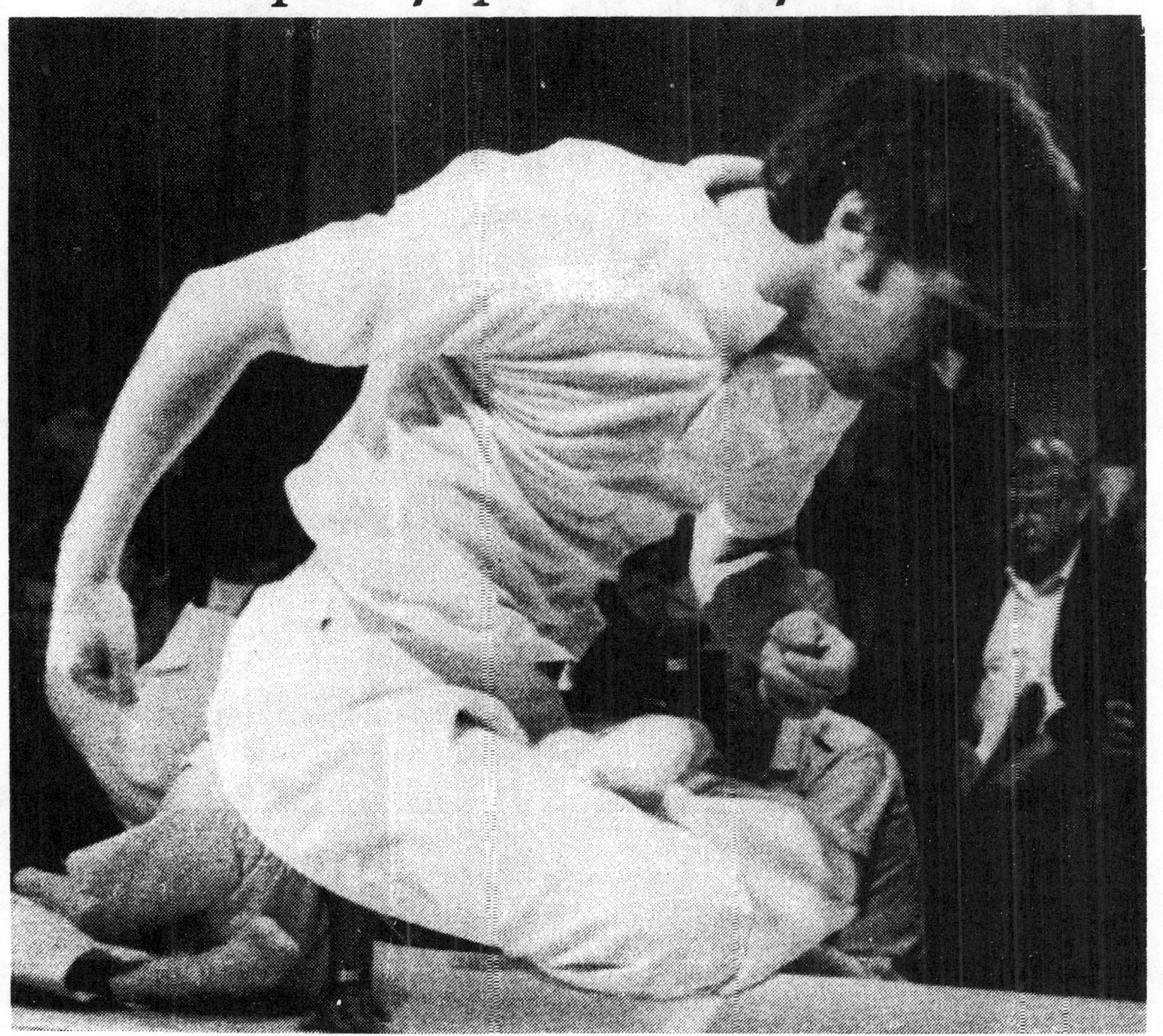

VI HOPPER OG HOPPER OG HOPPER

HARMONI OG ORDEN

Under udøvelsen af den 'yogiske flyveteknik' løfter kroppen sig fra underlaget og begynder at hoppe i det øjeblik, hvor hjernen befinder sig i en tilstand af maksimal kohærens, som betyder harmoni og orden. Den spreder sig fra den individuelle bevidsthed eller hjernefysiologi til Verdens kollektive bevidsthed og bevirker, at spændinger i den kollektive bevidsthed opløses.

Og så fortsatte det med påstande om, at sociologiske undersøgelser viste, at når bare 1 procent af en befolkning udøver TM, sker der en forbedring af livskvaliteten, bl.a. fald i kriminalitet, sygelighed og antallet af ulykkestilfælde. Al stress vil forsvinde hos den enkelte og i hele samfundet. Vi vil allesammen behandle hinanden ordentligt.

Derfor vil Maharashi danne en permanent gruppe på 10.000 sidha'er i Indien, der 15 minutter morgen og aften bl.a. dyrker 'yogisk flyvning' og på den måde skaber verdensfred.

Og Paradis vil være tilbage på Jord. Solen vil skinne mere, det vil regne mindre. Der vil være færre mord og selvmord, folk vil ikke mere køre så meget ind i hinanden mere osv, osv.

Og så kommer pointen i det hele. Vi andre skal bare skrabe 800 mill. kr. sammen til formålet. For renteafkastet af de penge, vil de 10.000 flyvende TM'ere kunne leve og ånde.

AF CHRIS WAMMEN

WORLD PEACE • GLOBAL INAUGURATION

PRESS REPORTS FROM EUROPE

Finland • *Aamulehti*
Perjantai 11 July 1986 (Finnish)

● Eddie Gob mietiskeli ilme tiukkana ilmassa Washingtonissa keskiviikkona.

Washingtonissa leijailtiin rauhaa

Washington — UPI

Washingtonissa järjestettiin keskiviikkona ensi kertaa julkinen näytös, jossa ihminen leijui ilmassa ajatuksen voimalla. Transsendentaalisen mietiskelyn harjoittijat halusivat tilaisuudella edistää maailmanrauhaa.

Mietiskelijät ottivat 'jooga-lennossa' mittaa toisistaan. Kanadalainen Blaine Watson ponnahti korkeimmalle istualtaan eli 57,15 senttimetrin korkeuteen. Eddie Gob Guadaloupesta voitti kultamitalit 25 metrin ja 50 metrin leijailussa sekä pituusponnahduksessa.

PRESS REPORTS FROM EUROPE

Finland • *Koillissanomat*

Kuusamo   15 August 1986   (Finnish)

Leipuri on saanut kutsun lehdistötilaisuuteen Helsinkiin.

Aiheena on Maharishi Mahesh Yogin Maailmanrauhan Ohjelma. Kutsun mukaan siellä esitellään ohjelma, jonka avulla lopetetaan terrorismi, sodat ja luodaan maailmaan ihana rauha.

Paljastan tässä etukäteen kutsukirjeestä kohdan, jossa lyhyesti ennakkoon kerrotaan miten se tapahtuu. Olkaapa tarkkana.

"Tieteellisissä tutkimuksissa on todettu, että yhdentyneen kentän Maharishi teknologian TM-Sidhi "Joogalento"-tekniikka luo koherenssia maailman tietoisuuteen. Tämä on perusta Maharishin ohjelmalle luoda ja ylläpitää pysyvästi maailmanrauhaa.

Joogalentotekniikan aikana keho lentää ilmaan ja liikkuu eteenpäin, kun aivotoiminnassa saavutetaan maksimaalinen koherenssi. Tietoisuuden ja materian välinen koherenssi kehossa ensimmäisen lentovaiheen aikana syntyy kaikkien luonnonlakien yhdentyneen kentän tasolla. Koska yhdentyneellä kentällä on äärettömän vuorovaikutuksen luonne, koherenssin syntyminen tällä tasolla välittömästi harmonisoi epäjärjestystä koko luonnossa. Koherenssi leviää ja neutralisoi negatiivisia pyrkimyksiä koko luomakunnassa."

Näin yksinkertaista se on. Ei muuta kuin kaikki koherenssia joogaamaan, mutta varokaa ettei jää sääret solmuun.

* * *

Finland • *Suomen Sosialidemokraatti*

Helsinki   29 August 1986   (Finnish)

Pompi rauhaa

Joogalentoa on kesän aikana harrastettu ympäri maailmaa. Tässä kuvassa lentävät amerikkalaiset mietiskelijät — rauhan puolesta.

WORLD PEACE • GLOBAL INAUGURATION

PRESS REPORTS FROM EUROPE

Finland • *Finnish television*

Helsinki   August 1986   (Finnish)

Can Terrorism and Wars be Eliminated by the Help of Yogic Flying?

(English translation)

Broadcaster: Last Friday, only two days after the Finnish Green Party's Linkola programme had been made public, Maharishi Mahesh Yogi from India announced his own world peace programme. According to Maharishi, the world is under the influence of so much stress that the only way to release the pressure from world consciousness is through quieting down all the individuals in the world and releasing their stress through the Transcendental Meditation programme. Maharishi did not choose the time to announce his programme arbitrarily. His teaching has existed in the Himalayas for thousands of years, but in his opinion, the world situation is now so serious that it is time to make it available everywhere.

Maharishi Mahesh Yogi announced his programme to the world press in press conferences organised simultaneously in over 100 countries around the world. The 'yogic flying' programme, by which terrorism and wars can be eliminated and lasting world peace created, was demonstrated to the general public for the first time in history.

The announcement was preceded by long-term planning and consideration. According to Maharishi, the world situation is now such that it is time for all responsible individuals to take responsibility for creating and maintaining world peace.

Maharishi: ... With the population of all the nations of the world violating the laws of nature, world consciousness can only be under a very strong influence of stress. Those who feel to be custodians of the world family must react to this stress in world consciousness. That is why we see the unfortunate policies of the superpowers.

Broadcaster: At the moment, the world peace programme is based in the techniques of the Maharishi Technology of the Unified Field. The influence generated through these techniques creates the phenomenon of coherence that will make peace on earth powerful, and power on earth peaceful.

Practically speaking, this technology of the unified field means the 'yogic flying' practise of the TM-Sidhi programme. 'Yogic flying' results in a higher state of expanded awareness which effectively removes stress from the world. During 'yogic flying', when maximum coherence in brain activity is achieved, the body lifts up and moves forward.

The coherence between consciousness and matter in the body experienced during the first stage of 'yogic flying' originates at the level of the unified field of all the laws of nature, because the unified field has the character of infinite correlation. An impulse generated from this level instantly harmonises discordant tendencies throughout nature and thus coherence spreads, neutralising negative tendencies in the whole creation.

According to the world peace programme of Maharishi, when the square root of one per cent of the population, which in Finland would mean 300 people, practises the 'yogic flying' programme together in one place, the quality of life improves in the whole society—crime rate goes down and accidents decrease. When 7000 experts practise the Maharishi Technology of the Unified Field together in one place, they create a ground for purification of the whole world consciousness. A group numbering the square root of one per cent of the population, rising to higher states of consciousness by practising the Maharishi Technology of the Unified Field for 15 minutes twice daily in one place in each city of every country, will maintain a high level of coherence in the city for unrestricted progress and fulfilment in every family, and smooth administration of the affairs of the city as a whole. This will create peace in every city in every country and perpetuate world peace. This is Maharishi Mahesh Yogi's programme for creating and maintaining world peace.

Finland • *Finnish television*
Helsinki   15 August 1986   (Finnish)

(English translation)

Broadcaster: In a series of rare Finnish championships there was a competition today in a new and special kind of event, 'yogic flying'. In fact, there were three events: high jump, long jump, and dash. But the ultimate goal is actual flying without wings, and that can only be achieved through Transcendental Meditation and the TM-Sidhi programme. In Finland there are 200 of these yogic hoppers, or 'yogic flyers'. Everyone can practise this event at home.

WORLD PEACE • GLOBAL INAUGURATION

PRESS REPORTS FROM EUROPE

Finland • *Suomenmaa*
Helsinki 21 August 1986 (Finnish)

Pomppimalla maailmanrauhaan

Kolme aikuista miestä pomppii matoilla lootusasennossa. Korkeutta, pituutta ja sileää.

Kysymyksessä ei ole sen vähäisempi asia kuin maailmanrauhan luominen. Siinä missä paneelit, seminaarit ja neuvottelut epäonnistuvat, onnistuvat joogalentäjät.

Espoon Dipolissa joogalennettiin Suomen TM-liiton järjestämässä tilaisuudessa. Näin esiteltiin menetelmä, jolla supervaltojen asevarustelukilpa ja kasvava kansainvälinen terrorismi voidaan pysäyttää.

Vastaavanlaisia tilaisuuksia järjestettiin yhtä aikaa 108:ssa maassa ympäri maapalloa.

Ryhmässä harjoitettuna joogalento aikaansaa nk. superradianssivaikutuksen joka harmonisoi koko kansakunnan kollektiivitajunnan. Tähän tarvitaan riittävä määrä ihmisiä, Suomessa 300, yhteen paikkaan kokoontuneena joogalentoa suorittamaan.

Teoreettinen pohja löytyy nykyfysiikan yhtenäisteorioista, joiden avulla tajunta selitetään aineen ja olemassaolon perustalla olevaksi luonnonvoimien yhdentyneeksi kentäksi.

TM-liikkeen maailmanrauhan ohjelman perustaja Maharishi Mahesh Yogi on kotona Intiassa tullut siihen tulokseen, että ainoa tie pysyvään maailman rauhaan on suora vaikuttaminen maailman kollektiiviseen tietoisuuteen, niin että ilmapiiriä hallitseva stressi poistuu ja mieliala vaihtuu pelosta ystävällisyydeksi.

Nyt nähty edusti 5000 vuotta vanhan Veda-perinteen mukaan joogalennon ensimmäistä vaihetta. Siinä ruumis lennähtää mielen voimalla ilmaan ja liikkuu eteenpäin pienen matkan.

Toisessa vaiheessa leijutaan ilmassa — tätä levitaatiota ei tiettävästi tällä hetkellä maailmassa esiinny, mutta Buddha harrasti sitä. Kolmannessa vaiheessa voitaisiin suorastaan puhua Veda-astronauteista, sillä siinä liikutaan ilmassa pidempiäkin matkoja. Jotkut pyhimykset ovat tähän pystyneet.

Tämänlaatuinen pomppiminen on suoraa vaikutusta kansojen kollektiiviseen tajuntaan.

Finland • *Helsingin Sanomat*
Helsinki 23 July 1986 (Finnish)

maailman ihmisiä

Lentäen rauhaan

99 mietiskelijää pomppi ja loikki kehäkukilla koristetulla Indira Gandhi -stadionilla Delhissä maanantaina järjestetyissä joogalennon olympialaisissa.

Miehet ja naiset 18:sta eri maasta yrittivät lentelyllään edistää maailmanrauhaa ja laannuttaa terrorismia sekä asevarustelua.

Mietiskelijät sanoivat, että ihminen pystyy lentämään, kun hänen aivoissaan kulkevat aallot ovat saavuttaneet mahdollisimman suuren harmonian. Kun useiden mietiskelijöiden harmoniset aallot yhdistyvät, ne pystyvät voimallaan poistamaan eripuraisuutta maailmasta.

Finland • *Kotilääkäri*

Helsinki 23 September 1986 (Finnish)

Markku irrottelee.

HEI ME LENNETÄÄN!

☐ »Minun on pakko kirjoittaa tästä jotain, ettei kukaan vain tähän usko», kuiskasi kollega vieressä.

Olimme saaneet kutsun joogalentonäytökseen. Paikalla oli myös pari tv-ryhmää. Lehdistötilaisuudessa vakavat miehet puhuivat transsendenttisesta meditaatiosta, Sidhi-tekniikasta, Maharishi Mahesh Yogin maailmanrauhan ohjelmasta, neliöjuurista ja kollektiivisesta tietoisuudesta.

Lehdistötilaisuuden jälkeen viisi miestä »lensi» pomppupatjoilla.

Näyttikö siltä, että he käyttivät lihasvoimaa, kyseli yksi järjestäjistä huolestuneena jälkeenpäin. Kyllä se vähän näytti, taisin vastata.

Ei se ihan totta ollut.

Vaikka miehet »lensivät» kilpaa, pompahtelivat kaikenkaikkiaan ehkä tunnin jalat ristissä täydessä lootusasennossa, suut eivät irvistelleet, hiki ei lentänyt niin kuin kovassa lihasponnistuksessa yleensä.

Ja entä heidän silmänsä! Niissä näkyi sellainen riemukas autuus ja auvo, joka ei ole mahdollista tuskallisen ponnistuksen aikana.

Kun niihin silmiin katsoin, saatoin aavistella, mikä tunne miehillä oli sisällään. Siitä en ole aivan varma, lensivätkö he todella vai tunsivatko vain lentävänsä. Mutta juuri sitä lentoon lähdön tunnetta minä jäinkin kadehtimaan.

Ja jos mennään itse pääasiaan: maailmarauhan kannlta nämä lentävät miehet ovat lentäjistä vaarattomimpia.

WORLD PEACE • GLOBAL INAUGURATION

PRESS REPORTS FROM EUROPE

France • *Le Méridional*

Marseille   16 August 1986   (French)

Hop ! Hop ! Hop !
Le "vol yogique" pour... la paix mondiale

Surprenante image : alors que tout Marseille est à la plage, dans une salle perchée au troisième étage d'une maison du cours Pierre-Puget, une dizaine de personnes font de la méditation transcendantale. Des adeptes du Maharishi Mahesh Yogi. Des hommes et des femmes de tous horizons, en tenue estivale mais bien habillés, dont le visage s'empourpre par les effets conjoints de la concentration et de la chaleur suffocante. Ils sont là pour s'initier à la technique de MT-Sidhi de "vol yogique" (le sidhi est un mot sanscrit qui signifie perfection) enseignée par le grand maître selon lequel, grâce à cette forme de lévitation, l'homme parviendra enfin à trouver son équilibre intérieur et à éliminer la violence et la guerre.

Déambulant d'une pièce à une autre, se faufilant entre chaises et tables, Jean-Pierre Amouyal muni de ses papiers, nous rejoint pour sa conférence de presse. La quarantaine distinguée, cheveux courts et soigneusement cravatée, ce "coordinateur" des oeuvres du Maharishi à Marseille est professeur de méditation transcendantale depuis six ans. S'il a invité les journalistes à assister à une démonstration de "vol yogique", c'est parce que dans 108 pays, cette journée du 15 août est consacrée à l'exégèse du programme Maharishi pour "créer la paix mondiale".

D'une voix calme, le professeur nous livre les clés de la MT-Sidhi : "**Il ne s'agit pas d'une philosophie mais d'une technique de développement mental**, insiste t-il. Une technique dont les effets sont irrésistibles. A entendre J.P. Amouyal, on a envie de rajeunir illico de dix ans. Foutaise ? Ecoutez donc ça : "**D'une part**, dit-il, **au niveau physiologique cette technique permet au corps d'évacuer les stress de la vie quotidienne, de s'apaiser deux fois plus profond que le sommeil profond, de renforcer le système nerveux, donc de recouvrer une meilleure santé, et même de rajeunir**". Eh oui ! On donne 60 ans à quelqu'un qui en a dix de plus et qui pratique le MT-Sidhi depuis cinq ans.

L'EFFET 1%.- Sur sa lancée, notre professeur évoque l'influence bénéfique de la MT-Sidhi sur l'esprit qui trouve fatalement sa cohérence dès lors qu'il est en harmonie avec le corps. Vieux précepte platonicien plus ou moins inspiré d'Epictète. Mais passons. Puisqu'il s'agit d'une technologie pour sauver la paix mondiale, on n'a aucune raison de contester le professeur quand il parle de "l'effet 1%".

Qu'est-à-dire ? C'est tout simple. Si on extrait la racine carrée de 1% de la population mondiale, on obtient 7000 personnes. A supposer que ces 7000 personnes éparpillées sur les cinq continents pratiquent la MT-Sidhi, l'agressivité innée chez l'homme disparaîtra au profit de la paix, grâce à la radiation des ondes émises par ces gens. Pour la France, il suffirait de 750 personnes.

Ainsi s'achève la conférence de presse. Reste maintenant la démonstration. Celle-ci a lieu dans une pièce voisine dont le plancher est recouvert de matelas. Lorsqu'on y pénètre, J.P. Amouyal et deux de ses collègues sont dans la position du lotus, assis les jambes croisées sous le fessier. Silence. Les regards convergent vers ces trois hommes qui, les yeux fermés et le torse bien droit, se préparent à faire le "vol yogique". Au bout de quatre minutes, retentit une clochette. Alors les uns après les autres, comme s'ils attendaient ce signal, les corps s'élèvent sous l'impulsion de la pensée maintenue au point zéro.

Pour les prosélytes du Maharishi, le miracle s'est produit quand s'est opérée la coordination entre le corps et l'esprit.....

G. Ch.

MAHARISHI'S PROGRAMME TO CREATE

PRESS REPORTS FROM EUROPE

France • *La Nouvelle République du Centre-Ouest*

Tours   17 August 1986   (French)

LES champions de l'U.L.M., qui s'affrontent jusqu'à la fin du week-end à Couhé-Vérac, ont failli être battus. Pourtant, leurs machines ultra-légères tiennent plus du sac à dos que de l'avion et il semble difficile de s'envoyer en l'air avec moins de matériel encore.

Eh bien, l'exploit a été tenté dimanche après-midi, à une trentaine de kilomètres de là. Au château de La Roche, à Asnois, des adeptes de la méditation transcendantale ont décollé par la seule force de leur esprit. Et même si leur lévitation ressemblait plus à un saut de puce qu'à un grand bond dans l'inconnu, l'histoire mérite d'être contée, car elle se place sous le signe de la paix...

Au fin fond de la campagne poitevine, quelques partisans de la « technologie Maharishi du champ unifié » étaient donc rassemblés hier. Parmi eux, un médecin et un ingénieur, chargés d'apporter les explications scientifiques. C'est pas simple, mais essayons. Sous certaines conditions, on peut augmenter les capacités d'un organisme. Exemples : le laser, mais aussi, chez l'homme, *« un état de conscience supérieure qui entraîne des modifications physiologiques »*.

En mettant de l'ordre dans la tête, la méditation fait du bien au cœur, à la vue, à la... Enfin à tout ! Et de cette accumulation de petits bonheurs individuels, naîtra l'harmonie universelle. C.Q.F.D.

D'ailleurs, les convaincus peuvent en apporter le témoignage statistique : dans une ville où 1 % de la population s'adonne à la méditation transcendantale, le stress général diminue, ainsi que les accidents... Il paraît même que les affaires reprennent !

La manifestation physique de cette panacée, c'est la « lévitation yogique »... Un spectacle auquel était convié, hier, un trio de journalistes en quête du scoop de l'été. Ils sont repartis perplexes.

Jambes croisées dans la position du lotus, les derviches du premier échelon ont, en effet, sautillé avec entrain, les yeux clos et le visage extatique. Une performance qui n'est pas à la portée du premier gymnaste venu. Mais, pour ce qui est de se stabiliser à un mètre du sol, bernique.

Pas démontés pour autant, les cultivateurs du Champ unifié ont précisé qu'au bout de six mois de pratique quotidienne, ils n'avaient atteint que la première phase. Pour le vol stationnaire et la navigation tous temps, il faudra revenir. Suffit d'avoir le moral, comme au bon vieux temps des pionniers de l'aviation.

A Couhé-Vérac, du côté des U.L.M., on respire : « Plus légers qu'eux, tu décolles pas encore ! »

Philippe RIVIÈRE.

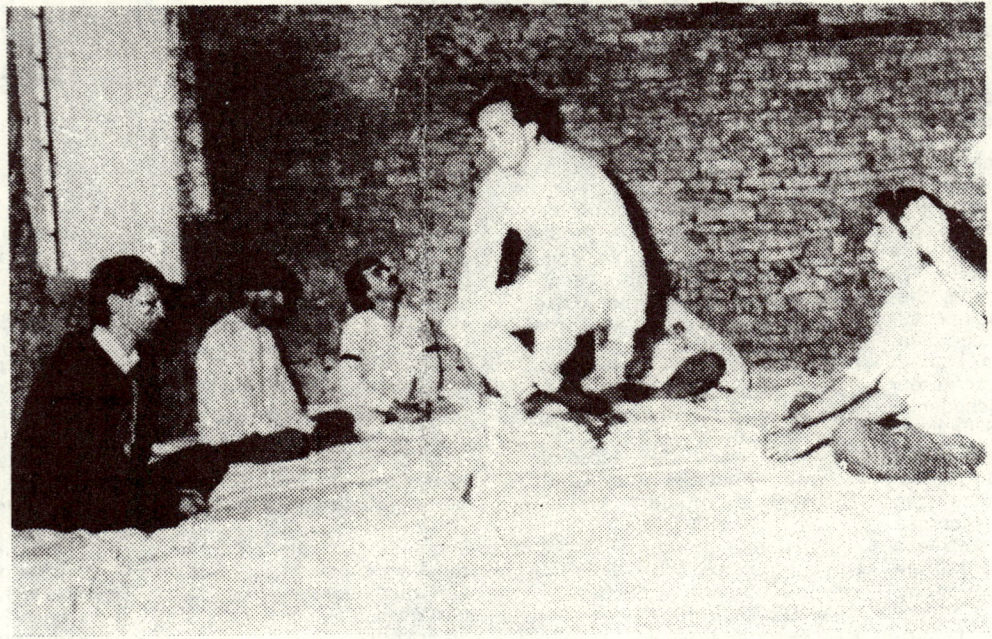

Un petit bond pour l'homme, un grand bond pour l'humanité...   (Photo « N.R. »)

WORLD PEACE • GLOBAL INAUGURATION

PRESS REPORTS FROM EUROPE

France • *Le Progrès*
Lyon   19 August 1986   (French)

MÉDITATION TRANSCENDANTALE
Léviter absolument

Photo Philippe Juste

Un groupe d'une douzaine d'adeptes de la Méditation Transcendantale tente de prouver à quelques journalistes présents que les lois de la pesanteur peuvent être vaincues grâce à « l'harmonie et la cohérence » de la conscience de chacun.
Ce phénomène est appelé « lévitation par les méditants » : ils en ont expérimenté le « stade n° 2 » qui consiste à laisser son corps faire une succession de bonds dans l'espace d'une pièce.
Cette photographie ne doit pas laisser croire à la suspension immobile des corps dans l'air ; elle n'est que l'image figée de mouvements de sauts rapides.

PRESS REPORTS FROM EUROPE

West Germany • *Lübecker Nachrichten*

Lübeck 11 July 1986 (German)

Den Yogi-Flug demonstrierte Eddie Gob, Anhänger des Yogi Maharishi Mahesh, in Washington. (Foto: ap)

WORLD PEACE • GLOBAL INAUGURATION

PRESS REPORTS FROM EUROPE

West Germany • *Frankfurter Rundschau*

Frankfurt   14 August 1986   (German)

Im Lotussitz zum Weltfrieden hüpfen

Beim Wettfliegen peilen Yogis große Ziele an

Der Einsatz der fliegenden Yogis für den Weltfrieden hat am 9. Juli in einer Washingtoner Flughalle begonnen. Zum ersten Mal durften etwa 1000 Zuschauer Zeugen einer bislang nur im Geheimen praktizierten Kunst werden: des Abhebens vom Boden aus eigenem Antrieb — leistungsgerecht in einen Wettbewerb mit vier Disziplinen verpackt: Hürden, Spurt, Weit- und Hochsprung.

Die Yogis erschienen in weißen Hosen und grünen Hemden. Sie falteten die Beine zum Lotussitz und versanken in transzendentaler Meditation. Nach fünf Minuten wich die völlige Bewegungslosigkeit der Wettkämpfer einem Zittern und Schütteln, offenbar handelte es sich um die Startvorbereitungen. Den Zeitpunkt für Sprung und Spurt durfte jeder Teilnehmer selbst bestimmen, da die Impulse der sogenannten Sidhi-Flugtechnik nicht bei jedem gleichzeitig einsetzten.

Das Schlüsselwort der Sidhi-Technik heißt Kohärenz: Das Bewußtsein verliert alle Begrenzungen und wird alles durchdringend, vollkommen rein und geordnet. Im Duden stehen gleich zwei Definitionen: 1. Zusammenhang, 2. Eigenschaft von Lichtbündeln mit gleicher Wellenlänge und Schwingungsart. Das kommt der Sache schon näher.

Die beim ersten Yogi-Wettfliegen erreichte Kohärenz ließ noch Wünsche offen. Der dreifache Goldmedaillengewinner Eddie Gob aus Guadeloupe legte mit 23,33 Sekunden über 50 Meter, 11,53 Sekunden im 25-Meter-Hürdenfliegen und 1,77 Meter im Weitsprung Ergebnisse vor, die mit konventioneller Technik leichter zu erreichen wären.

Dr. Bevan Morris, der Präsident der Maharishi-Technologie International University in Fairfield, Iowa, macht denn auch keinen Hehl daraus, daß es bis zur Vollendung des menschlichen Fluges noch ein weiter Weg sei. Gegenwärtig sei erst das Anfangsstadium, das Hüpfen im Lotussitz, erreicht. Das zweite Stadium sei das Schweben, das dritte endlich das freie, lenkbare Schweben.

Um den Weltfrieden herzustellen bedarf es aber nicht etwa des freien Fluges — das Anfangsstadium genügt. Nur ein Prozent einer Bevölkerung müsse nach Maharishi-Art meditieren, dann entstehe ein unüberwindlicher Schutzschild, der eine Nation unbesiegbar mache. „Genauso wie ein gesunder Körper Viren oder Bakterien zerstören kann, vermag eine Nation, die kulturell integriert ist, schädliche äußere Einflüsse zu neutralisieren und dadurch ihr Wohlergehen und ihren Fortschritt zu sichern", heißt es in einer Broschüre. Der „gesunde Volkskörper" soll auch auf seine Nachbarländer heilsamen Einfluß haben, wenn der „kohärente Einfluß" über die Landesgrenzen quillt.

Das „Entstehen von Kohärenz im kollektiven Bewußtsein" funktioniere ähnlich wie der „Quanten-Tunneleffekt" des Nobelpreisträgers und Ehrenprofessors für Physik an der Universität in Cambridge, Great Britain, Brian D. Josephon, der auch an Konferenzen der europäischen Maharishi Universität über Physik und Bewußtsein teilgenommen habe — mehr sei nicht verraten.

Am Freitag, 15. August, starten die Yogis auf dem Berliner Kurfürstendamm zum ersten deutschen Flugwettbewerb. Und was hat das alles, bitte schön, mit Frankfurt zu tun?

Erstens: Warum sollten mit Blick auf diese Veranstaltung Raum und Zeit als Koordinatensystem menschlicher Orientierung nicht ebenso überwunden werden wie die Schwerkraft? Und zweitens gibt es da das Frankfurter Institut für vedische Wissenschaft und Transzendentale Meditation, das just an jenem Freitag die Presse über die soziologischen und physiologischen Hintergründe des Yogi-Fliegens als „hochwirksames Mittel zur Beruhigung internationaler Krisenherde' aufklären möchte.

Im Moment freilich bereitet die Kohärenz dem Institut noch Mühe — es wird nach einer passenden Übersetzung gesucht.   ft

MAHARISHI'S PROGRAMME TO CREATE

PRESS REPORTS FROM EUROPE

West Germany • *Stuttgarter Zeitung*
Stuttgart 16 August 1986 (German)

Foto: Horst Rudel

West Germany • *Berliner Zeitung*
Berlin 16 August 1986 (German)

„Flug" für den Frieden reichte nur zum Hopser

"Yogisches Fliegen" sieht eher aus wie ein Hopser

Berlin, 16. August -ev Für den Weltfrieden wollten Yogis im Hotel Kempinski zeigen, wie man fliegt – doch es reichte nur zu Hopsern im Lotussitz. 13 Jünger der Transzendentalen Meditation setzten sich in Versenkung und behaupteten, durch Energie ohne eigenes Zutun „abzuheben". Nach Meinung der Veranstalter haben sie damit auch für steigende Aktienkurse, Gesundheit und Frieden auf der ganzen Welt gesorgt – denn sie würden negative Tendenzen in der Umwelt in positive verwandeln können. Wer's erlernen will: Der Kurs kostet zwischen 4000 und 6000 Mark.

WORLD PEACE • GLOBAL INAUGURATION

PRESS REPORTS FROM EUROPE

West Germany • *Volksblatt Berlin*
Berlin 16 August 1986 (German)

Yogis fliegen, und die Aktien steigen
„Gesellschaft für Transzendentale Meditation" hüpfte für den Weltfrieden

„Yogis fliegen für den Weltfrieden" war das Motto einer Veranstaltung der „Gesellschaft für Transzendentale Meditation" gestern im Hotel Kempinski. Die Organisation demonstrierte „yogisches Fliegen", das vom Inder Maharishi Mahesh Yogi gelehrt wird. 13 Anhänger dieser Meditationstechnik hüpften fünf Minuten lang im Lotussitz über eine Matratzenwiese. „Sie sehen, mit welcher Leichtigkeit das Hüpfen von stattengeht", kommentierte Veranstaltungsleiter Horst-Rainer Witt die sportlichen Leistungen. „In absehbarer Zeit werden wir auch die nächsten Stufen, das Schweben und Fliegen, erreichen können."

Die Anhänger Maharishis glauben, daß „yogisches Fliegen" den Weltfrieden wiederherstellen könne. Während der Körper in der Luft schwebe, würden sich Materie und Bewußtsein völlig vereinen. Der Meditierende erlebe ein starkes Glücksgefühl; negative Tendenzen in der Umwelt könnten neutralisiert werden.

„Wenn eine größere Gruppe dieses Programm aufführt, hat das ganz enorme Auswirkungen auf unsere Gesellschaft." Politiker würden freundlicher miteinander umgehen, Infektionskrankheiten und Verkehrsunfälle zurückgehen sowie Aktienkurse ansteigen.

Ein Zeitpunkt, wann Maharishis Anhänger das Hüpfstadium verlassen und auch das Schweben und Fliegen beherrschen, wurde von den Veranstaltern nicht genannt. Dies sei abhängig vom Bewußtseinszustand des einzelnen. „Wir wollten Ihnen mit dieser Demonstration heute zeigen, daß es überhaupt eine Technik zur Erreichung des Weltfriedens gibt", erläuterte Witt.

lbn

Yogis flogen in Berlin „für den Frieden". (Foto: dpa)

PRESS REPORTS FROM EUROPE

West Germany • *Frankfurter Rundschau*

Frankfurt 16 August 1986 (German)

Wo lang es denn, bitte schön, zu den fliegenden Yogis gehe? Der Empfangschef im feinen Westberliner Hotel Kempinski zögerte keine Sekunde: „Geradeaus, die Treppe hoch bis zum ersten Stock, im Schloßsaal." Dort waren vor dem Wandgemälde des Charlottenburger Schlosses zwei Dutzend weißbezogene Schaumgummimatratzen ausgelegt, links und rechts der Stuhlreihen vier Videogeräte aufgebaut. „Yogis fliegen für den Frieden" wurde auf den Schirmen angekündigt.

Das Ereignis finde weltweit in über tausend Städten statt, sagte Veranstaltungsleiter Horst-Rainer Witt, Anhänger „seiner Heiligkeit" des Maharishi Mahesh Yogi. Es handele sich um eine „Jahrtausendveranstaltung" und man habe sich bemüht, die „besten Flugtechniker hierherzubekommen". Ehe es soweit war, machte Horst-Rainer Witt seine gut hundert Zuhörer, die pro Kopf zehn Mark für die Eintrittskarte zahlen mußten, erst einmal mit seines Meisters „Programm für den Weltfrieden" bekannt.

Das Fliegen der Yogis solle die weltweiten Spannungen in Wohlgefallen auflösen. Es erzeuge, verkündete Witt ein „vereinheitlichtes Feld", das den Feindseligkeiten, dem Terrorismus, den Kriegen sowie den Infektionskrankheiten ganz einfach den Nährboden entziehe und zur Harmonie, zur totalen Ordnung und verstärkten Intelligenz führe.

Dieses zu Ehren des Meisters „Maharishi-Effekt" genannte Phänomen könne, so verrieten die Veranstalter, „sogar schon von einer Personenzahl, die der Wurzel aus einem Prozent der Bevölkerung entspricht, erzeugt werden". Voraussetzung sei nur, sie praktizierten das Programm gemeinsam an einem Ort. Die „Flüge für den Weltfrieden" sind allerdings nicht zum Spar-Tarif zu haben: 4000 bis 5000 Mark Kursusgebühr sind schon fällig, so war zu erfahren, um die Technik zu erlernen.

Zwei Massen-Flüge mit den nötigen 7000 Personen hätten in den vergangenen zwei Jahren bereits stattgefunden, in den USA und in den Niederlanden. „Danach gab es wirkliche Veränderungen im Weltbewußtsein", versicherte ... Franz-Theo Gottwald. Die Nachrichten über Aggressionen hätten deutlich abgenommen, die Staatsmänner in den Weltzentren hätten spürbar wohlwollender miteinander verkehrt, die Infektionskrankheiten und Verkehrsunfälle seien zurückgegangen, die Aktienkurse hingegen steil angestiegen. Nach etwa dreißig Tagen sei die Wirkung vorbei gewesen.

Damit das Phänomen ständig erhalten bleibt, will Maharishi Mahesh Yogi, Begründer der „transzendentalen Meditation", eine Truppe von 10 000 Personen im Yogi-Fliegen ausbilden lassen und einsetzen. Zur Verwirklichung dieses Ziels sind die „kreativen Menschen der Welt, die führenden und wohlhabenden Persönlichkeiten eingeladen, die dringende Notwendigkeit für Weltfrieden zu erkennen und den Maharishi-Weltfriedensfonds von 100 Millionen Dollar einzurichten".

Ehe es endlich ernst wurde im Schloßsaal des Hotels Kempinski, sahen sich die Veranstalter von der Gesellschaft für Transzendentale Meditation in West-Berlin allerdings noch genötigt, allzu weitgespannte Erwartungen zu dämpfen: Es sei „nichts Dolles für den Normalverbraucher zu sehen", erklärte man. Bislang sei das Ziel nicht erreicht, aber mit „steigendem Weltbewußtsein" werde man sich dem freien Flug nähern. „An unseren Flugübungen können Sie den Stand des Weltbewußtseins ablesen."

Die Kleinkinder wurden vor die Tür geschickt („dort ist ein Babysitter"), ein Glöckchen läutete fünf Minuten Schweigen ein, ein weiterer Glockenklang war Signal für das yogische Fliegen. Dreizehn Männer begannen im Lotussitz zu hüpfen, hielten ... inne und hüpften von neuem. Das Keuchen komme nicht von der Anstrengung, erklärte Teilnehmer Werner Opel (29) hinterher, sondern sei Ausdruck der in den Körper strömenden „großen Energie". Und wenn er selber jetzt „ein bißchen schwitze, dann ist das nur die Hitze".

BIRGIT LOFF (Berlin)

WORLD PEACE • GLOBAL INAUGURATION

PRESS REPORTS FROM EUROPE

West Germany • *Badische Zeitung*
Freiburg 16 August 1986 (German)

Anhänger der Transzendentalen Meditation in Freiburg:

Hopsen für den zukünftigen Frieden

Vorführung „yogischen Fliegens" im Hotel „Rheingold" – „Weltfrieden" hat seinen Preis

Von unserer Mitarbeiterin Margit Heyn

Ging es den Anhängern der Transzendentalen Meditation (TM) vor mehr als acht Jahren noch um die Unbesiegbarkeit der Nationen, so ging es ihnen und ihrem Anführer Maharishi Mahesh Yogi gestern um den Weltfrieden: wie angeblich in 30 Städten der Bundesrepublik und in 1000 Städten der gesamten Welt, so demonstrierten am Freitag TM-Lehrer vor einem kleinen Kreis auch in Freiburg das „yogische Fliegen". Den Interessierten sollte vorgeführt werden, wohin man mittels Transzendentaler Meditation kommen kann. Aber wirklich geflogen wurde dann doch nicht, und auch Schweben ist ein Ziel, das die hiesigen TM-Lehrer noch nicht erreicht haben.

Nach zehn Minuten absoluter Stille und Meditation vor dem Publikum wollten drei Anhänger der TM fünf Minuten lang das „yogische Fliegen vorführen und ihre Erfolge demonstrieren. Die absolute Stille wurde durch das Rauschen der Klimaanlage im „Ringsaal" des Hotels „Rheingold" gestört, und das ständige Klicken der Fotoapparate trug auch nicht sehr zur Stille bei. Nach zehn Minuten dieser relativen absoluten Stille demonstrierten dann Emil Treiber, Lothar Fink und Willi Kempe ihre Flugkünste. Im Yogasitz mit übergeschlagenen Beinen ging es über die Matten – Hospen oder Springen war es eher, und auch die Muskelkraft schien nicht ganz aus dem Spiel zu sein. Nach fünf Minuten – der eine hatte schon mal gen Publikum gelinst – kam schließlich das erlösende Klatschen des Publikums, und das „Fliegen" hatte ein Ende.

Sinn und Zweck dieser weltweiten Flugdemonstration: der Weltfrieden. Denn, so Emil Treiber, die Regierungen haben es bis heute nicht geschafft, Frieden herbeizuführen. Es herrschen ständig Angst und Rivalität zwischen den Supermächetn. Das Leben jedes einzelnen sei bedroht: Seit 1945 hätten immerhin 150 Kriege auf der Erde stattgefunden.

Konkretes Ziel der TM-Anhänger ist es nun, insgesamt 7000 Menschen gleichzeitig und ständig an einem Ort zu versammeln und gemeinsam in einer „Flughalle" fliegen zu lassen – auch wenn dies bis heute noch niemand gesehen hat. Fliegen nämlich ist das letzte angestrebte Stadium der Transzendentalen Meditation, davor liege Zittern und Schüttteln, Yoga-Hüpfen (dies Stadium wurde im „Rheingold" gezeigt), Schweben und schließlich Fliegen.

Wenn alle 7000 Anhänger gemeinsam hüpften, schwebten oder flögen, dann rücke der Weltfrieden näher: Das bedeutet für die Anhänger, daß die Kriminalitätsrate sinke, die Kriege würden beendet, die Verständigung auf der Welt zunehmen – und nicht zuletzt werden die Aktien dann steigen, versichert Emil Treiber. Überprüft hätten dies Wissenschaftler während eines Treffens von TM-Anhängern in den USA – damals waren kurzfristig genügend zusammengekommen, um die 7000 zu überbieten.

Maharishi Mahesh Yogi will mit seinem Programm zur Verwirklichung des Weltfriedens nichts weniger als die Ursachen von Terrorismus und Negativität in der Weltfamilie beseitigen – und das hat natürlich seinen Preis. Denn die 7000, die durch ihr Fliegen stellvertretend den Frieden sichern sollen, müssen von irgendetwas leben. Emil Treiber rechnet vor: 7000 (mindestens) benötigen jährlich drei Millionen Mark zu Leben. Und damit dies gesichert ist, greift er auf ganz einfache Methoden zurück – man möchte von den Zinsen leben. Dann benötigten die Anhänger von Maharishi Mahesh Yogi allerdings 100 Millionen Dollar.

PRESS REPORTS FROM EUROPE

West Germany • *Nord Stuttgarter Rundschau*
Stuttgart 16 August 1986 (German)

Stufe 1 des yogischen Fliegens: Start, Stillstand, Sturz

Bild: Uli Kraufmann

West Germany • *Die Tageszeitung*

Hamburg 16 August 1986 (German)

Ein Menschheitstraum mit langem Bart

Es ist möglich: Vor den Augen einer kritischen Jury demonstrierte Eddie Gob am 9. Juli 1986 im Washington Convention Center die Technik „Yogic Flying". Ein großformatiges AP-Foto, auch abgedruckt in der taz, zeigt ihn schwebend, im Yogi-Sitz.

Anders als in Süddeutschland, ... hob im Hamburger Interconti am 15. August tatsächlich jemand ab. Die taz war dabei. ...

Natürlich kann nicht jeder fliegen, ein ausgewählter und trainierter Maharishi-Anhänger muß man schon sein. Yogi-Fliegen ist auch mehr als Fliegen: Es leitet eminente, evidente politische Veränderungen ein. Der Mensch fliegt nicht für sich, er hebt ab zur Beseitigung der Ursachen von Terrorismus und Negativität.

Der Neue Weg lautet: Durch Meditation und Levitation werden Spannungen in der Welt neutralisiert. Levitation, so das Lexikon, kommt aus dem lateinischen und ist weiblich, heißt Leichtigkeit. ..... Von Mystikern und Medien behauptetes Phänomen: das physikalisch unerklärliche freie Schweben einer Person oder eines Objekts ... der psychologischen Interpretation zugänglich ist sowohl die objektive als auch die subjektive Levitation." Zur Subjektiven, führt das Nachschlagewerk aus, zählen vor allem Flugträume und Hexenfahrten.

Aber Lexikas sind keine Tageszeitungen und im vorliegenden Fall nicht auf dem neuesten wissenschaftlichen Stand. Erstens ist die Levitation männlich (jedenfalls bei längeren Flugleistungen) und zweitens konnte die EEG-Forschung die Grundeinheit für den Weltfrieden im menschlichen Gehirn lokalisieren. Durch maximale Kohärenz (Geordnetheit) der Gehirnwellenaktivität, schafft man die ideale Voraussetzung für den reibungslosen Fluß in Richtung Wunscherfüllung. Der Wunsch, dem sich tausende von Yogi-Jüngern im Interconti mit Heftigkeit hingaben: für den Frieden unter der Decke hängend.

In Hamburg beherrschen inzwischen 600 Menschen diese „flying ability". Unter den 600, die wiederum eine Teilmenge der 10.000 bilden, die in unserer Stadt die Transzendentale Meditation ausüben, befinden sich allerdings nur 50, die die Technik in vorzeigbarer Körper-Geist-Koordination vermitteln können.

Im Interconti wurden die männlichen Flieger, die sich schon vor der Flugdemonstration „erleichtert" hatten, der neugierigen Öffentlichkeit geschlagene anderthalb Stunden vorenthalten. Dies allerdings nicht aus Berechnung, quasi um die Spannung für die neugierigen Gäste zu steigern, sondern einzig und allein, um die späteren Flieger nicht wieder mit schwerwiegenden Spannungen aufzuladen.

90 Minuten mußten wir, „Menschen aus allen Bevölkerungsschichten und Berufssparten" auf die Befriedung unserer Neugier warten, Videos über Transzendentale Meditation verkürzten uns die Wartezeit, freundliche Ansprachen freundlicher TM-Anhänger halfen uns langsam aus der oberflächlichen Anspannung, unserer voyeuristischen Begierden in die tiefe Entspannung der Erwartungslosigkeit hinabzugleiten.

Die Ansammlung der Verdunkelungen, die uns nach unten zogen, hatten sich verflüchtigt, wir waren bereit, den Fliegern bei ihrem spannungslosen Flugversuch ohne „negative" Energie beizuwohnen. Jeder konnte es sehen: Wie sich im gleißenden Scheinwerferlicht 10 Demonstranten für den Frieden in die Luft erhoben. 1 cm, 2 cm, - hoffentlich fallen sie nicht gleich wieder runter ... 5 cm - dem Weltfrieden näher.

Plötzlich merke ich wie mein Begleiter neben mir immer kleiner zu werden droht. Ich kann ihn nur von oben herab anschauen. Ich war wohl selbst abgehoben. Mehr möchte ich über dieses, wenngleich öffentlich erlebte, aber mich doch in meinem Innern zutiefst verändernde Erlebnis an dieser Stelle nicht berichten. *ane*

PRESS REPORTS FROM EUROPE

West Germany • *Heilbronner Stimme*

Heilbronn 16 August 1986 (German)

Gestern in Heilbronn: Maharishis Anhänger zeigten fortgeschrittene TM-Technik

Meditierende: „Fliegen" für den Frieden

Von unserem Redaktionsmitglied Ulrike Bauer

Sechs dicke Matten liegen auf dem Wohnzimmerteppich. Drei junge Männer haben sich im „Lotussitz" darauf niedergelassen. Es wird um absolute Ruhe gebeten. Das „flugtaugliche" Trio beginnt zu meditieren. Sieben Frauen und ein Mann im Raum schließen ebenfalls die Augen und meditieren. In wenigen Minuten soll in der Frankenbacher Münchner Straße das „Yogische Fliegen" demonstriert werden.

Veranstalter ist das Heilbronner Zentrum für Transzendentale Meditation (TM), das in den letzten Jahren über 1000 Unterländer in diese besondere Entspannungstechnik eingewiesen hat, wie TM-Mitarbeiterin Ingeborg Glatzel mitteilt.

In 22 Städten der Bundesrepublik und in 108 Ländern der Welt wurden am gestrigen Freitag Presse und Fernseh-Teams eingeladen. Als Zeugen sollten sie der fortgeschrittenen Meditationstechnik, dem Sidhi-Programm beiwohnen. Gezeigt wurde das von „Seiner Heiligkeit" Maharishi Mahesh Yogi gelehrte „Yogische Fliegen". Nach Ansicht der TM-Leute ist das Fliegen nicht Selbstzweck, sondern sichtbarer Ausdruck einer inneren Harmonie.

Inzwischen haben die drei „Flieger" Antony Gawlikowski, Erhard Gehrke und Detlef Kramp einen gelöst-heiteren Gesichtsausdruck bekommen. Sie wiegen wie in Trance Kopf und Oberkörper, Zuckungen lassen ihren Körper erbeben, wie unter großer Anstrengung holen sie Atem und stoßen ihn wieder aus. Nach etwa fünf Minuten ist es soweit: die Körper im Lotussitz beginnen zu hüpfen. Erst zwanzig Zentimeter hoch, später wird Antony auf drei übereinander gelegte Matten springen. Mehrere Minuten dauert das Spektakel.

Fliegen? Geflogen im üblichen Sinne ist das nicht, bestätigen die TM-Leute. Es sei nur die erste Stufe davon. Bei Stufe zwei „schwebe" der Körper frei über dem Boden, bei Stufe drei führe er in der Luft Bewegungen aus. Die Einschränkung folgt auf dem Fuße: Stufe zwei und drei hat noch kein Mensch erreicht. Erst wenn „im Weltbewußtsein genügend Kohärenz erzeugt ist", sei es soweit.

„Im Zustand maximaler Kohärenz (Geordnetheit) der Gehirnwellenaktivität hebt der Körper vom Boden ab", das ist die These von Maharishi. Diese Kohärenz zwischen Bewußtsein und Materie im Körper entstehe auf der Ebene des „vereinheitlichten Feldes" aller Naturgesetze, so die Maharishi-Theorie. Das vereinheitliche Feld (so eine Art Urenergie) wiederum sei in der Lage, disharmonische Tendenzen in der gesamten Natur unmittelbar zu harmonisieren. Diese positive Kraft würde letztlich auch die Entwicklung von Natur und Menschheit beschleunigen.

Äußeres Zeichen einer inneren Harmonie – das „yogische Fliegen". Diese besondere Meditationstechnik wurde gestern weltweit vorgestellt, auch in Heilbronn.
Foto: HSt-Kleinknecht

WORLD PEACE • GLOBAL INAUGURATION

Was so akademisch-intellektuell klingt, hat in den Augen der TM-Anhänger praktische Anwendungsmöglichkeiten: Wo genügend Harmonie ist, könnten kein Krieg und kein Terror, keine Krankheit und keine Katastrophen mehr sein. „Der Mensch kann durch positive Gedanken Weltfrieden erzeugen", das ist der Wunsch Maharishis.

„Indem man die Völker der Erde in Angst versetzt, kann man keinen Frieden garantieren", sagt „Flieger" Antony Gawlikowski. Er ist 34 Jahre alt, wohnt in Rottenburg, betreibt seit 14 Jahren TM, ist von Beruf Sprachwissenschaftler und promoviert derzeit über Computerlinguistik.

Er erklärt, wie im Weltbewußtsein genügend Harmonie hergestellt werden könne: Mindestens 7000 Menschen müßten täglich zweimal gemeinsam unter einem Dach morgens und abends TM Maharishis yogisches Programm ausüben. Die Kohärenz, die sie erzeugten, sei dann so groß, daß sie über die ganze Welt ausstrahle und das gesamte „Weltbewußtsein reinige". Was diese 7000 in Gedanken an Positivem erzeugten, werde Auseinandersetzungen auf internationaler Ebene in Frieden umwandeln, und letztendlich den Weltfrieden erzeugen. Davon ist jeder TM'ler überzeugt.

Nur es fehlt an Geld. Um diese 7000, besser 10 000, täglich für die Menschheit Meditierenden zu unterhalten (sie sollen in der Nähe von Neu-Delhi in Indien wirken), braucht Maharishi Geld. Zehn Millionen Dollar jährlich. Um die zu kriegen, bedarf es eines Vermögens von 100 000 Millionen Dollar, angelegt mit einer zehnprozentigen Rendite. Es werden Spender gesucht ...

West Germany • *Kölnische-Rundschau*

Köln   16 August 1986   (German)

Das „jogische Fliegen"

Anhänger des indischen Jogis Maharishi Mahesh Yogi demonstrieren jetzt in Köln und Berlin das „jogische Fliegen." Mit Hilfe der „transzendentalen Meditation" soll es möglich sein, sich bei höchster Konzentration in die Lüfte zu erheben....

West Germany • *Westfälisches Volksblatt*
Paderborn 16 August 1986 (German)

Eine zehnminütige Meditation – dann hebt der Yogi ab . . .

Fliegen für den Weltfrieden

Die verblüffenden Experimente des Paderborners Eugen Lüchtefeld

Paderborn (wv). »Alle Ampeln waren rot«, entschuldigt sich das ältere Ehepaar, das einige Minuten zu spät kommt, »fliegen können wir nicht!« »Noch nicht«, hätte Eugen Lüchtefeld sicher gern ergänzt. Der 33jährige Heilpraktiker hat sich der Transzendentalen Meditation (TM) gewidmet und setzt diese weltweite Bewegung jetzt auch in Paderborn mit verblüffenden Experimenten fort. Im Zustand »maximaler Kohärenz«, wie die TM-Jünger es nennen, der totalen Vereinheitlichung von Körper und Geist, kann sich der Meditierende mit nur geringem Kraftaufwand vom Boden abheben.

Eugen Lüchtefeld machte es am Donnerstagabend vor: Lotussitz, eine Haltung ähnlich des Schneidersitzes mit extrem verschränkten Beinen, rund zehnminütige Meditation – und dann hebt der Yogi ab! Ohne sonderliche Kraftanstrengungen hüpft er mit leichtem Druck der Oberschenkel über eine rund vier Meter lange weiche Schaumstoffmatte in Ein-Meter-Sprüngen. Viermal hin, viermal zurück, drei bis vier Bahnen. Dann steht Lüchtefeld auf und tut, als wäre nichts gewesen. Keine Schweißperlen, keine erhöhte Herz- und Pulsfrequenz, die nach einem derartigen Kurs, der allein auf körperlichen Kräften beruht hätte, automatisch folgen müßte.

Aber das Fliegen ist für die TM-Freunde – inzwischen gibt es im Hochstift Paderborn rund 1500 – nur ein spektakuläres Beiwerk. Ihnen geht es um nichts Geringeres als die Herstellung des Weltfriedens! Und den versuchen sie mit ihrer Kohärenz zu verwirklichen. Nur ein Prozent der Bevölkerung müßte den Lehren »Seiner Heiligkeit Maharishi Mahesh Yogi« aus Indien folgen und die Bevölkerung könnte durch die glückliche zufriedene Ausstrahlung dieses Bruchteils der Menschen in totalem Frieden leben.

Auch für Paderborn hat Lüchtefeld schon Zahlen parat: »40 Bürger müßten sich finden, die regelmäßig morgens und abends gemeinsam meditieren und Paderborn wäre die friedlichste Stadt der Welt.«

Wenn dies erst erreicht ist, wird es sicherlich nicht mehr lange bis zum ersten Yogi-Wettfliegen in Paderborn dauern, eine Premiere, die am 9. Juli in New Dehli weltweit auf die TM-Bewegung aufmerksam machte: Dann geht es im Lotussitz im Spurt über 50 Meter, über 25 Meter Hürden, zum Hoch- und Weitsprung. Der Weltrekord steht übrigens bei 1,77 Weite und 61 Zentimeter Höhe . . .

Franz-Josef Herber

WORLD PEACE • GLOBAL INAUGURATION

PRESS REPORTS FROM EUROPE

West Germany • *Stuttgarter Nachrichten*
Stuttgart   16 August 1986   (German)

Wenn Menschen fliegen
Der Yogi als Friedenstaube

Nur fliegen sei schöner. Heißt es. Aber wer weiß es wirklich, von den Vögeln abgesehen, die nicht reden können? Niemand. Oder doch: Seine Heiligkeit Maharishi Mahesh Yogi weiß es, und seine Jünger in aller Welt sind drauf und dran, es zu lernen. Nach ihren ersten Erfahrungen ist fliegen nicht nur schöner, es befreit auch von Streß und vermittelt ein besseres Lebensgefühl. Alsdann, schwingt die Fittiche!

Von wegen. Mit den herkömmlichen Formeln der Physik läßt sich das nicht erklären, was beispielsweise den Computer-Linguisten Toni Gawrilowski bewegt, wenn er sich im Lotus-Sitz bewegt. Dann lupft's ihn aus der Gegenwart saubere 30 Zentimeter hoch in das „Vereinheitlichte Feld aller Naturgesetze" hinein, wo der fortgeschrittene yogische Flieger dann schwebend verweilt. Kraft der Kohärenz (Zusammenhang) zwischen Bewußtsein und Materie im Körper, versteht sich. Anfänger wie Gawrilowski und Kollegen, die am Freitag anläßlich der „weltweiten Einweihung von Maharishis Programm zur Herstellung des Weltfriedens" ihr fliegerisches Können demonstrierten, sind allerdings rein kohärenzmäßig auf keinem Radarschirm zu erkennen: Für sie gelten weiterhin die Gesetze der Schwerkraft.... Aber sind wir mal nicht so. Wenn's wirklich dem Weltfrieden hilft...

Bild: Uli Kraufmann

Stufe 1 des yogischen Fliegens: Start, Stillstand, Sturz

West Germany • *Saarbrücker Zeitung*

Saarbrücken 18 August 1986 (German)

Völlig losgelöst

Schweben aus dem Lotussitz

„Die ersten Flugzeuge sind am Anfang auch nur gehüpft" — so „Seine Heiligkeit Maharishi Mahesh Yogi" zur Sidhi-Technik des „yogischen Fliegens", der höchsten Stufe transzendentaler Meditation (TM). Begnügen muß sich der Mensch also vorläufig mit der ersten Stufe des „yogischen Fliegens", dem Hüpfen, das am Freitag von Mitgliedern der TM-Gruppe Saarbrücken im Rahmen einer weltweiten Aktion für den Frieden demonstriert wurde.

Im kleinen Konferenzraum der Kongreßhalle herrscht Stille. Drei Männer verharren, im Lotussitz meditierend, auf mehreren Matratzen, die nebeneinander auf dem Boden ausgelegt sind. Nach etwa 15 Minuten durchzuckt es ihre Körper und bald darauf hüpft schon der erste: mit den angewinkelten Beinen, froschähnlich, zieht es ihn im Schneidersitz ruckartig von der Matte. Die Hüpfbewegungen der beiden anderen folgen gleich im Anschluß.

Was hier vordergründig den Anschein von Scharlatanerie erwecken könnte, ist für den Laien, ohne meditative Hilfe, zumindest keine leichte Übung (wer's nicht glaubt, sollte es mal zu Hause probieren!). Doch es geht nicht um den Sensationseffekt, so beteuern die TM-Leute, sondern um die positive Wirkung der Meditation auf den einzelnen generell. Denn dessen innerer Friede, seine Erfülltheit und Harmonie ist gemäß der Lehre des Maharishi der wirksamste Beitrag zur Verwirklichung des Weltfriedens.

TM-Gruppenmitglied Astrid Wehrhahn stellte eine Reihe wissenschaftlicher Untersuchungen vor, die diese Wirkungsweise verdeutlichen.   mal

WORLD PEACE • GLOBAL INAUGURATION

PRESS REPORTS FROM EUROPE

West Germany • *Völklinger Stadtanzeiger*
Saarbrücken 20-21 August 1986 (German)

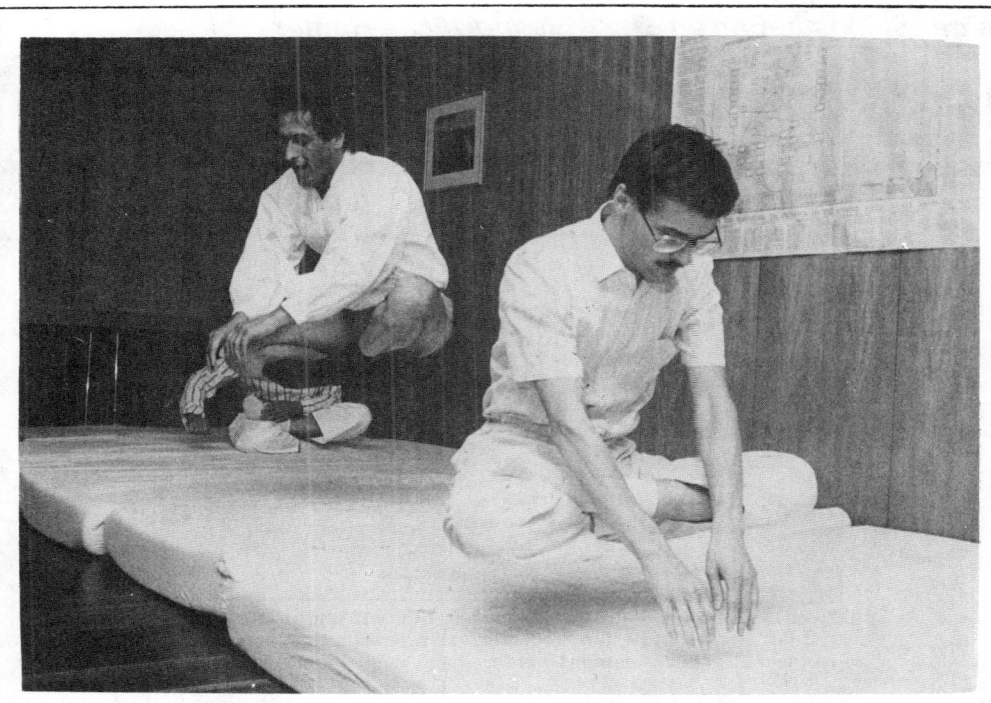

Nichts geringeres als den Weltfrieden haben sich die Anwender der „Transzendentalen Meditation" und der Aufbaustufe des „Sidhi-Programms" zum Ziel gesetzt. Um diese „Sidhi-Techniken" („Sidhi" ist Sanskrit und heißt auf gut deutsch „Vollkommenheit") ging es bei der Vorführung im Konferenzsaal der Kongreßhalle in Saarbrücken. Die Anwender, sogenannte „Sidhas", sollten fliegen, hieß es. Während dieser Meditationsmethode wird ein Bewußtseinszustand großer Geordnetheit im Gehirn erreicht, was auch von Wissenschaftlern aus aller Welt bestätigt wird. Ein „Nebenprodukt" dieser Technik ist, daß der Meditierende vom Boden abhebt, fliegt. Drei TM-Lehrer, Axel Bumb, Udo Redlich und Werner Klein, führten das vor. Bislang wurde dieser Effekt eher von der Öffentlichkeit ferngehalten.

Wer nun die Fähigkeiten von „Supermann" erwartet hatte, wurde enttäuscht. Vielmehr ähnelten die „Hopser" stellenweise eher denjenigen von Amphibien.

Der Demonstration war ein Vortrag der beiden TM-Lehrer Heiko Pilger und Astried Wehrhahn vorausgegangen, die sehr deutlich machten, daß dieses „Fliegen" kein Selbstzweck ist, sondern den erreichten Bewußtseinszustand widerspiegelt.

Die Veranstaltung lief gleichzeitig in 108 Ländern und 32 deutschen Städten. Weitere Informationen sind unter den Telefonnummern (0 68 98) 29 45 67, (06 81) 3 34 14 und (06 81) 6 14 59 erhältlich.

PRESS REPORTS FROM EUROPE

West Germany • *Neue Braunschweiger Zeitung*

Braunschweig 21 August 1986 (German)

Braunschweiger Sidhas heben ab • Zwölf sportliche Hüpfer

Fliegen für den Frieden der Welt

Zwölf Sprünge im Lotussitz — jeweils drei vor und drei zurück — sollten im Institut für vedische Wissenschaft (Campestraße) „yogisches Fliegen" demonstrieren.

Braunschweig (plo). Würden 50 Braunschweiger morgens und abends meditieren, ginge es mit unserer Stadt sogleich bergauf. Die Wirtschaft würde florieren, der Wohlstand der Braunschweiger sich mehren, Kriminalitäts- und Unfallrate sänken. Täten es weltweit 7000 Menschen am Morgen und am Abend, wären Wohlstand und Frieden für alle Menschen dieser Erde gesichert.

So hat es Mahesh Yogi, populärer Lehrer der transzendentalen Meditation (TM) verkündet und seine Mitarbeiter versuchen jetzt, es wissenschaftlich zu beweisen. Dazu haben sie die Theorie des vereinheitlichten Feldes entwickelt. Vereinfacht ist das ein Zustand absoluter Entspannung. Sämtliche Gehirnströme seien in diesem meditativen Stadium kohärent (gleichgeordnet) und würden riesige Energie freisetzen. Mit Hilfe dieser Energie ließe sich die Umwelt beeinflussen - zum Beispiel dahingehend, Frieden zu schließen. Das vereinheitlichte Feld erreiche man, so Maharishi, auf verschiedenen Wegen, effektiv sei ein Flug-Sutra. Bei diesem Programm, so will es die TM-Lehre, „fliegen" die Sidhas kraft Meditation.

Daß das funktioniert, wollten jetzt Braunschweiger Maharishi-Anhänger beweisen. Um es kurz zu machen: Mehr als zwölf - wenn auch recht flotte - Hüpfer kamen dabei nicht heraus. Sportlich bemerkenswert; gleich vom Fliegen zu sprechen, ist dick aufgetragen.

Fairerweise muß gesagt werden, daß die Sidhas selbst das Hüpfen als erstes Stadium des Fliegens betrachten, erst im dritten Stadium schwebt das Medium. Allerdings beherrscht zur Zeit niemand auf der Welt nachweislich dieses Stadium. Auch Mahesh Yogi ist den Beweis dafür noch schuldig.

WORLD PEACE • GLOBAL INAUGURATION

PRESS REPORTS FROM EUROPE

West Germany • *Lübecker Nachrichten*
Lübeck   27 August 1986   (German)

Yoga-Übung als ein Weg zum Weltfrieden

„Yogisches Fliegen" in seinem ersten Stadium, aber keine Sensation habe man in TM-Center Lübeck zeigen wollen. (Foto: Jo Marwitzky)

„Ein Sprung in die Luft nur mit Geisteskraft", LN vom 16. 8.

Ihren Artikel vom 16. 8. 86 möchten wir wie folgt ergänzen:
1. Es sollte keine Flugsensation, sondern das erste Stadium des „Yogisches Fliegens" gezeigt werden, das in einem Hopsen des Körpers besteht....
2. Gehirnwellenmessungen haben aber gezeigt, daß „Yogisches Fliegen" von maximaler Kohärenz (Geordnetheit) der Gehirnfunktion abhängt: Der Körper erhebt sich im Augenblick maximaler Kohärenz. Subjektiv wird dies als tiefste Ruhe, Glück, Freiheit und innerer Frieden empfunden.
3. Die Wirkung wird verstärkt, wenn größere Gruppen die Übung gemeinsam praktizieren. Die Kohärenz im Bewußtsein der Gruppe kann unmittelbar auf das größere kollektive Bewußtsein der Bevölkerung übergreifen, auch wenn die Gruppe verhältnismäßig klein ist. Eine Gruppe von 7000 reicht zum Beispiel aus, um auf der ganzen Erde einen Einfluß von größerer Geordnetheit und Positivität auszulösen und Weltfrieden zu bringen. Mehrere zeitlich begrenzte Versuche der letzten Jahre haben diese Theorie bestätigt.
4. Jeder verantwortungsbewußte Mensch fühlt heute, wie die gefährliche Rivalität der Supermächte und die blinde Gewalt des Terrorismus, der jederzeit und überall aufflammen kann, wachsen. Das einzige Mittel, dieser Gefahr zu begegnen, ist, das Bewußtsein des einzelnen und der Welt von Negativität und Aggressivität zu Geordnetheit und Harmonie zu entwickeln.

Die Technik dazu ist, weltweit sowie in jedem Land und jeder Stadt genügend große Gruppen aufzubauen, die regelmäßig gemeinsam unter anderem das „Yogische Fliegen" – in welchem Stadium auch immer – ausüben.

Darauf hinzuweisen, war der Zweck der weltweiten Vorführungen am 15. 8. 1986, und wir freuen uns, daß die „Lübecker Nachrichten" – soweit es ihnen möglich war – dazu beigetragen haben.

Dr. Claus Godbersen, Dipl.-Ing. Sabine Groth, Susanne Willnow, Dieter Zellweger

PRESS REPORTS FROM EUROPE

West Germany • *Schwäbische Donauzeitung*

Ulm   22 August 1986   (German)

Einfache und effektive Methode

Zum Artikel „Maharishis Anhänger hüpfen dem Weltfrieden entgegen" vom 18. August 1986: In Frieden leben – oder untergehen! Das ist die Alternative vor der wir heute stehen. Die Angst vor weltweitem Terrorismus und nuklearen Katastrophen hängt wie ein Damoklesschwert über Einzelnen und Nationen. Kann die Bedrohung noch größer werden?

Wenn Psychologen behaupten, daß der heutige Mensch höchstens fünf bis zehn Prozent seines geistigen Potentials nutzt, dann wundert es sicher niemanden, daß Unzulänglichkeiten aller Art unser Leben bestimmen. Frustration des Einzelnen, Ärger, Furcht, Fehlschläge und alle Ausprägungen von Negativität erzeugen Spannungen größten Ausmaßes im kollektiven Bewußtsein der Gesellschaft. Die Folgen der mit kollektiver Spannung angereicherten Atmosphäre sind z.B. Unfälle, Katastrophen, Terrorismus und kriegerische Auseinandersetzungen.

Wie die Erfahrung zeigt, ist es keine Lösung, einen immer größeren Gesetzeswald zu erstellen oder Polizeieinheiten zu verstärken. Auch die Aktivitäten der zahllosen Friedensorganisationen haben keinen nennenswerten Erfolg gebracht. Eine wirkliche Lösung muß an der Wurzel aller Probleme ansetzen. Jedes Individuum muß die Chance haben, endlich normal zu funktionieren, sein volles menschliches Potential zu nutzen.

Die Maharishi-Technologie des Vereinheitlichten Feldes, deren Grundlage die Technik der Transzendentalen Meditation ist und ihr vorläufiger Höhepunkt, das heute zumeist noch nicht perfekt beherrschte „Yogische Fliegen", ist – aller Kompliziertheit der Begriffe zum Trotz – die einfachste und natürlichste und deshalb schnellste Methode, das menschliche Bewußtsein voll zu entfalten.

Ich bin mir im klaren darüber, daß diese Aussage hohe Anforderungen an das Vorstellungsvermögen stellt. Im Hinblick auf die Dringlichkeit unserer weltweiten Lage sollte aber zu erwarten sein, daß verantwortungsbewußte Führer und Bürger der Gesellschaft wenigstens einmal frei von Vorurteilen hinsehen und hinhören, wenn ein Angebot dieser Art ergeht. Es steht zuviel auf dem Spiel, als daß wir es uns leisten könnten, eine Initiative zu belächeln und unbesehen beiseite zu legen, die den Weltfrieden sichern kann. Wie stichhaltig die Erklärung ist, daß ein Welt-Fonds von 100 Millionen Dollar es einer Gruppe von 7000–10 000 Experten dieser Technologie des Friedens ermöglicht, sich dauerhaft an einem Ort der Erde zu etablieren, um den Weltfrieden für alle Zukunft sicherzustellen, muß wenigstens nachgeprüft werden. Wenn die Sache hält, was sie verspricht, was bedeuten dann 100 Millionen Dollar als Gegenwert für dauerhafte Sicherheit, die auf innerer Geordnetheit und Harmonie der Menschen beruht? Konventionelle Mittel, unsere Lebensgrundlage zu sichern, sind nicht nur enorm teuer, sie haben auch versagt. Wenn wir wirklich Fortschritt auf der Basis von Frieden und Sicherheit und nicht den Untergang wollen, sind wir gezwungen, einen völlig neuen Ansatz zu wählen. Die Zeit drängt und das bedeutet, daß die Methode höchst einfach und effektiv sein muß. Diese bereits erprobte und wissenschaftlich belegte Methode heißt „Maharishi Technologie des Vereinheitlichten Feldes". Sie wurde am Freitag, dem 15. August 1986, in 108 Ländern in etwa 1000 Städten, darunter auch Ulm, vorgestellt.

Karin Guha,
Neu-Ulm

WORLD PEACE • GLOBAL INAUGURATION

PRESS REPORTS FROM EUROPE

Great Britain • *BBC TV*

Washington, D.C.   10 July 1986   (English)

Newscaster: Finally, an unusual addition to the summer's sporting program. The first games for practitioners of Transcendental Meditation have just opened. The organizers say they hope the event will bring peace… The venue…the United States.

Tim Sebastian: They call this the land of opportunity…On your mark, get set…This act of hopping is called 'yogic flying'—mind and body in close harmony…

Some of America's 3,000 flyers have come along to help set the mood, and one from Britain, too.

Guy Hardy (British expert in the Maharishi Technology of the Unified Field): I feel that I am with the whole world. I feel totally whole—there is nothing like it. It is just totally exhilarating. This is the best experience that anyone can have in life.

Tim Sebastian: Sports Day continued with the 50-meter hurdles—a headlong dash in the lotus position, the mind fully in gear and the body rolling behind. The judges from India and the nicest of motives.

Blaine Watson: It is beyond a shadow of doubt that world peace is the result of this, and that is why we do it.

Tim Sebastian: They collected their earthly prizes to add to their spiritual bliss, but there is more to come. This summer they will be flying to India…on an airplane.

PRESS REPORTS FROM EUROPE

Great Britain • WTN

New Delhi   22 July 1986   (English)

Reporter: Well, whatever fate might await the British teams at the Commonwealth Games there is one sport in which our competitors are proving themselves to be real high flyers. They have taken silver and bronze medals in the first-ever world championships of a sport that is really taking off....

Flying yogis came from all round the world to take part in the Olympics and to demonstrate a skill rarely seen in public—a leap into the air in the sitting lotus position as taught by the masters of meditation. The British team were confident of a place in the medals. After some brief meditating at the start of the 25-metre hurdles it was indeed an English surgeon who made the first lonely dash for the tape.

Each competitor had their own style, but some were more successful than others.

I have to talk in a stage whisper because to talk any louder might destroy their concentration, but I can tell you each time they leap a bubble of bliss is supposed to be released.

But can't this be done by any trained gymnast?

TM-Sidha: That point came up when we first started flying, and they spoke to a gymnastics expert in Oregon in the United States, and he said it just wasn't possible even for experienced athletes sitting in the lotus position to get that sort of leverage.

Reporter: ... how does it feel?

TM-Sidha: Ah, exhilarating! That's all I can say!...

Reporter: David Chater, News at One, in New Delhi.

WORLD PEACE • GLOBAL INAUGURATION

PRESS REPORTS FROM EUROPE

Great Britain • *LBC Radio*

London   15 August 1986   (English)

Broadcaster: World peace when, how, and if it comes will begin by sounding something like this. (Hopping sounds).

That's actually the sound of 'yogic flying', which is a form of meditation and, according to the Maharishi Mahesh Yogi, can bring world peace closer. All over Britain his followers have been demonstrating the technique, and Dr Geoffrey Clements, Vice-Chancellor of the Maharishi University of Natural Law in Buckinghamshire has been explaining all to Sue Brooks.

Dr Clements: This is a very significant demonstration of the mechanics of creating world peace through the programmes developed by His Holiness Maharishi Mahesh Yogi, and in essence this demonstration that we are seeing today has arisen because of the very acute need in the world for creating peace, particularly with the upsurge of terrorism, where even the superpowers are becoming involved with terrorism. We see that there is such an acute need for creating a coherent, stable, and harmonious world.

Interviewer: What's world peace got to do with four or five people hopping down some mattresses in the middle of a London hotel?

Dr Clements: The point about this is that we are looking at the principles by which peace is created. All the efforts that have been made to create world peace by governments and by responsible individuals in the past have failed because they have failed to address the unit of world peace, which is the coherent, orderly functioning of the individual in society.

Interviewer: You say 'flying technique' though. With the greatest respect, it actually seems as though you've got some very fit, agile people that are literally hopping, they are bouncing along mattresses—that's not flying.

Dr Clements: Now, this is a very good point you've brought up. There is a very clear definition. There are three stages in the development of this flying. The first stage is the one that we are seeing today, which is the level that most of the practitioners of this technique have reached, and that is that due to the consciousness reaching the coherent state, the body lifts up in the air but then comes down very quickly—it hops along these foam mattresses as you've said.

Interviewer: But I could hop....

Dr Clements: Yes, you could hop, but if you look at what is happening in the brain and also in the rest of the body you find that it is very, very different from physical jumping. If a person engages in physical jumping, particularly in this fully cross-legged position, the traditional position for this technique, usually one would find it is almost completely impossible and very fatiguing to do this, and certainly the brain functioning would not become more coherent. With this 'yogic flying' technique the whole body and mind-body co-ordination become very high. The body becomes very integrated, the brain functions very coherently and it goes without effort. The people you'll see are not fatigued at the end of the practice. I agree with you that we are still at a very early stage. In fact, we were really very shy in advance whether to do this or not, but we decided, and Maharishi felt himself, that it was important to demonstrate the mechanics by which world peace is created. The studies that have been performed when large numbers have been gathering together to produce this effect show that a global influence has been seen of increased harmony, decreased turbulence and violence in the whole world. All that is required is one group of about 7,000 to 10,000 people practising this technique morning and evening on a permanent basis to create a stable effect of world peace.

Interviewer: So move over Terry Waite and Bob Geldorf, let's all start hopping around and everybody will live happily ever after?

Dr Clements: Well, I think we fully appreciate the efforts of all the people who are working very hard to achieve world peace and integration in the world, but we see from the results of the past, that treaties or creating discussions between people do not produce any lasting effect. The United Nations was formed forty years ago; since that time there have been 80 wars in the world. In fact, UNESCO has as it's motto that 'war is created in the mind of man'. (Sounds of hopping).

Broadcaster: That's Geoffrey Clements talking there with Sue Brooks...

WORLD PEACE • GLOBAL INAUGURATION

PRESS REPORTS FROM EUROPE

Great Britain • *Radio Manchester*
Manchester 15 August 1986 (English)

Interviewer: Practitioners of Transcendental Meditation met earlier today to show the press 'yogic flying'—that's flying on your own. One of the flyers is from Manchester. His name is Phil Mitchell. I was talking to him, but first this tea-time I asked David Hughes, a lecturer in TM, what happened today.

David Hughes: The body lifts up in the air and comes straight down again, so we have half-a-dozen people demonstrating this procedure to members of the press this morning. This is the first time it's ever been demonstrated in public. It was part of a world-wide demonstration of this procedure that was going on around the world at the same time this morning.

The reason for it is that research has shown that TM itself, which is a very simple and effortless mental technique, practised by about 150,000 people in Britain, is capable of allowing the mind to settle down, and the body to settle down, and allowing a very deep state of rest to be gained.

Now, the individual benefits of that have been very well researched—greater energy and alertness, better health and so forth. It has also been found that society as a whole benefits from it in terms of reduced crime rate, reduced accident rate, reduced sickness, and more positive trends of life in cities where even just a small number of people are practising TM. It has been found that if just the square root of one per cent practise this 'yogic flying' technique together in a group, then a much more powerful impact of harmony and coherence and orderliness is generated in society.

... It's very easy to do this. It's very, very natural, and it's a means by which anyone can make a very powerful contribution towards harmony in the world,. When the mind settles down during meditation, it contacts a very silent level of restful alertness—a very pleasant experience. And a lot of scientists are suggesting that this experience is what they call the unified field of natural law, which is just a very fundamental level of nature.

If you watch the news or listen to the news and something is going wrong in the world, there are a lot of people with very good will who are wanting to put things right. But if orderliness and harmony are generated in that very basic, fundamental level of nature, the coherence created allows trends in society to become better, so it's something that anyone can practise and make a really significant contribution towards solving the problems in the world today.

Interviewer: You couldn't just do it to order though, could you—I mean, sit on the floor here outside and do it? You'd have to concentrate and it would have to be quiet, would it?

Phil Mitchell: Well, there's no concentration involved. What happened this morning is that we all had a five-minute meditation beforehand when we go down to a quiet level of restful alertness, and this is how it works.

Interviewer: Well, you can't just do it as a party trick?

Phil Mitchell: No.... Obviously now ... it's a good time to make it publicly known and to bring it to people's awareness in order to help combat the growing negativity and disharmony in the world. Not only are there problems with the two superpowers and the worry about nuclear weapons, but also there's an increasing concern over terrorism. So this seems to be a particularly good time to bring this to people's awareness and interest them more in it....

Interviewer: What's the highest that anyone can levitate to? Is that the right word?

David Hughes: Yes, you could say that. As Phil was mentioning earlier, this is only the first stage of yogic flying, and the tradition from which this TM and TM-Sidhi programme comes describes two subsequent stages—hovering in the air and what we would regard as directed flight. At the moment I think probably about a foot or two is about the highest.

Interviewer: Do you think this is where the old idea of flying carpets comes from?

David Hughes: It could well have been, actually, because this knowledge is very basic to human beings. Anyone can actually do this....

WORLD PEACE • GLOBAL INAUGURATION

PRESS REPORTS FROM EUROPE

Great Britain • *The Scotsman*

Edinburgh, Scotland   16 August 1986   (English)

World peace gets off to a flying start

By WILLIAM PAUL

Come fly with us, Transcendental Meditation Followers announced yesterday, and Utopia is just around the corner.

Edinburgh was one of 108 cities around the world to host a public demonstration of yogic flying. The idea is that world peace can be achieved through the collective willpower of the masses.

Four men bounced on 6in foam rubber mattresses in a hotel room. They called it flying. It looked more like hopping in the lotus position. Full levitation may follow, they said, and then proper flying as the technique achieves its full potential.

They said they felt much more refreshed at the end of a five-minute flight than when it started. But they needed ten minutes meditation to establish the right atmosphere.

"I wanted to go as high as I could." said computer consultant Mike Sullivan, "but something was holding me down...."

They said it was a state of consciousness in which there was "maximum brain-wave coherence." Individuals in this state would improve their health, they said; groups would improve their community's health, they said; and if the group was large enough there would be world peace....

There are plans for a community of 7,000 people in India to propagate this theory. A similar U S group tried it for three weeks in 1983, they said, and infectious diseases are supposed to have shown a worldwide decline, while stock prices showed unprecendented growth. When the goup broke up, things returned to normal.

To keep Britain on an even keel, 800 are due to take off in Skelmersdale. This number, they said, was based on the square root of 1 per cent of the total British population....

Everything is dependent they said, on the creation of a unified field which is at the most basic level of natural law, and which can be imposed by the coherent consciousness of a large enough percentage of the world population.

Dr Stephen Boyd, a registrar in psychiatry at the Crichton Royal Hospital in Dumfries, said: "There is a spread of coherent activity throughout all areas of the brain and at the point of maximum coherence the body leaves the ground."...

Picture by JACK CROMBIE
He has lift-off . . . David Rae could be called a flying instructor, but of a radically different kind.

WORLD PEACE • GLOBAL INAUGURATION

PRESS REPORTS FROM EUROPE

Great Britain • *The Guardian*

London   16 August 1986   (English)

PEACE EFFORT: A follower of his holiness the Maharishi Mahesh Yogi tackles the long jump during a yogic flying competition for world peace in London yesterday.   Pictures by Graham Turner

By Martin Wainwright

THE FIRST national yogic flying championships were held at a London hotel yesterday, with a promising notice in the front window.

"Transcendentals: please use main entrance," it said, suggesting that the more skilful meditators might be tempted to float in through an upper window.

In the event, the "flying" practised by followers of that timeless guru, the Maharishi Mahesh Yogi, proved to be a vigorous sort of hopping.... 10 competitors bounced along mattresses for up to 50 metres while retaining the lotus position.

This was impressive to watch, especially for someone who cannot attain the lotus position....

The contest, with medals for hurdling (over folded mattresses), high and long jumps (89 cms was yesterday's best) and the 50-metre "dash," launched a new initiative for world peace by the Maharishi.

His long-held belief that violence ebbs if sufficiently large numbers of people meditate is entering an ambitious new phase.

Although world leaders still seem to prefer climbing lighthouses and chasing dogs along beaches the Maharishi's men are optimistic about getting the square root of 1 per cent of the world's population to hop—the necessary quota for world peace.

PRESS REPORTS FROM EUROPE

Great Britain • *Daily Post*

Liverpool   16 August 1986   (English)

Flight of fancy for hoppers on yogic plane

by Roz Kay

THIS is yogic flying....

Primed with a few minutes of Transcendental Meditation, the "flyers," legs tucked up in the lotus position, hop or bound along thick foam mattresses, often laughing, wriggling and squealing with pleasure.

They say yogic flying is possible by a state of "maximum coherence in brain activity," lifting the body up so it begins to hop.

The six men demonstrating the technique at Edge Hill College, Ormskirk, all looked pretty fit, bouncing on the spot or along the mats.

They say it requires no physical effort whatsoever, and all at the demonstration claimed firm belief that someone would one day make the breakthrough to hovering and then true directed flight.

Their principal aim is to tackle terrorism and war by getting a Programme to Create World Peace off the ground, along with themselves, and to do it the hoppers are going public. The Ormskirk demonstration was organised by the Ideal Village Association of the Age of Enlightenment at Skelmersdale.

They claim scientific backing proves the "coherence" they create has the effect of producing mass harmony throughout nature, and if enough people - 7,000 - do it at the same time, wars, traffic accidents, crime, and Stock Exchange collapses will all cease.

The man behind it all, His Holiness Maharishi Mahesh Yogi, developed his philosophy for world peace because all other methods over the centuries have failed.

Anyone can practise Transcendental Meditation, and anyone who does that can become a yogic flyer - or even a champion one, because there are now competitions held in it.

But they need 100 million U.S. dollars to keep those 7,000 people hopping for peace.

In mid-hop — demonstrators take the first steps towards yogic flight

WORLD PEACE • GLOBAL INAUGURATION

PRESS REPORTS FROM EUROPE

Great Britain • *BBC Radio 4*
London   17 August 1986   (English)

Broadcaster: And now, as they say, to something very different; strange events have been taking place this week in Huddersfield, Ipswich, and Bournemouth to mention but three of a thousand locations world-wide. Flying for peace or, in the words of the organizers, 'Yogic Flying', a stage of Transcendental Meditation, is being pioneered by the Maharishi Mahesh Yogi as a way of generating world peace. His students throughout the world gathered on Friday to demonstrate the technique in public for the very first time. Trevor Barnes was among the audience at one of the events.

Trevor Barnes: Dr Geoffrey Clements, Vice-Chancellor of the Maharishi University of Natural Law, makes it all sound so simple that the wonder is that no-one's ever thought of it before.

Dr Clements: We are going to be seeing a demonstration of the mechanics of creating world peace. It's a very simple and innocent procedure, the goal of which is to rise in the air.

Trevor Barnes: Downstairs a foam rubber track dominates the hall. At one end four competitors in the 'yogic flying' games sit cross-legged in the lotus position under starter's orders as it were. Dr Bevan Morris explains the procedure as a hushed audience waits in the expectation for the Newtonian laws of gravity to be defied.

Dr Morris: When the person practises Transcendental Meditation their mind settles down to a completely silent state, a state of pure consciousness. Then they begin to practise a technique from the ancient Yoga Sutras of Patanjali which is supposed to produce flying. The brain becomes intensely coherent, and inside what you feel is an incredible surge of energy and great waves and thrills of bliss from head to toe and then the mind....

Trevor Barnes: I'll interrupt you here because there's the first one—the first one has started to hop towards us. It looks like a physical thing. He could just be propelling himself along with his hands.

Dr Morris: But you know it's at this time in the first stage, the hopping...internally the cause of that physical phenomenon is a completely unique and different state of brain functioning...

Trevor Barnes: That's all very well and here are a few more coming towards us now, but how can that possibly further the cause of world peace?

Dr Morris: The point is that world peace can be created only when individuals become peaceful.

Trevor Barnes: Flying on the radio is hard to get across, but I was helped by being able to pick up very definite sounds—those of the guru's disciples hitting the deck before launching again. For further explanation of this.. phenomenon I turned to Dr Clements.

Dr Clements: The connection between flying and world peace at first sight may seem remote, but the principles are actually very clear—that world peace depends upon coherence in the collective consciousness, that everybody functions in a coherent and integrated way—and the people that we have been seeing today are in the first stage of flying, but the effect even at this level is definitely there.

Trevor Barnes: Long-term practitioners of the flying technique, we were told, can keep terrorism, war, violent crime, and road accidents at bay. The square root of one per cent of the world's population—about 7,000 people—flying twice a day could pretty well guarantee world peace, and for that the organizers reckoned they'd need only $100 million to organize the man power. World peace, the Maharishi has confidently said, is only a matter of money. Meanwhile, those who did not have to leave for Dublin for another demonstration lined up for the medals.

Francis Chalmers: In the long-jump competition the third place was taken by Dr Geoffrey Mead with a distance of 73 centimetres....

Francis Chalmers: In the 25-metre hurdles competition the third place was taken by Mark Hersey with a time of 13.5 seconds. Unfortunately Mark cannot accept his medal in person because he's also flying to Ireland.

Broadcaster: But not under his own steam! Trevor Barnes was at the 'yogic flying games'.

WORLD PEACE • GLOBAL INAUGURATION

PRESS REPORTS FROM EUROPE

Great Britain • *Cambridge Evening News*

Cambridge 19 August 1986 (English)

Going up in the world while plugging in to peace in our time

SECURING global peace may seem a rather out of this world ambition, but a group in Cambridge is rising to the challenge — literally.

They are using meditation and what they claim is levitation in an attempt to cure the world of all its ills.

They say they are part of a "vibrant movement" that can bring peace to the world.

It may sound batty to the uninitiated, but members of the city's "Age of Enlightenment" group are convinced that their technique is the key to harmony.

By tapping a mysterious power, which they say is the source of everything, they claim to halt ageing, or even reverse it.

Plugging in to the power, they claim, can wipe out problems ranging from terrorism to divorce and fight illnesses.

Lifted

If their claims to be able to float in mid-air are anything to go by, they have found the key to cheap travel too.

It is done by sinking into deep meditation and finding inner tranquillity. Then, by introducing a thought — called a formula — one is forcibly lifted up, they say.

That is stage one. Stage two is being able to stay up without crashing to the floor and stage three is being able to hover around. No-one in the Cambridge group, however, has managed to get past stage one.

In a city centre house, Cambridge psychiatrist Dr Nick Argyle and a Peterborough engineer gave a demonstration.

They sat in the lotus position and suddenly jerked into life, bouncing furiously across the room.....

By Tim Curtis

To me it looked as if they could have simply pushed themselves into the air but Dr Argyle said they used no effort at all.

By measuring electronic impulses across the brain, scientists have proved that there is no body force used, he said.

"One is doing it without any intention. You don't fly in the same way that you try and do the high jump," he said. .

"Our whole culture is based on doing things with a lot of effort. In yogic flying you don't feel that you are being pulled, you just travel."

The basis of their claims for achieving world peace lies in radiating their peaceful thoughtwaves to the whole world.

An Indian guru, the Maharishi Mahesh Yogi, who founded the movement, claims that if 7,000 people use transcendental meditation at once the whole world will feel the effects.

The movement claims virtual miracles. It is claimed, for example, that during a three-week experiment when 7,000 followers practised TM, world stock market prices rocketed upwards unexplained while the amount of diseases in Australia and America plummeted.

Abuse

Dr Argyle told a meeting in Cambridge that as soon as a small group of villagers in Lebanon were taught the practice, artillery shells which fell on their village at the rate of about 100 a month suddenly stopped. Yet other villages around them still suffered bombardment.

Statistics gathered by researchers for TM claim smoking and alcohol abuse dropped along with crime and death rates in areas where TM was practised in sufficient numbers.

Dr Argyle, of Gwydir Street, who has been "levitating" for seven years but practising TM for 15, said: "It is like if you tried to explain to an aborigine how a TV works — he would not understand. The general public do not have the familiarity with modern science."...

It is by getting in step with the unified field through meditation, they say, that their concept works.

The Maharishi has launched a 100 million dollar appeal to set up a centre in India for 10,000 followers to practise TM and, they hope, to improve the world.....

MAHARISHI'S PROGRAMME TO CREAT

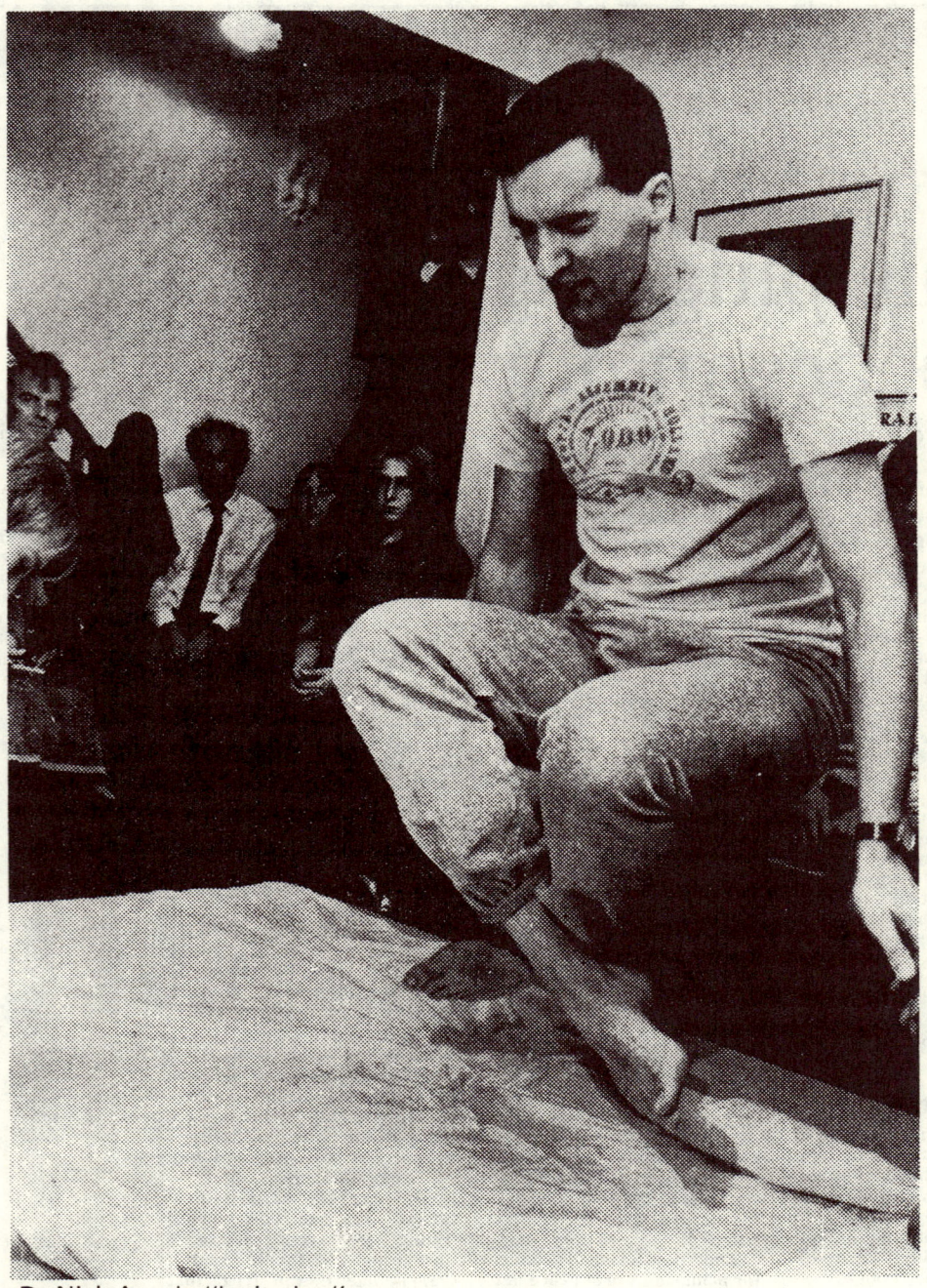

Dr Nick Argyle "levitating"....
Picture: Eddie Collinson

WORLD PEACE • GLOBAL INAUGURATION

PRESS REPORTS FROM EUROPE

Great Britain • *Bromsgrove Advertiser and Messenger*

Bromsgrove, Hereford and Worcester   21 August 1986   (English)

Bouncing back to happiness

HIGH-FLYING Paul Davies claims the only way to achieve world peace is through transcendental meditation.

And in one small corner of Hanbury, a small group of crusaders are literally bouncing back to happiness.

by Ross Crawford

Paul 38, and colleagues Peter Chandler, 29, and Mark Caves, 32, are all masters of what they call "yogic flying" — halfway towards complete levetation.

They claim the world would be a better place if we all meditated — and their long-term ambition is world peace.

"The important thing is this generation must have peace to survive, and TM relieves stress and reduces tension," said Paul, of West Lodge Farm, Hanbury, who has just returned from India.

Paul and his friends are followers of the Maharishi Mahesh Yogi, and they claim their 'flying' is a "blisfully induced" spontaneous movement.

The next stage is levitation, followed by controlled flight ....

● Picture by Julian Reynolds.

PRESS REPORTS FROM EUROPE

Great Britain • *Skelmersdale New Town Advertiser*

Skelmersdale, Lancashire   21 August 1986   (English)

Meditators show how it's done for TV

FOR THE first time Skelmersdale's TM meditators have revealed their techniques to the general public at an unusual press conference at Edge Hill College in Ormskirk.

The group are convinced that by use of a technique known as 'yogic flying' they can create a strong enough influence and radiate feelings of goodwill which will create peace.

'Flying' involves participants in reaching a high level of consciousness, which causes the body to 'hop' in the cross-legged 'lotus' position.

Six followers of the Maharishi Mahesh Yogi, including two from Skelmersdale, practised the technique in front of press cameras and television crews.

Spokesman for the movement, Mr. Stephen Whittle of Skelmersdale, said: "Our programme is very much a response to the needs of the time. The rivalry between the super powers has reached an unprecedented level, but there's an even worse threat of terrorism.

"The 800 people needed in the UK is the square root of one per cent of the population and it is gradually being gathered in Skelmersdale."

Eventually, through the setting up of a one hundred million dollar Maharishi Peace Fund, the organisation hope to establish a 7,000 strong community of yogic fliers.

Flying tonight?

IT'S VERY easy to be sceptical and scoff about things which you don't fully understand.

Imagine then the reaction in the Advertiser office when the news editor announced there was to be a display of 'yogic flying' at Edge Hill College in Ormskirk.

But after an hour spent with the people of the Ideal Village of the Age of Enlightenment — the followers of the Maharishi Mahesh Yogi — you tend to be a little less apt to snigger.

Based at the Ideal Village Association in Skelmersdale, the group were putting on a display of the technique which, it is claimed, is the only way left of achieving world peace and an end to terrorism....

Basically the group are all about Transcendental Meditation (TM) and the various alleged benefits attached to it.

Various speakers claimed that through achieving a high level of consciousness in meditation, practitioners of TM can radiate feelings of joy, goodwill and peace.

And they claim that if a community of 7,000 all practise the technique in one place, the resultant effect will affect a far greater number of people.

The Ormskirk effort was just one of more than a hundred taking place simultaneously around the world as part of the Maharishi's Programme to create World Peace.

Backed by a World Peace Fund of one hundred million US dollars, yet to be 'donated' by the wealthy of the world, the movement is very serious in their intentions.

They claim yogic flying — actually it's more like hopping in the cross-legged 'lotus' position — creates a feeling of fulfillment and relaxation....

Phil Mitchell is a 30-year-old interior design student from Manchester who was one of the demonstrators of the technique.

"The TM-Sidhi 'Yogic Flying' technique works on the same sort of level as ordinary TM but at a more increased rate.

One speaker even claimed that scientific evidence had proved that a large group of yogic fliers practising the technique in America had had an effect on the world's stock markets, causing the FT Index to soar!

WORLD PEACE • GLOBAL INAUGURATION

PRESS REPORTS FROM EUROPE

Great Britain • *Star*

Ormskirk, West Lancashire   28 August 1986   (English)

Bouncing up and down

How Transcendental Meditation can lead to world peace!

A Star special by Gordon Swindlehurst

BOUNCING around on a foam mattress may not seem to have much connection with the search for world peace.

But to those who practise transcendental meditation — or TM, as it is know- the connection is clear.

For they believe that TM can not only benefit the individual as far as health and physical performance are concerned, but that it also has far-reaching effects that can make the world a better place to live.

When practitioners of TM gave a demonstration of 'yogic flying' at Ormskirk's Edge Hill College, there was a serious message behind the rather strange sight of six grown men bounding about in the lotus position.

LIFE

Dave Gilbert, a 35-year-old publishing representative from Manchester, was one of the 'fliers'.

He told the Star, "I originally took up TM as a method of relaxation when I was driving to Scotland and back every day, and now it's part of my life, like cleaning my teeth or shaving."

He described the 'flying' as a result of 'an immense reflex surge' from within.

"When you meditate you find yourself getting this wonderful feeling, and you just leap around with the sheer joy of the thing," he said.

"The meditation extends your physical bounds, as well as quickening your reaction time," claimed Dave.

Graham Orr, Chairman of the Ideal Village Association of Skelmersdale, explained the further-reaching effects of TM.

"The concept of ideal villages is to allow practitioners of TM to live together.

PEACE

"We believe that if the square root of one per cent of the population of an area — be it a town, a nation or the world — can come together in meditation, we can achieve peace for that area," said Graham.

"So if we can get the square root of one per cent of the population of the world together to meditate, we can achieve world peace."

Graham claimed that squads of meditators had been sent into world trouble spots, and that there had been reductions in the death rate correspondent to

● FLIERS often bounce over two feet off the ground after transcendental meditation.

● JUMPING for joy......three exponents of yogic flying revel in the experience.

their stay in the area.

"We have also found that, when numbers as large as 7,000 meet together to meditate, the stock market reaches new highs, and road deaths in the immediate area of the meeting drop," said Graham.

Now the leader of transcendental meditators, Maharishi Mahesh Yogi, has set up the World Peace Fund to establish a 7,000-strong group in India, sponsored by some of the world's wealthiest men.

"We see yogic flying as a good demonstration technique to show just how powerful transcendental meditation can be," concluded Graham.

WORLD PEACE • GLOBAL INAUGURATION

PRESS REPORTS FROM EUROPE

Great Britain • *Redditch Advertiser*

Redditch, Worcestershire 28 August 1986 (English)

Hopping for World peace

Bouncing back to happiness

BOUNCING...may not seem the best way of furthering the cause of world peace — but for one group of Feckenham based meditators it could be mankind's only saviour.

by Ross Crawford

That's the claim of 38 year old Paul Davies and colleagues Peter Chandler, 29, and Mark Caves 32, who together have spent over ten years practicing the technique called the Transcendental Meditation Sidhi Programme.

They are all followers of the Maharishi Mahesh Yogi, the bouncing is called "hopping" or "yogic flying" and participants say it is a "blissfully induced" spontaneous movement.

And the Advertiser/Indicator had been invited along to see first hand the technique.

"We call it achieving the "finest level" of consciousness because TM aligns you with natural law, it relaxes you and relieves stress," said Paul, of West Lodge Farm, Hanbury, who has just returned from India.

The next stage of the technique after hopping is actual levitation, followed by controlled flight - although devotees admit they haven't got that far yet.

"The important thing is this generation must have peace to survive and TM relieves stress and reduced tension," said Paul.

PRESS REPORTS FROM EUROPE

Great Britain • *A.M. Weekend*

Manchester 29 August 1986 (English)

UPLIFTING!

WATCH OUT for unidentified flying objects in Withington.

For three local men have had an uplifting experience without the aid of wings or hot air.

Transcendental meditation expert, Nick Pullen claims he and two other practitioners of the relaxation technique can fly two feet above the ground.

"It is living proof of mind over matter," explained 42-year-old Nick of Parsonage Road, Withington.

"Anyone who has practised Transcendental meditation for three months can learn to fly.

"What makes it possible is a very high state of coherence in the brain when all parts are functioning with one another. "It is a very exhilarating experience."

Nick said he believes Yogic Flying — as it is termed — can bring about world peace because the individual's positive energy is picked up universally.

"I would recommend the experience to anyone. It is marvellous," said Nick.

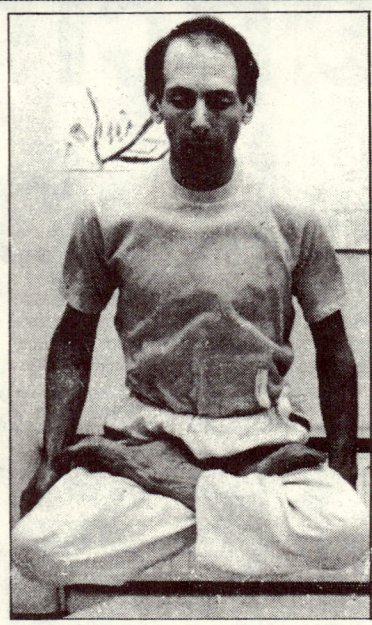

Flying high . . . Nick Pullen demonstrates Yogic Flying.
(FF110/75).

Great Britain • *South Manchester Reporter*

Manchester 22 August 1986 (English)

Flying on a different plane

FLYING for peace? That's the astonishing claim of three south Manchester men who believe they can achieve world peace.

They are practitioners of Yogic Flying, an advanced form of Transcendental Meditation in which the "flyer" bounces around in the lotus position while in a state of deep relaxation.

And at a special seminar in Ormskirk near Liverpool, they came together with other devotees to demonstrate the art.

Such is the power of Yogic Flying, they claim, that with only a limited number of people practising, dramatic changes in the environment take place.

"Scientific research has shown in cities where a group have been practising flying, the crime rate actually falls," says Nick Pullen, full-time teacher at the Withington TM Centre on Parsonage Road.

This, he claims, is due to all the natural forces being linked together and influenced by the advanced state of meditation and relaxation of the flyers.

And Nick now hopes to create a large enough group in Manchester to create more harmony and understanding here.

WORLD PEACE • GLOBAL INAUGURATION

PRESS REPORTS FROM EUROPE

Great Britain • *Western Mail*

Cardiff, Wales   11 September 1986   (English)

Art of flying by meditation is shown to public

By CHARLES HYMAS

AN ANCIENT form of "flying" made its public debut in Wales yesterday.

Up till now exponents of "yogic flying" — an advanced technique in transcendental meditation — have practised it in private.

"It has always been something we have kept to ourselves," said Mr Michael Beresford, a teacher of transcendental meditation based in Cardiff.

But at St David's Hall, Cardiff, yesterday, at the launch of the campaign to encourage more people to take up transcendental meditation, two transcendental meditation teachers, sitting in the Lotus position, gave a demonstration of the technique.

HOPS ALONG

"The body lifts off the ground completely effortlessly," said Mr Beresford, a mathematics and computer-science graduate from Reading University.

"There's no conscious effort to propel the body off the ground. It's completely spontaneous. Then it hops along."

Exponents, however, are still at the early stages of "yogic flying."

"The next stage is where the body is able to lift off the ground and stay there for an extended period of time," said Mr Beresford.

"The final stage is where you gain mastery of the air."

He admitted this would defy the laws of gravity, but in modern physics now a level of nature even more basic than those laws had been discovered.

In "yogic flying" people were "functioning at a level more basic than the law of gravity," he said.

It was not something new, and anyone had the ability to do it. "It's been around for thousands of years," said Mr Beresford.

It is one of a set of techniques in the TM-Sidhi programme brought out in 1977 by Maharishi Mahesh Yogi, ...

He was the founder of the transcendental meditation technique of which TM-Sidhi is a development.

Its exponents argue that by establishing a group of 10,000 practitioners of the advanced TM-Sidhi programme the possibility is there to create lasting world peace.

They say more than 300 scientific studies have shown that group practice of this technique produces a powerful effect of coherence and harmony throughout society.

Mr Beresford said that during the TM-Sidhi programme the functions of the brain become incredibly orderly and coherent.

"The whole thing is incredibly exhilarating and very good fun for the individual to do," he said. "It's that bliss quality and coherence generated in the individual which then radiates into the environment."

The aim of the campaign is to create a group of about 150 people practising the TM-Sidhi programme in Wales. At present there are about 50 exponents in the Principality.

PRESS REPORTS FROM EUROPE

Great Britain • *The Huddersfield Daily Examiner*

Huddersfield, Yorkshire 15 September 1986 (English)

Meditating on a high-flying ambition

Andrew Pearson discovers how meditation can be uplifting for both the individual and international peace

THREE blokes sat down in a lotus position and hopped up and down for ten minutes on foam mattresses.

"Many people," I pointed out, "must think you're a set of nutters."

Myself and chief photographer John Watson were guests of a Huddersfield meditation centre where we saw a demonstration of "yogic flying."

Where governments and peacemakers had failed since time immemorial, a group of meditators could succeed.

I was sceptical.

To the remark about nutters, centre chairman Alistair Bailey said that was exactly why they had invited the Examiner to see them in action.

"Through the press we can convey to the public the reasons and mechanics of 'yogic flying'," he said. "The display is just one of thousands taking place in over 100 countries.

"We believe we can bring world peace and we want to demonstrate the mechanics of gaining that peace."

The "we" also included Netherthong father and son Graham and Andrew Bull who have practised transcendental meditation for six years.

Stage one

"Yogic flying" is advanced TM—an outward expression of TM's peace and fulfillment, and "flying," they claim, is no misnoma.

The bouncing witnessed by John and myself was just stage one "flying."

"Directional flight is possible at a higher level," said Alistair "We are saying that man can actually fly.

"At present we are, if you like, at the Wright Brothers stage."

Like ordinary TM, "flying" is designed to reduce stress.

Relieving stress in many individuals, believe meditators, leads to the flushing of stress from others.

They believe that stress begets aggression so, with the obliteration of stress, there follows the extermination of local, national and international aggression.

"Studies," continued Alistair, "have proved that, if about 7,000 experts practice 'yogic flying' simultaneously in the same place, there is a reduction in world tension.

"So our mission is to provide the only possible way towards peace, and for that we need a permanent team of 7,000."

TM began in the late 50s, masterminded by Indian Maharishi Mahesh Yogi.

WORLD PEACE • GLOBAL INAUGURATION

Huddersfield transcendental meditation teacher Alistair Bailey displays 'yogic flying'

And, to fund his latest target—this 7,000 fleet, the Maharishi has approached many of the world's richest people to set up what he calls the World Peace Fund of 100m US dollars.

Superpowers

A movement handout says: "Government's have failed to create world peace.

"Today, with the onset of terrorism, they are not providing safety to the people in any part of the world.

"Even the superpowers are constantly in fear, and the rivalry between them is challenging the life of every individual.

"Now it is time for the responsible individuals in the world to take the responsibility for creating and maintaining world peace."

Created would be the Maharishi's ideal society when "Heaven will descend on earth."

PRESS REPORTS FROM EUROPE

Great Britain • *Kent and Sussex Courier*

Tunbridge Wells, Kent   19 September 1986   (English)

Yoga lovers aim to lift off for world peace

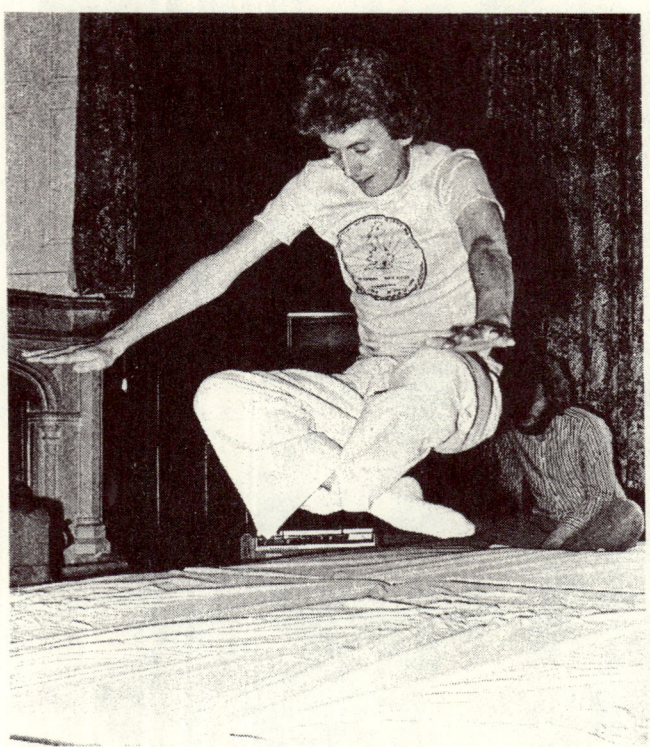

A CROSS-LEGGED "flyer" pictured during a demonstration at Royden Hall in East Peckham

TO THE average onlooker the sight of four men bouncing cross-legged on a collection of mattresses has little connection with world peace.

But this hopping, or "yogic flying" is, say its exponents a "physical manifestation of an internal experience that will save the world from itself".

For the first time, on Thursday of last week, the Age of Enlightenment centre in the luxurious Royden Hall, near East Peckham, flung open its doors to public gaze and public scepticism to reveal this Transcendental Meditation-Sidhi programme.

Reporters from the Courier who were invited to attend the "flying demonstration" were told they would only witness stage one of the programme.

"You will see the external manifestation of the lifting of the body," said Mr John Small, teacher and exponent of the art. "We cannot demonstrate the internal aspect, experiencing greater coherence, bliss and happiness. It will appear that we are simply hopping around."

HOVERING

Mr Small, who has studied yogic flying, admits that he has seen only one or two flyers reach stage two — floating.

He said: "Very few individuals repeatedly experience the stage of hovering. They are hindered by stress in the world consciousness. Some people may be practising stage one and then suddenly experience an extra long hop, or floating."

Stage three, directional flight, seems a long way off.

The Sidhi programme is explained as the natural extension of the transcendental meditation technique of mental relaxation. The aim is to achieve "the ultimate degree of coherence" and attain the level of the unified field — the home of all laws of nature where "all thought and action is perfectly in accord with natural law."

It is claimed that group practice of yogic flying will result in a decrease in negative tendencies in the world, leading to greater harmony and improved relations.

The aim of the students is to have a group of 7,000 people in permanent yogic flight to magnify their harmony across the world. Advocates of the order claim that these 7,000 people — the square root of one per cent of the population — together with specific groups for each town and country, would create "heaven on earth" — no accidents, no confrontations, no anger. At least 100 million dollars is said to be needed to help the group in India.

WORLD PEACE • GLOBAL INAUGURATION

PRESS REPORTS FROM EUROPE

Hungary • *Magyar Hirlap*

Budapest   16 August 1986   (Hungarian)

Jógabemutató – repüléssel?

Fotó: Habik Csaba

Tudósítónktól.

A sziddha végül is felemelkedett a talajról. Ötven éves, Szász Jánosnak hívják, Indiából érkezett Budapestre, és tegnapra, India nemzeti ünnepére időzítette bemutatóját, Maharishi Mahesh jógi világbéke programja megnyitásának részeként. Erre egyszerre 108 országban került sor. A békeprogram minden részletében az ismertetés ellenére sem vált előttem világossá. A bemutatón, a Fehérvári úti közösségi házban hívők és hitetlenek, orvosok, pszichológusok, pszichiáterek, fizikusok, rendszeres jógázók és meditálók, valamint kíváncsi érdeklődők vettek részt.

Többségünk a látványt nem röpülésnek érzékelte, de nagyon figyeltünk a magyarázatra: hogy a Maharishi guru által 30 éve kidolgozott transzcendentális meditáció rendszeres gyakorlása révén az emberben óriási energiák szabadulnak fel, belső béke teremtődik, ami nyugalmat sugároz a környezetre. Az ehhez vezető számos gyakorlat közül csupán az egyik — ez a konkrét emelkedés, amit ő a repülés első stádiumának minősített. A másodikhoz, az egyhelyben lebegéshez, valamint a harmadikhoz, az irányított repüléshez, nem elég érettek sem az egyének, sem a körülmények, bár Szász János meggyőződése, hogy Maharishi képes rá.

Mi ott, tízpercnyi meditálás után — amelyben a sziddhával együtt valamennyien csendben és mozdulatlanul maradtunk — azt láthattuk, hogy Szász János a magára csatolt rugalmas ülepvédőben többször felszökellt a földről, mintegy másfél-két arasznyira. Az ugrásszerű mozgást többen az összpontosításra, és gyakorlásra épülő izommunkának érezték. Szász János cáfolta ezt, és sajnálta, hogy nem értik. Hitét egyetlen szakember sem vonta kétségbe.

A jelenség (mutatvány?) tudományos értékelésére lapunk a közeljövőben megjelenő mellékletében még visszatérünk.

mse

PRESS REPORTS FROM EUROPE

Hungary • *Képés Hét*
Budapest 23 August 1986 (Hungarian)

BUDAPEST VENDÉGE

Jóga – repülés?

Jóga-repülésre kíváncsian gyűltünk össze múlt pénteken a Fehérvári úti közösségi házban. Az ötvenéves Szász János — 30 éve most látogatott először haza — 11 éve szegődött az indiai Maharishi Mahesh jógi hívévé. Elhatározta: tanítója — sziddhája — lesz. Maharashi 30 éve dolgozta ki a transzcentrális meditáció technikáját; ez képessé teszi a repülésre azokat, akik elsajátítják — mondta bevezetőjében Szász János.

Csaknem százan ültünk körben, némelyek padon, mások széken, többen jógaülésben a földön: orvosok, pszichológusok, pszichiáterek, rendszeresen jógázók-meditálók és kíváncsiak. A pódiumszerűen összetolt tornaszőnyegen tízperces, elmélyült meditációt láthattunk, melynek eredményeként felszabaduló belső erők emelkedni kezdenek a gerincoszlop mentén, s az ember — aki ilyen szintig fejlődött — megemelkedik.

Aki idvezült felemelkedést várt — nagyot csalódott. Szász János, amúgy nyakkendősen, pantallóban mezítláb, térdén átvetve magára csatolt, laticelszerű anyagból készült ülepvédőjét — fölszökkent a talajról, többször, sokszor egymás után, tíz percen át. Eközben erős rángás vonult át fején, nyakán, vállán, s ha ferde, ugrásszerű mozgásával eljutott a szőnyeg széléig, visszafordult. Mint utóbb, kérdésekre válaszolva elmondta: közben figyelt, az óráján meg azt nézte, mennyi van még hátra a tíz percből.

Maharishiék szerint az, amit láttunk — s ugyanilyet vetítettek le utóbb videón — ez a repülés első stádiuma; bár Szászé most laposabbra sikeredett. (Mivel nem elég hajlékony a jógaüléshez — tette ő hozzá — azért kell neki a párna, hogy ne üsse meg magát.) A második stádium — az egy helyben lebegés, a harmadik az irányított repülés, de az csak a megvilágosodottaknak adatik meg.

mse

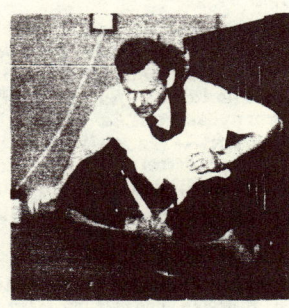

Iceland • *Morgunbladid*

Reykjavik   23 July 1986   (Icelandic)

Indland:
Jógar heyja „flugkeppni"

Nýju Delhi, AP.

FYLGISMENN jógans Maharishi Mahesh háðu á mánudag keppni í „flugi" jóga. Mikill fjöldi hindúa fylgdist með keppninni sem fram fór á Indira Gandhi-leikvanginum. Um 100 jógar frá 18 löndum kepptu til verðlauna í þessari sérkennilegu keppni. Veitt voru gull-, silfur- og bronsverðlaun.

Samkvæmt kenningum Maharishi Mahesh getur líkaminn lyfst frá jörðu og flogið stuttar vegalengdir sökum samstillingar bylgna í heila viðkomandi. Að sögn skipuleggjenda keppninnar eykst áhrifamáttur hugsunarinnar eftir því sem fleiri andlegir menn koma saman og geta þeir í krafti hugleiðslu dregið að sér orku alheimsins. Þátttakendur í keppninni voru beðnir um að einbeita sér að friði í heiminum.

Keppt var bæði í karla- og kvennaflokki og voru veitt verðlaun fyrir „langflug", „flughæð", og flug yfir grindur auk þess sem keppt var um hver yrði fyrstur til að fljúga 50 metra vegalengd. Bandaríkjamaðurinn Eddy Gobb sigraði í „langflugi" og náði 163 sm. Núgildandi met í „langflugi" er 1,8 metrar. Blaine Watson frá Kanada náði 60 sm „flughæð" og sigraði. Úrslit í kvennaflokki lágu ekki fyrir.

Til þess að ná flugi verður viðkomandi jógi að vera í djúpri hugleiðslu og sitja í „lótusstellingu", með krosslagða fætur. Hingað til hafa jógar stundað þessa iðju í einrúmi en hafa nú ákveðið að opinbera þessa hæfileika sökum vaxandi spennu í heiminum.

Maharishi Mahesh jógi.

Eddie Gob sigraði í „langflugi".

PRESS REPORTS FROM EUROPE

Ireland • *Evening Herald*

Dublin 13 August 1986 (English)

The flying Yogis get ready for their big Dublin lift-off

POWER OF THE MIND? . . . a yogi disciple goes lift-off.

A "YOGIC flying demonstration" using nothing but the power of the mind is to take place in a Dublin hotel on Friday.

Experts will literally hover above ground as they practice an extreme form of meditation, it has been promised.

Billed as the first demonstration of yogic flying in Ireland, the event has been organised by the Maharishi International University (Ireland) Ltd. which has been successfully promoting transcendental meditation in this country.

The technique of "flying" is practiced by advanced practitioners of TM.

"At the moment of maximum coherence in brainwave activity, the body lifts up and begins to hop. This is the first stage of flying. There are three stages in the development of the ability to fly: hopping, hovering and flying proper," a statement from the movement says.

The demonstration has been announced as part of the global inauguration of Maharishi's programme to create world peace and is taking place in 108 countries.

"As part of this inauguration, the mechanics to create world peace will be demonstrated. This technology to create coherence in world consciousness is the TM-Sidhi or "yogic flying technique," a press statement informs.

The TM movement in Ireland has thousands of followers, including business people and professionals, including lawyers, architects and journalists.

Most of these practice meditation as a form of relaxation to counter stress and medical tests have shown that in fact the body does enter a state of extreme rest during short periods of TM.

WORLD PEACE • GLOBAL INAUGURATION

PRESS REPORTS FROM EUROPE

Ireland • *The Cork Examiner*

Cork 16 August 1986 (English)

Fliers hop in peace

By EVELYN RING

FIVE men hopping on mattresses in a plush hotel in Dublin yesterday told journalists that this was the way to world peace.

The men call themselves "yogic flyers" and they told a sceptical media conference that this simple and basic technique was aimed at eliminating terrorism and war.

The group said that they were perfectly happy hopping about. They are all members of the Maharishi International University in Ireland, and are convinced that, but for world stress, they would be actually flying. In fact, they have just achieved the first stage of "yogic flying". The intermediary stage is hovering.

Dr. Bevan Morris, President of the Maharishi International University in the U.S.A., told the meeting in Buswells Hotel that a fund of 100 million dollars was needed to support 10,000 "yogic flyers" at a world peace centre just outside New Delhi in India. There are 2,000 there.

Dr. Morris explained that if the square root of one per cent of any population (in Ireland's case, the figure is 300) could experience a state of peace brought about by "yogic flying" all at the same time, disruptive influences in their society could be quelled. There was documentation to show this, he claimed.

Dr. Geoffrey Clements, a physicist with the Maharishi International University in Britain, said that people should not think that the "yogic flying" technique was a mystical or magical act. "It is brought about by acting upon the most basic level of natural law", he said.

The reader might not have noticed, but at about 5 p.m. yesterday evening an aura of peace enveloped Ireland as the "yogic flyers" prepared to do their thing. They sat down in the basic yogic position and when a little bell was rung they began to meditate.

Five minutes later, as their bodies began to jerk slightly, the little bell was rung once more and they were off hopping, on impulse, all over the mattresses and looking as if they were on cloud nine.

One of the "yogic flyers" was John Burns from Raheny, Dublin, who has been practising transcendental meditation for the past 11 years and is now an instructor. He has not yet, however, succeeded in getting beyond the hopping stage.

He explained that anyone could learn to become a "yogic flyer" in just a few months because it was a very simple thing to do. John said that the reason they had not gone beyond the first stage was that there were just not enough "flyers" about, and that was why they were at the press conference to promote it.

If they got 300 "yogic flyers" together in the one place in Ireland, who knows, maybe they could hover and even fly.

John said that two years ago he joined a group of 6,000 "yogic flyers" at a session in Holland. Alas, they did not take off.

Another "yogic flyer", Martin Cullen from Co. Wicklow, has been practising transcendental meditation for the past 15 years. He, too, was a qualified T.M. instructor. "Yogic flying", he said, was totally exhilarating.

PRESS REPORTS FROM EUROPE

Ireland • *Irish Independent*

Dublin 16 August 1986 (English)

There's less bother with a hover...or a hop

By BAIRBRE POWER

A "FLYING" WAY to decrease the Northern troubles and the countries unemployment and economic problems was unveiled yesterday with hopes and hopes.

The 'solution' would just involve 300 Irish people meditating twice a day using the Maharishis 'yogic flying' method, it was claimed, in Dublin, yesterday.

The TM-Sidhi yogic flying technique also has the mechanics to eliminate terrorism and war and create world peace, says the Maharishi International University (M.I.U.), promoters of Transcendental Meditation, who have launched a world peace programme.

Yesterday they called on the Irish Government to consider the technology of peace and encourage its use by paying unemployed people here to form groups to create coherence in world consciousness, meditating for 1-1½ hours twice a day.

This programme involves three steps of yogic flying, including hopping, hovering and then flying above a mattress. During yogic flying, at the moment of maximum coherence in brainwave activity, the body lifts up and begins to hop.

Five flyers 'hopped' in Dublin yesterday at the first public demonstration of the method here. And the M.I.U. are to undertake a series of T.M. and T.M.-Sidhi lectures in Dublin, Cork, Galway and Limerick in the next few weeks to promote the technology for world peace in every home.

The positive effects generated through the efforts of a group of 7,000 people worldwide—the square root of one per cent. of the population—could transform strife into peace on the international level, they claim.

A group meditation of 7,000 yogic flyers in America in December, '83, decreased hostile effects in the Lebanon and researchers found a decrease in violence and tension there that was extremely significant, Dr. Geoffrey Clements, psysicist, said.

Stock prices have risen, traffic fatalities have dropped, and infectious diseases have decreased as T.M.-Sidhi followers put into practice the programme of the Indian Maharishi, a man in his 60's.

The coherence created in world consciousness by group practice of the technology of the unified field will make peace on earth and power on earth peaceful, the Maharishi has predicted. A 100 million-dollar world fund peace has been launched to establish a permanent centre for a coherence creating group of 7,000.

Ireland's problems emerge from stress, says the Maharishi. But every problem is soluble because it is the people who make problems and everyone can be trained to think according to natural law through this technology, he says.

"Problems emerge, not from religion, but from stress and there is only one basic cause of stress, violation of natural law."

It is not the Catholics and Protestants who are flighting, but the stress and the basis of stress is the lack of education in natural law here, he says.

Ms. Maura McCann, PR for the MIU in Ireland, says the country's unemployed could be paid to train in yogic flying and to form coherence creating groups. Prisoners, too, could be trained and the beenfits resulting could be measured effectively.

● Dr. Geoffrey Clements (left) and Mr. Desmond Hourie, chairman of the press conference on Transcendental Meditation, in Dublin, yesterday.

WORLD PEACE • GLOBAL INAUGURATION

Perfect peace... in a flight of fancy

● Lift-off! Simeon Gillion of Blanchardstown Co. Dublin, demonstrated the technique of 'Yogic Flight' at a Transcendental Meditation press conference in Dublin yesterday.

MAHARISHI'S PROGRAMME TO CREATE

PRESS REPORTS FROM EUROPE

Ireland • *The Irish Times*
Dublin 16 August 1986 (English)

Mr Martin Cullen, Rathdrum, Co Wicklow, demonstrating the TM Sidhi "Yogic Flying" technique in Dublin yesterday at the Maharishi International University (Ireland) news conference for the global inauguration of Maharishi's programme to create world peace....
(Photograph: Matt Kavanagh)

WORLD PEACE • GLOBAL INAUGURATION

PRESS REPORTS FROM EUROPE

Ireland • *The Irish Press*

Dublin   16 August 1986   (English)

hopping hopefuls look up

By
MAOL MUIRE TYNAN

WORLD peace costs 100 millions dollars, several million rubber mats and a square root of one per cent of the earth's population jumping about like as many frogs.

So says the Maharishi Mahesh Yogi whose disciples launched his novel programme for world peace in a demonstration of "Yogic Flying" in Dublin yesterday.

According to the wise man's theory, if enough people perfect the art of taking to the air at the same time, the "last remnants" of world tensions can be eliminated.

However, in a Dublin hotel yesterday, five of his followers could only achieve the first stage of the process — hopping furiously six inches off the ground from a cross-legged position. There are in fact three stages in the development of the ability to fly-hopping, hovering and flying proper, according to the Maharishi.

"During the 'yogic flying' technique, at the moment of maximum coherence in brainwave activity, the body lifts up and begins to hop," said physicist Dr. Geoffrey Clements at yesterday's launching of the peace programme.

The highlight of the launching came as five young men, attired in white shirts and loose pants, settled themselves on thick foam mats and, legs crossed, slipped into a deep state of meditation.

After five minutes, and the tinkling of a bell, the men, eyes closed, threw themselves into a frenzy of hops. Bearing tranquil smiles, energetically up and down, always stopping short of the huddle of photographers poised at the end of the mats.

But, before these men can contribute to world peace, Dr. Clements said 100 million dollars must be raised to finance a little city of 7,000 full time Transcendental Meditation followers who can perfect the art of flying.

MAHARISHI'S PROGRAMME TO CREATE

HIGH FLYER... Simeon Gillan from Blanchardstown demonstrates Yogic Flying. Picture by Tom Hanahoe.

WORLD PEACE • GLOBAL INAUGURATION

PRESS REPORTS FROM EUROPE

Italy • *Il Giornale*
Milan 15 August 1986 (Italian)

Lo affermano dal Comasco i seguaci della filosofia Maharishi

Per raggiungere la pace nel mondo sembra che basti levarsi in «volo yoga»
Ma ci vogliono anche cento milioni di dollari

Como — A mezzogiorno in punto del Ferragosto 1986, sul colle di Brunate, a turisti e villeggianti tra il distratto e l'accalorato, ma in cerca di emozioni, un gruppo di esperti fornirà una dimostrazione che ha un po' del sensazionale: il volo yoga. Dopo qualche momento di meditazione trascendentale, quando la mente e il fisico raggiungeranno il massimo dell'armonia, anzi, in termine tecnico, della «coerenza», i corpi dei partecipanti alla dimostrazione si alzeranno da terra e cominceranno a saltellare da sé. E' la prima volta che viene data una dimostrazione pubblica del «volo yoga», una tecnica per armonizzare «le forze discordanti della natura», ed è stata scelta la giornata del 15 agosto perché oggi viene inaugurato il «programma di Maharishi per creare la pace mondiale», di cui il volo yoga è la base.

A Brunate, dal 1981, esiste una «capitale dell'età dell'illuminazione», che richiama migliaia di persone ogni anno, ispirata alla filosofia di Maharishi Mahesh Yogi, fondatore della meditazione trascendentale nel 1957, della scienza dell'intelligenza creativa, della tecnologia Maharishi del campo unificato, di varie università nell'Europa e negli Stati Uniti, di varie capitali dell'età dell'illuminazione e, naturalmente, del governo mondiale dell'età dell'illuminazione

L'anno scorso aveva preso avvio il programma per la «salute perfetta». Quest'anno invece l'obbiettivo dell'attività dei seguaci di Maharishi è la «creazione della pace mondiale». Infatti, oggi, in altri 108 Paesi del globo sarà eseguita la dimostrazione presentata a Brunate, uno dei centri italiani che ospitano la «capitale dell'età dell'illuminazione» in quello che fu il prestigioso albergo Milano.

«I governi hanno fallito nel creare la pace mondiale — dicono gli organizzatori del volo yoga di oggi — e con il diffondersi del terrorismo non sono più in grado di garantire sicurezza alla gente in nessuna parte del mondo. Trentuno studi sociologici, condotti negli ultimi dodici anni, hanno dimostrato che l'un per cento o più di una popolazione che pratica la teoria di meditazione trascendentale migliora la qualità della vita di tutta la società. Gli scienziati hanno chiamato questo fenomeno l'effetto Maharishi, in onore di Maharishi che lo predisse nel 1960.

«Dieci anni fa si scoprì che questo effetto può essere prodotto dalla sola radice quadrata dell'un per cento della popolazione che pratica insieme il programma in un solo luogo. Le ricerche scientifiche hanno ripetutamente dimostrato che quando settemila persone praticano insieme la tecnologia del campo unificato in un solo luogo generano un'influenza di coerenza sufficientemente forte da irradiarsi a livello globale e purificare l'intera coscienza mondiale».

Insomma, per perpetuare la pace, basterebbe che in un solo luogo per quindici-venti minuti al giorno, un gruppo corrispondente alla radice quadrata degli abitanti di una città sviluppasse stati di coscienza più elevati e mantenesse un alto livello di coerenza. Ma, visto che bisogna pur mantenere in un solo luogo settemila esperti della tecnologia del campo unificato, i seguaci di Maharishi lanciano un appello: «Le persone creative del mondo, i leader e le persone ricche sono invitate a rendersi conto dell'urgente necessità della pace mondiale e a creare il fondo Maharishi di cento milioni di dollari».

Maria Castelli

PRESS REPORTS FROM EUROPE

Italy • *La Provincia*
Como 17 August 1986 (Italian)

Presentato a Brunate il metodo dello «yogi» indiano Maharishi

Meditazione e... volo contro stress e guerre

BRUNATE — Viene dall'Oriente, ma non è la «solita» setta. Bisogna accostarvisi con fiducia per trarne beneficio, ma non è una religione. Ha un cospicuo fondamento filosofico, ma non occorre essere esperti di filosofia per capirne i principî-base. Per apprendere le tecniche avanzate occorre spendere un milione, ma imparare quelle fondamentali non costa nulla. Ha stretti legami con lo yoga, ma non è necessario assumere posizioni «strane» per praticarla. E chi ne studia i livelli avanzati può perfino volare....

Stiamo parlando della meditazione trascendentale, tecnica di riflessione messa a punto nel 1957 dall'esperto indiano d'yoga Maharishi Mahesh. A Brunate, nell'ex hotel Milano, ha sede la «casa madre» italiana dell'organizzazione creata da Maharishi per diffondere la pratica di questa tecnica e proprio qui la meditazione trascendentale è stata presentata ufficialmente a Ferragosto.

Nella conferenza introduttiva, riservata alla stampa, Angelo Ceglia, Elena Perrucchini e Franco Canteri, insegnanti di Mt a tempo pieno, e Carlo Galbiati, medico ed insegnante di Mt «part time», hanno spiegato a grandi linee di che si tratta ed anno esposto il programma, messo a punto da Maharishi, per cercare d'ottenere la pace nel mondo grazie alla diffusione delle tecniche da lui messe a punto.

Il nemico numero uno della meditazione trascendentale è lo stress. Per combatterlo la via proposta da Maharishi è insegnare alla gente a raggiungere un particolare stato di coscienza, detto «Coscienza trascendentale», in cui il corpo è quasi del tutto rilassato, come quando si dorme, ma la mente è totalmente cosciente, come quando si è svegli.

Il beneficio immediato quando si raggiunge questo stato, sostengono gli esperti di Mt, è la «messa in moto» di tutta la massa cerebrale contemporaneamente, e non a settori come nel normale stato di veglia. Ciò depura corpo e mente dallo stress accumulato nella vita di tutti i giorni ed è utile a prevenire parecchie malattie che si sa, provocate od aggravate dallo stress.

Già con le tecniche base della meditazione trascendentale, uno dei cui cultori è l'allenatore Liedholm si può raggiungere lo stato di coscienza trascendentale; meditando in questo stato (bastano due periodi quotidiani di 15-20 minuti) si ritiene possibile rendersi conto degli aspetti della vita del meditante che non sono in armonia con la natura umana e sono dunque fonti di stress.

Dal punto di vista della fisica (Maharishi non è il solito «guru» tutto Oriente, si è laureato in fisica e matematica) tutte le tecniche di meditazione trascendentale possono influire su quella che in linguaggio yoga ha il nome d'«energia vitale» e gli scienziati occidentali definiscono la forza elettromagnetica propria del corpo umano (uno dei maggiori studiosi di questa forza è il premio Nobel italiano Carlo Rubbia). Gli esperti di Mt, Maharishi in testa, credono addirittura che concentrando numeri fissi d'individui che praticano la Mt, due volte al giorno nei medesimi luoghi sia possibile creare, rinsaldare e rendere permanente la pace nel mondo con la creazione d'un «terzo polo magnetico», che ricicli gli influssi del polo Nord magnetico e del centro della Terra e modifichi l'agire umano.

E' quel progetto, chiamato «Utopia dei 7000» (il numero ritenuto necessario di meditanti da concentrare in un unico luogo per realizzare la prima fase del piano), che ha preso il via proprio a Ferragosto con conferenze, simultanee a quella di Brunate, in ogni angolo del mondo. Per mantenere questi 7000 è prevista una spesa di 100 milioni di dollari (circa 150 miliardi di lire), ma pare proprio che, a differenza d'altre categorie più tristemente note, quella di Maharishi non intenda arrivarci con la «mungitura» degli adepti, come vedremo.

Giungiamo ad uno degli aspetti più appariscenti della meditazione trascendentale, il cosiddetto «volo yoga». E' una tecnica avanzata di Mt in cui,

La conferenza stampa e la dimostrazione di... volo yoga

a detta dei relatori, la «manipolazione» delle forze elettromagnetiche arriva ad un punto tale da permettere al corpo di lievitare. A Brunate era in programma una dimostrazione, con meditanti al primo stadio di questa tecnica (la levitazione dura poche frazioni di secondo e si traduce in una serie di balzi), aperta al pubblico. Dopo cinque minuti di meditazione trascendentale preparatoria i dimostratori, seduti a gambe incrociate su materassi, sono entrati in azione. Secondo i relatori il «volo yoga» avviene sempre in completa rilassatezza muscolare, ma, mentre in alcuni soggetti ciò era evidente, era altrettanto chiaro che altri si muovevano grazie a robuste «spinte» di gambe o reni.

Che c'era sotto? Lo abbiamo domandato a Benedetto Valle, presidente della «Capitale dell'età dell'illuminazione» (come ufficiale del centro brunatese) e moderatore della conferenza. «Il volo yoga, tecnica avanzata di Mt che pratica in piena coscienza (altre richiedono ipnosi o stati di «trance»), ha il fine di disporre le forze elettromagnetiche in modo tale da creare con il suolo l'effetto di due calamite che si respingono. Da questo deriva l'impulso del volo, che si traduce in balzi, come qui, in levitazione un po' più prolungata — secondo stadio — od in «effetto tappeto volante» (terzo ed ultimo stadio). In qualcuno l'effetto è limitatissimo ed allora «ci marciano» per cercare di prolungarlo artificialmente. Ma è tutto inutile, si vede subito che è qualcosa d'artificioso»

«Negli Usa» — prosegue Benedetto Valle — «siamo addirittura arrivati a competizioni di volo yoga: «corsa» piana e ad ostacoli, salto in alto ed in lungo. A noi, però, questo pare uno snaturare l'essenza del volo yoga. Aggiungere lo stress della competizione a tecniche con cui ci vuole eliminare lo stress? Se questo non è perdere lo scopo... ci può star bene il volo yoga come sport, ma non certo con questi parametri».

Costa molto apprendere la Mt? «Non necessariamente» — risponde Valle — «Il corso di base, sette lezioni che non durano mai più di un'ora, è praticamente gratuito. Se si vuole apprendere tecniche avanzate, come il volo yoga, occorre partecipare ad un corso residenziale, quindici giorni in questo palazzo, a poco più di 50 mila lire al giorno (pensione completa). Costa come due settimane di ferie e rende molto di più!»

In chiusura due parole di Angelo Doneda, sindaco di Brunate ed ospite dell'appuntamento ferragostano: «Quelli della Mt hanno rilevato l'ex-hotel Milano nell'82. Condusse la trattativa, in Svizzera, Maharishi in persona. All'inizio erano circondati da indifferenza, ma ora sono piuttosto integrati: abbiamo capito che non sono la solita setta»

Maurizio Del Sordo

Si può imparare a casa o sul bus e apprendere le tecniche base non costa nulla Un ambizioso programma per favorire la tendenza alla pace nel mondo

Meditazione trascendentale a Brunate

E' contro lo stress il volo dello yoga

BRUNATE — Ferragosto all'insegna della meditazione trascendentale all'ex hotel Milano di Brunate, ora «casa madre» italiana dell'organizzazione che diffonde questa tecnica. I seguaci dell'esperto indiano di yoga Maharishi Mahesh hanno illustrato i principi della Mt, che combattendo lo stress si propone di migliorare la qualità della vita e agendo sulle forze elettromagnetiche del corpo mira addirittura a diminuire la tendenza umana alla guerra. Seconda parte dell'appuntamento dedicata a una dimostrazione di «volo yoga», una delle tecniche avanzate di meditazione trascendentale. I dimostratori, dopo cinque minuti di meditazione con le tecniche di base (quelle che l'allenatore Nils Liedholm è solito praticare), hanno cercato di creare un campo magnetico interno uguale a quello del suolo per venirne respinti e levitare, per qualche istante, senza darsi lo slancio. E qualcuno c'è pure riuscito.

PRESS REPORTS FROM EUROPE

Italy • *Corriere della Sera*
Milan 17 August 1986 (Italian)

Vicino a Como un centro per imparare la tecnica di levitazione

Quando il ragionier Brambilla vola senz'ali

DAL NOSTRO INVIATO SPECIALE

BRUNATE (Como) — Si vola nel salone belle epoque dell'ex Hotel Milano di Brunate, a strapiombo sul lago di Como. I nuovi ospiti, seguaci di Maharishi Mahesh Yogy, il guru dei Beatles, l'hanno destinato a base di prova delle straordinarie possibilità offerte al corpo e alla mente dalla MT, la meditazione trascendentale, già insegnata dagli antichi Veda indiani.

Non c'è legge fisica che tenga quando si entra in armonia con il CU, il campo unificato della coscienza universale: l'adepto sperimenta sublimi beatitudini e il corpo levita come piuma al vento.

Proprio il giorno di Ferragosto è stato scelto per la dimostrazione del volo Yoga nei 108 Paesi del pianeta che accolgono centri Maharishi, dove tra l'altro si fanno corsi per la salute psicosomatica....

Non occorre coltivare esoterismi, ascesi spirituali o culinarie. Basta seguire i corsi di MT e qualunque mortale può imparare a realizzare la perfetta aderenza al CU sfruttando energie sconosciute.

Ed eccoli i dimostratori del volo senza ali — professionisti, insegnanti, studenti, mana-

La «dimostrazione» (Foto Sioli)

gers, commercianti, tredici in tutto — entrare silenziosi nel salone per accovacciarsi sui materassini di gommapiuma in posizione «fior di loto», gambe incrociate alla Budda.

Il gran maestro della cerimonia suona il campanello e i tredici, insensibili ai clic dei fotografi, sprofondano nella meditazione dei sutra a occhi chiusi, rigidi come statue. Poi i loro tronchi si mettono ad ondeggiare come cavalli scalpitanti ai nastri e suona il secondo campanello. I tredici allora cominciano a balzare senza abbandonare la posizione di Budda.

Chi lo fa con estrema agilità, chi meno, ma in ogni caso più che voli sono salti di circa mezzo metro. Qualcuno ogni tanto tira il fiato, altri rimbalzano imperterriti come molle sui materassini come Roberto, un agente commerciale sui 40, di Firenze, il quale assicura che oltre alla felicità questa esperienza gli assicura creatività nel lavoro.

Dopo 10 minuti fine della dimostrazione. Un medico, Carlo Galbiati, spiega che i Veda avevano anticipato di millenni le scoperte della fisica quantistica di oggi che non crede più a leggi rigide. Sì, l'esibizione può aver deluso qualcuno; ma non si cercava l'effetto quanto rivelare che chiunque, con un po' di esercizio mentale, può se non proprio volare fare balzi sui materassi quasi senza accorgersi, e senza sforzo.

Dal grande quadro la barba di Maharishi sorride fiduciosa....

Andrea Biglia

WORLD PEACE • GLOBAL INAUGURATION

PRESS REPORTS FROM EUROPE

Italy • *Il Giorno*
Milan   17 August 1986   (Italian)

«Provare per credere» a Brunate: singolare esibizione nel centro Maharishi

Si librano in volo con lo yoga per portare la pace nel mondo

BRUNATE - L.M.) Il «volo yoga» crea coerenza nella coscienza mondiale, neutralizza le tendenze negative che esistono nella creazione, e di conseguenza determina la pace in tutto il mondo. Sono questi alcuni capisaldi del pensiero di Maharishi Mahesh Yogi, filosofo e santone indiano, a capo di un'organizzazione che conta centinaia di migliaia di seguaci nel mondo.

«Con la crescente onda di terrorismo e la pericolosa rivalità delle superpotenze è di vitale importanza creare immediatamente una fortissima influenza di coerenza nella coscienza mondiale» dice sempre Maharishi, ed ecco perciò la necessità di praticare il «volo yoga», del quale il giorno di Ferragosto è stata data una dimostrazione a Brunate, in uno dei centri «Maharishi, capitale dell'età dell'illuminazione». Una dimostrazione compiuta simultaneamente in 108 paesi del mondo e in oltre mille città. / Davanti agli occhi scettici di un gruppo di cronisti, e a quelli invece entusiastici di un centinaio di fedeli seguaci, ha avuto luogo una prova di levitazione collettiva, compiuta da 13 persone. Queste, nella classica posizione yoga (gambe incrociate e occhi chiusi), dopo cinque minuti di meditazione trascendentale, hanno cominciato a compiere balzi di 30-40 centimetri in altezza e anche di un metro in lunghezza. Dopo una decina di minuti sono tornate in sè e apparivano perfettamente riposate. / Attraverso la concentrazione, hanno spiegato gli esperti, si riesce a dimenticare il corpo. Se poi attraverso la meditazione si irradii una sorta di pozione magica che determina la pace mondiale, è un discorso a cui ognuno è libero di credere o meno. I seguaci di Maharishi ne sono certi al punto di pensare che la pace può essere assicurata dalla pratica della «tecnologia Maharishi del campo unificato per 15-20 minuti, due volte al giorno in un solo luogo», il che è in grado di sviluppare stati di coscienza più elevati e di mantenere un alto grado di coerenza, per il progresso e la realizzazione di ogni famiglia e per la tranquilla amministrazione delle città. L'efficacia sarebbe assicurata riunendo la radice quadrata dell'1% della popolazione mondiale (7mila persone), e per realizzare questo progetto si cercano fondi presso le persone creative, i leaders e i ricchi.

Osservatori a bocca spalancata durante l'esibizione di Brunate: uno dei discepoli di Maharishi si solleva da terra con la sola forza della sua concentrazione.

PRESS REPORTS FROM EUROPE

Italy • *La Notte*
Milan 18 August 1986 (Italian)

A COMO UNA SCUOLA DI YOGA INSEGNA LA LEVITAZIONE

Nel salone dell'hotel Milano di Brunate, tredici sequaci del guru Maharishi hanno dato una dimonstrazione di cosa si riesce a fare praticando la meditazione. Sollevati dalla forza del pensiero hanno compiuto piccoli balzi su soffici materassi. Anche Nils Liedholm, allenatore del Milan, crede nello yoga

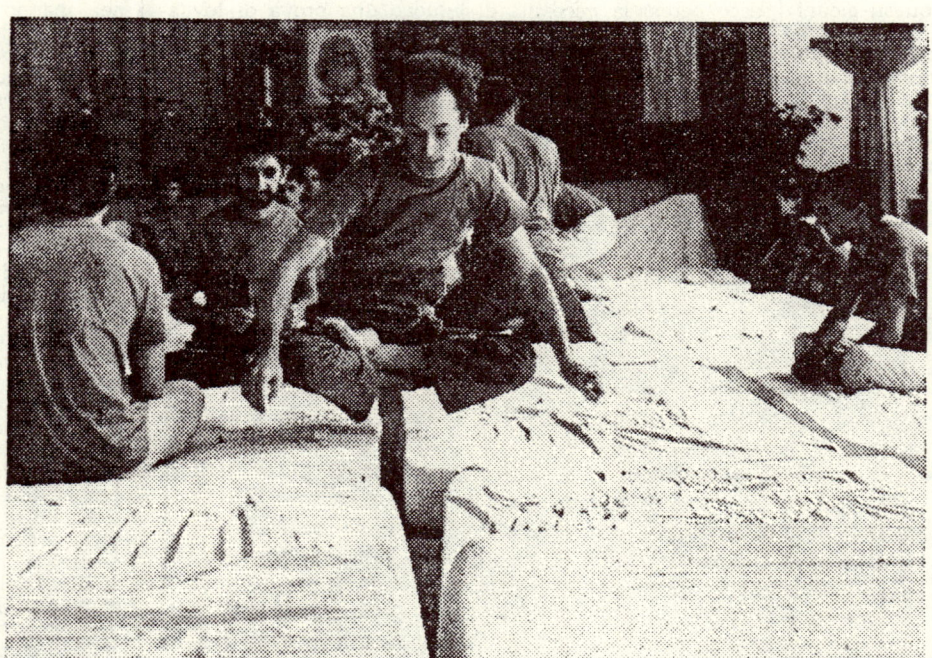

BRUNATE. Nel salone dell'Hotel Milano di Brunate, a strapiombo sul lago di Como, un gruppo di seguaci del guru indiano Maharishi, hanno dato dimostrazione di cosa si riesce a fare con la sola forza del pensiero e si sono «librati in volo» grazie alla levitazione, una facoltà che hanno appreso praticando lo yoga

di Marco Marelli

COMO. Erano in tredici a «volare» il giorno di ferragosto a Brunate, sopra Como, tredici seguaci di Maharishi Mahese Yogy, filosofo indiano, guru dei Beatles, oltre che fondatore del progetto Meditazione Trascendentale, dell'Intelligenza Creativa e del Governo Mondiale dell'Età dell'Illuminazione. Si è «volato» nel salone belle epoque dell'Hotel Milano di Brunate, dal 1982 «casa madre» italiana creata da Maharishi in persona, che trattò l'acquisto dell'imponente struttura che si erge a strapiombo sopra Como. La trattativa si svolse in Svizzera dove allora il santone abitava prima di tornare in India.

Sono riusciti, i seguaci di Maharishi, ad innalzare il loro corpo in aria anche se abalzi, tenendo le gambe incrociate e gli occhi chiusi

Una prova, quella eseguita il giorno di ferragosto, su confortanti materassi, che, così come è stato detto, si è svolta anche in altri 108 Paesi del mondo, e in oltre mille città.

Quello di Maharishi è un movimento imponente e, come sempre succede in casi pressoché analoghi, molto discusso. L'organizzazione certamente è in grado di radunare folle oceaniche. A centinaia di migliaia si contano gli adepti in tutto il mondo. Tra i più convinti in Italia troviamo l'allenatore del Milan, Nils Liedholm, il quale ha avuto occasione di dichiarare che *«fare venti minuti di meditazione non è tempo perso, anzi è tempo che guadagni dopo perché il benessere che provi è utile, specialmente per me che ho una certa età. Non dico che mi sento ringiovanito, ma sono più leggero, più chiaro e più lucido quando devo prendere le decisioni. Io posso consigliare la meditazione a tutti. Troveranno la serenità».*

Per qualcuno quella iniziata il giorno di ferragosto a Brunate è un'era nuova per il genere umano. Per combattere dell'incredulità, i tredici meditanti si sono posti dopo 5 minuti di meditazione in perfetta «armonia con il corpo unificato della coscienza universale» sperimentando così sublimi beatitudini, tanto da sentirsi leggeri «come una piuma» e levitare. Negli USA sono talmente bravi che già sono arrivati alle competizioni: «corsa» piana ed a ostacoli, salto in alto e in lungo.

Per levitare non è necessario coltivare filosofie particolari.

Il corso base, sette lezioni per un totale di altrettante ore, è gratuito. Se si vuole apprendere la tecnica del «yoga», occorre partecipare ad un corso che dura 15 giorni. Costa 750 mila lire, pensione compresa.

Italy • *La Repubblica*

Rome   17-18 August 1986   (Italian)

A Brunate l'esperimento dei discepoli di Maharishi Mahesh

Così si vola, grazie a Yogi

"Il nostro scopo non è aprire un circo", dice sorridendo Benedetto Valle, direttore della Capitale Maharishi dell'età dell'illuminazione, ossia dell'unica accademia di meditazione trascendentale in Italia (a Brunate, sul lago di Como). "E neanche far concorrenza all'Alitalia", gli fa eco il dottor Carlo Galbiati, suo assistente. "Assisterete al fenomeno del volo yoga: non è nulla di trascendentale — prosegue Valle con una punta di autoironia — ma dimostra come sia possibile, con la concentrazione mentale, una trasformazione anche fisica delle potenzialità umane".

Per testimoniare la bontà del metodo da loro insegnato, gli adepti di sua santità Maharishi Mahesh Yogi (filosofo indiano, fondatore del movimento, nonché del programma di Intelligenza Creativa e del Governo per la Pace Mondiale) a mezzogiorno di Ferragosto hanno aperto le porte del loro centro a increduli e scettici. Motivo dell'appuntamento con fotografi, giornalisti e operatori della Rai: un esperimento di volo yoga, cioè una serie di salti compiuti da dodici "sidha" (cioè di coloro che non sono più matricole dell'accademia), con le gambe incrociate nella posizione cosiddetta del loto. E per cinque minuti i sidha saltano tutti insieme sui materassi del salone centrale in stile liberty dell'ex-hotel Milano. Qualcuno fa balzi anche di un metro in avanti, alzandosi di una ventina di centimetri.

Intanto su un teleschermo scorrono grafici colorati con le percentuali di perdita (in stress) e di guadagno (in salute psichica), commentati da alcuni signori in inappuntabili completi di lino. Se non fosse per i grandi quadri raffiguranti il Maestro, potrebbe sembrare un borsino di provincia. Ad un tratto anche Nils Liedholm, allenatore del Milan, si materializza sul video per spiegare che, con il metodo Maharishi, "mi sento più leggero, più chiaro e più lucido quando devo prendere le decisioni". "Lo ha consigliato anche a Silvio Berlusconi", dice Galbiati. In vista del prossimo derby, il presidente dell'Inter Ernesto Pellegrini, il suo allenatore Giovanni Trapattoni e i tifosi nerazzurri sono avvertiti. *(Antonello Piroso)*

PRESS REPORTS FROM EUROPE

Italy • *La Stampa*

Turin 10 September 1986 (Italian)

Come mettere d'accordo anima e corpo

Il fast food della meditazione: professionisti e manager a scuola per combattere lo stress

In quattro ore insegnano come mettere d'accordo corpo e anima: un frullato di sapienza d'Oriente per il pronto consumo del frettoloso cittadino occidentale, una sorta di fast-food, con molte pretese, della filosofia yoga. In città come la nostra la ricetta pare avere buone probabilità di successo, già un migliaio di persone l'hanno sperimentata e il numero sembra destinato a crescere in tempi brevi. Tutto riferito ad uno spicchio dei movimenti ....

denominato Meditazione Trascendentale con sede in corso Moncalieri 72 e diretto da Ubaldo Cortinovis, tono pacato, occhio vispo, impegnato full-time a diffondere la tecnica del riposo interiore secondo la dottrina di Maharishi Mahesh Yogi.

E' una cosa seria? Non è comunque una faccenda da riderci sopra visto che i seguaci di Maharishi a Torino sono definiti in un recentissimo documento dell'Ires *«persone con alto livello di istruzione, appartenenti al ceto medio superiore, in prevalenza maschi e nella fascia di età tra i 30 e 45 anni con spiccato, precedente interesse per studi esoterici».* Ne ho incontrate alcune, medici, avvocati, preti, a Brunate di Como dove un vecchio albergo è diventato «capitale» del movimento. Lì Cortinovis con altri si è esibito per giornalisti, fotografi e simpatizzanti in una dimostrazione di volo yoga,

Una dimostrazione di volo

un mini-levitazione che si esaurisce in salti e saltelli, risultato della prevalenza della volontà sulla legge gravitazionale. Dicono che basta concentrarsi cinque minuti (traguardo che si raggiunge non certo nelle quattro ore di cui sopra) per annullare il peso corporeo: dopo di che sui materassi allineati nel salone dell'ex albergo una dozzina di iniziati comincia a ballonzolare avanti e indietro. Qualcuno mugola, altri sorridono: un su e giu frenetico, una sorta di gioco

«Provi lei, tenendo le gambe incrociate a fior di loto» incalza il prete, don Mario Mazzoleni di Zogno (Val Brembana), malattia renale piuttosto grave.

Non è facile dovendo spiegare razionalmente salti in lungo da 50 metri ed in alto da quasi un metro ottenuti nelle «olimpiadi» di volo-yoga che si tengono in America sotto l'occhio vigile e la candida barba di Maharishi Mahesh già laureato in fisica e matematica, poi rientrato ... sotto la guida illuminata dei maestro Shankaracharya. No, facile non è fare certe cose né spiegarle. Bisogna accettare l'evidenza e mettersi in un angolo ad ascoltare. Da un *videotape* giungono voci note. Nils Liedholm, allenatore del Milan: *«Fare venti minuti di meditazione non è tempo perso. Lo consiglierei ai tifosi prima di recarsi allo stadio».* Bruno Confortola, nazionale di sci: *«Sicuramente la MT mi ha aiutato molto nella pratica agonistica».* Lo stilista Luca Missoni: *«La meditazione aiuta lo sviluppo creativo».* Jack Basehart, attore: *«La MT mi ha fatto abbandonare gli psicofarmaci».* Seguono, commentate da Marisa Borroni, altre interviste: casalinghe, medici, professionisti, manager. Anche il sindacalista Uil, Stefano Morfino: *«La Mt consente una maggiore lucità negli interventi».*

Tutti possono cimentarsi con la «luce» e ricevere il premio della rivelazione. Senza limiti di età o di censo, né di religione. La porta è spalancata sul sogno dell'uomo oppresso dalla civiltà tecnologica, il messaggio coglie nel segno, promette ciò che ognuno in cuor suo desidera: via lo stress che uccide, salute mentale e fisica, potere e longevità, ore felici dietro l'angolo dell'angoscia quotidiana. Il colpo di genio di Maharishi è di aver capovolto ad uso e consumo dell'agitato Occidente il concetto dello yoga classico: questo richiede la disciplina del corpo per conseguire il dominio della mente, la Meditazione Trascendentale insegna in quattro e quattr'otto a dominare la mente per giungere col tempo, se uno vuole, a disciplinare il corpo. Mèta ultima la proiezione della pace individuale sul mondo intero: un'altra utopia, lo spiraglio per l'uomo che sente su di sé il peso della minaccia nucleare, della guerra senza vincitori o vinti.

Pier Paolo Benedetto

WORLD PEACE • GLOBAL INAUGURATION

PRESS REPORTS FROM EUROPE

The Netherlands • *De Volkskrant*
Amsterdam   12 July 1986   (Dutch)

Een opname van de eerste Noordamerikaanse „Yogic flying" wedstrijd, deze week gehouden in Washington. Beoefenaren van Trancendente Meditatie deden daar wie het hoogst kon vliegen. De winnaar kwam op 57,8 centimeter.
Volgens geestelijk leider Maharishi Mahesh Yogi kunnen zeer gevorderde meditatie-beoefenaren een staat van verlichtheid bereiken die dergelijke staaltjes mogelijk maakt. Toch heeft de kennelijke toestand van gewichtloosheid weinig te maken met meditatietechniek. De persoon zweeft niet, bleek tijdens de bijeenkomst, maar is aan het hoppen: op en neer hupsen met opgevouwen benen. Ook best wel moeilijk.

PRESS REPORTS FROM EUROPE

The Netherlands • *Nieuwe Noordhollandsche Courant*

Hoorn   23 July 1986   (Dutch)

Hoppen en stuiteren dat het een lust is

NEW DELHI *(AP).* — Levitatie tegen Terrorisme. Onder dat motto namen 99 aanhangers van de Indiase goeroe Maharisji Mahesj Yogi deze week deel aan het eerste wereldkampioenschap yogi-vliegen, in een poging de wereldvrede te bevorderen. Tijdens de eerste 'metafysische olympiade' hopten en stuiterden ze over de matrassen dat het een lieve lust was....

De yogi-vliegers kwamen uit in wedstrijden in het zogeheten eerste stadium van levitatie, waarbij de hersengolven in maximale harmonie met de lichaamsbewegingen moeten worden gebracht om te kunnen hoppen. Het tweede stadium zou zweven moeten zijn en in het derde stadium zou men echt moeten kunnen vliegen.

De aanhangers van de goeroe onder wie een populaire Amerikaanse goochelaar en diverse wetenschappers, zeggen dat zij door middel van transcendente meditatie (TM) eenverenigd veldvan universele natuurwetten kunnen activeren, waardoor zij geweld, negatieve gevoelens en stress kunnen uitbannen.

Als maar genoeg mensen hoppen, kan een eind worden gemaakt aan de rivaliteit tussen de supermachten en aan het terrorisme en wordt wereldvrede ons deel, aldus de TM'ers.

Zelfs als maar een klein percentage van de mensheid aan TM doet, is wereldvrede onvermijdelijk, aldus Blaine Watson, een 31-jarige TM-leraar uit Canada die 60 centimeter hoog hopte en daarmee de gouden medaille won.

De Maharisji heeft instituten over de hele wereld en duizenden aanhangers. Hij zegt dat ongeveer 7.000 mensen gezamenlijk moeten mediteren om een krachtig effect te sorteren op de wereldvrede.

In een groot centrum buiten New Delhi leidt hij ongeveer 2.000 jonge brahmanen, leden van de Indiase priesterkaste, op in de kunst van de meditatie. In totaal wil hij 10.000 mensen opleiden. Het is duidelijk dat politieke onderhandelingen, verdragen en het gebruik van wapens er nooit toe zullen leiden dat de wereld in een staat van duurzame vrede raakt, aldus de goeroe.

De vrouwelijke deelnemers aan het wereldkampioenschap hoppen werden door een groot gordijn gescheiden van de mannelijke hoppers. De vrouwen mochten niet worden gefotografeerd en er werden op de tribune van dat deel van het Indira Gandhi stadion alleen vrouwen toegelaten.

De Amerikaanse arts Nancy Lonsdorf zei dat haar leven meer in overeenstemming met de natuurwet is gekomen na 12 jaar TM. Ze won in elk geval de zilveren medaille op de 50 meter sprint-hop.

Sommige deelnemers schudden onder het hoppen met hun hoofd, en anderen stopten halverwege om eerst nog wat te mediteren voor zij verder hopten.

De Israelische student Jossef Jaakov stopte zeker acht maal tijdens de race over de 50 meter. Hij kwam als laatste binnen, maar vond het een geweldige ervaring. „In het begin vond ik TM wat vreemd, maar nu is het een deel van mijn leven. Ik ben tijdens de studie zo geconcentreerd dat alles gewoon op zijn plaats valt. Ik denk dat andere studenten harder hun best moeten doen. Ik kan minder doen en meer bereiken, precies zoals de Maharisji zegt, aldus de student.

WORLD PEACE • GLOBAL INAUGURATION

PRESS REPORTS FROM EUROPE

The Netherlands • *Trouw*

Amsterdam 16 August 1986 (Dutch)

Hoppend als een kikker op weg naar de wereldvrede

Een demonstratie 'hoppen', zoals die gisteren werd gegeven in het conferentieoord Soeria in Laag-Soeren, een techniek om zich bij transcendente meditatie een stukje van de grond te verheffen.
Foto APA

door Chris Bruijnius

LAAG-SOEREN – Zet zevenduizend mensen bij elkaar, laat ze twee keer per dag een tijdje flink hoppen en de wereldvrede is gered. Dat is ongeveer de boodschap die Marahishi Mahesh Yogi gisteren de wereld in heeft gestuurd.

Volgelingen van de Maharishi, die eind jaren vijftig de Transcedente Meditatie (TM) in zwang bracht, hebben gisteren in 108 landen met demonstraties hoppen de boodschap van de meester onder de aandacht gebracht.

TM-hoppen is natuurlijk niet zomaar hoppen. Op de TM-academie Soeria in Laag-Soeren, waar de Nederlandse demonstratie plaatsvond, belichtte cursusleider drs. M. C. ten Dam de achtergronden.

Het 'hoppen als een kikker' moet gezien worden als het eerste stadium van de TM-Sidhi vliegtechniek. Mensen die zich eraan wagen, dienen de transcedente meditatie onder de knie te hebben. Slechts dan zijn zij in staat geestelijk het 'verenigd veld' te bereiken.

Dat veld, een term uit de fysica, is het centrale thema, legde Ten Dam uit. Kan je de geest op dat niveau brengen, dan zit je als het ware aan het schakelbord van de schepping en heb je meesterschap over alle natuurwetten. Bovendien kan de mediterende invloed uitoefenen op het bewustzijn van andere mensen. Er moet een krachtige samenhang, *coherentie* in het wereldbewustzijn worden geschapen, luidt de boodschap van de Maharisje.

Wat hebben alle verdragen tussen landen, alle opgerichte organisaties en geperfectioneerde wapens nu bijgedragen aan de wereldvrede, was een van de hypothetische vragen waarmee Ten Dam de tientallen journalisten, fotografen en filmers bestookte, die waren afgekomen op het hopfenomeen. De Maharisja had, ziek geworden van de toenemende rivaliteit tussen de wereldmachten en het om zich heen grijpende terrorisme, besloten in te grijpen.

Minder ongelukken

De deelnemers aan TM hebben door de hoge frequentie van hun hersengolven, dus een grote uitstraling op hun omgeving. Honderden proeven hebben, aldus Ten Dam, aangetoond dat op plaatsen waar één procent van de bevolking mediteert het aantal verkeersongelukken en het misdaadcijfer terugloopt. Evenals de burenruzies. Wordt de Sidih-techniek beoefend, het hoppen, dan wordt de uitstraling nogeens zoveel sterker, dat het aantal deelnemers slechts de wortel van één procent van de bevolking behoeft te zijn om dezelfde resultaten te boeken.

Ten Dam kon wat krasse staaltjes noemen. Tijdens de burgeroorlog in Rhodesië was een groep hoppers naar dat land getrokken. Het aantal slachtoffers in het gebied waar ze verbleven liep binnen een dag terug van 35 naar 2. Toen zij na drie maanden weer vertrokken, lag het cijfer binnen de kortste tijd weer op 40. Ook in sommige Nederlandse plaatsen zijn groepen hoppers actief geweest, en met gunstige resultaten, kon de cursusleider verzekeren....

WORLD PEACE • GLOBAL INAUGURATION

PRESS REPORTS FROM EUROPE

The Netherlands • *NRC*
Rotterdam   16 August 1986   (Dutch)

Hop, hop, hop op weg naar de eeuwige wereldvrede

De deelnemers aan het hoppen. Rechts de Nederlandse kampioen F. Commandeur die de verwachting uitsprak binnenkort te kunnen vliegen. (Foto NRC Handelsblad / Freddy Rikken)

Door onze redacteur
MARCEL HAENEN

LAAG SOEREN, 16 aug. — Hoppend is gisteren in de Academie voor bewustzijnsontwikkeling Soeria in Laag Soeren een eerste stap gezet op weg naar de wereldvrede. Tegelijk met deze demonstratie van een transcendente meditatietechniek (TM) voor gevorderden, vond in nog 107 landen dezelfde bijeenkomst plaats. Vrijdag 15 augustus was door de ontdekker van TM, de Maharishi Mahesh Yogi, namelijk gekozen als beginpunt voor een programma dat moet leiden tot mondiaal geluk.

„Transcendente meditatie is namelijk de enige, let op de ènige methode om daadwerkelijk wereldvrede te scheppen", vermaande drs. M. ten Dam, directeur cursusbeleid van de academie. „De werking ervan is krachtiger dan die van verdragen, internationale organisaties of moderne defensieve wapens".

Schermend met zo'n 350 onderzoeken die de werking van TM volgens hem inmiddels afdoende hebben aangetoond, legde Ten Dam uit wat er precies te gebeuren staat. „Door TM kun je de menselijke geest contact laten maken met het Verenigd Veld of te wel de superzwaartekracht. In die situatie verwerf je meesterschap over alle natuurwetten en kun je ontwikkelingen in de maatschappij ten goede keren".

Om de nogal grofstoffelijk ingestelde sceptici te overtuigen van de mogelijkheden van TM werd gekozen voor een demonstratie van het Hoppen, de zogeheten TM-Sidhi techniek en eerste stadium van het yoga-vliegen. Ten Dam: „Niet omdat we zo graag variété-artiesten spelen maar omdat dit de meest effectieve reclame is".

Voor de demonstratie namen acht heren, onder applaus, in lotushouding plaats op een flinke verzameling matrassen. Na enige minuten stilte en bij het luiden van een koperen belletje zette het achttal zich hupsend in beweging. Zonder zich af te zetten, overbrugden zij snuivend, schokschouderend en soms lachend acht keer een afstand van zo'n 20 meter. Een indrukwekkend nummer, dat volgens arts C. Kiffmeyer, die met lichtbeelden een toelichting gaf, de deelnemers vooral innerlijk veel geluk verschaft. „Te vergelijken met het genot dat een baby aan de moederborst ervaart".

Het hupsen brengt echter niet alleen de hopper geluk, maar genereert een golf door de hele samenleving, aldus Ten Dam. Proefondervindelijk is gebleken dat in de omgeving van een groep mediterenden minder verkeersongelukken gebeuren, de mensen minder stress hebben, de misdaad daalt en betere politieke verhoudingen ontstaan. Mediterenden zelf ondervinden veel voorspoed. Reden waarom zij in de Verenigde Staten voor een ongevallenverzekering soms maar 70 procent van de premie hoeven te betalen, meldde Kiffmeyer.

Het streven van de TM-beweging is er nu op gericht één procent van de wortel van de totale wereldbevolking, zo'n 7.000 mensen, bij elkaar te brengen. Als deze groep permanent, op dezelfde plek, twee keer per dag hopt, dan is de wereldvrede bereikt. Ten Dam: „Het plan is een joint-venture te maken. Het westen levert het geld en India bijvoorbeeld de mensen". Binnen een paar jaar moet uit de nu al 55.000 hoppers in de wereld zo'n groep zijn geselecteerd, want als gevolg van het al maar erger wordende terrorisme, is haast geboden, gebood Ten Dam.

Wedstrijdhoppen

Tot besluit werden gisteren nog videobeelden getoond van een agressievere TM-tak, namelijk het wedstrijd-hoppen in de VS. Te zien was het 50 meter snelhoppen, de verre en de hoge hop en het spectaculaire hordenhoppen. Drs. Frits Commandeur, geograaf, haalde gisteren nog spontaan een zilveren medaille uit zijn binnenzak. Eremetaal dat hij enkele weken geleden behaalde bij het WK hoppen in New Delhi op het onderdeel verhoppen met een sprong van 1.61 meter (de kampioen had 1.63 meter). Commandeur, vroeger een matige voetballer, is tevens Nederlands kampioen hoppen met een tijd van 29 seconden over de vijftig meter. Hij hopt al acht jaar twee keer per dag, is 37 jaar oud, gelukkig getrouwd, van katholieken huize en heeft geen benedenburen.

The Netherlands • *De Limburger*

Maastricht 19 September 1986 (Dutch)

Door Joep Dohmen
Foto Frans Welters

Transcedente Meditatie en de Nieuwe Openheid
Vliegen voor de wereldvrede

De tijd is rijp om het stilzwijgen te verbreken. Immers, de wereldvrede is in gevaar. Hoogste tijd voor de beoefenaars van Transcedente Meditatie (TM) om de buitenwereld te vertellen dat zij dè oplossing hebben: Een positieve hersengolf die iedereen de wapens doet neerleggen. Transcedente Meditatie en het Maharishi-effect, de onverklaarbare invloed op de dollarkoers en de wereldkampioenschappen yogi-vliegen. En: De getuigenis van een eerlijk kunstschilder. „Ondanks TM zal ik nóóit een Rembrandt worden."

De deur van het TM-centrum aan de Alexander Battalaan in Maastricht staat open. Illustratief voor de Nieuwe Openheid. De Indiase goeroe Maharishi Mahesh Yogi, die in 1958 de TM-techniek lanceerde, gaf dit jaar een seintje dat de tijd rijp is om naar buiten te treden. Tot voor kort werd publiciteit angstvallig gemeden, nu kan alles. Zèlfs een demonstratie yogi-vliegen.

„De wereldvrede is namelijk in gevaar", openbaart TM-leraar Lambert Classens (29) op de eerste verdieping van het oude herenhuis. „De nood is hoog. Kijk naar het terrorisme en de oorlogen die ons omringen. Dat schreeuwt toch om een oplossing? Daarbij komt dat de Maharishi vindt dat de TM-beoefenaars de techniek nu zóver onder de knie hebben dat iedereen het mag zien. We hoeven niet meer geheimzinnig te doen."

Volgens de leraar is Transcedente Meditatie dè techniek om de geest tot rust te laten komen. Om af te dalen in de diepere regionen van de geest. TM is gebasseerd op oude Indiase meditatie-technieken die in 1958 werden 'herontdekt' door de Maharishi. In 1976 kwam de goeroe met een nòg intensievere meditatievorm: TM-Sidhi.

„Door de zeer diepe graad van geestelijke rust die met TM-sidhi wordt bereikt, kunnen we sterke hersengolven uitzenden", doceert Classens. „Met die golven gaan we de negativiteit in het collectieve bewustzijn te lijf. Dat is het Maharishi-effect. En hoe groter de mediterende groep, hoe krachtiger de uitstraling. We hebben berekend dat voor het positief beïnvloeden van de hele wereld een groep van 7.000 mensen nodig is".

Het 'wonderbaarlijke' Maharishi-effect zorgt en passant voor een afname van het aantal verkeersongevallen en een daling van de criminaliteit. En ook de economie blijft niet ongemoeid! Tijdens een TM-congres in de Verenigde Staten, waar enkele duizenden mensen aan het mediteren sloegen, zou de dollarkoers 'onverklaarbaar' omhoog zijn gesprongen.
De toepassingen lijken onuitputtelijk. In het TM-periodiek 'Volkomen gezondheid' wordt juichend geschreven over de mogelijkheid te verjongen ('vijf jaar TM en je bent twaalf jaar jonger'). En behalve wereldvrede, geeft TM ook hulp bij het afbouwen van stress, vermageren en afkicken ('twee Limburgse jongens kwamen er vanaf'). Last but not least dringt TM ook het ziekteverzuim in bedrijven terug.

Rembrandt

„TM geeft mij inspiratie en zelfvertrouwen", getuigt Gilbert Ramaekers (60), kunstschilder te Maas-

MAHARISHI'S PROGRAMME TO CREATE

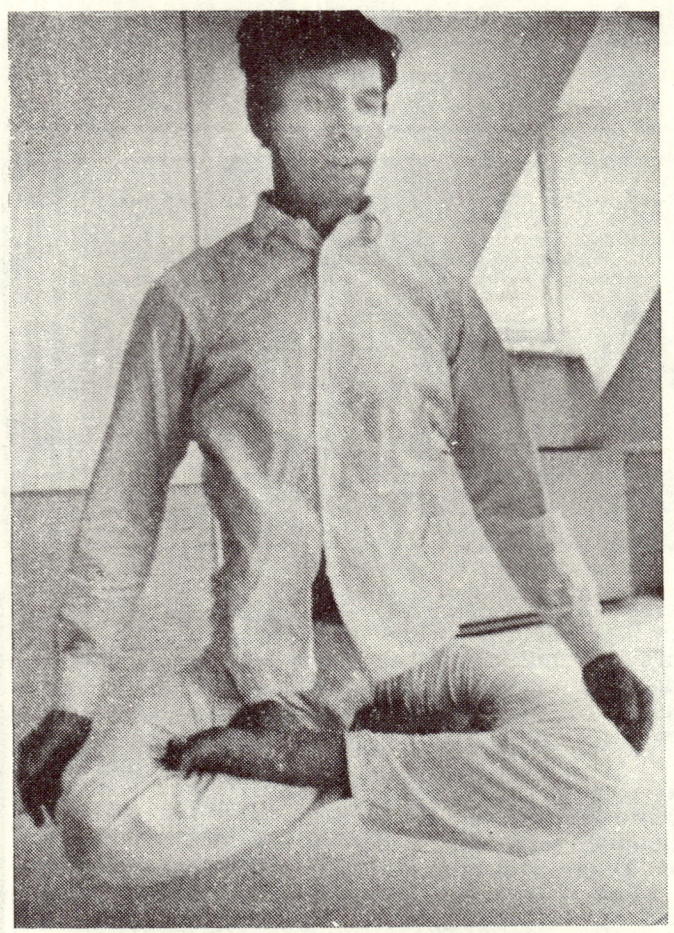

tricht. In het kantoor annex meditatieruimte vertelt de kunstenmaker dat meer dan tien jaar meditatie ('thuis doet iedereen het') hun vruchten hebben afgeworpen. „Niet dat ik door TM de absolute gave bezit. Een Rembrandt zal ik nooit worden. Maar wàt er inzit, haal ik er wel uit. En mijn gezondheid, natuurlijk! Dat gaat sinds de TM-oefeningen stukken beter. Vroeger had ik problemen met mijn longen. Nu niet meer."

Leraar Classens valt bij. Ook hij heeft 'persoonlijke positieve ervaringen'. Hij bekent. Dat hij in het dagelijks leven grafisch ontwerper is. Dat hij vroeger voor elke opdracht een 'enorme strijd' moest leveren om tot een 'creatief eindpunt' te komen. Dat dàt proces nu véél rapper gaat; leuke ideeën borrelen gewoon op. Dat hij veel minder dan vroeger aan zichzelf twijfelt. En, dat hij met zijn vader en moeder in harmonie leeft.

Meest spectaculaire onderdeel van de TM-techniek is het yogi-vliegen of hoppen. De diepe staat van rust van de TM-sidhi neutraliseert de zwaartekracht. Daardoor kunnen de TM'ers hun lichaam laten hoppen. „Het is de eerste stap op weg naar het echte vliegen", vertelt Frits Commandeur uit Dieren.

Hij werkt in het Maharishi Ayurvedic Prevention Centre, onderdeel van de TM-Academie voor Bewustzijnsontwikkeling in Laag Soeren (Veluwe). Ayurvedic is een oude Indiase geneeswijze die het lichaam reinigt. Commandeur is 's lands beste vlieger en bereidt zich in het herenhuis voor op een vliegdemonstratie.

„Bij het hoppen blijven we maar heel kort in de lucht. Vergelijk het met een kikkersprong", schildert de vlieger. „TM-sidhi wordt nu tien jaar beoefend. Nog niemand is het gelukt om echt te vliegen. Maar als we flink oefenen, kunnen we over een paar jaar langere tijd zweven. En nog weer later zullen we ons door de lucht kunnen verplaatsen. Vliegen dus."

Ver-hoppen

In de vernieuwde optiek van goeroe Maharishi passen ook de wereldkampioenschappen yogi-vliegen die in juli in India plaatsvonden. Honderd mediterende deelnemers uit alle delen van de wereld streden in New Delhi voor gouden, zilveren en bronzen vliegmedailles.

Hop-kampioen Frits Commandeur: „...Vliegen, een reëel perspectief..."

De deelnemers hadden de keus uit vijftig meter sprint-hoppen, vijfentwintig meter horden-hoppen, ver-hoppen en hoog-hoppen. Het record hoog-hoppen staat op 64 centimeter en het ver-hoppen op 1,63 meter. Nederlands hopkampioen Frits Commandeur, werd tweede bij het ver-hoppen met 1,61 meter.

Demonstratie

De demonstratie geeft Commandeur op de zolder van het TM-centrum. De vloer ligt vol matrassen

WORLD PEACE • GLOBAL INAUGURATION

waarop de vlieger in Lotushouding ontspant. Vier, vijf minuten duurt het, voor hij beweegt. In trance schudt Commandeur zijn hoofd, zwaait met zijn armen en snuift. Plots schiet hij de lucht in. Met zichtbaar gemak, dertig centimeter hoog. Hij landt één meter verder op de matrassen.

Dan veert de vlieger weer omhoog. Zo hopt hij moeiteloos door de ruimte.

„Ik mediteer acht jaar", zucht Commandeur na afloop. „Als ik zie wat ik nù al kan, is vliegen een reëel perspectief. Waarom ik wil vliegen? Niet om circusartiest te worden. Dat zal u duidelijk zijn. De geestelijke kracht die nodig is om te vliegen, kan ik ook gebruiken om mensen gezond te maken in het Mararhishi Ayurvedic Prevention Centre. En natuurlijk om de wereldvrede een stukje dichterbij te brengen."

The Netherlands • *Arnhemse Courant*

Arnheim 16 August 1986 (Dutch)

„Hoppen" voor de wereldvrede

(Van een onzer verslaggevers)
LAAG SOEREN — In 108 plaatsen in de gehele wereld werden gisteren hopdemonstraties gegeven die moeten leiden tot een stormachtige toeloop tot deze vorm van transcedente meditatie en uiteindelijk absolute wereldvrede moet brengen.

De hoppers zijn er van overtuigd dat als er zevenduizend mensen (de vierkantswortel van een procent van de wereldbevolking) op een plaats tegelijkertijd en tweemaal per dag deze oefeningen doen, de agressie uit de wereld zal verdwijnen. Dit wordt mogelijk doordat de hoppers, zo zeggen zij, meesterschap krijgen over alle natuurwetten. Hierdoor gaan alle mensen zich gelukkig voelen, waardoor terreur en onvriendelijkheid wordt uitgebannen.

In het academie voor bewustzijnswording Soeria in Laag Soeren werd gisteren voor de pers een demonstratie gegeven. Van het aangekondigde vliegen, zich door meditatie los maken van de grond en zodoende de zwaartekracht overwinnen, was geen sprake. Degenen die de demonstratie gaven hopten als kikkers in lotushouding over matrassen. Daaronder ook Nederlands kampioen drs. F. Commandeur die de vijftig meter in 29 seconden hopt en onlangs in New Dehli tweede in het verhoppen werd.

■ *Hoppen voor de wereldvrede in Laag Soeren. Links Nederlands kampioen vijftig meter hoppen drs. F. Commandeur.*

PRESS REPORTS FROM EUROPE

Norway • *Aftenposten*
Oslo 16 August 1986 (Norwegian)

En av de «flyvende» yogier som kom hoppende bortover skumgummimadrassen i dyp konsentrasjon under demonstrasjonen på Bygdøy i går. (Foto: Erik Berglund.)

WORLD PEACE • GLOBAL INAUGURATION

PRESS REPORTS FROM EUROPE

Norway • *Driva*

Sunndalsøra 30 August 1986 (Norwegian)

Flyging med tankekraft

— Kan mennesket flyge ? Ja !, meiner dei som praktiserer teknikken Transcendental Meditasjon (TM). Etter å ha møtt tvil og avvisning av denne påstanden i fleire år har TM-rørsla i sommar gått ut med demonstrasjonar i mange land verda rundt for å bevise at dei kan lette frå bakken under praktisering av det spesielle TM - Sidhi-programmet. Nyleg var turen komen til Norge, nærmare bestemt Sjøfartsmuseet på Bygdøy i Oslo. Eit stort oppbod av presse og kringkasting var tilstades. Lars Ranes frå Sunndalsøra var tilstades under demonstrasjonen i Oslo og gir her sine inntrykk i ord og bilde.

Tekst/foto: Lars Ranes

Fritt for «action» vart det ikkje på Bygdøy. Lette og luftige sprett om på skumplastmadrassane mangla det ikkje på. Høgdepunktet var «kappflyginga« på den 50 meter lange madrassen. Dei fem utøvarane av TM-Sidhi-programmet skulle her kappast om kven som først kunne tilbakelegge 40 meter med beina i kors og attlukne augo. Sittestillinga teke i betraktning var det reint imponerande å sjå kor radigt, lett og uanstrengt dei førti metrane vart tilbakelagt.

Skeptikarane uttrykte likevel tvil om det her ikkje snarare var inntrente fysiske øvelser ein hadde sett. På spørsmål om dette etter demonstrasjonen svara utøvarane at hoppa kjem utan nokon som helst fysisk anstrengelse. Altså kun ved praktisering av den mentale «Yogiske flygeteknikken» i TM-Sidhi-programmet. Dei la til at dei følte seg lette i kroppen idet dei spratt rundt på madrassane, samt at dei opplevde det som gledesfylt og behageleg.

Bakgrunn

Ei nærmare utgreiing om formålet med arrangementet og om mekanikken i TM-Sidhi-programmet generelt vart gitt på ein pressekonferanse før sjølve flygeteknikken vart demonstrert. Lærarar i Transcendental Meditasjon fortalte her at opprinnelsen til programmet ligg heile 2000 år tilbake i tida. På denne tida var det at den kjente yogafortolkaren Patanjali komponerte ei rekke mentale teknikkar, eller tankeformlar. Gjennom den rette praktiseringa av desse skulle ein kunne oppnå ei rekkje spesielle evner, som til dømes det å sveve i lause lufta.

Det er eit utval av desse teknikkane som utgjer TM-Sidhi-programmet, kor «Yogisk flygning» må seiast å vere den mest avanserte. Vidare vart det fortalt at ein viktig forutsetnad for at Sidhi-teknikkene skal virke er at dei blir praktisert ut ifrå det djupaste nivået i menneskesinnet. Transcendental Meditasjon er nettopp ein teknikk for å nå dette planet i seg sjølv.

Det blei fortalt at ein annan viktig forutsetnad for å oppnå den fulle verknaden av teknikkane var at nervesystemet måtte vere fritt for stress og spenningar. Så lenge ein har lagra stress og spenningar vil verknadene av teknikkane berre bli halvvegs, til dømes det at ein berre spratt lett omkring istaden for verkeleg å sveve. Ein understreka at det eigentlege formålet med TM-Sidhi-programmet var nettopp dette å løyse opp stress og spenning som vi alle har i oss, og slik gradvis utvikle hjarnens fulle potensiale. Vitskapen fortel oss at vi berre bruker 10-15% av hjarnens potensiale kunne TM-lærarane fortelje.

Kva med gravitasjonskrafta ?

Ein av journalistane som var møtt fram ville gjerne ha ein forklaring på korleis det kunne vere mogleg for eit menneskje å oppheve tyngdekrafta, for det måtte ein vel gjere om ein skulle klare å sveve. TM-læraren Harald Harung forklarte dette ved å ta utgangspunkt i dei siste teoriane innan fysikken. På linje med det som også vart hevda av den kjente fysikaren Albert Einstein fortel desse teoriane at alle naturlovene, inkludert gravitasjonskrafta, har opphav i et einhetleg kraftfelt. Dette feltet blir karakterisert som «ikkje-relativt», dvs. at det ligg bortanfor tid-og-romdimensjonen. Harung forklarte så at det også er dette ikkje-relative planet ein finn som det djupaste nivået i menneskesinnet, gjerne kalla tankens kjelde.

Det er dette planet ein etablerer kontakt med gjennom TM-teknikken. Når ein befinn seg på dette planet vil gravitasjonsfeltet lett kunne omformast til eit horisontalt bølgande felt. TM-Sidhi flygeteknikken er ein teknikk for å oppnå mellom anna dette, avslutta Harung.

Aller sist må det nemnast at lærarane i Transcendental Meditasjon fleire gonger understreka at hensikten med dette noko spesielle arrangementet ikkje var å lage show, men å rette søkjelyset på TM-Sidhi-programmet som virkningsfulle teknikkar, ikkje berre til å skape fredsfylte individ, men også til å skape harmoni i ein ellers så stressa og uroleg verden.

WORLD PEACE • GLOBAL INAUGURATION

PRESS REPORTS FROM EUROPE

Norway • *Bergens Tidende*
Bergen 16 August 1986 (Norwegian)

Sigbjørn Hanem — ikke svevende, men i et hopp

BT TEKST: PETTER LARSEN
FOTO: ENDRE JØRGENSEN

Folk som mediterer, kan bli i stand til å lette fra bakken. Dette er hva Maharishi Institutt for Kreativ Intelligens (MIKI Norge) ville demonstrere fro presse og spesielt innbudte på Hotel Norge i går kveld. Demonstrasjonen foregikk samtidig i 108 land....

PRESS REPORTS FROM EUROPE

Norway • *Adresseavisen*

Trondheim   13 August 1986   (Norwegian)

Det skjer i Oslo fredag?

Mennesker «letter» av egen kraft

ROLF W. THANEM

Fredag 15. august 1986 kan bli stående som en av de virkelig store merkedager i menneskehetens historie. Fredag er nemlig dagen da stor-yogi'en Maharishi har bestemt seg for å vise all verdens tvilere at mennesket kan fly, løfte seg fra bakken uten andre hjelpemidler enn full mobilisering av indre styrke. Begivenheten vil bl.a. finne sted på Bygdøy i Oslo, der «alminnelige» nordmenn ved hjelp av den såkalte Sidhi-teknikken vil lette fra bakken omkring klokken 20.

Man skal ikke være for skråsikker. De som har gått rundt og trodd at tyngdeloven gjelder for oss alle, kan oppleve et kraftig nederlag på Bygdøy fredag kveld. Maharishi må tydeligvis mene alvor når han i disse dager sender ut et varsel til 108 land om at nettopp fredag 15. august er dagen da tyngdekraften skal oppheves, i første omgang for noen ganske få.

I invitasjonen til media i sakens anledning legges det heller ikke skjul på at det dreier seg om en verdensbegivenhet. I brevet fra Maharishi Institutt for Kreativ Intelligens (heretter MIKI) som er sendt Adresseavisen og «endel VIP-personer», forhåndsbeskrives det som skal skje på Bygdøy ganske enkelt som en sensasjon.

Foran øynene på de inviterte skal altså mediterende som praktiserer TM-Sidhi demonstrere flyteknikken. De vil lette fra bakken bare ved hjelp av de indre krefter som eksisterer i ethvert menneske. Selv de største skeptikere skal ifølge brevet med egne øyne få se representanter for menneskerasen ta av.

Begivenheten er unik. Maharishi har varslet at det blir med dette ene vellykkede forsøket, som er å betrakte som en direkte oppfølging av den oppsiktsvekkende demonstrasjonen i Washington DC 9. juli i år, der 100 journalister og 14 TV-selskaper ifølge MIKI, overvar en masseflyvning under mottoet «First North American Yogic Competition». Her ble både største høyde og lengde målt for hvert svev. Om rekordene kan bli slått på Bygdøy, gjenstår å se.

Arrangørene håper begivenheten på Bygdøy ikke blir møtt med hån og latter på forhånd. Til det er arrangementet for seriøst. En av ildsjelene på lokalt plan er Erling Brekke, som selv ikke akter å fly på Bygdøy, men som ikke tviler et sekund på at forestillingen blir en begivenhet.

— Flyvningen er ikke målet i seg selv, sier Brekke. Når det er mulig for et menneske å lette fra bakken uten annen hjelp enn sin indre styrke, ja så er det et resultat av fullstendig samordning mellom kropp og sinn, noe som er bekreftet gjennom empirisk forskning. Det som skjer når kroppen letter fra bakken er at personen skaper koherens på et så dypt og fint plan at det ikke bare påvirker kroppen, men også omgivelsene.

Et meget godt eksempel på det har man fra et eksperiment i østen for en tid tilbake, der Brekke var en av 7000 mediterende, som gjennom Sidhi-teknikken samlet utløste så meget positivt overskudd at det resulterte i global stimulans.

WORLD PEACE • GLOBAL INAUGURATION

PRESS REPORTS FROM EUROPE

Poland • *Express Wieczorny*

Warsaw   28 July 1986   (Polish)

Konkurencja sportwa?

W Waszyngtonie odbyły się niecodzienne zawody w lewitowaniu. Eddie Gob uniósł swe ciało najwyżej.... Fot. CAF—AP

Poland • *Poland television*

Warsaw   August 1986   (Polish)

(English translation)

Interviewer: Welcome to our studio. Well, you have shown us that *you* can fly. Can you teach *us* to do it?

Dr. Stuckler: Certainly...

Interviewer: How long would it take?

Dr. Stuckler: It is very simple. Transcendental Meditation is learned in a 7-step course and afterwards, after some practice, you can learn the advanced stage—the TM-Sidhi programme—which includes 'yogic flying'.

Interviewer: What are you flying for?

Dr. Stuckler: I am flying for world peace. And how is this possible? World peace is a holistic, global phenomenon. To achieve it, we need the knowledge of natural law not only from the chemical, electronic and nuclear levels, but also on the level of the unified field of natural law—from where coherence can be developed in world consciousness. During Transcendental Meditation you settle down, your consciousness becomes very quiet, and you experience the unified field. With the experience of the unified field, which is a field of all possibilities and a field of infinite correlation, any impulse of thought, for example, 'I want to fly', immediately becomes a reality.

Interviewer: May I ask your profession?

Dr. Stuckler: I am a medical doctor.

Interviewer: You are a very practical man?

Dr. Stuckler: Yes, and this is a very practical programme.

Interviewer: Does a practical man fly occasionally?

Dr. Stuckler: No, we practice this flying twice a day for 20 minutes morning and evening.

Interviewer: May I ask when you are going to demonstrate your programme again?

Dr. Stuckler: We will demonstrate the programme tonight at 8 o'clock at the Intercontinental Hotel Vridorig.

Interviewer: Thank you very much.

WORLD PEACE • GLOBAL INAUGURATION

PRESS REPORTS FROM EUROPE

Spain • *El Diario Vasco*
San Sebastian 11 July 1986 (Spanish)

Yoga y levitación. Eddie Gob aparece en la fotografía haciendo una demostración práctica de levitación en el yoga, una de las técnicas más difíciles en la cada vez más popular técnica oriental del yoga. La demostración se llevó a cabo, ante miles de practicantes, en el Centro de Convenciones de Washington. Eddie Gob es discípulo, evidentemente aventajado, del Maharishi Mahesh Yogi, fundador de una de las escuelas de yoga más prestigiosas del mundo. (Foto Upi)

Sweden • *Skånska Dagbladet*

Malmö 16 August 1986 (Swedish)

Maharishi erbjuder fred genom frigörande av krafter

"Kom – låt oss flyga tillsammans och samtidigt skapa en bättre värld".

Så skulle man lite tillspetsat kunna beskriva gurun Maharishis senaste planer för världsfred i "upplysningens tidsålder".

I går lät nämligen Maharishi och hans lärjungar världen över presentera det totala programmet för global fred. Och inför massmedia i 108 länder visade speciellt utvalda lärjungar hur man med tankekraft utövar "yoga-flygning" och samtidigt skapar "harmoni i världsmedvetandet"

Denna historiska dag proklamerades även i Malmö.

I ett rum med golvet täckt av madrasser satt lärjungarna och samlade sina krafter. Snart skulle de inför den församlade pressen visa hur "Maharishi-teknologin för det Enhetliga fältet" bland annat kan få de initierade att flyga.

Och si. När samlingen var över och klockan pinglade, började männen studsa likt grodor över madrasserna – madrasser utlagda för att inte nedslaget skulle kännas alltför mycket i rumporna!

Ingen bluff

Men flög de verkligen...? Erik Säfsten var en av "yoga-flygarna" och transcendental meditatör sedan 1969.

– Detta är bara första stadiet i yoga-flygningen, menade han, men påpekade med stor bestämdhet att det faktiskt var medelst sinne- och tankekraft kroppen farit runt i rummet! Och absolut inte någon väl inövad bluff.

– De som verkligen behärskar tekniken kan sväva fritt i luften, hävdar han. Men i Malmö har vi ännu ingen som kommit så långt!

Nog pratat

Men vad handlar det hela om? Vad är syftet med denna för oinvigda spektakulära uppvisning?

Jo, att efter 3.000 år och 8.000 fredsföredrag äntligen uppnå världsfred. Och detta genom individens eget ansvar och frigörande av de universella krafterna. Kurth Larsson är TM-lärare och en av dem som nu vill förmedla denna praktiska lösning på ett urgammalt problem.

– Människan har i alla tider strävat efter fred, men ännu har ingen praktisk metod funnits till hands, menar han. Men nu finns en sådan och nu kan vi också skapa fred i världen över en natt!

Nu lär inte "flygningen" vara det primära målet, utan principerna bakom dessa frilagda krafter. Och här fick de församlade ta del av en föreläsning om "det enhetliga fältet", koherens (lär betyda ordning och harmoni) i världsmedvetandet och något som har med Einstein och kvantfysiken att göra.

WORLD PEACE • GLOBAL INAUGURATION

Yoga–flygning är bara det yttre, synbara tecknet på de inre krafter som frigörs med hjälp av "Maharishis teknologi för det Enhetliga fältet". Krafter som över natten skulle kunna ge världen den så hett efterlängtade världsfreden.

Foto: JAN CARLSSON

Tiden mogen

Att det nu är dags för denna globala invigning av Maharishis program för skapande av världsfred, lär bero på att tiden är mogen. Kunskapen och tekniken finns, och världen har aldrig varit i ett sämre utgångsläge inför framtiden.

– Vi kan inte längre skylla på något utanför oss själva, utan nu krävs ett personligt engagemang från var individ, säger Kurth Larsson. Man måste ha fred med sig själv för att kunna leva i och sprida fred.

Vilket ju är helt sant....

Ett fåtal räcker

Men det fina i kråksången när det gäller Maharishis plan för världfreden, är att endast ett fåtal egentligen behöver engagera sig! Deras goda kraft och vilja räcker åt oss andra, som inte orkar eller kan. Och här pratas det om kvadratrötter och procent.

– Det räcker med att 7.000 människor samlas på samma plats och tillsammans utövar Maharishi-teknologin för det Enhetliga fältet. Hävdar Lennart Eriksson, en annan av de närvarande TM-lärarna...

Men problemet är, enligt Lennart Eriksson, att det kostar pengar. Och detta lilla problem har alltså hittills legat i vägen för rådande harmoni i världen. För kompetens finns hos TM-anhängarna, menar Lennart.

– Vi skulle vilja samla dessa 7.000 i Indien, men utan pengar går det inte!

Men var pengarna ska komma ifrån, framgick inte riktigt.

MIKAEL ERICSSON

PRESS REPORTS FROM EUROPE

Sweden • *Trelleborgs Allehanda*

Malmö 16 August 1986 (Swedish)

Annorlunda program för världsfred

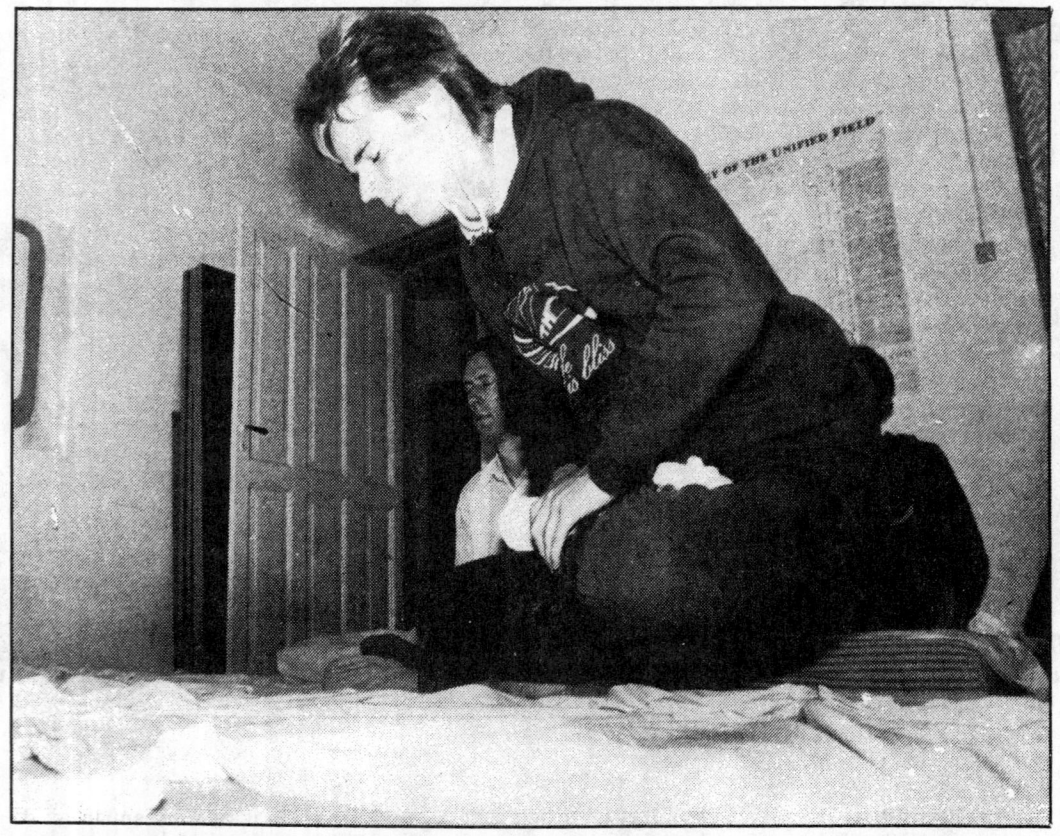

Erik Säfsten var en av sex yoga-flygare, som igår visade vad tankekraft kan åstadkomma.

Foto: JAN CARLSSON

I går presenterades världen över Maharishis program för skapande av världsfred. Så även i Malmö, där den väl representerade pressen fick bevittna ett inslag av "Maharishi-teknologin för det Enhetliga fältet" – nämligen yoga-flygning.

Ett antal TM-anhängare for på en given signal runt i ett rum, belagt med madrasser för rumpornas skull. Detta förflyttningssätt vill de initierade likna vid flygning, skapad av inre krafter avhängiga de universiella.

– Om vi bara får tillräckliga ekonomiska resurser, skulle vi kunna skapa fred över en natt, lovade en av de närvarande TM-lärarna.

Och detta enbart med hjälp av en grupp på 7.000 människor, samlade på ett ställe och med kraft nog att förändra världen till det bättre.

– SIDAN 17 –

WORLD PEACE • GLOBAL INAUGURATION

PRESS REPORTS FROM EUROPE

Sweden • *Swedish Daily News*

Stockholm 16 August 1986 (Swedish)

Hopp för fred på jorden

Foto: GUNNAR LUNDMARK

PRESS REPORTS FROM EUROPE

Switzerland • *Bote der Urschweiz*
Schwyz 18 August 1986 (German)

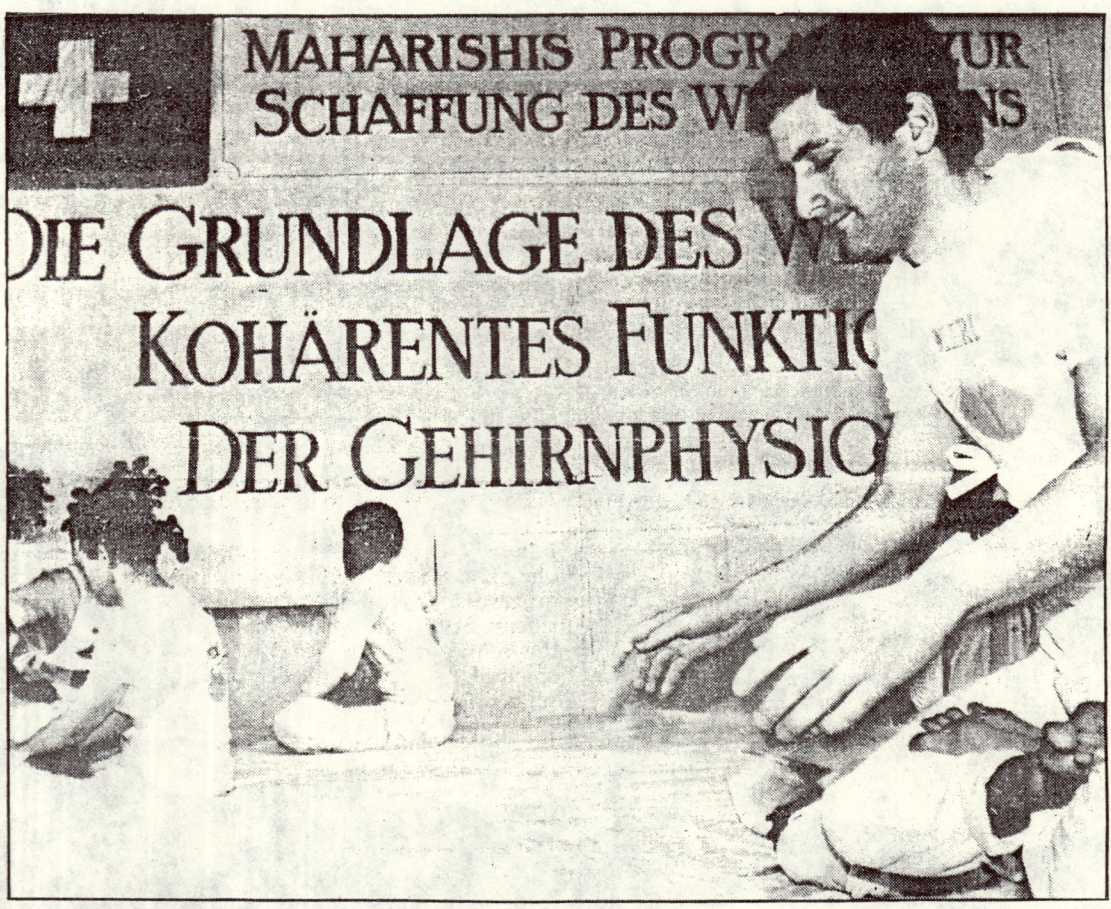

Seelisberg: Fliegen für Frieden

In einem ehemaligen Hotel in Seelisberg befindet sich das Zentrum der Transzendentalen Meditation (TM) seiner Heiligkeit, Maharishi Mahesh Yogi. Seine Anhänger meditieren für den Weltfrieden. Sozusagen als Abfallprodukt des Zusammenwirkens all dieser gleichzeitig aktivierten Hirnströme sei es möglich, in einen Schwebezustand zu gelangen. Mit diesem «Yogischen Fliegen» hat es am Freitag allerdings nicht ganz geklappt. Die Schüler brachten es nur zur ersten der drei Stufen, einer Art «Yogischem Hopsen». So muss wohl auch der Weltfrieden noch ein Weilchen auf sich warten lassen.   Keystone

WORLD PEACE • GLOBAL INAUGURATION

PRESS REPORTS FROM EUROPE

Switzerland • *Tribune de Genève*

Geneva   23 July 1986   (French)

Compétition mondiale : on lévite pour la paix

New Delhi : AP

Une centaine d'hommes et de femmes, venant d'une vingtaine de pays, se sont employés à sauter lundi dans une première compétition mondiale de lévitation, destinée à rétablir l'harmonie sur terre.

Les épreuves se sont déroulées sur une couche de matelas, au Stade Indira Gandhi, fleuri et empli du chant de mantras.

Un des plus célèbres hommes saints de l'Inde a présidé à ce que les organisateurs ont appelé le premier stage de la lévitation, dans le but de promouvoir la paix et l'harmonie dans le monde. L'Inde a été choisie comme lieu de la compétition, car c'est le pays des anciens rites védiques, qui enseignent la réalisation de l'harmonie avec l'univers.

Des médailles d'or, d'argent et de bronze ont été décernées dans quatre épreuves : 25 mètres haies, 50 mètres; saut en longueur et saut en hauteur.

Le Martiniquais Matt Bourtin et l'Américaine Susan Waterson ont enlevé les médailles d'or du 25 mètres haies, avec, respectivement, des temps de 14 secondes 81 et de 23 secondes 65. Le Guadeloupéen Eddy Gibb a gagné le saut en hauteur avec 1 m 63, le Canadien Blaine Watson a triomphé dans le saut en hauteur, avec 60 cm, et Bourtin a gagné le 50 mètres.

Ce n'est pas un miracle

« Nous ne faisons rien de miraculeux, a déclaré Watson, 31 ans, moniteur de méditation transcendantale. Voler est un sentiment parfait, mais on peut réussir au bout de six mois. »

« C'est le mécanisme de la paix mondiale, a-t-il ajouté. Seule une nouvelle semence et une nouvelle approche donneront une nouvelle récolte d'harmonie et de fraternité. »

Les concurrents sont des pratiquants de la méditation transcendantale, qui enseigne que « voler » est possible lorsque le corps s'élève et commence à sauter, au point culminant de l'harmonie des ondes cérébrales. Il faut sauter avant de pouvoir voler. La deuxième étape, disent-ils, est la lévitation, la troisième le vol véritable.

Lorsque d'importants groupes de personnes méditent ensemble, leurs ondes cérébrales se synchronisent, ajoutent les organisateurs : elles puisent à une source d'énergie universelle et sont en mesure d'exercer une force puissante pour combattre la discorde, le terrorisme international et même la rivalité entre les superpuissances.

« C'est magique »

« Durant des milliers d'années, l'homme a essayé de réaliser la paix par des traités, un désarmement, des organisations internationales, la course aux armements. Toutes les méthodes ont échoué et, aujourd'hui, le besoin est pressant », a déclaré le professeur Bevan Morris, président de l'Université internationale de Maharishi, à Fairfield (Iowa).

« C'est véritablement magique, a déclaré Doug Henning, un magicien de Los Angeles, qui a pris part à la compétition. Pendant des années, j'ai pratiqué la lévitation par le truchement de l'illusion. Mais c'est la plus grande chose que le monde ait jamais vue en matière de magie. »

« Voler, c'est comme être emporté par un ascenseur, a déclaré Yossef Yaakov, un étudiant israélien en informatique aux Etats-Unis. C'est un sentiment de perfection. L'esprit dit au corps : envole-toi, et le corps s'envole. »

PRESS REPORTS FROM EUROPE

Switzerland • FAN Feuille d'Avis de Neuchâtel-L'Express

Neuchâtel 16 August 1986 (French)

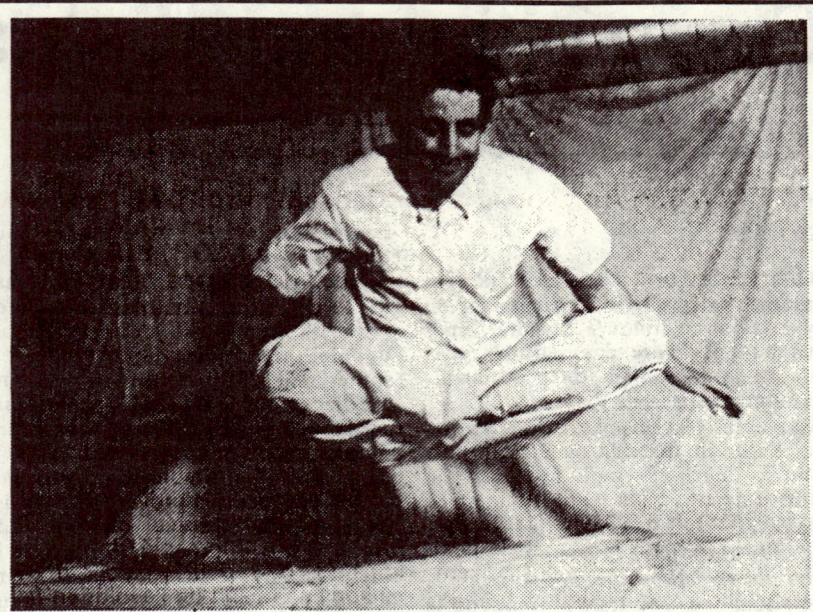

Un yogi au décollage. (Keystone)

Yogis volants

DELHI (AP) – Cela va voler haut, c'est promis. Des milliers d'adeptes de la méditation devaient se prêter hier dans 108 pays à une lévitation simultanée, afin de contribuer à la paix mondiale et à lutter contre le terrorisme.

Ces «yogis volants» appliquent la méthode enseignée par Maharishi Mahesh de Méditation transcendantale, selon laquelle la paix peut être obtenue dans le monde en ordonnant une activité au cerveau humain grâce à une profonde méditation.

Ses adeptes affirment que 7000 yogis - soit 1% de la racine carrée de la population mondiale - se livrant ensemble à la méditation, en un même lieu, peuvent obtenir des effets significatifs sur l'environnement, la réduction des maladies, la criminalité et d'autres problèmes.

Le Maharishi avait lancé son programme pour la paix mondiale à Delhi, en juillet, avec une manifestation de yogis volants, durant laquelle les participants avaient quitté le sol, apparemment en sautillant. Le Maharishi affirme que si la méditation permet de sautiller, elle peut déboucher sur le vol et ses adeptes pensent pouvoir un jour voler vraiment dans une direction donnée.

WORLD PEACE • GLOBAL INAUGURATION

PRESS REPORTS FROM EUROPE

Switzerland • *24 Heures*

Lausanne 16 August 1986 (French)

Démonstration à Seelisberg
Les yogis savent léviter

Les yogis de Seelisberg (UR) ont enfin montré en public qu'ils savent léviter ! Devant de nombreux représentants de la presse, ils ont fait une démonstration de leur art. A leurs yeux, la lévitation est une technique permettant de créer la cohérence mentale nécessaire pour combattre le terrorisme et la guerre.

SEELISBERG
Lin KRIEGER

C'est dans leur superbe siège central, la Maharishi European Research University, qui surplombe le lac des Quatre-Cantons, que les adeptes du programme de méditation transcendantale, mis sur pied par leur gourou Maharishi Mahesh Yogi, ont dévoilé leurs secrets. Cette démonstration de lévitation était coordonnée avec des manifestations semblables se déroulant le même jour dans 108 différents pays du monde.

Sous les caméras

Dans une salle comble, où caméras de télévision et flashes ont créé l'atmosphère des grands jours, huit yogis, tous vêtus de blanc, ont fait leur entrée dans un silence total. Ils se sont assis sur une grande surface matelassée — toute blanche elle aussi — pour commencer leur démonstration par dix minutes de méditation. Au son d'une clochette, les hommes assis les jambes croisées, ont tout d'un coup

Un premier stade. Keystone

commencé à sauter, en s'élevant d'une trentaine de centimètres, tout en gardant « la position du lotus ».

Leurs sauts, ou lévitations, ont bien duré huit minutes, et les huit hommes ont à plusieurs reprises traversé l'espace à disposition. Si leur effort musculaire s'est bien traduit par quelques gouttes de sueur, ils n'en ont pas moins gardé un sourire radieux... A la fin de leur démonstration, ils ont chacun été récompensés par une rose blanche.

Six mois d'entraînement

Selon la théorie des yogis, ces sauts sont possibles quand l'harmonie des ondes cérébrales, obtenues par la méditation transcendantale, atteint un point culminant. Les sauts, qui demandent au moins six mois d'entraînement, ne seraient pourtant qu'un premier stade de la lévitation yogique décrite dans les textes védiques. Le deuxième stade consisterait à planer, le troisième à voler à travers les airs.

Synchronisation cérébrale

Les pratiquants de la méditation transcendantale estiment que lorsque d'importants groupes de personnes méditent, elles synchronisent leurs ondes cérébrales et arrivent ainsi à créer une force puissante capable de combattre le terrorisme et la rivalité entre les superpuissances.

L. K.

PRESS REPORTS FROM EUROPE

Switzerland • *Il Dovere*
Bellinzona   August 1986   (Italian)

E i seguaci del santone levitarono...

E' accaduto a Brunate in una seduta a cui hanno assistito alcuni increduli cronisti

Como - Quello di levitare, alzarsi in aria con balzi, è un esercizio che, soprattutto d'estate, vede cimentarsi centinaia e centinaia di persone. Levitare è riuscito nel giorno di Ferragosto, a Brunate, sopra Como, a tredici seguaci di Maharishi Mahesh Yogi, filosofo indiano, fondatore del progetto «Meditazione Trascendentale», dell'«Intelligenza Creativa del Governo Mondiale dell'Età dell'Illuminazione».

Sono riusciti a «saltare», ad innalzare il corpo in aria con balzi incredibili di 30-40 centimetri d'altezza e un metro circa di lunghezza, a gambe incrociate ed occhi chiusi, dopo cinque minuti di meditazione, nel corso dei quali è parso di cogliere fremiti che attraversavano il corpo dei tredici meditanti, che hanno eseguito la loro prova, la prima in Italia, sotto gli occhi abbastanza increduli di alcuni cronisti e occhi entusiastici di un altro centinaio di seguaci del santone indiano. Una prova che, così è stato sostenuto, si è svolta, nello stesso giorno, in altri 108 paesi del mondo, in oltre mille città.

Quello del santone indiano è un movimento imponente .... Un' organizzazione in grado di radunare folle oceaniche. Centinaia di migliaia di adepti in tutto il mondo. Fra i più convinti in Italia, si è appreso a Brunate, attraverso un video, c'è Nils Liedholm, allenatore del Milan, il quale ha avuto occasione di dichiarare che «fare venti minuti di meditazione non è tempo perso, anzi è tempo che guadagni dopo perché il benessere che provi è utile, specialmente per me che ho una certa età; non dico che mi sento ringiovanito, ma sono più leggero, più chiaro e più lucido quando devo prendere le decisioni». Altre testimonianze sono state illustrate a Brunate da parte anche di medici e sacerdoti.

Ecco dunque il levitare collettivo, riuscito secondo gli organizzatori. Com'è possibile questo saltare, o meglio questa tecnica del «volo yoga»? Attraverso la concentrazione che porta, si sostiene, a dimenticare il corpo, ricevendo perciò impulsi che fanno levitare. Per qualcuno questo non solo è possibile, ma irradia e neutralizza le tendenze negative in tutta la creazione. Insomma, seguendo il filo di questo discorso, non più guerre, terrorismo, distruzione, ma solo pace. Ecco perciò l'importanza di meditare.

«La meditazione trascendentale — è stato sostenuto a Brunate, prima del salto collettivo, alla quale hanno partecipato non solo giovani ma anche persone di una certa età — è una tecnica per combattere lo stress, ridurre l'ansia, abbassare la pressione sanguigna, e ridurre l'abuso di fumo, droghe e psicofarmaci. Tutti motivi che, sempre più spesso causano morte e tante guerre». Per qualcuno quella iniziata il giorno di Ferragosto a Brunate e in altre mille città del mondo è un'era nuova per il genere umano. Per combattere gli strali dell'incredulità a Brunate tredici seguaci di Maharishi, a gambe incrociate e ad occhi chiusi hanno innalzato il loro corpo in aria con balzi incredibili.

WORLD PEACE • GLOBAL INAUGURATION

PRESS REPORTS FROM EUROPE

Switzerland • *Corriere del Ticino*

Lugano   18 August 1986   (Italian)

A Brunate dimostrazioni di «volo yoga»

Meditazione trascendentale per pacificare il pianeta

BRUNATE (Como) – Nel 1982, lo «yogi» Maharishi, gran teorico contemporaneo della *meditazione trascendentale*, dalla Svizzera trattò l'acquisto dell'hotel «Milano», polo della villeggiatura milanese, a cavallo del secolo, ma nel frattempo degradato, nonostante l'incantevole posizione a picco sul Lario, dai nuovi riti estivi. La trasformazione dell'albergo in Centro Maharishi, in una *capitale dell'età dell'illuminazione* è stata indolore per Brunate, anche perché i seguaci dello yogi non hanno portato eccessivo folclore – o peggio – nel paesino arroccato sopra Como. Al contrario, si sono integrati, offrendo vacanze alternative, a prezzo ragionevole, a chiunque voglia liberarsi dallo «stress», tramite il raggiungimento di quella padronanza di sé che non ha bisogno di eccessivi ancoraggi ai limiti fisici umani.

Ma la quiete con se stessi non basta al gran maestro Maharishi: nell'incalzare degli eventi politici internazionali, egli vuole costituire una pacifica «terza potenza», aggregando le forze magnetiche di settemila adepti, da riunire in un solo luogo stabilmente per *creare immediatamente una fortissima influenza di coerenza nella coscienza mondiale* determinando, quindi, la pace planetaria. Il progetto – *Utopia 7000* – ha i suoi costi, un centinaio di milioni di dollari e, per sensibilizzare la Terra della necessità della pratica della *tecnologia Maharishi* proprio il giorno di Ferragosto è stata avviata in più di un centinaio di nazioni del Globo e in oltre mille città la campagna dimostrativa dei risultati che si possono conseguire con la *meditazione trascendentale*. A Brunate, una dozzina di cultori di quello che viene chiamato *volo yoga* dopo qualche minuto di concentrazione, occhi chiusi e gambe incrociate, nella canonica posizione «fior di loto», ha cominciato a saltare, con balzi di mezzo metro, talvolta ripetuti, in apparenza senza sforzo.

Non è proprio quel che si intende per «levitazione», ma i responsabili del Centro Maharishi l'hanno indicato come primo stadio verso ben altri traguardi, dove, tuttavia, più che il fenomeno paranormale interessa la pacificazione mondiale, ottenibile, sostengono con convinzione a Brunate, per sola forza di *meditazione trascendentale*.

PRESS REPORTS FROM EUROPE

Switzerland • *Tages-Anzeiger*

Zürich   19 August 1986   (German)

Hopsen für den Weltfrieden

Abheben im Seelisberger Zentrum der Transzendentalen Meditation

VON ROLF WESPE, SEELISBERG

Unter einer goldgesäumten Schweizer Flagge sitzen acht wie Turner weissgekleidete junge Männer auf Matratzen. Sie meditieren während zehn Minuten, und es herrscht Stille im Saal des ehemaligen Hotels Sonnenberg in Seelisberg. Wir befinden uns in der «International capital of the age of Enlightenment», dem Zentrum der Transzendentalen Meditation (TM) von «Seiner Heiligkeit Maharishi Mahesh Yogi».

Maharishi weilte seit 1983 nicht mehr hier, sondern in Neu Delhi, und Seelisberg ist eigentlich nicht mehr Hauptstadt der TM-Bewegung. Früher waren pro Tag bis zu 1500 Kursteilnehmer hier. Heute sind es nach Angaben seiner Anhänger noch 150.

★

Aber zurück zu unsern Meditierenden auf den Matratzen: Sie sitzen im sogenannten Lotussitz mit geschlossenen Augen vor uns. Das ist ein Schneidersitz, bei dem die Füsse auf die Oberschenkel gelegt werden.

Die Stille erhöht die Spannung, bis der angekündigte Glockenton erklingt und das Yoga-Fliegen beginnt. Bei einzelnen ist eine Vibration und ein Zucken am Körper zu sehen, und dann hüpfen sie – in der Lotusstellung verharrend – ein wenig in die Luft und landen dann wieder, wobei sie sich beim Landen zum Teil mit Hilfe der Hände abstützen. Auf Phasen des Hüpfens folgen Momente der Ruhe. Dann geht es wieder los. Auf den Gesichtern der Hopsenden ist nach dem Landen ein Anflug von Verzückung, Lachen oder Lächeln zu beobachten.

Die Vorführung wird durch die anwesenden TM-Anhänger mit Applaus quittiert. Er fühle einen Bewegungsimpuls, Glück und Freude, erzählt Adrian Hug nachher über sein Erleben des Hopsens. «Man setzt sich auf die Matte und meditiert, und plötzlich macht man eine völlig neue Erfahrung», erinnert sich Mithopser Thomas Heumann an seine ersten Gumpversuche. Inzwischen habe er den Impuls unter Kontrolle bekommen, und daher habe man auf das Signal des Glockenklangs gemeinsam hopsen können. Heumann hat aber trotz allem noch das Gefühl, «dass ich das nicht so richtig unter Kontrolle habe».

★

Handelt es sich um einen echten oder einen faulen Zauber? Sind das Muskel- oder Geistesathleten? Für mich als Zuschauer lässt sich das beim besten Willen nicht beurteilen. Ich suche nach Schweisstropfen auf den Stirnen der Hopser und sehe keine. Hug sagt nachher, gelegentlich müsse man dabei «auch automatisch tief und schwer atmen, es sei mög-

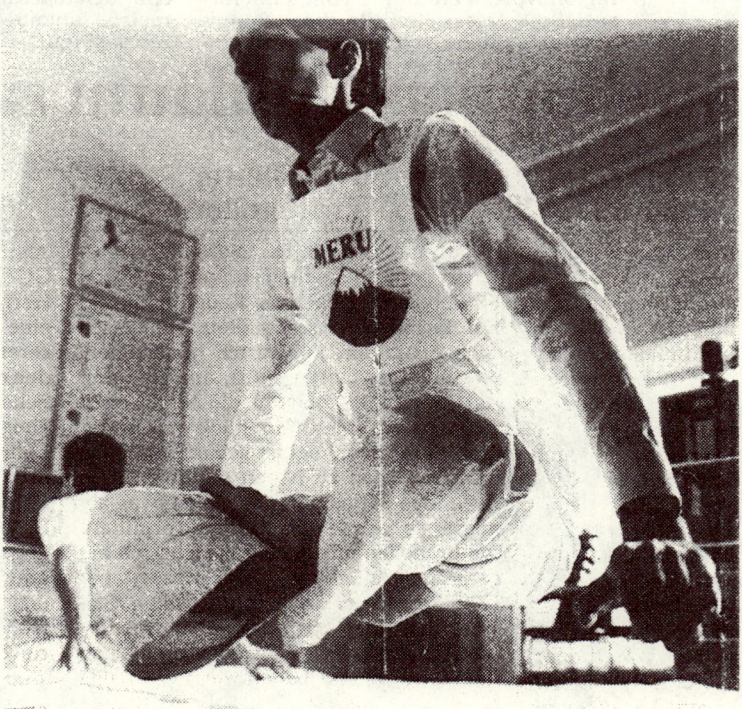

Nach der Konzentration im Lotussitz der erhebende Augenblick.
(Bild Emanuel Ammon)

lich, dass man unbewusst mit der Muskulatur nachhelfe».

★

Vielleicht stehe ein noch unbekanntes Naturgesetz hinter dem Phänomen, meint ein TM-Anhänger. Hopsen ist nur die erste von drei Stufen von Schweben und Fliegen, welche durch Meditation erreicht werden sollen. Schweben und Fliegen kämen allerdings seltener vor. Der einzige Weg der Nachprüfung für Skeptiker wäre wohl der, es selbst zu probieren. Nach sechs Monaten intensiver Ausbildung und Praxis der Transzendentalen Meditation soll man so weit sein, dass man in dieses höhere Programm der Flug-Sutra einsteigen kann.

★

Gemäss Darstellung der TM-Leute ist das Yoga-Fliegen eine Folge des geordneten Zusammenwirkens (Kohärenz) der Hirnströme. Dies werde auf der feinsten Ebene des Selbst, auf der Stufe des reinen Bewusstseins erreicht. Dann habe das Bewusstsein keinen Inhalt mehr, sondern sei nur noch für sich selber da.

Der gleiche geistige Prozess soll aber nicht nur das Hopsen auslösen, sondern auch den Weltfrieden bringen. Eine geordnete Evolution bilde auch Voraussetzung für den Weltfrieden. Diese Kohärenz könne auch erreicht werden, wenn 7000 TM-Jünger am gleichen Ort gemeinsam hopsen.

★

Maharishi sucht gegenwärtig 100 Millionen Dollar für seinen Friedensfonds, um diesen Ausstrahlungsprozess in Neu Delhi in Gang zu bringen.

Switzerland • *Le Courrier*

La Neuveville 19 August 1986 (French)

Ils sont soixante dans le canton
Genève décolle !

L'Institut Maharishi, spécialisé dans l'enseignement de la méditation transcendentale, a présenté en fin de semaine dernière à Genève – en même temps que dans une centaine de pays – son programme de «lévitation yogique pour la paix mondiale». Au cours de cette réunion, une démonstration de lévitation a été effectuée par deux Romands.

Selon le groupe, si 7000 personnes lévitent ensemble sous un même toit, les ondes qui s'en dégagent produisent un effet mesurable de part et d'autre de la planète. Une expérience a déjà été tentée entre le 17 décembre 1983 et le 6 janvier 1984 sur le campus de l'Université internationale Maharishi, dans l'Iowa (USA). Selon les responsables, l'économie, la santé, la vie sociale et l'état général du monde s'en sont trouvés nettement améliorés durant cette période. Pour se dégrader à nouveau par la suite...

C'est pourquoi l'institut nourrit un projet ambitieux : rassembler 10 000 experts en vol yoguique (lévitation) et assurer une permanence de 7000 personnes vouées à l'établissement et au maintien de la paix. Un pareil groupe est en train de se constituer en Inde près de New Delhi, où ont eu lieu récemment les premières compétitions internationales de vol yoguique (saut en hauteur et en longueur, 25 et 50 mètres haies, etc.).

Switzerland • *Teuschers Presse-Dienst*

Zurich September 1986 (German)

Neues Denken und Handeln ist gefragt

Dass die grossen Religionen oder die sozialpolitischen Weltanschauungen den Weltfrieden auch nur ein Stückchen näher gebracht hätten, zu behaupten, wäre wohl etwas voreilig. Was man mit unerhörten Geburtswehen und Kosten fertigbrachte, ist, dass ein Gleichgewicht des Schreckens erzielt wurde, auf dem für Europa—eine 'Friedenspause' von 40 Jahren eintrat. In den vergangenen 3000 Jahren wurden über 8000 'Friedensverträge' abgeschlossen und gebrochen, von denen jeder im Durchschnitt nicht länger als neun Jahre dauerte, obwohl sie langfristig angelegt, wenn nicht gar für 'ewig' besiegelt wurden. Angesichts dieser erfolglosen Bemühungen, der immer wieder demonstrierten Ohnmacht der UNO und der heutigen nuklearen Bedrohung dürfte es klar sein, dass es der Menschheit an einem grundlegenden Wissen mangelt, Weltfrieden zu schaffen und zu erhalten. Nur ein neues Wissen kann Weltfrieden schaffen, so wie nur ein neuer Samen eine neue Ernte bringen kann.

Um das Friedensheil bemühen sich die Religionen und Weltanschauungen, die ständig von Frieden reden. Im Namen Gottes wird Stärke, Macht und Waffengewalt demonstriert und die Friedensansicht des Anderen wird verneint. Maharishi sagt, dass der Weltfriede in unserer Hand liegt. Wissenschaftliche Forschungen haben gezeigt, dass 7000 Menschen, 'Welche die Maharishi-Technologie des Vereinheitlichten Feldes am Morgen und am Abend zusammen an einem Ort ausüben, einen starken Einfluss von Ordnung und Kohärenz im ganzen Weltbewusstsein erzeugen und dadurch überall lebensunterstützende Tendenzen fördern.'

Am Sitz der Maharishi European Research University in Seelisberg wurde dieser Tage das Prinzip des TM-Sidhi-Flugprogramms vorgeführt, mit dem der Weltfrieden von der grundlegenden Funktionsebene der Natur aus verwirklicht werden kann. 'Angesichts des zunehmenden Terrorismus und der gefährlichen Rivalität der Supermächte ist es äusserst wichtig, unverzüglich einen unüberwindlichen Einfluss von Kohärenz im Weltbewusstsein zu schaffen.'

Yogisches Fliegen

Nach Meinung von Maharishi kann durch 'yogisches Fliegen' Kohärenz und Geordnetheit im Weltbewusstsein erzeugt werden. Während der Ausübung der 'Yoga-Flugtechnik'' im Moment, wo in der Gehirnaktivität maximale—durch das EEG gemessene—Kohärenz eintritt, hebt der Körper vom Boden ab und beginnt zu hopsen. Die Kohärenz zwischen Bewusstsein und Materie im Körper, die während dieses ersten Stadiums des 'yogischen Fliegens' erfahren wird, entsteht auf der Ebene des vereinheitlichten Feldes aller Naturgesetze. Da das vereinheitlichte Feld die Eigenschaft unendlicher Wechselwirkung besitzt, bringt ein Kohärenz-Impuls, der auf dieser Ebene erzeugt wird, entgegengesetzte Tendenzen in der ganzen Natur sofort in Einklang. So breitet sich Kohärenz aus und neutralisiert negative Tendenzen in der ganzen Gesellschaft.

Drei Schritte für den Weltfrieden

Der erste Schritt ist dem Frieden auf internationaler Ebene gewidmet, der zweite Schritt dem Frieden auf nationaler Ebene und der dritte Schritt dem Frieden im Familienbereich.

Unfangreiche wissenschaftliche Forschungsprojekte verdeutlichten, dass die Maharishi-Methode funktioniert. Der Körper, der im Augenblick maximaler Gehirnwellenkohärenz vom Boden abhebt, ist der Zeitpunkt maximaler Körper-Geist-Koordination. Körper und Geist weisen eine Einheit auf, in der die Gedanken im Trancezustand sich miteinander vereinigen und auf diese Weise zu einem Kraftfeld grossen Ausmasses werden, die 'etwas' zu bewegen vermögen. Das Hopsen oder Fliegen ist hier sichtbarer Ausdruck, dass man sich in der geistigen Kohärenz befindet.

An der Vorführung der Methode in Seelisberg wurde von den Mitmachenden bestätigt, dass das 'Fliegen' ein unaussprechliches Erlebnis sei und mit physischer Kraft nichts zu tun habe.

Würdigung aller Friedensbemühungen

'Es gibt Hunderte von Friedensorganisationen auf der ganzen Welt. Der Friede wird auf verschiedenen Ebenen angestrebt. Wir würdigen jede Bemühung für den Weltfrieden' sagte Maharishi. 'Unser Ansatz zur Schaffung des Weltfriedens ist ganzheitlich und grundlegend. Es kommt von jener grundlegenden Funktionsebene der Natur, wo ewige Stille die lebendige Grundlage der unaufhörlichen Dynamik des Universums ist. Dies ist mit sich selbst in Wechselwirkung stehende Dynamik des vereinheitlichten Feldes des Naturgesetzes, wo der Friede die Dynamik aufrecht erhält. Deshalb gewährleistet der Weltfriede, der von dieser Ebene des vereinheitlichten Feldes des Naturgesetzes her geschaffen wird, immerwährenden Fortschritt fur die ganze Menschheit.'

Switzerland • *Züri Woche*

Glattbrugg 5 September 1986 (German)

Friedenssicherung mit Transzendentaler Meditation?

In der «Züri Woche» vom 14. August nahm Sigmund Widmer als Historiker das Phänomen der Armeefreundlichkeit unter die Lupe. Die These von der Friedenssicherung durch die Armee akzeptiert einer unserer Leser nicht:

«Sigmund Widmer befasst sich im Artikel ‹Volk und Armee› mit der Frage, warum die Schweizer Armee in den letzten Jahren in der Bevölkerung an Ansehen verloren hat.

Die Gründe liegen wohl noch anderswo, als es vom Autor dargestellt wird. Das Bedürfnis nach Frieden und Freiheit war wohl selten so stark und weitverbreitet wie heute. Im weiteren leben wir glücklicherweise in einer sehr aufs Praktische ausgerichteten Zeit. Nicht nur die jüngere Generation hinterfragt Dogmen mehr und mehr auf ihre praktischen Auswirkungen. So fragt man sich auch, wie Frieden und Freiheit realisiert und aufrechterhalten werden können. Jahrtausendealte Erfahrung der Geschichte und vor allem die heutige Situation militärischer Bedrohung zeigen folgendes Bild: Militärische Rüstung bringt die Möglichkeit (insbesondere mit den heutigen Massenvernichtungsmitteln), nicht nur einen Gegner, sondern die Erde als Gesamtheit mehrere Male zu zerstören. Gleichzeitig aber ist kein Land – ob Supermacht oder klein wie die Schweiz – fähig, sich selber zu verteidigen. Ferner zeigt der Terrorismus, welchem Staaten sowohl mit minimaler als auch mit maximaler militärischer Rüstung etwa gleich ohnmächtig gegenüberstehen, dass der Friede auch im Inneren eines Landes nicht mit militärischen Mitteln erhalten werden kann. Diese Einsichten und die praktischen Folgerungen daraus sind wohl der Hauptgrund, warum die Armee auch in der Schweiz je länger je mehr als inadäquates Mittel zur Sicherung von Friede und Freiheit entlarvt wird.

Die pragmatische Zeit, in der wir leben, bringt aber nicht nur die Ernüchterung, was den militärischen Einfluss auf Frieden und Freiheit angeht, sondern gleichzeitig tiefgreifende wissenschaftliche Erkenntnisse, wie diese beiden Grundbedürfnisse eines jeden Individuums und einer jeden Nation befriedigt werden können. Friede und Entspannung oder Spannungen und Krieg hängen von der Qualität des kollektiven Bewusstseins einer Nation oder sogar der ganzen Welt ab. Durch die Ausübung der Technik der Transzendentalen Meditation und der TM-Sidhis wächst das Bewusstsein nicht nur des Individuums, welches diese Technik praktiziert, sondern zugleich wird das kollektive Bewusstsein der Umgebung beeinflusst. Wissenschaftliche Untersuchungen zeigen, dass eine Gruppe von 7000 Experten dieser Bewusstseinstechnik, die das TM- und TM-Sidhi-Programm – vor allem die Technik des Fliegens – gemeinsam an einem Platz ausüben, das gesamte Weltbewusstsein an Harmonie und Kohärenz bereichert, was die Grundlage für dauerhaften Frieden bildet.

Es ist nun nach tausenden missglückter Versuche zur Realisierung und Erhaltung des Friedens auf der Welt an der Zeit, diese neuen Erkenntnisse in die Tat umzusetzen und damit allen Kriegsschrecken und der Bedrohung durch Terrorismus ein Ende zu setzen.»

Jürg Wenger, 8041 Zürich

WORLD PEACE • GLOBAL INAUGURATION

PRESS REPORTS FROM EUROPE

Switzerland • *St. Galler Tagblatt*

St. Gallen 6 September 1986 (German)

Demonstration des Meditationszentrums Vorarlberg in Bregenz

Im Stadium des «yogischen Fliegens»

GÜNTHER STEIERT

Im Bregenzer Festspielhaus konnten am Donnerstag einige Besucher eine Demonstration des «yogischen Fliegens» bestaunen. Zu der Demonstration lud das Meditationscenter für Vorarlberg. Der Übertitel der Veranstaltung lautete: «Wie das yogische Fliegen Kohärenz im Weltbewusstsein erzeugt». Die Veranstalter sind der Überzeugung, dass durch bestimmte – im menschlichen Körper entstehende Strahlen – die Umwelt positiv beeinflusst wird.

Während der Technik des «yogischen Fliegens» hebt der Körper zum Zeitpunkt maximaler Kohärenz (Zusammenhang) der Gehirnwellenaktivität vom Boden ab und fängt an zu hüpfen. Die Grundvoraussetzung dafür ist, Yoga sehr gut zu beherrschen. Der Geist muss den Körper dirigieren können.

Seit einigen Jahren, so der Vortragende, Ludwig Krenner, wird das «yogische Fliegen» von ernstzunehmenden Wissenschaftlern – die meisten davon in Amerika – untersucht. Beim «yogischen Fliegen» in der Gruppe, wie grösser die Gruppe, desto besser, so Ludwig Krenner, entstehen Schwingungen oder Strahlungen, welche das Umfeld positiv beeinflussen. So breite sich Kohärenz aus und neutralisiere negative Tendenzen in der gesamten Schöpfung. Diese Auswirkungen wären schon seit Jahren bekannt.

Grundsätzlich für jedermann möglich

Im Prinzip könnte jeder, der Yoga sehr gut beherrscht, das Stadium des yogischen Fliegens erlangen. Die drei, die das Fliegen im Lotussitz vorführten, erzählten im Anschluss, dass es im Moment, wenn sie sich vom Boden lösen würden, ein Gefühl höchsten Glückes sei. Ein neuer – alter Weg, den Traum des Menschen vom Fliegen Wirklichkeit werden zu lassen? Um den Weltfrieden herzustellen, bedarf es aber nicht des freien Fluges – das Anfangsstadium würde schon genügen. Wenn nur ein Prozent einer Bevölkerung nach Maharishi-Art meditiere, dann entstehe ein unüberwindlicher Schutzschild, der eine Nation unbesiegbar mache. Genauso wie ein gesunder Körper Viren zerstören kann, so könne eine Nation, die kulturell integriert ist, schädlichen äusseren Einflüssen widerstehen.

Weiter heisst es in der Broschüre: «Das Entstehen von Kohärenz im kollektiven Bewusstsein funktioniere ähnlich wie der Quanten-Tunneleffekt des Nobelpreisträgers und Ehrenprofessors für Physik D. Josepfon. Dieser habe auch an Konferenzen der europäischen Maharishi-Universität über Physik und Bewusstsein teilgenommen – mehr würde nicht verraten.

***

Der Leiter des Meditationszentrums Vorarlberg, Ludwig Krenner.

Das dauernde Schweben gelingt in dieser Stufe nicht, es sind nur kurze Sprünge bis rund 30 cm über die Matte, deren Antriebskraft allerdings kaum Muskeln sein können.

Bilder: G. Steiert

PRESS REPORTS FROM EUROPE

Switzerland • *Journal du Jura*

Bienne 15 September 1986 (French)

Lévitation yoga

Des Romands, pratiquant la technique de méditation transcendantale ainsi que le programme avancé MT-sidhi, ont fait la démonstration de la première étape de la lévitation «yoguique».

Comment l'espoir de guérir notre monde malade du stress et de la guerre peut-il exister à l'heure d'aujourd'hui?

«Les techniques sidhi, dont la lévitation est l'aspect le plus spectaculaire, figurent au cœur du nouveau programme de Maharishi pour créer la paix mondiale, poursuit M. Jean Matter, responsable de l'information du bureau suisse du Parlement pour la paix, l'instance organisatrice de cette démonstration.

«Ces techniques MT-sidhi sont de formidables outils d'évolution qui augmentent en puissance avec le nombre d'individus les pratiquant. L'essentiel est de former un grand groupe et d'exercer une influence à l'échelle mondiale».

Une expérience isolée a déjà montré que 7000 personnes lévitant ensemble sous un même toit produisent un effet mesurable de part et d'autre de la planète. Toute tentative pour établir la paix est à saluer. En voici une ambitieuse: rassembler 10 000 experts en vol «yoguique» et assurer une permanence de 7000 personnes vouées à l'établissement et au maintien de la paix.

Réalisation

Un pareil groupe est en train de se constituer en Inde près de New-Dehli,

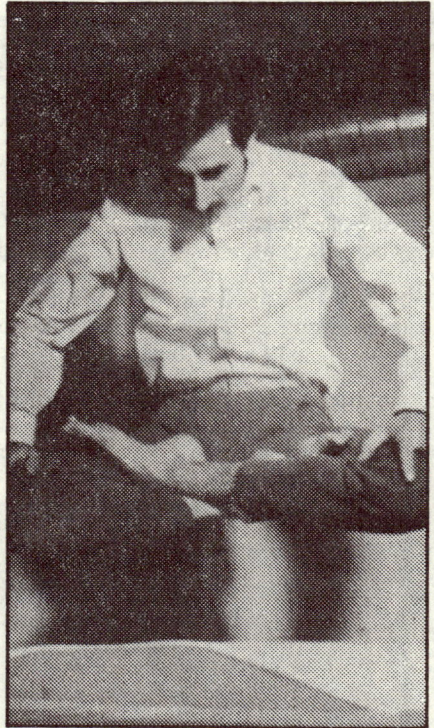

Un expert en lévitation «yoguique» démontre comment les programmes de méditation transcendantale et de MT-sidhi permettent d'éliminer le terrorisme et d'établir la paix mondiale. (f)

où ont eu lieu récemment les premières compétitions internationales de vol «yoguique».

Qui financera l'existence de ce groupe? Tous ceux qui souscrivent à ce projet, banques, industries, individus, sociétés etc. sont invités à participer à un fonds de soutien.

Performances

Selon Mme Yvette Jardin, responsable de l'enseignement de la MT à Genève, «les adeptes du vol «yoguique» ne démontrent actuellement que la première étape de la lévitation: des bonds de 50 cm à 1 m 60 de longueur, en position assise (position du lotus).

Ces bonds sont produits par une impulsion émise dans la tranquillité intérieure: l'esprit apaisé dit au corps pleinement détendu «envole-toi» et le corps s'envole.

Ces bonds donneront lieu plus tard à des expériences de suspension du corps dans l'espace, la lévitation proprement dite, puis finalement à une maîtrise complète du vol dirigé. Gageons que cette deuxième et troisième étapes seront pour bientôt! Elles témoigneront d'une nouvelle qualité de vie sur terre où l'homme vivra libre de toute souffrance, problèmes et échecs, en paix complète avec lui-même et son environnement». (jm)

WORLD PEACE • GLOBAL INAUGURATION

PRESS REPORTS FROM EUROPE

Yugoslavia • *Politika*

Belgrade   16 August 1986   (Serbo-Croatian)

СИНОЋ У „САВА"-ЦЕНТРУ
**Покушај необичне демонстрације
— извођења „Јоги-летења"**

Синоћ је у „Сава"-центру у организацији „ТВ новости" и „Новости 8" одржан разговор на тему „Моћи психичке енергије". Повод за разговор је био покушај једне необичне демонстрације — извођења „Јоги-летења", а о његовој атрактивности сведочила је и препуна сала „Сава"-центра.

После првог дела програма, у којем су о историји и достигнућима трансцеденталне медитације говорили Бранко Чичић, учитељ програма трансцеденталне медитације из Београда и Лазар Вош, магистар политичких наука из Загреба, наступило је „оно главно". Седморица младића су приказала нешто што не личи на летење, а што су присутни назвали „скакутањем" Међутим, објашњење стручњака из ове области је да је реч о првој фази „Јоги-летења" и да је то — то.

Приказан је и филм на исту тему и са сличним демонстрирањем, снимљен пре месец дана у Америци, а своје мишљење о моћима психичке енергије дали су и неуропсихијатри Никола Видев и Петар Станцедић.

Оцене о оном што се видело, своја искуства и размишљања, изнели су и појединци из публике...

С. Митраковић

Yugoslavia • *Novosti*

Belgrade   17 August 1986   (Serbo-Croatian)

»Јоги летење«

ДВОРАНА „Сава" центра у Београду била је прексиноћ препуна знатижељника који су дошли да виде необичну демонстрацију „јоги летења". Али, уместо „левитирања" посетиоци су могли да виде само скакутање седморице јогина. То је названо „првом фазом јоги летења".

Скуп у Сава центру, иначе, првенствено је био прилика за разговор на тему „Моћи психичке енергије". О историјату и достигнућима трансцеденталне медитације говорили су **Бранко Чичић**, учитељ трансцеденталне медитације из Београда и **Лазар Вош**, магистар политичких наука из Загреба.

Приказан је и филм на тему „јоги летења" снимљен недавно у Америци, а у занимљивој расправи у којој су учествовали и гледаоци, своје мишљење о моћима психичке енергије изнели су и неуропсихијатри **Никола Видев и Петар Станковић**.

PRESS REPORTS FROM EUROPE

Yugoslavia • *TV Novosti*
Belgrade   22 August 1986   (Serbo-Croatian)

ПРВА ДЕМОНСТРАЦИЈА ЛЕВИТАЦИЈЕ У БЕОГРАДУ

ЧУДО СЕ ДОГОДИЛО!

У организацији нашег листа, у Центру „Сава" су седморица младића покушала да изведу „јоги-летење" снагом властите психичке енергије ★ „Видео сам једног вежбача како се уздиже са тла без икаквог напора, у појединим тренуцима 50, чак и 70 сантиметара изнад душека" — сведочи један очевидац

Београд не памти, то добро знају они који посећују његове трибине, да је на једно предавање дошло више хиљада људи. Прошлог петка се то догодило у препуној дворани Сава-центра. Око 2.000 Београђана присуствовало је разговору о моћима психичке енергије који је, заједно са колегама из редакције „Новости 8", организовала наша редакција.

Према изјави **Зорана Јакшића**, радника Контроле безбедности Центра „Сава", више од **500 грађана** је морало да се врати кућама, јер за њих није било места у сали.

Огромну знатижељу изазвала је пре свега најављена атракција вечери — покушај демонстрације такозваног јоги-летења, прве фазе левитације, то јест лебдења људи на валстити погон.

УСПЕЛО ЈЕ!

Левитација подразумева да човек искључиво снагом своје психичке енергије савладава силу гравитације, издиже се изнад земље у јоги-положају (прекрштених ногу са стопалама на горњим деловима бутина) и лебди у ваздуху извесно време, коју секунду.

Пред почетак демонстрације, готово невероватно, на молбу организатора у сали је седам минута владала апсолутна тишина, чуло се само зујање еркондишна и шкљоцање фото-апарата. За то време седам младића из разних крајева земље, које су обукле Робне куће „Београд", на душецима „Прве искре" из Барича, склопљених очију, покушало је да се макар накратко „искључи" из овог света, сконцентрише у медитацији, „олакша" своје тело, тако да се искључиво под дејством психичке енергије – одвоји од земље.

Кретања многих демонстраната подсећала су на жабљи скок, Те покрете „скакутања" су можда и могли да изведу врхунски мајстори партерне гимнастике и јоги-веш- тина, како су тврдили неки присутни.

„Чудо" се ипак догодило. Тројица њих, што су упућени с разлогом прижељкивали, без икаквих кретњи тела, кукова и бутина, праве кичме у јоги-положају, у једном тренутку „праснула" су као кокица на ватри. Уздизали су се, спуштали на под, без икаквог напора, мирног лица као у трансу, у пуној концентрацији. Питање је само да ли су сви присутни, у препуној дворани, успели то и да запазе, јер је експеримент трајао десетак минута, а привремена сцена је, због непокретне говорнице, морала да буде разбијена на два дела. Зато је поглед присутних лутао час лево, час десно, од једног до другог вежбача....

Иако су за људе Истока то сасвим обичне ствари и нису никаква чуда, јавност је код нас још подељена око тога могу ли се искључиво психичком енергијом савијати гвоздене виљушке, померати предмети /телекинеза/ преносити мисли на даљину /телепатија/, лечити људи биоенергијом, (додиром, без лекова и скалпера), левитирати у ваздуху....

ИСТОРИЈСКИ ЗНАЧАЈ

Да су којим случајем ови младићи заиста успели да лебде изнад наших глава, сасвим је сигурно да те вечери не би били са нама, него би као светска атракција крстарили континентима, јер права левитација, њен трећи и последњи ступањ, када тело заиста неко време лебди у ваздуху, нкада нигде није јавно изведена! О томе постоје само појединачна сведочења из живота пустињака са Хималаја – тибетанских лама.

За оне пак упућеније у психичке моћи човека и експерименте са њима, ово „скакутање" је имало – „историјски значај", како су нам сами саопштили. Ако су гледаоци и посумњали у искреност четворице, верујући да се ради о каквој врхунској партерној гимнастици, јер се заиста видело трзање бутина и кукова, преосталима је успело да изведу право „чудо".

Тројици Југословена пошло је, дакле за руком да изведу „јоги-летење", на првој јавној демонстрацији код нас, и у Европи. Прва у свету одржана је пре месец дана у Америци. Свега седам минута концентрације, трансценденталне медитације, иако су годинама тренирали да у то стање „чисте свести" улазе тек после пола сата медитације, било им је довољно.

Ево шта о томе сведоче двојица присутних грађана:

– Назвати то скакутањем заиста је бесмислено и смешно и поништава напоре тих младића. Пре би се могло рећи да се ради о вибрирању тела – каже Александар Павловић, снимател и ликовни уметник из Београда. – Пажљиво сам посматрао десни подијум и приметио да је само један од четири вежбача успео да се „спусти" у дубоку медитацију, и наједном је као у трансу почео да се диже и спушта на земљу. Изводио је то са невероватном лакоћом, миран, равне кичме без икаквих контракција мишића, бутина и кукова. Има црну брадицу, округло лице, носи наочари. Честитајте том момку у моје име!

– Штета је, замерам организаторима што са двојицом најбољих нису поновили експеримент! Овако, бојим се да нису сви успели да виде оно што сам видео ја. Тог тренутка сам био поред саме бине са леве стране и видео једног вежбача како се уздиже са тла без икаквог напора. У појединим тренуцима 50, чак и 70 сантиметара изнад душека! Имао је наочари, дужу косу, висок је. Годинама пратим сва парапсихолошка истраживања и експерименте, и код нас и у свету. Ради ове демонстрације сам дошао чак из Битоља и не осећам се превареним – рекао нам је Ристо Билимбиловски, судија Окружног привредног суда у Битољу.

ТО ЈЕ ТО: Јосип Шћурец, Ервин Шимић и Владо Томљеновић

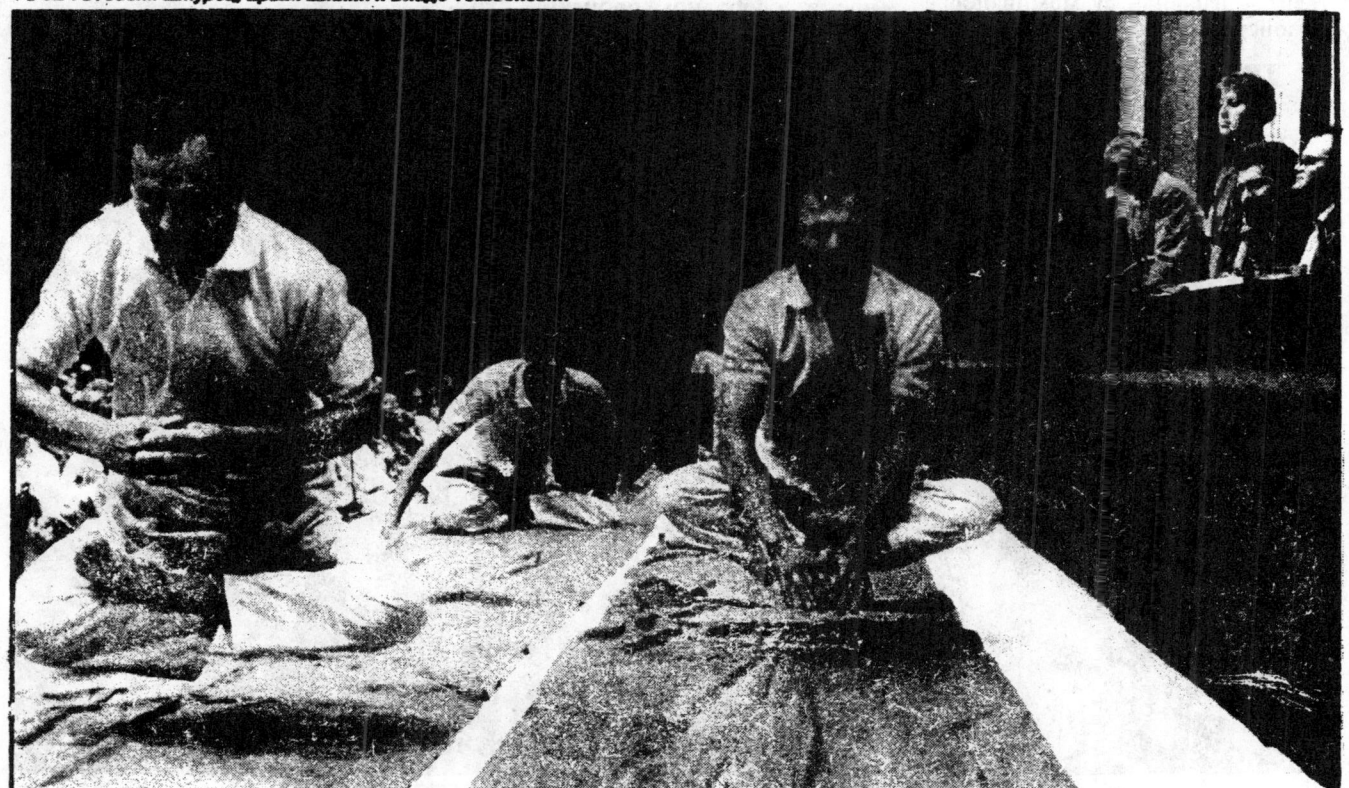

Аутор ових редова је видео и трећег, с разлогом можемо рећи — шампиона „летача". Пажња нам је била сконцентрисана углавном на њега, јер су нас претходно упозорили његови другови да је он један од врснијих мајстора ове технике. Био је то **Давор Станчић,** учитељ трансценденталне медитације из Паланчана крај Загреба.

Идентификовали смо, према опису посматрача, и другу двојицу. Били су то **Владо Томљеновић,** наставник физичке културе који такође живи у Паланчанима крај Загреба, и **Жарко Тришић,** инжењер електротехнике из Београда. И они су учитељи трансценденталне медитације.

У експерименту су још учествовали **Ото Шереги,** апсолвент Више техничке школе из Сенте, **Ервин Шилић,** дизајнер из Београда, **Јосип Шћурец,** зидар из Загреба, и **Јован Цакић** ...итељ трансценденталне медит...е из Београда. „Били смо узбуђени видевши оволику масу света, али никада се тако лепо нисмо осећали, чини нам се да никада тако добро нисмо летели" — изјавили су момци после демонстрације.

ТРАНСЦЕДЕНТАЛНА МЕДИТАЦИЈА

О моћима психичке енергије, која може позитивно и негативно да делује на наше здравље, говорили су те вечери неуропсихијатри **др Петар Станковић** из Београда и **др Никола Видев** из Битоља, после чега се заподенуо у сали занимљив разговор.

Многи су желели да сазнају још више о трансцендентној медитацији, иако су о њеном историјату, техникама и теорији у току програма говорили **Бранко Чичић,** учитељ трансценденталне медитације из Београда, и **Лазар Вош,** магистар и асистент на Факултету политичких наука у Загребу.

Хиљадама година две културе, источна и западна, развијале су се једна крај друге, готово и не дотичући се. Трансцендентална медитација је један од тих „мостова" сусрета два света. Проширила се по Европи и Америци пре нешто више од две деценије, заслугом познатог индијског филозофа **Махаришија.** Инспирисани тим идејама, многи наши, нарочито млади људи, почели су да упражњавају трансценденталну медитацију. Рачуна се да је кроз курсеве прошло, према слободној процени, око 10.000 Југословена.

Не треба заборавити да су многе источњачке технике и филозофије последњих деценија постале права духовна атракција на Западу. Оне неуротичном човеку данашњице нуде најчешће мир и духовну равнотежу.

Практиканти трансценденталне медитације тврде да после пет дана курса ту технику могу да изводе сами, два пута по 20 минута у току дана. Успевају најчешће толико да се опусте, и психу и тело, да им овај тренинг може заменити најчвршћи сан од неколико сати. Опуштено тело и глава без мисли из којих су „извучени" и стресови дневних и прошлих догађаја, једна је од основних научних формула на које се ослања теорија трансценденталне медитације. Успоставља се организму хармонија животне енергије, биоенергије која је веома битна за здравље и максимално коришћење менталних и креативних потенцијала.

Како незванично сазнајемо, Будва је позвала ове младиће да на Словенској плажи репризирају београдску представу.

Наташа МАРКОВИЋ

ЗА НЕКЕ „СКАКУТАЊЕ", ЗА ДРУГЕ ЧУДО: са демонстрације у Центру „Сава"

WORLD PEACE • GLOBAL INAUGURATION

PRESS REPORTS FROM EUROPE

Yugoslavia • *Vikend*

Zagreb   5 September 1986   (Croato-Serbian)

KAKO NAUČITI LEBDJETI

Petsto Jugoslavena koji vježbaju Maharišijevu tehniku jedinstvenog polja na jednom mjestu (studenata, vojnika, mladih umirovljenika, štićenika kazneno-popravnih domova... mogli bi proizvesti skok u kvaliteti života cijele zemlje. Smanjila bi se inflacija, ubrzao bi se znanstveni, ekonomski i kulturni napredak, kriminala bi bilo manje, a zdravlja više. Manje bi moglo bit oboljelih, smanjila bi se stopa smrtnosti i broj nesreća s tragičnim posljedicama. Prijavljivalo bi se više znanstvenih otkrića, što bi utjecalo na kreativnost cijele zemlje. Sve su to promjene koji određuju kvalitetu života suvremenih društava.

I ne trepnuvši izjavio je to **Lazar Voš**, magistar političkih znanosti iz Zagreba, na skupu »Moći psihičke energije« u prepunoj središnjoj dvorani »Sava centra«. Skup je održan 15. kolovoza u Beogradu.

Dan uoči skupa najslušanije beogradske radio-stanice »Studio B« i »202« najavljivale su ga kao prvorazrednu senzaciju. **Branko Čičić**, učitelj transcendentalne meditacije, rasplamsavao je maštu slušalaca riječima: »Nakon više od deset godina skrivanja iza zatvorenih vrata, Maharishi Mahesh Jogi dopustio je javnu izvedbu joginskog letenja. Svi koji dođu u »Sava centar« moći će vidjeti kako ljudi, pokrenuti isključivo unutrašnjom mentalnom energijom, uzdižu svoje tijelo 10, 20, 30 ili više centimetara od tla i prenose ga na drugo mjesto, prkoseći zakonima sile teže.«

Magistar Lazar Voš — meditacijom protiv inflacije

Prepuna dvorana znatiželjnika

To što se dogodilo u »Sava centru« zacijelo nije isprazan trik. Ali, je li samo skok u meditativnom transu dovoljan da bi se uvjerilo prisutne u Maharišijev plan ostvarenja svjetskog mira pomoću tehnike jedinstvenog polja? Potrebno je za to još i stotinu milijuna dolara

Bez traga napora na licu

■ SAMO DVAPUT NA DAN

U dvorani koja inače primi 1500 posjetilaca, bilo ih je ovaj put barem dvije tisuće. Svi su prostori između redova bili prepuni, rijeka ljudi ostala je pred zgradom uzalud moleći čuvare da ih puste. Mnoštvo Beograđana htjelo je vidjeti najavljeno čudo nad čudima. Ali, lebdenje nije bilo glavni razlog okupljanju tolikog broja ljudi. Organizator je lebdenje iskoristio samo kao potkrepu mogućnosti ostvarenja svjetskog mira po planu Mahareši Maheš Jogija.

Cijelu je manifestaciju vrlo profesionalno vodila **Nataša Marković,** novinarka »TV-novosti«. Ona je izgovorila kratak uvod, a prvi je govornik bio Branko Čičić. Svojski se potrudio uvjeriti prisutne da su transcendentalna meditacija i TM-sidhi program, koji je njezina dopuna, mogućnost rješenja svih teškoća u životu pojedinca i društva. Po njemu, transcendentalna meditacija razvija inteligenciju, pamćenje, osjetnost, kreativnost, liječi anginu pektoris, bronhijalnu astmu, visoki tlak, reumatoidni artritis, gastritis i bezbroj drugih psihosomatskih bolesti, čuva zdravlje, jer je idealan način sprečavanja bolesti.

Oni koji meditiraju sretniji su u braku, bolje se slažu s djecom i roditeljima, s kolegama na poslu, imaju bolje poslovne rezultate, a narkomani, zatvorenici i ostali iz svijeta besprizornih vraćaju se u normalne društvene tokove. Da bi čovjek sve to ostvario, potrebno je da samo dvaput na dan meditira po dvadesetak minuta — ostalo dolazi samo od sebe. Sve je to, kaže Branko Čičić, znanstveno proučeno i dokazano.

■ SAMO JEDAN POSTO

Lazar Voš govorio je o sociološkim aspektima transcendentalne meditacije, međunarodnim teškoćama i Maharišijevoj formuli za ostvarenje svjetskog mira.

Dovoljno će biti, rakao je Voš, da samo jedan posto ljudi u nekom gradu, zemlji ili na svijetu vježba transcedentalnu meditaciju da bi se smanjili stopa kriminala, automobilskih nesreća, broj oboljelih i smrtnost. Istodobno, poboljšalo bi se ekonomsko stanje društva, vrijednost akcija na svjetskim burzama bi rasla, a političke razmirice među zemljama bi se razriješile.

Za to je potrebno ostvariti koherenciju u kolektivnoj svijesti društva. To je moguće samo ako se prije ostvari koherencija u svijesti dovoljno velikog broja pojedinaca. Koherencija u svijesti pojedinaca plod je vježbe Maharišijeve tehnike jedinstvenog polja, koja obuhvaća već spomenutu transcendentalnu meditaciju i TM-sidhi program.

Prema znanstvenicima koje je Voš citirao, potreban broj pojedinaca za taj neobičan efekt je magičnih jedan posto od broja svih članova društva. Jedan posto je kritična masa osoba bilo koje velike društvene cjeline nužne za fazni prijelaz u glavnim društvenim kretanjima. Štoviše, taj je broj moguće smanjiti, ako na jednom mjestu i u istom trenutku meditanti zajednički izvode Maharišijevu tehniku jedinstvenog polja. U tom je slučaju, tvrdi se, dovoljan broj osoba koji se dobije kad se iz broja jedan posto populacije izvadi drugi korijen, a efekt bi mogao biti i veći. Stručnjaci to nazivaju »efekt superzračenja«.

Koherencija u mozgovnim valovima, koja se inače zaista postiže meditativnim tehnikama, pa i transcendentalnom meditacijom, očituje se kao sinhronizacija bioelektrične aktivnosti različitih područja kore velikog mozga. Meditanti tvrde da se, kad ih ima jedan posto od ukupnog broja članova društva, efekt prenosi na one koji ne meditiraju, a pojačava se »efektom superzračenja«.

SAMO OD KAMATA

Da bi ostvario svjetski mir, što nikom dosad nije pošlo za rukom, Mahariši se upustio u golem pothvat. Pokraj Delhija gradi se cijeli grad za 10.000 Maharišijevih učenika koji bi zajednički prakticirali njegovu tehniku jedinstvenog polja i zračili mir u duše manje smirenih stanovnika Zemlje. Za to su potrebne i goleme svote novca. Osnovan je fond u koji treba skupiti ni manje ni više nego 100 milijuna američkih dolara. Stanovnici novoosnovanog grada živjeli bi samo od kamata, a glavnica se ne bi dirala. Pozivaju se vlade i bogataši da pridonesu stvaranju svjetskog mira. Ali ako bajka i ne uspije, ostaje činjenica da ipak nečeg ima u onome što smo vidjeli u »Sava centru«.

Joginsko letenje, koje je prikazano i koje je glavni dio Maharišijeve tehnike jedinstvenog polja, iznenadilo je mnoge u dvorani. Tko god je očekivao Petra Pana koji leti iznad glava gledalaca zacijelo se razočarao. S druge strane, gotovo je nedvojbeno da fenomen nije prevara. Krajnje je teško zamisliti da bi se ti mladi ljudi (bila su i dvojica na pragu šestog desetljeća) mogli čisto fizičkim naporom u tradicionalnoj lotos-pozi dizati i cijelih 70 cm uvis, ne pokazujući pri tom nikakve znakove napora.

Nakon pet minuta meditacije, koja im je poslužila »da bi ušli u transcendentalnu svijest«, iz koje je moguće te tehnike izvoditi, mladići u žutim majicama i bijelim hlačama pokazali su tzv. prvi stupanj joginskog letenja, koji podrazumijeva dizanje tijela od tla samo mentalnom energijom. Druga je faza, tvrde, lebdenje, a treća — letenje. Istodobno kažu da ne poznaju nikog tko je tim fazama sasvim ovladao, ali vjeruju da će marljivim vježbanjem jednog dana oni to postići.

Bilo kako bilo, dobili su zaslužen aplauz za ono što su prikazali, a Nataša Marković im je u ime organizatora darovala — po jednu crvenu ružu.

Viđeno su komentirala i dvojica domaćih neuropsihijatara **dr Nikola Videv** iz Bitolja i **dr Petar Stanković** iz Beograda, autor glasovite »Božanske medicine«. Njih dvojica su s prilično simpatija opisala ono što su demonstratori prikazali, ukazujući na tradiciju parapsholoških fenomena i poruke mitoloških predanja drevnih kultura Indije, Grčke i drugih naroda. Skup je završen spontanim pripovijedanjem pojedinaca iz publike o iskustvima što su stekli kroz primjenu raznih tehnika kojima se bave.

Kad su se približila 22 sata, svjetla velike dvorane počela su se polako gasiti. Bio je to znak da je manifestacija završena. Nataša Marković je još jednom pozdravila prisutne i najavile nove teme iz ciklusa »Moći psihičke energije«.

R. Š.

Mahariši Maheš Jogi — zračio bi mir po uznemirenom svijetu

PRESS REPORTS FROM EUROPE

Yugoslavia • *Reporter*
Belgrade 5 September 1986 (Serbo-Croatian)

DUHOM PROTIV MATERIJE: TM za zapadnjake željne letenja

IKARI IZ NASEG SOKAKA

Nekada su to radile lame sa nedostupnih tibetanskih visova, jogini iz neprohodnih šuma Indije. Sada je red na samoupravljače iz naših mesnih zajednica.
* *Da li ono što se dešava u glavi jednog coveka može da utiče na sve ljude?*
* *Može li se levitacija objasniti uz pomoć kvantne mehanike?*
* *Treba li leteti, leteti, leteti... da bi se postigao mir u svetu, ili ćemo našu brigu za mir, ponovo prepustiti drugima?*

Ko su savremeni naslednici Petra Pana?

Jovan CAKIĆ

Priča počinje 30 godina ranije. U pećinama snežnih Himalaja i tišini prirode, prekidanoj samo žuborom potoka i cvrkutom retkih ptica, daleko od uzbudenja života, zaronjen duboko u meditaciju, jedan jog **po imenu Mahariši Maheš, odlučio je da svetu podari mir. Na svetu se 30 godina kasnije, na žalost, i dalje puca, a terorizam buja nesmanjenom žestinom. Pa ipak, Mahariši i njegovi sledbenici veruju da su na pragu ostvarenja vekovnog sna – tvrde da su konačno otkrili formulu kojom mogu već u ovoj generaciji ostvariti svetski mir.**

Kada je daleke 1957. godine Mahariši Maheš Jogi sišao s Himalaja i krenuo u svoju misiju koja je trebalo da pojedincima pruži sreću, a svetu mir i sigurnost, malo je ko verovao da će uspeti. Svi su znali da potiče iz najdrevnije tradicije čuvara vedskog učenja, bilo je tačno i to da su ova učenja oduvek predstavljala "deblo" iz kojeg su crple život sve grane indijske filozofije i religije i da se na njemu zasniva celokupno duhovno nasleđe ove neobične zemlje. Njegov učitelj je bio Svami Brahmananda Sarasvati, dagadguru (vrhunski guru) reda Šankaračarija, još za života slavljen kao "inkarnacija vedante", kome su na poklonjenje išle vodeće ličnosti tek oslobođene Indije. Dr Raždendra Prasad, prvi predsednik Indijske Unije i dr Servapali Radakrišnan, njen drugi predsednik i jedan od najvećih filozofa 20. veka bili su medu njegovim štovateljima. Sve je to bilo tačno, pa ipak, mudri ljudi Indije sa zebnjom oko srca, ispratili su Maharišija na Zapad, Jer, govorili su: "stara indijska poslovica kaže Žedni idu k izvoru, a ne izvor k žednima".

Prekinuvši s tradicijom prema kojoj je učenik trebalo godinama da se dokazuje da bi **dobio ma i homeoptaske doze tajnih znanja** koja vode ka "prosvetljenju", Mahariši je napravio razlaz i sa drugim dotad važećim "pravilom": znanje je ponudio običnom coveku sa ulice i to znanja koja su vekovima bila apsolutna privilegija odabranih, koji su napustivši roditeljski dom, i zadobivši poverenje svog učitelja stekli status i ekskluzivna prava učenika vrhunske realnosti....

Duge crne kose i uredno negovane brade, obučen u beli doti, sa koralnom ogrlicom oko vrata i cvetom u ruci, uvek nasmešen i s porukom "instant" prosvetljenja, Mahariši je brzo privukao pažnju masovnih medija. Njegov metod, poznat kao "transcendentalna meditacija", naprečac je osvojio mlade. **Bitlsi** su medu prvima naučili "transcendentalnu meditaciju". **Rolingstonsi** nisu hteli da zaostanu, a **Mia Farou, Bob Dilan i Donovan** predvodili su meditantski džet-set sa druge strane Atlantika. Ceo svet je pričao o neobičnoj tehnici koja dolazi sa Istoka i donosi njenim praktikantima "unutrašnji spokoj i mir". Euforija je trajala kratko, a onda su stvari poprimile mirniji tok. TM-pokret je ipak rastao, krajem šezdesetih, bilo je već više od milion ljudi na svetu koji su upražnjavali ovaj metod samorazvoja, tvrdeći da je usled ovog "njihovo mišljenje jasnije, da su kreativniji, psihički stabilniji i fizički zdraviji" sasvim dovoljno da se naučnici zainteresuju.

Godine 1970. dr R. K. Valas sa Harvardske medicinske škole, jedne od najautoritativnijih naučnih ustanova u SAD, objavljuje rezultate svojih istraživanja, navodeći da su svest i fiziološko stanje koje vežba transcendentalne meditacije proizvodi sasvim različiti od obične budnosti, sanjanja ili dubokog sna. Ovo novo stanje Valas naziva "budno hipometaboličko stanje", u kojem je svest maksimalno **budna**, dok se telo istovremeno maksimalno odmara. Budući da je svest u ovom stanju "prazna", oslobođena sadržaja, Valas je naziva "transcendentalna ili čista svest", smatrajući da se radi o kvalitativno novoj formi ljudske svesnosti..

Bio je to signal za brojne zapadne psihologe, psihijatre i lekare najrazličitijih specijalnosti da otpočnu sa intenzivnim proučavanjem transcendentalne meditacije i njenih efekata. Istraživanja su sledila jedno drugo. Svaki novi eksperiment otvarao je vrata za sledeći, a utvrđeni efekti množili su se geometrijskom progresijom: transcendentalno meditiranje blagotvorno deluje u slučajevima srčanih oboljenja, normalizuje visoki krvni pritisak, stišava napade bronhijalne astme, povoljno utiče na tok hipertireoze, dijabetes i gastritis, ublažava reumatične upalne procese, jača imuni sistem itd. Psihijatri tvrde da uklanja neuroze i anksiozna stanja, ublažava migrene i depresije, a psiholozi da razvija spoznajne sposobnosti i crte ličnosti... Broj istraživanja popeo se na blizu 400, a preko 160 vodećih svetskih naučnih institucija angažovalo se u opsežnim ispitivanjima sa ciljem da se ustanove različiti aspekti njenog psihološkog, medicinskog i socijalnog potencijala. I kada je već izgledalo da je transcendentalna meditacija konačno stekla svoj akademski status, uklopivši se u redovne tokove nauke i njene institucionalne primene, istovremeno gubeći ponešto od svog prvobitnog šarma, Maharaši je izašao pred svet sa potpuno novim setom tehnike za razvoj svesti i pozvao svoje učenike da nauče – leteti!

NASLEDNICI PETRA PANA

Bio je to šok. Iako je oduvek govorio da „živimo u polju svih mogućnosti", nikome u potpunosti nije bilo jasno što Mahariš stvarno misli pod tim, a još manje da će tehnike za oživljavanje ovog polja u vlastitoj svesti učiniti dostupnim i zapadnom čoveku.

U tom trenutku, hiljade meditanata pohrlilo je u Selisberg, mestašce pored jezera Lucern, jednog od najlepših u čitavoj Švajcarskoj, na Maharišijev Evropski Istraživački Univerzitet, da bi naučilo tehnike kojima je moguće „leteti, postati nevidljiv, saznati prošlost i budućnost, profiniti svoja čula i postići sva ostala čula koja Patanđali obećava u svojim poznatim „Joga sutrama".

Još u jesen 1974. američki naučnici Landrit i Borland objavili su rezultate sociološke studije 24 američka grada od kojih je 12 imalo 1% građana koji su vežbali transcendentalnu meditaciju. U ovim gradovima, kako tvrde Borland i Landrit, došlo je do pada kriminala za čitavih 8,2% u poređenju sa gotovo istom stopom porasta u drugim kontrolnim gradovima. Ovi neverovatni rezultati ukazivali su na fantastičnu hipotezu – da individualna i kolektivna svest nisu dve različite stvari. Drugim rečima, sve ono što se zbiva u glavi jednog čoveka ima nekog uticaja na svest svih drugih članova društva, i obrnuto – promene u kolektivnoj svesti odražavaju se u svesti i ponašanju pojedinaca.

Kada je čuo za ove rezultate, Mahariši je

Maharishi Mahesh Yogi, osnivač Transcendentalne meditacije

rekao „Sada imamo formulu za svetski mir". Zadatak je sada postao neuporedivo lakši, pa ipak, tek sa otkrićem efekta „superzračenja" njegove šanse da ostvari svoj „plan za mir". dobile su realnu osnovu. Grupa fizičara sa Maharišijevog internacionalnog univerziteta, došla je, na osnovu analize ponašanja izvesnih fizičkih sistema, do pretpostavke da će za „efekat 1" biti potreban daleko manji broj pojedinaca, ukoliko zajedno, na jednom mestu i u jedno vreme, praktikuju već pomenute TM-sidhi tehnike, od kojih je svakako najjača tehnika „joginskog letenja". Budući da tehniku vežbaju **zajedno** i **istovremeno** stvara se vrsta izuzetno snažnog mentalnog zračenja koje prenosi koherenciju sa grupne na kolektivnu svest društva.

Eksperiment koji je izveden u periodu od 17. 12. 83-07. 01. 84. u laboratorijama Maharišijevog internacionalnog univerziteta pokazao je da je kritičan broj takve grupe koja je u stanju da izazove fazni prelaz u životu zemlje kvadratni koren iz 1 od ukupne populacije. Tokom 21 dana koliko je eksperiment trajao, više od 7000 ljudi (kvadratni koren iz 1% svetske populacije) zajednički je vežbalo ono što je danas poznato pod nazivom Maharišijeva tehnologija jedinstvenog polja. Rezultati, ako su tačni, zaista su fascinantni. Zvanične statistike pokazuju da je u navedenom periodu došlo do drastičnog smanjenja kriminala u mnogim zemljama, da se smanjila stopa obolelih, baš kao i broj vazdušnih, automobilskih i drugih saobraćajnih udesa, da se kreativnost nacija povećala izraženo većim brojem prijava patenata u istom periodu, da je broj sukoba u ratom zahvaćenim područjima, kao što je Liban - značajno opao, da se međunarodna saradnja trenutno poboljšala i da su ekonomski trendovi, indicirano simultanim rastom vrednosti akcija na svetskim berzama - pri čemu su na nekim dostigli najviše vrednosti u istoriji - vrtoglavo krenuli napred.

Od tog trenutka, ideja da okupi 7000 meditanata na jednom mestu postaje Maharišijeva osnovna preokupacija.

OSNOVA ZA SVETSKI MIR

Svoju zvaničnu inauguraciju, „Maharišijev program za stvaranje svetskog mira", kako se plan zvanično zove, doživeo je sredinom jula ove godine u Vašingtonskom konvenšn centru. Nekoliko stotina novinara iz čitave Amerike, reporteri nacionalnog radija i vodećih televizijskih kompanija, akreditovani izveštači međunarodnih pres-agencija, kao i brojni članovi diplomatskih misija koji borave u Vašingtonu skupili su se u Konvenšn centar da vide čudo neviđeno. Magnet za sve njih bila je najava demonstracije „joginskog letenja" u okviru Prvog severnoameričkog takmičenja u ovoj ni malo običnoj veštini.

Ceremonija je počela inauguralnom adresom, u kojoj se Mahariši prisutnima obratio sledećim rečima:... „Naš pristup stvaranju svetskog mira je holističan. On izvire iz najfundamentalnijeg nivoa prirodnog zakona, jedinstvenog polja svih zakona prirode - tog polja odakle svi različiti zakoni prirode proizlaze i koje održava sve različite vrednosti univerzuma... Želim naglasiti da je priroda jedinstvenog polja u potpunosti evolucionarna. Destrukcija je nepostojeća u jedinstvenom polju. Oni koji jedinstveno polje poznaju iz sopstvenog iskustva, oni koji praktikuju TM-sidhi program, razvijaju ga u sopstvenoj svesti, a kada tehnike praktikuju grupno, stvaraju harmoniju i evolucionarni uticaj u svetskoj svesti. Razvijajući koherenciju u svetskoj svesti, oni spontano eliminišu destruktivne trendove i tendencije u životu. Stanje svetskog mira biće trajno kada jedinstveno polje bude oživljeno u svim različitim aspektima dnevnog života svih ljudi na zemlji. Za ovo, biće potrebno ostvariti uticaj koherencije u svetskoj svesti..."

Da bi objasnio mehanizam stvaranja ovog uticaja koherencije, dr Džon Hegelin, jedan od najdarovitijih fizičara sveta mlađe generacije, bivši saradnik Evropskog centra za nuklearna istraživanja u Ženevi i istraživač Stendfordskog univerziteta, koji je „prešao" u Maharišijev tabor pre nepune tri godine, rekao je: „Koherencija je glavna karakteristika kvantno-mehaničkih fenomena... `Joginsko letenje', u suštini, predstavlja demonstraciju istog fenomena koherencije na fundamentalnijem nivou funkcionisanja prirode, na nivou samog jedinstvenog polja. Klasične teorije gravitacije, teorije kao što su Njutnova gravitacija i Ajnštajnova opšta relativnost, ne mogu da objasne „joginske letenje".

Kvantna gravitacija, međutim, može...

A onda je sledilo „glavno".

KO ĆE BRŽE, KO ĆE DALJE

Sa urođenim smislom za spektakl, Amerikanci su se potrudili da demonstracija joginskog letenja, ne bude obično prikazivanje tehnike. Umesto toga, organizovali su takmičenje u četiri discipline joginskog letenja: **trka na 25 m s preponama; skok uvis; skok udalj"** i **"sprint" na 50 m**.

Čak tri zlatne medalje pripale su izvesnom Edi Gobu, sa rezultatima 11.53 sekunde za

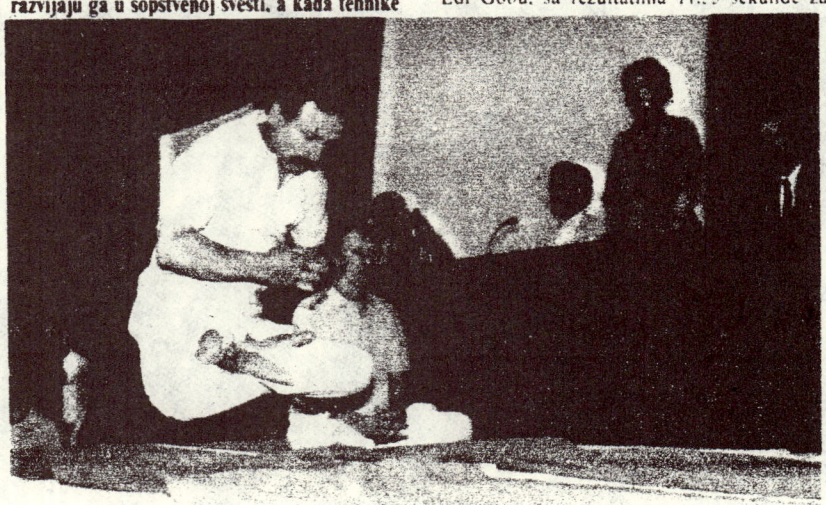

Meditanti u vazduhu: mir je na pomolu

trku 25 m sa preponama, 23.33 sekunde za "sprint" i 1,80 za skok udalj.

Zlatna u skoku uvis pripala je Blejn Votsonu iz Kanade koji je leteo 63 cm uvis.

Svi rezultati su postignuti u klasičnom lotus položaju, dakle sedeći na tlu prekrštenih nogu, koristeći kao pogon isključivo mentalnu energiju kojom pojedinac raspolaže. Bila je to, kako su naučnici objasnili, prva faza joginskog letenja. Druga predstavlja lebdenje ili plutanje u vazduhu, a treće pravo letenje kao Petar Pan.

Na žalost, ove druge dve faze nismo mogli videti.

Isti scenario ponovio se 15 dana kasnije u Nju Delhiju, kada su održane i prve Olimpijske igre u joginskom letenju, sa takmičarima iz 36 zemalja! Jogi olimpijadu je otvorio sadašnji Šankaraćarija, Svami Višnu Devanand, u prisustvu članova diplomatskog kora (bili su i naši!) i 10.000 gledalaca koji su se okupili na stadionu "Indira Gandi" da vide - kako ljudi lete!

Predstava je uspela, i premda Petar Pan ni ovog puta nije bio prisutan, gledaoci su se razišli zadovoljni - čovek je pokazao da njegov duh, bar za trenutak, može da savlada silu gravitacije.

Domaća repriza se odigrala 15. avgusta o.g., istovremeno kad i u 108 drugih zemalja. U "Sava centru" u Beogradu 7 Jugoslovena je prikazalo da ni malo ne zaostaje za svojim inostranim kolegama. Uz to, od Lazara Voša, naučnog asistenta na Fakultetu političkih nauka iz Zagreba, čuli smo da bi grupno letenje 500 Jugoslovena na jednom mestu i u isto vreme moglo rešiti neke ključne društvene probleme zemlje, uključujući "inflaciju, ekonomski, naučni i kulturni progres, kolektivno zdravlje i dr.", što je publika pozdravila aplauzom ....

Svaki let prema nebu, pa i ovaj, uvek predstavlja pokušaj ljudskog duha da se uzdigne iznad sivila svakodnevice i bezizlaza života. Pa čak i ako ne uspe, ostaće činjenica da je pre 30 godina, jedan jog, po imenu Maharisi Maheš, čistog srca, sišao sa snežnih visova Himalaja i pokušao da svetu podari mir. Koliko više od perspektive nuklearnog sukoba koji nam nudi na blokove podeljeni svet! ■

PRESS REPORTS FROM EUROPE

Yugoslavia • *Dvoje*

Belgrade   18 September 1986   (Serbo-Croatian)

Ljudi koji „lete"

Beograd, krajem avgusta 1986. Centralna hala „Sava centra". Tačno je 19 časova. Prvi Jugosloveni pokušaće nemoguće. Pokušaće da lete.

Blizu dve hiljade ljudi okupilo se u „Sava centru" da vide čudo neviđeno. Centralna sala se za čas popunila. Podignulo se jedno krilo i otvorilo se još nekoliko stotina mesta. I ona su se popunila. Zatim se diglo i desno. Ponovo isto. Reka ljudi popunila je prolaze između redova. Stotine znatiželjnih ostali su pred zatvorenim ulazom. Svi su hteli videti svojim očima. A sretni koji su došli i uspeli da uđu – nisu zažalili! Dan pre toga, radio je javio: „Nakon više od deset godina letenja iza zatvorenih vrata, Mahariši Maheš Jogi odlučio je da dozvoli javnu demonstraciju joginskog letenja". Svi oni koji dođu sutra u „Sava centar" moći će videti kako ljudi, pokrenuti isključivo unutrašnjom psihičkom energijom, uzdižu svoje telo 10, 20, 30 ili više santimetara od zemlje i prenose ga na drugo mesto, prkoseći zakonima gravitacije." Kada smo ušli u salu, pola sata pre početka predstave, bila je već dupke puna. Ljudi, a bilo ih je svakakvih – intelektualaca, profesora univerziteta, domaćica, studenata, radnika i učenika – pažljivo su pratili sve što se dešavalo.

U ime organizatora, skup je otvorila Nataša Marković, novinar. Počelo je govorom. Branko Čičić, učitelj programa Transcendentalne Meditacije upoznao je prisutne sa prirodom ove metode samorazvoja i zadržao se poduže na njenim efektima, rekavši: „Prema dr Hansu Selijeu, jednom od najpoznatijih istraživača problema stresa, stanje najmanje fiziološke pobuđenosti koje se postiže vežbom Transcendentalne Meditacije, upravo je dijametralno suprotno sindromu stresa. Karakterističan relaksacioni sindrom koji tehnika TM sistematski pobuđuje, osnova je iz koje proizlaze svi

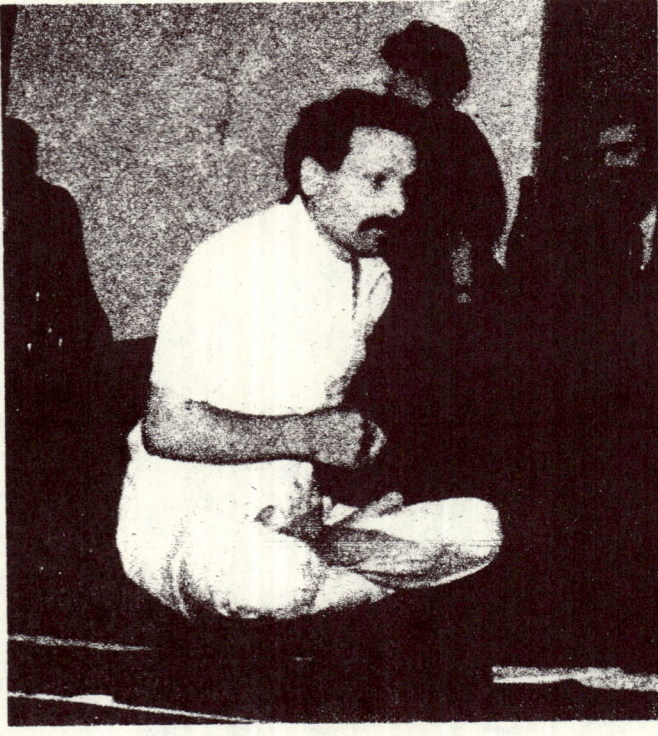 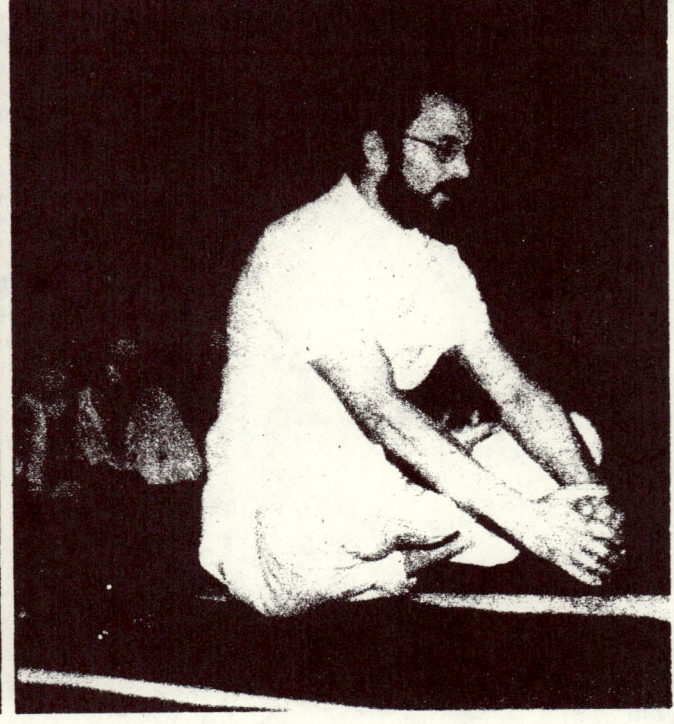

njeni efekti na čovekov mentalni, fiziološki i socijalni status." Navodeći rezultate više od 360 studija o prednostima ove metode koje su istraživane u više od 160 vodećih međunarodnih naučnih institucija, on je kazao: „Transcendentalne Meditacije razvija intelektualne sposobnosti, ličnost, percepciju, donosi bolje zdravlje, utičući blagotvorno na anginu pektoris, visoki krvni pritisak, bronhijalnu astmu i druge psihosomatske bolesti, ona poboljšava socijalne odnose i rehabilituje zatvorenike. Ali to nije ono ", rekao je Čičić, „zbog čega smo se ovde sastali. Mi danas tvrdimo da Transcendentalna Meditacija i TM-sidhi program, poznati pod zajedničkim imenom 'Maharišijeva tehnologija jedinstvenog polja", mogu da donesu svetu mir".

Na koji način i koliko, ostavio je sledećem govorniku, Lazaru Vošu, magistru političkih nauka iz Zagreba.

Teorija jedan odsto

U svom referatu, Voš koji priprema doktorat iz socioloških uticaja Transcendentalne Meditacije, rekao je: „U osnovi, svest jedinke i društva, nisu dve različite stvari... Promene u kolektivnoj svesti društvenih celina, odražavaju se u ponašanju članova društva – i obrnuto. Rast ili regresija individualne svesti direktno menjaju tokove kolektivne svesti i praktično ponašanje čitavog društva". Da bi dokumentovao ovu tvrdnju, Voš je naveo brojne sociološke studije koje ukazuju da su članovi svakog društva na jednom dubljem nivou svesti povezani. Istraživanja vršena u SAD pokazuju, prema njemu, da u onim gradovima gde jedan odsto ljudi praktikuje Transcendentalnu Meditaciju, stopa kriminala pada. Druga istraživanja su našla da i neke druge varijable, kao što su broj samoubistava, stopa nesreća, broj obolelih itd., takođe padaju u gradovima sa 1% meditanata. I ne samo to, u tim sredinama dolazi do značajnih poboljšanja u ekonomskim tokovima, stišavaju se političke razmirice, redukuju se ratni sukobi i terorističke akcije. Do sada postoji više od 30 studija da to jeste tako. Prema Vošu, najnovija istraživanja pokazuju da je za isti efekat potreban svega kvadratni koren iz jedan odsto ukupne populacije, pod uslovom da metodu vežbaju zajedno, na jednom mestu i u isto vreme.

Objašnjavajući na primeru Jugoslavije, što bi to značilo, Voš je rekao: „500 Jugoslovena koji vežbaju Maharišijevu tehnologiju jedinstvenog polja na jednom mestu (studenata, vojnika, mladih penzionera, štićenika kaznenopopravnih domova ili bilo koje druge društvene ustanove) mogli bi da dovedu do faznog prelaza u kvaliteti života zemlje. Ove promene bi, obuhvatile: pad inflacije (što su prisutni burno pozdravili!), brži naučni ekonomski i kulturni progres, nižu stopu kriminala, bolje kolektivno zdravlje – manju stopu obolelih, nižu stopu smrtnosti, manji broj svih nesreća sa fatalnim ishodom, veću kreativnost zemlje izraženu većim brojem prijava naučnih otkrića, dakle sve one promene koje bitno određuju kvalitet života savremenih društava... Ono što ćete sada videti jeste mehanizam stvaranja jednog takvog društva, mehanizam stvaranja svetskog mira. Značaj fenomena letenja nije u njegovoj površnoj manifestaciji, već u onom što on donosi onome koji ovu tehniku izvodi i društvenoj zajednici kao celini".

Ljudi kao kokice

A onda je Branko Čičić zamolio prisutne da se utišaju. Da bi letači mogli pokazati šta znaju, potreban je potpuni mir, kazao je. 2000 judi se utišalo. Čulo se samo jedva primetno zujanje er-kondišna. Oči prisutnih bile su prikovane na sedmorici mladića obučenih u bele pantalone i žute majice, koji su mirno sedeli na dvadesetak santimetara debelim sunđerima, specijalno izrađenim za ovu prili-

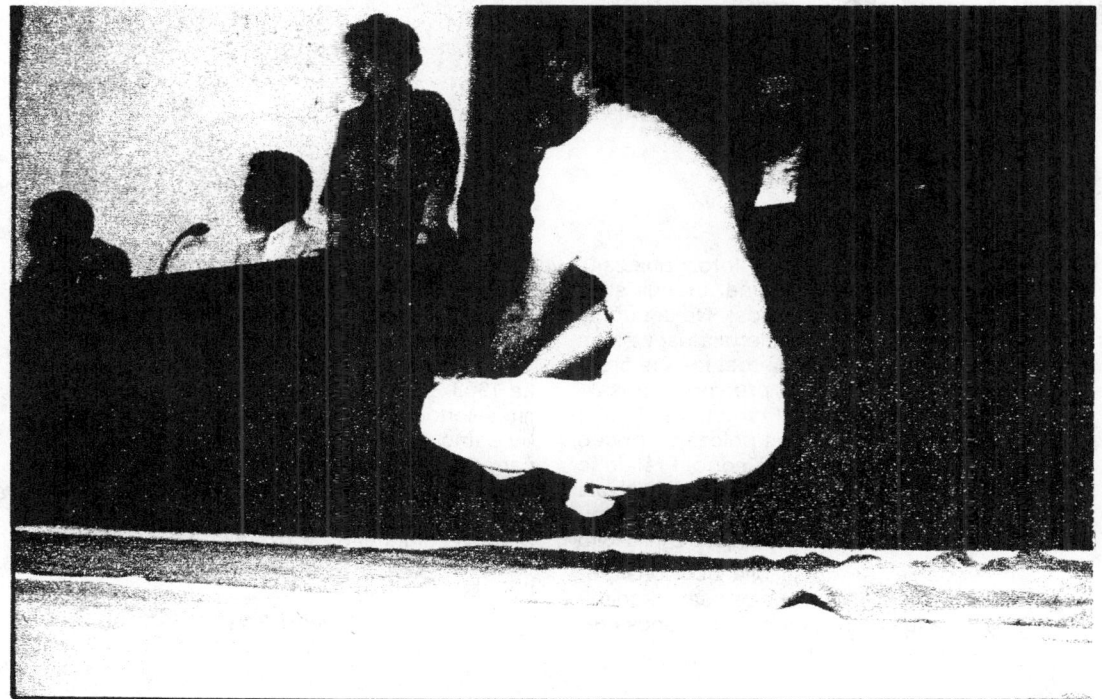

MAHARISHI'S PROGRAMME TO CREATE

ku. Nogu prekrštenih u lotos položaju, karakterističnom za jogine, utonuli su u meditaciju. U sali napetost. Neka čudna, ali sasvim konkretna energija osećala se u vazduhu. Tišina i napetost koja je pretila da se svakog trena pretvori u prasak. A onda – eksplozija. Prvi letač je kao iz katapulta izletio u lotos položaju i počeo – hopsati! A onda svi zajedno. Prštalo je na sve strane. Tela mladića odskakivala su od podloge kao kokice. Skoro pet minuta. Ne, to nije bilo letenje. To nije bilo ni lebdenje. Ali, to je bila očevidna potvrda da ljudski duh suočen sa zakonima materije ipak može da pobedi, njihova tela su se odizala i po 70 santimetara od podloge u elegantnim skokovima i premeštala se za još toliko napred. Kao prvi avion.

Kada su braća Orvil i Vilbur Rajt daleke 1903. godine u Kiti Hoku preleteli svojim avionom 285 m i zadržali se u vazduhu samo 59 sekundi, svet je bio skeptičan. Hoće li ta naprava ikada moći bolje leteti, pitao se? Danas znamo odgovor. Avioni nas prenose sa kraja na kraj sveta, povezujući narode i zemlje. Meditanti tvrde da će oni to jednog dana umeti još bolje ■

Snimio: Rade KRSTINIC

WORLD PEACE • GLOBAL INAUGURATION

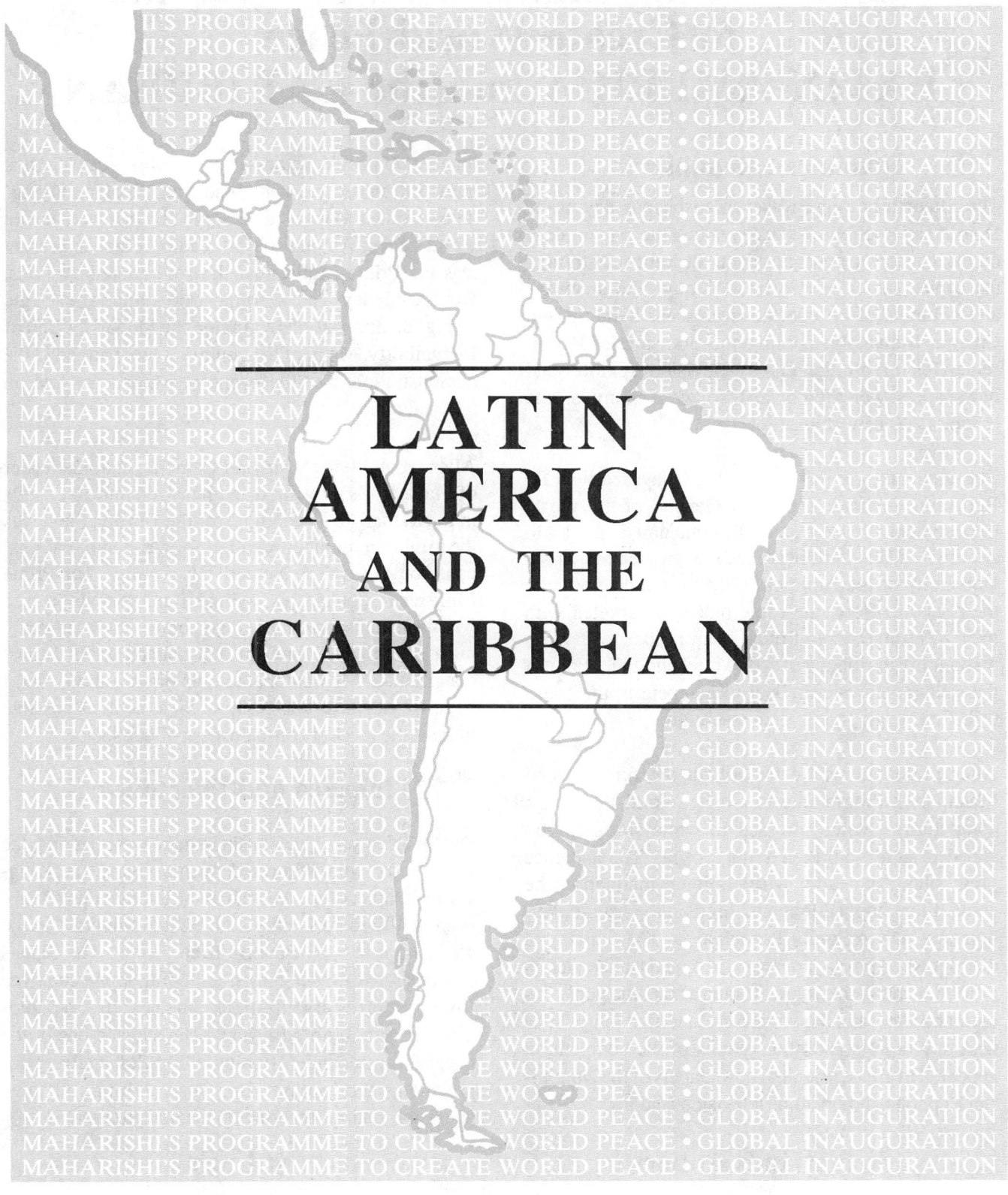

LATIN AMERICA AND THE CARIBBEAN

Inaugurating Maharishi's Programme to Create World Peace
LATIN AMERICA and the CARIBBEAN

Dominican Republic

The fifteenth of August was an auspicious day in the Dominican Republic—one day before the inauguration of the country's new president. In **Santo Domingo**, the capital, a sea breeze blew through the archways and columns of an enormous crescent building, the Colegio Maharishi, cooling the 300 guests. Representatives of all the city's television stations and newspapers were there, and so were many of the school's 200 new graduates.

The students were excited. Three days earlier, Dr Benjamin Feldman, Governor General of the World Government of the Age of Enlightenment for Latin America and the Caribbean, had inaugurated Maharishi University of the Americas (UMA) in a ceremony at their school. Now, the same hall was carpeted with over 700 square feet of thick foam rubber, with lanes marked off in ribbons of red, white, and blue. Four of their classmates were about to compete in the country's first 'yogic flying' demonstration.

After presentations by faculty on the principles of Maharishi's Programme to Create World Peace, the competitors entered, dressed in white shirts emblazoned in gold with their school's seal. The audience grew silent, and after a five-minute meditation the competitors hopped long and high on the way to their honours. Dr Antonio Panochia, a TM-Sidha and distinguished physician, awarded medals to the victors of four events—the yogic 50-metre race, the yogic 25-metre hurdles, and the yogic long and high jumps. The next day reports and photographs of the competition appeared in all the principal newspapers of the Dominican Republic and on all its television stations.

Netherlands Antilles

Four hundred miles south across the Caribbean, more than 1,000 people witnessed a similar spectacle. Nine men in shirts marked 'Curaçao, Yogic Flying' demonstrated Maharishi's simple mechanics to create world peace. Among the 30 leading citizens present was the Prime Minister of the Netherlands Antilles, His Excellency Don Martina, who started the 'yogic flying' demonstration by ringing the Maharishi Bell of Invincibility. Many of the country's press attended the demonstration, and the event was broadcast live on national radio.

After 'yogic flying', Mr Carl Camelia, national leader of Maharishi's movement, emphasized that 50 experts in the Maharishi Technology of the Unified Field was the minimum number required for a coherent national consciousness in the Netherlands Antilles. The Prime Minister responded by saying, 'I am very impressed by this demonstration. I will go home convinced that I must spend more time on this phenomenon. I must congratulate Mr Camelia and his organization, and I hope we can have this group of 50 as soon as possible to raise the level of consciousness of our society.'

Jamaica and Puerto Rico

Doctors, lawyers, and businessmen were among the 250 guests who witnessed 'yogic flying' at **Kingston's** Tropical Inn. At Maharishi International Caribbean, a 400-room facility high on a promontory at the western end of Puerto Rico, five TM-Sidhas demonstrated for 40 guests, including representatives from nine press organizations. The next day, a photograph in **San Juan's** *El Nuevo Dia* showed one of the television cameramen filming a TM-Sidha 'flying for peace', as the caption said. That evening, all three television stations reported on the inauguration.

St Lucia

Television also brought Maharishi's Programme to

WORLD PEACE • GLOBAL INAUGURATION

INAUGURATING MAHARISHI'S PROGRAMME TO CREATE WORLD PEACE—LATIN AMERICA AND THE CARIBBEAN

Create World Peace to all the people of St Lucia in the Windward Islands. A one-hour film made from the press conferences and 'yogic flying' competitions in Washington and New Delhi was aired twice on national television. An article in the national newspaper began, 'Up and away with yogic flying', and concluded, 'The road to a cool and harmonious state of affairs in St Lucia and around the globe will need a liberal stock of foam mattresses on which yogic flyers can practise their art while driving away inner tensions and the stress of the world.' A series of four more articles followed, giving an in-depth account of Maharishi's programme. 'TM's benefits have been verified,' read one headline.

Guadeloupe and Dominica

Martinique sent Governor of the Age of Enlightenment Matt Boutrin to the First International 'Yogic Flying' Competition in New Delhi, where he won two gold medals. It was, he said, 'the proudest moment of my life, because I knew that through gaining these two medals I was participating in the demonstration of the mechanics of how to create world peace.' Said Guadeloupian Eddie Gob, winner of three gold medals in Washington, 'It is doubly fulfilling: you feel fulfilled inside while you are flying, and you know you are contributing maximum to create world peace.'

The first demonstration in Guadeloupe itself, held at the Salako Hotel, was attended by 40 people, including the Mayor and General Counsel of Capesterre, Guadeloupe's third largest city. The event was introduced by five TM-Sidhas seated beneath a gold-lettered banner announcing 'Programme de Maharishi pour Créer la Paix Mondiale' ('Maharishi's Programme to Create World Peace'). Three other TM-Sidhas hopped across foam mats beneath a second banner that read 'Démonstration des Méchanismes pour Créer la Paix Mondiale' ('Demonstration of the Mechanics to Create World Peace'). According to the organizers, journalists from *Antilla*, Radio Eclair, and Radio Intité accepted the reality of the flying and showed great enthusiasm to see stages two and three—hovering and controlled flight.

On neighbouring Dominica, a press conference and demonstration of Maharishi's programme was held on 15 August. On 13 September, 200 people attended a second demonstration of 'yogic flying' on Guadeloupe at the Hotel Novotel. A journalist from R.F.O. Radio came and invited the speakers to hold a one-hour radio conference on the Transcendental Meditation programme, which took place two days later. The following day a long article on Maharishi's programme appeared in the newspaper *France Antilles*.

Trinidad and Tobago

At the southern end of the Caribbean chain, in Trinidad and Tobago, a demonstration of 'yogic flying' was held on 7 September at the Fatima College auditorium in **Port-of-Spain**, the capital city. Beneath a banner that read '7000 in the Republic of Trinidad and Tobago, a Unified Field Based Perfect Civilization', the Permanent Secretary of the Ministry of Sports, Culture, and Youth Affairs formally opened the events. Trinidad's Prime Minister was represented by his private secretary.

In an article headlined, 'Men who fly', *Sunday Punch* wrote, 'Could you believe that humans are able to fly? Not in an aeroplane or with the aid of engines, but with sheer mental strength. This was the case when the International Meditation Society demonstrated the yogic flying technique last weekend.' Noting that 4,000 Trinidadians practise the Transcendental Meditation technique, a number that is growing rapidly, the article said, 'What seems to attract participants is the enormous inner peace that is attained after Transcendental Meditation.'

Panama

'Peace is not something to discuss; it must be experienced and enjoyed,' said Mercedes Appin, national leader of Maharishi's movement in Panama, following the demonstration in **Panama City**. Many of the 75 guests who saw a TM-Sidha fly effortlessly up onto a two-foot-high stack of foam mattresses were inspired to follow Mrs Appin's advice. Reports in the national papers and a national television broadcast fueled their enthusiasm, not only for Transcendental Meditation, Mrs Appin reported, but also for Maharishi Ayurveda.

El Salvador and Guatemala

Articles in El Salvador's *La Prensa Grafica* and *El Mundo* gave advance notice of the demonstration at the Chamber of Commerce in **San Salvador**, which was organized by the Maharishi Institute of Natural Law.

In Guatemala, 100 people witnessed 'yogic flying' in **Guatemala City's** National Theatre. After the demonstration, Gustavo Martinez, a leader of Maharishi's movement in Guatemala, told the audience that 'This is something the whole world needs urgently, especially Central America. We have seen that there exists a technique to accomplish peace and that any country can use it.'

An interviewer from *Prensa Libre* asked other members of the Guatemalan Association for Transcendental Meditation how the TM-Sidhi technique helps 'in these turbulent times.'

One TM-Sidha replied that 'The turbulence of today's world is due to the tension and stress in world consciousness, which is a reflection of individual consciousness. If we are not at peace with ourselves, we cannot be at peace with other people. The TM-Sidhi technique eliminates stress in the individual and the environment. The programme generates such a high degree of coherence in brain activity that, according to scientific studies, only 7,000 people practising it together in one place are needed to radiate coherence to the whole world.'

The published interview included three photographs of the 'yogic flying' demonstration. On 22 August, a second article appeared in *El Grafico*.

Mexico

In **Mexico City**, a banner reading 'Apoyo de la Ley Natural' ('Alliance with Natural Law') stretched across the wall of the Polyform Cultural Siqueiros, the hall in which a large audience had heard Maharishi speak in 1977. On 15 August, 600 people filled the hall to capacity as five TM-Sidhas flew for peace, their red shirts decorated with a world map on which lines of coherence radiated out from Mexico to all other nations. National television devoted five minutes to the event, and two of Mexico's leading daily newspapers, *Excelsior* and *El Universal*, published pictures and full accounts. One month later, similar demonstrations were held in **Puebla**, where 100 people came, and **Guadalajara**, where 70 guests and several radio and press journalists attended.

Chile

In Chile, four national daily newspapers—*El Mercurio, La Tercera, Ultimas Noticias,* and *La Cuarta*—published reports of the 15 August demonstrations in **Santiago** and **Viña del Mar**, as did National Television and Catholic University Television in both Santiago and Valparaíso. The newspaper *El Sur* and local television reported on the demonstration in **Concepción** on 24 September, and University of Chile Television produced two specials covering all aspects of Maharishi's Programme to Create World Peace.

Argentina, Uruguay, and Bolivia

The inauguration in **Montevideo**, Uruguay, was held on 15 August. On 26 September, other demonstrations were held in **Buenos Aires** and **Cordoba**, Argentina, and in **La Paz**, Bolivia.

Ecuador

On 15 August, 50 Ecuadorians came to the Liceo Alpha, the academy for the Transcendental Meditation programme in **Guayaquil**. Three television stations reported, and the leading national paper, *El Universo*, published the news that 'by mere intention alone, the mind can make the body lift up in the TM-Sidhi programme, and the coherence this creates can create world peace.'

Colombia, Venezuela, and Suriname

In **Bogota**, Colombia, and in **Caracas**, Venezuela, many members of the local press attended demonstra-

WORLD PEACE • GLOBAL INAUGURATION

INAUGURATING MAHARISHI'S PROGRAMME TO CREATE WORLD PEACE—LATIN AMERICA AND THE CARIBBEAN

tions. Among the 50 other guests at the Caracas Hilton were engineers, lawyers, writers, industrialists, and publishers. The Bogota demonstration was held at the Tequendama Hotel, and the guests included a Colombian Chamber of Congress Representative, the Chairman of the International Academy for Human Dignity, and other prominent citizens. The director of one of Colombia's most respected television programmes, 'El Mundo Hoy y Mañana' ('The World Today and Tomorrow'), was among the journalists present, as were reporters from 'El Noticiero Cinevision' ('Cinevision News') and *El Tiempo*, one of Colombia's national papers. And on 6 November, eight TM-Sidhas demonstrated 'yogic flying' in **Paramaribo**, Suriname.

Peru

In **Lima**, Peru, a national senator and other leading politicians and government officials as well as members of the diplomatic corps, eminent physicians, top businessmen, and university professors were among a distinguished audience of 120 people at the demonstration on 15 August at the Miraflores Cesar's Hotel. A second demonstration for 50 people was given on 9 September in the auditorium of the Ministry of Education, and journalists from 10 newspapers and magazines attended.

The newspaper *El Comercio* reported, 'In an unprecedented exhibition, two Peruvian "Sidhas", supported by the power of their minds, "flew" innumerable times before astonished reporters across hard foam mattresses stretched out on the floor .... "Yogic flying" ... consists of the body lifting up and moving in fairly long leaps upon attaining maximum mental co-ordination. It is a plainly amazing spectacle.'

Students at Colegio Maharishi, the largest building in the Dominican Republic, where a demonstration of Maharishi's Programme to Create World Peace was held on 15 August 1986.

MAHARISHI'S PROGRAMME TO CREATE

INAUGURATING MAHARISHI'S PROGRAMME TO CREATE WORLD PEACE—LATIN AMERICA AND THE CARIBBEAN

'Yogic flying' at the Maharishi School of Santo Domingo.

A smiling champion is congratulated on his success in Santo Domingo.

Dr Benjamin Feldman, Governor General of the World Government of the Age of Enlightenment for Latin American and the Caribbean (second from right) and Dr Antonio Panochia, a distinguished physician (far left), with the champions at the Dominican Republic 'yogic flying' competition.

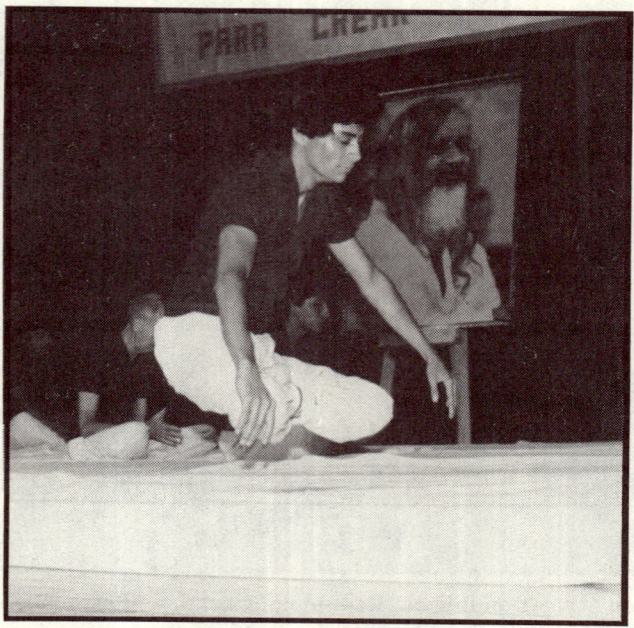
'Yogic flying' in Guatemala City, Guatemala.

'Yogic flying' for world peace in Lima, Peru.

WORLD PEACE • GLOBAL INAUGURATION

INAUGURATING MAHARISHI'S PROGRAMME TO CREATE WORLD PEACE—LATIN AMERICA AND THE CARIBBEAN

The Curaçao demonstration drew more than a thousand spectators.

The Curaçao TM-Sidhas.

H E Don Martina (left), Prime Minister of the Netherlands Antilles, and Mr Errol Cora, President of the Workers and Teachers Unions, at the Curaçao demonstration.

Meditating before the demonstration in Guadeloupe.

The inauguration in Trinidad and Tobago.

MAHARISHI'S PROGRAMME TO CREATE

INAUGURATING MAHARISHI'S PROGRAMME TO CREATE WORLD PEACE—LATIN AMERICA AND THE CARIBBEAN

Group meditation precedes the demonstration of 'yogic flying' in Venezuela.

Governors of the Age of Enlightenment (left to right) Silvia Martinez de Wolfermann, Professor Abdón Ricardo Hernández Trujillo, Alvaro Hipólito Salinas Contreras, and José A. Alayón Ramos inaugurate Maharishi's Programme to Create World Peace at the Caracas Hilton.

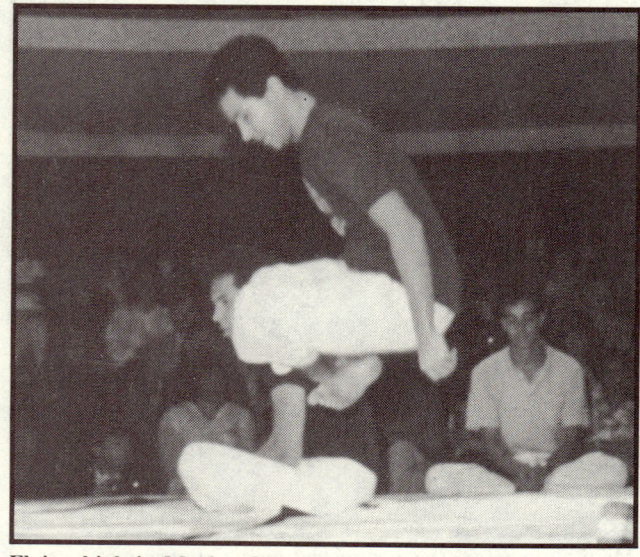

Flying high in Mexico City.

WORLD PEACE • GLOBAL INAUGURATION

PRESS REPORTS FROM LATIN AMERICA AND THE CARIBBEAN

Chile • *La Cuarta*
Santiago   13 July 1986   (Spanish)

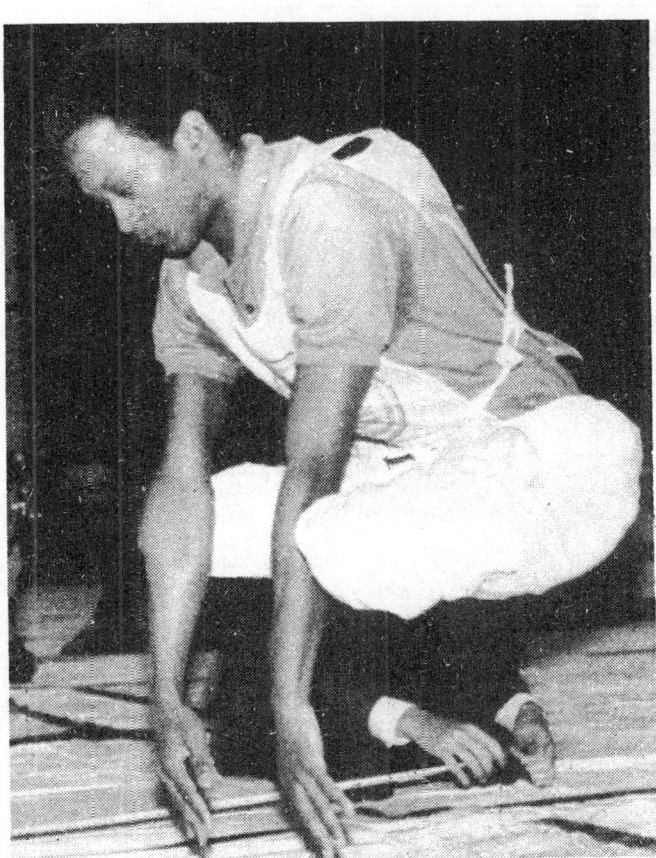

Después de ver esta foto, usted seguramente creerá todo lo que le digan acerca del yoga. Según los iniciados, el yoga no es sólo una manera de perfeccionar el cuerpo, sino también el espíritu. Por eso le dan mucha importancia a la relajación mental y corporal. Pero el negrito de la foto se pasó. Eddie Grob hizo esta demostración sensacional en el Centro de convenciones de Washington. Fotógrafos, periodistas y curiosos vieron cómo se elevaba del suelo mostrando la técnica del llamado "Vuelo Yoga". usted puede comenzar a practicarlo en su casa (AP).

PRESS REPORTS FROM LATIN AMERICA AND THE CARIBBEAN

Chile • *La Estrella*

Valparaiso 14 August 1986 (Spanish)

Espectacular demostración harán "capos" de la meditación trascendental.—

Levitación y vuelos con fuerza mental en Viña

Una demostración de avanzadas técnicas que permiten a las personas levitar e incluso desplazarse por el espacio sin ningún apoyo, efectuarán mañana en Viña del Mar expertos del Instituto de Meditación Trascendental (IMT).

Según se explicó a La Estrella, la práctica de la denominada "Técnica SIDHIS" ofrece al individuo la oportunidad de desarrollar capacidades físico-mentales que se encuentran latentes en la persona.

Representantes del IMT señalaron que la práctica de la técnica SIDHIS proporciona al individuo alternativas eficaces para lograr un reordenamiento interior mental y, a la vez, una forma efectiva de dar solución a problemas y conflictos.

En nuestro país, las técnicas básicas de levitación son practicadas actualmente por alrededor de 500 personas, mientras que la práctica de la Meditación Trascendetal ha sido asumida ya por más de 22 mil personas.

Según se indicó, el ser humano vive con un 10 por ciento de su capacidad mental y física, a menudo en desorden, pudiendo lograr una armonía de hasta más de un 90 por ciento a partir de la práctica de técnicas como la SIDHIS.

En países como Estados Unidos, la práctica de las técnicas de levitación se encuentra en un avanzado grado de desarrollo. Incluso, en algunas universidades norteamericanas, se han efectuado verdaderas competencias entre levitantes en las que varios de ellos han logrado desplazarse a más de 70 metros de distancia por el aire.

Diversos antecedentes sobre la meditación trascendental y las técnicas de levitación serán dados a conocer mañana, en el hotel San Martín de Viña del Mar, en una reunión a la que han sido invitados autoridades y representantes de los medios de comunicación social de la zona.

Durante la reunión, los instructores de meditación trascendental Luis Aparicio y Rafael de la Puente harán una demostración de levitación, mientras que el profesor de la USM, Luis Paredes, se referirá a los aspectos científicos de la mencionada técnica.

WORLD PEACE • GLOBAL INAUGURATION

PRESS REPORTS FROM LATIN AMERICA AND THE CARIBBEAN

Chile • *El Mercurio*

Santiago 16 August 1985 (Spanish)

Movimiento por la Paz Mundial:
Exhibieron Técnica del "Vuelo Yógico"

■ En céntrico hotel los seguidores del Maharishi mostraron modalidad de meditación trascendental que -afirman- servirá para desterrar guerras y el terrorismo.

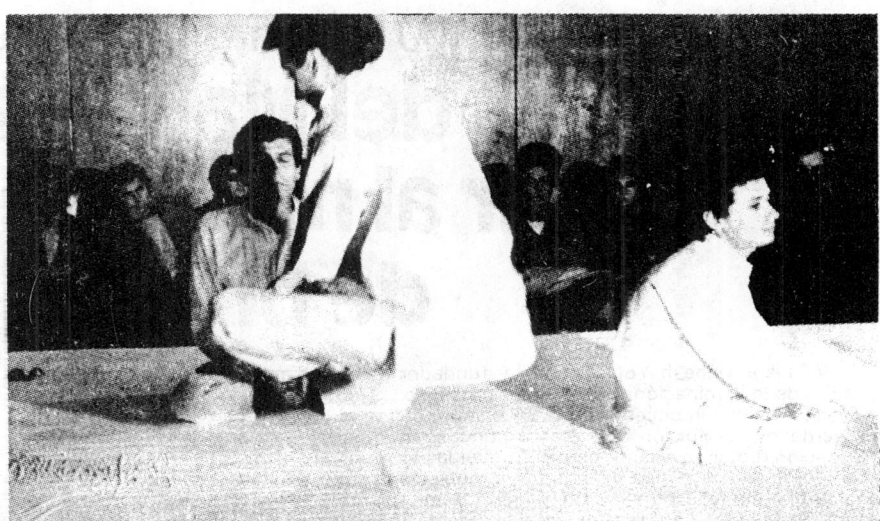

Una demostración de la técnica del "vuelo yógico", a través de la meditación trascental, se realizó ayer en un céntrico hotel de la capital. Aunque la fotografía hace aparecer a este joven en estado de meditación, lo cierto es que él y otros tres meditadores mostraron ayer la primera fase de esta técnica y que equivale a una serie de saltos con las piernas entrecruzadas (en posición de loto).

Una exhibición de la milenaria técnica del "vuelo yógico" hizo ayer en esta capital un grupo de seguidores chilenos de la "Tecnología Maharishi del Campo Unificado".

Tras una extensa charla acerca de los objetivos de esta técnica de meditación trascendental, que apunta a lograr la paz mundial, cuatro varones, vestidos de impecables trajes blancos, hicieron una demostración ante un centenar de espectadores.

Ellos mostraron la primera etapa del "vuelo yógico", una de las expresiones de la técnica Sidhis MT. Sentados en la posición de loto, y tras cinco minutos de quieta y silenciosa meditación —interrumpida sólo por el ruido de los flashes de los reporteros gráficos— los cuatro meditadores comenzaron a saltar sentados y con las piernas entrecruzadas.

La presidenta de la Asociación de Damas del Instituto de Meditación Trascendental, Astrid Cáceres, dijo que esta técnica permite una plena armonía entre mente y cuerpo.

Sostuvo que en esta reunión sólo se exhibió la primera fase del "vuelo yógico", que corresponde a una serie de saltos en posición de loto, algunos de los cuales pueden a llegar a los 50 centímetros de la superficie.

Las otras dos fases -ya más avanzadas, según explicó- corresponden a una especie de flotación y a "poder volar y desplazarse por el aire", las cuales -reconoció- aún no se logran entre los chilenos que cultivan esta técnica.

Al resumir los objetivos de la experiencia, hecha sobre una bien acolchada superficie blanca, dijo que "la demostración científica ha demostrado que a través de esta técnica los individuos pueden crear coherencia en la conciencia mundial" e irradiar armonía "para evitar los conflictos y desastres mundiales"

Relató que tras una experiencia realizada en 1984, en Estados Unidos, se reunieron 7 mil expertos en esta técnica y se demostró que en el mundo bajaron los índices de conflictos bélicos, homicidios, suicidios y "creció la positividad y armonía en el mundo".

Señaló que la cifra de 7 mil personas no fue elegida al azar. Equivale a la raíz cuadrada del uno por ciento de la población mundial. Este movimiento estima que si esa cantidad de personas se reúne, en forma permanente, a practicar la meditación trascendental, incluyendo la técnica del vuelo yógico, habrá una armonía global que fomentará la paz mundial.

La demostración de ayer corresponde al inauguración simultánea en 108 países del programa "Maharishi para crear la Paz Mundial". La idea, según se explicó casi al final de la charla, es reunir 100 millones de dólares en aportes para que, mediante los intereses que devengue esa cantidad, se pueda sustentar a 7 mil practicantes de esa técnica que -se afirmó- "meditarán por la paz del mundo en un lugar de la India".

PRESS REPORTS FROM LATIN AMERICA AND THE CARIBBEAN

Chile • *La Cuarta*
Santiago 16 August 1986 (Spanish)

Buscan ayudita de 100 millones de dólares para sus maestros
Discípulos del Maharishi quieren salvar al mundo a punta de brincos

El Maharishi Mahesh Yogi, profeta y fundador del "Gobierno Mundial de la Era de la Iluminación", debe estar orgulloso... Cuatro de sus pupilos en Chile, vestidos impecablemente de blanco, dieron al mediodía de ayer una verdadera exhibición de saltos o brincos sin impulso -paso previo a la levitación (flotar en el aire)- para promover la paz mundial.

Con la presencia de los medios de comunicación y de un centenar de seguidores -entre ellos la actriz Jael Unger-, estos "canguros" del Programa Meditación Trascendental y Dishis-MT hicieron su demostración huacha, para dar a conocer los alcances de su movimiento, en el Salón Montt del Hotel Crowne Plaza.

Estos místicos chiquilines, que suman varios miles a través del mundo, están segurísimos de crear al cabo de algunos años una sociedad ideal, a través de un programa que provee la tecnología para desarrollar el pleno potencial del individuo, mejorando de esta forma la calidad de la vida. Cháchara o realidad, los instructores Héctor Oberg y Astrid Cáceres, el físico Luis Paredes y el psicólogo Ignacio Rossel -oradores en la conferencia- hablaron maravillas de la "tecnología del campo unificado", que desarrolla la potencia mental, mejora la salud y crea un potente comportamiento social.

Como los discípulos del Maharishi -ciudadano indio (de la India) y amante de las flores-, resaltan que su programa está científicamente probado, y también se atreven a decir que el "Efecto Maharishi", el fenómeno que resulta de la influencia de orden y coherencia propagada en la conciencia colectiva de la sociedad cuando el uno por ciento de la población practica la meditación trascendental, contribuye poderosamente a la Humanidad.

SUPER-HOMBRES

Con las tejas corridas o no -hay quienes no aceptaron este tipo de ondas-, los maharishis inauguraron el amanecer de la Era de la Iluminación para todos los continentes, el 12 de enero de 1975, en el lago Lucerna, Suiza, cuando se dieron cuenta de la funcionalidad del "Efecto Maharishi". Luego, el caperuzo de la organización decretó el Gobierno Mundial de la Era de la Iluminación y extendió su soberanía en el ámbito de la conciencia.

La meditación trascendental y Sidhis-MT permite, a juicio de sus expertos, que el alumno tenga un descanso más profundo; posea mayor orden del funcionamiento cerebral, creatividad y recuperación fisiológica más rápida; un funcionamiento más eficiente del sistema nervioso; mejor adaptación a los ruidos y estímulos de tensión; mejor presión arterial; que no tenga insomnio; reacciones más rápidas y mejor coordinación de la mente y el cuerpo, y mayor desarrollo de la personalidad, productividad e inteligencia.

ETAPAS DEL VUELO

En el programa de meditación están contemplados tres tipo de vuelo, en los cuales aumenta la coherencia en las ondas del cerebro y una armonía perfecta entre mente y cuerpo.

En la primera etapa los muchachos pueden saltar o brincar sin impulso (en Chile hay unos 300 "canguros"), en la segunda se puede levitar y,

El Maharishi predica pura paz y amor, asegurando que uno no está para sufrir en la tierra, sino que para pasarlo harto bien. Es el fundador del Programa Meditación Trascendental y Sidhis-MT.

en la tercera, desplazarse libremente y volar por los aires, cuestión que sólo pueden lograr los grandes maestros indios.

Luis Aparicio, Marco Antonio López, Carlos Amhed y Pedro Ugalde, los demostradores chilenos del brinco, dejaron con la boca abierta al respetable con una meditación trascendental y posteriormente saltos, que los dejó absolutamente felices, porque así colaboraron con la paz mundial.

Según la teoría del campo unificado, que tuvo su máxima expresión en enero de 1984 con una asamblea de 7.000 expertos en vuelos, se puede lograr una sociedad ideal con la fuerza mental que efectúan miles de personas en el mundo por medio del programa. Así, por ejemplo, se verificó a través de un experimento que ciudades con mayor cantidad de discípulos de Maharishi tienen menos crímenes y menos enfermedades que ciudades de otro tipo.

AYUDITA DE 100 MILLONES

El programa de Maharishi tiene planificada una ciudad en la India para unos 10 mil expertos que ayuden al mundo a través del "campo unificado", en forma permanente. Pero como no todo puede ser sacrificio y trabajo, se creó un Fondo Internacional para recibir donaciones hasta completar ¡100 MILLONES DE DOLARES! para que estos 10 mil niños puedan subsistir sin problemas.

Tremendos saltos se pegaron cuatro discípulos chilenos del Maharishi, gracias a la meditación trascendental. De paso ayudaron con sus ondas cerebrales -que se unen a otras del extranjero- para formar un campo de paz. Estos "canguros" funcionan en Las Torcazas 103, de Santiago.

Obsérvese el brinco que da este señor sin ayuda de nada más que de su potencia mental. Las manos están apretadas y las piernas muy cruzadas. Todavía no logran en Chile la levitación.

MAHARISHI'S PROGRAMME TO CREATE

PRESS REPORTS FROM LATIN AMERICA AND THE CARIBBEAN

Chile • *La Estrella*

Valparaiso   16 August 1986   (Spanish)

Asombrosa exhibición en Viña

ESTOS YOGAS VUELAN

WORLD PEACE • GLOBAL INAUGURATION

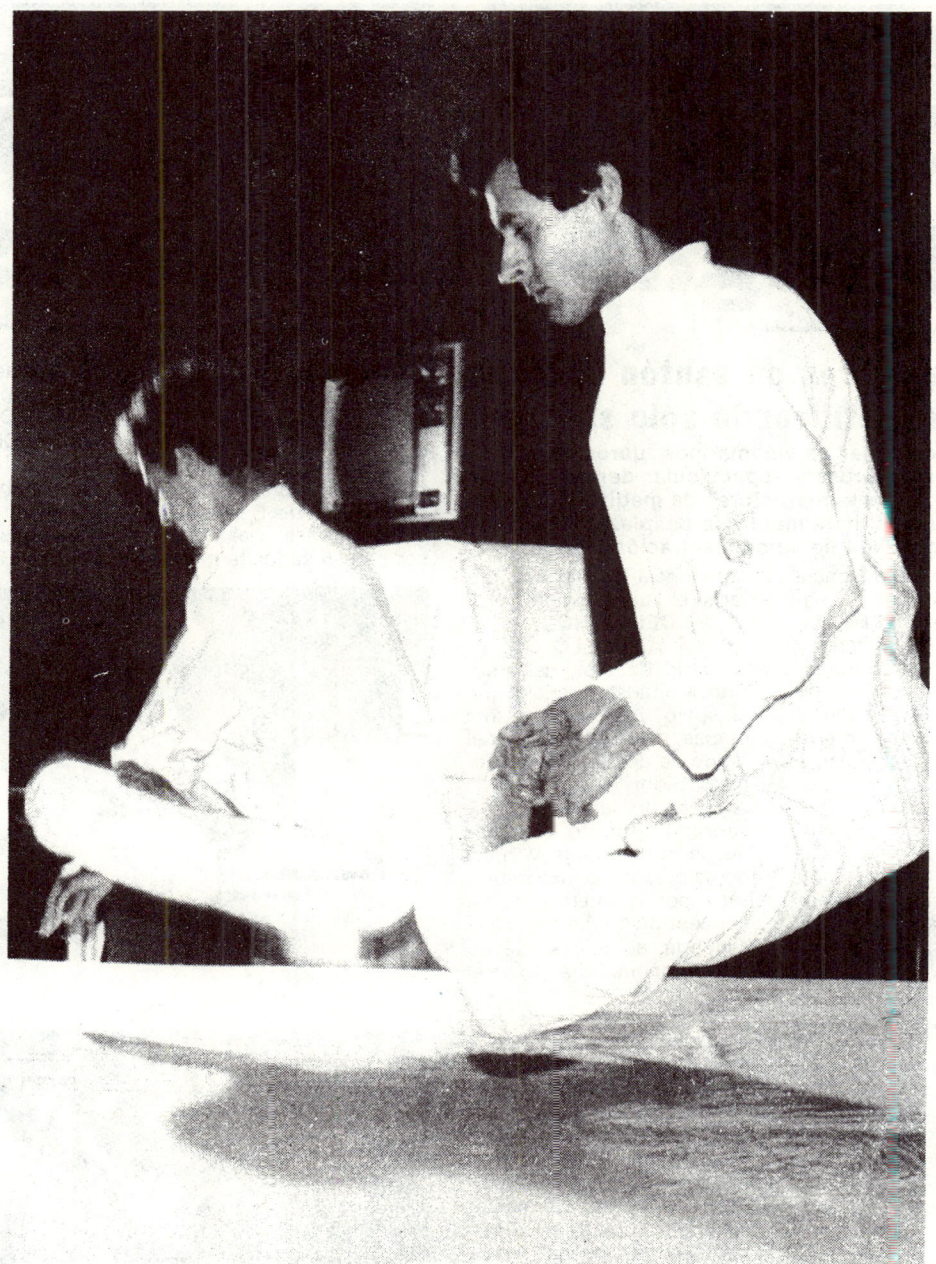

Seguidores santiaguinos y viñamarinos del santón hindú Maharishi Mahesh Yogi han desarrollado una increíble técnica que les permite desplazarse por el aire y volar, utilizando sólo su concentración mental. La técnica, denominada "Sidhis", hace que el individuo levite y vuele al alcanzar el máximo punto de coherencia entre la mente y el cuerpo. En la fotografía, Luis Aparicio y Pedro Ugalde en pleno vuelo durante la espectacular demostración de anoche ante un centenar de atónitos testigos.

Anoche, en Viña del Mar.—
Asombrosa exhibición de yogas "voladores"

* Seguidores de santón hindú se desplazan por el aire, utilizando sólo su concentración mental

Más de un centenar de viñamarinos fueron testigos anoche de la asombrosa y espectacular demostración efectuada por yogas e instructores de meditación trascendental, quienes literalmente se desplazaron por el aire sin otro impulso que su concentración mental.

La singular experiencia tuvo lugar en uno de los salones del hotel San Martín, donde cuatro instructores y practicantes de la denominada técnica "Sidhis" de meditación trascendental volaron a su gusto ante el sorprendido público presente.

La técnica "Sidhis", que posibilita el denominado "vuelo yógico", está basada en la teoría del Campo Unificado desarrollada por el Maharishi Mahesh Yogi, santón hindú que es el líder mundial de una cruzada que busca establecer la paz universal permanente, a través de la masificación de la "Sidhis" en 108 países del mundo.

Luis Paredes, físico de la Universidad Santa María, señaló que el vuelo yógico es un fenómeno posible de explicar a través de la física cuántica.

Dijo que la coherencia alcanzada entre mente y cuerpo es cada vez mayor según el tiempo de práctica de la meditación trascendental y la técnica "Sidhis". Así, el punto más alto de coherencia se alcanza durante el vuelo yógico.

DEL BRINCO AL VUELO

Astrid Casaret, del Instituto Maharishi, señaló que el vuelo yógico tiene tres etapas, determinadas por el grado de dominio de la técnica "Sidhis".

En la primera etapa, alcanzado el punto de coherencia entre mente y cuerpo, la persona brinca impulsada por la energía de su concentración mental. En la segunda, el individuo levita y se mantiene flotando en el aire.

La tercera etapa, de perfección absoluta, permite al individuo **volar**, desplazarse a voluntad en distancias de hasta varios metros.

A principios del pasado mes de julio se realizó en Washington, Estados Unidos, la Primera Olimpiada de Vuelo Yógico, en la que participaron competidores de distintos países.

Las pruebas cumplidas durante la Olimpiada fueron realmente increíbles. Eddie Gob, de las islas Guadalupe, **voló** una distancia de 50 metros en 23,3 segundos. Lo mismo hicieron Blair Butterfield, de Bermuda, y el canadiense Blaine Watson, destacados entre los supervoladores de la olimpiada.

VOLADORES CRIOLLOS

La exhibición realizada anoche en Viña del Mar estuvo a cargo de los instructores Luis Aparicio, Pedro Ugalde, Carlos Ahmed y

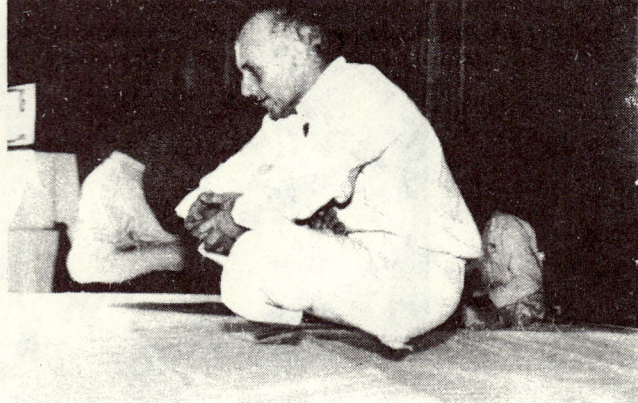

Carlos Ahmed permanece en el aire, en pleno vuelo, impulsado por su concentración mental. Abajo, un aspecto del público que presenció la asombrosa exhibición.

Marcos Schuller.

Sentados en posición de meditación sobre un colchoneta de lona blanca, los cuatro voladores iniciaron un breve proceso de concentración mental.

Cuatro o cinco minutos después, uno de los meditantes comenzó a elevarse y luego voló cayendo un metro y medio más adelante, para enseguida volver a elevarse y desplazarse por el aire otro trecho similar.

Uno a uno, los meditantes fueron incorporándose a los vuelos, sumidos en un estado de concentración absoluto en el que alcanzaron la plena coherencia entre sus mentes y cuerpos.

Los asistentes a la espectacular exhibición siguieron con gran interés cada una de las evoluciones de los hombres-voladores quienes incluso efectuaron giros en el aire sin mayor problema.

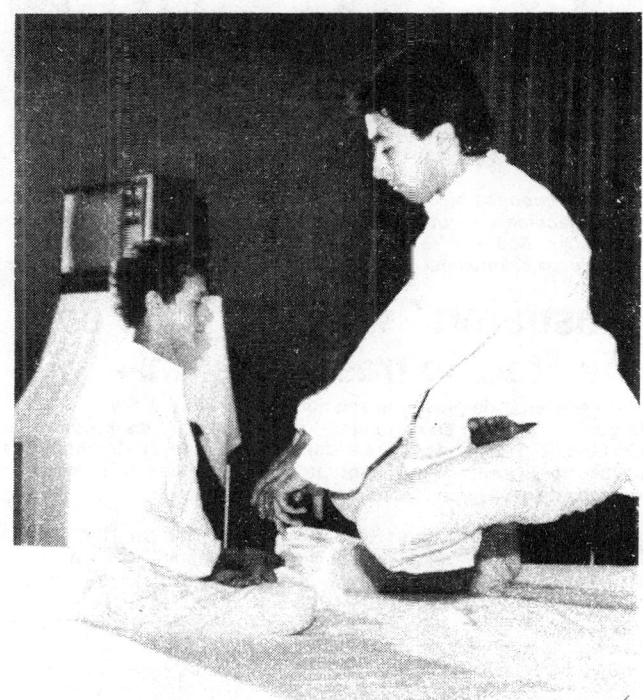

Marcos Schuller se eleva e inicia su vuelo, mientras, en segundo plano, Luis Aparicio se prepara para hacer lo mismo.

PRESS REPORTS FROM LATIN AMERICA AND THE CARIBBEAN

Chile • *Tercera de la Hora*

Santiago   16 August 1986   (Spanish)

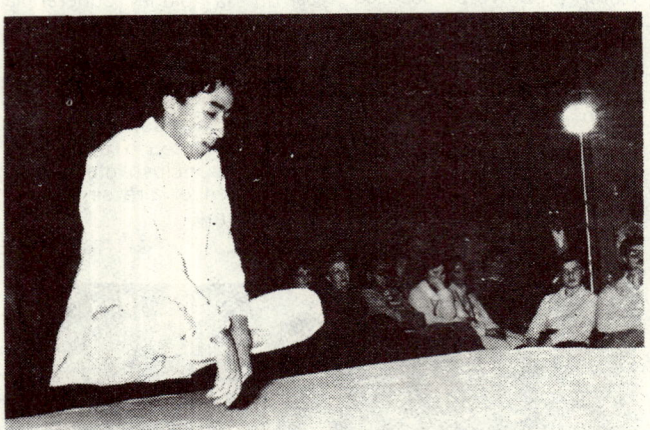

Cuatro personas hicieron demostración de saltos, en el marco de la técnica de vuelo yógico de los Sidhis, fundada por el Maharishi Mahesh Yogi. Aquí, sobre una gran colchoneta, en uno de los salones del Hotel Crowne Plaza.

Mostraron "vuelo yógico" con meditación trascendental

Un centenar de personas asistieron en el Hotel Crowne Plaza a lo que en principio se denominó "vuelo yógico", del Instituto de Meditación Trascendental. La demostración de cuatro hombres se centró finalmente en la etapa de saltos, después de cinco minutos de meditación trascendental.

El llamado programa de Maharishi para crear paz mundial se inició con la exposición de algunos profesionales adherentes a la entidad, quienes dieron sus puntos de vista para fundamentar la demostración que se haría posteriormente. Héctor Oberg explicó finalmente que la demostración del vuelo yógico no se haría, sino en su primera etapa, a cargo de cuatro alumnos destacados: Luis Aparicio, Marco Antonio López, Carlos Amhed y Pedro Ugalde.

Oberg explicó que la meditación trascendental permite la elevación de un individuo, hasta su desplazamiento en el aire, al final de tres etapas de acción. Estas son: saltar, levitar y desplazarse en el aire. En la ocasión, los cuatro expositores sólo saltaron, sobre una amplia colchoneta que se desplegó en una de las salas del Hotel Crowne Plaza.

Asimismo se pidió colaboración para concretar la meta de reunir cien millones de dólares, con el fin de financiar, con los intereses, la permanencia de 7.000 expertos en meditación trascendental en una ciudad, que preside el Maharishi Mahesh Yogi.

WORLD PEACE • GLOBAL INAUGURATION

PRESS REPORTS FROM LATIN AMERICA AND THE CARIBBEAN

Chile • *El Sur*
Concepcion   28 September 1986   (Spanish)

Uno de los participantes en la demostración de levitación o "saltos".

Aseguran que la levitación terminará con el terrorismo

Una demostración de levitación, como expresión máxima del equilibrio entre la mente y el cuerpo, hizo el Instituto de Meditación Trascendental en Concepción. José Herrera y Astrid Cáceres, impulsores de esta técnica, explicaron que este es un método para crear una efectiva paz mundial e incluso terminar con el terrorismo.

"El vuelo yógico -dijo Astrid Cáceres- genera ondas positivas, al igual que una bomba atómica crea ondas destructivas que alcanzan más allá del lugar mismo de la explosión".

Previo a la demostración de levitación, que estuvo a cargo de dos cultores de esta técnica, José Herrera y Astrid Cáceres explicaron a los asistentes los alcances del programa de maharishi para crear paz mundial. También entregaron detalles de las investigaciones científicas que se han realizado para probar que esto no tiene truco alguno y que sólo obedece a reglas de la física y del equilibrio entre la actividad de la mente y del cuerpo.

En la actualidad, por lo que informó Astrid Cáceres, hay más de 300 investigaciones serias realizadas en este campo. En Chile la primera se hizo en 1978 con internos de la Penitenciaría de Santiago. El experimento estuvo a cargo de sicólogos de Gendarmería y el año pasado se hizo algo similar en el Centro de Readaptación Social de Colina. "Se está usando la meditación trascendental como medio de rehabilitación", dijo.

El principio básico general de este proyecto para lograr la paz mundial se basa en que si se logra el equilibrio entre el cuerpo y la mente en cada persona se puede lograr un equilibrio en la conciencia colectiva de las naciones y del mundo.

La demostración de levitación se hizo arriba de una colchoneta de espuma regalada por una fábrica local y Carlos Ahmed y Pedro Ugalde -dos meditantes- efectivamente saltaron del suelo y flotaron en más de una ocasión, luego de cinco minutos de concentración.

José Herrera dio a conocer que hay "tres etapas de vuelo" consistentes en levitación, flotación y vuelo. Dijo también que ya se han hecho competencias lográndose vuelos horizontales de 60 metros a 50 centímetros del suelo.

"Dentro de poco esto estará incluido en las olimpíadas", finalizó.

PRESS REPORTS FROM LATIN AMERICA AND THE CARIBBEAN

Columbia • *El Tiempo*
Bogota   19 September 1986   (Spanish)

Vuelo yógico

El vuelo yógico se logra a través de la meditación trascendental, una forma de disminuir los latidos del corazón y la cantidad de oxígeno, se dijo en conferencia que sobre el tema se dictó en el Hotel Tequendama. De acuerdo con los promotores, ésta constituye una vía para buscar la paz.

Ecuador • *Expresso*

Guayaquil 15 August 1986 (Spanish)

En Guayaquil y otros países del mundo:

Vuelo yogi a través de la meditación trascendental

Gracias a las instrucciones impartidas por expertos en Tecnología Maharishi del Campo Unificado Programa MT y MT-Sidhis, en 108 países del mundo hoy se realizará (incluyendo a Guayaquil), una demostración del Vuelo Yogi a través de la Meditación Transcedental, técnica traída a Occidente por Maharishi Mahesh Yogi, un científico indio, especializado en física, que a principios guardaba celosamente el secreto pero que, a medida que pasó el tiempo creyó conveniente hacerla conocer para evitar en el hombre las enfermedades de adaptación, por que si el cuerpo humano no recibe suficiente descanso para restaurar el equilibrio, los efectos perjudiciales del stress se cumulan y crean una condición crónica, que va destruyendo el bienestar físico emocional.

En nuestra ciudad, precisamente en Arguelles 409, entre Rosendo Avilés y O'Connor, se encuentra el Instituto de la Ciencia de la Inteligencia Creativa, que dirige el señor Washington Ruales, quien nos dispensó una gentil visita para hacernos partícipe el programa que hoy se realizará, cual es, la demostración de la primera fase del vuelo yogi. Estuvo acompañado del señor Ernesto Bruzual, un venezolano que se encuentra de paso por nuestra ciudad, y que está relacionado también con la técnica del maestro Maharashi.

En la gráfica los distinguidos visitantes Washington Ruales, Director del Instituto de la Ciencia y la Inteligencia Creativa de Guayaquil, y Ernesto Bruzual, que presidirá esta noche la demostración de la primera fase del vuelo yogi, que se realizará en Arguelles 409, al igual que en 107 países del mundo.

El señor Ruales, nos comentó que los días jueves por la noche, en su local realizan charlas demostrativas, para profesionales, estudiantes, ejecutivos y personas interesadas en aprender la técnica para mejorar la facultad de adaptación a la vida actual, porque a través de la meditación trascedental se logran niveles de relajación más profundos que el sueño.

Ecuador • *El Universo*

Guayaquil 19 August 1986 (Spanish)

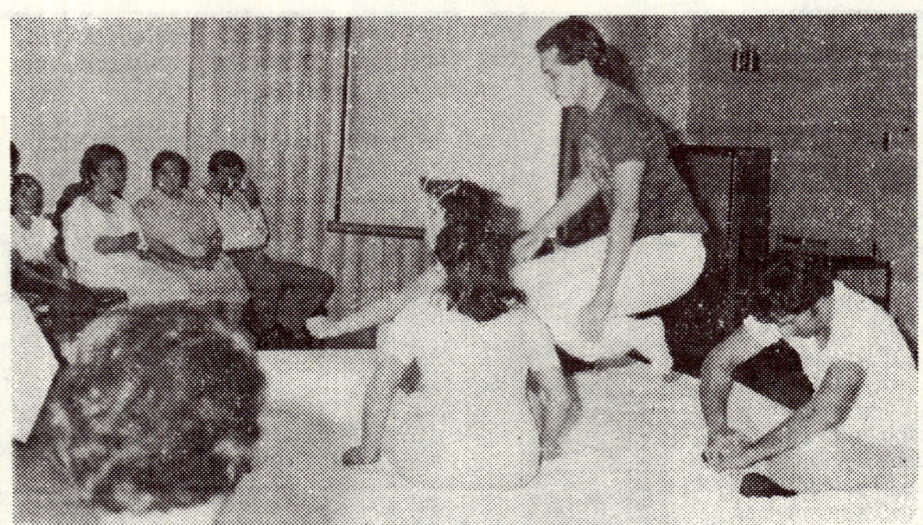

Demostración de vuelo yoqui

La Universidad Internacional Maharishi, con sede en Estados Unidos, dio a conocer en 108 países incluyendo el nuestro en la ciudad de Guayaquil, una demostración del "vuelo yoqui" logrado a través de la práctica de la Meditación Trascendental, teniendo el propósito de que los líderes de todas las sociedades y miembros de la prensa observen uno de los logros que se consiguen con esta técnica que permite una máxima coherencia en la fisiología cerebral del ser humano. Esta demostración la realizó el instructor venezolano de paso por esta ciudad, Ernesto Bruzuel, a quien vemos suspendido en el aire, junto a otros seguidores, ante la curiosidad de los asistentes.

WORLD PEACE • GLOBAL INAUGURATION

PRESS REPORTS FROM LATIN AMERICA AND THE CARIBBEAN

El Salvador • *La Prensa Grafica*
San Salvador   15 August 1986   (Spanish)

Conferencia de métodos hindúes para crear la paz

Hoy a las seis de la tarde en la Cámara de Comercio, habrá una demostración de "vuelo yogi" y conferencia sobre cómo eliminar la guerra y crear la paz.

El Instituto Maharishi de Ley natural, informa que en otros 107 países y con la misma demostración y conferencias se inaugura el Programa de Maharishi para crear la paz mundial.

En esta capital, expertos salvadoreños en la tecnología del Campo Unificado, demostrarán la técnica de "vuelo yógico" Sidhis-MT, fundada por Maharishi Mahesh Yogi.

La investigación científica, expresan, ha demostrado que a través de esta técnica los individuos pueden crear coherencia en la conciencia mundial. Este hecho es la base del programa para establecer y mantener la paz mundial.

Durante la técnica del "vuelo yógico", en el momento de máxima coherencia en la actividad cerebral como lo indica el eléctroencefalograma, el cuerpo se eleva y comienza a dar saltos.

Los organizadores de esta demostración, dicen, que los gobierno han fallado en crear la paz mundial.

Hoy en día, con el surgimiento del terrorismo, ellos no proveen seguridad a los habitantes; aún las superpotencias están constantemente con miedo y la rivalidad entre ellas amenaza la vida de cada individuo. Es ahora el momento para que los individuos tomen responsabilidad de crear y mantener la paz mundial. Sobre este tema, versará la conferencia que ofrecen hoy en la Cámara de Comercio.

El Salvador • *El Mundo*
San Salvador   15 August 1986   (Spanish)

INVITAN. Señorita Patricia Vásquez, izquierda, y María Elena Aguirre, invitan a la Inauguración Mundial del Programa de Maharishi "Para Crear La Paz Mundial", acto que se efectuará mañana a las 6 p.m. en el auditorium de la Cámara de Comercio e Industria de El Salvador. Explicaron que se darán demostraciones del "vuelo yogi", que es la tecnología para crear coherencia en la conciencia mundial y eliminar la violencia y la guerra. El evento se celebrará simultáneamente en 108 países.

PRESS REPORTS FROM LATIN AMERICA AND THE CARIBBEAN

Guadeloupe • *France – Antilles*

Pointe-à-Pitre   30 August 1986   (French)

« Seule une nouvelle graine produira une nouvelle récolte »

« Avec la montée du terrorisme et la dangereuse rivalité entre les super puissances, il est vital de créer immédiatement une infuence invincible de cohérence dans la conscience mondiale.

Il y a des centaines d'organisations dans le monde qui s'occupent de la réalisation de la paix sur terre. De nombeuses personnes essayent de créer la paix mondiale à partir de niveaux d'approche différents et variés.

Nous, à l'Institut Maharishi de la Loi Naturelle (I.M.L.N.), apprécions tous les efforts en cours pour la réalisation de la paix.

Cependant, « Seule une nouvelle graine produira une nouvelle récolte », seule une nouvelle philosophie et de nouveaux efforts fondés sur une nouvelle connaissance, réaliseront le vieux rêve des sages d'un monde en paix.

Notre approche de la paix mondiale, à l'Institut Maharishi de la Loi Naturelle, est plus holistique et fondamentale. Elle se fait à partir du niveau le plus profond du fonctionnement de la nature, où le silence éternel lui-même est la base vivante de la dynamique éternelle de l'univers : la dynamique auto-interactive du Champ Unifié de la loi naturelle, où la paix soutient le dynamisme.

C'est la raison pour laquelle la paix mondiale, créée à partir de ce niveau soutiendra un progrès illimité pour toute l'humanité.

La Technologie Maharishi du Champ Unifié, enseignée par Maharishi Mahesh Yogi, dont l'une des composantes est la Technique de Méditation Transcendantale, entraîne l'esprit humain à opérer à partir de la dynamique auto-interactive du champ unifié de toutes les lois de la nature qui est la source et le dirigeant de toutes les valeurs de l'univers. Puisque le champ unifié possède la caractéristique de corrélation infinie, une impulsion de cohérence générée à partir de ce niveau, harmonise instantanément les tendances discordantes partout dans l'environnement.

La recherche scientifique a montré que 7.000 individus (la racine carrée de 1% de la population mondiale) pratiquant la Technologie Maharishi du Champ Unifié ensemble en un même lieu, créent une influence puissante de cohérence dans toute la conscience mondiale, produisant une vague montante de directions et tendances positives de la vie partout.

Avec ce groupe de 7.000 Experts, « La paix sur terre sera puissante, et la puissance sur terre sera paisible ».

Afin de créer un groupe important pour animer le champ unifié de la loi naturelle, nous vous invitons tous : individus, élus, leaders d'organisations et d'associations, responsables à tous les niveaux de la société, à contacter l'Institut de la Loi Naturelle de la Guadeloupe pour une présentation des mécanismes permettant de créer la paix mondiale, grâce à la Technologie Maharishi du Champ Unifié ».

Les adresses de l'Institut :
A POINTE A PITRE : 86 rue Frébault, 1er étage. Tél. **82.74.44.**
A BASSE TERRE : 41 rue Baudot, 2ème étage. Tél. **81.37.90.**

Guadeloupe • *France-Antilles*

Pointe-à-Pitre   16 September 1986   (French)

Les Adeptes de la méditation transcendentale partent en guerre contre le terrorisme

Les responsables : « Nous voulons arriver à établir la paix mondiale ».

Samedi après-midi, les responsables locaux du « programme de Méditation Transcendentale Sidhis pour créer une paix mondiale » selon les préceptes du Maharishi Mhesa Yogi, avaient convié leurs adhérents et les représentants de la presse à une démonstration de la dite méthode, effectuée dans les salons de l'hôtel Novotel à Gosier.

Les praticiens de la Méditation Transcendentale seraient en Guadeloupe au nombre de 2000 personnes. Ils sont dirigés par M. Joseph Vespasien. Leur siège social se trouve au 86 de la rue Frébault à Pointe-à-Pitre. Ils sont implantés dans le département depuis 1977. Relativement discrets, bien qu'abreuvant de temps en temps les médias locaux de prospectus sur les avantages de leur « méthode », ils tenaient cette conférence à la suite du lancement mondial, effectué depuis l'Inde par le Maharishi lui-même, d'une campagne de promotion du « Programme de Méditation Transcendentale Sidhis pour la Paix Mondiale ».

SEPT MILLE PERSONNES POUR LA PAIX

Devant une assistance relativement nombreuse (près de 200 personnes), les dirigeants de la M.T. Sidhis ont donc débuté leur conférence vers 16h00. Différents intervenants allaient prendre tour à tour la parole pour souligner les bienfaits de la Méditation qu'ils préconisent. Selon eux, la M.T. Sidhis possède tellement davantages que l'on se demande pourquoi tout le monde ne la pratique pas. Elle ressemble en effet fort à la panacée universelle, aussi bonne pour l'individu que pour les nations.

Pour la personne qui la pratique, la méditation apporte de multiples dons : — diminution du stress, — repos plus profond que le sommeil normal, capacité intellectuelle accrue, réflexes plus rapides... Soit « le développement de plein potentiel de l'individu ».

Plus intéressante peut être, la possibilité d'utiliser la méditation transcendentale collective pour supprimer la violence et l'agressivité dans le monde, et en influant sur la conscience collective par l'intermédiaire du « champ unifié ». Ce dernier engloberait les domaines physiques de la science moderne, comme le nucléaire ou l'électronique pour atteindre par l'intermédiaire du cerveau humain, les lois mêmes de la nature.

Selon les dires des conférenciers, apparaît un autre fait remarquable : — à savoir que le chiffre nécessaire pour rétablir la paix dans un endroit donné du globe correspondrait à la racine carrée de un pour cent de la population ; soit pour le globe, un total de 7.000 personnes. L'on comprenait alors l'argumentation du préambule portant sur « le rétablissement de la paix dans le monde et la disparition du terrorisme : **«Nous cherchons à avoir en permanence un groupe de 7.000 personnes en méditation de par le monde. D'où la nécessité de notre campagne »**, précisait M. Vespasien.

Une fois ce chiffre atteint, l'agressivité dont notre civilisation est trop souvent victime disparaîtrait comme par enchantement...

La méditation avant le saut yogique.

LA TECHNIQUE DE L'ENVOI YOGIQUE

Finalement, on arrivait à ce qui promettait d'être le plus passionnant : — la démonstration de « l'envoi yogique », soit la possibilité de l'éviter par l'utilisation de la méditation transcendentale, en manipulant le « champ unifié ». Technique apparemment possible pour tout être possédant un cerveau, cet « envoi » avait attiré l'attention de l'auditoire qui, à l'annonce de son déroulement commençait à s'agiter, alors qu'il avait été jusque-là d'un calme olympien.

En effet, ce n'est pas tous les jours que l'on pouvait espérer voir des gens se promener dans les airs seulement par la force de leur cerveau et de leur volonté. La respiration des personnes présentes s'interrompaient alors que cinq jeunes gens, **« les techniques »**, faisaient leur apparition dans la pièce, revêtus d'un pantalon blanc et d'une chemisette vert pâle. Les pieds nus, ils s'asseyaient dans la position lotus sur les matelas disposés devant l'assistance, alors que l'un des responsables expliquaient que la démonstration n'allait concerner que la première phase de l'enseignement, la seconde phase consistant en la lévitation proprement dite et la troisième dans le déplacement aérien, « comme le foufou », précisait même M. Vespasien. ...

WORLD PEACE • GLOBAL INAUGURATION

PRESS REPORTS FROM LATIN AMERICA AND THE CARIBBEAN

Guadeloupe • *France – Antilles*

Pointe-à-Pitre   3 October 1986   (French)

Les adeptes de la méditation transcendantale s'envolent pour le bon motif

Pendant le première compétition de vol yogique.

> La race des soucougnans, les vampires humains des Antilles, serait en voie de disparition, mais le ciel de la Guadeloupe pourrait néanmoins se couvrir bientôt d'un nuage d'hommes-volants. 83 d'entre eux ont été vus voici deux semaines voguant entre sol et plafond, dans les salons de l'hôtel Novotel. Fox Bravo a été voir du côté de la Méditation Transcendantale ce que signifient ces drôles d'escadrilles.

La méditation transcendantale, tout le monde croit savoir un peu ce que c'est. En tout cas, chacun sait ce que signifie méditer. Un sympathique sage indien, le Maharishi Mahesh Yogi, dont l'un des premiers mérites retentissants dans le monde occidental fut d'intéresser les célèbres Beatles à sa science et à sa philosophie dans les années 60, a recueilli et restitué dans sa pureté une antique tradition védique. C'est elle que l'on connait aujourd'hui sous le nom de Méditation Transcendantale, ou MT pour les initiés.

« Au debut, il a choisi de s'installer aux Etats Unis pour faire connaître sa technique au monde, car c'est un pays de grande créativité » m'expliquent Jocelyne Jolivère et Fred Maya, professeurs de MT à la Guadeloupe. Et le gourou qui se double d'un homme de science à l'occidentale, puisqu'il est aussi physicien, demande à tous les savants du monde de venir vérifier ses découvertes. Des électrodes sont branchés sur des pratiquants de MT, et les savants découvrent avec stupeur que, lorsqu'ils sont plongés en méditation, leur consommation d'oxygène s'abaisse de

MAHARISHI'S PROGRAMME TO CREAT

Le Maharish Mahesh Yogi, premier initiateur et grand maître de la Méditation Transcendantale.

16 %, soit deux fois celle d'un homme plongé en sommeil profond !... Et le reste est à l'avenant, « notre santé morale et physique s'améliore. Nous parvenons à un état de santé telle que nous analysons plus vite les données soumises à notre sagacité et que, libérées des angoises du monde moderne, toutes nos facultés s'améliorent progressivement » me disent encore Fred et Jocelyne. « Sur le plan personnel, le but est de parvenir à la perfection. Sur le plan général, le but est de parvenir à la paix mondiale ». ....

J'expose tous mes doutes à Jocelyne et à Fred, et ils affinent la pensée transmise par le Mahatishi : « Les tensions mondiales et la paix commencent par des états individuels. Nous dégageons tous des vibrations qui créent une atmosphère bonne ou mauvaise. Einstein avait pressenti la théorie du champ unifié que fait constater le Maharishi Mahesh Yogi... Pour parvenir à établir la paix sur terre, il veut aujourd'hui établir partout des groupes de 7.000 personnes. 7.000, c'est la racine carrée de la population. 7.000 personnes qui émettent des ondes pacifiques cela suffit à établir l'harmonie dans un lieu donné ».

A la Guadeloupe, l'on recense 2.500 pratiquants de MT. Mais, en raison de la grande liberté que leur laisse l'institution, il est impossible de savoir si ces 2.500 adeptes méditent régulièrement et positivement deux fois par jour, comme il est préconisé. En tout cas, 83 d'entre eux sont parvenus au premier stade de la MT (Shidi, ou MT de la perfection. Ces 83 individus sont capables de se maintenir en état d'apesanteur pendant quelques secondes. Quel que soit leur poids, leurs corps s'élèvent puis il retombe. C'est le premier stade du vol yogique.

« Quand on parvient à une maitrise parfaite, on est non seulement capable de s'élever du sol mais de voler véritablement et de se diriger où l'on veut, comme le fait le Maharishi. »

C'est le Guadeloupéen Eddy Gob qui a remporté la première compétition mondiale de vol yogique organisé à Washington le 9 juillet dernier. Hugues Voutrin, un Martiniquais, s'est aussi classé parmi les meilleurs. Pour les adeptes du Maharishi, cette double victoire serait la confirmation du don énigmatique des Antillais pour les sciences et les techniques traditionnelles venues d'Asie. Jocelyne et Fred me rappellent que Montama puis Pinda ont dominé le karaté mondial, en devenant champions toutes catégories. Faut-il en déduire que nous serions les plus doués pour faire tout leur usage des connaissances transmises par les Japonais et les Indiens ?... Qui vivra verra.

Si, en tout cas, les techniques de la MT et de la MT Shidi vous intéressent, vous pouvez vous rapprocher de l'Institut de la Loi Naturelle, 86, rue Frébault, à Pointe-à-Pitre. Il y a une permanence, et le téléphone est le 82.74.44. ....

Eddy Gob et Hugues Voutrin, dit Mat, après leur victoire à Washington.

WORLD PEACE • GLOBAL INAUGURATION

PRESS REPORTS FROM LATIN AMERICA AND THE CARIBBEAN

Guatemala • *Prensa Libre*

Guatemala City   25 August 1986   (Spanish)

MECANICAS PARA CREAR PAZ MUNDIAL

La Meditación Trascendental (MT) y el programa avanzado Sidhis-MT son técnicas simples que pueden ayudar a eliminar el terrorismo y la guerra en el mundo. El fundador de estas técnicas es MAHARISHI MAHESH YOGUI. En una breve entrevista que tuvimos con las profesoras de MT Sritas. Magda López y Lucrecia Martínez, y con el Ing. Gustavo Martínez, todos miembros de la Asociación Guatemalteca de Meditación Trascendental, nos contaron algo acerca de estas técnicas:

P. Pueden decirnos por favor en que consiste esta técnica?
R. Meditación Trascendental es una técnica mental fácil y simple que se practica por 15 ó 20 minutos dos veces al día. Decimos que es fácil y simple, porque es natural, esto quiere decir que no requiere de esfuerzo alguno para practicarla y no implica cambio de costumbres, ideas, dietas, etc.
Durante la práctica de la M. T. se obtiene un descanso profundo a nivel físico y mental, éste es un estado especial para nuestro sistema nervioso, por medio del cual es posible la eliminación de tensiones y fatiga de una manera agradable y sencilla; ya que se ha comprobado que el descanso es el medio más efectivo para ello.

P. Hay alguna restricción por la cual esta técnica puede ser practicada sólo por un determinado grupo social, o está disponible para todos sin importar la raza, religión, edad y condición económica?
R. No hay ninguna restricción, cualquier persona puede aprender y practicar la técnica M. T. fácilmente. Lo único que se necesita es la capacidad natural de la mente de tener pensamientos, y no nos referimos a un pensamiento científico o complicado sino que al pensar común y corriente. Así que el único requisito para practicar la técnica M. T. es tener el deseo de aprender.

P. Uds. hablaron acerca del efecto Maharishi del 1o/o. ¿Podrían explicar detalladamente este punto?
R. El efecto Maharishi del 1o/o ha sido comprobado por varios estudios científicos realizados en Estados Unidos. En uno de estos estudios se tomaron 22 ciudades similares en número de habitantes, clima, localización y estadísticas delictivas previas. En 11 de estas ciudades el 1o/o de la población eran meditadores. En la otras no. Después de un año de observación las estadísticas mostraron que en las ciudades con el 1o/o de meditadores había disminuido considerablemente el ingreso a hospitales, el consumo de drogas, los accidentes automovilísticos, la criminología, etc. Por el contrario en las 11 ciudades control, estos parámetros aumentaron en un alto porcentaje.

P. Creen Uds. en realidad que ésta técnica Sidhis-MT pueda hacer algo en estos tiempos tan controversiales que estamos viviendo?
R. Definitivamente sí. La controversia en el mundo actual se debe a las tensiones producidas en la conciencia mundial, la cual es reflejo de la conciencia individual.

Si no estamos en paz con nosotros mismos no podemos estar en paz con los demás. Esta técnica permite la eliminación de tensiones del individuo y como resultado automático las del medio ambiente que le rodea.
Este programa genera tan profunda coherencia en las ondas cerebrales que según estudios científicos solamente se necesitan 7,000 personas practicándolo en un mismo lugar para irradiar coherencia a todo el mundo. Esta es una de las razones por las cuales se hizo la demostración en público el día 15 de agosto pasado. Existe una mecánica simple y positiva para alcanzar la paz mundial: el programa Sidhis-MT.

P. Existe alguna evidencia de que la técnica Sidhis-MT ayuda a mejorar el medio ambiente y la situación mundial en general?
R. Si, a finales del año 1,983 se llevó a cabo el primer experimento del programa de Maharishi para crear paz mundial en Fairfield, Iowa, U. S. A. En esta ocasión se reunieron 7,000 expertos practicantes del programa Sidhis-MT durante tres semanas. En este período, estudios científicos verificaron la coherencia creada en la conciencia mundial. Los conflictos internacionales disminuyeron de 20o/o a 30o/o en relación a su situación

Parte de la concurrencia que asistió al Teatro de Cámara el Viernes 15 de agosto del presente año, para presenciar la demostración de las mecánicas para crear Paz Mundial.

Ricardo Mérida, guatemalteco, practicante del programa Sidhis MT, durante la demostración de la primera etapa del "Vuelo Yóguico"..

previa a la asamblea. Hubo un incremento simultáneo en los principales índices de la bolsa de valores alrededor del mundo.

Estudios realizados en Australia y Estados Unidos mostraron una disminución en la incidencia de enfermedades infecciosas. En general hubo un descenso en las tendencias negativas y un incremento en la positividad en los campos internacionales de la política, economía y salud.

P. Si a nuestros apreciables lectores les interesara aprender esta técnica ¿Cuáles son los pasos a seguir?

R. Primero deben asistir a una Conferencia Informativa en la cual se explicará qué es la M. T., cuáles son los beneficios, mecanismos y requisitos para aprenderla. Estas conferencias se imparten todos los jueves a las 12:30 y 19:00 horas en nuestro Centro Nacional. Luego de aprender la M. T. y practicarla por algún tiempo, el paso siguiente será tomar la técnica avanzada Sidhis-M.T. Quisiéramos aprovechar esta oportunidad para extender una cordial invitación a los amables lectores de Prensa Libre quienes serán bienvenidos a nuestra Asociación localizada en Ruta 4, 6-32, Zona 4, Teléfono: 63983.

El Ing. Gustavo Martínez dirigiéndose a la concurrencia en la Inauguración del Programa Maharishi para crear Paz Mundial.

Guatemala • *El Grafico*

Guatemala City   22 August 1986   (Spanish)

Programa de Maharishi para la paz mundial, inaugurado en 108 países

El programa de Maharishi Mahesh Yogi para crear paz mundial fue inaugurado simultáneamente en 108 países, incluyendo a Guatemala, en donde se realizó el respectivo acto el pasado viernes 15, en el Teatro de Cámara del Centro Cultural, ocasión en la que fueron demostradas las mecánicas para crear paz mundial. Esta tecnología para crear coherencia en la conciencia mundial es la técnica Sidhis-MT de "Vuelo Yógico", un aspecto de la Tecnología Maharishi del Campo Unificado.

"Esta tecnología para crear paz mundial está siendo demostrada ahora a causa de la urgente necesidad de crear una influencia indomitable de coherencia en la conciencia mundial. La historia es testigo de la inhabilidad de los gobiernos para crear paz mundial, y hoy en día, con la embestida del terrorismo, los gobiernos son incapaces de proveer seguridad a la gente en cualquier lugar del mundo. Aun las superpotencias están constantemente en temor, y la rivalidad entre ellas está poniendo en peligro la vida de cada individuo", manifestó la señora Lucrecia de Martínez, director de la Asociación Guatemalteca de Meditación Trascendental, quien a continuación expresó que: "Ahora es el momento para que los individuos responsables del mundo asuman el papel de crear y mantener la paz mundial. Como Maharishi ha dicho, la Paz Mundial es un requerimiento personal e inmediato para cada hombre importante en el mundo de hoy.

"La investigación científica ha demostrado repetidamente que 7,000 expertos, practicando la técnica Sidhis - MT "Vuelo Yógico" juntos, en un solo lugar de la tierra generan una influencia de coherencia suficientemente fuerte para irradiar globalmente y purificar la conciencia de todo el mundo. Esta super radiancia de coherencia global es la inspiración y la base científica para el Programa de Maharishi para Crear Paz Mundial.

Este es un nuevo enfoque que crea físicamente la paz mundial. Durante la técnica Sidhis MT "Vuelo Yógico", en el momento de máxima coherencia en el funcionamiento cerebral, tal como indica el FEG, el cuerpo se levanta en el aire y primer estado de "Vuelo Yógico" se origina en el nivel del campo unificado tiene el carácter de infinita correlación, un impulso de coherencia generado desde este nivel, armoniza instantáneamente las tendencias discordantes en toda la naturaleza. Así, la coherencia se distribuye, neutralizando las tendencias negativas en el ambiente.

El Programa de Maharishi para Crear Paz Mundial es una oportunidad para que aquellos que están más interesados en el futuro de la Humanidad, hagan algo que realmente funcione. Está siendo inaugurado con una conciencia profunda de la necesidad de acelerar el crecimiento de la paz verdadera sobre la tierra, y con una gran apreciación por todos los esfuerzos que se han hecho hasta este momento, por la paz mundial.

En las palabras de Maharishi, "hay cientos de organizaciones para la paz alrededor del mundo. La gente está tratando de crear la paz desde varios niveles diferentes de enfoque. Nuestra apreciación va hacia todos los esfuerzos que están siendo realizados en favor de la paz mundial".

"Nuestro enfoque de la paz mundial es completo y muy básico. Es desde ese nivel más básico del funcionamiento de la naturaleza, donde el silencio eterno mismo es la base viva de las dinámicas eternas del universo —las dinámicas interactuantes del campo unificado de la ley natural— donde la paz sostiene al dinamismo.

Es por eso que la paz mundial creada desde este nivel sostendrá un progreso infinito para toda la humanidad.

"Conocimiento sobre este programa que tiene el potencial de cumplir al fin la aspiración de paz mundial que ha sido acariciada por los sabios a través de los siglos" concluyó la señora de Martínez, puede obtenerse en la sede de la Asociación Guatemalteca de Meditación Trascendental, en sus oficinas de la Ruta 4 y Vía 6-32, zona 4 teléfono 63983.

WORLD PEACE • GLOBAL INAUGURATION

PRESS REPORTS FROM LATIN AMERICA AND THE CARIBBEAN

Mexico • *Excelsior*

Mexico City   21 September 1986   (Spanish)

Se Inauguró Programa Para Crear la paz Mundial

El 15 de agosto pasado se inauguró en la ciudad de México y en otras 108 ciudades de diferentes países del mundo el Programa de Maharishi para crear paz mundial, el cual fue seguido de una demostración de un mecanismo capaz de generar coherencia y armonía en la conciencia colectiva: el "vuelo yóguico" Sidhis-MT.

En la ciudad de México, se realizó en el Polyforum Cultural Siqueiros. Asistieron más de 600 personas, entre las que se encontraban periodistas y reporteros de los principales medios de comunicación del país.

La concurrencia escuchó las explicaciones de un equipo de profesores del Instituto Maharishi de Ley Natural: licenciado Armando Pascacio, ingeniero José Barbosa y licenciado José Gordon, que hablaron de una nueva tecnología para crear máxima coherencia en el funcionamiento cerebral, que, a la vez, produce armonía en el ambiente. Señalaron que la investigación científica había demostrado que cuando siete mil expertos han practicado la técnica de "vuelo yóguico" Sidhis-MT, simultáneamente en un mismo lugar, se genera una influencia de coherencia suficientemente fuerte para irradiar armonía en todo el planeta, y de esta manera purificar la conciencia mundial. La comprobación científica de esta superirradiación de coherencia —afirmaron— fue la base que inspiró al Programa de Maharishi para crear paz mundial.

Explicaron al público los mecanismos físicos que intervienen en este proceso. Durante la técnica de "vuelo yóguico" Sidhis MT, en el momento de máxima coherencia en el funcionamiento cerebral —tal como se registra en los electroencefalogramas (EEG) —; el cuerpo se levanta en el aire y comienza a saltar. Esta es la primera etapa del "vuelo yóguico", de la cual ya gozan decenas de miles de personas. En 1903 el primer avión se elevó 36 metros en el aire, durante sólo 12 segundos. Muchos de los espectadores se mostraron poco impresionados; no podían llamar a eso volar como un ave. Sin embargo el corto vuelo de los hermanos Wright probó que era posible vencer la fuerza de la gravedad. Esto es el principio que sustenta la historia de la aviación, y culmina, en nuestros días, con los vuelos interplanetarios. De manera similar, los profesores del Instituto Maharishi señalaron que se iba a mostrar en dicha reunión un fenómeno que se encontraba en su primera etapa; pero cuyas consecuencias y trascendencia son sin duda de amplitud incalculable. Al detallar lo que ocurría durante el "vuelo yóguico" plantearon que depende de una máxima coherencia entre mente y cuerpo, es decir, entre conciencia y materia. Cuando la mente llega a su estado de mínima excitación —y el cerebro funciona en su forma más integrada— se identifica con el campo unificado de todas las leyes de la naturaleza; el nivel básico de la creación, desde donde surgen todos los campos de materia y fuerza (incluyendo la de la gravedad).

Debido a que el campo unificado —explicó uno de los profesores— tiene la característica de correlación infinita, un impulso de coherencia generado desde ese nivel armoniza instantáneamente las tendencias discordantes en la naturaleza. De esta manera, la coherencia se difunde y neutraliza las tendencias negativas en el ambiente."

Los profesores informaron que el doctor John Hagelin, uno de los físicos a la vanguardia en el conocimiento del campo unificado ha desarrollado una teoría que explica como es posible vencer la fuerza de la gravedad y, a la vez, irradiar armonía en el entorno: "las teorías clásicas de la gravedad, por ejemplo la de Newton y la de Einstein, no podrían explicar el "vuelo yóguico". Sin embargo, la teoría de la gravedad cuántica sí nos permite entender este fenómeno. Esta teoría se aplica en la escala del campo unificado, y en este nivel se genera dinámicamente la geometría del espacio tiempo. Mediante la generación de una influencia sostenida de coherencia desde este campo, es posible modificar la curvatura de la geometría del espacio tiempo, de tal forma que el cuerpo puede elevarse y subir en cualquier dirección.

"Exactamente estos son los mecanismos que se requieren para crear una influencia global de coherencia que funcione como base para la paz mundial. Para propagar coherencia en la sociedad a grandes escalas de distancia, son insuficientes las explicaciones que consideran los efectos de carácter electromagnético. Se vuelve necesario recurrir a un entendimiento de la naturaleza más básico que el de la geometría del espacio-tiempo. Este es precisamente el nivel del campo unificado."

Después de terminada la exposición de los profesores del Instituto Maharishi, los fotógrafos y camarógrafos se reunieron alrededor de una área cubierta con colchones de hule espuma, en donde se llevó a cabo la demostración del "vuelo yóguico".

El salón del Polyforum Cultural Siqueiros estaba en completo silencio. Cinco meditadores se encontraban sentados sobre los colchones en posición de flor de loto. Después de que ellos practicaron durante cinco minutos la meditación trascendental, se oyó un leve rumor. Un salto y luego otro y luego otro y otro y otro. Con ligereza y gracia los cuerpos se levantaban en el aire y volvían a caer una y otra vez. El silencio sólo era interrumpido por los "clicks" de las cámaras y los "flash". En el ambiente se percibía una atmósfera delicada y suave. Los rostros de los meditadores rebosaban felicidad.

Posteriormente el licenciado Armando Pascacio explicó la naturaleza de este fenómeno extraordinario de coordinación mente-cuerpo. En un estudio en el que se compararon saltos voluntarios con la práctica del "vuelo yóguico", se encontró que el "vuelo yóguico" produce una gran coherencia en el funcionamiento del cerebro y aumenta el nivel de energía del meditador después de que lo practica; en cambio, los saltos voluntarios tienen un efecto extenuante.

El ingeniero Gustavo Cerna —uno de los meditadores que participó en la demostración— comentó:

"Cuando el cuerpo salta uno se siente con una gran plenitud interna... con una gran felicidad. Es realmente glorioso... El propósito no es demostrar el vuelo por sí mismo; más bien se trata de mostrar las po-

Técnica del vuelo yóguico Sidhis MT

sibilidades que brinda la coherencia máxima en el funcionamiento del cerebro individual: la unidad básica de la paz mundial".

Demostraciones similares se llevaron al cabo en diversos países del mundo, además del nuestro, para alertar sobre las posibilidades y potencialidades del ser humano en una época tan crítica y llena de peligros, se está difundiendo la existencia de una tecnología que opera a niveles más profundos y poderosos que los descubiertos en los niveles electrónicos y nucleares: la Tecnología Maharishi del Campo Unificado, la cual puede generar coherencia, armonía y paz desde el nivel básico de funcionamiento de la naturaleza.

WORLD PEACE • GLOBAL INAUGURATION

PRESS REPORTS FROM LATIN AMERICA AND THE CARIBBEAN

The Netherlands Antilles • *Beurs en Nieuwsberichten*

Willemstad 14 August 1986 (Dutch)

Levitatie-demonstratie in SDK

7000 MEDITERENDEN HELPEN WERELDVREDE

WILLEMSTAD - Om een positieve invloed te kunnen uitoefenen op de situatie van onrust, oorlog en terrorisme, waar de wereld in leeft, heeft Maharishi Mahesh Yogi op 7 juli dit jaar in New Delhi zijn programma voor wereldvrede, wereldkundig gemaakt. De Maharishi maakte bekendheid met zijn Transcedente Meditatie, en ook met de techniek van "levitatie", waarbij men zich --in meditatieve staat-- losmaakt van de aantrekkingskracht. Een delegatie van de TM-Sidhi beoefenaars, van de Maharishi's Technology of the Unified Field, zal vrijdag om 4 uur 's middags in Centro Deportivo een demonstratie geven van deze bevrijdende meditatie-techniek.

"Wereldvrede is een persoonlijke onmiddellijke noodzaak voor iedere persoon van belang in de wereld van vandaag" is een uitspraak van de Maharishi. Tijdens de lezing die in New Delhi (India) opgenomen werd en die ook bij de bijeenkomst van de "World Assembly on Vedic Science in Washington DC ten gehore werd gebracht, maakte de oosterse wijsgeer duidelijk, dat groepen van 7000 transcendent mediterenden, verspreid over de wereld, voldoen aan de noodzaak om de gevaarlijke spanningen van onze tijd tot het minimum te verminderen. Om deze mening te onderstrepen maakte de World Assembly on Vedic Science, (die op 9 juli gehouden werd) melding van een (eigen) onderzoek, waaruit bleek dat tijdens de meditaties, tussen 9 en 17 juli gehouden in de Verenigde Staten, enkele opvallende constateringen werden gedaan.

Zo meldde de "Assembly" een duidelijke vermindering in internationale conflikten --minder infektieziekten-- minder branden en veel meer toegepaste patenten. Ook de op de effektenbeurzen van zowel de VS als de totale wereld, werd een zekere hausse bemerkt.

Eigen vijand

"Ons programma tot het verkrijgen van harmonie in de wereld vanuit een basis van het totaal potentieel der natuurlijke wetten, kan niet anders dan verzachtend werken voor alle naties", zei de Maharishi tijdens zijn toespraak.

"Het kan slechts vervullend werken voor iedere natie. En dat is onze vreugde, dat het programma dat wij lanceren er een is, dat elk land verheft, door die evolutionaire invloed van de natuurlijke wetten". Er is dan ook geen mogelijkheid tot destruktie in het programma. En zo vindt Maharishi een mogelijke oplossing voor de supermachten, en voor de bewapening: Elk wapen is immers nutteloos, als de eigenaar ervan vredelievend is? Het zijn niet de wapens, die het gevaar in zich dragen – het is het niveau van bewustzijn waar de mens in leeft. De voortdurende schending van de natuurwetten is de oorzaak van de druk, die voortdurend veroorzaakt wordt in het bewustzijn van de wereld.

"Het zijn deze slachtoffers van stress waarvan wij weten, dat een tegenmiddel ze moet verzachten", volgens de Maharishi.

"Wat wij nodig hebben is een paar groepen van 7000 personen, die deze techniek van het "verenigde veld" (van energieën) in praktijk brengt, om de evolutionaire invloed van de natuurlijke wetten --in het wereldbewustzijn-- in het leven te roepen. Hierbij wordt een natuurlijke situatie gecreëerd, waarbij negatieve invloed en verwoestende symptomen zich gewoon niet aandienen".

Om deze gedachte ook op Curaçao te introduceren geven enkele afgevaardigden van de "TM-Sidhi practise of the Maharishi Technology of the United Field"een demonstratie, waarbij wellicht ook de levitatie, een staat van totale bevrijding getoond zal worden. Vrijdagmiddag om 4 uur, Sentro Deportivo Korsou.

The Netherlands Antilles • *Ultimo Noticia*
Willemstad   14 August 1986   (Papiamento)

DEMOSTRASHON DI E TECNICA YOGIC FLYING DI SIDHI-MT
E mecanismo pa elimina terorismo i guera i crea pas mundial

WILLEMSTAD.-- Mayan atardi den Sentro Deportivo Korsou, lo tuma lugar inaugurashon di e programa di Maharishi pa crea pas mundial, cu un demostrashon publico di e tecnica di Sidhi-MT "Yogic Flying," cu ta e mecanismo pa elimina terorismo i guera i crea pas mundial.

Ta asina cu e tecnica aki ya a ser demostra den luna di juli na Washington, Estados Unidos i dos siman despues na New Delhi India, pero e intenshon ta cu mayan e evento aki lo tuma lugar den 128 pais simultaneamente den un esfuerso concentra pa busca pas mundial.

Esnan cu ta eherce e mecanismo aki di "bula" of "zweef" ta siguidornan di Maharishi Mahesh Yogi, fundador di TM.

Bulamentu den pasado tabata un asuntu priva, pero organisadornan di e evento a disidi di bai den publico cu ne pa motibu di aumento di amenasa di terorismo i e necesidad urgente pa atakele cu pensamentu sublime i positivo.

Segun cientificonan di TM, si 7.000 hende ta bula huntu riba un lugar, esaki lo crea coherencia den consenshi mundial. I segun nan, esaki ta un manera efectivo pa establece i mantene pas mundial.

Nan ta di opinion cu den cada continente, pais i famia hendenan mester practica bulamentu TM i promove armonia.

Mayan atardi 4'or publico lo haña e oportunidad di mira e tecnica aki di TM personalmente den Sentro Deportivo Korsou, caminda Korsou, huntu cu 127 otro pais rond mundu lo ta cooperando den e mecanica di Mararishi di trata na yega na eliminashon di terorismo i guera i crea pas mundial.

WORLD PEACE • GLOBAL INAUGURATION

PRESS REPORTS FROM LATIN AMERICA AND THE CARIBBEAN

The Netherlands Antilles • *NOBO*
Willemstad 16 August 1986 (Papiamento)

WILLEMSTAD —. Riba e foto d.r.p.d. nos lectornan po mira Señoresnan Heinz Ietswaari (docente wiskunde, natuurkunde di Radulphuscollege), Carl Camelia (Presidente di N.A. Stichting Onderwijs i-d Wetenschap der Creatieve Intelligentie), Dr. Axson, kendenan diabierne último atardi a ofrecé un conferencia di prensa na S.D.K., pa inauguración di "MAHARISHI" y su programa pa crea paz mundial. NOBO ta recomendá tur ciudadano yu di Corsou cu ta interesá den Maharishi, pa tuma contacto cu Sr. Camelia na telefon numero 623160. Aki ta trata di un organisación di técnica SIDHI-MT "Yogic Flying", y esnan cu practiké ta adkiri hopi conocimiento pa desaroyá nan mes den un forma amplio den tur loke nan haci.

MAHARISHI'S PROGRAMME TO CREATE

PRESS REPORTS FROM LATIN AMERICA AND THE CARIBBEAN

Netherlands Antilles • *Beurs en Nieuwsberichten*

Willemstad 16 August 1986 (Dutch)

Yogi's geven demonstratie in SDK

NAAR VREDE IN WERELD DOOR MASSA-MEDITATIE

WILLEMSTAD - Een geest van positivisme manifesteert zich wanneer een groep mensen in onze onrustige tijden een ongekend alternatief als het mediteren durft aan te bieden. De TM-Sidhi/Yogic Flying Yogi's getuigen van een visie, die probeert een ommekeer teweeg te brengen in het gevestigde denken, waarin de Overheid zorg moet dragen voor de vrede (maar daar in de 3000 jaar die achter ons liggen, niet in slaagde). Zij ontwikkelden een techniek, waarin de wetten van Newton en Einstein niet hebben voorzien: Door meditatie moet het mogelijk zijn tot zweven te komen.

Om aan deze gedachte bekendheid te geven, werd door de heer Carl Camelia, voorzitter van de N.A. Stcihting Onderwijs in de Wetenschap der Creatieve Intelligentie, gistermiddag een persconferentie gegeven in het SDK, gevolgd door een demonstratie in de levitatie techniek.

Curacao hoort in deze bij de voorlopers - in '108 landen tegelijk werd het programma dat leidt tot coherent denken van de Maharishi Mahesh Yogi aangeboden. Dit programma is bedoeld als een alternatief op de gespannen situatie in de wereld.

Dat het niet gaat om een ongegronde gedachtengang toonde men aan met wetenschappelijke gegevens, waaruit onder meer bleek, dat in 27 landen 325 studies gedaan zijn - onder andere bij 160 universiteiten die 4 boekwerken gevuld hebben. Ook op Curacao zijn medici als Dr. Ciro Axson (sekretaris van de "World Medical Association for perfect Health) en de longarts Dr. Ignacio (penningmeester van deze Vereniging) betrokken bij deze tak van Transcendente Meditatie. Dat de wetenschap belangstelling heeft voor de levitatie techniek, bleek ook uit e woorden van de heer Heinz Ietswaard, leraar Natuurkunde aan het Radulphus College.

Coherentie

De meditatie techniek richt zich op het bereiken van een perfekt evenwicht, waarbij de werkzaamheid van de hersenen in absolute coherentie moet plaatsvinden. Dit heeft een concentratie van energie tot gevolg die, gebundeld, kan leiden tot de levitatie, die gedemonstreerd werd. Het is echter niet de opheffing van het lichaam, die de doelstelling van de meditatie is. De demonstratie zal dan ook niet herhaald worden - het is niet als show bedoeld - Veel meer tracht men een groot publiek te bereiken, zodat meer mensen tot de meditatie overgaan.

Effect

Door een aantal mediterenden te verzamelen, gelijk aan de wortel van 1 procent van de bevolking, kan men het "Maharishi effekt" bewerkstelligen. De meditatie van dit aantal mensen (dat zou voor Curaçao op 40 à 50 mensen neerkomen, en voor de wereld op groepen van 7000) kan een harmonie, en een ordelijkheid in de rest van de samenleving teweegbrengen, waardoor misdaden en ongevallen verminderen, terwijl er tegelijkertijd een verbetering in de positieve trends van de maatschappij opmerkbaar wordt. Dit alles berust op het principe, dat wanneer een aantal mensen het individuele bewustzijn bevordert, de gehele samenleving het uitstralend effect hiervan ondervindt. Als feit dient ook aangemerkt te worden, dat deze methode op geen enkele manier destruktief kan zijn. Voor de beoefenaars van de levitatie-meditatie zelf geldt bovendien volgens de informanten, dat hun algemene gezondheid met sprongen vooruit gaat, en dat spanningen verminderen, doordat ze in hun staat van evenwicht niet de verkeerde be-

WORLD PEACE • GLOBAL INAUGURATION

sluiten zullen nemen. De bloedcirculatie, de hormoonfunktie alsmede de hersen funktie worden positief beinvloed, wat het verouderingsproces tegengaat, en resulteert in een uitstekende gezondheid.

Yogic flying

In 1980 werd de eerste basis cursus in deze meditatie techniek gegeven. Sindsdien worden jaarlijks twee cursussen van drie weken gegeven, waarna men zelf verder oefent. De cursussen hadden een opkomst van minimaal 20 man. Nu zijn er op Curacao zo'n 150 mensen, die deze meditatie-techniek van de TM-levitatie beoefenen. In New Delhi heeft men zelfs een groep zover gekregen, dat er een wedstrijd 'hoppen' georganiseerd werd. Op de vraag, of dit wel strookt met het hooggestelde doel van de Wereldvrede, kregen wij te horen, dat de wedstrijd ten doel had, bekendheid te geven aan de levitatie techniek. Dit geldt ook voor de demonstratie in het Sport Centrum: Het is geen show-programma, maar een introduktie bij het publiek.

De techniek van het mediterend zweven is onderverdeeld in drie fasen: het "hoppen" (sprongetjes maken), dan de fase van hovering (in langere sprongen zweven) en ten slotte het doel waar men naar streeft: de totale verheffing (levitatie).

Voor een aantal genodigden, onder wie ook de Minister President, toonden 9 beoefenaren van de levitatie techniek hun kunnen. Er was ook op de tribune veel belangstelling voor het fenomeen.
Kijkend naar de demonsstratie, kon men inderdaad het feit, dat de 9 jongemannen sprongen maakten, geen afbreuk doen.
Eerlijkheidshalve dient daarbij aangemerkt te worden, dat het moeilijk aantoonbaar zal zijn, of deze sprongen inderdaad voortkomen uit een dieptemeditatie, die energie verzamelt, zodat men tijdelijk de lucht in gaat. Moet de levitatie niet voortkomen uit de spontane beleving van de beoogde co-herentie, inplaats van via eenbelletje – van buitenaf? Dit zijn vragen, die ons niet losieten tijdens de demonstratie.

Hetgeen geen afbreuk hoeft te doen aan het initiatief. Als de theorie van Maharishi Mahesh Yogi ondersteund wordt door wetenschappelijk onderzoek, en als men daarbij met grafieken verantwoording kan afleggen over de behaalde resultaten, dan is het de moeite waard, om kennis te nemen van deze wetenschap waaraan óók op Curaçao vooraanstaande artsen en deskundigen op verschillende gebieden hun steun verlenen. Wellicht schuilt er waarheid in het geen zegsman Carl Camelia gistermiddag herhaalde: Om Orville en Wilbur Wright werd ook gelachen toen ze enige meters vlogen. Het gevolg van hun eerste vlucht is nu alom merkbaar.

De demonstratie was een symbool van de goede wil, die velen momenteel beheerst, om vanuit de eigen beleving te kunnen bijdragen tot een betere wereld.

Op onze kritische kanttekeningen ten aanzien van de getoonde "hopping" demonstratie was het commentaar van de heer Carl Camelia -- voorzitter van de Stichting, Onderwijs in de Wetenschap der Creatieve Intelligentie het volgende:
"Wij hebben met nadruk gewezen op de ondergeschiktheid van het fenomeen.
Opzienbaren en veel belangrijker is namelijk het feit, dat wetenschappelijk is vastgesteld, dat tijdens de beoefening van deze meditatie een volledige synchronisatie van het functioneren van de hersenen plaats vindt. Dit is een doorbraak in de menselijke capaciteiten.
Het belletje gebruiken wij als coordinatiemiddel bij de gezamenlijke meditatie, als teken dat we kunnen beginnen. Tot dit begin komen we, door het toepassen van een formule om te komen tot het leviteren.
Het verschil in hersengolfcoherentie (via de E.E.G.) tussen iemand, die vrijwillig een sprong maakt, en iemand die de techniek van Yogic-Flying toepast, heeft aangetoond, dat deze techniek veel fundamenteler is, dan vrijwillig springen."

Voor informatie: Stichting Onderwijs in de Wetenschap der Creatieve Intelligentie -- tel. 623160.

PRESS REPORTS FROM LATIN AMERICA AND THE CARIBBEAN

The Netherlands Antilles • *La Prensa*
Willemstad 18 August 1986 (Papiamento)

WILLEMSTAD/-- Ayera den Sentro Deportivo Korsou a tuma luga un demostrashon di e loke nan ta jama teknika di Sidhi-MT. "YOGIC FLYING". Esaki a ser proba ku ta un berdat na momentu ku miembronan di e sekta tabata medida profundamente y na e momentu ey a kuminsa lanta for di suela y bai kasi 50 sentimeter for di suela. E foto ta mustra momentu ku algun miembro di e sekta ta meditando. Meta di e demostrashon aki ta pa yuda krea pas na mundu.

WORLD PEACE • GLOBAL INAUGURATION

PRESS REPORTS FROM LATIN AMERICA AND THE CARIBBEAN

Panama • *La Estrella de Panama*

Panama City   14 August 1986   (Spanish)

Programa Maharishi por la paz mundial

Maharishi Mahesh Yogi...conocido como el fundador del programa Meditación Trascendental, ahora anuncia su programa para crear paz mundial.

Maharishi dijo: "Con el aumento del terrorismo, la rivalidad peligrosa entre las superpotencias, es vital crear inmediatamente una influencia indominable de coherencia en la conciencia mundial".

El 15 de agosto los expertos en la tecnología Maharishi del campo unificado de Panamá demostrarán la técnica SIDHI-Meditación Trascendental del "vuelo yoguístico" fundada por Maharishi Mahesh Yogi.

Investigaciones científicas han demostrado que a través de esta técnica los individuos pueden crear coherencia en la conciencia mundial. Esto es la base del programa del Maharishi para establecer y mantener permanentemente la paz mundial.

La exhibición se llevará a cabo en el Centro de Convenciones ATLAPA a las 11:00 a.m.

Todos los medios de comunicación están cordialmente invitados a este acto.

Para mayor información llamar a los siguientes teléfonos: 69-0520, 69-0158 o escribir a SIMT, apartado 6-3216 El Dorado, Panamá.

PRESS REPORTS FROM LATIN AMERICA AND THE CARIBBEAN

Peru • *Dominical*

Lima   10 August 1986   (Spanish)

El vuelo del YOGA

En una exhibición sin precedentes, dos "sidhis" peruanos tomando su fuerza mental como punto de apoyo, "volaron" innumerables veces sobre extendidos y duros colchones, ante atónitos periodistas del DOMINICAL.

Ambos "sidhis" son practicantes del sistema universal de Meditación Trascendental (MT) que preconiza el Maharishi Mahesh Yogi, fundador de la Tecnología Maharishi del Campo Unificado y de la Universidad de la Era de la Iluminación. El Maharishi estuvo en Lima hace algunos años y aquí publicamos una información sobre su trabajo.

Un arquitecto y un profesor de inglés que practican la MT desde hace algunos años, siguieron luego, el siguiente curso, para convertirse en "sidhis", es decir personas que mientras meditan pueden elevarse y desplazarse en el aire, no por su voluntad, sino cuando la coordinación entre la mente y el cuerpo alcanza su plenitud.

Afirman que "El principio de mínima acción que gobierna todas las actividades en la naturaleza y usa la destreza de la naturaleza para lograr todo silenciosamente, está disponible en su totalidad cuando la coherencia de las ondas cerebrales es máxima y la conciencia está en su estado más simple".

(En literatura especializada se dice que "bajo el nombre de "sidhis" se agrupan toda una serie de sorprendentes experiencias (levitación, invisibilidad, etc.) descritas en el Sistema de Yoga (Yoga Sutras) de Pantajali (Siglo III a. de C.) uno de los 6 sistemas de la Filosofía Hindú que elabora el conocimiento de los Vedas. La experiencia de los "Sidhis" se obtiene mediante un fácil procedimiento conocido técnicamente con el nombre de "Sanyama" y descrito en los citados Yoga Sutras).

Esta primera etapa de levitación, porque las otras dos consisten en quedarse en el aire y desplazarse, respectivamente, se practica en todo el mundo. Aquí, en el Perú hay, aproximadamente, un medio centenar de meditadores que lo hacen. Pero, de acuerdo a directivas del gurú Maharishi, esto no tiene por qué convertirse en prueba pública ni menos espectacular. Es una práctica que pertenece a la satisfacción espiritual de cada individuo.

Sin embargo, el famoso yogui hindú, está ansioso porque la paz y la felicidad reinen sobre el mundo y según él, sólo se conseguirá cuando el hombre restablezca el equilibro mental que lo tiene perdido. Un medio para ese restablecimiento

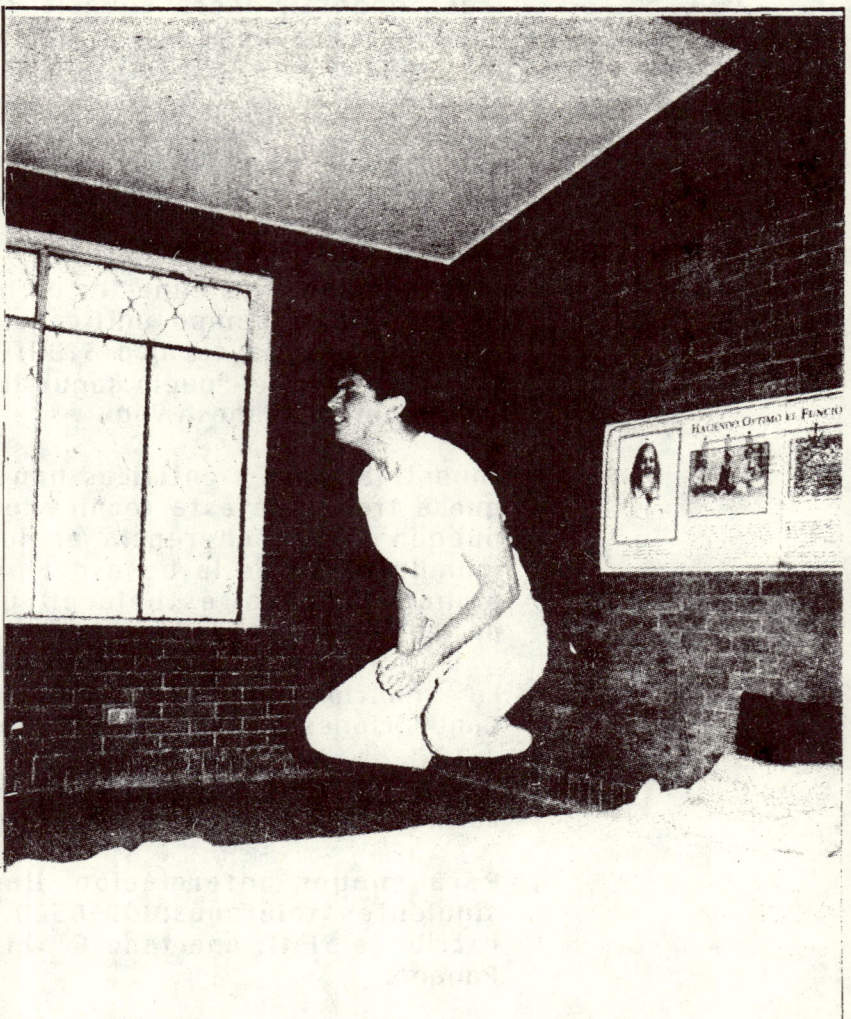

Los Sidhis vuelan con apoyo de su fuerza mental.

sería ése.

Así, para demostrar gráficamente que sus enseñanzas no pertenecen al reino de la charlatanería ni a la mentira en la que han caído muchas sectas practicantes de yoga, ha ordenado abrir las compuertas de su propio código y mostrar lo que antes era una secreto.

Por esta razón, el arquitecto Javier Ortiz y el profesor Santiago Reynaga en compañía de otros miembros de la MT local, van a ofrecer una conferencia de prensa el próximo viernes 15, ante invitados especiales entre los que figuran conocidos políticos, médicos y filósofos. Allí explicarán los beneficios de la doctrina del Maharishi. Durante tal acto, realizarán el llamado "vuelo del yoga", que consiste en elevar el cuerpo y desplazarlo en trancos más o menos largos, luego de alcanzar el máximo de coordinación mental. Un espectáculo, llanamente asombroso.

Esto mismo estará sucediendo simultáneamente en 108 países del mundo donde hay practicantes de MT, según se nos ha informado. Hace un mes, hubo una gigantesca demostración en los Estados Unidos de Norteamérica. El "Washington Times" entre otros diarios, informó que 3 mil meditadores a nivel de "sidhis", se habían reunido en la Capital norteamericana para realizar públicamente sus experiencias. Fue un acontecimiento, dice el diario.

La reunión en la India fue más reciente. Y, según publicaciones, resultó apoteósica. Por esta razón especial es que el Maharishi ha decidido fundar una ciudad a 50 kilómetros de Nueva Delhi, en la que vivirán unas 20 mil personas dedicadas a la meditación, para lograr, según su teoría, un **campo unificado** que permita el enseñoreamiento de la paz mundial. Como se sabe, la MT está muy difundida y ha logrado aceptación en los medios científicos. Hay verdaderos centros universitarios en muchos países como los EE.UU., Holanda, Suiza, etc.

Aunque la palabra **panacea** ha sido, prácticamente, borrada de todos los diccionarios del mundo, para el Maharishi, la MT es un remedio

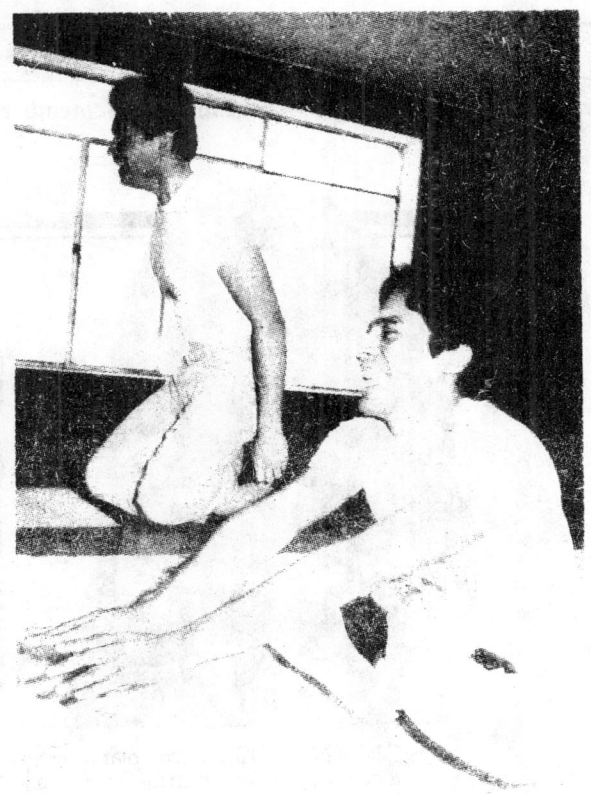

Los Sidhis consiguen no sólo experiencias de levitación sino también de invisibilidad y otras.

capaz de curar todos los males que padece nuestra civilización incluyendo el terrorismo y las amenazas de una Tercera Guerra Mundial.

Seguramente, la próxima exhibición que realizarán los "sidhis" peruanos en Lima, va a permitir el auscultamiento y la discusión de una técnica que, según ellos, sirve para la solución de problemas trascendentales y no solamente para curar el "stress". **(MJO)**

PRESS REPORTS FROM LATIN AMERICA AND THE CARIBBEAN

Peru • *Oiga*
Lima   1 September 1986   (Spanish)

LLEGO A LIMA

El vuelo de los Yoguis

Maharishi Mahesh Yogui: la Tecnología del Campo Unificado, —asegura— puede contribuír a lograr la tan ansiada paz en el mundo.

CONVENCIDOS que, mediante sus técnicas, pueden contribuír a lograr la paz en el mundo, existen diseminados en todo el mundo miles de seguidores del Maharishi Mahesh Yogui, fundador de la llamada Tecnología Maharishi del Campo Unificado. En el Perú, numerosos adeptos se han dedicado, desde la década del '70, a la meditación trascendental. Pero hace pocos días, llegó a nuestro país la SIDHI-MT, que es nada menos que una forma de lograr lo que parece imposible: flotar en el aire a voluntad. Se trata de una técnica que el Maharishi Mahesh Yogui practica desde 1983. Según sus seguidores, la levitación no solo contribuye al desarrollo físico y espiritual de las personas, sino que también puede contribuír a lograr la tan ansiada paz mundial. Para ello, debería practicar la técnica SIDHI-MT —que consta de tres etapas— un grupo que ascienda a la raíz cuadrada del 1% de los habitantes de cada ciudad del planeta. En un hotel miraflorino, un grupo de seguidores del Maharishi mostró sus progresos en materia de levitación, en su primera etapa (el cuerpo se eleva, pero cae de inmediato). La segunda fase se alcanza cuando el levitador puede permanecer elevado el tiempo que desee. La tercera —no alcanzada hasta ahora por nadie— consiste en desplazarse en el aire sin caer. ¿Se anima? (Texto y fotos: Felipe de Rivero). ■

 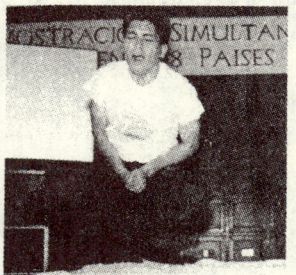

SIDHI-MT se llama la técnica para aprender a levitar. Consta de tres etapas. En el Perú ya tiene seguidores (en la primera etapa). Foto izq.: levitadores en los EE.UU.

WORLD PEACE • GLOBAL INAUGURATION

PRESS REPORTS FROM LATIN AMERICA AND THE CARIBBEAN

Peru • *La Crónica*

Lima   10 September 1985   (Spanish)

ESPECTACULAR DEMOSTRACION
ANTE PERIODISTAS

Yogas criollos levitaron en sorprendente prueba

● ¡Asombroso! ... Un arquitecto y un profesor convertidos en yogas, se elevaron ayer en el aire desde el escenario del teatro Felipe Pardo y Aliaga hasta un metro, más o menos, de altura, en una de las demostraciones de levitación más espectaculares realizadas en la capital.

El prodigioso experimento, al que fueron invitados periodistas y científicos de las universidades limeñas, fue el acto inaugural en el Perú, del Programa del Gurú Maharishi, para crear la Paz Mundial.

Los reporteros gráficos de los medios de comunicación y camarógrafos de la TV, subieron al escenario del teatro para verificar la autenticidad del fenómeno, que se produce como resultado de la aplicación mental de las técnicas del Yoga Patanjali.

Los científicos al no poder, asimismo, explicar lo que veían sus ojos esgrimieron diversas teorías, pero el secreto de los Sutras, que permiten la levitación, es accesible a todos, mediante prácticas místicas en bien de la paz mundial, señalaron los yogas.

El arquitecto Javier Ortiz y el profesor de secundaria Santiago Raynaga, protagonistas del fenómeno, revelaron que, al inicio del experimento, el yoga entra en estado de meditación, sentado en la posición del asana de loto, con los pies sobre los muslos.

Acto seguido, comienza a operar en su mente con una fórmula establecida por el sabio Patanjali, que vivió en la India hace miles de años....

Vestidos con una camiseta celeste, y un pantalón blanco, los místicos criollos dieron una extraordinaria demostración sobre colchonetas de color azafrán, dispuestas sobre el escenario del mencionado teatro. Las fuerza espiritual de la meditación mística, que compararon a la de la electricidad, los hacía experimentar estados de éxtasis y los impulsaba en el aire ante los estupefactos reporteros gráficos, que una vez más demostraron su profesionalismo tomando instantaneas del fenómeno.

"Debido al aumento del terrorismo y la peligrosa rivalidad entre las superpotencias, es vital crear de inmediato una influencia poderosa de coherencia de la conciencia mundial", señala una de las enseñanzas de Maharishi, que sustentan el vuelo yógico, o tecnología del Campo Unificado como este movimiento, denomina a las prácticas de levitación.

Las técnicas de Patanjali, sostuvieron de otro lado sus practicantes, permiten al individuo experimentar un estado mayor orden, equilibrio, paz, un cambio placentero de la condición física y mental.

"La coherencia creada en la conciencia mundial por la práctica grupal de la Tecnología del Campo Unificado hará que, la paz de la Tierra, sea poderosa y que, el poder de los gobiernos sobre la Tierra, sea pacífico", destacaron.

PRESS REPORTS FROM LATIN AMERICA AND THE CARIBBEAN

Peru • *Gente*
Lima 18 September 1986 (Spanish)

EL PODER DE LA MENTE

Frente al caos y la violencia que crecen y se extienden en el mundo, surgen simultáneamente y se multiplican en muchos lugares del planeta esfuerzos profundos y vastos del hombre y los gobiernos, dirigidos a contener la inmensa ola del desastre que amenaza destruirnos.

Uno de los movimientos más espectaculares y que ha atraído considerablemente la atención mundial en los últimos años es el que gira en torno de la llamada Tecnología Maharishi del Campo Unificado.

Creada por Maharishi Mahesh Yogi, su fundador en 1983, dicha tecnología aliada a la Meditación Trascendental Maharishi (1958) consigue según su fundador y sus seguidores "que el equilibrio perfecto de la naturaleza, su eficiencia suprema, poder organizador infinito y creatividad ilimitada estén disponibles en la vida diaria".

Aplicada a la administración se afirma , dicha tecnología ofrece a todo gobierno la eficiencia suprema con la que la naturaleza rige el universo, sin alterar las características de ese sistema de gobierno. De este modo "se produce un desarrollo equilibrado y se logra la creación de una sociedad ideal en un tiempo tan corto como se desee".

Maharishi explica que todo gobierno, independientemente de su sistema, es un espejo inocente de su nación y que dado que el gobierno deriva su inspiración y extrae su vitalidad de la conciencia colectiva de la población, "es indispensable que el gobierno haga lo que pueda para mantener la conciencia nacional en su nivel más elevado".

El movimiento ha creado, en este sentido, el Gobierno Mundial de la Era de la Iluminación, que tiene asociaciones en muchas ciudades del mundo y también en nuestro país.

El 9 de setiembre, precisamente, la Asociación Peruana para la Era de la Iluminación ofreció una conferencia de prensa y para demostrar su eficiencia, hizo uso de la tecnología y la meditación que nos ocupan y produjo un "vuelo yóguico", que sólo se obtiene en el momento de máxima coherencia de la actividad cerebral.

En estas páginas ofrecemos vistas de dicho "vuelo" conseguido por gente del grupo nacional de un movimiento que cuenta, también, con varios centros de la nominada Universidad Internacional Maharishi. ■

Maharishi Mahesh Yogi: "La paz mundial es una necesidad inmediata y personal de cada hombre importante del mundo de hoy..."

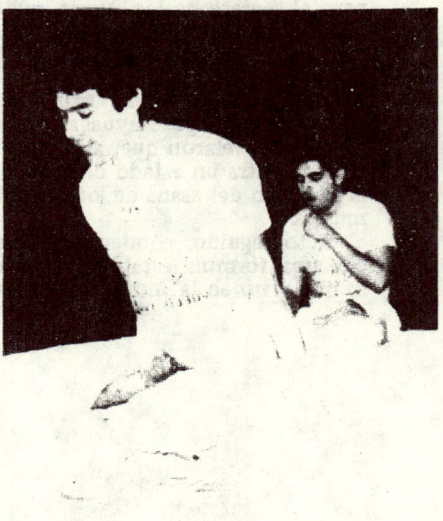

Concentrado, el discípulo de Maharishi se eleva en silencio.

WORLD PEACE • GLOBAL INAUGURATION

¡Sorprendente! La técnica del Sidhi—MT no tiene truco alguno.

Fotos: JORGE GALVEZ

"EL VUELO YOGUICO"

● Según Maharishi Mahesh Yogi, la investigación científica ha demostrado repetidamente que siete mil expertos que practiquen la técnica del Sidhi-MT de "Vuelo Yóguico" juntos, en un lugar de la Tierra, generarán una influencia suficientemente fuerte de coherencia para ser irradiada mundialmente y armonizar toda la conciencia mundial. Esta super-irradiación de coherencia es la inspiración y base científica del Programa de Maharishi para crear Paz Mundial.

"Durante la Técnica del Sidhi-MT de "Vuelo Yóguico", en el momento de máxima coherencia del funcionamiento cerebral, como lo indica el electroencefalograma, el cuerpo se eleva en el aire y empieza natural y espontáneamente a saltar. La coherencia entre mente y cuerpo que se expresa en esta primera etapa del "Vuelo Yóguico", se origina en el nivel del campo unificado de todas las leyes de la naturaleza, generado desde este nivel se armonizan las tendencias negativas del medio ambiente".

PRESS REPORTS FROM LATIN AMERICA AND THE CARIBBEAN

Peru • *Vision*
Lima   21 September 1986   (Spanish)

VUELO DE LA PAZ

Debido al aumento del terrorismo y la peligrosa rivalidad entre las superpotencias es vital crear de inmediato una influencia poderosa de coherencia en la conciencia mundial".

Esta es al parecer la filosofía que motivó al Maharishi Mahesh Yogi para crear paz mundial a través de la técnica del Sidhi-MT de "vuelo yóguico", que muy bien podría ser aplicada en nuestro medio, tan convulsionado por la violencia y por una tendencia tanática enfermiza. ¿Pero en qué consiste este "vuelo" que según la técnica del Maharishi puede dotar a nuestra sociedad de la paz? Muy sencillo. Solamente dando saltitos o lo que se conoce como levitación, la cual —previa meditación— ejerce en los individuos una disminución del nerviosismo y de todas las cargas emocionales que son las que generan la violencia. Al final de la conferencia de prensa en la que se dio a conocer esta nueva técnica científica, muchos de los presentes se preguntaron si ésta no podría ser aplicada también a algunos miembros de nuestro Parlamento.

No es truco... en realidad está volando y según el Maharishi, este "vuelo" puede crear paz mundial.

Peru • *Gente*
Lima   11 September 1986   (Spanish)

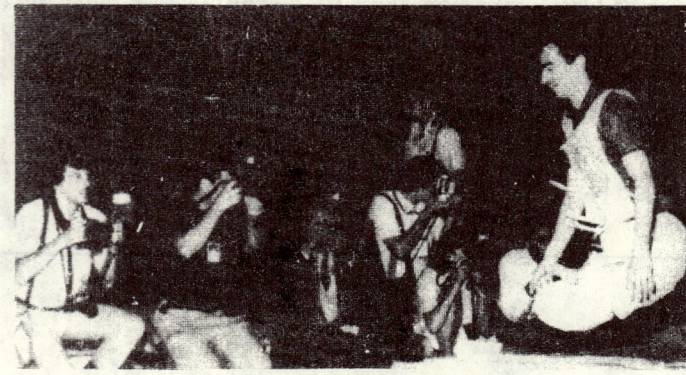

EL VUELO DE LA PAZ

● Si lográramos que siete mil personas juntas efectúen el "Vuelo Yóguico" en cualquier lugar de la tierra, esa integración de fuerza mental que permite al ser humano elevar su cuerpo por sí mismo, generaría la fuerza pacífica que tanto requiere el mundo. Es increíble pero cierto, aseguran los iniciadores de la Técnica del Sidhi MT que participan en el Maharishi Mahesh Yogi, lo que no se ha dicho es si será tarea de iluminados o de gentes comunes y corrientes como los mortales.

WORLD PEACE • GLOBAL INAUGURATION

PRESS REPORTS FROM LATIN AMERICA AND THE CARIBBEAN

Puerto Rico • *El Nuevo Dia*

San Juan   17 August 1986   (Spanish)

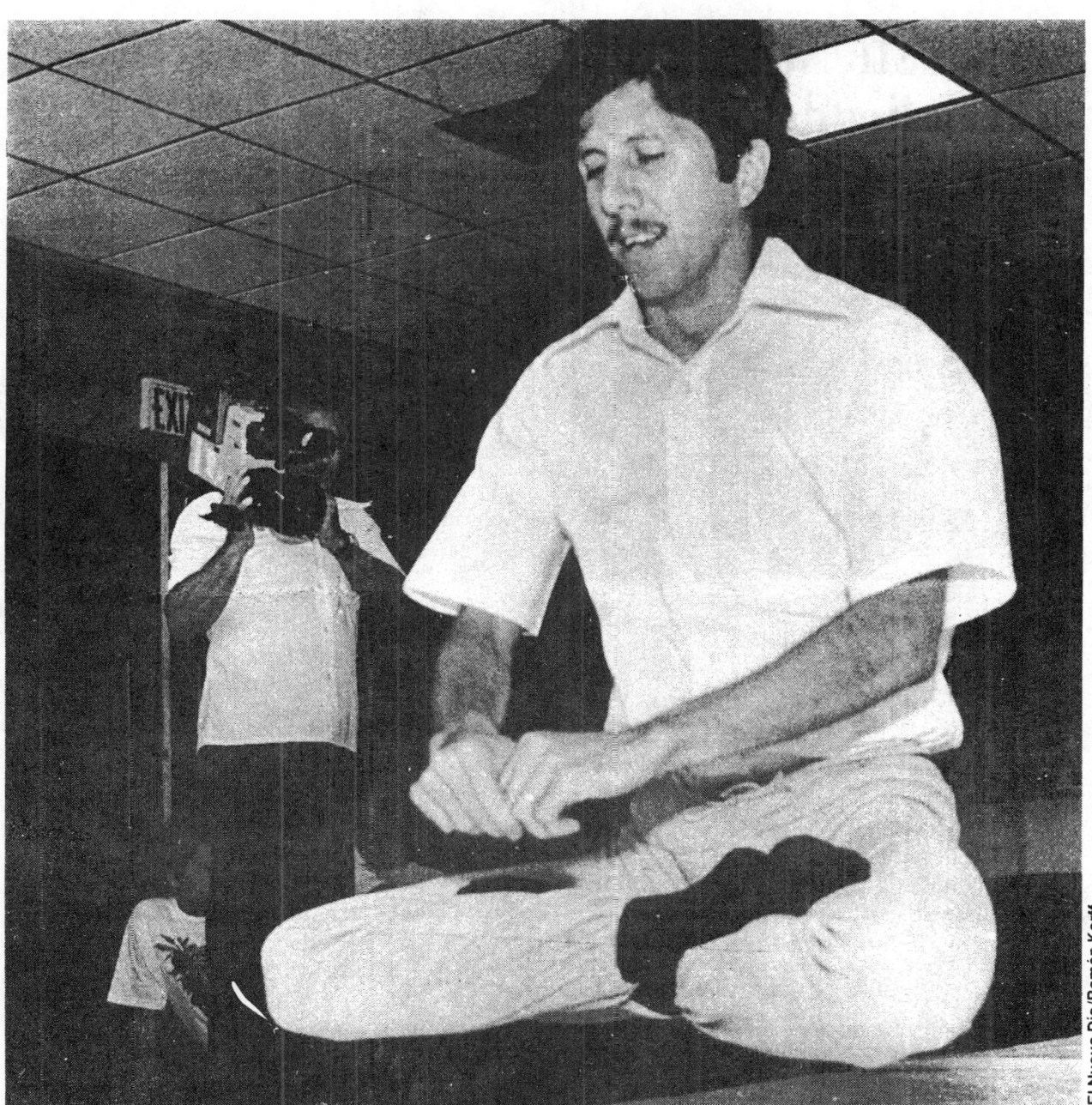

Vuelo por la paz Puerto Rico acaba de participar en un programa mundial de meditación trascendental, mediante un "vuelo yóquico" de expertos en "Maharishi", en un intento por colmar de paz al mundo. La actividad se efectuó a la misma vez en 108 naciones.

PRESS REPORTS FROM LATIN AMERICA AND THE CARIBBEAN

Suriname • *De West Van Zaterdag*
Paramaribo 8 November 1986 (Dutch)

Eerste Nationale Yoga-vliegdemonstratie in Suriname

Het Transcedente Meditatie Programma werd voor 5 minuten beoefend voordat het Yoga-vliegen gedemonstreerd werd door deze 8 T.M. Siddhi beoefenaars.

(Een woord van de organisatie)

In de vroege vooravond van donderdag jl. hebben 8 Surinaamse yogi's voor het eerst in de Surinaamse geschiedenis een publieke demonstratie gegeven van hun kunnen, namelijk Yoga-vliegen, het programma om wereldvrede te creëren. Dit geschiedde in de aanwezigheid van topfunctionarissen in de Surinaamse Medische Wetenschap, Rechterlijke Macht, Onderwijs Inspectie en Persmedia. Ook waren hoge vertegenwoordigers uitgenodigd van alle nationale vredesorganisaties, onder ander de Jaycees, het Nationaal Comité Jaar voor de Vrede en ook kerkelijke autoriteiten.

Yoga-vliegen is een van de aspecten van de van het T.M. Siddhi programma, dat gebaseerd is op de vermaarde Yoga Sutra's van Patanjali. Wetenschappelijk onderzoek bewijst dat het lichaam de grond verlaat op het moment van maximale coherentie (ordelijkheid) van de hersengolven in de verschillende areas van het menselijke brein.

Ook is aangetoond dat deze coherentie gerelateerd is aan de mate van Creativiteit, Intelligentie en Ordelijkheid in het menselijke bestaan, hetgeen onze gehele natie ten goede komt en de basis vormt voor vrede in Suriname.

Wij, Surinamers, mogen er erg trots op zijn dat vanuit de Persmedia veel belangstelling bestond en wilde daarom ook dank uitbrengen aan al degenen die spontaan hun medewerking hebben gedaan tot het welslagen van dit belangrijke evenement in Suriname.

Ondanks dit grote succes willen wij ook nog een beroep doen op het overige deel van de Persmedia in Suriname om wat meer tijd te besteden aan dit programma dat daadwerkelijk, zonder omwegen, vrede zal creëren in ons geliefd Suriname. Dit schrijven wij omdat dezer dagen er veel te veel tijd wordt verknoeid aan negativiteiten en het vertonen van allerlei wrede, levensbedreigende films aan het volk. Ook dit zal moeten veranderen want alles wat wij aan het volk geven zullen

WORLD PEACE • GLOBAL INAUGURATION

wij terugkrijgen.

Voor dit belangrijke evenement waren tevens uitgenodigd onze geliefde Leiders van ons Suriname.
Wij van de Internationale Meditatie Societeit vragen de aandacht van de Leiders van de republiek Suriname om wat meer tijd te besteden aan het verhogen van het bewustzijnsniveau van het volk.

Bewustzijn is de basis van het leven. Educatie zal er op gericht moeten worden om de mensen te leren leven volgens de natuurwetten; en dit zal alleen maar kunnen door op ene spontage, moeiteloze wijze het bewustzijn te doen ontwikkelen. Het Maharishi Programma om wereldvrede te scheppen is wetenschappelijk bewezen het programma om zo snel mogelijk, doch zo natuurlijk mogelijk, het bewustzijn van het inidividu tot ontwikkeling en zodoende het collectief bewustzijn te verrijken.

Terrorisme wordt geschapen door opstapeling van collectief bewustzijn. Met de Transcedente Meditatie en het T.M.S. - Siddhi Programma kunnen wij alle facetten van de Overheid maximaliseren, alle verenigingsdoelen vervullen en zodoende het beste geven aan het volk.
Wij zijn in staat om samen te werken met elke overheidsinstantie en elke organisatie in Suriname voor meer voorspoed en welvaart in Suriname.
Momenteel is de organisatie bezig te werken aan een maandelijks televisie programma om meer informatie over dit programma te verspreiden. Hiervoor is echter veel geld nodig.

MAHARISHI'S PROGRAMME TO CREATE

PRESS REPORTS FROM LATIN AMERICA AND THE CARIBBEAN

St. Lucia • *The Voice*

Castries   13 September 1986   (English)

Up, Up And Away With
YOGIC FLYING

THE higher they go, the happier they become. Over-flowing with bliss the competitors, including Eddie Gob of Martinique, third from right, spontaneously hop together.

A global effort to create world peace organized around the teaching of Transcendental Meditation and its connection to the unified field of all the laws of nature has switched the spotlight to a coherence creating phenomenon called "yogic flying."

Experts claim that widespread group practice of the "flying" technique involving as little as the square root of one percent of the world's population guarantees a positive influence on the quality of life in society.

Actually, this contention has formed part of the TM teaching for a number of years and social scientists at leading research institutions and research centres around the world have been able to validate the suggested field effect in a variety of replicated studies.

What is really new is the fact that TM international and its founder Maharishi Mahesh Yogi, have opted to go public with a growth of consciousness technique previously confined to strict privacy.

Accordingly, local TM officials have moved their lecture presentation emphasis to explanations of "yogic flying" with the assistance of a video-taped version of the first ever Flying Yogis Olympiad staged in Washington in July.

They say that rising terrorism and other world problems have made it necessary to show the public just how an influx of coherence in the individual's life can lift his mind-body coordination to the pure consciousness state, described by TM practitioners as the basis of world peace.

Teachers at the Laborie St. centre explain that "yogic flying" is currently at level one, where practitioners hop around on foam mattresses sitting in a cross-legged position. The second and third levels are said to be hovering and directed flight.

TM boss Maharishi Mahesh Yogi insists that all that is needed to do it right as far as national harmony and world peace are concerned, is the right number of people super-radiating in a state of transcendental meditative bliss.

Turns out that the magic number is just a little more than 7000 ... calculated as the square root of one percent of the world's five billion population.

Local exponents of the mental technique believe that this many people involved in TM and its advanced procedures like "yogic flying," can ensure daily doses of purification for world consciousness and thereby make life easier for ongoing efforts to secure a happy and prosperous world family.

Along these lines they cite the published results of a number of scientific research studies documenting reduced crime, sickness, accidents and drug abuse along with greater productivity and booming stock prices in communities under the influence of group practice of TM.

Twenty two competitors sat in on the recent Yogic Flying Olympiad at the Washington Convention Centre in the American Capital, but the day belonged to 27-year-old Ecie Gob from the french caribbean department of Guadeloupe.

The slender frenchman out-did his yogic hopping competitors in three events to cop a trio of gold medals and a rare chance in the glare of stardom. His closest rival, Canada's Blaine Watson grabbed top honours for rising to the highest level.

The stewards of the international movement say this intensification of their efforts to usher in a world at peace has been inspired by a long history of failures with other approaches.

They claim that "since 1000 BC there have been over 8000 peace treaties, each one lasting an average of nine years." They speak too, of the failure of the league of nations (founded in the aftermath of world war one) and the United Nations (born after world war two) to put an end to strife among nations.

In fact the TMers note that since 1945 there have been more than 150 wars and they submit, "it is clear that political negotiations, treaties and use of arms have never and can never create a lasting state of world peace."

Their new thrust suggests that the road to a cool and harmonious state of affairs in St. Lucia and around the globe will need a liberal stock of foam mattresses on which yogic flyers can practice their art while driving away inner tensions and the stress of the world.

Trinidad and Tobago • *Trinidad Guardian*

Port-of-Spain   5 September 1986   (English)

Peace meeting

MINISTER of Sport, Culture and Youth Affairs Muriel Donawa-McDavidson will officially open the Maharishi's Programme to Create World Peace on Sunday afternoon, September 7, at 4 p.m. at the Fatima College auditorium.

The programme is being put on by the International Meditation Society and Maharishi College of Natural Law. The organisation says that it will be demonstrating the actual mechanics to physically create world peace.

MAHARISHI'S PROGRAMME TO CREAT[E]

PRESS REPORTS FROM LATIN AMERICA AND THE CARIBBEAN

Trinidad and Tobago • *Sunday Punch*

Port-of-Spain 14 September 1986 (English)

Men who fly

Story and picture by
CISSLYN RAMDEO

COULD you believe that humans are able to fly?

Not on a aeroplane or with the aid of engines, but with sheer mental strength.

This was the case when the International Meditation Society demonstrated the Yogic flying technique last weekend.

The auditorium of the Fatima College in Mucurapo was crowded with curious onlookers as they had their eyes fixed on the two yogis.

Ian Persad and Ruthvyn Forte sat with legs folded as they meditated while the audience was asked to remain silent.

But after the yogis had meditated for five minutes, the crowd broke out in gasps of surprise as the men began to fly.

With their legs folded, they were hoisted up in the air and carried for several yards.

According to David Lee Shen Tin, president of the Society, the men got the strenght to fly from their minds.

He also stated that by transcendental meditation, (T.M.) the mind is able to order the body to do anything and succeed.

This type of meditation was founded by His Holiness Maharishi Mahesh Yogi of India and has been practiced in Trinidad for the past 20 years.

The Meditation Society of Trinidad has a membership of more than 4,000 and is growing rapidly.

What seems to attract participants is the enormous inner peace that is attained after transcendental meditation.

Believers are convinced that T.M is the only solution to terrorism and war.

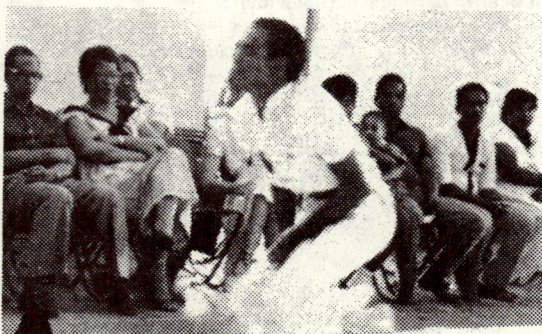

Yogi **RUTHVYN FORTE**, as he flys through the air after meditating.

WORLD PEACE • GLOBAL INAUGURATION

PRESS REPORTS FROM LATIN AMERICA AND THE CARIBBEAN

Uruguay • *El Pais*
Montevideo   11 September 1986   (Spanish)

En Procura de la paz Mundial
La Levitación, Práctica de Yoguis Avanzados es Exhibida en Montevideo

Una demostración de levitación será concretada ante autoridades nacionales y prensa en general, por parte de seguidores del Maharishi Mahesh Yogui, como parte de su campaña para crear la Paz Mundial que se viene concretando simultáneamente en 108 países.

En ese sentido, visitó la redacción de EL PAIS, Angel Haro, quien mañana a partir de las 15:00 horas en la Asociación Cristiana de Jóvenes, 7° piso de Colonia 1870, realizará las prácticas levitatorias originadas según el mismo expresa en la "Técnica Sidhis-M.T. del Vuelo Yógico", agregando que "las investigaciones científicas han demostrado que a través de esta técnica las personas pueden crear coherencia en la conciencia mundial, base para establecer y mantener de forma permanente la paz mundial".

Durante el "vuelo yógico", según explicitó su practicante, el cuerpo se eleva y comienza a saltar debido a la coherencia que se imprime a la mente. 'La expansión de la coherencia se expande, neutralizando las tendencias negativas en toda la creación" afirmó el levitador.

Paralelamente reseñó que las personas que se encuentran en el entorno, autoridades y prensa en este caso; podrán apreciar diversas modificaciones en su sentir momentáneo e incluso experimentar diversas sensaciones físicas.

Con respecto a las prácticas que lleva adelante el Instituto Maharishi de Ley Natural, su Directora en Uruguay, Doris Stenger afirmó que "treinta y un estudios sociológicos realizados alrededor del mundo durante los pasados doce años han mostrado que el uno por ciento o más de una población practicando la técnica de la Meditación Trascendental mejora la calidad de vida en la sociedad". En la actualidad los interesados pueden dirigirse los lunes a partir de las 19:30 a las charlas informativas que se concretan en Tristán Narvaja 1513.

Agregó la seguidora de Maharishi que durante la realización de estas demostraciones semi-públicas que se han comenzado en el mundo, en La Haya, y Norteamérica, se constató tras su concreción una variante positiva a nivel de la pacificación e incluso de las economías locales. Sólo resta aguardar entonces los eventuales a suceder en nuestro medio, tras la práctica levitatoria.

El uruguayo Angel Haro, que levitará mañana en nuestra capital, junto a Doris Stenger, Directora del centro de nuestra capital, dialogan con EL PAIS, sobre la experiencia.

PRESS REPORTS FROM LATIN AMERICA AND THE CARIBBEAN

Uruguay • *El Pais*

Montevideo   15 September 1986   (Spanish)

Levitación, pero en cómodas cuotas

Concretada la experiencia de levitación, anunciada por los seguidores del Maharishi Mahesh Yogui en nuestra capital, los diferentes medios presentes se mostraron algo asombrados, y hasta escépticos, sobre la serie de breves saltos sentados efectuadas sobre esponjosos colchones en la Asociación Cristiana de Jóvenes, que cediera su local para la experiencia. Previo a la ejecución se brindó una disertación explicativa de la "Técnica Sidhis —M.T. del vuelo Yóguico", a través de un excelente video tape efectuado en los Estados Unidos, en donde los levitadores concretan **competencias**, en estadios cerrados, casi similares en las olímpicas, en donde en una posición "de loto" recorren distancias en breves saltos, con vallas, efectuan tornos de levitación en altura

El acontecimiento tuvo su razón en el inicio de la campaña para crear la paz mundial, que se viene concretando simultáneamente en 108 países.

LA LEVITACION CRIOLLA

Iniciada la conferencia tres representantes del organismo se intercalaron para efectuar explicaciones ante la nutrida concurrencia presente. Posteriormente se desarrolló la televisación del video-tape; en el que se exhibían las competencias en Estados Unidos, donde numerosos levitadores cumplían con sus "salto-largo"; "Salto alto"; carreras en distancia; y recibiendo las preseas, ante el aplauso general del estadio, que hay que reconocer estaba prácticamente colmado.

Luego de ello, el uruguayo Angel Haro, tras ser extendidos dos colchones de poliuretano en el suelo del salón, y cubrirlo con un manto naranja, procedió a concentrarse acompañado de otros "pensadores" que colaboraron con su meditación. En determinado momento Haro, sentado sobre el extremo de un colchón experimentó algo similar a temblores, y con las manos sobre sus rodillas "levitó" en breves saltos de una punta a otra de los colchones, girando al llegar al extremo.

Luego de cuatro minutos aproximados de saltos, el meditador finalizo su labor, reseñándose que esto es simplemente una primera etapa evolutiva de la levitación que llevará en el futuro a lograr trasladarse en el espacio y por el aire.

WORLD PEACE • GLOBAL INAUGURATION

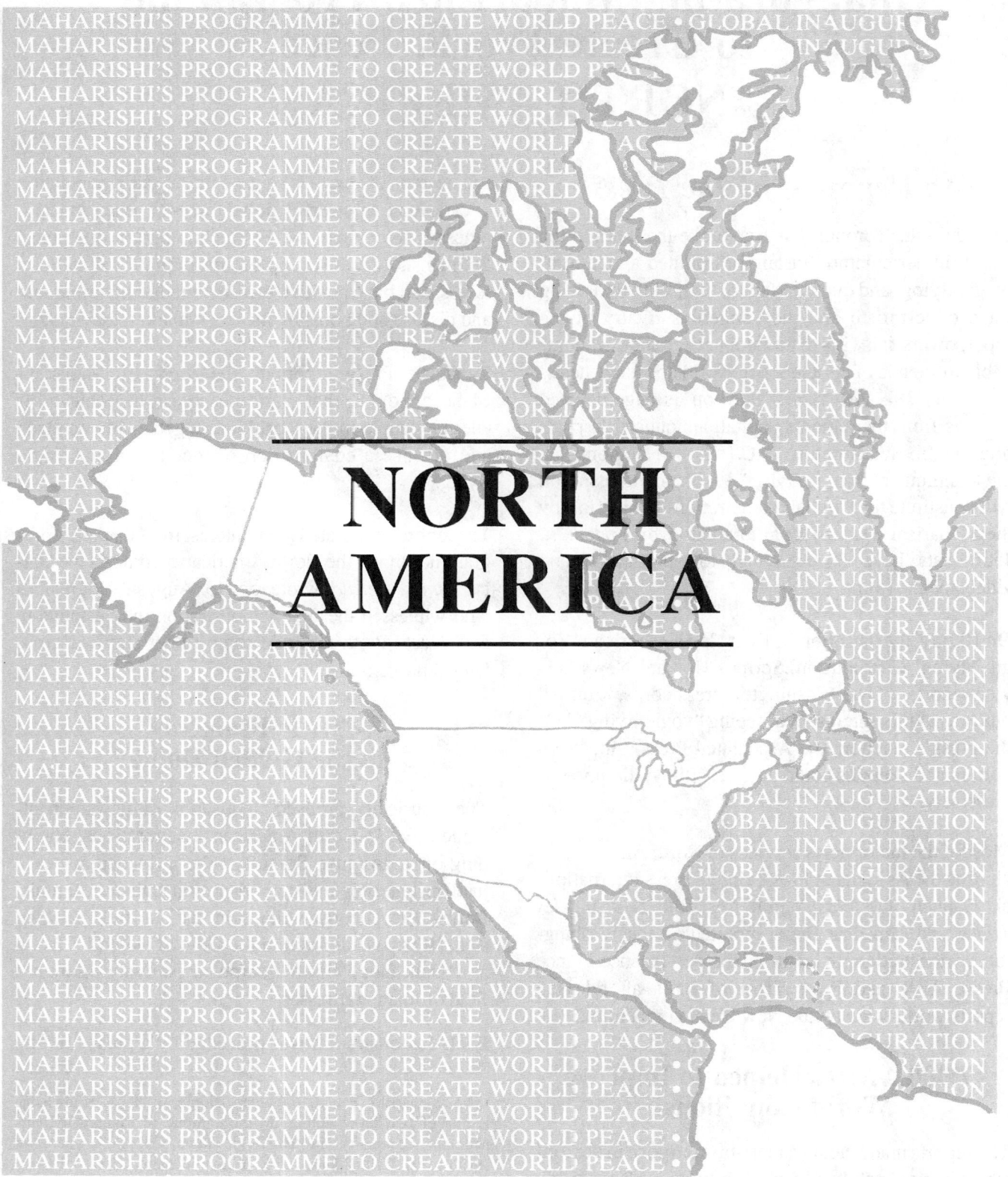

NORTH AMERICA

Inaugurating Maharishi's Programme to Create World Peace
NORTH AMERICA

As Reported by the Press

On 7 July the Toronto *Star* first broke the news to the world. In her column, Susan Ford printed a picture of 'yogic flying' and quoted Maharishi: '[With the] rising wave of terrorism and the dangerous rivalry of the superpowers, it is vital to immediately create an indomitable influence of coherence in world consciousness.' On 8 July *The New York Times*, on its page devoted to news from the nation's capital, announced 'a press briefing [in Washington, D.C.] ... [to] demonstrate the technique of "yogic flying".... The demonstration will constitute the "global inauguration" of an effort by the Maharishi Mahesh Yogi to create world peace.... Journalists have been invited to photograph and videotape the event.'

On 10 July, the day after the First North American 'Yogic Flying' Competition, Scripps Howard News Service reported, 'The Washington press corps, it turned out, was avidly interested in seeing "yogic flying".' Of the press's reaction, the Associated Press said, 'Supporters and skeptics could agree ... [they] did hop impressively.'

Most of the major news services in North America, including the Associated Press, United Press International, Gannett, the *Washington Post*, the *Los Angeles Times*, and Canadian Press, reported on the Washington demonstration. In addition, the AP, Agence France Presse, UPI, and Press Trust of India all released reports world-wide on the New Delhi competition.

'7,000 ... Has Helped to Improve World Conditions'

The reports made clear Maharishi's purpose in demonstrating 'yogic flying'. On 21 July, the AP reported, 'TM organizers say that about 7,000 people—the square root of one per cent of the world's population—can create a powerful global force for peace and happiness if they apply the TM technology in one place. Studies show that similar groups on national and city levels also have positive effects in reducing crime rate and disease and boosting the stock market, they say.'

Canadian Press reported 'the view of Maharishi Mahesh Yogi ... that world peace can be achieved if enough people in the world join together in one place and practise a combination of meditation and yogic flying.'

The reports stimulated great interest in Maharishi's programme among the North American media. As the Dallas *Times Herald* wrote on 15 August, 'Journalists who witnessed the first demonstration in Washington, D.C., last month reported some rather startling cross legged hops....'

'It Is Peaceful in the Golden Dome'

Their curiosity aroused, thousands of newsmen attended the 72 North American inaugurations, beginning on 15 August. Some felt the influence of peace just on entering the demonstration halls. Columnist Bobby Lowenberg, writing in the Fairfield *Ledger*, said, 'It is peaceful within the Golden Dome.* I feel it as I walk along the red-carpeted pathway through a field of foam mattresses.'

Each demonstration was preceded by a press briefing

---

*The Maharishi Patanjali Golden Dome of Pure Knowledge is one of two large domes on the campus of Maharishi International University in Fairfield, Iowa, U.S.A., where at least 1,600 TM-Sidhas have been practising the Maharishi Technology of the Unified Field together for the past four years.

WORLD PEACE • GLOBAL INAUGURATION
INAUGURATING MAHARISHI'S PROGRAMME TO CREATE WORLD PEACE—NORTH AMERICA

in which Maharishi's principles and practical programme to create world peace were explained. The *Washington Times* quoted Dr Morris: 'This technique can create world peace ... and the decision for this display was impelled by a need for world peace.'

'Peace in the Making'

Following the briefings, journalists waited silently as the demonstrators meditated for five or ten minutes and then started 'yogic flying'.

'Suddenly', said the Stockton *Record*, 'it was future peace in the making, in a burst of energy that opened eyes and lifted heads....'

A headline in the *Indianapolis Star* reported, 'Boing! Crocco just up and flew.'

People magazine's comment, next to a photograph of two happy 'yogic flyers', was, 'Wreathed in beatific smiles, they hopped and they hopped.'

After the 'yogic flying', which lasted for about 10 minutes, the journalists eagerly asked the demonstrators about their experiences.

'There's a sense of being superfluid,' Sally Mattoon told the San Diego *Tribune*. Eddie Gob told *People*, 'You feel such wonder, such joy ... and then you're flying.... I'm not surprised my body lifts up.... I'm surprised it comes back down.' Bill Van Zandt said to the Quad City *Times*, 'You just can't imagine the bliss and exhilaration you feel.' The newspaper commented, 'Boy could these guys hop.'

Flowers were given to the TM-Sidhas following the demonstrations, recognizing not so much their physical feat as its effect—the influence of coherence created in world consciousness. As the *Washington Post* noted, 'What better laurel for a victorious yogic flyer than a red rose?'

Many journalists wanted to know when the hopping would become hovering and free flight. Dr Bevan Morris's answer, quoted in the Hartford *Courant*, was, 'In the years ahead the hops will be longer and higher and this will be the parameter of the expanding world consciousness.'

Newsmen asked guests what they thought of the demonstration. Fairfield City Councillor Ruth Ewart told the *Ledger*, 'It was dramatic and I was glad to be here.'

The San Francisco *Examiner's* reporter called the Berkeley demonstration 'one of the most charming, good-natured demonstrations for peace ever held in this ... community.'

'World Peace Will Be a By-product of People Creating Bliss'

The press couldn't help but feel the bliss. 'They fly the blissful skies of Maharishi's meditation,' said a headline in the Lakewood, Ohio *Sun Post*. *People* reported on 'the blissful flight of the Maharishi's yogic hoppers'. One interviewer wrote in the Forest City, Pennsylvania *News* about a TM-Sidha: 'Whatever Pat Hirsch radiates is good, because this interview was one of the most pleasurable I've had the occasion to do.'

The media was also closely attuned to the significance of the demonstrations. Gannett News Service asked, "Did you feel more peaceful on Wednesday? Maybe it was because of 22 flying yogis....' The Winnipeg, Manitoba *Sun* began its article, 'If your world was more peaceful than usual Friday, thank the Maharishi Mahesh Yogi.'

The San Diego *Tribune* reported '"Yogic flying" launches Maharishi peace plan.' The Southfield, Michigan *Eccentric* said, 'They "fly" in the air for the sake of peace on earth.' Said the Madison, Wisconsin *Capital Times*, '... Peace will come if we just hop.' The headline in the San Francisco *Chronicle* said, 'Bouncing the global blues away'. In the Grand Rapids, Michigan *Press:* 'Hopping for peace—Maharishi's disciples believe meditation can allay world's violence.' The *Northern Nevada Communicator* quoted Maharishi: 'The group practice will make peace on earth powerful

(Continued on page 440)

MAHARISHI'S PROGRAMME TO CREATE

REPORTING THE DEMONSTRATIONS OF 'YOGIC FL
HEADLINES FROM NORTH AMERICAN NEWSP

'Yogic flying' gets off the ground

Yogi unveils those amazing young men and their flying

'Yogic Flying' introduced to public for first time

Yogic 'Olympics' Off To A Flying Start

Maharishi's men show off talents

Up, up and away

Practitioners going public with 'yogic flying' displays

'Yogic Flying Competition' proves uplifting

And Awaaaaaaaay We Go

That's Incredible

Levitation Through Meditation Amazes Crowd

'Yogic Flying' contest gets off the ground

Can't afford plane? Try 'yogic' flying

Blissful Yogic flyers meditate, hop high ... and awaaaay they go

Newest Maharishi Mahesh Yogi Practice: Bliss-Induced Flying

Yogis 'superradiate' to end world's woes

'Yogic flying competition' called a hopping success

Wanted: 7,000 TM Flyers to Secure World Peace

Maharishi's men demonstrate ability to 'fly' without wings

Maharishi's men find 'flying' quite blissful

Yogic convention 'flies'

TM 'fliers' hop to it

Yogic flyers won't sit still for world's mounting problems

WORLD PEACE • GLOBAL INAUGURATION

'ng'—The Mechanics to Create World Peace
ers • July, August, and September 1986

Flying yogis hop for world peace

Levitation the path to peace

Yogic olympics has flying start

'Yogic flyers' wow reporters

Meditators go for the gold

Yoga flying: seeing is believing

Yogi's followers rise to new heights in 'flying' competition

3-2-1...Bliss off!
'Yogic flyers' use heads instead of jet engines

Bouncing the Global Blues Away

Yogis Have Hopping Good Time

No license required:

Up, up and awaaaaaaay

Yogic fliers claim bliss-induced flight

Followers of yogi 'fly' in blissful meditation

22 flying yogis make a hop at bringing peace to the world

'Yogic Flying' Students Get a Jump on Bliss

Okay everybody! Let's fly!

Yogi fliers 'levitate' in bounds

Maharishi's men up in air at convention

'Yogic flying' is an eye-catcher

Rising to the occasion

Bliss-fueled flight starts with a hop

Up, up and away with 'yogic flying'

Maharishi meditators: 'I think, therefore I fly'

Maharishi's Followers 'Fly' With The Greatest Of Ease

Yogi's followers hopping for world peace

Yogi Followers 'Fly' to Ease World's Stress

Yogis Say They're a Hop, Skip and Jump From Flying

439

and power on earth peaceful.' The *Denver Post* put it simply: 'Peace Postures'. The Honolulu *Advertiser* was more expansive: 'Yogi's disciples try levitating to help calm a troubled world.' The Dubuque, Iowa *Telegraph Herald* said, 'Enjoy life and fight terrorism.' In that report on 17 August, United Press International wrote, 'When it comes to ending terrorism and promoting world peace, followers of Transcendental Meditation say they are ready to hop to it.'

UPI went on to say that the appeal of the programme is to the individual. Quoting one TM-Sidha, the news service wrote, '"What we need to let the individual know is, yes, there is something he can do" to end world terrorism … world peace will become a by-product of people "creating joy individually in their own lives."'

'Thank You, Maharishi'

The report in the Burlington, Vermont *Free Press* began, 'Steve Birkett … and Andy Cozzens … spent a little piece of Friday conquering terrorism, crime, war, and a sluggish stock market. They did their part by sitting yoga-style and hopping down 30 feet of foam mat…. Vermont TM leader Bill Powers explained that meditation creates maximum brain wave coherence. That allows the hoppers to get off the floor. The coherence also spreads from the individual through the world, rinsing out stress like a washing machine.'

Some alert reporters checked the news of the day to see if even the demonstration had created some more coherence in society. KCRA-TV 3 in Stockton, California, reported, 'The stock market fluctuated throughout the day, but toward the closing bell, about the time the flying yogis lifted off their mats, well, it shot up by more than ten points. Now, we're not sure this was a direct result of their efforts. However, maybe some people here at Paine Webber [a stock brokerage house] are saying, "Thank you, Maharishi."'

In New Haven, Connecticut, the *Register* reported, 'Even though no one soared Friday, the demonstration may have had a tranquilizing effect anyway. Cromwell police said Friday was as calm and quiet a day as they've seen all summer.'

A reporter for the Honolulu *Advertiser* wrote, 'Lift-off occurred at 1:07 p.m. In Beirut at that moment, according to the World Desk of United Press International, there were no reports of terrorist activity. It was probably only a coincidence … but … [TM-Sidhas believe that] hopping helps to reduce world stress.'

A television report of the demonstration in Davenport, Iowa, began, 'Where world leaders have failed, TM followers say they can succeed.'

The Minneapolis *Star and Tribune* reported one TM-Sidha as saying, 'The participation of global leaders isn't essential to the success of yogic flying for world peace…. "Maharishi estimates that [if] about 7,000 can get together in a permanent facility and practise [this] twice daily, that would be a powerful enough influence of coherence and evolutionary positive trend to establish world peace."'

'World Peace Today Is Just a Matter of Money'

In fact, declared the Rock Island, Illinois *Argus* in a headline on 16 August, 'Yogic "fliers" could achieve world peace for $100 million.' The article began, 'The U.S. budget could be balanced quickly; the U.S. deficit could be wiped out in a few years. The mechanism would cost $100 million, quite a savings from the Reagan Administration's proposed $320 [billion] defense budget for 1987. It's the Maharishi World Peace Fund, which would maintain, permanently in one place, a group of 7,000 persons expert in Maharishi Mahesh Yogi's technology of the unified field…. The technology is to create coherence in world consciousness and eliminate terrorism and war.'

Newspapers throughout North America quoted Dr Morris's statement: 'World peace today is just a matter of money.'

'Utopia for the World'

On 10 July, the *Washington Post* said, 'If yesterday's

WORLD PEACE • GLOBAL INAUGURATION

INAUGURATING MAHARISHI'S PROGRAMME TO CREATE WORLD PEACE—NORTH AMERICA

competition was any indication, the road to world peace is paved with rubber mats, divided into five lanes and populated by would-be hoppers neutralizing their own and the world's stress.' On 16 August, a Burlington *Free Press* headline declared, "Yogic flyers" hopping path toward utopia for the world.'

Inaugurations throughout the Continent

Not only the press, but thousands of North Americans from every walk of life came on 15 August to learn about Maharishi's uniquely effective programme to create world peace. From Vancouver to Florida, at hotels and Capitals of the Age of Enlightenment in more than 70 cities, fascinated audiences listened to the scientists and watched the demonstrations of man's most powerful technology.

U.S.A.

At the Hilton Hotel in **Melbourne, Florida**, not far from the site where man first rocketed to the moon, 100 people witnessed the first stage of a more profound kind of rocketry—one designed by nature to boost the world to peace. Beneath a banner proclaiming, 'First Space Coast Yogic Flying Demonstration', three TM-Sidhas showed the mechanics to create world peace to journalists and local leaders, who included executives and scientists from the National Aeronautics and Space Administration and Lockheed Aircraft. Radio brought the news to many more people locally, Orlando television broadcast it throughout central Florida, and the newspaper *Florida Today* made it available state-wide.

Paul Gelderloos, Assistant Professor of Psychology at Maharishi International University in Iowa, who presented Maharishi's programme in Melbourne, described the event as 'perfect'.

'The audience's main question afterwards was, "What do you want us to do?",' he said.

Further south, the **Miami** area had its own demonstration in the Sheraton Hotel in Boca Raton. In **Atlanta, Georgia**, several hundred miles to the north, reporters from two television stations and Atlanta's major daily newspaper came to the event at the Capital of the Age of Enlightenment.

One of the Atlanta television teams was called away on another assignment before the 'yogic flying' had been demonstrated. To prepare their story for the 6:00 p.m. news, the reporters took scenes from the Boston, Massachusetts, demonstration, 1,000 miles away, that had been filmed by an affiliated station and transmitted by communications satellite. Three weeks later, a television network based in Atlanta produced for national broadcast a half-hour documentary on Maharishi's Programme to Create World Peace.

In **Philadelphia, Pennsylvania**, the demonstration was attended by reporters from the *Inquirer* and several smaller papers. In **Baltimore, Maryland**, 15 TM-Sidhas created what organizers described as 'a very wonderful, powerful feeling in the room.'

WABC television, the Associated Press, *Newsday*, Gamma (the international news photo service), and the *New York Post* all sent journalists to **New York City, New York's** Capital of the Age of Enlightenment to witness and record 'yogic flying'. That evening, ABC Eyewitness News, one of the most widely watched evening news programmes in the U.S.A., reported that 'the demonstration will quiet skeptics.'

Elsewhere in New York, Maharishi's programme was inaugurated in **Suffolk** and **Westchester** counties, and people from throughout upstate New York joined residents of **Rochester** to see a demonstration of 'yogic flying' at a local college there.

Spectators and journalists from central **New Jersey** came to **Montclair**, while those from the southern part of the state attended a demonstration at the South Jersey Capital of the Age of Enlightenment in **Collingswood**. There, the journalists asked so many questions that the conference continued for two-and-a-half hours.

MAHARISHI'S PROGRAMME TO CREAT[E]

INAUGURATING MAHARISHI'S PROGRAMME TO CREATE WORLD PEACE—NORTH AMERICA

Large Audiences in New England

In **Connecticut**, one television station used a film clip of 'yogic flying' throughout the day to promote that evening's news programme. The station broadcast a report on the inauguration in **New Haven** to more than one million people throughout the state. The broadcast featured six TM-Sidhas, each wearing in bold letters on his shirt the name of his home town. The next day, another million people in Hartford, New Haven, and Bridgeport read newspaper reports of the demonstration. In the words of one Sidha, 'Our whole state came together for this.'

Faculty from Brown University were among the guests at the **Providence, Rhode Island,** Capital of the Age of Enlightenment, in one of the city's suburbs. ABC Channel 12 television, with the largest viewing audience in the state, featured the demonstration on its 6:00 p.m. news.

The TM-Sidhas in **Cambridge, Massachusetts,** wore shirts proclaiming, 'Flyers for Peace', and demonstrated beneath a 20-foot banner that read, 'Maharishi's Programme to Create World Peace'. Journalists from WGBH-TV, one of America's best-known and most highly respected public television stations, as well as United Press International, *Harvard Magazine*, and other media attended, as did Harvard faculty and the presidents of several high technology companies in the Greater Boston area. A *Middlesex News* columnist counted 300 spectators. An Associated Press reporter said he 'could feel the hopping'. 'Yogic flying' was the lead story on Boston's NBC Channel 4 television news. That same evening another station interviewed Dr Deepak Chopra, President of the American Association for Ayurvedic Medicine, on the relationship between 'yogic flying', world peace, and global health.

The Transcendental Meditation teaching centres in **New Hampshire** jointly organized a demonstration in the city of **Manchester**, while in neighbouring **Vermont** journalists from throughout the state congregated for the inauguration at the **Burlington** Capital of the Age of Enlightenment.

Inaugurations in the Midwest

Sixty people filled the lecture room at the **Cleveland, Ohio,** Capital of the Age of Enlightenment to hear Dr David Orme-Johnson, world authority on the Maharishi Effect, present scientific research showing that the TM-Sidhi 'yogic flying' technique creates a strong influence of coherence and peace in society. Ohio's largest newspaper, the *Plain Dealer*, as well as *Cleveland Magazine*, two television stations, and National Public Radio all sent reporters. The journalists asked many questions of Dr Orme-Johnson and the TM teachers present, who said it was 'the most fulfilling experience of our teaching careers'. In September, three TM-Sidhas presented Maharishi's programme in **Canton**. Their demonstration was reported at length in the principal newspapers of both Canton and Akron.

In **Indiana**, two demonstrations were held, one in the state capital, **Indianapolis**, and a second at a private home in **Muncie**. In Muncie, where 50 people attended, the hostess said, 'So many people responded to our invitation that some had to sit in the entryway and on the stairs.' Local journalists were among the audience, and the Muncie *Star* printed a long report of the inauguration on the national and global news page. The Muncie *Evening Press* put its story on the front page with a photograph. Later, the *Evening Press* reporter wrote to the hostess, 'I don't know how others felt, but I could really feel the energy and the joy bubbling up, which caused me to laugh and feel really good…. I feel so clear, even now.'

The demonstration in **Detroit, Michigan**, also inaugurated the city's new Capital of the Age of Enlightenment. Among the 40 guests were journalists from several newspapers and radio stations as well as a camera crew from Detroit's largest television station. That evening a popular Detroit sportscaster featured 'yogic flying' as the national event of the day. In **Grand Rapids,** the demonstration at the Amway Grand Plaza Hotel drew local press and many guests, and, according to the organizers, stimulated great public interest in learning the Transcendental Meditation technique.

WORLD PEACE • GLOBAL INAUGURATION

INAUGURATING MAHARISHI'S PROGRAMME TO CREATE WORLD PEACE—NORTH AMERICA

At the Holiday Inn in **Chicago, Illinois,** four professors from Maharishi International University presented the principles of 'yogic flying', and five TM-Sidhas demonstrated for an audience of 50 people. Channel 5 TV photographed one of the competitors in the yogic high jump hopping over two feet high. One hundred miles south, in **Champaign-Urbana,** all three television stations, the local newspaper, and University of Illinois radio reported on the presentation, describing in detail Maharishi's Programme to Create World Peace and the Maharishi World Peace Fund.

Milwaukee and **Madison, Wisconsin,** and **Minneapolis, Minnesota,** all hosted presentations by members of the MIU faculty. In Madison, the event was held at the University of Wisconsin. At the Business Technology Center in Minneapolis, journalists had many questions: What is the least excited state of consciousness? When will you hover? That night, the answers were reported on the 6:00 p.m. and 11:00 p.m. television news, and the next day the Minneapolis *Star and Tribune* carried a full report.

In **Fargo, North Dakota,** the *Forum* printed an article and photograph of the 'yogic flying' demonstration held there in early September.

Iowans Master Natural Law

Maharishi International University in **Fairfield, Iowa,** played an important role in demonstrations throughout North America, sending TM-Sidhas and faculty to 14 cities to help the local people present Maharishi's Programme to Create World Peace. In Fairfield itself, a thousand people filled MIU's Maharishi Patanjali Golden Dome of Pure Knowledge for the presentation on 15 August. The guests included the mayor, the Executive Board of the Chamber of Commerce, and seven news teams from around the state.

KGAN TV's 'Iowa Tonight' showed scenes from the press conference at MIU's Carnegie Hall, in which Dr Geoffrey Wells, Dean of the College of the Science of Creative Intelligence, explained the three stages of 'yogic flying'—hopping, hovering, and directed flight.

The report showed two TM-Sidhas hopping onto a stack of foam as the broadcaster said, 'These practitioners believe each flight is a step towards peace.' One TM-Sidha told the interviewer, 'The coherence that's generated in the individual naturally radiates in society. Through the structuring of coherent, happy, peaceful individuals, we structure world peace.' The reporter commented, 'That means peaceful people make a peaceful world.'

On 29 August, MIU students demonstrated 'yogic flying' to Iowa student government leaders and the media at MIU's First Student 'Yogic Flying' Competition. In the yogic high jump, So Kam Tim, a psychology and government major, set a new world's record on his way to winning three gold medals. Michelle Beausoliel, bronze medalist in the ladies' 50-metre race, said, 'The competition was blissful for everyone. There was not a sense of a winner or a loser, but a sense of unity among the participants.' Another competitor, Claude Windenberger, commented, 'What I felt was probably one of the deepest silences since I started practising Transcendental Meditation.

On 15 August at the Savery Hotel in **Des Moines,** TM-Sidhas competed in 'yogic flying' on 600 square feet of foam marked off by ribbons in three long lanes. The Associated Press, United Press International, two Iowa newspapers, and two television and four local radio stations all sent reporters to the event. The AP quoted MIU faculty member Dr Ron Openshaw as saying of 'yogic flying', 'It's not defying natural law.... It's just raising human life to its dignity as master of natural law.' Dr Openshaw summarized the presentation: 'We have a practical technique to bring enlightenment to the individual and peace to the world.'

The Quad City *Times* began its report of the event in **Davenport** with a photograph of a TM-Sidha flying a foot above a hurdle. Next to the picture was a quotation from Maharishi: 'They are all up in the air, inviting everyone who still has their feet on the ground to join them in ushering in the sunshine of the Age of Enlightenment.'

INAUGURATING MAHARISHI'S PROGRAMME TO CREATE WORLD PEACE—NORTH AMERICA

Guests at the demonstration in **Kansas City, Missouri,** said that 'the feeling in the room was marvellous.' Two television stations and the two principal newspapers of the city sent reporters. Another journalist from National Public Radio sat on the foam with the TM-Sidhas after their demonstration and asked them how they felt. MIU student Trung Tran replied, 'It's a very blissful experience ... it's one of great unboundedness, of real peace within yourself.'

In **St. Louis**, reporters came from all the newspapers in the city and from two television and three radio stations. Several weeks later a half-hour television special brought news of Maharishi's programme to all the people of the region.

On 6 October, three TM-Sidhas presented Maharishi's programme at **Nashville, Tennessee's** Vanderbilt Plaza, one of the city's finer hotels. Four journalists attended the demonstration. In a report the next day, *The Tennessean* quoted one of the TM-Sidhas: 'In this age of terrorism and threats to world peace, we need a technology that will neutralize stress and create coherence in world consciousness....'

That same week, at a private home in **Birmingham, Alabama,** three TM-Sidhas demonstrated the mechanics to create world peace for members of the press. The city's largest newspaper, the *Post-Herald*, printed an article covering two-thirds of a page and including two photographs of 'yogic flying'.

And in **Baton Rouge, Louisiana**, on 15 August, MIU faculty presented Maharishi's programme at Louisiana State University.

Demonstrating Maharishi's Programme in the Southwest

Dallas, Houston, and **Austin, Texas,** held simultaneous inaugurations at 11:00 a.m. on 15 August. The TM-Sidhas in Austin demonstrated at the Hyatt Regency Hotel beneath long banners that said, 'Coherently Functioning Brain Physiology, the Unit of World Peace'. After the 'yogic flying', scientists measured the increased coherence of the Sidhas' brain activity. The Dallas *Times Herald*, the Dallas *Morning News*, and the Fort Worth *Star Telegram*, as well as television and radio all reported on the demonstration in Dallas. In Houston, both major television stations devoted four minutes on the evening news to scenes of 'yogic flying'.

In **Albuquerque, New Mexico,** Maharishi's programme was introduced at a news conference, while in **Denver, Colorado; Reno** and **Las Vegas, Nevada;** and **Tucson** and **Phoenix, Arizona,** 'yogic flying' was demonstrated. The event in Phoenix, held at Arizona State University, was reported by two television stations and Arizona's largest newspaper. At the end of a television report on the demonstration in Reno, the reporter, referring to 100 helium balloons that were released at the conclusion of 'yogic flying', said, 'Some day, they say, they will be able to fly just as high and just as easily as the balloons.'

'Yogic Flying' along the Pacific Coast

Demonstrations in the Pacific Northwest were held in **Portland, Oregon,** and **Seattle, Washington**. TM-Sidhas from Tacoma, Bellevue, and Bremerton joined those from Seattle in a competition that was reported by the Associated Press, two television stations, and seven newspapers.

In **Sacramento, California**, directly across the street from the State Capitol, 'yogic flyers' demonstrated the technique for coherence in state, national, and world consciousness. Both Sacramento newspapers published reports, and Channel 3 television showed scenes of the demonstration held at the same time in nearby **Stockton**.

Marin County TM-Sidhas convened a news conference. An inauguration for the entire San Francisco Bay Area was held in **Berkeley**, where 13 Sidhas demonstrated 'yogic flying' for several hundred guests, including many of the major television and radio stations, the Oakland *Tribune*, and the San Francisco *Chronicle*. The *Chronicle* called it 'a rare public display of mind over gravity'. In one press interview, a 68-year-old TM-Sidha was asked, 'How far do you

WORLD PEACE • GLOBAL INAUGURATION

INAUGURATING MAHARISHI'S PROGRAMME TO CREATE WORLD PEACE—NORTH AMERICA

hop?' He replied, 'Oh, I don't know, I just feel the bliss and go up.' Wrote a reporter in the Martinez *News-Gazette*, 'His eyes twinkled and he laughed.... [He] is a happy man.'

One guest who saw a report on ABC television said that 'At the end, a scene from the demonstration was slowed down and played along with classical music to show the grace of "yogic flying". Then the motion stopped on one TM-Sidha floating in the air in bliss. It was beautiful.'

In **Palo Alto**, 130 people came to the Cubberly Theatre, the auditorium of the Stanford Linear Accelerator Center, to witness the meeting of ancient and modern science in Maharishi's mechanics to create world peace.

Elsewhere in California, inaugurations were held in the **Santa Clara Valley**, **Santa Rosa**, **Santa Barbara**, and **Orange County**. In **San Diego**, scientists from the local state university took EEG measurements after the demonstration of 'yogic flying'.

The inauguration at the National Capital of the Age of Enlightenment near **Los Angeles** was held in a large tent pavilion on a bluff overlooking the Pacific Ocean. TM meditators and Sidhas from throughout the Los Angeles area were joined by many guests. The mayor of Los Angeles sent a representative to see first-hand what the organizers had meant when they told him, 'We will turn Los Angeles into a city of angels.'

UPI, NBC, CBS, the *Herald Examiner*, the *Daily News*, and the *LA Weekly* were among the many press organizations represented. According to the organizers, one journalist was 'very impressed with the inner experience she felt during the demonstration. She said that normally she is hyperactive, but that she was happy and peaceful when she left.'

Soon after the demonstration in Los Angeles, NBC television began using a promotional tape for its evening news broadcast that included the statement, 'Some people run, some hop, and some fly,' and showed scenes of 'yogic flying' with the words, 'some hop'.

Far across the Pacific in **Hawaii**, 40 guests and journalists from three television stations and the *Star Bulletin* attended the inauguration at the Hotel Ilikau in **Honolulu**. After Maharishi's Programme to Create World Peace was explained, TM-Sidhas from three different islands demonstrated 'yogic flying'. 'We all felt very strong within ourselves during the exhibition,' one said. Afterwards, according to one guest, 'They appeared radiant.' The press response to Maharishi's programme, the Sidhas said, was 'great—very positive'. After the demonstration the Honolulu Capital of the Age of Enlightenment hosted a World Peace Banquet.

CANADA

In 1975, Maharishi had inaugurated the dawn of the Age of Enlightenment for North America at **Ottawa, Ontario's** Chateau Laurier, adjacent to the Canadian Parliament building. Again the venerable hotel was chosen, this time for the Canadian national inauguration of Maharishi's Programme to Create World Peace on 15 August.

Dr Ashley Deans, a Canadian physicist at Maharishi International University, explained the mechanics to create world peace to an audience of 80, and then eight TM-Sidhas demonstrated 'yogic flying'. The event was reported by CBC and CTV national television, CJOH TV, local CBC TV, CBC radio (in both French and English), several local radio stations, the Ottawa *Citizen*, the Toronto *Star*, and United Press International.

Elsewhere in Canada, demonstrations were held in **Vancouver**, **Victoria**, **Saskatoon**, **Winnipeg**, **Calgary**, **Edmonton**, **Sarnia**, **Toronto**, **Montreal**, **Québec City**, and **Halifax**.

Fifty people came to the demonstration in **Victoria, British Columbia**, which was given by three TM-Sidhas. A journalist from the Victoria *Times* attended, and Victoria television reported on the evening news. The *BC Engineer*, a magazine that circulates to 20 countries, published a feature article on 'yogic flying'.

The demonstration at the **Calgary, Alberta** Palliser

Hotel drew 25 journalists and resulted in extensive coverage by the Calgary *Herald*, two television stations, and local radio. Two experts in the Maharishi Technology of the Unified Field demonstrated in **Saskatoon** for journalists and leaders of **Saskatchewan** society. In **Winnipeg, Manitoba**, all three local television stations sent reporters to the demonstration, as did one newspaper, which devoted two-thirds of a page to its report.

In **Toronto, Ontario**, Canada's largest city, the Toronto *Globe and Mail*, Canada's premier newspaper, and Global Television, City Television, and CFMT-TV all reported on the demonstration by 12 TM-Sidhas.

Two television stations featured the inauguration in **Montreal, Québec.**

The **Halifax, Nova Scotia**, demonstration was held at Dalhousie University. Reports appeared on radio, on the front pages of both Halifax daily newspapers—the *Daily News* and the *Mail Star*—and on the evening CBC television news.

Of the demonstration in **Québec City, Québec**, *Le Journal de Québec* said on 16 August, 'In silence broken only by the sound of cameras— smiling from ear to ear—these people are giving the first Canadian demonstration of flying done by practitioners of Transcendental Meditation.' The article continued, 'Our three "yogis" were far from exhausted. They were full of energy and serenely calm. They even looked disappointed that the demonstration didn't last longer. The most important point in the flyers' message was "peace in the world". The road to universal harmony should be paved with foam mattresses—thick white foam mattresses on which at least 7,000 experts could hop together daily!'

'World Peace Begins with Personal Peace'

In many cities, the 15 August inauguration was followed several days later by a newspaper announcement offering every individual the opportunity to participate in Maharishi's Programme to Create World Peace. The headlines read, 'How You Can Help Create World Peace', and 'World Peace Begins with Personal Peace'. The text said, 'Learning Transcendental Meditation is a significant step to contribute to world peace while growing in vitality yourself.'

Thousands of North Americans who had been interested in Maharishi's programme from seeing 'yogic flying' or reading about it attended lectures on TM. Many began the practice, and many more who were already practising the TM technique were inspired to take the next step, learn the TM-Sidhi programme, and begin to create greater coherence in the collective consciousness of North America and the world. □

WORLD PEACE • GLOBAL INAUGURATION

INAUGURATING MAHARISHI'S PROGRAMME TO CREATE WORLD PEACE—NORTH AMERICA

TM-Sidha 'yogic flyers' from different towns in Connecticut at the New Haven demonstration.

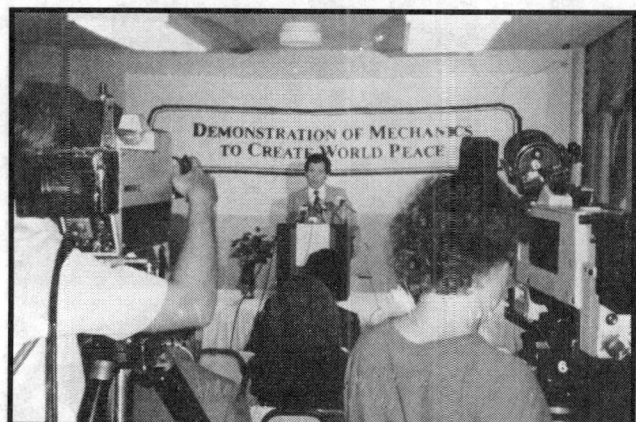

Iowa television records the Des Moines inauguration.

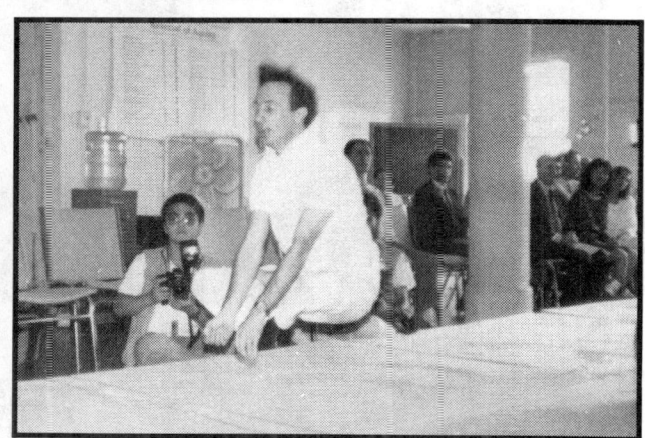

'Yogic flying' in New York City.

MAHARISHI'S PROGRAMME TO CREATE

INAUGURATING MAHARISHI'S PROGRAMME TO CREATE WORLD PEACE—NORTH AMERICA

The yogic high jump in Melbourne, Florida.

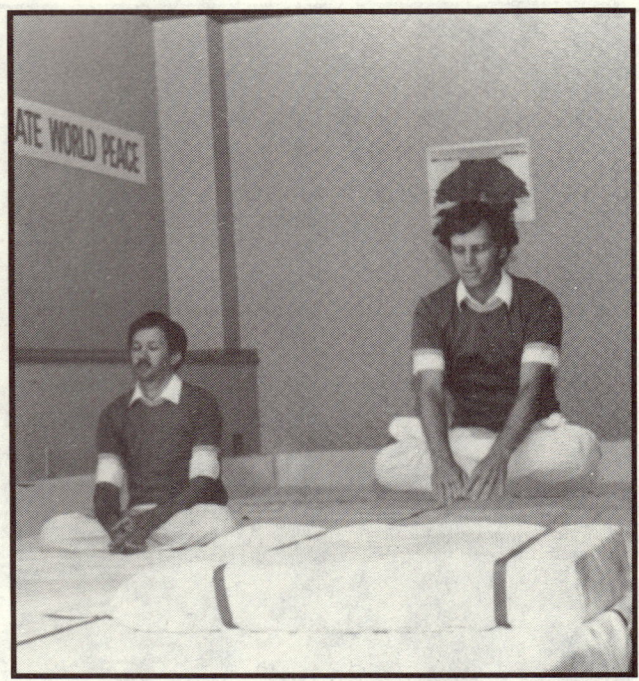
At the demonstration in Saskatoon, Canada.

Inauguration of Maharishi's programme at the Chateau Laurier Hotel, Ottawa, Canada.

WORLD PEACE • GLOBAL INAUGURATION

PRESS REPORTS FROM NORTH AMERICA

Canada • *The Canadian Press*

Washington, D.C. 9 July 1986 (English)

Yogis hop, skip and jump for world peace

WASHINGTON (CP) — The competitors, dressed in baggy white cotton pants and numbered shirts, tucked their feet over their thighs, began to meditate and at the sound of a chime began to lift off one by one.

What followed was 11 men hopping along a foam track with a series of raised bumps. The event was the men's 25-metre hurdles in the first North American Yogic Flying Competition.

Then there was the high-jump, long-jump and finally the 50-metre dash, all conducted from the same yoga sitting position and observed by more than 1,000 people.

The display, perhaps more accurately described as yogic hopping, had many trappings of a regular track-and-field competition. There were timers and judges. There were cheers and applause. And there was an award for each winner, a single red rose.

The winning times: 11.53 seconds in the 25-metre hurdles and 23.33 seconds in the 50-metre dash. The longest jump was 70 inches, or almost 1.8 metres; and the highest jump, by Blaine Watson of Elmira, Ont., was 24.75 inches or about 60 centimetres. Watson is a student at the Maharishi International University College of Natural Law in Washington.

But competition was not the only reason for the event. It was used primarily to promote the view of Maharishi Mahesh Yogi of India and his followers that world peace can be achieved if enough people in the world join together in one place and practise a combination of meditation and yogic flying.

The magic number, the Maharishi has said, is 7,000 people engaging together in what he labels the Technology of the Unified Field. They will, he said, generate a sufficiently strong influence of coherence to radiate globally and purify the whole world consciousness, which is the basis of world peace.

Believers say studies have shown the combination, when perfectly practised, has reduced killings in Lebanon, resulted in lower crime rates in the Netherlands and the United States and improved stock-market trends.

Bevan Morris, president of Maharishi International University in Fairfield, Iowa, told reporters the group decided on such a public display of the yogic-flying technique at this time because of rising world tensions, including recent terrorist outbreaks.

Governments, treaties and international peace organizations have failed to reduce tensions, he said.

The Maharishi teaches war is caused by the build up of stress in the collective consciousness of countries, Morris said.

Meditation is known to relieve stress for individuals and the idea is meditation by more people who also practise the yogic-flying technique can relieve collective stress, he said.

People who practise yogic flying say the body spontaneously lifts off from the ground at the point of the maximum coherence of brain waves, spreading a "super radiance" effect to people who are not participating in the joint meditation.

The Maharishi's program to create world peace calls for raising $100 million U.S. to permanently maintain a group of 7,000 experts practising his technology in India.

PRESS REPORTS FROM NORTH AMERICA

Canada • *Le Nouvelliste*

Trois-Rivières, Québec   8 August 1986   (French)

Le Trifluvien Périgny participe à une démonstration du 'Vol yogique'

par Jean CAUMARTIN

WASHINGTON— Les experts et instructeurs de Méditation transcendantale n'ont pas choisi pour rien la capitale américaine comme lieu d'intervention. Pour eux, il s'agit d'un endroit stratégique où les grandes décisions influencent la paix mondiale.

Le 9 juillet dernier, c'est à Washington que Messieurs Ken Matthews de Montréal et Roger Périgny de Trois-Rivières, instructeurs de Méditation Transcendantale, accompagnés de 3,000 autres experts de la Technologie Maharishi du Champ Unifié ont fait une démonstration d'une méthode ancienne mais validée scientifiquement pour établir la paix à travers le monde entier: la technique de MT-Sidhi appelée "Vol yogique".

Selon Ken Matthews, la recherche scientifique a démontré que la technique de Méditation Transcendantale élimine les tentions, augmente la créativité et améliore la santé. De plus, selon le docteur David Orme-Johnson, chef du Département de psychologie de l'Université internationale Maharishi à Fairfield, Iowa (E-U), la technique du "Vol yogique" améliore le degré d'intelligence, la capacité d'apprendre, la santé et promouvoit la longévité.

Plusieurs études ont démontré qu'au moment où 7000 experts, soit la racine carrée d'un pour cent de la population mondiale, effectuent ensemble la technique du "Vol yogique", ils produisent une influence de cohérence qui neutralise les tentions et tendances négatives, puis renforcit la positivité dans toutes les sociétés du monde.

Il y a eu, dans le cadre d'une " Assemblée Mondiale pour la Promotion d'une Santé Parfaite", une toute première compétition nord américaine du 4 au 13 juillet à Washington D.C.

Les finalistes chez les hommes ont atteint une hauteur de 61 centimètres dans la catégorie du saut en hauteur, une distance de 1,80 mètres pour le saut en longueur, et des temps de 23,33 secondes dans la course de 50 mètres et de 11,83 secondes dans la course à la haie de 25 mètres. Tous les experts étaient assis, les jambes croisées dans la position yogique et concentrés sur le finalistes. Ceux-ci, hommes et femmes, assisteront aux finales internationales au Stade Indira Gandhi à New Delhi en Inde. Parmi les finalistes de l'amérique du Nord, nous retrouverons Mlle Jacqueline Benoit qui a étudié à Sherbrooke et enseigne présentement l'éducation physique à l'Université internationale Maharishi et Mlle Jocelyne Comtois de la région de Québec.

Selon Monsieur Périgny, il est très évident que les gouvernements semblent impuissants à établir une paix mondiale. Cette responsabilité revient à l'individu qui doit utiliser son plein potentiel en développant la cohérence du fonctionnement cérébral par la technique de MT-Sidhi (Vol yogique). Il augmentera donc la cohérence dans la conscience collective et mondiale. Ce serait-là la vraie méthode pour établir la paix mondiale.

M. Roger Périgny irradie la joie de la première étape du "Vol yogique", moment où la cohérence des ondes cérébrales est à son maximum et où le corps bondit vers l'avant. Il fait ici la démonstration d'une technique qui vise à établir le fondement de la paix mondiale: la cohérence dans la conscience individuelle et mondiale.

WORLD PEACE • GLOBAL INAUGURATION

PRESS REPORTS FROM NORTH AMERICA

Canada • *CBOF-TV*

Ottawa, Ontario   15 August 1986   (French)

Commentateur: Les adeptes de la Méditation Transcendantale, à l'occasion des fêtes de la méditation dans 108 pays, se sont prêtés aujourd'hui à des lévitations de groupe afin de contribuer à la paix mondiale et à la lutte au terrorisme. Au Château Laurier ce matin, une centaine de personnes se sont livrées à l'expérience.

Reporter: La méditation est surtout connue pour son effet de relaxation. Donc, tout rassemblement qui se respecte se caractérise par le calme absolu. Et aujourd'hui, on nous a promis une primeur, un aperçu d'une technique que seuls les initiés connaissaient jusqu'ici.

Méditant: On va démontrer aujourd'hui le mécanisme pour créer la paix mondiale avec cette technique de 'yogic flying', 'le vol yogique.'

Reporter: ...Et lorsque 7000 personnes dans le monde volent ainsi, simultanément, leurs bonnes vibrations réduiraient le stress des gens ordinaires et apporteraient la paix. Mais la grande question est la suivante: c'est pour quand la vraie lévitation, le vrai vol de yogi?

Méditant: La raison pour laquelle on ne peut pas encore flotter, c'est aussi une raison de conscience collective. Il y aurait encore trop de négativité présentement dans la conscience collective pour nous permettre justement de flotter ou de voler.

Reporter: ....Michel-Denis Poitevin à Ottawa.

PRESS REPORTS FROM NORTH AMERICA

Canada • *Global News*

Toronto, Ontario   15 August 1986   (English)

Reporter: They call it 'yogic flying', and they claim it can eliminate war from the face of the earth. The man behind the theory is Maharishi Mahesh Yogi. He introduced Transcendental Meditation, or TM, to the world in the 1960's. He explains what 'yogic flying' can do.

Maharishi: To bring a soothing influence in the world consciousness, whereby the fear generated by the dangerous rivalry of the superpowers can be neutralized and all the nations could be freed from a continuous state of fear.

Reporter: Studies done by his followers claim that 'yogic flying' has had profound effects on world events. Among other things, the stock market rose dramatically, and traffic accidents decreased. Today in Toronto, followers of Maharishi demonstrated the technique in the first global 'yogic flying' competition. First they had five minutes of meditation, sort of like a warm up, to, as they say, bring the mind and body into harmony. And then they were off in the first event, the 50-metre dash. Next came the long jump. Each jump was carefully measured by stern-faced judges. The final event was the demanding high jump. Some made it look easy. Others show they have more work to do. Followers describe what it feels like to fly.

First TM-Sidha: It's really being alive. It is the point in the day when you really feel that you're living.

Second TM-Sidha: I'm generally a happy person, but the act of levitation is blissful.

Reporter: This is only the first stage. They say the third and final stage is actual flying, not the hopping we see here. The Maharishi says 7,000 people practising the technique in one place will bring an end to world tensions, and he claims that will cost $100 million.

TM-Sidha: In terms of where the money comes from, it might come from industry, it might come from concerned individuals, some philanthropist, some government that wants to take the initiative and say, 'Let's experiment with this, let's try it because it looks like it has possibilities.'

Reporter: Hamlin Grace, Global News.

WORLD PEACE • GLOBAL INAUGURATION

PRESS REPORTS FROM NORTH AMERICA

Canada • *Le Journal de Québec*

Québec 16 August 1986 (French)

ENTRE LE VOL ET LE SAUT

Yvon Pellerin

Dans le silence traversé seulement par les bruits de caméra, les trois hommes, enfermés dans la position du lotus, les yeux clos, le sourire fendu jusqu'aux oreilles, sautent et rebondissent sur les matelas de mousse....

Pendant trois minutes, les «hommes volants» ont sauté et rebondi sur les matelas. Pas bien haut, faut bien le dire. A peine un pied ou un pied et demi à chaque fois. Et ils retombaient lourdement quelques pieds plus loin, comme poussés par un ressort qui se serait brusquement relâché au moment du décollage. Volent-ils vraiment ou sont-ils d'excellents sauteurs?

«Pas très convaincant comme démonstration», chuchotait un journaliste qui s'attendait à quelque chose comme l'Ascension.

En fait, si personne ne nous avait préparé par une petite conférence suivie d'un film vidéo illustrant le phénomène de «haute cohérence cérébrale» atteint au moment du décollage, survenant alors comme une impulsion spontanée irrésistible, on croirait volontiers qu'ils font un effort considérable pour y arriver.

«Si c'était le cas, explique M. Michel Nadeau, un instructeur qui présidait la séance, on les aurait retrouvés épuisés ou en sueurs au bout de trois minutes.» Or, il a dû les arrêter, un peu comme le prof de maternelle doit intervenir quand les jeux se prolongent au delà de la limite, et nos trois «yogis» ne tiraient pas la langue. Ils resplendissaient d'énergie et de calme serein. Ils semblaient même déçus que ça n'a pas duré plus longtemps.

«ASPIRÉ...»

«Non, ce n'est pas difficile. On ressent comme une urgence involontaire, une sensation de poussée le long de la colonne vertébrale, qui nous aspire vers le haut et l'on suit le mouvement. C'est tout!», expliquait plus tard un des trois, Claude Médieu, un dessinateur de 46 ans qui, entre les sauts du matin et soir, travaille dans un bureau d'architectes dans la région de Québec.

Il explique qu'il pratique ces bonds depuis maintenant six ans, de même que la méditation transcendantale, et qu'il en retire un bien être indéfinissable. «A chaque fois que je saute, c'est différent. Mais il reste toujours cette joie au creux de l'estomac qui me pousse à recommencer.»

Michel Nadeau explique sans sciller que la technique du «vol» pratiquée par les disciples de Maharishi Mahesh Yogi, «dans plus de 108 pays», n'est que le premier stade d'un long apprentissage pour un jour arriver à léviter véritablement, c'est-à-dire pouvoir rester en l'air à volonté et voler là où l'on veut.

Ces techniques sont apparues en 1977, entourées du plus grand secret. Aucun photographe ou cinéaste n'était alors autorisé à filmer l'évènement privé. Mais aujourd'hui, les choses ont changé et le groupe a même organisé en juillet, pour la presse de Washington, les premières «Olympiques nord-américaines du vol yogique», remportées d'ailleurs par un Canadien qui a bondi à un peu plus de deux pieds en l'air.

M. Nadeau explique le phénomène antigravitationnel par la théorie complexe du champ unifié de la physique quantique... . «Mais ça ne se pourrait pas autrement», dit-il.

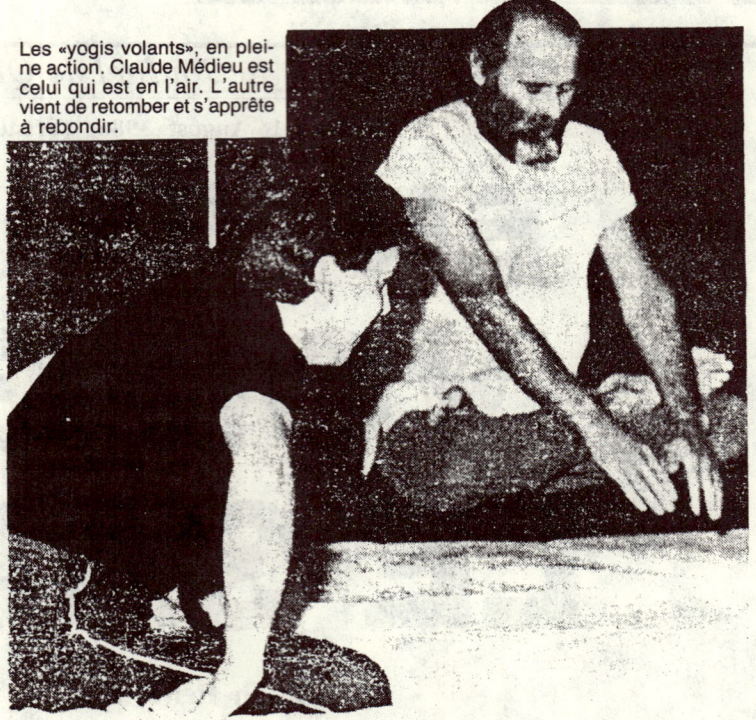

Les «yogis volants», en pleine action. Claude Médieu est celui qui est en l'air. L'autre vient de retomber et s'apprête à rebondir.

(Y.P.) — Le plus important du message des sauteurs n'est cependant pas la lévitation ou ce qu'elle procure individuellement, assure-t-il. Selon lui, en sautillant ainsi, on travaille pour la paix dans le monde.

La route vers l'harmonie universelle devrait, selon lui, être pavée avec des matelas de mousse. Des milliers de matelas blancs sur lesquels sauteraient quotidiennement, en même temps, au moins 7 000 pratiquants!

M. Nadeau, qui applique la formule de la «racine carrée de 1% de la population mondiale», le chiffre magique pour déstresser toute le terre, croit que c'est la solution idéale pour que l'Utopie se réalise.

Le Maharishi, qui a lancé toute cette campagne de relations publiques (les démonstrations avaient lieu en même temps dans 108 pays) voit d'ailleurs à ce que ce jour de grâce arrive enfin.

Il annonce qu'il vient de créer un «fonds Maharishi» pour la paix mondiale, dans lequel sont invitées à souscrire les personnes fortunées.

Le but est d'amasser pas moins de $100 millions américains pour permettre d'entretenir en un même endroit sur terre le groupe permanent des «7 000 experts».

«Grâce à ce programme, estime-t-il, dans son communiqué, «la paix mondiale n'est plus maintenant qu'une question d'argent!»

WORLD PEACE • GLOBAL INAUGURATION

PRESS REPORTS FROM NORTH AMERICA

Canada • The Daily News
Halifax, Nova Scotia 16 August 1986 (English)

YOGIS HOP FOR PEACE

by ELIZABETH HANTON

THE two young men seem unaware of the noises around them: cameras clicking, lights being set up.

Barefoot, dressed in t-shirts and drawstring pants, they sit silently on foam rubber mats with their legs folded into the lotus position and eyes closed.

Then, as if on some silent command, they begin to hop. They keep hopping for 10 minutes, still folded into that pretzel-like position.

The two — 30 year-old Ian Temple of Halifax and 29 year-old Gilles Bigras of Montreal — are followers of the Maharishi Mahesh Yogi. They're giving a demonstration of yogic flying, part of the Transcendental Meditation Sidhi.

They're at the first stage of yogic flying — the hopping stage. Stage two is hovering while stage three is flying. This flying leads to a feeling of bliss, if not vertigo, and generates coherence between the consciousness and physical matter.

Their hopping demonstration was part of a session on TM yogic flying, held Friday in Halifax.

If it all seems like a way of showing off mind over matter techniques, practitioners say it has a serious purpose. War is caused by a collective build-up of stress among nations, you see. A group of, say, 7,000 doing the yogic flying technique in one place will create "coherence" in the world consciousness.

That, in turn, can mean less international conflict, crime, infectious disease and accidental death. Sound like the '60s? Listen to this: "We've been able to measure certain changes in the body," says Dr. **David Sanders**, a Dartmouth general practitioner. "Some very sophisticated studies show interesting biochemical and hormonal changes among people practising TM."

It is possible for anyone to hop like the two young men — provided you can get your legs in that configuration. But the point of the exercise, explains the panel, is to end their demonstration without being exhausted. The time they spend meditating before starting to hop also lowers the amount of oxygen their bodies will use.

During the demonstration Bigras did seem to be breathing hard and making a sniffing sound. After, though, his pulse rate appeared normal.

"You move the mind and the body follows," he said.

He feels rested after a session, says Ian Temple, who's been practising TM for four years ....

GILLES Bigras demonstates the first stage of yogic flying — that is, hopping. (Ducklow)

PRESS REPORTS FROM NORTH AMERICA

Canada • *The Winnipeg Sun*

Winnipeg, Manitoba 17 August 1986 (English)

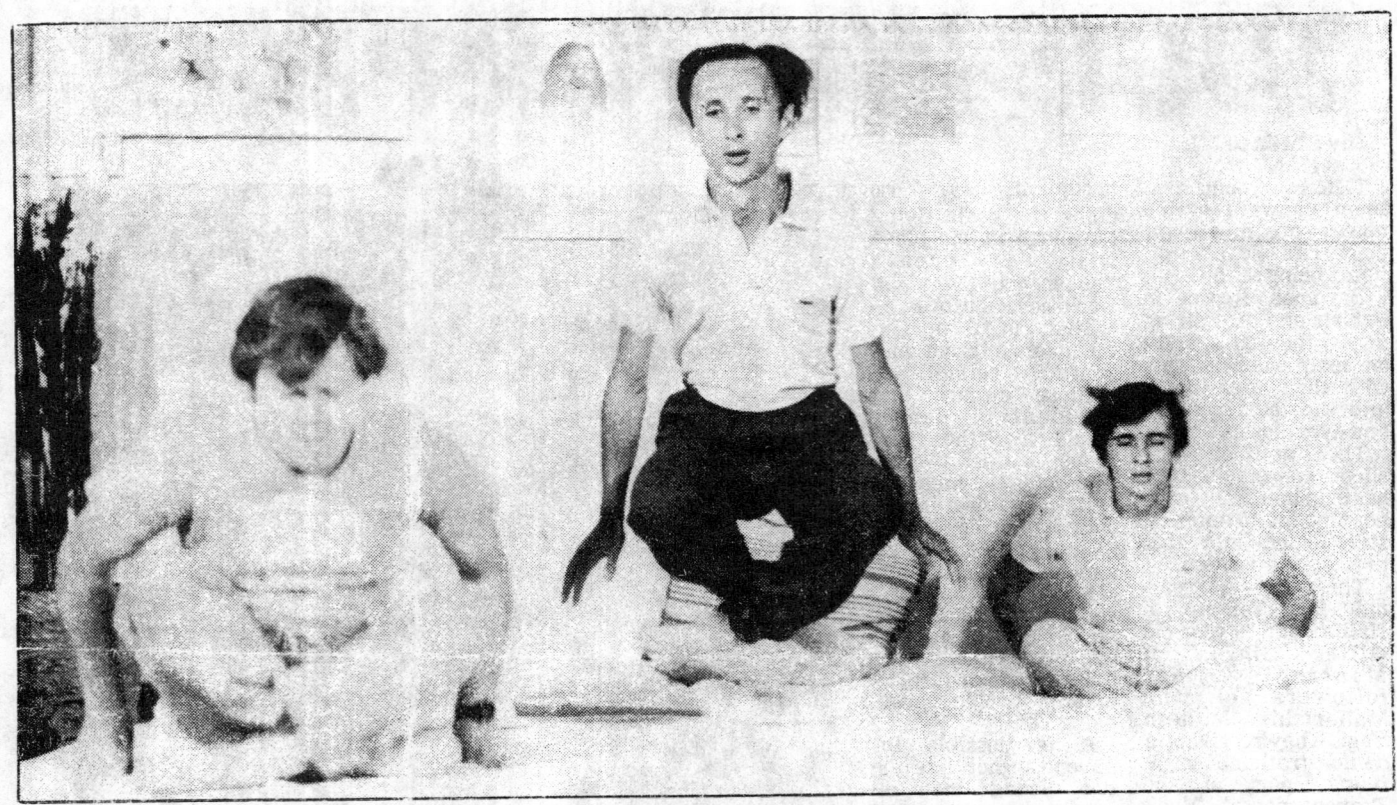

By DARRYL STERDAN
Sun Staff Writer

Yoga students give levitation their best shot.

If your world was more peaceful than usual Friday, thank the Maharishi Mahesh Yogi.

Followers of the Indian Maharishi say the founder of Transcendental Meditation has developed a technique that can create spiritual happiness, bolster the stock market and save the world from war.

It's called yogic 'flying,' and last week, local media got an explanation of how it works and a demonstration.

However, the display turned out to be something which might be more accurately described as yogic hopping.

Three men sat cross-legged on sheets of foam, calmly meditating. Then, one by one, they began to bounce as if on trampolines, slowly at first, then higher and faster, until they were hopping about like giant frogs.

Later, Dr. Mark Novak of the University of Winnipeg explained the bouncing is only the first stage of yogic flying. The second stage is hovering, he said, and the third is being able to fly.

But he added, "no one's been able to do stage two or three yet."

Novak, a sociology professor, said the technique is "based on mental coherence."

The body spontaneously lifts off the ground when a person's brain waves reach maximum coherence during meditation, he said.

This 'coherence' radiates outward and destroys 'negative influences' in the world, eliminating war, murder and accidents while at the same time creating peace and raising the stock market, he explained.

According to the Maharishi, 7,000 people practising the technique twice daily would rid the world of all negative influences....

Reprinted from The Winnipeg Sun

WORLD PEACE • GLOBAL INAUGURATION

PRESS REPORTS FROM NORTH AMERICA

Canada • *Maclean's*

Toronto, Ontario   8 September 1986   (English)

What goes up usually comes down—unless it is **Blaine Watson**, a 31-year-old transcendental meditation (TM) teacher from Welland, Ont. Watson is a proponent of yogic flying, an activity which apparently defies gravity: participants hop into the air from a cross-legged seated position, then progress to hovering and eventually to free flight. Watson says that yogic flying occurs when an advanced TM technique is used. "The technique stimulates greater use of the brain and lift-off takes place at the moment of maximum coherence." This summer Watson won a gold medal at the first international yogic flying competition in Washington, D.C., with a hop of 24¾ inches and later in New Delhi he beat his own record with a hop of 25¼ inches. Watson says that he expects to be flying within a few months.

United States • *The New York Times*

New York, New York   8 July 1986   (English)

WASHINGTON TALK

Briefing

'Yogic Flying'

At a press briefing tomorrow, several hundred adepts will demonstrate the technique of "yogic flying" at the Washington Convention Center.

According to the Age of Enlightenment News Service, the demonstration will constitute the "global inauguration" of an effort by the Maharishi Mahesh Yogi to create world peace through transcendental techniques. The demonstration will consist of the first stage of yogic flying, in which, the news service says, the "body lifts up and begins to hop at the moment of maximum brain wave coherence." Journalists have been invited to photograph and videotape the event.

PRESS REPORTS FROM NORTH AMERICA

World-wide • *The Associated Press*

Washington, D.C.   9 July 1986   (English)

AND AWAAAAAAAY WE GO

By Robert Furlow

More than a dozen followers of the Maharishi Mahesh Yogi bounded down a foam-rubber track and high-jumped onto stacked-up mattresses Wednesday—all the while in sitting positions—in what they described as bliss-induced 'yogic flying.'

The Maharishi's supporters have for years contended that advanced practitioners of his transcendental meditation can 'fly,' but such exhibitions have been conducted only in private.

However, organizers said, rising terrorism and other world problems have made it necessary to work harder at spreading the word of such practices, which the Maharishi and his followers say can positively influence trends in society.

The 'flying' is an involuntary bodily response to a person's achieving high levels of coherence in brain functioning, they say.

Actually, they declared Wednesday, current experts have achieved only the first stage of flying—a kind of hopping—with hopes that they eventually can reach the second and third stages: hovering and then directed flight.

Supporters and skeptics could agree Wednesday on at least one point: Participants in what was billed as 'The First North American 'Yogic Flying' Competition' did hop impressively. Their propulsion could still be debated.

The students—all relatively young men in apparent good physical condition—meditated while sitting on foam-rubber mattresses, their feet tucked in what is commonly known as the yoga position, their hands resting lightly on the mattress in front of them.

After a while, the men began hopping in place, and then—still in the yoga position—they went bouncing down track lanes laid out at the Washington Convention Center.

According to the organizers, winning performances in four events were 11.53 seconds for the 25-meter hurdles—over humps of eight inches or so—23.33 seconds for the 50-meter dash, 70 inches for the long jump and 24.75 inches for the high jump.

Eddie Gob, of the Caribbean island of Guadeloupe, winner of the two races and the long jump, said afterward of his flying experiences: 'You do not feel tiredness and boredness. You just want to go on and on.'

He and the others were closely watched by reporters, photographers and more than 1,000 transcendental meditation students who cheered exuberantly—but only after all the competitors had finished and there was no danger of breaking concentration.

(This release from the Associated Press and the AP photograph on the next page appeared in hundreds of newspapers throughout the world.)

WORLD PEACE • GLOBAL INAUGURATION

AP Laserphoto

Eddie Gob demonstrates 'yogic flying' at the Washington Convention Center Wednesday. Gob won a 25-meter race, a 50-meter race, and did a 70-inch long jump, all using "Maharishi technology."

PRESS REPORTS FROM NORTH AMERICA

World-wide • *United Press International*

Washington, D.C.   9 July 1986   (English)

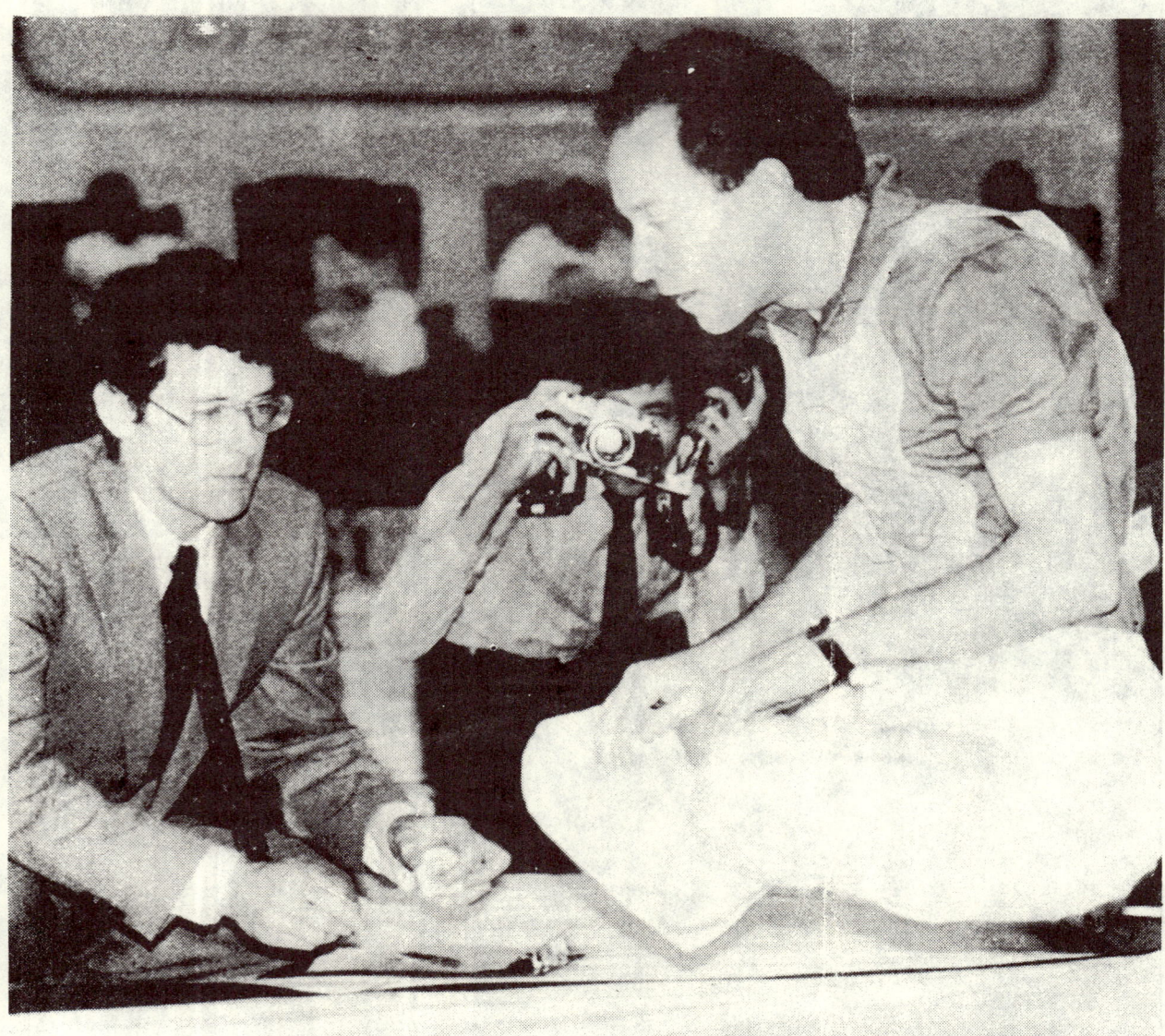

Michael Dillbeck of Fairfield, Iowa, participates in "The First North American Yogic Flying Competition," Wednesday in Washington as a competition official measures his height above the mat. The winner of the event, Blaine Watson of Canada, attained the height of 22.75 inches.

(This photograph from UPI appeared in many newspapers throughout the world.)

WORLD PEACE • GLOBAL INAUGURATION

PRESS REPORTS FROM NORTH AMERICA

United States • *The Associated Press*

Des Moines, Iowa 9 July 1986 (English)

Meditators who 'fly' set contest to find the best

Associated Press

After years of saying they can fly, adherents of transcendental meditation are ready to go for the gold.

Meditators will have a chance to compete in a "yogic flying" competition during a conference in Washington, D.C., this week.

"Anyone who's in the TM-Sidhis Program can enter," said Richard Schneider, public relations director for Maharishi International University in Fairfield, Iowa. "Judges will observe during a regular meditation session, and 11 men and 11 women will go on to India for the First International Yogic Flying Competition."

People from around the world are expected at that competition, set for July 21 in India.

Transcendental meditation is billed as a scientific technique for reducing stress. Meditators claim advanced TM techniques can help bring about world peace and improve social conditions.

During the practice of the advanced techniques, they say, they levitate.

Maharishi Mahesh Yogi, who founded the technique, says yogic flying is the only way to world peace.

Schneider, who is in Washington for the event, said the technique will be demonstrated to the news media by 20 men today during the group's convention at the Washington Convention Center.

A DEMONSTRATION of the "coherence" the mind and body attain during meditation also is planned.

Schneider said the public can view the demonstration.

"We want to attract people who are concerned with world peace, who are willing to see this as an alternative that has not been fully explored," he said.

During previous meetings, MIU officials have claimed the gathering of as many as 7,000 meditators in one place has helped to improve world conditions.

"We're only expecting 2,500, so I wouldn't make any predictions on the worldwide level," said David Orme-Johnson, a director of the psychology and neuroscience programs at MIU who will monitor the conference. "But things should improve in the U.S.

"Based on past research, we expect a reduction in infectious diseases. In the past, the stock market has gone up, so we predict that again. We predict a reduction in traffic fatalities and we predict a reduction in the crime rate."

PRESS REPORTS FROM NORTH AMERICA

United States • *The Washington Post*

Washington, D.C. 10 July 1986 (English)

At the Hop:
The Flying Yogis' Olympiad

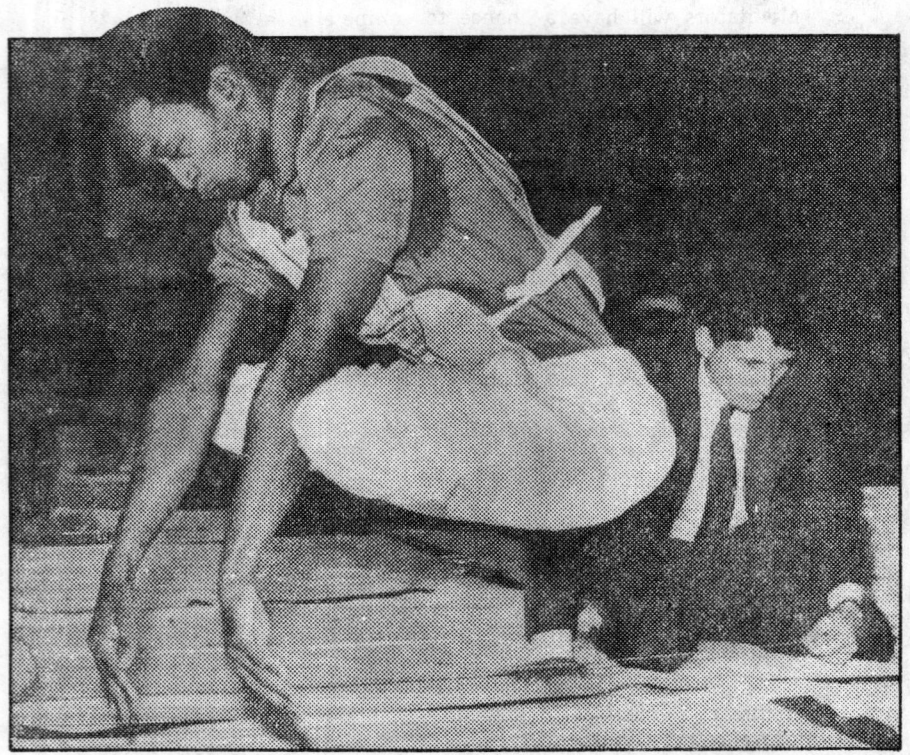

BY MARGARET THOMAS—THE WASHINGTON POST

Yogic flier Eddie Gob competes in the long jump as judge Tom Shira measures distance.

By Victoria Dawson
Special to The Washington Post

In a silence broken only by clicks of cameras and the gentle hiss of ventilated air, the First Olympics of the Age of Enlightenment began something like the way kernels of corn begin to pop.

The 22 male "Olympians"—finalists in yesterday's First North American "Yogic Flying" Competition at the Washington Convention Center—were advanced practitioners of Transcendental Meditation, here as part of a week-long World Assembly on Perfect Health sponsored by followers of the Maharishi Mahesh Yogi.

Wearing identical uniforms of white drawstring pants, green T-shirts and bare feet, the Olympians sat motionless, their legs crossed in a yogic twist, meditating. Inert and as full of promise as unpopped corn.

At first, nothing. Not a motion.

Then a tremor. A sizzle. A shiver.

And, at last, minutes having passed, a POP! Up went the first cross-legged

WORLD PEACE • GLOBAL INAUGURATION

Michael Busch, left, and Richard LaMarita.

PHOTOS BY MARGARET THOMAS—THE WASHINGTON POST

Chad Warren in the hurdle race.

kernel. The first meditator was off and—hopping!

This particular Olympiad was open only to assembly participants and the press. Reporters had been invited for an unprecedented bring-your-video-camera, bring-your-skepticism demonstration of the TM-Sidhi "yogic flying" technique.

"War is caused by a buildup of stress in the collective consciousness of nations," said Bevan Morris, president and chairman of the board of trustees at Maharishi International University in Fairfield, Iowa, explaining the ultimate purpose of the stress-relieving exercise. Morris stood in front of a portrait of Maharishi Mahesh Yogi as he presided over a press briefing yesterday morning at the convention center.

"Levitation" is the usual term for what the meditators would try to do—but the word is misleading. "Yogic flying," as it is more properly called, comes in three distinct stages—and today's contestants were only attempting Stage One.

They aren't hovering or floating yet. That will be Stage Two. They aren't flying through the air yet. That will be Stage Three. For now, the Transcendental Meditators are concentrating on the Hopping Stage, propelled, they say, by nothing more than their own spiritual awareness.

"The press is on their way up," said TMer Paul Tarnoff, holding a walkie-talkie in front of his mouth, as the briefing ended. And the press corps filed up to the cavernous second-floor hall in the Convention Center, where the competition was to take place.

"So, have you ever seen anything like this before?" muttered one cameraman to another.

And on the escalator, in a haze of post-briefing bewilderment, a reporter tried to assimilate the TM argot. "I don't suppose you know what a unified field is?" he asked meekly.

If yesterday's competition was any indication, the road to world peace is paved with rubber mats, divided into five lanes and populated by would-be hoppers neutralizing their own and the world's stress.

A sea of mats, covered with white sheets and divided by red ribbon into hopping lanes, spread across the room. On the far side, a row of solemn dignitaries sat in golden wing-back chairs. In the middle chair was a turbaned B.D. Triguna, president of the all-Indian Ayurveda Congress (practitioners of an ancient natural health care system).

Across the way, Tiers O, P, Q and R were filled, row after row, with yogic fliers who had not made it to the finals. Walls were bedecked with large banners conveying TM slogans: "Alliance with Natural Law" and "Enlightenment to the Individual. Invincibility to Every Nation."

To a standing ovation, the finalists appeared and settled down on a mat, legs crossed and eyes shut.

"Gentlemen, let the competition begin," Morris intoned.

Some were smiling. Some were rocking back and forth. Some were bouncing up and down. Lined up as they were for the five-lane, 25-meter hurdles, it seemed as if the eager competitors in the back rows would hop right into the still-sedentary front row.

But in a TM minute, all the front-row hoppers were flopping down the foam rubber rows, balancing themselves with their arms, bouncing into other lanes, rocking back and forth, pursuing the Olympic dream.

A corps of TM referees, bearing clipboards and stopwatches, wearing earnest looks and conservative business suits, ran alongside the sitting hoppers, charting their progress.

When they crossed the finish line, they just kept hopping. Wiggling. Squirming. Hopping deftly and not-so-deftly around and into the photographers.

It was the rare hopper who got up and walked to his next destination.

=

The high jump began at 40 centimeters. Each contestant composed himself, took a hopping start and sprang up onto the elevated mattress, leg fold still intact. Yogic Flyer No. 37 made the hop. Then No. 57. Then No. 11. And just as it threatened to settle into routine, No. 7 sprang onto the mattress and, glory in sight, hopped around in 180-degree turns.

When No. 20 wasn't hop-jumping onto the mattress, he was giggling. Blaine Watson by name, he said later that he's been smiling "all my life, but it became more prominent with TM. I'm not blissed out, just happy and content." The 31-year-old TMer is here in Washington studying "Natural Law" (consciousness). While he is experiencing "maximum brain wave coherence," which manifests itself by involuntary hopping, Watson "sort of sits back and watches it. You enjoy the ride. One hundred percent wide-awakefulness—it's sort of fun."

Centimeter by centimeter the high-jump mattress was raised: 55 centimeters . . . 57 centimeters . . . 59 centimeters . . . all the way up to 63.

Hopper No. 7, twitching and bouncing, fresh from a jump, looked at the next contestant, No. 40, and gave him the thumbs-up signal. Go for it. But No. 40 missed, hit the edge of the mattress, rolled onto his back and had to settle for hopping around at ground level.

=

When the final race, the 50-meter dash, was completed, the contestants were utterly animated. While the audience rose to its feet in applause, the hoppers remained seated, hopping vigorously among themselves, mixing and mingling with spiritual energy and good feeling. Finally they got up, walked over to the front of the arena and stood in formation, awaiting the announcement of the winners and the distribution of the laurels.

And what better laurel for a victorious yogic flier than a red rose?

Eddie Gob, the man with the most roses, was the only yogic flier wearing socks in a line of bare feet. He walked off with four roses (three "gold" and one "bronze") and warm toes. Gob, who comes from Guadeloupe, completed the 25-meter hurdles in 11.53 seconds, long-jumped 70 inches, high-jumped 21⅝ inches and hopped off 50 meters in 23.33 seconds.

The 27-year-old champion, who says he discovered Transcendental Medication by accident, says that to hop is to "feel so full inside. So happy. It's really blissful."

© 1986—*The Washington Post;* reprinted by permission

WORLD PEACE • GLOBAL INAUGURATION

PRESS REPORTS FROM NORTH AMERICA

United States • *Washington Times*
Washington, D.C. 10 July 1986 (English)

Eddie Gob from the island of Guadeloupe demonstrates the ultimate in "yogic flying" technique as he wins gold medals in both the 25-meter hurdles and 50-meter dash yesterday at the Washington Convention Center

3,000 meditators assemble, seeking peace, soft landing

By Lucy Keyser
THE WASHINGTON TIMES

Bouncing on their bottoms down foam-mattress racing lanes, contestants in the First Olympics of the Age of Enlightenment demonstrated here yesterday the techniques of an unusual strategy for world peace.

The peacemakers are advanced "transcendental meditators," followers of Maharishi Mahesh Yogi.

The practiced meditators' frog-like "yogic flying" is part of their Leader's program for generating "coherence in world consciousness, the basis of world peace."

Theoretically, a yogic flyer has very orderly brain waves, fluid coordination between mind and body. Consciousness and matter become completely integrated, and all this "coherency" — a favorite term among meditators — can spread around the world if enough meditators gather at the same place and time.

About 3,000 meditators are together for 10 days in Washington for their annual conference. They are working to get 7,000 of themselves together next year — the number needed for world peace, which is exactly the square-root of 1 percent of the world's population, according to the theory.

"Maharishi feels the world could really collapse, there could be a nuclear war," said Bevan Morris, master of ceremonies at the yogic flying demonstrating and president of Maharishi International University in Fairfield, Iowa.

Usually, Maharishi has closed the flying sessions to the the press. But with the rise in terrorism and the tension between world powers, Maharishi — who in the 1960s taught meditation to the Beatles — agreed to this first public yogic flying demonstration, Mr. Morris said.

"We've found clearly that this technique can create world peace... and the decision for this display was compelled by a need for world peace," Mr. Morris said.

The display started with 22 green-shirted, trim and fit men parading onto the soft 6-inch-thick track at the Washington Convention Center. About 1,000 meditating colleagues — men from around the nation who didn't make it to the olympic finals — rose to their feet in the stands for a long and boisterous ovation.

The rest of the demonstration was silent, punctuated only by Mr. Morris's gentle whispering into a microphone — "Let the games begin" — and the sound of the flyers ... flopping across the foam-mattress floor.

Before each event, contestants warmed up, meditating for about five minutes in the classic cross-legged lotus position ....

Eddie Gob, from the Caribbean, was the froggiest in the 25-meter hurdles (11.53 seconds) and the 50-meter dash (23.33 seconds). He sprung forward lightly and rhythmically, rocking forward and pushing off from his knees, swinging his arms for leverage. He won the gold medal for both events.

"It's so blissful and exhilarating," Mr. Gob told the crowd. "You just want to go on and on. When I first learned, they had to tell me 'OK, OK, you can stop now.'"

A student at the Maharishi campus here, Jeff Klein, 35, won the bronze medal in both the long jump (65¼ inches) and high jump events (21⅝ inches).

Mr. Klein has been practicing Transcendental Meditation for 14 years and the more advanced flying technique for eight years. He teaches the technique and studies natural law at the university.

"The laws of nature organize and you just go!" he said, showing no signs of fatigue or irritation when asked about the validity of the technique. "If it was strictly physical, you'd find people sweating, gasping and panting at the end. And if you did it on your own, you wouldn't want to continue."

"I was skeptical about it, too, at first," said Dean Anderson, 28, who teaches the meditation technique to employees of computer and chemical firms in Austin, Texas. "I tried two or three hops without the technique and I was exhausted."

Practicing since he was 16, meditation has improved his creativity, intelligence, school grades and ability to get along with his parents, Mr. Anderson said.

bombs will see there is no similarity between the two."

sults of TM were the most satisfying and the research on it was good," he said. "It's so exhilarating. When they talk about unbounded awareness and bliss — that's concrete."

"I feel like a child but my mind feels wise," said Tim Bernstein, 36, who earned a master's degree in business administration at the Maharishi's Iowa university and now teaches. He used to be a loan officer in California but 14 years of meditation and nine years of yogic flying twice a day changed his outlook on life.

"My heart feels innocent. It doesn't feel old. I just feel happy, whether I'm ironing my shirt or talking to you," Mr. Bernstein said.

Reprinted with permission from the Washington Times

WORLD PEACE • GLOBAL INAUGURATION

PRESS REPORTS FROM NORTH AMERICA

United States • *Scripps Howard News Service*

Washington, D.C.   10 July 1986   (English)

Yogic olympics has flying start

By Ann McFeatters
Scripps Howard News Service

WASHINGTON — While Moscow witnesses the Goodwill Games, Washington hosted the North American Yogic Flying Competition.

Never before held, the yogic flying contest Wednesday at the Washington Convention Center was aimed at getting the press to announce the Marharishi Mahesh Yogi's "global inauguration" of his program for world peace.

It worked.

The Washington press corps, it turned out, was avidly interested in seeing yogic flying. Such a skill, until now not publicly demonstrated, involves leaping about in the sitting lotus position while practicing transcendental meditation. It's very hard to do.

But the First Olympics of the Age of Enlightenment really wasn't much of a contest. It was Eddie Gob of Gaudaloupe and Blaine Watson of Ontario all the way.

In front of more than 1,600 hushed spectators — all said to be able to "fly" — the 21 competitors in their green shirts looked somewhat like lean frogs as they prepared for such events as the 50-meter dash and the two-feet high jump.

Although the World Assembly for Perfect Health runs through Sunday, its yogic flying competition took only 49 minutes. In 23.33 seconds the 27-year-old Gob hopped on his buttocks with his legs crossed in front of him 50 meters across muslin-covered polyurethane mattresses for a rose and a gold medal.

It took Gob 11.53 seconds to do the 25-meter hurdles in a sitting position for a second gold medal. His third gold medal was for a 70-inch long jump. The only other gold medalist was Watson who hopped up 24 and 3/4 inches in a lotus position.

The exuberant crowd of slender, business-suited yuppies cheered Gob loudly. "Beautifully done," they exulted.

Susan Dillbeck, wearing a beige linen suit and a great deal of gold jewelry, said followers of the Maharishi Mahesh Yogi dress well because they believe in the dignity of the program. She said she has a doctorate in education from the University of California at Berkeley and is dean of education at Maharishi International University in Fairfield, Iowa.

Bevan Morris, 37, president and chairman of the board of trustees at MIU, explained the Maharishi Mahesh Yogi "thought carefully for a month" before permitting the Yogic Flying Olympics. The real need for world peace and the growth of terrorism convinced him, Morris said.

The Maharishi teaches that if 7,000 people — the square root of 1 percent of the world population — all meditate at the same time, the world will be at peace because of the "coherence on all levels of mind, body, and environment." He wants to fund a group of 10,000 regular meditators.

MAHARISHI'S PROGRAMME TO CREATE

PRESS REPORTS FROM NORTH AMERICA

United States • *Daily News*

New York, New York   10 July 1986   (English)

'YOGIC FLYING' was demonstrated in Washington yesterday by Eddie Gob of Guadeloupe (l.) and Blain Watson of Canada

HARRY HAMBURG/DAILY NEWS

WORLD PEACE • GLOBAL INAUGURATION

"Followers of yogi do the bounce"

by Frank Van Riper

Washington, July 10, 1986—

They call it yogic flying and they demonstrated it at the District of Columbia Convention Center yesterday.

"They" are followers of Maharishi Mahesh Yogi.

Bevan Morris said that yogic flying—achieved after deep meditation—creates "higher levels of moral judgement" and can influence outside events.

R. Keith Wallace, a Ph.D. scientist who teaches at Maharishi International University in downtown D.C., claimed that there is a relationship between yogic meditation and good things happening in the world.

"War is caused by the buildup of stress in the collective consciousness of nations," Morris said. Yogic flying's "super radiance effect" is good for the whole population, he said.

The yogic flying demonstration was like watching kernels heating up in a corn popper.

A dozen or so athletic young men meditated until they achieved what they called "optimal coherence" so they could begin to "spontaneously" bounce.

Yogic flying, it turns out, is not really flying. To be absolutely accurate it simply involves bouncing up and down in the lotus position on a 6-inch foam rubber mattress. But the Maharishi's followers insisted its the last best hope for world peace.

Morris and his colleagues say this was just the beginning.

Despite the law of gravity, they declared, it would not be long before yogic flyers achieved enough "coherent brain function" to levitate and stay aloft "as long as they want."

United States • *Los Angeles Times*

Los Angeles   10 July 1986   (English)

"Yogis Say They're a Hop, Skip and Jump From Flying"

Washington, July 10, 1986—

You assume a yoga position and then hop down a foam-rubber track, high-jumping onto stacked mattresses. Described as bliss-induced "yogic flying," the hopping by the followers of the Maharishi Mahesh Yogi in "The First North American Yogic Flying Competition" was supposed to demonstrate that practitioners of transcendental meditation can fly. Actually, the Maharishi's supporters acknowledged that they only achieved the first stage of flying—a kind of hopping—but said they have hopes of reaching the second and third stages: hovering, and then directed flight. Canadian Blaine Watson bounced—or levitated, depending on one's point of view—to a height of 24 ¾ inches to win the high-jump event at the Washington Convention Center. Dr. Bevan Morris, president of Maharishi International University in Fairfield, Iowa, said that yogic flying can bring peace to the world. . . .

PRESS REPORTS FROM NORTH AMERICA

United States • *San Francisco Chronicle*

San Francisco, California   11 July 1986   (English)

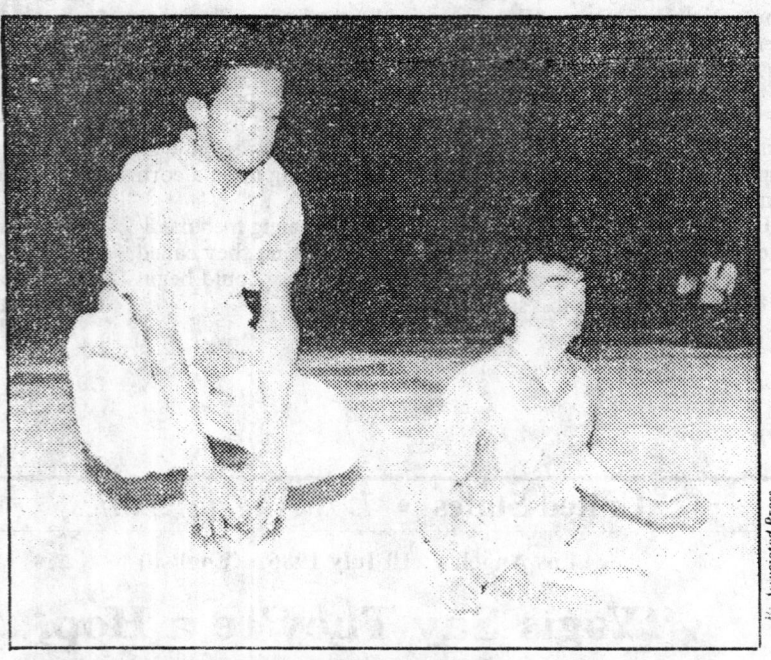

Bouncing the Global Blues Away

More than a dozen followers of the **Maharishi Mahesh Yogi** participated in the First North American Yogic Flying Competition in Washington this week.

They sat — in the yoga position, of course — on foam mattresses and bounced up and down, sideways and forward and back. They said this was flying.

They said the purpose of this demonstration was to combat terrorism and other world problems.

The high jump winner of the competition raised himself 24.75 inches off the mattress.

WORLD PEACE • GLOBAL INAUGURATION

PRESS REPORTS FROM NORTH AMERICA

United States • *National Public Radio*
Washington, D.C.   11 July 1986   (English)

In Washington, D.C., this week—an unusual mind over matter athletic event. Races, hurdle jumping, and attempts at levitation through meditation at the First North American 'Yogic Flying' Competition. NPR's Alex Vanoss could not resist watching.

Alex Vanoss: I've always wanted to fly, on my own, without tickets or seat belts. And in my dreams as a child I did fly. I would climb a tree, jump, and float back to ground and sometimes with the right uplift to the chin, I would even rise up over the trees at the end of the yard and the fields beyond and on up into the hills far away.

One Christmas, I asked for a Superman suit, and it came with a note attached saying that of course, only the real Superman suit with its red cape could make you fly.

Dream on, Alex. And I have, these three decades. And I thought my dreams might come true this week when I got a leaflet from the World Assembly on Perfect Health, meeting at the Washington, D.C., Convention Center. It invited members of the media to a demonstration of what they called 'yogic flying.' There was a photo of two smiling young men in white shirts, practitioners of Maharishi Mahesh Yogi's Transcendental Meditation. They were sitting cross-legged in the photo, sitting in lotus position and a good foot-and-a-half off the ground. Superman, move over!

A couple of thousand spectators sat in the bleachers in the convention hall, and there were visiting dignitaries in turbans. There were dozens of photographers and camera technicians. And in one corner, a couple of meditators, with wires attached to their heads, surrounded by video monitors and people in white lab coats. The floor of the hall was a field of polyethylene foam pads covered with sheets and marked off in lanes just like and indoor race track.

At a press conference, spokesmen displayed graphs and gave out lists of scientific research papers saying that Transcendental Meditation, TM, when performed by enough people, had been shown to reduce the crime rate in a community, the number of auto accidents and suicides, and even raise stock prices.

Meanwhile, Bevan Morris, President of Maharishi International University in Iowa, said that through TM, when the brain waves are most coherent, the body can lift off the ground. The point of TM and yogic flying is to promote greater brain wave coherence and hence coherence in world consciousness, the basis of world peace. Governments have failed to do this, he said, the world is a mess; and that made it necessary to have this public demonstration, at least of the first stage of yogic flying.

Dr Bevan Morris: Yogic flying is supposed to start with hopping of the body and then later on develops into floating or hovering in the air, and finally into the actual ability to fly around anywhere. Today what we'll see is that first phase. This is how far we have developed in our practice of this technique, this hopping stage.

Alex Vanoss: A couple of dozen competitors, all youngish, dressed in green shirts, and white pants, sat at the end of the track, meditating, swaying a little, or smiling. A few twitched their shoulders. The audience grew quiet, the photographers grew quiet, then came the get ready signal. And they were off! One after another, they took off down the foam track.

Then came the other events—the dashes, the long jump, and the high jump.

Dr David Orme-Johnson: What we want to do is repeat the experiment. Measure him sitting meditating and then show what the effect is when everybody starts meditating.

Alex Vanoss: Can you tell me what we're looking at on the screen here?

Dr David Orme-Johnson: We're looking at the top of the brain. These are different frequency bands. So, delta, theta, alpha, and beta. We are measuring an individual here while he is meditating, and what we see is that when the whole group is meditating together his brain becomes much more coherent. Part of this is the collective effect. I don't know if you could feel that. I could sort of feel the whole atmosphere becoming very settled and quiet.

Alex Vanoss: The winners of the competition got red roses as prizes and go on to compete in the First World Olympics of Yogic Flying in New Delhi later this month. I don't think I'll be there, but I came away satisfied from this first exposure. To be sure no one at the convention got beyond the hopping phase of yogic flying or even knew of anyone at stage two of levitation or three—free movement through the air. But it doesn't matter, they say. The techniques are thousands of years old and there have been many masters in that time, surely. Perhaps some will appear at the Olympics in New Delhi. I came away satisfied with a thought that when thousands of people gather, if only to meditate, if only to hop together, how could this not help but improve humanity's collective disposition. As for flying itself, it is a fact that in a certain field in Maryland thirty years ago, there was a boy who dreamed of flying through the rows of corn. He wore a Superman suit, with a red cape, and he was happy.

For National Public Radio, I'm Alex Vanoss.

United States • *The Journal*

Winston-Salem, North Carolina   12 July 1986   (English)

An Impressive Exhibition

Maharishi Mahesh Yogi (remember him?) believes that if you get really good at his transcendental meditation, you can fly. Some followers put on a demonstration this past week. Sitting in the yoga position, these people competed in the dash, the hurdles, the high jump and the broad jump. Track and field records remained intact, but the broad jump winner went almost six feet and the high jump was won with a spring of better than two feet. No threat to commercial airlines service, perhaps, but an impressive exhibition of mind over matter. Skeptical? You try jumping with your legs crossed and your feet atop your thighs.

WORLD PEACE • GLOBAL INAUGURATION

PRESS REPORTS FROM NORTH AMERICA

United States • *Watertown Sun*

Watertown, Massachusetts   1 August 1986   (English)

—Rising resident—

Watertown resident Steve Balyosian Jr., 41, is photographed floating in mid air during a recent Washington, D.C. demonstration of yogic flying under His Holiness Maharishi Mahesh Yogi's Program to Create World Peace. Yogic flying occurs during transcendental meditation, Balyosian says, when "the body lifts up and moves forward a few feet at the moment of maximum brain wave coherence."

PRESS REPORTS FROM NORTH AMERICA

United States • *People*

New York, New York   28 July 1986   (English)

Says Eddie Gob (left, with Blaine Watson): "I'm not surprised my body lifts up... I'm surprised it comes back down."

WORLD PEACE • GLOBAL INAUGURATION

IT'S A BIRD—IT'S A PLANE— IT'S THE BLISSFUL FLIGHT OF THE MAHARISHI'S YOGIC HOPPERS

Photograph by Stanley Tretick

It was one of the odder Olympiads in memory: Twenty-two finalists wearing identical green T-shirts and white drawstring pants were seated cross-legged on thick foam mats at the Washington Convention Center, meditating before a hushed crowd of about 1,000 happy spirits who had failed to make the cut. After an official had commanded, "Gentlemen, let the competition begin," nothing happened. For a moment—then a longer moment—there was only the sound of one hand clapping. Then the competitors began to twitch. And shake. And twist. And lo, they propelled themselves into the air, bouncing ever higher. Wreathed in beatific smiles, they hopped and they hopped—powered only by their belief in a universal consciousness. Or so they said.

While it may not have been the sort of event to attract major network coverage and six-figure sponsorship from, say, Bud Light, the first North American "yogic flying" competition in Washington, D.C. was a milestone for followers of the Maharishi Mahesh

475

Yogi. India's venerable proponent of Transcendental Meditation (and erstwhile Beatles guru), the Maharishi Mahesh Yogi revived a centuries-old yogic technique in 1976 and disclosed the mysteries of hopping to his devotees. He contends that "brain-wave coherence" can liberate one from the bonds of gravity, but rarely has anyone beyond his TM circle ever been invited to witness such wonderments. Not, that is, until the Maharishi meditated on the alarming rise in terrorism and the rumblings among world powers.

As Dr. Bevan Morris, president of the Maharishi International University in Fairfield, Iowa, explains it, yogic flying produces positive energy that can defuse dangerous stresses between nations. The Maharishi concluded that a public demonstration might serve as a kind of call to arms for the world's pacifists. Accordingly, the press was invited to watch as advanced practitioners demonstrated their prowess in Stage One, hopping. Yet to be viewed in public are Stage Two, hovering, and Stage Three, free flight—something the Maharishi "could do if he wanted to," says Morris.

Blaine Watson, a 31-year-old TM teacher from Canada, was rewarded with a red rose for his record-setting high jump of 24.75 inches. The feat seemed easier to achieve than to explain. "At the moment of maximum coherence in brain-wave activity brought about by meditation, the body effortlessly lifts up," Watson said. "At the top of a hop, the energy bubbles up inside. You feel such wonder, such joy . . . and then you're flying."

Eddie Gob, 27, a TM teacher from the Caribbean island of Guadeloupe, was the yogis own Carl Lewis—winning no fewer than three events out of four. After a few minutes of meditation, he lifted off and hopped over six-inch foam hurdles to finish a 25-meter course in 11.53 seconds. Legs tightly folded in the lotus position. he also took the 50-meter dash at 23.33 seconds and the long jump at 70 inches. "You do not feel tiredness or boredness," he said later. "You just want to go on and on."

Watson, Gob and other followers of the Maharishi will participate in an international yogic flying competition in New Delhi later this month, and they say that Stage Three—if not world peace—is just a shadow away. "It will happen soon, very soon," Watson predicts. "I'll be flying in the next few weeks or months." — MARIA WILHELM

United States • *Newsweek*

New York, New York   21 July 1986   (English)

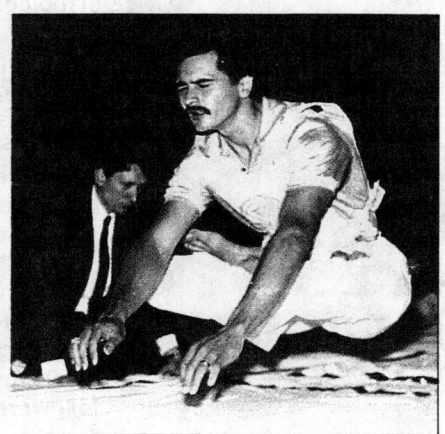
PAM PRICE

WORLD PEACE • GLOBAL INAUGURATION

PRESS REPORTS FROM NORTH AMERICA

United States • *Democrat and Chronicle*

Rochester, New York   4 August 1986   (English)

No wings, no wires, just meditation helps yogis fly

Practitioners believe it reduces stress, brings world closer to peace

By Michelle Fountaine Williams
Democrat and Chronicle

William Taylor is learning how to fly.

You can see him now, right? The 29-year-old University of Rochester librarian in the air with nothing but blue skies, cottonballs for clouds and down below they really do look like ants.

You can see him, right?

Well, if you do you see him, wrong, because William Taylor isn't learning how to fly a plane.

William Taylor, you see, is learning how to fly William Taylor — just like countless other transcendental meditators worldwide who say they are learning how to fly.

Yessirree, without ropes or magic, Taylor is able to lift himself in the air while sitting in the lotus, or cross-legged, position.

Go ahead. Laugh. You are in the minority, Taylor says.

"We just haven't found bizarre skepticism. (Flying) has been met with pretty good inquiry."

The proof, he said, was in the newspapers earlier this month. More than 3,000 meditators gathered in Washington, D.C., for their annual conference on world peace, which included the first North American Yogic Flying Competition. The latter event was open to journalists.

"We had no idea what the press would think or what they would write," Taylor said. But the headlines, according to Taylor, were kind.

"They didn't read: '3,000 whackos think they can fly. They weren't *National Enquirer* headlines at all.'"

Taylor has been practicing transcendental meditation, a form of yoga, for seven years. He's been flying — known as TM-Sidhi, an advanced form of TM — for three.

Taylor hops, the first of three stages of yogic flight. The next level is hovering, best described as a sustained hop, followed by flying, which is a moving hover.

"Right now we have the capability to totally fly," Taylor said. "But what prevents us is the stress in the (body and mind's) system and stress in the world."

As the stress goes, the body is better able to be airborne, he said.

"As you meditate day by day, you're losing more stress. What happens is you're very deeply rested and your mind says, 'Lift off the ground' and your body responds."

Taylor said he did not participate in the flying competition earlier this month because flying to him is "personal." Still, he was glad to see fellow fliers compete in the Olympic-type 25-meter hurdles, 50-meter dash, long jump and high jump. The winner of the high jump leaped more than 22 inches off the ground.

"Seeing how far other people could fly induced other fliers to go a bit farther," Taylor said. It also made the public less doubting.

Why do they do it?

"We don't fly for flying's sake," Taylor said, "although it is fun. When you fly, it's a blast."

He said once flying is achieved, "there's unbounded potentiality."

Taylor and other followers of Maharishi Mahesh Yogi believe that with flying, the deepest form of meditation, comes a coherence of the left and right sides of the brain. This, in turn, produces a calmness within fliers that they believe "radiates into society."

Because they believe the larger the number of people flying together, the larger the number of non-fliers affected, group meditations, such as the one in Washington, are held twice a year.

What they are striving for, he said, is world peace.

"It's sort of like, in a way, smile and the whole world smiles with you."

United States • *Baltimore Chronicle*

Baltimore, Maryland 6 August 1986 (English)

Yoga: Flying High

At left, in the air, is Eddie Gob of Guadeloupe as he "hops" 24 inches in the air during the Yogic Flying competition. Jeff Klein, from Washington, D.C., is also hopping. These men and others in the event used transcendental meditation techniques to lift up and move their bodies from a cross-legged, seated position.

A Report on the First Annual Yogic Flying Competition

by Maryellen Graybill

Whatever "happened" to Transcendental Meditation (TM) and physicist Maharishi Mahesh Yogi? Well, things are hopping: literally. The First Yogic Flying Olympics of the Age of Enlightenment was held July 9 in the Washington Convention Center, drawing the largest group of reporters (100) in the history of the TM movement. The olympics was attended by over 1,500 TM practitioners from 28 countries.

A highlight of the event occurred when, in the hushed silence of the convention center, 22 contestants wearing numbered green and white outfits "flew" in the "Yogic Flying Competition." "Levitation" would be the usual term for the activity of "yogic flying," which is an ability that comes in three stages: hopping, hovering, or floating. The contestants demonstrated only the first stage of levitation, hopping on their haunches.

Winners of this First Yogic Flying Competition will proceed to New Delhi, India to perform in a 25,000 seat facility. At the Washington competition, Eddie Gob of Guadeloupe won three red roses for his scores of 11.53 seconds for the 25 meter hurdles, the 70-inch high jump, and 50 meter hop, all events performed in the lotus sitting position.

Steve Gardner, a meditator for 12 years who witnesses the "yogic flying" event, said, "It reminds me of the Wright brothers—the pictures I have seen of their period. It was, at that time, just a 'hop' of a plane, but the mechanics were there and it was enough for people to believe it was the onset of something great, the onset of a new technology."

Dr. Bevan Morris, president of Maharishi International University in Fairfield, Iowa, explained the "how" and "why" of the hopping to reporters. According to Dr. Morris, the unified field of all the laws of nature—termed "the supersymmetric unified field theory"—has been discovered by scientists to be more refined than the electronic field. It allows the body to lift up at the point of maximum coherence of brain waves.

The human brain, according to Dr. Morris, is so sophisticated that, during the practice of TM, this unified field of all the laws of nature is enlivened. Having an infinite correlation, it can actually neutralize discordance throughout nature, preventing the build-up of stress in both the individual and the environment.

In the TM view, the individual is the basic unit of society. When individual coherence is high, then society will function with great coherence. In this way, world peace can be attained.

"Now we have scientific evidence that we can create peace," Dr. Morris stated at the press conference. "And, with the threat of terrorism and international rivalry growing, world peace is dearer to us than anything."

It would take the square root of one percent of the world's population practicing the TM Sidhi Program to create world peace, Dr. Morris said.

TM is not considered a joke or a fraud by western medical practitioners. In fact, the "yogic flying" competition was part of a nine-day Assembly on Perfect Health that was attended by leading medical professionals from all over the world.

With more than 350 studies from 24 countries compiled at over 160 independent research centers and universities, the TM program has achieved some scientific validation. The results of the studies have been published in four volumes of 700 pages each by the Age of Enlightenment News Service (*Scientific Research on the Transcendental Meditation and the TM-Sidhi Program*, Maharishi European Research University Press, Vlodrop, Holland.

The unique characteristic of TM-Sidhi "yogic flying" is the presence of alpha and theta brain activity which is not seen during ordinary jumping. The term "TM-Sidhi Yogic Flying" means performing a mental technique while the mind is settled in the simplest state of awareness—the state of transcendental consciousness. During the "yogic flying," the inner state of integration of the mind is maintained along with the activity of the body, radiating the harmonizing influence of the unified field of the environment.

Beneficial changes that have been attributed to TM include a reduction in drug and alcohol abuse, crime, hospital admissions, and aging. More than one million TM practitioners have reported feelings of increased happiness and fulfillment as a result of their meditation practices.

Who knows? The first stage of "yogic flying" is now being practiced. Perhaps in the future we will also see meditating TM practitioners hover and float. And then, someday, people may really fly.

Mary Ellen Graybill, a resident of Northeast Baltimore, was a social worker with the Department of Social Services for 12 years. She has practiced TM herself for 14 years.

PRESS REPORTS FROM NORTH AMERICA

United States • *Fairfield Ledger*

Fairfield, Iowa   13 August 1986   (English)

'Yogic flying' event Friday at dome

Transcendental meditators in Fairfield will open their "yogic flying" experience to public view in a demonstration of the technique Friday morning in the men's dome at Maharishi International University.

Demonstrations will be held simultaneously Friday in major cities throughout the United States and in Des Moines and Davenport, according to Richard Schneider, MIU director of public affairs.

Schneider said about 75 area media representatives and guests have been invited to a press conference and orientation at 10 a.m. in Carnegie Hall on the campus here.

The group will move on to Patanjali Golden Dome to see the actual exercise by five to ten local meditators.

The concurrent demonstrations are a take-off from the first major demonstration of the mechanics of yogic flying carried out in Washington, D.C., July 9. Billed as the first North American Yogic Competition and conducted along the lines of an Olympics event, the demonstration was followed by an international competition in India.

Dean Gabbert, formerly of Fairfield, was the first non-meditator to observe and report on TM levitation, which he described as "hopping" in his May 31, 1977 account in the Ledger.

WORLD PEACE • GLOBAL INAUGURATION

PRESS REPORTS FROM NORTH AMERICA

United States • *Quad-City Times*

Davenport, Iowa   14 August 1986   (English)

Be on the lookout for flying people

By Rae Dixon
QUAD-CITY TIMES

Followers of the Maharishi Mahesh Yogi will demonstrate the "yogic flying" technique in Davenport Friday as part of a worldwide inauguration of the technique.

The levitation technique was demonstrated publicly for the first time last month in Washington, D.C. The Davenport demonstration will be 10 a.m. in the Bix Room of the Blackhawk Hotel.

Lynn Coriell of the Davenport Transcendental Meditation Program, 322 Brady St., said five people will participate in the levitation demonstration. She said some will be from Maharishi International University in Fairfield, Iowa.

Coriell said demonstrations will be held in other locations in the United States and 107 other countries Friday to bring attention to the technique as a way to world peace.

The Maharishi and his follow-

> **Coriell said the group believes world peace could be achieved if 7,000 people practiced transcendental meditation in one place.**

ers have contended for years his advanced transcendental meditation methods could achieve such brain wave coherence that they could — in groups — lower wartime death tolls, raise the stock market and generally improve the world's quality of life.

Coriell said the group believes world peace could be achieved if 7,000 people practiced transcendental meditation in one place.

Coriell said "flying" is the advanced form of Maharishi meditation. She said only about 10 people in the Quad-City area practice it.

She said about 200 people in the area practice transcendental meditation and more are learning the technique all the time. "It's the one thing they see they can do to create world peace."

Coriell said those who want to learn the advanced technique are required to practice transcendental meditation for at least six months.

MAHARISHI'S PROGRAMME TO CREAT

PRESS REPORTS FROM NORTH AMERICA

United States • *The Associated Press*

Boston, Massachusetts 15 August 1986 (English)

AP

Peace Flight

Merle Brakey of Hancock, N.H., demonstrates what is called "yoga flying" in Cambridge, Mass., Friday at an event staged to promote world peace. He's not really flying, though. He's bouncing off a mat, but at heights and distances he says are aided by yoga techniques.

WORLD PEACE • GLOBAL INAUGURATION

PRESS REPORTS FROM NORTH AMERICA

United States • *WCAX-TV*

Burlington, Vermont   15 August 1986   (English)

Broadcaster: Creating world peace is an ambitious project, but that's just what the followers of the Transcendental Meditation movement are aiming for. Today in Burlington they offered a demonstration of how they're going to achieve their goal, and Ward Lasso witnessed it.

TM-Sidha: What we will see today is a display of the technology that can bring world peace.

Reporter: These two people are demonstrating the art of 'yogic flying'. It's the key to a world peace programme sponsored by the followers of Maharishi Mahesh Yogi, who practise Transcendental Meditation. Today's demonstration in Burlington is part of the global inauguration for this world peace plan. These two Vermonters are only at the first level of 'yogic flying', which looks kind of like hopping. Actual levitating doesn't come until the next two stages.

TM-Sidha: Until the world gets to a point where it's functioning very coherently, you probably won't see too many people floating.

Second TM-Sidha: Once your body gets used to this kind of experience, it likes it. It likes to do it over and over again. [The experience] has great benefits. Every time you do it, a lot of stress is being released.

Reporter: The idea behind the world peace plan is to get 10,000 people in India practising 'yogic flying' all together on a daily basis. This practice is believed to reduce stress, and with so many people doing it at once, the Maharishi's followers say the world consciousness should become more coherent and be improved.

TM-Sidha: This is a large enough group to affect the entire world. Just by establishing this group we can significantly cut down on terrorism, war, and violence around the world.

Reporter: The global inauguration of the world peace programme is occurring in 108 countries, and it includes a videotaped message from the Maharishi himself.

Maharishi: The whole world family has been under fear continuously for decades in the past.

Reporter: Of course, establishing this 'yogic flying' community in India will cost money. The Maharishi's followers estimate that they'll need 100 million dollars to set it up and keep it going, but they say it's a small price to pay for world peace.

TM-Sidha: Now 100 million dollars sounds to me like a lot of money, but it's a very small percentage of what the world, or actually what the U.S., spends on defense. We will take donations but we don't want people to necessarily feel they have to financially support this with ten dollars here and ten dollars there. That's not the purpose of this inauguration. It's just to let people know what's going on.

Reporter: There will be an open house on Tuesday night at the Transcendental Meditation center for anyone who wants to find out more about their world peace programme. Ward Lasso, Channel 3 News, Burlington.

United States • *WPTZ-TV*

Burlington, Vermont   15 August 1986   (English)

Reporter: Transcendental Meditation. The vehicle is people—7,000 of them all meditating for world peace.

TM-Sidha: Just by establishing this group, we can significantly cut down on terrorism, war, and violence around the world.

Reporter: A non-believer, you say? Well, just watch this. This is called 'yogic flying'. It happens just after meditation when the brain achieves maximum coherence....

TM-Sidha: This technique is a lot of fun and very enjoyable, and we all practise it here ourselves. The main benefit of this is it creates coherence in the individual. And this coherence in the individual spreads throughout creation.

Reporter: The Maharishi wants to put 10,000 people in India, have them meditate twice a day, perform this, and let the world relax. Studies show TM can really affect the community.

TM-Sidha: It's very enjoyable—a very easy, very soft, and very powerful feeling....

WORLD PEACE • GLOBAL INAUGURATION

PRESS REPORTS FROM NORTH AMERICA

United States • *KGAN-TV*

Cedar Rapids, Iowa   15 August 1986   (English)

Broadcaster: Coming up, MIU students say they are making the world a better place.

Reporter: Some people in Fairfield say not only can they fly, but their doing so will make the world a better place. Ann Irvin shows you how they do it.

Reporter: Ken Allen is an expert at the fine art of 'yogic flying'....

Ken Allen: It's bliss. I do it all for the bliss.

Reporter: According to Allen, that happy feeling comes from inner harmony, not hopping. He achieves both peace of mind and the ability to fly by meditating before the bounce. This man, hooked to an EEG, shows how meditation makes peace in your brain. Instructors at Maharishi University think hopping is only the first step.

TM-Sidha: The second is that the body lifts up and stays up. It floats.... And then the third stage is that movement through the air is possible.

Reporter: Dr Geoffrey Wells speculates flyers will achieve the next two stages within a couple of years. Meanwhile, these practitioners believe each flight is a step toward world peace.

TM-Sidha: The coherence that's generated in individuals naturally begins to be generated in society. Through the structuring of coherent, happy, peaceful individuals, we structure world peace in the environment.

Reporter: Translated, that means peaceful people make a peaceful world. Maharishi followers say if they can get $100 million they can support enough full-time meditators to create and keep world peace....

Broadcaster: Followers of the Maharishi say they believe group meditation can help everything from the stock market to the crime rate.

PRESS REPORTS FROM NORTH AMERICA

United States • *KCRG-TV*

Cedar Rapids, Iowa   15 August 1986   (English)

Broadcaster: If we could achieve world peace by spending $100 million, it may be worth the price. Well, that's the amount the followers of the Maharishi Mahesh Yogi say they need to bring lasting peace to the world. They made their pitch today in 108 different countries around the world, and Eyewitness News reporter Ed Tibbits says that included an unusual show in Fairfield, Iowa.

Reporter: This is it. The Transcendental Meditation 'yogic flying' technique. These people aren't praying for peace; they're letting it come to them. When it does, they say they'll radiate it to the rest of the world, and then, peace for all.

TM-Sidha: We're in a position now to offer real hope for the world, not in some fanciful way, not in some imaginary way, but in an extremely practical way.

Reporter: …The same technique they say will create peace will also, they say, allow them to fly. Yes, fly….

TM-Sidha: It's an experience of unboundedness, experience of lightness, and an experience of fullness and bliss.

Reporter: Whether they're hopping or flying, these are some of the best at it. They're medal winners in the first North American 'yogic flying' competition, held in Washington, D.C., last month. If they can get that 100 million dollars, they say they'll be well on their way to creating peace, eliminating famine, and flying even higher….

WORLD PEACE • GLOBAL INAUGURATION

PRESS REPORTS FROM NORTH AMERICA

United States • *KCCI-TV*

Des Moines, Iowa   15 August 1986   (English)

Interviewer: We had a difficult time getting this remote put together technically, but we did it at the very last second and these two people stayed totally calm and stress-free. That is because they are meditators, and instructors in Transcendental Meditation, and they have welcomed us to the centre here at 1210 37th Street—Cheryl Crest and Marcus Crane.

For anybody who may not have been listening the last twenty years or so in America, Marcus, what is Transcendental Meditation?

Marcus Crane: Transcendental Meditation is just a very simple, natural, effortless mental technique that we practise for 15 to 20 minutes morning and evening, and it has a very profound effect on our life. The benefits include reduced stress, improved health, better social relationships, more inner happiness....

Interviewer: And it is, as you say, non-denominational; it is not religious in nature. Anyone can practise it, is that right?

Cheryl Crest: Priests, ministers, rabbis practise TM. It is a universal procedure for bringing deep rest and the benefits that Marcus has just mentioned. It doesn't involve any conflict with religion.

Interviewer: Does it make you live better, and easier, and do your work more efficiently?

Marcus Crane: Yes, naturally, when a person is more stress-free, it has an effect on our daily lives.

Interviewer: The fact that stress has become the health buzz-word of this decade has got to have helped with introducing this to people, because they understand what the need is.

Cheryl Crest: Absolutely. And that is why people come and learn Transcendental Meditation: for the benefits that TM has in reducing stress and improving cardiovascular efficiency, relief from insomnia and so forth. There are over 350 scientific research studies verifying the effects of TM, and one important one is that the TM programme provides rest and relaxation twice as deep as any other form of meditation....

Interviewer: You have taught about 100 people since you opened in March, and one of them is Richelle Larkridge.... Richelle is a home maker, a mother, and soon to be a student at Iowa State University. Why did you decide to do this?

Richelle Larkridge: I decided because I had seen the benefits that my husband had after a week of taking TM, and I knew that this was for me. It has helped in the stress's of my life so much. I have two pre-schoolers and waking up at night is a very common occurrence. Getting up in the morning now is not so hard. I'm able to go about my life in a normal pattern very efficiently.

Interviewer: Did you find it very difficult to learn?

Richelle Larkridge: No. It was very simple. I kept thinking that it has to be harder than this.

Interviewer: The fact that it is so simple is what is hard for people to understand. There is one aspect that I think has caught people's interest and imagination lately. The fact that you cannot defy gravity but certainly change our concepts of gravity by levitating. Is that right? And this was introduced recently as shown to the press in Washington?

Cheryl Crest: And this we call the 'yogic flying' technique. What you see here is the person practising the 'yogic flying' technique. And the purpose of this technique is to increase the orderliness in the brain. It is not so much to demonstrate this supernormal ability. It is just the fact that someone is using more laws of nature than we are normally used to using.

Interviewer: And this comes about as a result of meditating after a certain amount of time. I understand you have to do it for 20 minutes twice a day. Is that right?

Cheryl Crest: Yes, that is correct.

Interviewer: And that is all you have to do? And there is a quieting of the mind that is the result.

Marcus Crane: Yes. During Transcendental Meditation we experience that the mind becomes less and less active. The mind settles down. We experience the mind in its simplest form.

Interviewer: How long does it take to learn and actually start to practise? I mean, could I start today, for instance?

Cheryl Crest: It takes about five to seven days. We have an introductory lecture, and that is the first step. We explain the benefits of TM. Then we have a few meetings where we instruct the person, then we have the follow-up, and then a person is an expert meditator....

WORLD PEACE • GLOBAL INAUGURATION

PRESS REPORTS FROM NORTH AMERICA

United States • *Des Moines television*

Des Moines, Iowa   15 August 1986   (English)

Reporter: It's touted as spreading world peace. It's not religion, but a technology. It's called the TM-Sidhi 'yogic flying', and it's all part of the Maharishi's programme to create world peace.... The followers of the Maharishi say this is tied to world peace by making individuals more peaceful. They say war is the result of stress, and by eliminating stress we eliminate war. 'Yogic flying' reportedly happens when the mind makes the body start hopping.

TM-Sidha: The technique itself is very pleasurable to do. There's this great exhilaration that comes up into the body, and so it's natural that when you're doing it you're happy and laughing.

Reporter: The meditators say they've been working on this 'yogic flying' for nearly 12 years, but the recent wave of terrorism has pushed them to bring it to the public's eye. They claim if 10,000 people practise 'yogic flying' all at the same time, it would generate world peace.

PRESS REPORTS FROM NORTH AMERICA

United States • *WHBF-TV*

Rock Island, Illinois   15 August 1986   (English)

Reporter: Today followers of a man called the Maharishi Mahesh Yogi demonstrated something called 'yogic flying'. The Maharishi, known to this area through his university in Fairfield, Iowa, believes that the mental process that gives rise to 'yogic flying' can also bring world peace.

How can this [film of 'yogic flying'] bring an end to this [film of war]? The explanation offered by the Maharishi Mahesh Yogi and his followers is based on a physics theory, a theory that says everything in the universe is inter-connected. Every molecule, every individual is bound by a common force. So, they believe, when people throughout the world are feeling stress, anger, and hatred, it creates an atmosphere of stress that leads to terrorism and war. But, the Maharishi says ... through Transcendental Meditation the world would find peace....

This is stage one of 'yogic flying', the hopping stage. Stage two, the body hovers in the air. Stage three, the body flies through the air. No one has yet reached stages two or three.

TM-Sidha: There's a great surge of energy and exhilaration. It's a feeling of bliss. And you just can't sit still. The body wants to move somewhere.

Reporter: And the Maharishi wants more people to practise it to use the positive powers of the mind to wipe out negative forces in the world. Where governments have failed, he says, individuals must succeed.

WORLD PEACE • GLOBAL INAUGURATION

PRESS REPORTS FROM NORTH AMERICA

United States • *KITV-TV*

Honolulu, Hawaii   15 August 1986   (English)

Broadcaster: Followers of Maharishi Mahesh Yogi say they have just the exercise for total relaxation, and June Grasso went to a demonstration of the so-called 'yogic flying' today in Honolulu.

Reporter: First there were five minutes of complete silence and meditation. Then, on cue, it began.... It's called 'yogic flying' and it's part of the Transcendental Meditation technique founded by the Maharishi Mahesh Yogi. The flyers, or Sidhas, say this hopping occurs spontaneously when the mind achieves coherence.

TM-Sidha: It's a spontaneous feeling. You just have to hop.

Reporter: The Sidhas maintain it is not achieved through physical means.

TM-Sidha: The reason I do it is not to lift up and hop. I can do that, too. I can do it two or three times and then I'm tired. I can do this twenty or thirty times, and the more I do it, the better I feel. It's an inner calm which, at the time of the lift-off, begins to spread and expand and just goes out in all directions.

Reporter: According to the Maharishi, this calm will minimize the stress and tensions of the world if the square root of one per cent of the population engages in 'yogic flying'. Now I admit I tend to be skeptical, and they say this is only the first stage of 'yogic flying'. Next comes hovering, and then comes flying about at will. But, at this stage, no one has demonstrated stage two or three.

TM-Sidha: The reason for that is that there's still too much stress in world consciousness, and that's why we want to have as many people practising the 'yogic flying' as possible....

PRESS REPORTS FROM NORTH AMERICA

United States • *KHON-TV*

Honolulu, Hawaii   15 August 1986   (English)

Broadcaster: Followers of the Maharishi hope and hop for world peace.... Followers of the Maharishi Mahesh Yogi ... believe they've got the means to achieve peace. And, as Chris Parsons reports, people who practise the technique find it an uplifting experience.

Reporter: No, it's not an aerobics class. It's the advanced Transcendental Meditation technique of 'yogic flying'.

TM-Sidha: You feel radiant, and your energy expands in all directions. With that there is an increase of your subjective bliss and fulfilment that's indescribable.

Reporter: It's part of the Maharishi Mahesh Yogi's Technology of the Unified Field....

TM-Sidha: Individually, when you do the TM-Sidhi 'yogic flying' technique, what happens is that you bring greater coherence to your own mind. After you bring this greater coherence to your own mind, the effect radiates to the entire world around you.

Reporter: The more people who fly together the more the stress in the world is supposed to fade. As evidence, the Maharishi's followers point to the effect they saw during a gathering of 7,000 'yogic flyers' in 1983.

TM-Sidha: We saw first of all an increase in the world stock markets.

Reporter: Not only that but the TM folks claim things got better in Lebanon. And car accidents went down, and there was less disease....

WORLD PEACE • GLOBAL INAUGURATION

PRESS REPORTS FROM NORTH AMERICA

United States • *KCUR Radio (National Public Radio)*

Kansas City, Missouri   15 August 1986   (English)

Reporter: Maharishi Mahesh Yogi, head of the practice of TM, has a new plan for world peace. Maharishi says the practice of 'yogic flying' could end terrorism and war. All it would take is 7,000 people lifting up off the ground at the same time, in the same place. Today followers of Maharishi had press conferences in 108 countries—70 major cities in the U.S., including Kansas City.

TM-Sidha: We hope to give you a glimpse today of the potential of the Maharishi Technology of the Unified Field for creating maximum coherence in brain functioning and, on that basis, coherence in the whole world consciousness as the foundation for permanent world peace.

Reporter: Here's the theory: War is caused by the build-up of stress in the collective consciousness of nations. TM reduces stress. TM'ers in the advanced Sidhi programme have for years been rising into the air. That's called 'yogic flying'. TM advocates claim during meditation there's a high degree of synchronization between all the different parts of the brain. They call that 'coherence' and they say it makes 'yogic flying' possible. Followers of the Maharishi demonstrated the technique for the first time in Washington, D.C. at the First North American Yogic Flying Competition. They say governments can no longer ensure peace.

TM-Sidha: This experience is the experience of the heart of perfect silence, infinite dynamism, the essence of peace within us. So this practice of TM and 'yogic flying' not only enlivens peace in the individual practitioner but also radiates peace throughout the environment on a very basic and universal level of life.

Reporter: The TM'ers say if 7,000 people practise the technique at once it will bring world peace. 7,000 is the square root of one per cent of the world's population. The plan is to have a few thousand extra just to be safe.

TM-Sidha: What individuals can do is participate in coherence-creating groups practising the TM and TM-Sidhi programme and contribute to the Maharishi World Peace Fund to maintain a group of 10,000 'yogic flyers' practising together to sustain world peace.

Reporter: Maharishi says he needs $100 million to keep those 10,000 flyers up in the air and thus keep the world at peace.

After explaining all of this, Maharishi's followers took the press into another room for the demonstration. They cautioned, what we are about to see is the first stage of 'yogic flying'. The final stage would be levitation. The flyers begin by sitting cross-legged and meditating. A small bell tinkles. One by one their bodies rise. The flyers begin to bounce like human popcorn on the white foam mats.

It's not exactly flying, not floating, not hanging suspended in the air; but it's also not something just anyone can do. Try it. Sit cross-legged on the floor. Without using your hands or your legs, without rocking, hop a foot off the floor and propel yourself across the room that way. That's what the 'yogic flyers' did.

Interviewer: What do you feel like when you're flying?

TM-Sidha: It's a very blissful experience. Most people don't understand what bliss is because they don't experience very much ... happiness in day-to-day life; but [this experience] is one of great unboundedness, real peace within yourself.... That's the whole beauty of the TM-Sidhi programme. You practise it, and you are able to function from that level.

Interviewer: You know when you get to the end of the mat?

TM-Sidha: Right. There's still that awareness of the outside world, you could say.

Interviewer: Is it harder to do this technique when there are people in the room?

TM-Sidha: It's OK. When I go into the unified field there's only my Self....

Interviewer: The demonstrators have promised to invite the press back to witness the next stages of 'yogic flying'.

WORLD PEACE • GLOBAL INAUGURATION

PRESS REPORTS FROM NORTH AMERICA

United States • *WVIT-TV*

Cromwell, Connecticut   15 August 1986   (English)

Broadcaster: If you're looking for a way to end all wars, some folks believe that levitating or floating in the air is the answer. Harlin Levy has more.

Interviewer: Yogic hopping is the answer, according to Connecticut students of Transcendental Meditation, who demonstrated their abilities today in Cromwell. They believe if enough people get hopping all together, world tension will gradually disappear. How to do it? You start with deep meditation.

TM-Sidha: ...and inside you can feel a wide range of emotions, from just a quiet sort of happiness to a tremendous surge of energies seconds later...and the body starts doing that hopping.

Second TM-Sidha: ...a lot of energy pulsating through my nervous system. And I just feel that I have to just lift off and take off.

Interviewer: ...There are two further stages—'yogic floating' and the highest, 'yogic flying'.

TM-Sidha: ...when the mind is is the deepest state of awareness—this settled state—we put into the mind, at that time, a particular formula for the body to rise. And that's what happens.

Interviewer: Now, in case you're wondering when you'll get a chance to see stage two—floating and hovering, and stage three, flying—well, the answer is, soon.

TM-Sidha: Well, I'd hope within the next year, but we don't know. But you'll be the first to know.

Interviewer: And this may be what it will look like. What about gravity you say? Well, these folks believe there are other laws of nature. Have you ever hovered?

TM-Sidha: No. I want to and I will someday. It can happen anytime, I guess....

United States • *WOTV-TV*

Grand Rapids, Michigan   15 August 1986   (English)

Interviewer: ...followers of the Maharishi Mahesh Yogi demonstrated 'yogic flying', and as we see on the Freeman File tonight, they're trying to reach a lofty goal.

Interviewer: These Transcendental Meditators believe stress sometimes makes people hopping mad. To relieve stress they practise TM, and what they call 'yogic flying'. Do you have any fear that you are going to bump your head on the ceiling?

TM-Sidha: No, because I'm aware of what I'm doing.

Broadcaster: TM'ers say individual peace begins from within. And then it is just a short leap to creating world peace.

TM-Sidha: We can now realistically promote a soothing influence of coherence, neutralizing the negative trends and tendencies in society, and therefore establishing this technique as the basis of world peace.... It is effortless. It is so hard to explain, and even to look at it looks a little bit out of the ordinary, but it really is effortless. And my body does go up, and it does come down, you know. And the only thing is, when I'm up in the air I sometimes wonder if I am going to come down.

Broadcaster: TM'ers want to get a group of 7,000 people together, maybe even here in Grand Rapids—people who would meditate, hope, and hop for peace and have fun doing it. Who knows, maybe people will jump at the chance to do it in Grand Rapids. Bill Freeman. News 8.

United States • *KIRO-TV*

Seattle, Washington 15 August 1986 (English)

Broadcaster: Ever thought about flying without using an airplane? Well a group of Seattleites are trying to do just that.

Interviewer: (sounds of flying on foam) It may look just like a lot of hopping around to you but it's a form of flying to these guys, all of them practising an advanced form of Transcendental Meditation or TM.

TM-Sidha: It's very blissful. It's a very beautiful feeling inside.

Second TM-Sidha: It's very exhilarating. The body just lifts off the foam.

Interviewer: Their goal is to eventually hover in the air, then fly round the room....It's not a stunt for Westbush and not an attempt to set any record.

TM-Sidha: What we're trying to do is develop perfect mind-body coordination to be a fully realized individual, an enlightened person—basically to be very happy and successful in our lives.

Interviewer: It's a technique they want to share. These folks believe that wars and crime, poverty and sickness can all be blamed on a build-up of stress in the world. Stress that could be eliminated if more people practised TM.

TM-Sidha: When these more powerful techniques are practised by people together in groups, research shows that a more coherent and orderly collective consciousness in society is created.

Interviewer: The TM people also claim the good effects of all this hopping around can spread to others. They are planning to put 7000 TM practicioners in each continent of the world to neutralize the tension and stress generated by everyone else.

TM-Sidha: I am absolutely sure that this is a very excellent way to create a positive influence in the environment.

Interviewer: So it is much more than an exercise for these people. It's a hop they say, for world peace.

Broadcaster: Well, when they start hovering and flying around the room, we will return with our cameras and bring that to you.

WORLD PEACE • GLOBAL INAUGURATION

PRESS REPORTS FROM NORTH AMERICA

United States • *KCRA-TV*

Stockton, California   15 August 1986   (English)

Flying Yogis

Broadcaster: Now, some people who fly through the air with the greatest of ease; not the man on the flying trapeze, but the flying yogi.

Across the country today students of the Maharishi Mahesh Yogi popped into the air, and who was there? Channel 3's Rich Iberra, who says it was all in the name of world peace.

Interviewer: These are students of Transcendental Meditation and the Maharishi Mahesh Yogi. The Maharishi is convinced that his students hold the answer to world peace, one not yet solved by arms talks or the United Nations.

Dorothy Nicolas: It is not how many weapons we have or what kind of weapons we have that make war. It is always the consciousness of the individual.

(Scenes from the flying demonstration)

Interviewer: This bouncing or flying, as it's called, is supposed to reduce world stress and results from a consciousness-raising, a power in the universe....Basically the idea is that good vibrations emanate from this, affecting everything for the better

Will Nicolas (demonstrator): Prosperity, happiness, fulfillment...that's everyone's right.

Interviewer: And the stock market might go up?

Will Nicolas: It will go up, sure!

Interviewer: And crime rate will go down...

Will Nicolas: It'll go down. And don't you want crime to go down and the stock market to go up?

Interviewer: The stock market fluctuated throughout the day, but toward the closing bell, about the time the flying yogis lifted off their mats, well, it shot up by more than 10 points. Now, we're not sure that this was a direct result of their efforts. However, maybe some people here at Payne Weber are saying, 'Thank you, Maharishi!'

PRESS REPORTS FROM NORTH AMERICA

United States • *KCRL-TV*

Reno, Nevada   15 August 1986   (English)

Broadcaster: ...Their goal is peace on earth. But the followers of the Maharishi Mahesh Yogi have a rather unnorthodox way of bringing that about. The yogis believe that not only their personal lives but the state of the world around them improves when they engage in Transcendental Meditation. A few Maharishi followers held a free lecture today, and a demonstration of what they call 'yogic flying'. Now it may look like hopping to you and me, but the yogis insist they're being propelled off the ground because of the relationship of a different kind of gravity. When they fly, the yogis say, they're achieving maximum brain coherence, and that, they say, is the way to peace....

TM-Sidha: If by doing some technique of flying twice a day I can become a better individual, not only as far as feeling much better, but being a better individual able to do more with my mind, then that's worth doing, and that is what the TM and TM-Sidhi programme does.

Interviewer: He says that the phenomenon is based on the laws of physics. He says it is an exhilarating experience for him, and it also has an influence on the entire community.

TM-Sidha: Statistical studies show that when we have large groups of people doing this they also have an effect on the environment around them. Crime goes down when we have a sufficient number of people, and all aspects of the environment improve. This is just because we are all united on the unified field level of creation. The experience itself is beyond anything I've ever experienced doing before, especially at the point of lift-off. To have the body become so light that it lifts off the ground—you can imagine that must be an exhilarating and blissful experience....

WORLD PEACE • GLOBAL INAUGURATION

PRESS REPORTS FROM NORTH AMERICA

United States • *The Associated Press*

Des Moines, Iowa   15 August 1986   (English)

Meditators hop to Des Moines

DES MOINES, Iowa (AP) — Followers of the Maharishi Mahesh Yogi brought their "yogic flying" show here Friday, claiming they're on the road to mental coherence that will someday enable them to fly through the air.

"What they will experience is just an impulse from deep inside to lift off," Thomas Niederman told reporters before leading them into a meeting room at the Hotel Savery where six meditators sat cross-legged on foam rubber cushions covering an area of the floor.

After five minutes of silence to allow the meditators to coordinate their minds with their bodies, they began hopping on the cushions. Most reached eight inches to a foot in the air, and all quickly returned to the floor subject to the force of gravity.

"At the present, we've only developed to this first stage of 'hopping,'" said Ron Openshaw, a professor of physics at Maharishi International University in Fairfield.

Openshaw said meditators hope to reach the second level — levitation — before reaching the third level of actual flight through the air.

"The fact that it can happen is a quite certain thing," added Niederman, another practitioner of the maharishi's form of transcendental meditation.

"It's not defying natural law," said Openshaw. "It's just raising human life to its dignity as master of natural law."

The followers of the maharishi did their hopping in private until last month, when they held "The First North American Yogic Flying Competition" in Washington, D.C. Billed as the flying olympics, the event was chronicled by many of the nation's major media.

On Friday, hopping exhibitions were held in Des Moines and other sites throughout the world. Meditators said they are going public because they believe that if enough people start meditating around the world, violence will end.

"If we want to get rid of war, we have to get rid of stress in individuals," Openshaw said. "This is really the only way to prevent war."

The maharishi is trying to raise $100 million to fund a permanent population of 10,000 transcendental meditators in a single location near New Delhi, India.

That group would be able to reach a coherence of mind that "spreads throughout nature" and makes the world a peaceful place, Openshaw said.

"What this is all about is maharishi's plan for world peace," Niederman said. "There is violence sprouting up in a very localized way, so that no one can really say that they're safe."

PRESS REPORTS FROM NORTH AMERICA

United States • Times-Herald
Dallas, Texas   15 August 1986   (English)

A lift for lives of stress

Yogic flying hailed as route to peace

By JIM BRADY
Staff writer

In the interest of world peace and inner tranquility, transcendental meditators have launched a nationwide campaign to publicize their private remedy to stress.

Yogic flying.

In fact, the world would be a better place if more people would just sit down, bend their legs into the lotus position and levitate, says local disciple Tom Proudfoot.

"It happens inside," said Proudfoot. "There's this integration of mind and body, and you just lift off the ground."

And for ye of little faith, a demonstration was scheduled for this morning at the Marriott Park Central Hotel.

"When you see it, you might feel, 'That guy is not flying,'" said Proudfoot.

And he probably won't be, unless world karma dramatically improves by morning. Bad vibes, it seems, present a counterforce that keeps the 3 million followers of the Maharishi Mahesh Yogi from advancing past the first stage of flying — Yogic hopping.

"The first stage is hopping, the second is hovering and the third is Master of the Skies — free flight," Proudfoot explained.

And for ye of even less faith, journalists who witnessed the first demonstration in Washington, D.C., last month reported some rather startling cross-legged hops — one 24.75 inches high and another 70 inches long.

The concept of yogic flight is somewhat difficult to grasp for non-disciples, Proudfoot conceded before trying to explain.

Basically, when meditating, the mind and body merge on a single thought that carries a state of awareness — and inner tranquility — deeper and deeper, until it is part of the Unified Field, a body of energy. "Flight" comes when the meditators merge mind, body and the Unified Field.

"It's kind of abstract," he said.

Dallas Times Herald

Connie and Tom Proudfoot advocate Yogic flying.

But practitioners say the world has so many problems, it's time to take the trouble to sway nonbelievers.

True believers say if enough people practice transcendental meditation at the same time and place, something akin to good vibrations will calm strife in the world.

"When people are coherent in themselves (that is, meditating), it radiates into the environment," said Carol Stansberry, a spokeswoman for Maharishi International University in Fairfield, Iowa.

And as the vibes improve, so do the believers' chances of soaring higher.

"As there is less stress in world consciousness," said Connie Proudfoot, Tom's wife, who helped coordinate the local demonstration. "We will be free to hop higher."

WORLD PEACE • GLOBAL INAUGURATION

PRESS REPORTS FROM NORTH AMERICA

United States • *The Associated Press*

New York, New York   15 August 1986   (English)

Four Men Bounce For World Peace

NEW YORK (AP) — In a loft in lower Manhattan on Friday afternoon, four men bounced for world peace.

The men, followers of the Maharishi Mahesh Yogi, India's proponent of Transcendental Meditation, believe a large group of people bouncing in one place produce enough positive energy to defuse stress between nations and improve the world's quality of life.

The bouncing — or as they call it, "yogic flying" — occurs when "brain-wave coherence" liberates people from stress and gravity, allowing them to pop like corn kernels in a hot pan.

The technique was demonstrated simultaneously in 70 cities throughout the United States and 108 countries around the world on Friday, said John Lloyd, president of the New York Association of Professionals Practicing the TM Program.

The demonstrations were held to introduce people to the technique in an effort to raise $100 million. The money will be used to permanently maintain a group of 7,000 people who will meditate, bounce and help achieve world peace together, Lloyd said.

"Stress cannot rise in communities, nations or in the world unabated forever before negative tendencies begin to arise; the prime rate increases, wars break out and terrorism occurs," he said.

John Graff, 36, a computer programer from Brooklyn, sat on the edge of a row of five mattresses, meditating, his legs crossed in lotus position. A bell rang and suddenly, with a broad smile on his face, he began to bounce in froglike jumps down the length of the mattresses.

He did a broad jump of about 50 inches, a high jump of 18 inches, and then he hopped to the top of a pile of three stacked mattresses.

"It's a spontaneous phenomena," Graff explained afterwards. "I have no sense of effort when I'm rising. I get a great deal of exhilaration and fulfillment. It's a purification of the nervous system."

Bouncing is not all such meditation can achieve. The second and third stages of yogic flying are hovering and actual flight, said Lloyd.

"We're at the level where the Wright Brothers were some 80 years ago," he said. With a little more practice he believes, flying is a definite possibility — and so is world peace.

MAHARISHI'S PROGRAMME TO CREATE

PRESS REPORTS FROM NORTH AMERICA

United States • *United Press International*
Los Angeles, California   15 August 1986   (English)

Just practicing
Devotees of Transcendental Meditation hopped atop mats in Los Angeles yesterday in a demonstration of 'yogic flying.' The TM people said it's the first stage of levitation — a hopping where they are propelled by their own spiritual awareness. They hope to get to the final stage, flying.

WORLD PEACE • GLOBAL INAUGURATION

PRESS REPORTS FROM NORTH AMERICA

United States • *The Muncie Star*

Muncie, Indiana   15 September 1986   (English)

You Have to Hop Before You Fly

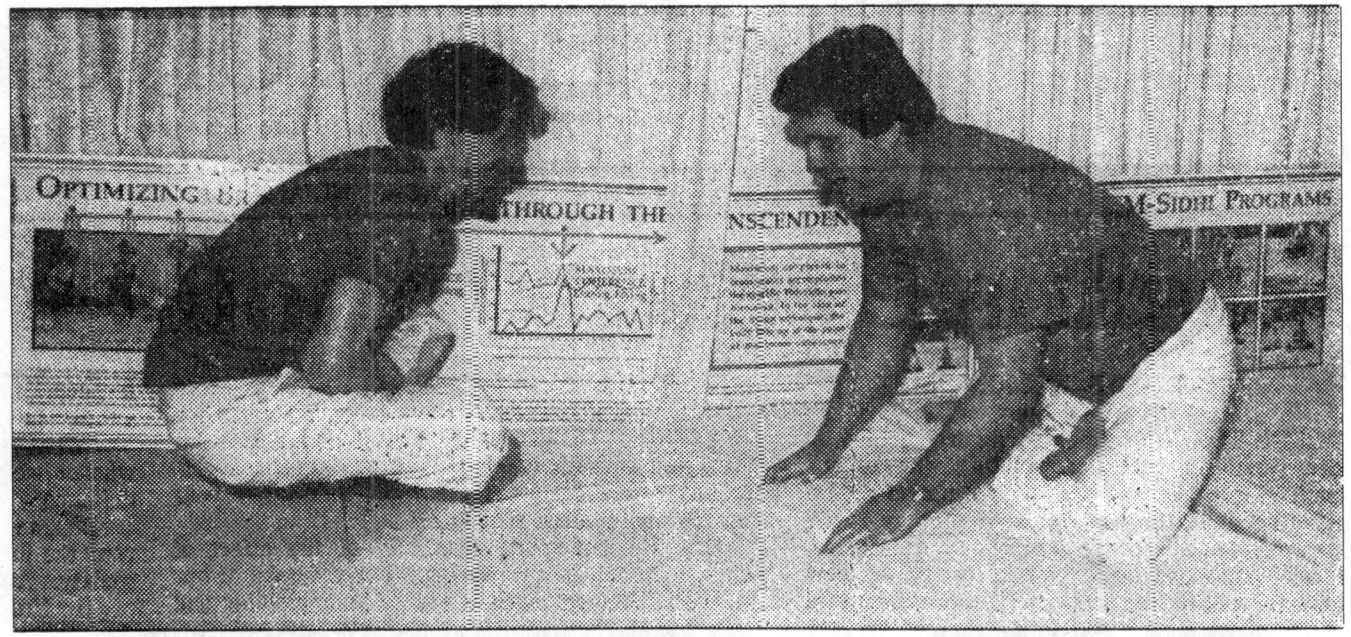

Star Photo by Jeff Mastin

Mind Over Matter

Dr. John Peterson, 304 Alden Road, and Charles Watkins of Indianapolis demonstrate the first step toward flight, according to Maharishi Mahesh Yogi, the founder of the Transcendental Meditation movement. The meditation that allowed Peterson and Watkins to take short, flying hops through a method called "Yogic Flying" can lead to world peace, Peterson said at the Sunday demonstration in his home.

By KRISTI STONE
Star Staff Reporter

Jumping on mattresses was a no-no for most children, but about 30 people gathered Sunday to watch three men do just that.

The men jumped, or more acurately hopped, across the widths of three mattresses on the floor of Dr. John C. Peterson's home to demonstrate the first level of "Yogic Flying," a meditative achievement that can lead to world peace, according to Marharishi Mahesh Yogi, the founder of the Transcendental Meditation movement.

Peterson and his wife, Vicki, a 12-year teaching veteran of TM, invited friends, students and the media to their home at 304 Alden Road, to describe the techniques that they said in future years could lead to world peace and people flying "like Peter Pan."

TM works to develop inner peace and harmony, Vicki Peterson said. The meditation reaches a field of pure consciousness which is the source of "strength, creativity and intelligence."

Peterson described meditation as a "frictionless flow of awareness toward a fulfillment of desire."

Because each person is a unit in the universe, as more people have inner peace there will be world peace, Peterson said. If people unite in meditation and reach that level of pure consciousness, it affects the rest of the world because, like force of a magnet has an effect on metal, the force of meditation has an effect on the world.

"In cities with more than 1 percent of the population practicing TM; the crime rates, the hospital rates, the accidents rates went down," Peterson said.

According to Maharishi Yogi, flying reaches the level of consciousness that came before gravity, so when people reach that level they not only can fly, they can affect the world conciousness.

"That's why I got into TM," Peterson explained, "I wanted to do something about the world situation...."

© *The Muncie Star; reprinted with permission*

United States • *Sacramento Union*

Sacramento, California   16 August 1986   (English)

LARRY BRISKIN, left, and Kevin Cook were among four advanced students of Transcendental Meditation who demonstrated techniques for achieving peace on Friday.

WORLD PEACE • GLOBAL INAUGURATION

PRESS REPORTS FROM NORTH AMERICA

United States • *The Burlington Free Press*

Burlington, Vermont 16 August 1986 (English)

'Yogic Flyers' Hopping Path Toward Utopia for the World

Free Press Photo by ROB SWANSON

Andy Cozzens of Burlington, left, does some 'yogic flying' as Steve Birkett, also of Burlington, is at rest on the mat between hops as the pair demonstrates the first stage of a form of meditative flying for the cause of world peace.

MAHARISHI'S PROGRAMME TO CREATE

PRESS REPORTS FROM NORTH AMERICA

United States • *Courier-Post*

Camden, New Jersey   16 August 1986   (English)

Demonstration of yogic flying has Maharishi's followers hopping

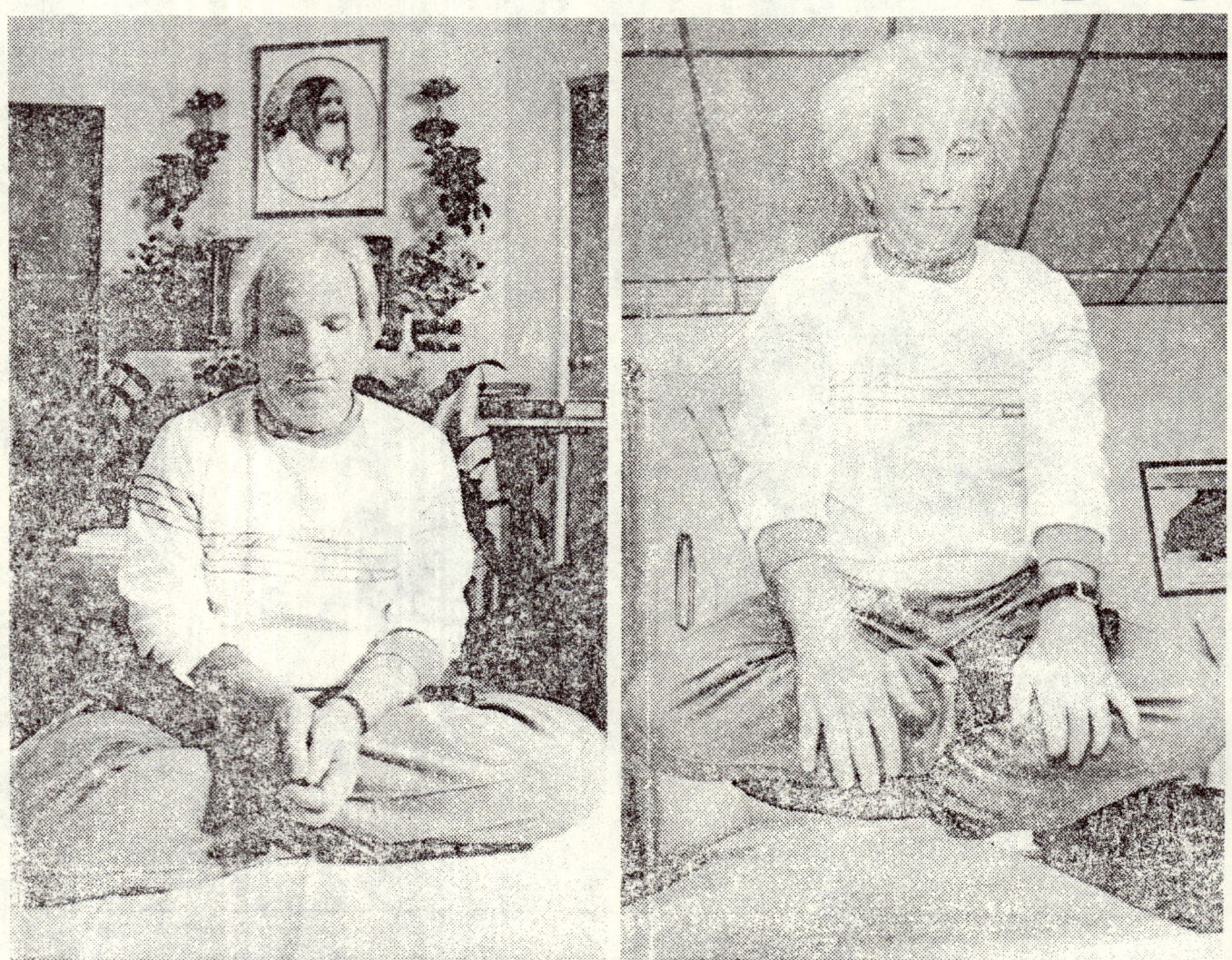

Jack Boles meditates (left) before starting to hop in a demonstration of yogic flying yesterday.

WORLD PEACE • GLOBAL INAUGURATION

By BERNIE WEISENFELD
Of the Courier-Post

COLLINGSWOOD — In a post-hop interview here, Transcendental Meditation teacher Jack Boles said he is a 42-year-old ex-Marine, "hovering" around 200 pounds and practicing "yogic flying" daily.

Well, flying eventually, hopping for now.

Yogic flying is an advanced meditation technique done by followers of the Maharishi Mahesh Yogi as part of his plan for world peace, Boles said.

In what they said was one of 200 worldwide demonstrations of "unified field technology" yesterday, Boles and fellow teacher Dan Bolling shed navy business suits at the Transcendental Meditation Center, and in athletic garb leaped frog-like from a cross-legged lotus position on a line of foam mats. This followed a few minutes of silent meditation in the center at 322 White Horse Pike.

"When you are doing this with the technique involved it is effortless," Boles told reporters earlier. "You don't really want to stop."

Instruments that record brain wave activity show "tremendous coherence" during yogic flying, he said.

"You've never seen that in any waking, sleeping or dreaming."

Practitioners are still held down by stress and can only hop, Boles said. But "hovering" is expected in stage two and finally, flight, he said.

"What you see now is not going to be near as grand as when we can hold the body up in the air."

Asked if anyone had attained the flight stage, Boles responded with "a shaded no. There are such people, but I don't think you have access to them."

When practiced in a group of about 7,000, yogic flying can restore balance to nature, Boles said. The number represents the square root of one percent of the world population.

"Then spontaneously, life will be lived in the tidal waves of harmony on earth."

A $100 million world peace fund is being gathered to support a standing group of yogic flyers in India, Boles said.

"We are actually getting together 10,000 (flyers) as in that way we'll have the security that we'll always have 7,000 in the meditation hall every day."

Meditator-levitators could come from 50,000 around the world now, Boles said.

"As soon as you see this group has been established, this is what the press is going to start reporting: that international conflicts such as the Iran-Iraq war will cease.

"Cordiality will prevail in all international relations. Terrorism will vanish from the face of the earth.

"This is not speculation. We have been doing these global research projects with 7,000 Sidhas (advanced meditators) flying together . . . and we have been predicting ahead of time the positive things that would emerge as a result of those technologies, and those things did happen.

"We know that we are on very, very solid ground."

Boles said the hopping stage was not intended to be seen, but "the press has been urging us for almost 10 years to 'show us.' "

"We didn't want to show this hopping technique because we thought they don't know what's going on internally."

But the Maharishi decided now was the time because "the Maharishi feels the bursting point of nature is very, very close," Boles said.

"All the strategies of government today has only created greater fear in the world."

Last month, public hopping began with a competition in Washington, D.C. The program had high jumps, dashes and hurdling events.

Hovering is not far off, Boles predicted. "When we call you back in, which I don't think will be much longer, we will demonstrate that technique for you."

Courtesy of Courier

MAHARISHI'S PROGRAMME TO CREATE

PRESS REPORTS FROM NORTH AMERICA

United States • *Plain Dealer*

Cleveland, Ohio   16 August 1986   (English)

If Scott Walmsley is right, his performance of yogic flying is the answer to disease, war, and other problems.

Straighten up and fly yogic, we are urged

By TIMOTHY PUIN
STAFF WRITER

If three flying men can help cut the deficit, then voodoo economics should yield to guru economics. No question about it — levitation is more fun than tax increases.

But fun doesn't describe the half of it, say followers of Maharishi Mahesh Yogi, who demonstrated yogic flying last night at their headquarters in Lakewood.

"It's just a rush of energy and bliss, and you just go. It's a wonderful feeling," said Robert Oates, who doffed his suitcoat and tie before performing the first stage of this flying — hopping.

None of the thousands of people worldwide who practice yogic flying are past that first stage, according to a videotape shown before the demonstration to the more than 40 people assembled.

But, said the tape, the hopping stage should be surpassed when the world consciousness is completely at peace ....

David Orme-Johnson, a professor at Maharishi International University in Fairfield, Iowa, said 32 studies had proved yogic flying made the world a better place.

Whenever 7,000 yogic fliers perform simultaneously, Orme-Johnson said, crime rates drop, patent applications increase, wars cease, diseases are cured and world peace is fostered.

Last night, yogic fliers practiced in hundreds of cities in 108 countries. But that isn't enough, Orme-Johnson said. What the world needs is a community of full-time yogic fliers, headquartered in India.

To accomplish that, Maharishi's followers must first raise $100 million, according to a group pamphlet. No contributions were solicited during the demonstration, however.

After the videotape, Oates said he was not a world-class yogic flier. He asked the crowd to meditate for five minutes, as he and his two partners sat cross-legged, in the lotus position, on a foam rubber mattress.

Then he began twitching and hopped across the mat. Neither he nor Walmsley, both of whom said they taught transcendental meditation in Dayton, matched the flying capacity of Tim Casey, however.

The crowd cheered Casey, who said he was a rooms division manager for Marriott Hotels here. As attendants stacked four mattresses, Casey prepared for the high jump onto the pile, and he executed it on his second try.

Walmsley said he hadn't met any skeptics yet, except, perhaps, his mother, who was present. "I think my mom always wondered what that bumping was in the room," he said. "So I couldn't demonstrate when I visited her."

Regardless of skeptics, Oates said, "The whole thing is going forward organically."

United States • *WQAD-TV*

Moline, Illinois   15 August 1986   (English)

Broadcaster: ...[A group] in Fairfield, Iowa, launched a unique campaign for world peace today, and Rae Martin was there.

Reporter: This probably looks like hopping, and it is, but it's also what Transcendental Meditation backers call an alternative method to produce everlasting world peace: 'yogic flying'.

Today in one thousand cities, representatives from Maharishi International University in Fairfield, Iowa, brought their 'yogic flying' before the public. They claim practising this form of TM can decrease the amount of terrorism and war in the world.

TM-Sidha: When enough people get together in one place and practise this technique together, it turns out that the effects are even greater than they would be if each of those individuals were practising separately.

Reporter: The TM'ers are trying to get the square root of one percent of the world's population to practise 'yogic flying'. They claim that if they do, there will be world peace. Rae Martin, Active 8 News, Davenport.

MAHARISHI'S PROGRAMME TO CREATE

PRESS REPORTS FROM NORTH AMERICA

United States • *Florida Today*

Cocoa, Florida   16 August 1986   (English)

Meditation for peace

Jeff Thompson, FLORIDA TODAY

NO FEAR: Bob Bowser is a Transcendental Meditation student visiting Melbourne.

'Yogic fliers' hop and flop in Melbourne for crusade

By Billy Cox
FLORIDA TODAY

The so-called Maharishi Effect descended upon Melbourne Friday afternoon as three "yogic flyers" sitting in the cross-legged lotus position bounded frog-like across foam mattresses on the first leg of a crusade to end warfare and terrorism.

Paul Gelderloff of the Netherlands joined Bob Bowser

WORLD PEACE • GLOBAL INAUGURATION

and Dee Booth of Washington, D.C., at the Rialto Place Hilton as part of a campaign —reportedly conducted in 108 countries and more than 70 U.S. cities simultaneously — to unveil what Ava Kennedy described as "a new technology for attaining world peace."

Kennedy, co-director of the Space Coast Association of Professionals Practicing The Transcendental Meditation Program, told a small media audience that the "flying technique" about to be unveiled was an element of the Maharishi Effect last observed when 7,000 people convened to meditate in December and January of 1983 and 1984.

Using their minds to tap into the Unified Field Theory, the physical law of unity which eluded Einstein all his life, the TM flyers, Kennedy said, were able to lower the collective global stress levels from Dec. 17 to Jan. 6. "Studies showed drops in violence, automobile accidents, hospital admissions, and stock markets rose everywhere," Kennedy said.

Taking five-minute silent meditation breaks between events, Gelderloff, Bowser and Booth proceeded to hop and flop down 25 meters of foam runway, long-jumping, high-jumping and sprinting all the way. None flew or levitated.

"This is only the first stage," said Bowser, a 10-year TM student. "Eventually we will progress to floating, and then to free flight. Maharishi says the only reason we're not hovering now is because stress levels around the world are so high."

Bowser referred to Maharishi Mahesh Yogi, the TM founder who contends that world peace can be achieved when the square root of 1 percent of the Earth's population — or about 7,000 people — gather in one place to practice yoga.

The group has a free public lecture at the Melbourne Hilton Tuesday at 7:30 p.m.

United States • *KGMB-TV*

Honolulu, Hawaii   15 August 1986   (English)

Reporter: You, too, can learn to hop, fly, and make the world a better place. That's the message of a local branch of a Transcendental Meditation group. The Honolulu Capital of the Age of Enlightenment says meditation causes 'yogic flying', or at least hopping. They say this eventually results in decreased violence and disease and increased economic activity.

TM-Sidha: We feel that when the level of violence and stress is reduced substantially in the world, as it would be if we had a large group of 7,000 to 10,000 people doing their TM and TM-Sidhi programme together, we enliven world consciousness so people can actually fly on a regular basis. Hover first, and then actually fly at will.

Reporter: But hopping is still just the first step. Thirty-five year old Honolulu chiropractor Lawson Cannon has been doing it for nine years.

Lawson Cannon: I'd say the mental picture is one of moving through the air, or feeling just light so that you come off the ground. And the emotional feeling is one of just total fulfilment or bliss.

Reporter: They say if enough people do it, you get the Maharishi Effect.

Maharishi: To bring a soothing influence in the world consciousness, whereby the fear generated by the dangerous rivalry of superpowers can be neutralized and all the nations could be freed from a continuous state of fear....

PRESS REPORTS FROM NORTH AMERICA

United States • *The Dallas Morning News*

Dallas, Texas   16 August 1986   (English)

'Yogic flying' aficionados go to a hop for world peace

By Ed Timms
Staff Writer of The News

David Sharp is a 33-year-old Austin school bus driver. He earned a black belt in karate at 16, but attains inner peace at work and at home through meditation.

John Hopkins, 29, is a graduate student studying mathematics at Texas Christian University, an aficionado of Pythagorean principles and a pianist. He, too, found fulfillment in the teachings of Maharishi Mahesh Yogi, the guru of Transcendental Meditation.

On Friday, Sharp and Hopkins went to the hop. They were hopping for world peace.

The main event for the day was "Yogic flying." Sharp and Hopkins, their legs locked in the lotus position, would hop up and down on five mattresses on the floor of a meeting room in the Marriott Park Central Hotel.

But before the show came the message.

Tom Proudfoot, a local leader in TM, explained that through meditation the two fliers would "lift off" when "optimal coherence of brain function occurs."

Proudfoot told more than 50 people that the demonstration was part of the maharishi's program to end war and hatred caused by a "lack of coherence of the collective consciousness of society."

"You have all come here to see Yogic flying," he said. "But I'm here to talk about world peace. It's a very weighty subject not to be taken lightly."

Proudfoot told the audience that meditation can help many ills, including high blood pressure and cholesterol levels, as well as stress. He maintained that with enough people meditating, world problems can be remedied.

And recent research, he added, "even indicates a reversal of the aging process and stress" in long-term meditators whose biological ages are years younger than their chronological ages.

As he spoke, a fidgeting toddler on her father's lap was a brief distraction. "She's 47 years old," her father quipped.

After two short films, it was time for Sharp and Hopkins to do their stuff. First came five minutes of meditation. At the sound of the bell, they were off, leaping up and down on the mattresses in a froglike motion, rising inches into the air. Afterwards, Sharp described the hopping as "relaxing," a pleasant experience.

"A couple of times I felt I was so high I was going to fall off the mat," he said.

Hopkins, after the demonstration, also revealed one of his techniques for safe hopping.

"You have to keep your eyes open once in awhile," he said, "to keep from running into things."

WORLD PEACE • GLOBAL INAUGURATION

PRESS REPORTS FROM NORTH AMERICA

United States • *Quad-City Times*

Davenport, Iowa   16 August 1986   (English)

Yogi fliers: Hopping for peace

They are all up in the air, inviting everyone who still has feet on the ground to join them in ushering in the sunshine of the Age of Enlightenment.
— Maharishi Mahesh Yogi

By Jeff Hunt
QUAD-CITY TIMES

Well, they didn't exactly fly around the room. They didn't hover, either. But boy could these guys hop.

Three devotees of the Maharishi Mahesh Yogi Friday gave the first Quad-City demonstration of the "yogi flying" technique at the Blackhawk Hotel as part of a worldwide inauguration of the technique, which practioners believe can bring world peace.

Three men demonstrated the technique on a 40-foot foam pad in the Hotel's Bix Beiderbecke Room. Demonstrations were held Friday in 1,000 other cities to kick off the Maharishi's "Program to Create World Peace."

AS BIX STARED down from framed posters on the wall, Charles Egner, a building contractor from Fairfield, Iowa; William Koppel, an accountant also from Fairfield; and DeArmond Briggs, a former Rock Island High School basketball star, leap-frogged around the pad.

The three men, clad in white pajama pants, polo shirts and white socks, sat in the traditional yoga position and meditated for five minutes before performing each athletic event.

There were four events: The hurdles (they jumped over two 8-inch styrofoam dividers), the long jump, high jump and dash.

The demonstration was billed as a "levitation," but the two dozen or so people who watched it did not see anyone suspended in air. For those who practice transcendental meditation, that was not surprising.

Yogi flying is comprised of three distinct stages, explained Lynn Coriell, of the Davenport Transcendental Meditation Program.

STAGE ONE, at which the demonstrators appeared quite proficient, is hopping. That's where through transcendental meditation the mind reaches such coherence that the body involuntarily hops around.

Stage Two is hovering, a feat that meditators have yet to achieve, according to Bill Van Zandt, a doctorate candidate in neuroscience at Maharishi International University, Fairfield.

However, Van Zandt said that during mass meditations in the "Golden Domes" on the Maharishi campus, if you open your eyes and peek, some fellow meditators appear to be "quite light."

Stage Three is flying. This is the peak experience for a meditator, where his or her mind has achieved maximum coherence, and, according to the Maharishi literature, "the practitioner experiences waves of exhilaration and a profound stabilization of this silent level of awareness."...

CORIELL SAID Maharishi followers have for years refused to demonstrate the flying yogi technique in public. However, rising world violence has made it necessary to spread the word of such

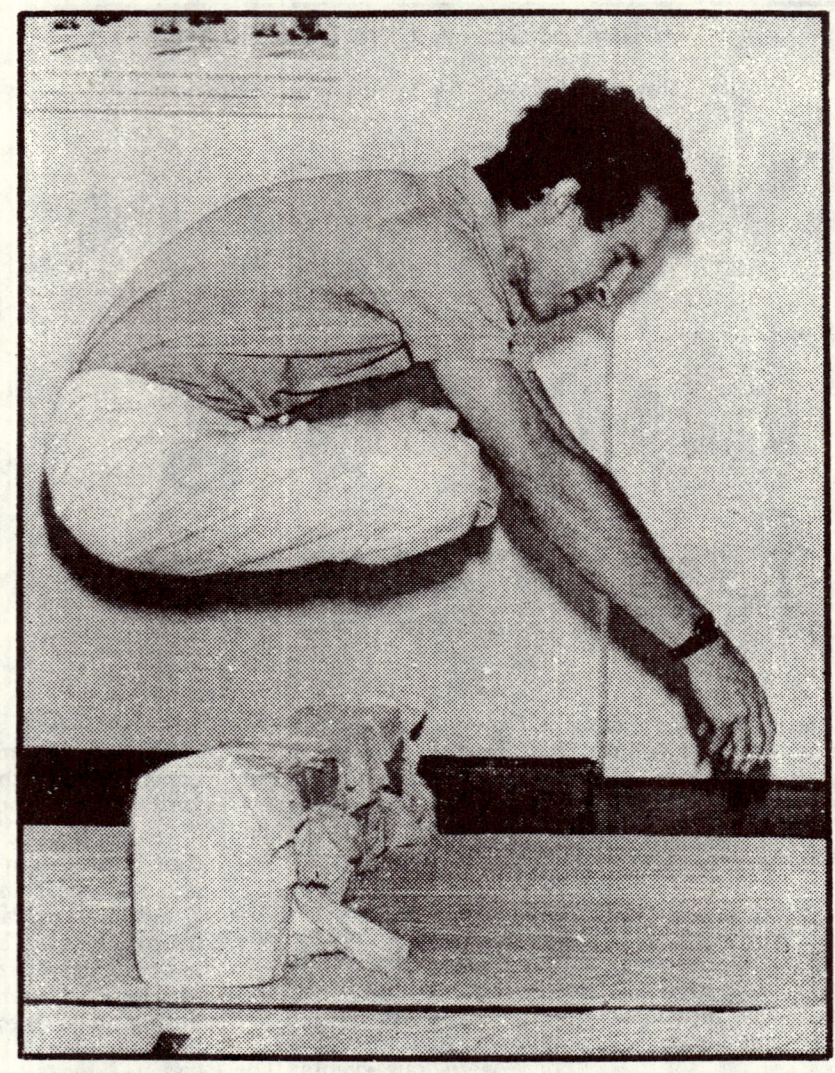

Demonstrating the "yogic flying" technique is William Koppel, an accountant from Fairfield, Iowa. (Times photo by Don Jones)

practice, which the Maharishi says can result in harmony throughout the world.

Van Zandt said world peace could be achieved if 7,000 people (a figure arrived at by taking the square root of 1 percent of the world's population) practiced transcendental meditation in one place.

"Your first flight, you just can't imagine the bliss and exhilaration you feel," said Van Zandt, a yogi flyer himself.

WORLD PEACE • GLOBAL INAUGURATION

PRESS REPORTS FROM NORTH AMERICA

United States • *The Denver Post*

Denver, Colorado   16 August 1986   (English)

The Denver Post / Brian Brainerd

PEACE POSTURES

Transcendental meditators, from left, Robert Wofford; Bruce Padgett, in background; Dave Lupberger, in air; and Bob Wampler, with his back to camera, demonstrate advanced Sidhi meditation, which is said to promote peace. Maharishi Mahesh Yogi has calculated that 7,000 people meditating in this fashion could bring peace to the world.

MAHARISHI'S PROGRAMME TO CREATE

PRESS REPORTS FROM NORTH AMERICA

United States • *United Press International*

Des Moines, Iowa   16 August 1986   (English)

UPI Photo

Flying high

When it comes to ending terrorism and promoting world peace, followers of transcendental meditation say they are ready to hop to it. Tim Ko San (left) and David Pasco joined four other Iowans in Des Moines to demonstrate the "yogic flying" technique practiced by advanced meditators.

WORLD PEACE • GLOBAL INAUGURATION

PRESS REPORTS FROM NORTH AMERICA

United States • *Fairfield Ledger*
Fairfield, Iowa   16 August 1986   (English)

Meditators put on 'yogic flying' show

YOGIC 'FLYING' — Christopher Streicher is shown in stride during the demonstration of the dash competition as part of MIU's demonstration of 'yogic flying' Friday afternoon. Six other meditators participated in the four-event demonstration in the men's dome on the campus as members of the community and school witnessed the event. — LEDGER PHOTO by John Gaines

By MARNI MELLEN

A sampling of city officials and Fairfield business people went to Patanjali Golden Dome at Maharishi International University Friday to watch seven men sitting in the lotus position on an expanse of six-inch foam rubber and, at the signal of tinkling bells, pop upward as much as 24 inches into the air.

Local transcendental meditators said the demonstration of the first stage of yogic flying — more commonly recognized as "hopping" — was only a physical manifestation of the mental coherence the meditators had achieved. More significant, they said, is that with the brain functioning on this level of deep understanding, stresses which create disharmony in the world will be eliminated and world peace created.

For the Fairfield audience, the lofty goal of peace translated into a 24-inch high jump in the dome — just three quarters of an inch short of the record jump at a North American yogic flying competition in Washington, D.C., last month.

Quietly supporting the men in their demonstration were about 1,000 other members of the Sidha community of mediators sitting on the sideline. All of them participate in the same kind of program in the dome twice daily and joined in the five minutes of meditation which proceeded the broad jumps, high jumps and hurdles.

Performers were Richard Anonsen, Manitoba, Canada; Ken Allen, Lincoln, Neb., who was a silver medal winner in Washington, D.C.; Arthur Pons, Philippines;

Jeff DeRuvo, New York City; Christoph Streicher, Germany; and James Davis and Michael Necessary, both of Fairfield.

Streicher described his experience as an "upsurge of energy through the muscles." Although hopping appeared to be a purely physical feat, Streicher said the movement was involuntary and effortless.

Non-meditators generally defined the morning event as "interesting." City council member Ruth Ewart said, "It was dramatic and I was glad to be here."

Robert Silverman, president of J & B Plastics Inc., compared it to Einstein's theory of relativity: "I've read it, but I still don't know what it means."

Masters of ceremony were Mario Orsatti, co-chairperson of the MIU Development Council, and Dr. Geoffrey Wells, dean of the College of Creative Intelligence.

Calling the day "auspicious," Orsatti said that 10,000 TM practitioners were carrying on similar demonstrations Friday throughout the world.

A total of 108 countries and more than 70 cities in the United States with TM centers were a part of the international project to try to publically explain the mechanics of how meditation is expected to put the brain into a fundamental stage of "least excitation." At that stage, TM officials say, the mind can identify with the "unified field" of all nature and do things it couldn't do otherwise.

Hopping is just one way in which mental coherence can be harnessed, Wells said.

Buttressed by EEG pictures of brain waves, Wells said brain activity while hopping is unique, unlike brain waves in ordinary hopping or any other kind of physical activity.

To demonstrate the point, a meditator was wired to an EEG machine in the dome where he sat lotus-style throughout the half-hour the seven men were hopping. Any skeptic who could read an EEG machine could observe and question.

One big question of the day was whether the presence of an audience had disturbed the seven demonstrators. The men said no — they found support in an audience.

United States • *Ottumwa Courier*

Ottumwa, Iowa   16 August 1986   (English)

Fly-in gets MIU message off the ground

By DAN NIERLING
Courier photographer

FAIRFIELD — Make no mistake about it, the place was hopping.

For about 75 residents of Fairfield and members of the press, the "yogic flying" demonstration Friday at Maharishi International University provided the first opportunity to witness the much-talked about levitating that goes on in the golden domes.

The event was part of a simultaneous demonstration in more than 1,000 cities and 108 countries around the world.

MIU students, like those in the program around the world, are taught to fly as part of their study of transcendental meditation-Sidhi. TM, as it is commonly referred to, is a method of meditation used to eliminate stress.

Modeled after the "First North American Yogic Flying Competition" in Washington, D.C., July 9, MIU's "fly-in" featured individuals demonstrating the flying technique in four competitive categories: Hurdles, long jump, high jump and 50 meter dash.

No scores were kept Friday, but the demonstrators were definitely world-class caliber.

The goal of the demonstration, however, was not to show-off the athletic, or aerial, abilities of the demonstrators, according to Mario Orsatti, co-chairman of the MIU Development Council.

"We want to highlight the effect of flying on world peace," Orasatti said.

Orsatti and his counterparts contend that the hopping is a result of using the brain's physiology to coordinate the mind and the body into a maximum coherence.

At the moment of this unification, the body hops, defying the law of gravity as we know it. The theory is that if this maximum coherence of the individual's ability is possible to create such phenomena, then a group consciousness can create much greater achievements.

Orsatti cited a variety of achievements, of the Maharishi Technology of the Unified Field Conference in which 7,000 people gathered in Fairfield in December 1984 in an attempt to help lessen the world's problems. Included in these achievements were a reduction of drunk driving arrests in Des Moines and a sharp rise in the stock market, he said.

Friday's simultaneous meditation was held because, according to the Maharishi, "it is vital to immediately create an indomitable influence of coherence in world consciousness."

WORLD PEACE • GLOBAL INAUGURATION

PRESS REPORTS FROM NORTH AMERICA

United States • *Morning-Star Telegram*

Fort Worth, Texas   16 August 1986   (English)

You gotta hop to it if you want peace

By JIM JONES
Star-Telegram Writer

DALLAS — Followers of Maharishi Mahesh Yogi hopped for world peace Friday....

Texas Christian University student John Hopkins, 21, took part in the "yogic flying" exercise as cameras flashed in the Plano Room of the Marriott Park Central Motel in Dallas.

The hopping event began in silence as Hopkins and the other yogic flier, David Sharp of Austin, sat motionless in a period of meditation.

A leader of the Transcendental Meditation movement ... asked a woman to take her baby out of the room so the silence could be complete.

About 50 practicing meditators among the spectators closed their eyes and concentrated on secret mantras, which are specially assigned words. They say the mantras

> "At the point of liftoff you get the maximum coherence of brain waves."
> — Tom Proudfoot

allow them to meditate and tie into a "unified field" of energy that they believe has great power.

The same power was supposed to bubble up in the yogic fliers and allow them to defy gravity and bounce down a lane of foam mattresses set up on the floor.

At first nothing happened.

Then Sharp, sitting in the cross-legged yoga position, popped into the air without using his hands and arms. He hopped forward along the foam mattress track all the way to the end. Somehow, he wore a smile during the entire series of hops.

Hopkins was close behind.

His carrot-colored hair bounced neatly as he flopped half way down the track. Then he stopped. He sat motionless as if waiting for more power. He looked like a giant frog waiting for an unsuspecting fly.

During a "yogic flying" exercise John Hopkins begins to hop.

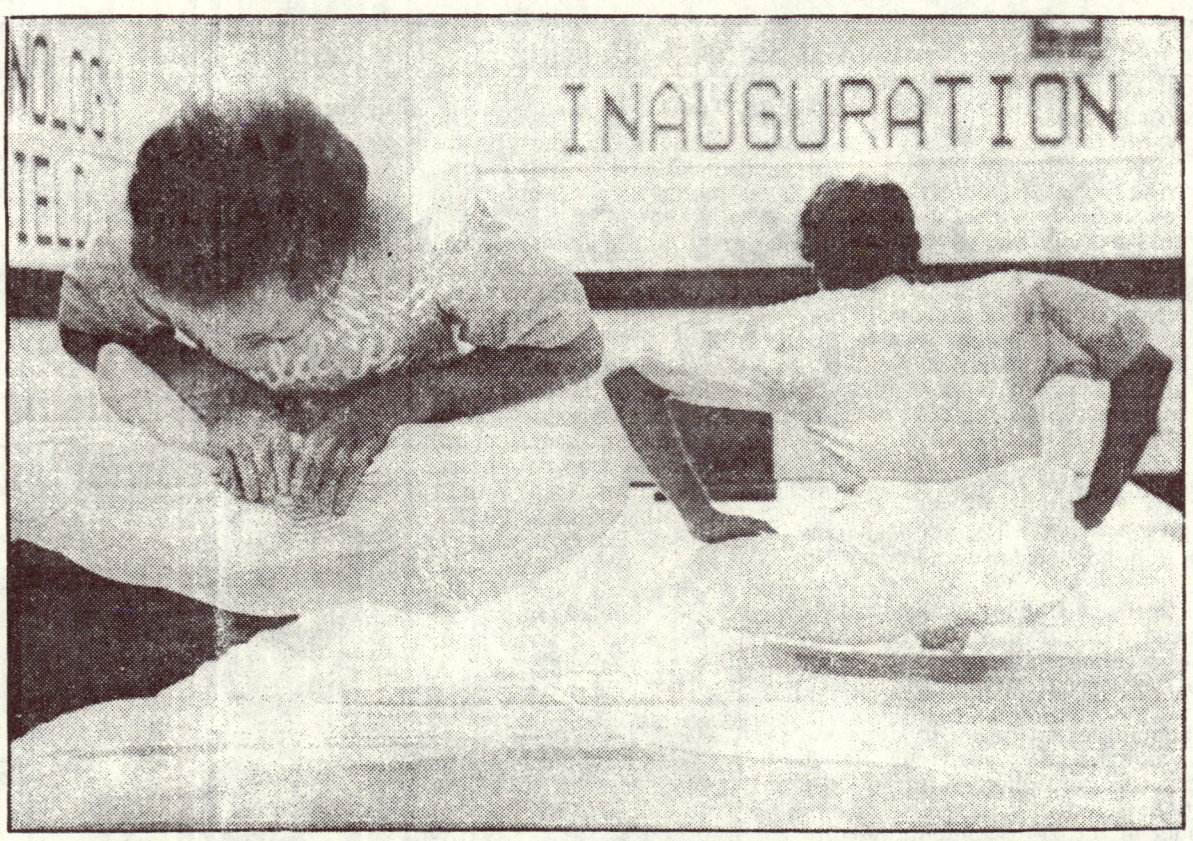

Star-Telegram/JOYCE MARSHALL

John Hopkins and David Sharp, back to camera, move faster down the mattresses.

Believers hopping for peace

Then Hopkins took off again with even more spirit. He seemed to be laughing at one point.

"It was just the joy bubbling up inside of me," Hopkins, a math major at TCU, said later....

Sharp, who holds two college degrees but currently is driving a bus for the Austin school district, said that when he first tried yogic flying he had a hard time lifting off.

"I could feel the energy, but I would just rock a lot and not get off the ground," he said.

Tom Proudfoot, the Transcendental Meditation leader, explained the theory that if enough of this kind of hopping can be experienced the world will eventually be at peace.

"Our goal is to have 7,000 people on every continent practicing this," said Proudfoot. "We hope America can be first."

Only about 50 hoppers are now operating in the Fort Worth-Dallas area.

Using Transcendental Meditation as a way of promoting peace is not new. The maharishi, in the early 1980s, said if enough people started meditating it could bring about peace.

Practitioners believe the brain waves of the meditators would affect the human consciousness of individuals around the world and reduce hostility and warlike feelings.

The hopping is a new wrinkle on the world peace plan.

Proudfoot said that those who practice yogic flying have very orderly or coherent brain waves. To prove his point, he showed pictures of brain scans that he said were made of persons engaging in yogic flying.

The squiggly lines on the brain wave photos were not explained, but presumably they showed peaceful brain waves.

"At the point of liftoff," said Proudfoot, "you get the maximum coherence of brain waves."

If enough people begin hopping, the coherent brain waves will begin to spread around and have an effect, he said.

Proudfoot said it would be impossible for the yogic fliers to hop with such ease if they were doing it with their own physical strength.

Before the event began, he told what was about to happen. The two yogic fliers, he said, would at first begin meditating.

"Then they will feel a tremendous upsurge of energy, a bubbling of bliss, and with no conscious effort will begin to jump up in the air and forward."

Proudfoot said skilled gymnasts who have tried the hopping technique who were not mediatators were quickly exhausted.

True yogic fliers, he said, move effortlessly and are not exhausted after a hop, but feel more energy than before.

"The body, by itself, jumps down the foam carpet," he said.

The hopping is just a glimpse of the power available, said Proudfoot.

"The first stage of yogic flying is hopping," he said. "The second stage is hovering, lifting off and staying in one position, and the third stage is free flying." The second and third stages have not been accomplished yet.

Proudfoot says he expects skepticism, but he said scientific proof is available to show that the techniques do produce coherent brain waves.

He showed a videotape of the First Olympics of the Age of Enlightenment held in Washington, D.C., last month in which the most proficient yogic fliers, both men and women, took part in hopping competitions.

The long jump winner hopped 70 inches and the high jump winner hopped 24.75 inches, Proudfoot said.

"The hops will be longer and higher as stress settles in the world," he said.

After their hopping exhibition, Hopkins and Sharp were each given a single red rose, and they quickly left the room.

A reporter went looking for them to see if they were breathing hard. They had disappeared.

Both Hopkins and Sharp came back to the room a short time later and granted interviews. They didn't seem tired.

PRESS REPORTS FROM NORTH AMERICA

United States • *Birmingham Post-Herald*
Birmingham, Alabama   16 October 1986   (English)

Meditation is their way to unleash potential
They believe yogic flying helps cut down on stress

By Bill Ingram

George Beals, left, meditates to free his body from the forces of gravity as Wayne Foster demonstrates the effects of the meditation

WORLD PEACE • GLOBAL INAUGURATION

PRESS REPORTS FROM NORTH AMERICA

United States • *Philadelphia Inquirer*

Philadelphia, Pennsylvania   18 August 1986   (English)

Directing their minds toward peace, and flight

Maharishi Mahesh Yogi and promoters of his transcendental meditation (TM) say they can, in groups, achieve a level of brainwave coherence strong enough to improve world harmony and the quality of life. Toward that aim, TM centers worldwide, including the Capital of the Age of Enlightenment in Philadelphia, conducted demonstrations Friday of the advanced form of meditation called yogic flying. Expert practitioners of yogic flying are said to have achieved only the first stage — a kind of hopping from a seated yoga position — with hopes of eventually reaching the second and third stages: hovering and directed flight.

Inquirer photograph
by J. Kyle Keener

Placentra, in yogic flying's first stage, hops from a seated position while Milles meditates.

PRESS REPORTS FROM NORTH AMERICA

United States • *Honolulu Advertiser*

Honolulu, Hawaii   16 August 1986   (English)

Yogi's disciples try levitating to help calm a troubled world

Advertiser photo by Bruce Asato

From left, Robert Standard and Lawson Cannon were among the four who hopped for peace

WORLD PEACE • GLOBAL INAUGURATION

PRESS REPORTS FROM NORTH AMERICA

United States • *Journal Inquirer*

Manchester, Connecticut   16 August 1986   (English)

Some small leaps for world peace, from the people who created TM

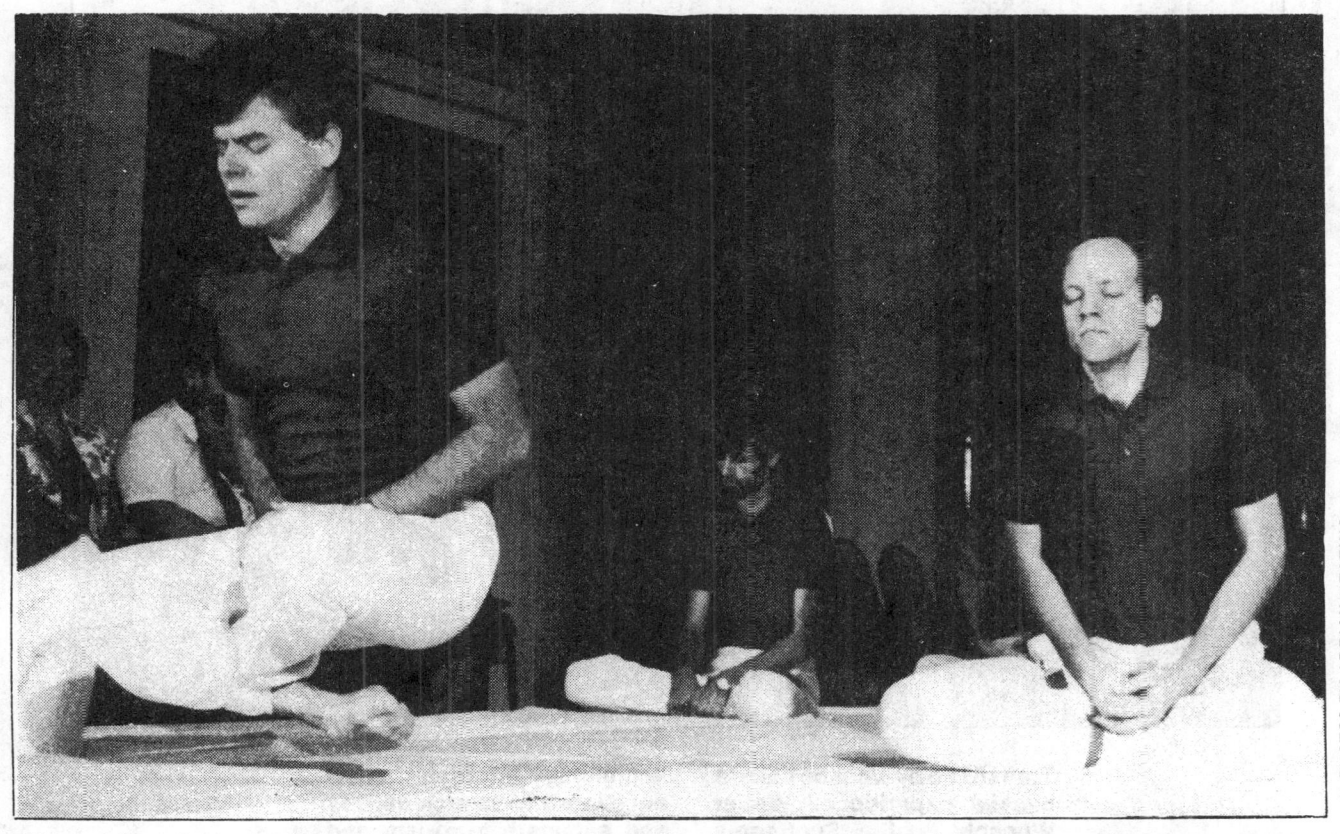

Gerard Frechette of New London hops past David Theriault during the meditation exercise.

MAHARISHI'S PROGRAMME TO CREATE

PRESS REPORTS FROM NORTH AMERICA

United States • *Mesa Tribune*

Mesa, Arizona 16 August 1986 (English)

Staff photos by Gary O'Brien

Transfixed by what he calls 'a blissful experience,' Walter Wunsch of Scottsdale demonstrates TM (transcendental meditation) — Sidhi 'yogic flying' — during a press conference at ASU Friday. Ten followers of the Marharishi Mahesh Yogi demonstrated the technique, a fundamental part of his 'technology to create coherence in world consciousness and eliminate terrorism and war.' According to followers, if 7,000 believers were to practice the technology simultaneously in the same location, 'their coherence would radiate globally and purify the whole world consciousness.'

WORLD PEACE • GLOBAL INAUGURATION

PRESS REPORTS FROM NORTH AMERICA

United States • *The Middletown Press*

Middletown, Connecticut   16 August 1986   (English)

The Flight of the Seven Sidhas

By KENNETH FODOR

CROMWELL — The seven sidhas sat cross-legged on the thick foam mats, apparently deep in meditation. Their only movements were an occasional head bobbing or twitching. The only sounds, the clicking of camera shutters and the low hum of the air conditioner.

Then, at the sound of a bell — almost as if on cue — the seven men dressed in blue polo shirts and white, drawstring pants began hopping, some wildly with arms flailing and heads twisting.

The men, all from Connecticut and followers of the Maharishi Mahesh Yogi, were demonstrating the Transcendental Meditation-Sidhi Yogic Flying Technique as part of the "global inauguration of the Maharishi's program to create world peace."

Richard Dalby, co-director of the New Haven City Capital of the Age of Enlightenment and one of the hopping sidhas, explained that the demonstration here yesterday at the Treadway Cromwell Hotel was one of similar demonstrations being held that day in 108 countries throughout the world.

"We are here not simply to demonstrate yogic flying, but to generate world peace," he said.

The connection between "yogic flying" and world peace, the sidhas explained, goes something like this.

The Maharishi Mahesh Yogi's global effort to promote world peace came to Cromwell yesterday, giving Richard Dalby (above and left, airborne) and David Therault a chance to demonstrate the all-but-forgotten art of yogic flying.
(Staff Photos by Skip Weisenburger)

MAHARISHI'S PROGRAMME TO CREATE

(Staff Photo by Skip Weisenburger)

An overall view of the proceedings Friday at the Treadway Cromwell Hotel during a demonstration of the Transcendental Meditation-Sidhi Yogic Flying Technique conducted by the followers of the Maharishi Mahesh Yogi. The demonstration in Cromwell yesterday was all part of the Yogi's ongoing "program to create world peace."

The Marharishi, founder of the World Government of the Age of Enlightenment, teaches that when a person reaches the level of meditation needed to induce the flying, his or her brain reaches a state of "maximum coherence" — or in other words, its most orderly state. Not only does this state cause the person to spontaneously hop or "fly," it also causes more order or coherence in what the Marharishi calls the "unified field of natural law." Since the unified field of natural law affects all of nature, the coherence spreads to the world consciousness, eliminating stress, harmonizing discordant tendencies and creating peace in the world.

"It's absolutely the only way world peace can be established," said Gail Dalby, the other co-director of the New Haven City Capital of the Age of Enlightenment, the sponsor of the day's demonstration.

The Maharishi teaches that in order for the world peace to be achieved, a group of 7,000 persons — the square root of 1 percent of the world's population — must practice the meditation together. Dalby said the organization is trying to establish two such groups of "pandits" in the United States who would practice the meditation twice a day — part of a larger plan to establish groups of 7,000 persons in all the countries of the world....

WORLD PEACE • GLOBAL INAUGURATION

PRESS REPORTS FROM NORTH AMERICA

United States • *Moline Dispatch*
Moline, Illinois 16 August 1986 (English)

To hop, perchance to fly

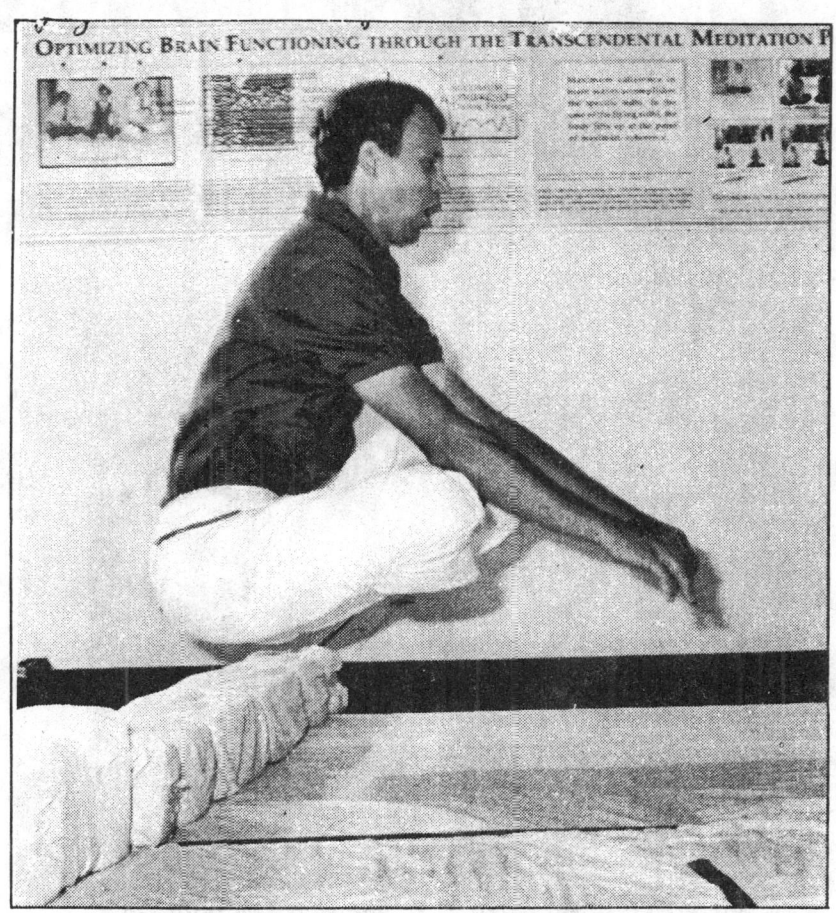

— Dispatch photo by Gary Krambeck

A transcendental meditator demonstrates hopping, the first stage of levitation through meditation. The TM practitioners at the Blackhawk Hotel Friday said deep meditation allowed them to hop down a foam runway over foam hurdles.

MAHARISHI'S PROGRAMME TO CREATE

PRESS REPORTS FROM NORTH AMERICA

United States • *Daily Record*

Morristown, New Jersey 16 August 1986 (English)

Uplifting experience

Daily Record/STAN GODLEWSKI
John Graff of Brooklyn, N.Y., showing TM-Sidhi Yogic Flying Technique, Montclair Capital of the Age of Enlightenment.

WORLD PEACE • GLOBAL INAUGURATION

PRESS REPORTS FROM NORTH AMERICA

United States • *Arizona Republic*
Phoenix, Arizona   16 August 1986   (English)

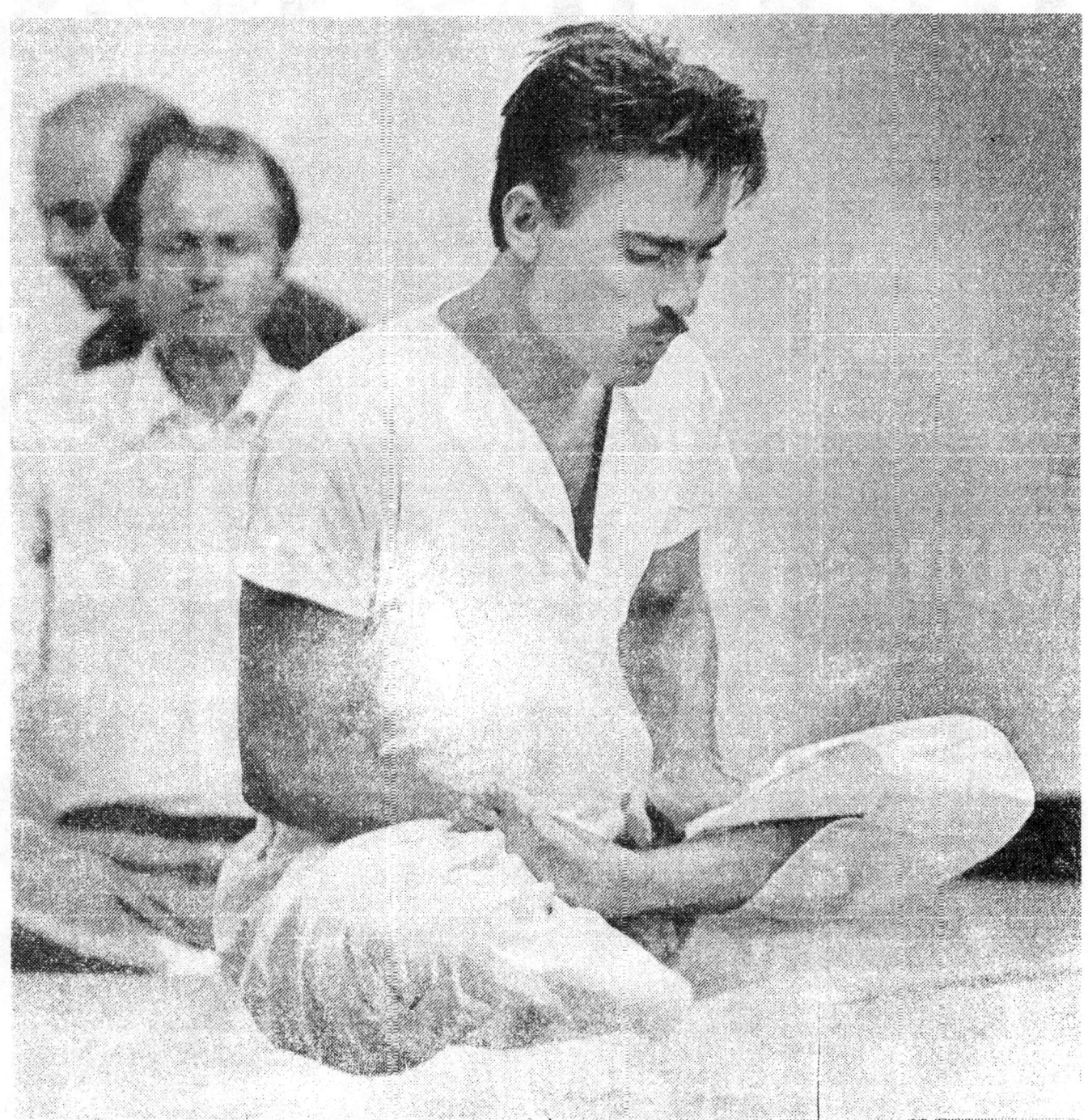

Wayne Kernodle of Mesa "flies" while others meditate between flying events Friday at Arizona State University's Memorial Union.

Peter Schwepker/Republic

Hopping to it
Meditators strive to 'fly' for a higher purpose

By HOLLY D. REMY
The Arizona Republic

The uninitiated can call it mind over matter.

The Valley's followers of the Maharishi Mahesh Yogi program of Transcendental Meditation call it "bliss-induced flying," and Friday they showed for the first time in the Valley how it is done.

Ten men, one of them still in the shirt and tie he had worn to the office, took cross-legged positions on thick, foam mattresses that covered a stage in a conference room at Arizona State University's Memorial Union.

They closed their eyes. For five minutes, punctuated only by the sound of deep breathing, they meditated.

Then the tinkle of a small brass bell announced it was time for transcendental aviation.

It began in a small way, the men bobbing like popcorn about to pop.

Within seconds, the action exploded. The men laughed as they hopped across the stage, still cross-legged and with their eyes closed.

Some of them careened into one another. Some came perilously close to a vase of roses near the lectern. Some reached heights of about a foot. None of them appeared to be straining for altitude; they made it look effortless.

When the brass bell announced the end of flight, the men became quiet, opened their eyes and smiled at the sparse audience.

"If you didn't see it, you wouldn't believe it," said Phyllis Hume of Phoenix, who follows the maharishi's Transcendental Meditation program on a level that does not result in flying.

Even so, it looked a lot like hopping.

It is a lot like hopping, the men explained, but it is hopping with a higher purpose.

Flying, they said, is an involuntary response to exceptional achievement in meditation — the kind of achievement that, if reached by groups of people, can radiate into the environment, lowering the crime rate, halting terrorism and bringing peace to the world.

Flying was first demonstrated openly in July in Washington, D.C. The Valley event was one of 100 smaller exhibitions held around the world Friday.

When it was over, flier Ken Hagan of Chandler took a breather outside the conference room.

"I feel blissful, very settled but very dynamic," said Hagan, who flies to relieve the stress of his job as general manager of a Mesa dental laboratory. "It's a feeling of exhilaration, like I might have run five miles."

"It's kind of like dancing in a cross-legged position," explained Don Sherbondy, a Phoenix architect.

However, Sherbondy added, flying isn't all that new. He learned in 1978, and he is ready to vouch for the calming effect that group flying has on the environment.

"In 1978, the maharishi sent a group of us to San Salvador," he said. "We were there for a little over 30 days, and we noticed a significant effect, a decrease in the amount of violence in the area where we were staying."

Flying was top-secret stuff until this year. Non-fliers were not allowed to see it. Even now, men and women are not permitted to fly together unless they are married to each other.

The maharishi explained on a videotape shown at the demonstration that he has brought flying to the public this year because of terrorism.

"The only thing that could rescue mankind today is the rise of a power greater than that now being displayed by the superpowers," he said.

That power is the power of group meditation, which he has claimed can radiate into society, favorably influencing even those people who do not meditate.

To put the power to use, the maharishi wants to form a group of 7,000 people in India who will meditate and fly together.

Someday, he has said, followers of his meditation techniques will achieve still higher bliss. More blissful than flying will be hovering, and after hovering will come directed flight.

"I think Step 2 is definitely possible, considering the way I'm feeling today," Hagan said.

© 1986—Phoenix Newspapers, Inc. Reproduced by permission. Permission does not imply endorsement by the newspaper.

WORLD PEACE • GLOBAL INAUGURATION

PRESS REPORTS FROM NORTH AMERICA

United States • San Diego Tribune

San Diego, California 16 August 1986 (English)

'Yogic flying' launches Maharishi peace plan

By Bill Callahan
Tribune Staff Writer

In what may become the ultimate test of mind over matter, followers of the Maharishi Mahesh Yogi plan to use their powers of transcendental meditation to radiate a harmonious influence they believe will bring peace to a world threatened with destruction.

To that end a group of local TM practitioners demonstrated the "yogic flying" technique yesterday at the Pacific Beach center of the Maharishi City Capital of the Age of Enlightenment in San Diego.

The demonstration here was part of a worldwide inauguration of the Maharishi's new peace program coordinated yesterday by nearly 50,000 of his followers in 108 countries.

"With the rising wave of terrorism and the dangerous rivalry of the superpowers, it is vital to immediately create an indomitable influence in world consciousness," said the Maharishi in a statement released at each of the demonstrations.

The TM movement, which has kept a relatively low profile in recent years, will now devote much of its energy to promoting peace, said Sally Mattoon, a local official.

"We've been sort of in the closet before because we didn't think the world would be able to understand what we are trying to do (in TM)," she said. "But it's getting late. We couldn't wait any longer."

The Maharishi, who in the 1960s taught TM to the Beatles, believes use of the powers of meditation funneled through brain waves into a positive consciousness will be powerful enough to spread around the world.

This consciousness will improve the quality of life and reduce stress and strife enough that the elusive goal of world peace can be reached, say leaders of the movement.

To draw attention to the movement the Maharishi has been opening to the press demonstrations of the controversial "yogic flying," in which believers supposedly use the powers of their mind to propel their bodies.

Four young men participated here, meditating for five minutes before launching themselves cross-legged across a floor covered with mattresses in tests of how far, high and fast they could "fly."

Each participant, in turn, would gather himself in deep concentration, often twitching and rocking or smiling as if enjoying some private joke, and then lurch forward in leapfrog style with legs locked inward.

To some observers it was difficult to tell whether the "flying" actually was powered by the men's minds or by pairs of powerful, skilled limbs.

However, each of the men appeared sincere and none of them were sweating, despite spurts of strenuous efforts

"That's one of the criteria we use to determine if the proper level of consciousness is achieved," said Priscilla Bazan, who has been a "flying" judge. "The effortlessness is one way of telling if someone is muscling their way through or is using their mind."

Mattoon, who said she has "flown" but did not participate yesterday, said she is filled "with a sense of energy before takeoff," when she does "fly."

"It's not simply a case of going from point X to point Y. The impulse comes and I spontaneously lift off. There's a sense of being super fluid."

MAHARISHI'S PROGRAMME TO CREATE

PRESS REPORTS FROM NORTH AMERICA

United States • *The Sacramento Bee*

Sacramento, California   16 August 1986   (English)

Jumping for joy may lead to flying for peace

Bee/Richard Gilmore

As a prelude to Yogic flying, Ramiro Garcia practices hopping, hoping to eventually bring world peace. ...

WORLD PEACE • GLOBAL INAUGURATION

PRESS REPORTS FROM NORTH AMERICA

United States • *San Francisco Chronicle*
San Francisco, California   16 August 1986   (English)

BY FREDERIC LARSON/THE CHRONICLE

Taking off in Berkely

This is called flying. Followers of the Maharishi Mahesh Yogi demonstrated it yesterday in Berkely. Twelve men, in a rare public display of mind over gravity, bounced along a long row of mattresses....

MAHARISHI'S PROGRAMME TO CREATE

PRESS REPORTS FROM NORTH AMERICA

United States • *Seattle Times*

Seattle, Washington   16 August 1986   (English)

Alan Berner / Seattle Times

Fledgling flight: Transcendental meditators Bruce MacCracken, left, Dave Rider and Robert Arnold demonstrate what they call the first stage to yogic flying — hopping — at the Westin Hotel. Next summer TM'ers hope to present the second stage, hovering. They believe yogic flying produces a super radiance effect, relieving stress and creating peace. The goal is to have 7,000 trained yogic fliers in a quest for world peace.

WORLD PEACE • GLOBAL INAUGURATION

PRESS REPORTS FROM NORTH AMERICA

United States • *The Indianapolis Star*
Indianapolis, Indiana   17 August 1986   (English)

Boing! Crocco just up and flew

Dan Carpenter

David Crocco was the first to fly.

It happened quite suddenly. David was sitting cross-legged on a sheeted mattress, eyes closed, head bobbing, lips quivering with meditative rapture. His friends, Jeff Shaffer and Steve Underwood, squatted next to him, sharing the state. A dozen other men and women, four from the news media, watched the three in silence

Watched and waited. Waited for . . .

BOING! BOING! There he came, right toward the audience, his folded, athletic body springing across six feet of the mattress in two leaps, as if he were a legless frog in a giant corn popper.

BOING! There went Shaffer. BOING! There went Underwood. Slowly at first, just a bounce here and a bounce there, then building to a riot of spasmodic, directionless jumps, like a pot of water coming to full boil.

The only sounds were nasal breathing and occasional giggles — not from the cynical press, but from the fliers and their fellow followers of His Holiness Maharishi Mahesh Yogi. One giggles, it was later explained, because flying under one's own power fills one with happiness.

BOING! BOING! BOING!

So it went Friday night at the Age of Enlightenment house, a majestic tile-roofed mansion at 3434 Washington Boulevard, where the Maharishi's disciples teach and learn his Theory of the Unified Field.

According to Vicki Ann Crocco, David's wife, the Maharishi had directed that shows such as this one be given for the press all over the world on Friday.

The flying was put forth as evidence of something much bigger, "Maharishi's Technology to Create Coherence in World Consciousness and Eliminate Terrorism and War."

Now, the skeptical observer might regard this demonstration of Yogic Flying Technique as mere hopping around a mattress. That observer is trapped in the classical physics of Newton, Einstein and the like. In the Maharishi's physics, hopping is the first of three stages of unaided human flight.

Presumably, the next two stages — hovering and full flight — would be much more impressive than the first. Unfortunately, no one has attained these levels of coherence between their nervous systems and the forces of nature.

When, then?

"We don't know. We hope very soon," Mrs. Crocco replied. "Maharishi has people practicing all over the world."

But that's not the point, she added. The point is not to make people fly, but to avert nuclear war. The only way to do that is

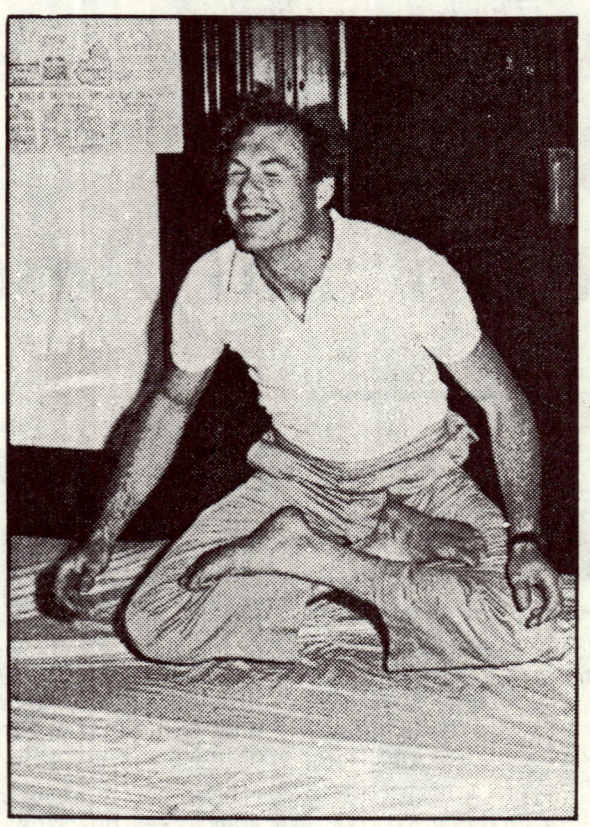

STAR STAFF PHOTOS

David Crocco (above) giggles from the feeling of taking flight under one's own power.

through elevated consciousness, whose power is shown in elevated bodies.

"People flying around isn't going to bring world peace. We fly around in airplanes now. What will bring world peace is people in harmony, in synchrony."

It's a lot for a bunch of coffee-swilling, buck-chasing reporters to absorb; but previous Yogic Flying hop-ins have enjoyed friendly, if bemused, treatment in the media.

"We weren't just born yesterday," Vicki Ann Crocco said. "We know this looks odd. But it works."

If nothing else, Friday's performance was an excellent opportunity to ask the media's favorite question:

How do you feel?

"Bliss," David Crocco said, looking truthful.

"Elation," Steve Underwood said. "Nature rises up in you and gives you elation. It lifts you in the air."

The media, we were promised, will be notified of future public flights.

WORLD PEACE • GLOBAL INAUGURATION

Jeff Shaffer (left) bounces off a mattress during demonstration of His Holiness Maharishi Mahesh Yogi Theory of the Unified Field, while Steve Underwood shows concentration.

MAHARISHI'S PROGRAMME TO CREATE

PRESS REPORTS FROM NORTH AMERICA

United States • *Minneapolis Star and Tribune*

Minneapolis, Minnesota   17 August 1986   (English)

'Yogic flying' proves to be a short hop

Staff Photo by Duane Braley

Sam Farling demonstrated the hopping component of "yogic flying," a technique that some say could help promote world peace.

By Cheryl Johnson
Staff Writer

As an Olympic event, "yogic flying" is barely off the ground.

First you have to hop, and meditate, then hover and meditate, then much later begin cutting into airline profits.

During a demonstration Friday, three disciples of the Maharishi Mahesh Yogi demonstrated the hopping — and only the hopping — component of this transcendental technique, which they believe could lead to world peace.

Bob Boyer, a psychologist who works at Maharishi International University in Fairfield, Iowa, moderated yesterday's demonstration at the Minneapolis

WORLD PEACE • GLOBAL INAUGURATION

St. Paul Transcendental Meditation Program, 511 11th Av. S.

Boyer said he didn't know when this fledgling event would be part of the Olympics, but that it ought to be, since some form of yogic flying has been possible since before the Olympics started 2,700 years ago. The first national yogic flying competition was held in Washington, D.C., this summer.

"This is a new technology that does seem to have the power to generate a much more harmonious, orderly world that is the basis for world peace," said Boyer.

But really. Can Boyer see Ronald Reagan, Ayatollah Khomeini and Moammar Khadafy going so deeply into trances that they are hopping around like frogs in the lotus position?

"I can see them doing it," said Boyer. "Sure, yeah. They'd personally enjoy it."

Boyer said, however, that the participation of global leaders isn't essential to the success of yogic flying for world peace. Not even the Maharishi, who Boyer credits with reviving the technique, has been seen practicing it.

"Maharishi estimates that (if) about 7,000 people can get together in a permanent facility and practice (this) twice daily, that would be a powerful enough influence of coherency and evolutionary positive trend to establish world peace."

Boyer, who said he is accustomed to the words of skeptics, said there have been more than 360 studies on the positive effects of transcendental meditation (TM) on concerns such as crime, auto accidents and economic indicators.

"There are very clear logical connections that have a strong scientific, empirical basis that does seem to suggest that the release of stress and tension produced in the individual and spreading to the environment is powerful enough to generate world peace," he said.

Yogic flying is part of a relatively new area of TM — which has been well known in America since the 1950s — known as TMS, for transcendental meditation sidhi. "One aspect of the TMS is yogic flying," said Boyer, "and the connection between yogic flying and world peace is the ability during yogic flying to produce the maximum amount of brain coherence."

Barry Ruzek, a Sperry Corp. software designer, Sam Farling, an inventor and investor, and Lee Fergusson, a college lecturer in fine art, all claimed their yogic hopping exercises were the most effortless of endeavors.

Dressed in blue-and-white T-shirts and white loose-fitting pants, the three men looked as though they were showing off powerful gluteus maximus muscles as they participated in the hop, long jump and high jump. Every now and then they would laugh and smile, indicating the "bubbling bliss" that accompanies TM.

Before and during their demonstration atop eight foam mattresses covered with fitted sheets, the men meditated. When they needed a break, they would meditate some more and the audience of about 30 TM followers would join in, sending more energy to them.

Then the games would begin anew.

"Hopping like a frog and soon, soon, hopefully hovering and then flying through the air and really discounting air rates," Boyer told the audience.

United States • *United Press International*

Davenport, Iowa   15 August 1986   (English)

Enjoy life and fight terrorism

When it comes to ending terrorism and promoting world peace, practitioners of Transcendental Meditation say they are ready to hop to it.

To that end, followers of the teachings of Maharishi Mahesh Yogi are embarking on a global effort to counter terrorism and other negative forces in the world through positive brain waves.

"What we need to let the individual know is, yes, there is something he can do" to end world terrorism, said Bill Van Zandt of Muscatine, who is studying for a doctor's degree in neuroscience at Maharishi International University in Fairfield.

What each individual can do is "enjoy life to the fullest," generate positive thoughts and practice stress management techniques, which will help contribute to a unified field of consciousness, Van Zandt said. World peace will become a by-product of people "creating joy individually in their own lives."

PRESS REPORTS FROM NORTH AMERICA

United States • *Daily Californian*

Berkeley, California   18 August 1986   (English)

Hopping to fly
Berkeley meditators rise to new heights

William Martinez takes off as 12 transcendental meditators try to fly

Staff photo by David Yee

By TOM SCHMITZ
STAFF WRITER

His face a mask of intense concentration, Drew Zavatsky sighed. He shuddered. He shook. And then, rising from his lotus position, Drew Zavatsky flew.

His flight lasted one second, and carried him two feet. It was followed by another, and another, transporting Zavatsky down a 50-foot padded runway as flashbulbs popped and TV cameras panned. After his 10th takeoff, Drew Zavatsky made a final landing, his features breaking into a satisfied grin.

To the untutored observer, Zavatsky's flying looked suspiciously like a

SEE PAGE 8

Flying

FROM FRONT PAGE

series of short, froglike hops. But Zavatsky and 11 other "sidhas" of the Berkeley Transcendental Meditation program say their bouncing is the first stage of "yogic flying," a form of levitation powered by a mental union with nature's most basic forces.

"We're not good enough to really stay in the air yet," said Michael Thune, director of the Berkeley center. "But eventually, our coherence will be so great that the individual will be able to move around in the air as he chooses."

Successful or not, the 12 men who demonstrated the technique for members of the press and public Friday took their efforts very seriously. At Thune's summons, the fliers filed into the hall like a squad of Olympic gymnasts, dressed identically in blue t-shirts and loose-fitting white trousers.

The crowd observed a five-minute silence as the fliers took up positions at the end of the runway and began their meditations. Some sat perfectly still, while others lolled their heads and shrugged their shoulders in preparation for takeoff.

"As the flier approaches total brain coherence," Thune explained, "he feels a tremendous surge of energy and an explosion of awareness. Then they involuntarily lift and begin to move down the foam."

A bell chimed, clearing the group for flight. A sidha in the front of the squadron began to tremble, his head shaking violently as he popped into the air. He was followed immediately by another flier farther back in the pack, and suddenly the air was filled with bouncing yogis.

A German shepherd in the audience whined and howled in alarm. The fliers, however, were ecstatic. Many smiled from ear to ear as they leapfrogged along, and one seemed to gasp with joy at each liftoff.

"I feel an expanded, unbounded awareness when I fly," said Bruce Smith, a former chemical research assistant. "The impulse to fly comes from deep within; there is no conscious effort. When I first did it, I realized not only could I do this, I could do anything."

The flying demonstrations are part of a program of "Mechanics for World Peace," inaugurated last month by the sidhas' guru, Maharishi Mahesh Yogi. The Maharishi and his followers say they have become concerned about the rising level of terrorism and conflict in the world, violence they attribute to a lack of "coherence in world consciousness."

According to the Maharishi's teachings, yogic flying is accomplished through the experience of a "unified field" of natural laws, resulting in "total brain coherence." This individual coherence in turn acts to calm disturbances in the world consciousness by "radiating a harmonizing influence out to the rest of society."

By holding mass meditation and flying sessions to reduce psychic stress, the Maharishi and his followers claim they can affect everything from the number of hospital admissions and war casualties to stock prices on Wall Street and smog levels in Los Angeles.

"We who know the antidote must rise and lessen this stress in world consciousness," the Maharishi said in a videotaped message....

The sidhas claim they have practiced the technique in secret for years, inspired by the writings of ancient sages who could hover at will.

"We've always kept this thing private," Smith said. "We haven't wanted to make it a circus situation."

But according to Dr. Bevan Morris, president of Maharishi International University, the level of violence in the world has risen to the point where the sidhas must come forward "to inspire strong people to come forward and support the creation of world peace."

At times however, the demonstration more closely resembled a sporting event than a spiritual one. After the initial flying exhibition, Thune announced that the sidhas would perform "the long jump."

An assistant marked a starting line on the mats with silver tape. One by one, the fliers bounced up to the line, gathered their concentration, and flew for all they were worth.

"2-feet-4!" the assistant called out, measuring the distance from takeoff to landing with a carpenter's rule. "2-feet-6!"

The longest jump of the day was that of Woody Barlettani, 68, a retired electrician from Martinez and winner of the "over 50" flying competition. He flew 5 feet 2 inches.

"I never thought I'd take off from the ground. I thought I'd just stay home and baby my arthritis," said Barlettani, who first started practicing transcendental meditation 12 years ago. "I feel light as a feather. I've had a lot of three-point landings, but at first I landed on my head."

Then came the "high jump." Several of the mats were stacked on top of each other to form an 11-inch platform. Several of the sidhas sat in front of the platform and tried to fly up onto it.

Some managed the feat. Others struck the front of the stack and fell back, or worse, tipped forward, plowing face first into the foam. None seemed to mind.

The dog, however, did. Its whines increased with each yogic jump, prompting its master to drag it from the room.

"I'm surprised she feels so uncomfortable," said Vicki Voss, the dog's owner. "I guess it's all the energy in this room. She's done it before in situations where the energy is really high."

Following the demonstration, the fliers were asked if the day's flying would produce any visible effects. After a brief conference, center member Devorah Belilove stepped forward to announce that the fog cover over Berkeley had broken two hours earlier than normal.

Were the fliers responsible for clearing the air?

"It's possible," Thune said. "It's definitely possible."

Daily Californian Staff Writer Jim Herron contributed to this report.

MAHARISHI'S PROGRAMME TO CREAT

PRESS REPORTS FROM NORTH AMERICA

United States • *Atlanta Journal*
Atlanta, Georgia   18 August 1986   (English)

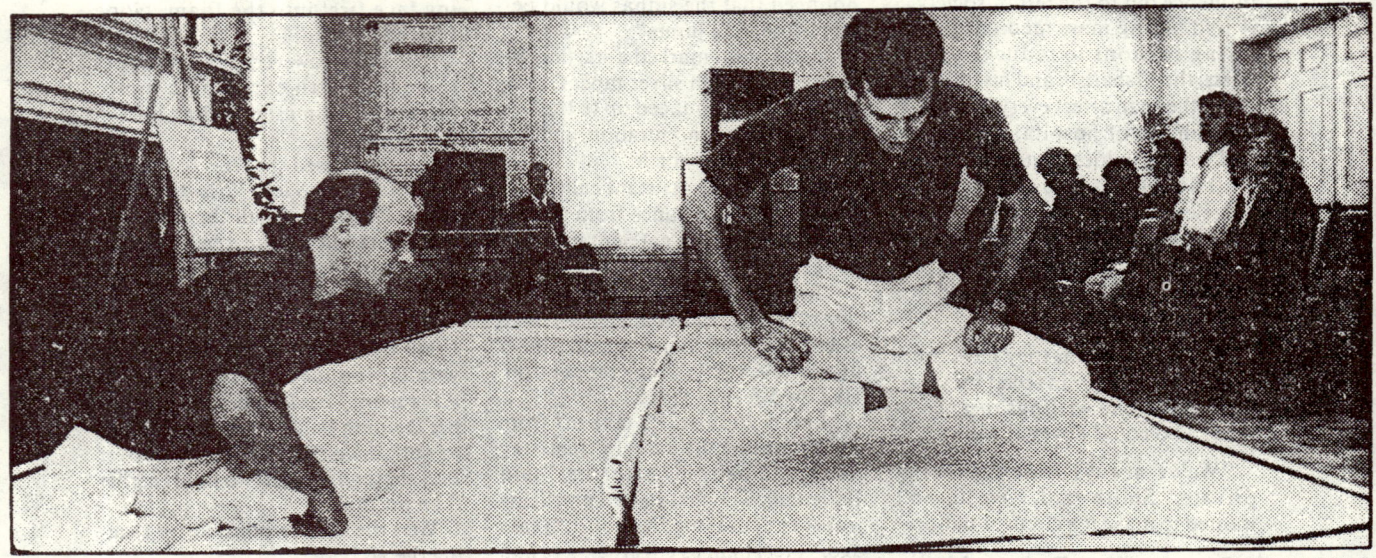

NEIL McGAHEE/Staff

FIRST STEP: Wayne Foster, left, and Dale Stephens demonstrate "yogic flying" to a group at the TM center.

United States • *Palisadian Post*
Pacific Palisades, California   21 August 1986   (English)

See how they fly

MEDITATION AT THE START

WORLD PEACE • GLOBAL INAUGURATION

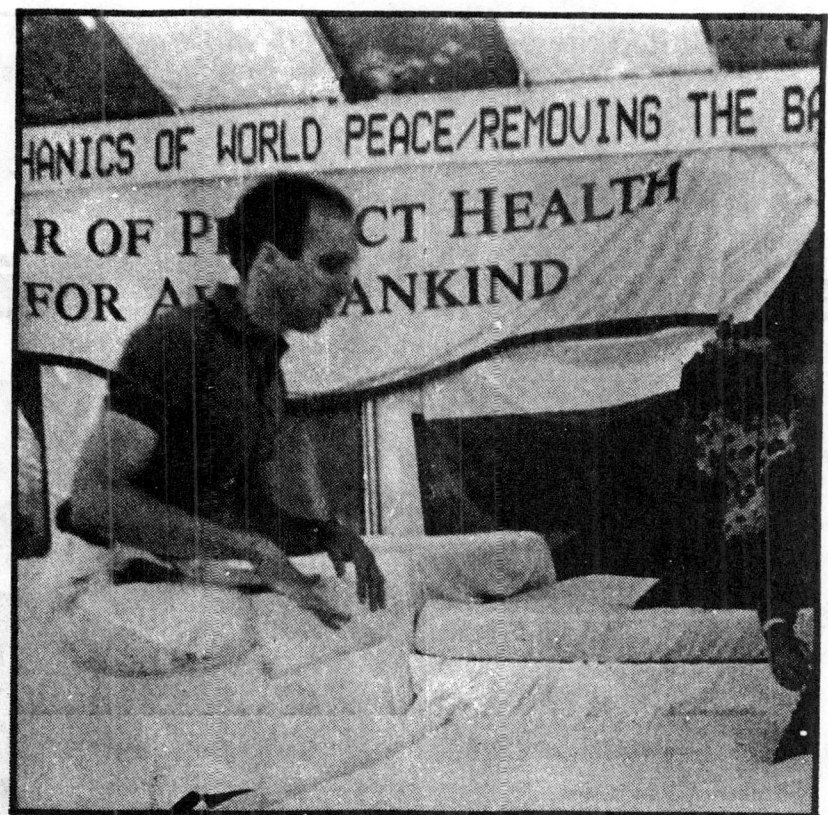

GETTING OFF THE GROUND

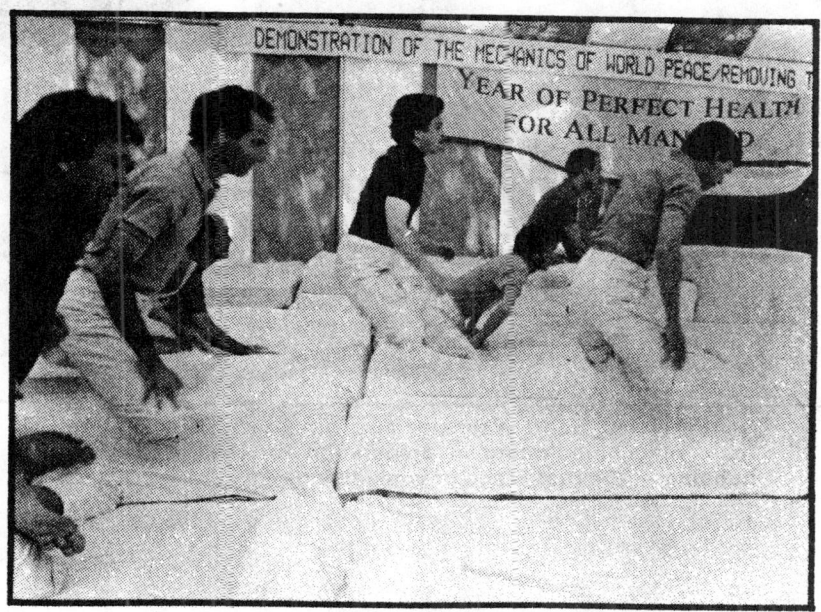

DOING THE HIGH JUMP

PRESS REPORTS FROM NORTH AMERICA

United States • *Lakewood Sun Post*

Lakewood, Ohio   21 August 1986   (English)

They fly the blissful skies of maharishi's meditation

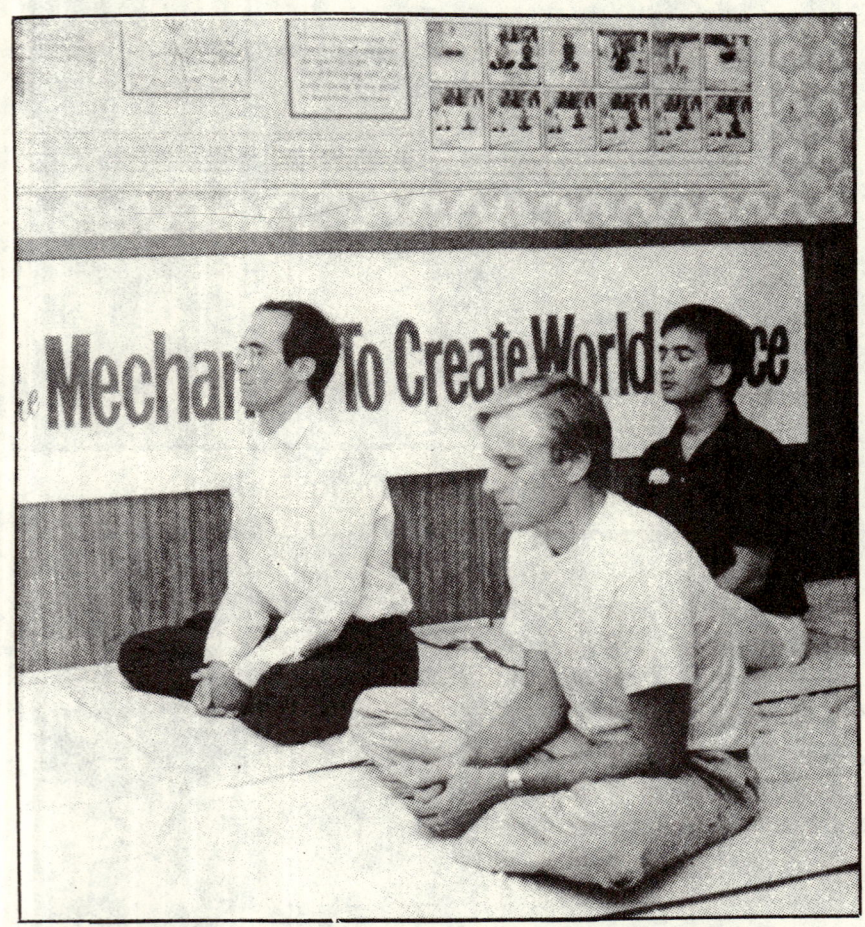

Robert Oates, Scott Walmsley and Tim Casey sit quietly on foam mats, meditating in preparation for their display of hopping — the first Stage of yogic flying.

WORLD PEACE • GLOBAL INAUGURATION

Sun photos by Carol Calabrese

Scott Walmsley, a transcendental meditation teacher in Dayton, is airborne in the first stage of yogic flying. As the banner on the wall proclaims, the technique can lead to world peace — if enough people do it at the same time.

MAHARISHI'S PROGRAMME TO CREATE

PRESS REPORTS FROM NORTH AMERICA

United States • *Southfield Eccentric*

Southfield, Michigan   21 August 1986   (English)

They 'fly' in air for the sake of peace on earth

By Jackie Klein
staff writer

Staff photos by Dan Dean

"They are all up in the air, inviting everyone who has his feet on the ground to join them in bringing in the rising sunshine of the age of enlightenment." — Maharishi Mahesh Yogi

With the rising wave of terrorism and the dangerous rivalry of the superpowers, it is vital to immediately create an indomitable influence of coherence in world consciousness.

With these words by the Maharishi, two experts in the "technology of the unified field" demonstrated yogic flying for world peace Friday....

'The coherence created in world consciousness by group practice of the technology of the unified field will make peace on earth powerful and power on earth peaceful.'
— Maharishi Mahesh Yogi

Members of the audience close their eyes in meditation.

"Scientific research has shown that through this technique, individuals can create coherence in world consciousness," said John Viviano of the meditation staff.

"It is the basis of Maharishi's program to establish and permanently maintain world peace."

PRACTICING TM-SIDHI, advanced, accelerated Transcendental Meditation, the bodies of yogic flyers Steve Poke and Charlie Parker, at the moment of maximum coherence in brain activity, were said to lift up and begin to hop.

WORLD PEACE • GLOBAL INAUGURATION

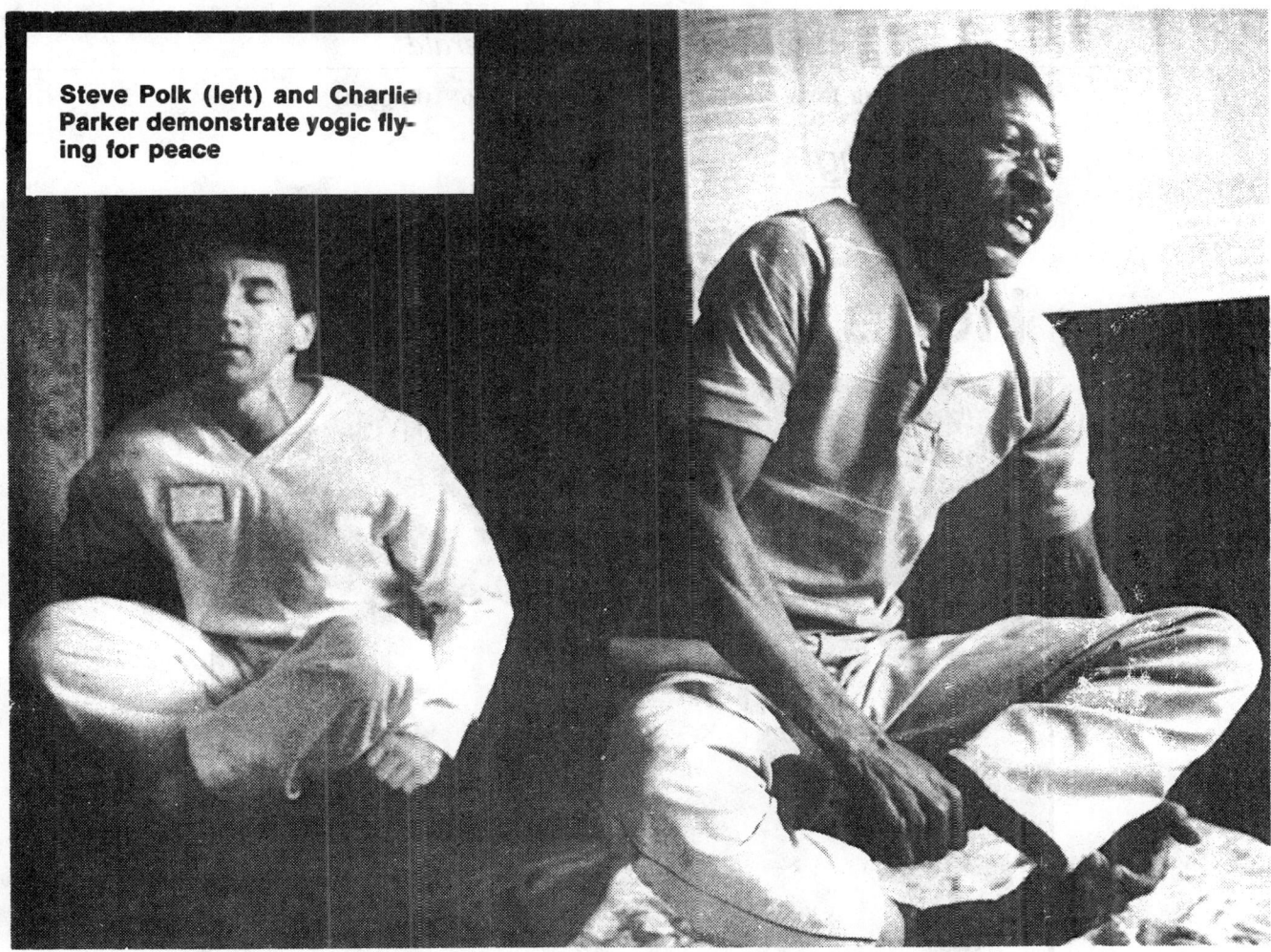

Steve Polk (left) and Charlie Parker demonstrate yogic flying for peace

The two men, sitting in the lotus position on a mat, raised their bodies off the mat. It was unclear whether the spirit moved them or they moved themselves.

The coherence between consciousness and matter in the body, which is experienced in the first stage of yogic flying, originates at the level of the unified field of all laws of nature, Viviano said.

"The coherence created in world consciousness by group practice of the technology of the unified field will make peace on earth powerful and power on earth peaceful," the Maharishi has said.

THE EVENT in Lathrup Village was part of a global inauguration of the program to create world peace and was held simultaneously in 108 countries.

Sociological studies conducted throughout the world during the past 12 years have shown that one percent or more of the population practicing the transcendental meditation technique improves the quality of life throughout society, Viviano said.

Scientists have named this phenomenon the Maharishi effect in honor of Maharishi Mahesh Yogi, who predicted it in 1960, he said.

Viviano didn't specify which sociological studies or how scientists made their determinations.

"Ten years ago it was found that the Maharishi effect can be produced by as little as the square root of one pecent of the population practicing the TM-Sidhi program together in one place," Viviano said.

ACCORDING TO the Maharishi, scientific research has shown that 7,000 experts practicing the technolngy in one place generate a sufficiently strong influence of coherence to radiate globally and purify the whole world's consciousness.

Simultaneously, groups equivalent to the square root of one percent of the population practicing the Maharishi technology in every country will bring peace to the nation by creating coherence in the national consciousness, he said.

PRESS REPORTS FROM NORTH AMERICA

United States • *News Herald*

Santa Rosa, California   26 August 1986   (English)

Yogic Flying

Can Cross-Legged Hops Save the World?

Blaine Watson of Toronto, Canada demonstrates yogic "flying."

BY SIMONE WILSON

Can levitating meditators put a crimp in terrorism and make the world more peaceful? That was the vaunted claim of TM followers in Santa Rosa recently who demonstrated a meditation technique they believe will lead to world peace. The Transcendental Meditation disciples, followers of Maharishi Mahesh Yogi, met at the Sheraton Round Barn Inn August 15 to demonstrate the technique of yogic flying, a practice they say will lead eventually to greater harmony and peace in the world.

Santa Rosa TM teacher Chris Johnson said he and about 30 other TM students in the area have been perfecting their yogic flying abilities in the past few years. Now that terrorism is increasing throughout the world, says Johnson, Maharishi Mahesh Yogi has decided to demonstrate the technique publicly.

In July, 22 yogic jumpers and their supporters gathered for the first "Yogic Flying" competition in Washington, D.C., competing in the yogic hurdles, high jump and long jump. At least one meditator rose some two feet off the floor and another bounded cross-legged over foam hurdles. Another traveled some 70 feet in a cross-legged hop. In Santa Rosa, John Wooster, a TM teacher from a retreat at Cobb Mountain in Lake County, demonstrated the same technique.

Wooster sat amid a dozen other TM meditators, who helped clear the atmosphere and create a calm climate in the room. No orange robes in this bunch: everyone was dressed in suits and ties or in clean-cut yuppie garb.

After a few minutes Wooster began to smile and then executed a series of hops and flops, propelling himself around the foam mattresses spread out on the floor. After a dozen hops, all performed cross-legged, he announced he was finished and lay down to rest.

Wooster explained that the hopping is the first of three phases of yogic flying. In the second phase, people will hover, and in the highest phase they will be in flight.

"Phases two and three are not commonly achieved yet and are not being shown," said Johnson.

Although the hops looked like a lot of work, Wooster said the leaping is an effortless performance. "An impulse rises that takes the form of flying," said Wooster. "It's not fatiguing; it's exhilarating."

Dee Johnson, another TM follower, said that electroencephalograms (EEG's) of people practicing yogic flying show changes that are very different from those during normal exercise. "The EEG shows they're in a mental state comparable to deep sleep," she said.

Yogic flying, at least as it has been publicly demonstrated, doesn't quite compare with the lift and loft of a 747, or even with the halting efforts of a fledgling pigeon. But TM practitioners have demonstrated the ability to leave the ground quite aggressively while sitting cross-legged on the floor.

There's strength in numbers in this technique, claim TM hoppers. A change in global antagonism is predicted to occur when a sufficient number of people are airborne, according to the Maharishi. The change in the world's hostility quotient, a shift TM people call "the Maharishi Effect," takes place when 7,000 or more people are engaged in TM flying. The 7,000-person threshold is the square root of 1 percent of the earth's population. Apparently that's enough to have a positive effect on the rest of the world's inhabitants. Terrorism and war will abate, the theory goes, and harmony and peace will result.

A trial run took place in late 1983 when about 8,000 TM disciples gathered at the American headquarters in Iowa for two weeks of intense practice. During that time, claimed Chris Johnson, "there was a lessening of international conflicts," as well as an upsurge in world stock markets.

"The effect is for the entire world," said Dee Johnson, who added that a major TM center in India is close to having the critical number of meditating fliers needed.

Skeptics may scoff at unassisted human flight, but if TM fliers are capable of injecting some serenity into a world torn by tension, who's to argue? □

MAHARISHI'S PROGRAMME TO CREATE

PRESS REPORTS FROM NORTH AMERICA

United States • *Martinez News–Gazette*

Martinez, California   August 1986   (English)

Yogic Flyer Aims At World Peace

By JIM CAROOMPAS
News-Gazette Staff Reporter

Woody Barlettani, a lifelong Martinez resident and a retired electrician, has a new calling these days.

He wants to bring peace to the world, and while his method may seem unusual, he is convinced that it will work. If only more people would give it a chance.

Barlettani, 68, is a yogic flyer. Actually, he and fellow flyers hop while in a cross-legged position.

But what appears to be merely hopping is actually something far more significant, he says.

Barlettani got involved with Transcendental Meditation techniques 12 years ago through his son. He is now a follower of the Maharishi Mahesh Yogi ....

Now the Maharishi runs the School of the Age of Enlightenment, based in Iowa, and has followers around the world.

Barlettani said that the key to yogic flying is blending the powers of the conscious and unconscious mind. Through such a blending, he said, can come the goal of "unbound awareness."

During a demonstration for the press last week in Berekely, Barlettani and 11 other students showed off their abilities. One at a time, the flyers would hop down the length of a mat. Barlettani managed a jump of 5 feet, 3 inches, the longest jump of the day.

"If we can get 10,000 people doing this at the same time," he said, "we can have world peace. I'm not doing this for my own ego. I'm doing it because we're all seekers, and I have found something."

Barlettani believes we "live in a world with tunnel-vision. Everyone's so negative. Meditation creates an unbound awareness."

Barlettani has been practicing his beliefs for 12 years, but the Maharishi followers have avoided the press until now.

"The world wasn't ready for this three or four years ago," he said. "But with terrorism and other problems we're going through now, the Maharishi feels it's time people found out about this. The time is right for exposure."

Barlettani did not start out flying. He practiced the Maharishi's form of meditation for two 20-minute sessions daily, and worked his way up, so to speak, from there.

Now, he says, he meditates 45 minutes in the morning, and 45 minutes in the evening. The next step after hopping, according to the Maharishi, is hovering. After that, it's full-fledged flying.

"The Age of Enlightenment started 10 years ago," Barlettani says. "It will only get better and better. The ones doing this will get the full value. The ones not involved will get a diluted value."

His eyes twinkled and he laughed. No matter what one may think of his ideas, it's clear that Barlettani is a happy man.

WORLD PEACE • GLOBAL INAUGURATION

PRESS REPORTS FROM NORTH AMERICA

United States • *Northern Nevada Communicator*

Reno, Nevada August-September 1986 (English)

'Yogic Flying' Demonstrated in Reno

RENO--The media and public were invited, on Friday, August 15, to the global inauguration of Maharishi Mahesh Yogi's Programme to Create World Peace, which was held around lunchtime simultaneously in 108 countries.

Thirty-one sociological studies conducted throughout the world during the past 12 years have shown that one percent or more of a population practicing the Transcendental Meditation technique improves the quality of life throughout society.

This research has repeatedly shown, states the Maharishi, that 7,000 experts practicing one aspect of the TM-Sidhi program, called the "flying" technique, or the Technology of the Unified Field, together in one place can generate a sufficiently strong influence of coherence to radiate globally and purify the whole world consciousness.

In Reno, the first stage of the "flying" technique (called hopping) was demonstrated by three area residents, Jim Bydolek, Craig Dale and Tony DeMasi. They sat on mats on the floor, and after five minutes of quiet and meditation in the room, began to hop, or lift off the floor. Often, one would start and this would seem to cause the others to join in.

What these men were experiencing was explained in this way: Optimum brain functioning, as indicated by maximum coherence (orderliness) in brain wave activity creates the perfect conditions for the 'principle of least action', the center which governs all activity in nature and quietly accomplishes everything. As the body of a "flyer" begins to lift off and hop, the person experiences waves of exhilaration and, in this way, the "flying" technique accelerates evolution to enlightenment. Matter and consciousness are completely integrated. One group of 7000 persons will generate a sufficiently strong influence of coherence to radiate globally and purify the world consciousness.

Blaine Watson, of Toronto, Canada, demonstrates the mechanics of "yogic flying" in New Delhi, India in July.

When asked why the 'yogic flying' must be publicly demonstrated, the Maharishi has said that our governments have failed to create world peace. Today, with the onset of terrorism, they are not providing safety to people in any part of the world. Even the superpowers are constantly in fear and the rivalry between them is challenging the life of every individual. Now it is time for responsible individuals in the world to take the responsibility for creating and maintaining world peace. The group practice will make peace on earth powerful and power on earth peaceful.

More information on Transcendental Meditation is available by calling the office at 323-6291.

PRESS REPORTS FROM NORTH AMERICA

United States • *The Weekly*

Santa Barbara, California   4 September 1986   (English)

Never far from mission control, this flying yogi approaches apogee.

At the Hop

THE MAHARISHI MAHESH Yogi, who founded the Transcendental Meditation movement more than 10 years ago, purports to know the way to create world peace. The bulwark of the Maharishi's program to eliminate terrorism and war is what's known as the TM-Sidhi "Yogic Flying" technique. It was publicly demonstrated on August 15 at the Santa Barbara Capital of the Age of Enlightenment, the sobriquet for the SB TM Center at 125 E. Victoria St.

Colloquially known as levitating, yogic flying involves three stages—hopping, hovering, and flying. During this process, the prospective yogic flyer attempts to marshal a coherence between consciousness and matter in the body. According to TM philosophy, this link originates at the level of the unified field of all the laws of nature. At the point of maximum coherence of brain waves, the body lifts off the ground.

Since, for the meditators, flying is the very apex of consciousness, the more hoppers who practice the discipline, the greater the chance of achieving a world consciousness. Exponents of the movement at the Maharishi International University predict that if 7,000 people practice the program in one place simultaneously, international tension will be greatly alleviated.

—*Mark Terlesky*

WORLD PEACE • GLOBAL INAUGURATION

PRESS REPORTS FROM NORTH AMERICA

United States • *Repository*

Canton, Ohio   14 September 1986   (English)

Hopping for universal tranquility
3 TM instructors give public 'yogic flyer' demonstration

By DEBBIE BLAKE
Repository staff writer

JACKSON TWP. — Aloft, they smiled blissfully. They even giggled.

Three men — "yogic flyers" — hopped on foam pads on the floor while seated in a cross-legged position. They hopped high, and they hopped sideways.

And unless you've studied Transcendental Meditation-Sidhi Yogic Flying, "you can't do this without great gymnastic ability," explained David Kidd, a Canton TM instructor.

The demonstration, Saturday at the Belden Village Holiday Inn, was sponsored by Canton-Akron TM Center at 3935 Everhard Rd. NW. The press was invited to witness the demonstation, which Kidd said showed, "a breakthrough in human consciouness."

What's more, he claimed, if the square root of one percent of the world's population — about 7,000 people — got together daily to practice these techniques, world peace would be achieved.

A video tape and a brief talk preceded the demonstation. Kidd explained that it has been 10 years since the Maharishi Mahesh Yogi has been training teachers and meditators in the sidhi techniques. Public demonstrstions are being held in cities throughout the United States to help accomplish a goal of training more sidhas.

Kidd said there are eight sidhas — those who practice TM sidhi — in the Canton area, adding, "we'd like to have 50." He said there are 1,600 Canton area residents practicing TM in some form.

About 25 meditators or friends of meditators attended Saturday's demonstration.

After hopping comes hovering, Kidd said. He's never seen anyone hover, "but I've heard reports that it's happened."

"The point of TM and yogic flying is to promote greater brain wave coherence and hence coherence in world consciousness," explained a brochure Kidd handed out.

It also said, "with each stroke of the TM Sidhi practice, the awareness goes deeper into the unified field level of consciousness . . . mind-body coordination is maximum; with each intention to fly, the mind propells the body up into the air."

The long hops didn't look too different than the vertical hops. The high hops, onto a stack of as many as four foam pads, propelled the yogis about two feet off the ground.

"It's fun," said Kidd.

After the demonstrations he said, "OK, this is where you can applaud if you're going to."

He added that just watching the demonstration, "shakes you inside. It makes you want to take off too."

He claims the technique, which costs $3,000 to learn when practiced in groups of 7,000, not only brings inner harmony to the practitioners, but also reduces stress worldwide and causes good things to happen, such as declining crime rates.

"If society as a whole begins to accept this," he claimed, the power generated could cause, "everyone — not just the TM practicers — to begin flying."

Reproduced by permission

PRESS REPORTS FROM NORTH AMERICA

United States • *The Muncie Evening Press*

Muncie, Indiana 15 September 1986 (English)

Muncie has its first yogic flying demonstration

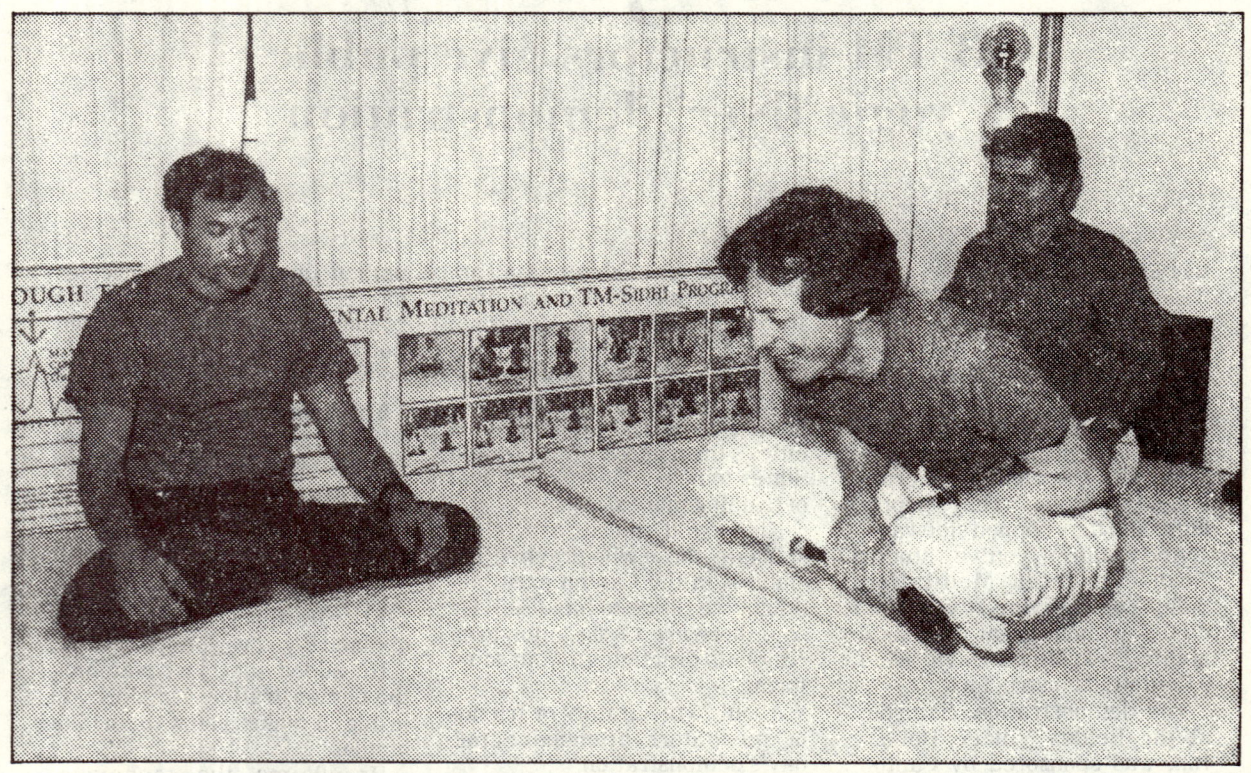

MIND OVER MATTRESS . . . Dr. John Peterson of Muncie (center) achieves liftoff during a yogic flying demonstration in his home Sunday. He and fellow TM Sidhi meditators David Crocco (left) and Chuck Watkins, both of Indianapolis, are students of techniques developed from ancient Indian vedas, meaning "knowledge." They believe flying occurs when all parts of the brain reach coherence in function and that it can create world peace through individual peace. — Evening Press photo by Jeff Mastin.

By PAT MILLS
evening Press reporter

The three men in green T-shirts and loose trousers sat on foam mattresses, their legs folded in the lotus position, soles of feet upward. Deep in meditation, one twitched and wriggled all over. Another rolled his head as if loosening tension. The third sat quietly. Suddenly, with quickened, snorting breaths, they exploded off the mats in hops of three to four feet in length.

Muncie's first yogic flying demonstration had begun. For five minutes Dr. John Peterson of Muncie, with fellow meditators David Crocco and Chuck Watkins, both of Indianapolis, showed the progress they've made in the first stage of the Maharishi Mahesh Yogi's technique.

Peterson and his wife Vicki, a TM instructor since 1973, were hosts to a group of meditators and media representatives Sunday night in their home. Yogic flying, Vicki Peterson said, is a technique for "creating world peace, which comes from individual peace."

Practitioners of TM, she said, reach a state of pure consciousness which is "different from waking, sleeping or dreaming" and contacts "the unified field, the field from which all natural laws arise," she said. "It precedes gravity."

The Petersons are students of advanced techniques known as TM Sidhis, an Indian word meaning "perfections." According to the instructor, "The peacefulness and coherence of the Sidhi techniques are much stronger than with plain TM."

She showed a videotape of the North American Yogic Flying Games, held in July in Washington, D.C. Physicians and physicists speaking on the tape said the flying occurs at the point where the meditator reaches the greatest "coherence of different parts of the brain working together" as measured on EEGs. Charts and graphs were shown.

"The influence of the mind settling down radiates out from the person as an invisible influence," Vicki Peterson said, and has "a powerful influence on society."

Followers of Maharishi, who developed the practices from ancient Indian writings, believe that if the square root of 1 percent of the world population were trained in and practiced the advanced Sidhi techniques, world peace could be maintained through a change in consciousness.

The Petersons showed literature detailing sociological studies in which the "Maharishi effect" improved the quality of life in cities where this ratio of meditators existed. They cited decreases in accidents and violent crime, as well as a rise in the stock market.

After the demonstration, spectators asked the "flyers" to describe their sensations. "I experienced deep silence, waves of bliss bubbling up," Watson said. "Extreme happiness exudes out of the whole physiology. It is very enlivening. I felt complete easiness, lightness. It creates peace in the individual."

John Peterson added he often feels he is " really flying through space, but the body lingers here and goes plop."

His wife added that since the practice causes "a perfect state of order" meditators come to lose any desires that are not "life-supporting" and "spontaneously act more in accord with the laws of nature."

The Muncie physician and TM instructor said there are only half a dozen currently practicing the advanced Sidhis in Delaware County. They have studied them for eight years.

There are 150 persons on her active TM meditator list, Vicki Peterson added, and the number of Sidhi meditators needed for the "Maharishi effect" would be 30. "My goal is to have 30 flyers in Muncie," she said, laughing.

What about the next stages of the technique, which include hovering and then flying through the air? According to the Petersons, no one they know has achieved them yet. They quoted Maharishi, who said that "physiology is not perfected yet" and cited "world stress, a massive violation of natural law" as a force holding down would-be flyers.

But, Watson added, "How did the Wright Brothers start out? With a series of hops."

PRESS REPORTS FROM NORTH AMERICA

United States • *Harvard Magazine*

Cambridge, Massachusetts November-December 1986 (English)

Flying a Peace Mission

Gerald Geer lifts off at the Cambridge TM Center.

With customary artlessness, a press release went out from the Cambridge Transcendental Meditation Center announcing the "Global Inauguration of Maharishi's Program to Create World Peace." Six "expert flyers," selected from among three hundred advanced meditators in the area, would demonstrate their ability to transcend gravity and thereby unveil, for press and assorted guests, the "mechanics to create world peace." One of the six, Gerald Geer, was a Harvard man, Class of '72, and we went to watch him fly.

The demonstration was at Longy School of Music's recital hall, and the place was packed. Most in the audience were meditators, some were flyers themselves. One cheery woman flyer had driven from New Hampshire to attend. A single parent of two, she confessed that her teenagers thought her flying "weird." Preflight preparation included a briefing by Maria Lasagna '73 and endocrinologist Deepak Chopra, past chief of staff of New England Memorial Hospital, both of whom practice the TM-Sidhi flying yogic technique. Then six men, wearing T-shirts that said "TM Flyers for Peace," took the stage and assumed the lotus position. There was a five-minute meditative interlude, which ended with the "ding" of a little bell, and peaceful silence was replaced with a suspenseful, anticipatory one.

At first, nothing. Then, within a minute or so, each flyer, still locked in a cross-legged position, popped up in the air—as effortlessly as toast from a toaster. They lifted off and bounded away. Bouncing startlingly high and surprisingly far, they boinged across the stage and boinged back again. One man repeatedly caught his breath as if at some delightful surprise. Another kept giggling. It wasn't what you'd call sustained flight, but they did seem to be having a wonderful time.

Flyer Geer, who teaches TM in his down time, talked about what happens when he practices this mental technique: "For me there is a wonderful upsurge of energy and vitality and happiness, a great feeling of clarity and awareness. The outward expression is that the body rises up in the air and comes down." Dr. Chopra offered a more clinical description. He maintained, using graphs measuring brain-wave activity before and during flying, that lift-off occurs at a moment of "intense peak brain-wave coherence," a highly desirable state, free of stress, full of joy, and right now, ephemeral. Citing descriptions in ancient Vedic texts, he and the other flyers are confident that eventually they will be able to "hold the impulse," and hopping will give way to hovering and, then, directed flight.

The yogic flyers say the effect of this exercise will have global consequences. "If innocence can do this, which is physically impossible, maybe innocence can go even further," Huntley '69 says. Dent, a writer who has been flying for three years, explains how the peace program works. "The idea is to take a large problem and break it down into small problems. We feel the world will be peaceful when the people in it are peaceful, and people become peaceful only at the level of their own peace of mind."

But as with dropping a pebble into a pond, the meditators say, the effect of one man hopping influences the whole field of global consciousness. They get out the EEG pictures to prove it.

"Brain-wave coherence is not present only in the people who are doing the flying," says Chopra. "It is present and can be measured in the surroundings. Our coherence goes up even though we are not flying ourselves. Taken far enough—given a large enough group of flyers—this is the basis for world peace."

TM practitioners say that when one percent of a population meditates, the effects manifest themselves in the environment: the crime rate drops, the stock market rises. According to them, the TM-Sidhi technique is such powerful meditation, its environmental effects are felt when a much smaller group practices. To initiate his program for world peace, Maharishi hopes to gather ten thousand flyers who, by constant practice, will enliven the collective consciousness and neutralize negative tendencies. "People who are very sophisticated have not stopped war," says Dent. "We hope people who are very innocent can."

At the end of the demonstration the flyers received roses, and thanks for generating so much coherence in themselves and in the environment. The crowd began to disperse. The cheery woman went back to New Hampshire, and we left Longy with something to ponder: These meditators are trying to fly. They're trying to create world peace. One may seem as hard to achieve as the other, but we hope neither proves impossible.

—*Gretchen Friesinger*

© 1986—*Harvard Magazine*; reprinted by permission

APPENDICES

Appendix A

The following summary in 61 points is reprinted from *Maharishi's Programme to Create World Peace—Ensuring Permanent Success through a World Peace Fund.*

MAHARISHI'S PHILOSOPHY OF WORLD PEACE

Role of Invincibility

1. Invincibility is the key to world peace.

2. Invincibility to every nation is the only ground for permanent peace in the world.

3. Lack of invincibility even in one country will render world peace fragile.

Need for a Holistic Approach

4. It must be emphasized that invincibility for every nation is the only effective means for permanent peace on earth. Lack of invincibility even in any one nation will render world peace fragile. Therefore, we have to take a holistic approach.

5. The only approach that will be holistic is one that will simultaneously raise all nations to the level of invincibility.

6. Again, that approach will be holistic which will bring peace to the individual along with world peace.

Role of Natural Law

7. Just as everything in the world is basically governed by natural law, similarly all aspects of life of the individual are basically governed by natural law.

Natural law is that one element which can be utilized to influence all nations and all individuals in the world simultaneously.

8. Skilful use of natural law will establish peace on all levels—individual, national, and international.

Natural Law Maintains Eternal Peace in Nature

9. Peace is eternal in nature, because everything in nature is progressive. Everything in nature is progressive because it moves under the direct influence of the evolutionary power of natural law.

10. If man does not violate natural law, he will not generate stress around him. Stress generated by the violation of natural law causes strained trends and tendencies in the environment.

This is the basic cause of all negativity, violence, terrorism, and national and international conflicts.

11. The whole population of the world is violating the laws of nature because

WORLD PEACE • GLOBAL INAUGURATION

MAHARISHI'S PHILOSOPHY OF WORLD PEACE

people are not trained to not violate natural law.

Sickness and suffering, problems and failures in the life of all the people are signs of violation of natural law.

Education does not train the people to think and act spontaneously according to natural law.

12. As long as people in the world continue to violate the laws of nature, perfect health will be non-existent, and peace and invincibility will not be found in any nation.

Role of Perfect Health

13. Invincibility of a nation is characterized by an integrated, self-sufficient quality of collective consciousness, where all the different trends of different groups in the country are supported by the evolutionary power of natural law and no group remains frustrated in the state of unaccomplishment or non-fulfilment.

This will characterize perfect health of the nation. Only a perfectly healthy nation will enjoy self-sufficiency and invincibility.

Invincibility is really the state of perfect health. Therefore, it is obvious that peace has its basis in perfect health.

World Peace on the Ground of Perfect Health

14. For perfect health, mind-body co-ordination of the individual and also the co-ordination of the individual with his environment and society are needed.

It is fortunate for all mankind and all nations in the world today that all these different areas of perfect health are simultaneously served through the Maharishi Technology of the Unified Field[*][‡], the effectiveness of which has been verified by extensive scientific research conducted around the world during the past 17 years.

World peace on the ground of perfect health is now going to be a reality of our scientific age. What is needed is a quick establishment of the holistic approach through the Maharishi Technology of the Unified Field.

Life in Accordance with Natural Law

15. Now, with the Maharishi Technology of the Unified Field of all the Laws of Nature, which identifies human intelligence with the cosmic intelligence on the level of the unified field of natural law, it is possible to train the people to not violate natural law and to generate a very strong influence of coherence in one place on earth.

---

[*]Maharishi, through his Technology of the Unified Field, has recently restored Ayurveda—the ancient science of perfect health—to its supreme dignity and universal utility, offering perfect health and invincibility for every nation.

[‡]The Maharishi Technology of the Unified Field is Maharishi's programme of Transcendental Meditation, its advanced techniques, and the TM-Sidhi programme.

MAHARISHI'S PROGRAMME TO CREATE

MAHARISHI'S PHILOSOPHY OF WORLD PEACE

This influence will radiate throughout the world and continue to neutralize stress in the whole world consciousness caused by continuous violation of natural law by the whole population of the world day by day.

This is Maharishi's principle of creating permanent world peace.

Peace Is Based on Progress

16. Peace can be permanent only on the basis of unshakable satisfaction. Satisfaction depends upon progress and evolution.

Lack of progress at any one level, or stagnancy of life at any one level, will create frustration, for the simple reason that the nature of life is to grow and evolve.

If world peace is to be a reality, life must be lived under the direct influence of the evolutionary power of natural law. This is Maharishi's insight into the mechanics of creating and maintaining world peace.

17. Reinforcement of evolutionary power in world consciousness is the only effective way to neutralize all kinds of negative trends in the world and maintain world consciousness on a high level of purity.

Role of Higher States of Consciousness

18. Having higher states of consciousness means that one has increasingly broad vision and comprehension and increasing ability to accomplish things.

This results from increasing purity of consciousness, which stimulates spontaneous use of finer levels of natural law, leading ultimately to the use of the full potential of natural law in unity consciousness, which is the highest state of consciousness.

19. Development of higher states of consciousness[*] is vital to establish world peace, because it is the narrowness of vision and inability to accomplish one's desires that cause uncertainties, fears, and loss of self-confidence, leading to frustration and all unwanted values in life, which make life cry for peace.

20. Only individuals rising to higher states of consciousness can restructure the destiny of the nation and the world.

Perfect Means for World Peace

21. Just as world peace has its basis in the invincibility of every nation, peace of the individual has its basis in the ability to fulfil all his desires, and this ability rises spontaneously with the development of higher states of consciousness.

22. It is clear that natural law is that one effective element which can make every nation invincible and every individual capable of accomplishing anything. Therefore, it is wise to conclude that the use of natural law is the perfect

---

[*]Scientific research has shown the spontaneous development of higher states of consciousness through the Maharishi Technology of the Unified Field.

WORLD PEACE • GLOBAL INAUGURATION

MAHARISHI'S PHILOSOPHY OF WORLD PEACE

means for creating world peace on a permanent basis.

Role of Governments

23. Governments have an age-old history of failure to create world peace.

24. Governments have not succeeded in creating world peace because in principle they are not competent to do so.

This is no reflection on the high dignity of government, because it is always the supreme authority of the nation and deserves all respect and appreciation.

25. Government is not an independent entity. It depends upon the collective consciousness of the nation.

Every government, regardless of its system, is an innocent mirror of the nation. Whatever is the quality of the collective consciousness of the nation, that only can be the quality of its government.

26. Government is silently governed by the collective consciousness of the people.

27. Whatever a government does, it is the doing of the collective consciousness of the nation, in the same way as anything done by the body is the doing of the mind.

28. Wherever there is violence in the collective consciousness, the governmental mood is overtaken by violence and governmental performance displays violence—a mirror can only reflect whatever falls on it.

Government— Motivated by Collective Consciousness

29. Governmental activity, motivated by collective consciousness, is like the activity of a machine which is run by power. Just as a machine cannot do anything to the power, in the same way the government cannot do anything to the quality of the collective consciousness of the nation.

30. Dependence on the collective consciousness of the nation is the unavoidable element in the nature of government.

31. The destiny of government is designed by national consciousness. The incapacity of a government to design a new destiny for the nation is evident.

32. The destiny of a nation depends upon that which is at the basis of the collective consciousness of the nation. That is the consciousness of the individual.

Role of Collective Consciousness

33. In principle and in practice, a government can only react to the situation created by the collective consciousness.

34. There is no government in the world that knows how to handle the collective consciousness of a nation or of the whole world, simply because there has been no holistic concept of life, due to the lack of knowledge of the

MAHARISHI'S PHILOSOPHY OF WORLD PEACE

total potential of natural law.

It needed a scientific age to discover the holistic value of natural law in the unified field and to realize that basic level of creation from where everything emerges and from where everything could be controlled.

Now, with the knowledge of this field, world peace is at hand. It is clear that world peace could not be achieved in the past because there had been no holistic knowledge to produce it.

Collective Consciousness— a Reality of All Times

35. The holistic concept of handling the collective consciousness of a nation is the most ancient Vedic concept.* When Veda went out of fashion in India, the world lost sight of this holistic concept of life.

36. The technology of handling collective consciousness was recently brought to light by Maharishi during the formulation of his Vedic science.

Government Rising to Perfection

37. The concept of collective consciousness has clarified the status of government with regard to its relationship with national consciousness, and this has provided a highway for every government now to rise to perfection and govern from the level of nature's perfect government.

38. Maharishi's insight into the functioning of government on the basis of collective consciousness promises to raise any nation to invincibility and any government to self-sufficiency.

On this basis it offers to create a permanent state of world peace—the perpetual sunshine of the Age of Enlightenment for all mankind.

Role of Individual Consciousness

39. The unit of collective consciousness is the consciousness of the individual. Through the individual consciousness alone can the collective consciousness be improved.

40. Improvement in the quality of consciousness of the individual is a direct way to improve the performance and achievement of the government and make the nation invincible, and finally make government competent to maintain world peace.

41. World peace, once created by individuals, can certainly be maintained spontaneously by governments.

42. The continued failure of governments to create world peace has alerted creative individuals not to place their hopes on governments for creating peace in the world. Reliance on governments for world peace is a complete waste of human concern.

---

*The concept that the collective consciousness of the whole universe is in one's own single awareness, Aham Brahmasmi—'I am the totality'.

WORLD PEACE • GLOBAL INAUGURATION

MAHARISHI'S PHILOSOPHY OF WORLD PEACE

Role of the Leaders and the Wealthy

43. Those individuals whose activities are global and whose personal interests are spread over different countries, it is their duty for their own pleasure and for their own survival and progress to formulate a successful plan and action for world peace and create and maintain world peace in every generation.

44. That is why the call is being made to individuals to join hands and soon create world peace. They can fulfil their responsibility through Maharishi's programme to create world peace, which will bring about a new awakening of evolutionary, positive influence in world consciousness.

45. The quality of the collective consciousness of a nation depends upon those creative individuals who take it upon themselves to employ large numbers of people and enjoy raising the national economy through their efforts.

These creative individuals, on whom the whole population of the country depends, stand at the basis of the collective consciousness of their people.

46. These wealthy individuals, who can command the quality of the collective consciousness of the nation, rightfully have the responsibility to create and sponsor this programme for world peace, which is going to create a supreme level of positivity in world consciousness.

Need Is Urgent

47. Everyone should realize that the need is urgent for today, and the need is urgent for every tomorrow.

Every wise and responsible man in the world is feeling increasing pressure from the dangerous rivalry of the superpowers and the unpredictable violence of terrorism, which is known to burst out at any time in any place.

The need is urgent to eliminate these dark patches of ignorance from our modern civilization.

Modern Science and Ancient Vedic Science

48. The practical application of Maharishi's philosophy of world peace is through natural law, which governs the universe and nourishes all life in the most orderly way.

49. What is encouraging is the availability of the invincible evolutionary power of natural law everywhere.

Both modern science and ancient Vedic science, through their respective angles, authenticate the availability of the full creative potential of natural law at every point in creation.

Everything is possible from this level of nature. Anything can be created, anything can be transformed into any other thing, and any situation can be changed into any other situation. All this is just a matter of knowing how to function from this unified level of natural law.

50. The Maharishi Technology of the Unified Field of All the Laws of Nature

MAHARISHI'S PHILOSOPHY OF WORLD PEACE

is the means to raise the level of individual consciousness and collective consciousness.

51. The qualities of the unified field—self-referral, self-interacting dynamics, the spontaneous dynamical sequential symmetry breaking process of creation described by supersymmetric quantum field theories, and the qualities of the unified field described by the superstring theories of modern physics—are the same as those demonstrated to be qualities of the Samhita of Rig Veda.

The unified level of natural law from the platform of modern science is the same as the unified field level of natural law from the platform of Maharishi's Vedic Science. Whether we say the Maharishi Technology of the Unified Field or Maharishi's Vedic technology, the basic meaning is the same.

Peace through the Creative Power of Natural Law

52. Peace in the world has been shattered due to the knowledge and application of the destructive powers of natural law on the electronic and nuclear levels of nature's functioning.

Peace can easily be established through the knowledge and application of the creative powers of natural law, which lie at more fundamental levels than the electronic and nuclear levels of nature's functioning.

When we want world peace to last permanently, we must establish it through the knowledge and application of the most fundamental and most creative level of nature's functioning—the unified field of all the laws of nature.

Unified Field— the Ultimate Basis of Peace

53. At any isolated level of creation, natural law could be used in a creative or destructive manner, according to one's ability and desire, but the holistic value of natural law at the level of the unified field, being the source of all the laws of nature, can be used only for creative purposes.*

It can never be used for destructive purposes, because the quality of destruction is non-existent in the eternal continuum of the self-interacting dynamics of the unified field.

54. Because the dynamics of the unified field are self-interacting, nothing from outside can influence it. The unified field is self-evolutionary, and anything which can identify itself with the unified field spontaneously gains the evolutionary character.

When approached by human awareness, the unified field stimulates human awareness in the evolutionary direction, and only in the evolutionary direction.

When human awareness comes in attunement with this level of nature, all negative tendencies are spontaneously neutralized. It stands pure, fully awake

---

*Please refer to the chart on page 5.

WORLD PEACE • GLOBAL INAUGURATION

MAHARISHI'S PHILOSOPHY OF WORLD PEACE

within itself in the state of the unified field of natural law.

Ten Thousand Experts

55. Ten thousand experts* in the Maharishi Technology of the Unified Field, practising in one place, will generate a very strong influence of positivity to purify world consciousness day by day. This will neutralize negativity prevailing in world consciousness, which is the basis of all terrorism and the dangerous rivalry between the superpowers.

Glorious New Status for Every Government

56. World peace, arising from the growing purity of world consciousness, will enliven and release all the evolutionary power of natural law which is dormant in world consciousness.

This will bring about the full blossoming of positivity and infinite creativity in the national consciousness of every country.

With this, the governments of all countries will rise to their supreme dignity, which they have always deserved, and will enjoy self-sufficiency and freedom from limitations.

57. This clear perspective about the relationship of a government with its national consciousness and with world peace makes it clear why the governments or the heads of state, with all good intentions, have not succeeded in establishing world peace.

Now is the time to create a new history of government and give a new glorious status to every sovereign government in the world by directly creating world peace through the efforts of the individual.

58. Maharishi's programme to create world peace will enliven the evolutionary power of natural law in national consciousness and thereby raise the status of every government to the level of the government of nature.

59. Every government, functioning in full alliance with natural law, will begin to enjoy its due supreme dignity, authority, freedom, self-sufficiency, and invincibility.

Invincibility and Peace—One Reality

60. It is interesting to see that the first point of Maharishi's Philosophy of World Peace states that invincibility of every nation is the only ground for permanent world peace, but from the conclusion of the previous point (no. 59), it is obvious that world peace is the basis of invincibility of every nation.

The truth is that there is no contradiction between these two elements of the

---

*Seven thousand is the square root of one per cent of the world's population today (1986). The square root of one per cent of a population practising the Maharishi Technology of the Unified Field together has been found, through many years of scientific research, to be the formula required to create coherence in the collective consciousness of a given population. Ten thousand are to ensure 7,000 at all times.

philosophy, because the level of world peace and the level of invincibility are not two different levels.

World peace and invincibility of every nation are two values of one level of reality—the unified field of natural law.

The Maharishi Technology of the Unified Field, enlivening this level of natural law in world consciousness, is going to establish world peace and invincibility of every nation simultaneously.

Supreme Philosophy of World Peace

61. What places Maharishi's Philosophy of World Peace on the supreme level of human thought, the supreme level of wisdom, is the fact that invincibility, which has a ring of power, is enlivened on the level of peace.

The result is that world peace, established on the basis of Maharishi's philosophy, will be invincible—peace on earth will be powerful, and power on earth will be peaceful. □

Appendix B

THREE STEPS TO PERMANENT WORLD PEACE—THE GLOBAL MAHARISHI EFFECT

Maharishi has outlined three steps to permanent world peace.

First Step

The first step, he said, is to create coherence in world consciousness. This can be achieved through one permanent group of 7,000 people practising the Maharishi Technology of the Unified Field together in one place.

Maharishi has also set forth the criteria by which we would know when world peace had been created.

'We will ring the bell of success for our first step,' he said, 'when international conflicts, such as the Iran-Iraq war, cease to exist; when cordiality prevails in international relations; when terrorism has vanished; when the dangerous rivalry of the superpowers has gracefully come to an end; and when international trade and industry gain unrestricted growth.'

WORLD PEACE • GLOBAL INAUGURATION

THREE STEPS TO PERMANENT WORLD PEACE

Second Step

The second step to permanent world peace is to create coherence in national consciousness in every country. For this, a group numbering the square root of one per cent of the country's population is required. This will create an armour of invincibility for every nation, creating national peace in every country and strengthening world peace.

'We will ring the bell of success for our second step,' Maharishi said, 'when the national consciousness of every country is integrated; when different groups in the country do not weaken themselves through mutual conflicts but rather strengthen the nation, enriching national life and increasing national resources through their own philosophies and angles of approach; when the systems of education, health, administration, agriculture, rehabilitation, and defence are established on the basis of the infinite organizing power of natural law and enrich all areas of the life of the individual and the nation on a permanent basis; and when national trade and industry gain unrestricted growth.'

Third Step

The third step to permanent world peace is to create coherence in city consciousness in every country. For this, groups of the square root of one per cent of the population of every city of every country in the world are needed. These groups would practise the Maharishi Technology of the Unified Field regularly morning and evening, maintaining a high level of coherence for the city and thereby bringing unrestricted progress and fulfilment for every family and the smooth administration of the affairs of the city as a whole. Peace in every city will perpetuate world peace.

'We will ring the bell of success for our third step,' Maharishi said, 'when progress and fulfilment prevail in every city and peace prevails in every home of every country in our world family; when the administration of all areas of city life is smooth, harmonious, and successful; when every member of the family is an integrated personality and has a high level of mind-body coordination; when every man on earth lives his daily life in enlightenment; when no one violates the laws of nature and the thoughts and actions of every individual are in full accord with natural law, as indicated by fulfilling success in every field of daily life; and when no one creates stress and everyone is always behaving positively and in an evolutionary direction.' □

Appendix C

EXPERIENCES AND ACCOUNTS OF FLYING

The history of flying is both ancient and modern. In the oldest records of human experience, the Vedic literature, we find detailed descriptions of both the phenomenon and the technique of flying. In reports from this century, witnesses from several countries describe people repeatedly levitating.

Butler's Lives of the Saints reports that 'Levitation, the name given to the raising of the human body from the ground by no apparent physical force, is recorded in some form or other of over two hundred saints and holy persons (as well as of many others)....'

Despite the many instances of levitation over the centuries, flying was remote from modern life until the late summer of 1986. Then, for the first time in history, hundreds of people demonstrated the first stage of 'yogic flying' in front of thousands of witnesses while millions more watched the performance on television in their own homes.

Experiences of 'Yogic Flying' in July, August, and September 1986 by TM-Sidhas from around the World

When my body lifts up into the air, I feel a great strengthening of the physiology, and my mind is filled with a feeling of joy, vitality, and brilliance.
—N.G., **Britain**

There is an awareness of the whole body becoming lively and alert, along with a unique sharpness and purity of mind. This builds up to a joyful sense of expansion, freedom, and bliss.
—S.L., **Greece**

When I practise the 'yogic flying' technique, I experience tremendous energy and immeasurable bliss emerging from within me.
—B.T., **India**

The subjective experience of 'yogic flying' is a feeling of the body being composed of bliss, or pure joy, rather than some heavy material substance.
—T.S., **Dominica**

During the practice of the 'yogic flying' technique, I feel very light, strong, and invincible. The more silence I experience inwardly, the higher is the flying and the greater the bliss.
—A.R., **Czechoslovakia**

The experience during 'yogic flying' is one of complete silence and peace followed by very powerful thrills of bliss that literally propel the body into the air.
—P.B., **Switzerland**

The act of 'yogic flying' is totally automatic and effortless. When the mind is completely calm, just the smallest intention to fly is enough to lift my body up and propel it forward on a wave of energy and happiness.
—J.K., **U.S.A.**

During the demonstration, there was a feeling of great expansiveness, as though the consciousness had filled the hall. The whole time it seemed as though I were moving about very freely and effortlessly in that feeling. This expansiveness completely dominated the experience. I was not so much aware of the body except

WORLD PEACE • GLOBAL INAUGURATION

EXPERIENCES AND ACCOUNTS OF FLYING

to know that it was very light and moving about in a very blissful, energetic, and silent manner.

—B.W., **Canada**

To hop is to experience complete happiness, freedom, harmony, and infinite waves of bliss. You have the feeling that anything can be accomplished when you are functioning from that level of infinite correlation, the unified field. —C.M., **Guatemala**

Flying is bliss. —R.K., **Lebanon**

There is nothing that compares to this happiness, this bliss. —R.Z., **Israel**

When my body lifts up in the air, I feel an enormous inner peace and integration of heart, mind, body, and surroundings. There is a feeling of togetherness with everyone and everything. —G.K.P., **Norway**

The more people around me practising the TM-Sidhi 'yogic flying' technique, the more I can enjoy it.

—T.P., **Finland**

Accounts of Flying down through the Ages

Asia

When the Yogi, though remaining in Padmasana [sitting position] can rise in the air and leave the ground, then know that he has gained Vayu-siddhi (success over air), which destroys the darkness of the world. . . . It destroys decay and death.

—from *The Siva Samhita,* trans. Raj Bahadur Srisa Chandra Vasu (India: Sat Guru Publications, 1984)

He was sitting on a mat, like all the others, in the usual Buddha position. Suddenly, he sprang off his seat into the air, easily two-and-a-half to three metres high, at least well above my head—I am 1.91 metres tall—and then relatively slowly, certainly much more slowly than a man landing from a jump, he landed again in his Buddha position. I was very much surprised, for it was absolutely clear that this was no usual jump, but a true but quick levitation.

—translated from *Magier, Mächte und Mysterien,* Wilhelm Moufang (Heidelberg: Keysersche Verlagsbuchhandlung, 1954)

When one sits in meditation, the fleshly body becomes quite shining like silk or jade. It seems difficult to remain sitting; one feels as if drawn upwards. . . . In time, one can experience it in such a way that one really floats upward.

—from *The Secret of the Golden Flower, A Chinese Book of Life,* trans. Richard Wilhelm (London: Kegan Paul, Trench, Trubner & Co., Ltd., 1962)

Europe

Rapture is generally irresistible. . . . it sweeps upon you so swift and strong that you see and feel yourself being caught up in this cloud and borne aloft as on the wings of a mighty eagle. . . . Even at times my whole body has been lifted from the ground.

—translated from the words of St Teresa of Avila, in *St Teresa of Avila,* Stephen Clissold (London: Sheldon Press, 1982)

I found myself lifted up completely by the very soles of my feet, just as the magnet draws up a fragment of iron, but with a gentleness that was marvellous and most delightful. . . . I knew that I was raised some distance above the earth, my whole body being suspended for a considerable space of time. Down to last Christmas eve (1618) this happened to me on five different occasions.

—translated from the words of Sour Maria Villani, in *The Physical Phenomena of Mysticism,* Herbert Thurston, S.J., from *Vita della V. Serva di Dio Sour Maria Villani,* D.M. Marchese (London: Burns & Oates, 1952)

St. Richard, then chancellor to St. Edmund, Archbishop of Canterbury, one day softly opening the chapel door, to see why the archbishop did not come to dinner, saw him raised high in the air, with his knees bent and his arms stretched out. . . .

—from *The Origins of Culture,* Sir Edward Burnett Tylor (New York: Harper & Row, 1958)

MAHARISHI'S PROGRAMME TO CREATE

EXPERIENCES AND ACCOUNTS OF FLYING

One effect of Thomas's amazing concentration in prayer was that several times, as he prayed, his body was seen lifted off the ground, as if it followed the movement of his mind. . . .

—from 'The Life of St. Thomas Aquinas', Bernard Gui, in *The Life of Saint Thomas Aquinas: Biographical Documents,* trans. and ed. Kenelm Foster, O.P. (Baltimore: Helicon Press, 1959)

Dominic of Jesu Maria . . . is said to have been raised above the ground in the presence of King Philip II of Spain and his Queen. . . . On another occasion the same holy Carmelite when rising in the air was caught hold of by a sceptical witness who believed these ecstasies to be a trick. The critic was carried up along with the Saint, and becoming afraid, loosed his hold, so that he fell to the ground. . . .

—from *The Physical Phenomena of Mysticism,* Herbert Thurston, S.J., after *Vita dell V.P. Domenico di Gesu Maria,* Filippo della S. Trinità (London: Burns & Oates, 1952)

He [St. Joseph of Copertino] at once flew about a dozen paces over the heads of those present to the foot of the statue. Then after paying homage there for some short space and uttering his customary shrill cry he flew back again and straightway returned to his cell, leaving the Admiral, his wife, and the large retinue which attended them speechless with astonishment.

—translated in *The Physical Phenomena of Mysticism,* Herbert Thurston, S.J., from *Acta Sanctorum, Sep. Vol. V,* Angelo Pastrovicchi (London: Burns & Oates, 1952)

During the seventeen years he [St. Joseph of Copertino] remained at Grottella over seventy occasions are recorded of his levitation. . . .

—from *Butler's Lives of the Saints, Complete Edition,* edited, revised and supplemented by Herbert Thurston, S.J., and Donald Attwater (New York: P.J. Kenedy & Sons, 1962)

From these accounts it is clear that flying is natural, effortless, and universal. It is the same exhilarating experience of deep silence and lively bliss, of lightness of body and unbounded awareness, irrespective of the era or culture in which it occurs and regardless of the language used to describe it.

Many of the accounts of flying reflect the Vedic science description of its three stages—hopping, hovering, and flight. But only Vedic science provides insight into flying as a procedure for developing full human potential to the state of enlightenment. And only Vedic science, as brought to light by Maharishi, provides the systematic technique to develop the ability of 'yogic flying'.

Maharishi explains that flying is a reality of all ages because of the eternal relationship of consciousness and matter. All matter, including the senses and objects of the senses, is expressed in sequence from pure consciousness, the self-interacting unified field of all the laws of nature, which is the Self of every individual. Once one is able to think from the level of the Self, from the level of the unified field, the total potential of natural law supports one's intentions. Therefore, the technique that cultures the ability to think from the level of the unified field naturally increases one's ability to fulfil desires, including the impulse to fly.

Today, with the rise of Maharishi's Vedic Science, more than 50,000 people throughout the world are practising the TM-Sidhi programme and experiencing the first stage of 'yogic flying' as part of their daily routine. Theories of quantum physics are beginning to explain the phenomenon, and the instruments of modern science are measuring its effects.

WORLD PEACE • GLOBAL INAUGURATION

EXPERIENCES AND ACCOUNTS OF FLYING

The benefits of TM-Sidhi 'yogic flying' to individual life are numerous. The enhanced co-ordination of mind and body promotes health, happiness, and well-being. Since flying is possible only by enlivening the unified field of natural law, through 'yogic flying' all thought, speech, and action become more and more in accord with all the laws of nature, and the individual grows in the ability to live life free from mistakes, problems, and suffering.

Because the unified field has the quality of infinite correlation, the benefits of 'yogic flying' extend to the whole environment. Maharishi Patanjali describes 'yogic flying' in the *Yoga Sutras* and states, 'Tat Sannidhau Vairatyagah' ('In the vicinity of coherence [Yoga], hostile tendencies are eliminated'). Scientific research has confirmed that 7,000 people practising TM-Sidhi 'yogic flying' together in one place create coherence in world consciousness, the basis of world peace.

The individual lifting up against gravity towards the heavens is inspiring, but more important is that now we know how to create a powerful influence of coherence to neutralize all negativity in the world and bring the descent of heaven on earth. Through the Maharishi Technology of the Unified Field, the responsible people of this generation can open all possibilities for the world by creating world peace. This will be the springboard to happiness and harmony for all, and will usher in the full sunshine of the Age of Enlightenment. In Maharishi's words, 'We'll soon have it.' □

TEACHER GUIDE

9th–12th Grade | Includes Student Worksheets | Apologetics

- Weekly Lesson Schedule
- Student Worksheets
- Tests
- Answer Key

Cultural Issues Vol. 1: Creation/Evolution and the Bible

General Editor:
Ken Ham

Master Books Creative Team:

Editor: Craig Froman

Design: Terry White

Cover Design: Diana Bogardus

Copy Editors:
Judy Lewis
Willow Meek

Curriculum Review:
Kristen Pratt
Laura Welch
Diana Bogardus

First printing: January 2015
Seventh printing: April 2022

Copyright © 2015 by Master Books®. All rights reserved. No part of this book may be reproduced, copied, broadcast, stored, or shared in any form whatsoever without written permission from the publisher, except in the case of brief quotations in articles and reviews. For information write:

Master Books, P.O. Box 726, Green Forest, AR 72638

Master Books® is a division of the New Leaf Publishing Group, Inc.

ISBN: 978-1-68344-003-1
ISBN: 978-1-61458-578-7 (digital)

Unless otherwise noted, Scripture quotations are from the New King James Version of the Bible.

Printed in the United States of America

Please visit our website for other great titles:
www.masterbooks.com

For information regarding author interviews,
please contact the publicity department at (870) 438-5288.

Permission is granted for copies of reproducible pages from this text to be made for use with immediate family members living in the same household. However, no part of this book may be reproduced, copied, broadcast, stored, or shared in any form beyond this use. Permission for any other use of the material must be requested by email from the publisher at info@nlpg.com.

Your reputation as a publisher is stellar. It is a blessing knowing anything I purchase from you is going to be worth every penny!

—Cheri ★ ★ ★ ★ ★

Last year we found Master Books and it has made a HUGE difference.

—Melanie ★ ★ ★ ★ ★

We love Master Books and the way it's set up for easy planning!

—Melissa ★ ★ ★ ★ ★

You have done a great job. MASTER BOOKS ROCKS!

—Stephanie ★ ★ ★ ★ ★

Physically high-quality, Biblically faithful, and well-written.

—Danika ★ ★ ★ ★ ★

Best books ever. Their illustrations are captivating and content amazing!

—Kathy ★ ★ ★ ★ ★

Affordable
Flexible
Faith Building